™

**Agenda, Lotus, Metro**, and **1-2-3** are registered trademarks of Lotus Development Corporation.

**dBASE II, dBASE III**, and **dBASE III PLUS** are registered trademarks of Ashton-Tate.

**Harvard Project Manager** and **PFS: Professional File** are trademarks of Software Publishing Company.

**IBM** and **PC DOS** are registered trademarks of International Business Machines Corporation.

**Microsoft** and **MS-DOS** are registered trademarks of Microsoft Corporation.

**Notebook** is a trademark of Pro/Tem.

**Paradox** is a registered trademark of Ansa Software.

**Q & A, Ready!**, and **ThinkTank** are trademarks of Synmantec Corporation.

**Quattro** is a trademark of Borland International.

**R:BASE** is a trademark of Microrim, Inc.

**SuperProject** is a registered trademark of Computer Associates International, Inc.

**WordPerfect** is a trademark of WordPerfect Corporation.

**ZyIndex** is a trademark of ZyLAB Corporation.

Published by **Windcrest Books**
FIRST EDITION/FIRST PRINTING

**Library of Congress Cataloging-in-Publication Data**

Ottensmann, John R.
    Working with Lotus Agenda / by John R. Ottensmann and Jan Neuenschwander.
        p.    cm.
    Includes index.
    ISBN 0-8306-3161-5 (pbk.)
    1. Agenda (Computer program)  2. Business—Data processing.
I. Neuenschwander, Jan.  II. Title.
HF5548.4.A35O88  1988
005.75′65—dc19
                                    88-7783
                                       CIP

TAB BOOKS Inc. offers software for sale. For information and a catalog, please contact TAB Software Department, Blue Ridge Summit, PA 17294-0850.

Questions regarding the content of this book should be addressed to:
**Windcrest Books**
**Division of TAB BOOKS Inc.**
**Blue Ridge Summit, PA 17294-0850**

Ron Powers: Director of Acquisitions
Marianne Krcma: Technical Editor
Katherine Brown: Production
Jaclyn B. Saunders: Series Design

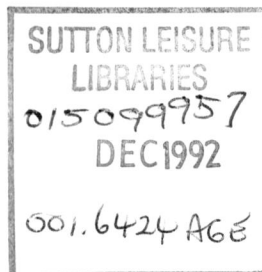

# Contents

# ACKNOWLEDGMENTS

We would like to thank Sue Jensen at Lotus Development Corporation for her continuing assistance in providing information and making available the different versions of Agenda. The figures illustrating the operation of the Agenda program have been reproduced with the permission of Lotus Development Corporation. The screen images are copyright Lotus Development Corporation. Used with permission.

We would also like to thank Ron Powers at TAB BOOKS for making it possible for us to obtain an early version of Agenda and to pursue our work with Agenda in writing this book.

Above all, our daughter Sandra served as a constant source of inspiration. We have to thank her for her patience as we kept telling her that we had to work on the book.

# INTRODUCTION

Agenda is a personal information manager—a program that enables you to manage the diverse information that you work with every day. The program allows you to enter information and organize it in many different ways. Agenda is very flexible and very powerful.

Agenda's flexibility and power can be illustrated by considering how you could use it to keep track of the tasks that you have to do. You could enter a brief description of each task—each of these descriptions would be an *item* in the Agenda database. Agenda items can range in length from a short phrase to several sentences. Initially, you would enter the items into sections displayed on the screen. Each section could correspond to a different type of task, such as a section for all tasks related to Meetings. When you entered items into the Meetings section, Agenda would automatically assign the items to the Meetings category. This assignment of items to categories is the source of Agenda's flexibility and power.

Because your tasks may involve one or more projects for different clients, each item you enter into an Agenda database can be assigned to one or more different project categories. Any time you want to look at the work that has to be done for a particular project, you can display a view of your Agenda database that groups the task items for that project.

Agenda includes very sophisticated capabilities for handling dates. If you enter an item that says a task is to be completed by "tomorrow" or "next

Thursday,'' Agenda will determine the date to which you are referring. These date capabilities let you select and sort items by date.

Anyone confronted by many tasks can make effective use of Agenda to organize activities. Organizing tasks is likely to be the single most popular application of Agenda, but it is effective for many additional applications as well. Agenda's capabilities for managing activities can be extended to generate sophisticated appointments calendars and to manage complex projects with large numbers of interrelated tasks.

If you regularly deal with large numbers of different people as clients, sales prospects, or employees, Agenda can assist in organizing information about those people. Agenda gives you flexibility because it lets you organize (and reorganize) the information at any time—you don't even have to decide in advance how you are going to organize the information. Managers responsible for assigning many tasks to many different people within an organization will find Agenda to be a powerful management tool. Indeed, Agenda can even be used to develop an organizational structure.

Agenda is also valuable to anyone who wants to keep track of large numbers of things having diverse characteristics. Agenda can be used to manage the information, enabling you to organize and locate what you need. Such an application is useful for businesses providing diverse mixes of products or services, as well as for hobbyists who need to organize their collections.

For many people, including researchers and students, dealing with large amounts of information is nearly an overwhelming burden. Agenda can be used to manage and organize such information so you can use it effectively. You can enter the bits and pieces of information you encounter every day in memos, magazines, newspapers, and so on. Later, you can use Agenda to organize this information. Once you have entered information into an Agenda database, you can find what you need, when you need it. Those who conduct research and write papers and reports will want to use Agenda to store the information gathered in their research. They can then use Agenda to organize the information for the preparation of the report.

Using Agenda is not difficult. The basic operations can be mastered within several hours, so you can be up and running, using Agenda effectively right away. (If your goal is to use Agenda as quickly as possible, an outline for learning the bare essentials is presented at the end of the first chapter.) Mastering the many features of this powerful program will, of course, take longer. Learning the advanced features, however, can be done while you are using Agenda for productive work.

This book provides all you need to use Agenda. The first part of the book introduces Agenda and describes the basics for getting started. In the second section, you learn how to use Agenda, acquiring all of the fundamental skills necessary to apply the program to your personal needs. The third section addresses advanced features of Agenda that you can learn as you work to extend your mastery over the program. The final section of the book shows how Agenda can be used in a wide variety of applications. Specific applications for Agenda are illustrated. The principles underlying these applications are explained so that you can use these examples as points of departure for designing your own Agenda applications.

*To Sandy*

# 1
## INTRODUCING AGENDA

LOTUS refers to Agenda as a "personal information manager." Agenda is a new category of software that gives users the capability to manage text flexibly and powerfully. The program provides sophisticated capabilities for organizing the information entered, yet does so in a simple, intuitive way.

Agenda provides the capabilities for managing information in ways never before possible. It allows you to create a database by entering simple statements representing ideas, things to do, or any other information. You can then manipulate and examine this information in a limitless number of ways. These very general capabilities allow you to use Agenda for everything from keeping track of and managing projects and people to organizing the information and ideas associated with different tasks.

The key to the power of Agenda is its flexibility. The program does not require specifying or adhering to rigid formats like other data management software. You are always free to organize the information in a database in new ways. Agenda allows you to work with ideas—with text—in the flexible way in which an electronic spreadsheet program such as Lotus 1-2-3 allows you to work with numbers.

## THE NATURE OF AGENDA

You enter information into an Agenda database as free-form text. Each entry is called an *item*. An item can be a phrase of text or several sentences. An example of such an item is

Prepare report on the Walker project by next Thursday.

An Agenda database can be made up of hundreds of such items. New items can be added to a database at any time.

You organize the information by assigning the items to *categories*. For example, the item above might be assigned to a ''Reports'' category, which would include all items referring to various reports. The item might also be assigned to the ''Walker'' subcategory of a ''Projects'' category, since the item refers to the Walker project.

Agenda allows you to display the information in a variety of different *views* based upon the category assignments. All of the items referring to reports could be assigned to the Reports category displayed together in one view. A Project view might show the items referring to specific projects, grouped by the name of the project. The example item above would be listed under Walker in the Project view, along with all of the other items referring to the Walker project. Dates associated with any of the items can also be displayed in any view.

The power of Agenda comes from the flexibility with which items can be assigned to categories. Items can be assigned to categories as they are entered into the database. In addition, new categories can always be created later, and items then can be assigned to those new categories. This enables you to recognize the information in the Agenda database and look at it in new and different ways.

Agenda provides a great deal of assistance in assigning the items in the database to categories. You can always create categories and explicitly specify that any item is to be assigned to any given category. If you start typing in a category assignment, and Agenda recognizes that the entry matches an existing category, it gives you the opportunity to accept that category without typing the entire name. For example, when assigning an item to the Walker project category, Agenda might display Walker as soon as you typed the W. You can then accept this category and make the assignment without typing in the entire category name.

Agenda can also recognize that new items belong to certain existing categories and make the assignment automatically. Suppose that the Walker project category had already been created. When you enter a new item referring to the Walker project, Agenda will assign the new item to the Walker category.

Perhaps the most impressive capability of Agenda is its ability to understand references to dates. When the item including the text ''next Thursday'' was entered, Agenda would have recognized that this was a date reference, determined the appropriate date for next Thursday, and made the appropriate When Date entry.

Agenda provides many more capabilities for managing categories and assigning items to categories. Categories can be rearranged and restructured. Items can be assigned automatically to new categories based upon existing category assignments. These features enable you to organize the information in an Agenda database flexibly and easily, in whatever manner you desire.

Agenda likewise gives you the capabilities to create views to display precisely the information desired. You select the categories of information to be displayed in any view. Columns can be added to the displayed information to indicate other categories to which each item is assigned, and to display any dates associated with the item. You can then select the items to be displayed in a view by specifying various category assignment and date criteria. You can then arrange the items in a view as desired.

Agenda can import files of text from other sources into an Agenda database. This enables you to use Agenda to sort through and organize information obtained from other sources, including electronic mail and online databases.

Like Lotus 1-2-3, Agenda allows the creation and use of *macros* to automate repetitive tasks. You can create macros in Agenda by simply recording the sequence of keystrokes used when performing an operation. Additional macro commands allow the creation of more elaborate and powerful macros.

## AN AGENDA APPLICATION

A simple example will best illustrate the features and capabilities of Agenda. Suppose that a manager uses Agenda to keep track of tasks to be performed—reports to prepare, meetings to attend, telephone calls to make. Many of these tasks are related to projects for specific clients. And always, there are deadlines.

The process begins by starting Agenda and setting up section heads to serve as the categories. For example, tasks could be grouped under the section heads "Reports," "Meetings," and "Phone Calls." Under each of these section heads, the manager then enters individual items describing the various tasks to be accomplished. Figure 1-1 shows the Agenda display after several items have been entered into the database.

Recognizing that the information should also be organized in other ways, the manager can create columns for designating the project to which the item refers and the date by which the item is to be completed. This is illustrated in Fig. 1-2. Agenda automatically recognizes the date references in the items and displays the appropriate dates in the When column. The project names will have to be entered for the existing items in the database and for any additional projects. Now, however, Agenda is prepared to take on most of the work of assigning newly entered items to the appropriate categories.

```
File: C:\AGFILES\TASKS                              03/09/89    13:17
View: Initial View
════════════════════════════════════════════════════════════════════

Reports
    · Prepare report on Walker project by next Thursday.

Meetings
    · Meeting to discuss project for James next Monday.
    · Meet with Jim to discuss report on the Peters account.

Phone Calls
    · Call Ron Smith at Walker by Tuesday to discuss the progress of the
      project.
    · Call Adam Baker at James Wednesday to get his reactions to our proposals.




══F1══╤══F2══╤══F3══╤══F4══╤══F5══╤══F6══╤══F7══╤══F8══╤══F9══╤══F10══
 Help ║ Edit ║ Copy ║ Done ║ Note ║ Move ║ Mark ║Vw Mgr║Cat Mgr║ Menu
```

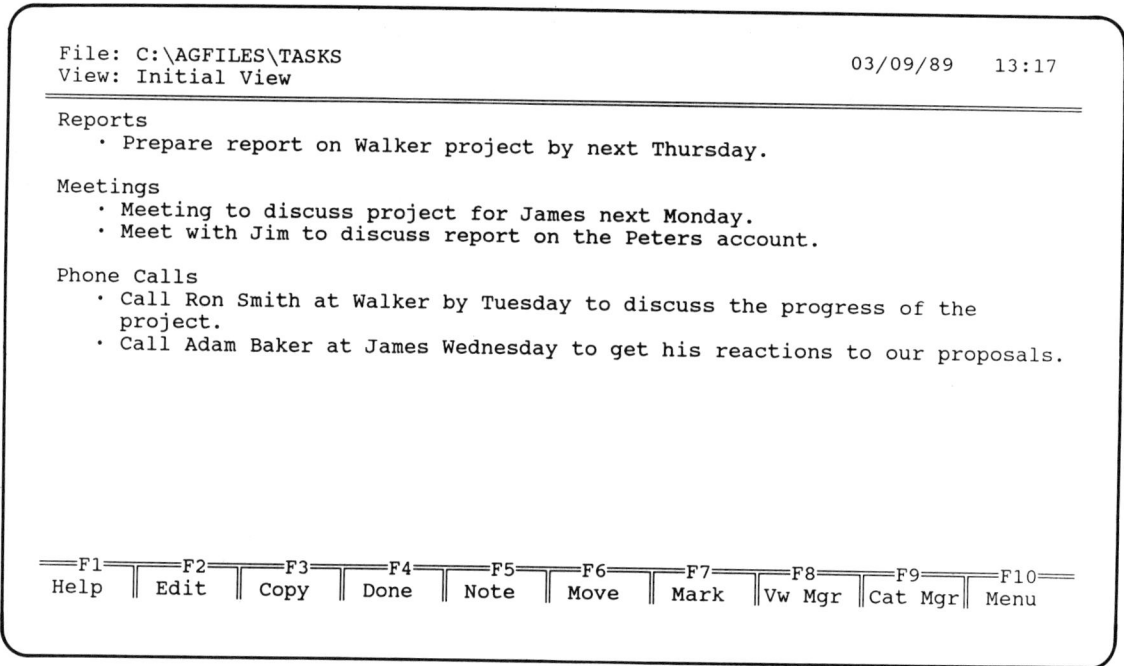

Fig. 1-1. *The initial entry of items for the tasks to be accomplished.*

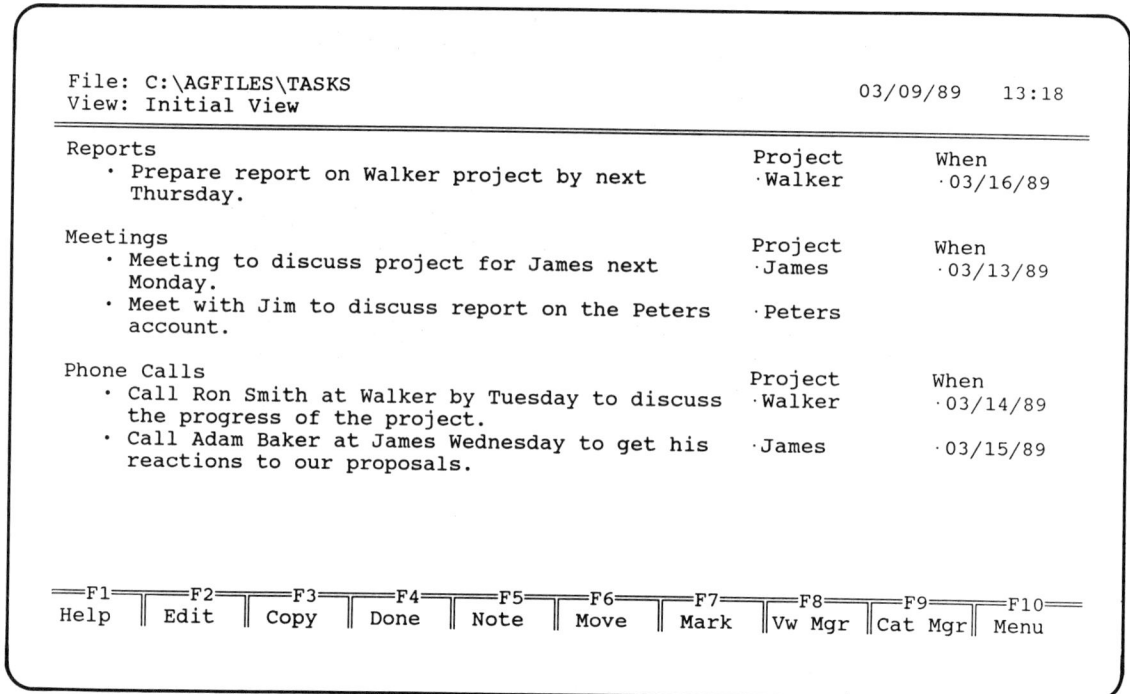

```
File: C:\AGFILES\TASKS                              03/09/89    13:18
View: Initial View
════════════════════════════════════════════════════════════════════

Reports                                    Project      When
    · Prepare report on Walker project by next   ·Walker      ·03/16/89
      Thursday.

Meetings                                   Project      When
    · Meeting to discuss project for James next  ·James      ·03/13/89
      Monday.
    · Meet with Jim to discuss report on the Peters ·Peters
      account.

Phone Calls                                Project      When
    · Call Ron Smith at Walker by Tuesday to discuss ·Walker   ·03/14/89
      the progress of the project.
    · Call Adam Baker at James Wednesday to get his  ·James    ·03/15/89
      reactions to our proposals.




══F1══╤══F2══╤══F3══╤══F4══╤══F5══╤══F6══╤══F7══╤══F8══╤══F9══╤══F10══
 Help ║ Edit ║ Copy ║ Done ║ Note ║ Move ║ Mark ║Vw Mgr║Cat Mgr║ Menu
```

Fig. 1-2. *The addition of Project and When Date columns to the view with the tasks.*

Assume that the first item entered into the database is

Prepare report on Walker project by next Thursday.

The manager then assigns this item to the Walker project category by typing in Walker in the Project column. Later, the manager enters the following item:

Call Ron Smith at Walker on Tuesday to discuss the progress of the project.

Because of the reference to "Walker," Agenda recognizes immediately that the item should be assigned to the Walker project category. It makes the entry in the Project column automatically. Agenda also determines that Tuesday's date is 3/14/89 and makes this entry in the When column. Thus, as the database is being created and organized, Agenda can take on more of the work for the user.

Given that the manager's activities are focused upon many different projects, an obvious next step is to display the various tasks organized by project. This just requires creating a new view of the information in the Agenda database. Figure 1-3 illustrates this view of the data by project. The manager can switch back and forth between the Project view of the data and the Initial view in which the items were entered. New items can be entered, edited and assigned to categories in either view.

Agenda is not limited to simply providing different views of the entire database. The user can also make very specific selections of the information to

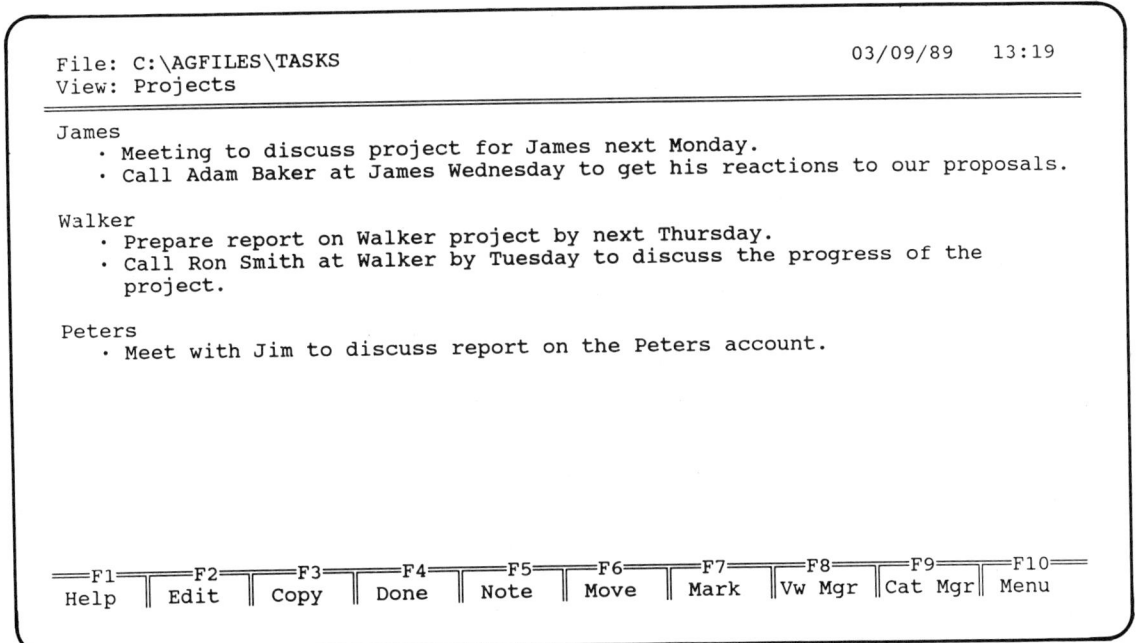

```
File: C:\AGFILES\TASKS                          03/09/89    13:19
View: Projects
================================================================

James
   · Meeting to discuss project for James next Monday.
   · Call Adam Baker at James Wednesday to get his reactions to our proposals.

Walker
   · Prepare report on Walker project by next Thursday.
   · Call Ron Smith at Walker by Tuesday to discuss the progress of the
     project.

Peters
   · Meet with Jim to discuss report on the Peters account.




  =F1=    =F2=    =F3=    =F4=    =F5=    =F6=    =F7=    =F8=    =F9=    =F10=
  Help  | Edit | Copy | Done | Note | Move | Mark |Vw Mgr|Cat Mgr| Menu
```

Fig. 1-3. *The Projects view of the database showing the tasks grouped by project.*

```
 File: C:\AGFILES\TASKS                                    03/09/89   13:22
 View: Walker & James, Next Week       (When date: 03/13/89 - 03/19/89)     ‡
════════════════════════════════════════════════════════════════════════════
 Walker                                                      When
    · Call Ron Smith at Walker by Tuesday to discuss the progress  ·03/14/89
      of the project.
    · Prepare report on Walker project by next Thursday.    ·03/16/89

 James                                                       When
    · Meeting to discuss project for James next Monday.      ·03/13/89
    · Call Adam Baker at James Wednesday to get his reactions to   ·03/15/89
      our proposals.




════F1════╤════F2════╤════F3════╤════F4════╤════F5════╤════F6════╤════F7════╤════F8════╤════F9════╤═══F10════
  Help    ║  Edit    ║  Copy    ║  Done    ║  Note    ║  Move    ║  Mark    ║ Vw Mgr  ║Cat Mgr║  Menu
```

Fig. 1-4. *A view showing the tasks associated with the Peters and Walker projects to be completed in the following week, in order by date.*

be displayed to address virtually any question. Suppose some problems have arisen on the James project, and the manager needs to devote the entire following week to working on that project. The tasks due to be completed on the Peters and Walker projects for that week have to be assigned to an assistant.

Identifying and displaying these tasks involves creating another view of the database. This view displays those items assigned to the Peters and Walker projects. In addition, only those items with When dates during the following week, the period through 3/19/89, are to be displayed. Finally, the items are ordered within each category by the date. Figure 1-4 shows the resulting view of the database. The manager can print out the information in this view to give to the assistant when making the assignment of responsibilities for the following week.

This very simple example only begins to illustrate the power of Agenda to organize and manage information. Obviously, the more items there are in the database, the more important it is to organize this information in different ways and display exactly the information desired.

## THE LOGIC OF AGENDA

Using Agenda is easier if you have a clear understanding of the structure of the program and the way it handles information. This section describes the basic elements of Agenda—items, categories and views—and how they are related.

An item is the basic element of information entered into Agenda. Items are short text entries, ranging in length from a single word to several lines of text. Items are displayed on the screen in a view preceded by a bullet (either a dot or some other symbol). For example, the first item entered into the database discussed in the previous example is

Prepare report on Walker project by next Thursday.

Items represent brief statements of the information to be organized using Agenda. Each item may have an optional *note* attached, containing additional information relating to the item. A note can be several pages long. These notes are available for reference at any time.

Items are assigned to categories in an Agenda database. Each item must be assigned to at least one category, and an item can be assigned to as many categories as desired. The item above was assigned to the Reports category and the Walker category. By assigning items to categories, you provide a structure for the information contained in an Agenda database.

Items may be assigned to existing categories as they are entered into the Agenda database. In such cases, Agenda can provide assistance in making the assignment. For example, Agenda can determine that when an item contains the word "Walker," it should be assigned to the Walker project category.

Items in Agenda are displayed in views. Every view includes one or more categories as *section heads*, with items assigned to those categories listed under the section heads. For example, the first view of the example database, shown in Fig. 1-1, included section heads for the categories Reports, Meetings, and Phone Calls.

Agenda allows for the creation of many views of the database, displaying the information in different ways. Items can be entered or changed only while in a view. A new item is entered by inserting it in a section, under a section head, in a view. When an item is entered into a section, the item is assigned to the category represented by the section head. Since an item must be entered within a section, an item is always assigned to at least the one category represented by the section head.

Views may also include *columns*, which indicate the additional categories to which an item is assigned. Figure 1-2 shows the Initial view, which includes two columns. Column heads are always categories. The information displayed in columns under the column heads may be other categories to which the items are actually assigned. In the example, James, Peters, and Walker are the categories in the Project category column. These are actually subcategories, called *child categories*, of the Project category.

Alternatively, the information displayed in columns under the column heads may relate to the assignment of the item to the category represented by the column head. In the example, the When column displays the date associated with the assignment of the items to the When category. Columns can display other information as well, such as a Yes or No, indicating whether or not an item is assigned to the category represented by the column head.

New views may be created and views may be changed at any time. Creating or changing views involves specifying the categories to be displayed within the view, either as sections or as columns. The categories specified may be existing categories within the database, or they may be totally new categories.

Views can include *filters* that provide for the display of only those items meeting certain criteria. The final view displayed in the example in Fig. 1-4 uses a filter to display only those items with When Dates in the following week. Items may also be sorted within the sections of views.

The Category Manager in Agenda allows the direct manipulation of the categories in a database. You can use the Category Manager to add or delete categories, and to rearrange or restructure them. The Category Manager also lets you set conditions and actions that make category assignments for items.

This is just a brief overview of the logic of Agenda. The ways in which these elements are used are explained in detail in the following chapters. Only by using Agenda will you fully appreciate the structure of the program.

## AGENDA VERSUS OTHER SOFTWARE

Agenda is a personal information manager, one of the first entries in this new category of personal computer software. As such, Agenda is very different from other types of personal computer applications software. Understanding Agenda, however, can be enhanced by examining the differences between it and some of the other major types of software. Such a comparison is also important for understanding the types of applications for which Agenda is best suited, as well as the types of applications for which other types of software are more appropriate.

Agenda is an information manager, and thus should be compared with the traditional database management software available for personal computers. Database management programs range from the simpler single-file database management programs such as Q & A and PFS: Professional File to very sophisticated relational database management programs such as dBASE, R:BASE and Paradox. The key difference between these database managers and Agenda lies in the flexibility and the amount of structure imposed upon the information entered.

Database management programs require that the structure of the information be established prior to the entry of any information. Specific fields must be defined and information must be entered into those fields. Changing the structure of such a database is extremely difficult. Agenda, on the other hand, allows the information to be entered without any prior structuring. Items can be assigned to categories at any time, providing for complete flexibility in organizing the information in the database.

For managing information with a very regular structure, such as a mailing list or information on customer accounts receivable, the traditional database managers are the software of choice. They provide powerful capabilities for handling multiple, repeated clusters of information such as name and address records or customer accounts. On the other hand, for organizing and managing the diverse types of information that cross your desk every day in dealing with complex problems, the flexibility of Agenda makes it the program to choose.

Traditional database management software is inappropriate for the management of unstructured textual information. Another category of personal computer software, the so-called *free-form text databases*, have been developed in response to this need. To some extent, such programs are aimed at the same problem that Agenda addresses. The difficulty with the free-form text databases is that they impose either too much structure on the information in the database or too little.

Notebook II, for example, can handle extensive amounts of text, unlike the database management programs, but it requires the prior specification of categories and the entry of the text into these categories. The program lacks the flexibility of Agenda in entering information and then assigning that information to categories. You are forced to create blank categories when entering items to allow for the subsequent categorization in different ways.

A program such as ZyIndex, on the other hand, allows text to be entered without structure. The text can be searched, and selected based upon the results of such searches. The limitation with ZyIndex, however, lies in the user's inability to impose sufficient structure on the information in the database once the information has been entered.

While the free-form text database programs may be useful for certain applications, Agenda will generally be the more powerful and useful tool for managing such information.

Outline processors such as ThinkTank and Ready! provide very powerful and flexible structuring of information in the form of outlines. They give the user the power to create and change the structure of the information entered. They are not, however, information management programs. The outline processors require you to develop a structure, move the information into the structure, and organize the information into it. They do not have the powerful capabilities to automatically assign information to categories, nor do they provide for multiple views of the information entered. For creating a simple outline, the outline processors are useful tools. For managing more substantial quantities of information, including the development of a hierarchical structure for this information, Agenda is the more powerful tool.

Project management software, such as SuperProject and Harvard Project Manager, provide for the sophisticated, quantitative management of the interrelated tasks associated with complex projects. Agenda is definitely not a substitute for such project managers. However, when managers need the capability to manage random items of information about projects, including dates, without the complexity of the project management software, Agenda can serve as a valuable tool.

Of all of the common types of applications software, Agenda seems to differ most from the electronic spreadsheets such as Lotus 1-2-3. The spreadsheets deal primarily with numbers; Agenda deals primarily with text. Yet despite this fundamental difference, Agenda shares some aspects with the spreadsheets. Both are the most flexible tools for managing their respective types of information. Both are extremely valuable for looking at different possibilities existing in the information. A spreadsheet program allows the user to ask ''what if'' questions to determine what would happen if a value were changed, simply by changing that value. Agenda also provides for answering certain types of ''what if '' questions by assigning the information to new categories and displaying the information in different views.

## LEARNING AGENDA

As with any powerful piece of software, Agenda contains many operations and commands to implement a diverse range of capabilities. Because of these possibilities, the sheer bulk of the Agenda documentation can be intimidating to new users. Do not be put off by this apparent complexity.

Using Agenda—and using it productively—requires the mastery of only a few basic skills. You need to be able to enter items into an Agenda database. You need to assign items to categories, which are used as section heads and in columns in your views of the database. And you need to be able to create new views of the information in the database. Once you have mastered these skills, you can begin taking advantage of the organizational capabilities of Agenda. Then, as you work with Agenda, you can gradually learn about and use the more powerful features of the program.

This book is designed to facilitate learning Agenda gradually. The next chapter presents the basics needed to get started running Agenda: installing the program, starting Agenda, and performing some basic operations that are required throughout the program.

The second section of the book gets you into using Agenda. Chapters 3 through 6 present the fundamental operations, including entering items, attaching notes, assigning items to categories using sections and columns, and examining information by creating views. These are the fundamental skills necessary to use Agenda effectively.

The remaining chapters in the second section address additional capabilities of Agenda that new users will soon wish to master. Chapter 7 describes the use of the Category Manager to manage the category hierarchy. Chapter 8 explains how to print out information, and Chapter 9 covers the management of Agenda database files. After working through the topics covered in the second section, you will be a skilled user of Agenda.

The third section of the book addresses advanced features of Agenda. Chapter 10 examines Agenda's capabilities for using dates and describes their use. Advanced category assignment features, such as conditions and actions, are covered in Chapter 11. Chapter 12 explains how to import existing text files into an Agenda database and how to export information from one Agenda database to another. Chapter 13 discusses two accessory programs that make it easier to import information into Agenda databases. Macros, which provide capabilities for automating repetitive tasks, are introduced in Chapter 14. The final chapter in the third section covers special features, including those for customizing the operation of Agenda for specific applications.

Once you are familiar with using Agenda, you will be interested in learning how to develop a wider range of applications for the program. The final section of the book shows you how to develop Agenda applications for a variety of problems. Specific examples are provided of the ways in which Agenda can be employed to deal with a wide range of problems. This section provides ideas and specific examples of ways to use Agenda to effectively manage the information with which you regularly work.

The information in the chapters is organized to serve as a useful reference for the user of Agenda as well as a tool for learning how to use the program. For example, Chapter 6 explains how to create views to examine the information in an Agenda database. As you work with Agenda, if you encounter questions during the creation of views, you can turn to this chapter to see explanations and examples that answer your question.

To get the quickest possible introduction to Agenda, use the book in the following manner:

1. Work through Chapter 2 to learn the necessary information required to run Agenda.
2. Work through the first part of Chapter 3 on entering and editing items.
3. Work through the first two parts of Chapter 4 on creating and changing sections and placing items in sections.
4. Work through the first part of Chapter 5 on creating and using columns.
5. Work through the first two parts of Chapter 6 on creating and using views.
6. Work through the first part of Chapter 8 on printing views.

These sections provide the absolute basics required to effectively begin using Agenda. The remainder of those chapters and the additional chapters can be read as the need arises.

The chapters in the second section of the book on using Agenda explain the use of the program by addressing a problem. You will learn the most by working through the example as it is presented in these chapters, actually creating, using, and modifying the Agenda database as instructed. There is no substitute for actually using the program to learn its operation.

A number of typographical conventions are used throughout the following chapters to highlight the instructions on the use of Agenda. Information that is to be typed in is shown in different, narrow letters, such as the following:

Prepare report on Walker project by next Thursday.

Instructions to press a special key on the keyboard, such as ENTER or PGUP are shown in small capital letters. When pressing a special key is indicated as part of the entry of other text, the name of the key is displayed in angle brackets, such as the following:

<ENTER>

Thus, the instruction to enter the text shown above and press the ENTER key would be

Prepare report on Walker project by next Thursday.<ENTER>

Finally, Agenda command settings and options are always displayed in italicized type. Thus, *Column type:* would be one of the settings made when creating a new column with the Category Column New command.

# 2

# RUNNING AGENDA

GETTING started with any program involves setting up the program for operation, learning how to start it and exit from it when you are through, and understanding the basic operations that are performed throughout the program. This chapter gets you started running Agenda. The first section describes installing the Agenda program. The second section explains the process of entering and exiting Agenda so you can begin working with the program. The final section shows how to perform basic operations required throughout Agenda, such as getting help, using function keys, entering commands, and responding to prompts for information.

## INSTALLING AGENDA

Installing Agenda is a simple procedure handled by a special program that comes with Agenda. Most users will be installing Agenda on hard disks. Some users will be able to use Agenda on floppy disk systems, but they must follow a special installation procedure.

To use Agenda, you need an IBM PC compatible computer running the MS-DOS or PC DOS operating systems, versions 2.0 or later. The Agenda documentation states that a hard disk is required for Agenda. However, if you have a floppy-disk based system with disk capacity of at least 720K (such as many laptops), you can also use Agenda. The documentation also states that a minimum memory size of 640K RAM is needed for Agenda. Agenda can operate in 512K of RAM, but then you will not be able to use the accessory programs at the same time you use Agenda.

When installing Agenda, you must enter your name and company name. These are permanently recorded in the program to identify the copy of Agenda as yours. After you do this, Agenda is no longer copy-protected. You may freely copy the files on the Agenda disks using the normal DOS commands.

This section describes the installation of Agenda on hard disk systems and floppy disk systems. Instructions are also provided for the installation of the optional accessory programs.

## Hard Disk Installation

The entire process of installing Agenda on your hard disk is handled by a special installation program, which does all the work for you. You simply run the program, respond to the prompts, and change the disks as instructed. The procedure is as follows:

- Start DOS and change the default to the floppy disk drive you will be using for installation. For example, if you will be using the A: drive, type in A: and press ENTER.
- Place the Agenda Install Disk into the selected floppy disk drive. If you are using the 5¼-inch disks, the disk will be labeled Install and Utility Disk. If you are using the 3½-inch disks, the disk will be labeled the Install, Program, and Utility Disk.
- Run the Agenda installation program by typing install and pressing ENTER.
- Follow the instructions presented by the installation program. You will be prompted to enter your name and your company name to permanently identify your copy of Agenda. If you are using Agenda as an individual, enter your name twice.
- When prompted for the hard disk onto which Agenda is to be installed, you can press ENTER to accept installation on the C: drive, which is the default. Otherwise, you need to type in the letter designating the hard disk drive.
- When prompted for the directory into which Agenda is to be installed, you can press ENTER to accept installation into a directory named AGENDA. Otherwise, you need to type in the name to be given to the directory. The installation program will use an existing directory or create the directory if it does not yet exist.
- The installation program now copies files from all of the Agenda disks to the specified directory. Change disks as instructed by the program.

This completes the installation of Agenda onto your hard disk. The program is now ready to run. The Agenda program files are not copy-protected. They may be copied and the hard disk may be backed up with any software.

An optional but useful addition when installing Agenda on a hard disk is the inclusion of a DOS PATH command to enable Agenda to be started from any drive or directory. If Agenda were installed in a directory named AGENDA, the PATH command

PATH C: \ AGENDA

would allow the program to be started from any directory.

The PATH command can be included in an AUTOEXEC.BAT file so that it will be executed whenever the system is started. If you already have a PATH command for programs in other directories, the path designation

C: \ AGENDA

can be added to that command so that the AGENDA directory is included in the list of paths which DOS searches for executable files.

## Floppy Disk Installation

The Agenda documentation states that a hard disk is required to run Agenda, but you can run Agenda on some floppy disk systems. You need to have floppy disk drives with capacities of at least 720K. Users of traditional machines with two 360K floppy disk drives will thus be unable to use Agenda, but those with large capacity floppies can use Agenda. In particular, laptop users with two 720K 3½-inch drives can readily use Agenda on their machines.

The Agenda installation program copies all of the files on the Agenda disks to a single large directory on a hard disk. All of these files will not fit on a floppy, but all are not needed to run Agenda. The installation program thus cannot be used to perform the entire installation of Agenda on a floppy disk system. Instead, a two-part procedure requires using the installation program to place your identification into the program and then using the DOS COPY command to copy individual files.

To enter your identification into the Agenda program, follow these steps:

- Start DOS and select the A: drive as the default drive. If necessary, type in A: and press ENTER.
- Place the Agenda Install disk into the A: drive. If you are using the 5¼-inch disks, the disk will be labeled Install and Utility Disk. If you are using the 3½-inch disk, the disk will be labeled the Install, Program, and Utility Disk.
- Run the Agenda installation program by typing install and pressing ENTER.
- Follow the instructions presented by the installation program. You will be prompted to enter your name and your company name to permanently identify

your copy of Agenda. If you are using Agenda as an individual, enter your name twice.

- When you are asked whether you want to install Agenda on your hard disk, type N and press ENTER. This concludes the operation of the installation program.

Now create your Agenda program disk by following this procedure:

- Place a blank, formatted disk into the B: drive.
- With the Install and Utility Disk (5¼-inch) or Install, Program, and Utility Disk (3½-inch) still in the A: drive, copy the file AGENDA.RI to the B: drive with this command:

    copy agenda.ri b: < ENTER >

- Copy the printer definition file or files you need to use to the B: drive. The printer definition files begin with the name of the printer and have the extension .PDF. Use the DOS directory command to examine the list of .PDF files on the disk in the A: drive and select the file or files you wish to copy. If you cannot find a file for your printer, you can copy the generic printer definition file named PRINTER.PDF. Copy the file or files to the B: drive using commands of this form:

    copy printer.pdf b: < ENTER >

- If you are using 5¼-inch disks, replace the disk in the A: drive with the Agenda Program Disk. If you are using 3½-inch disks, leave the Agenda Install, Program, and Utility Disk in the A: drive.
- Copy the Agenda program file to the B: drive using this command:

    copy agenda.exe b: < ENTER >

- Replace the disk in the A: drive with the Agenda Help Disk (5¼-inch) or the Agenda Applications, Help, and Demo Disk (3½-inch).
- Copy the Agenda help file to the B: drive using this command:

    copy agenda.hlp b: < ENTER >

This completes the installation of Agenda onto the floppy disk in the B: drive. You can now use this disk to run Agenda. Place the disk into the A: drive, and at the A > prompt, type in agenda and press ENTER. You will store your Agenda database files on floppy disks in the B: drive.

Every time you open an Agenda database which is stored on a floppy disk, Agenda will display a message warning you not to remove the disk with the Agenda database while you are working with that database. Since Agenda routinely accesses the database files during Agenda execution, removing or changing disks could create problems.

The installation procedure for floppy disks copies the basic files required for the operation of Agenda to your new Agenda program disk. Special utilities and all of the applications database files are not copied. If you wish to use special utilities, they may be copied from your original Agenda disks to your Agenda program disks. For example, importing ASCII text files into Agenda, described in Chapter 12, requires the use of the TXT2STF.EXE conversion program. This may be copied from the Utility Disk to your Agenda program disk. If you want to use any of the example applications database files, copy the desired files to another disk and place that disk into the B: drive to work with those databases.

## Accessory Installation

Agenda includes two accessory programs which may be executed and then called up in other programs to aid in transferring information to Agenda. These are the Items accessory and the Clipboard accessory, and Chapter 13 describes how they are used. If you wish to install the accessory programs now, follow this procedure:

- Start DOS and change the default to the floppy disk drive you will be using for installation. For example, if you will be using the A: drive, type in A: and press ENTER.
- Place the Agenda Install disk into the selected floppy disk drive. If you are using the 5¼-inch disks, the disk will be labeled Install and Utility Disk. If you are using the 3½-inch disk, the disk will be labeled the Install, Program, and Utility Disk.
- Determine the hard disk drive on which the accessories are to be installed. For most users, this will be drive C:. (The accessory programs are not very workable on a floppy disk system.)
- Execute the ITEMS.BAT batch file by typing the file name followed by the hard disk drive on which you want the accessories installed. To install the accessories on the C: drive, for example, type

    items c: <ENTER>

The batch file creates the required directories and copies the necessary files. The accessory programs are now ready to use. Information on executing and using the accessories can be found in Chapter 13.

## STARTING AND EXITING AGENDA

The procedure required to run the Agenda program depends upon whether or not you have entered a PATH command that specifies the AGENDA directory.

If such a path has not been specified, you must first change to the directory in which the Agenda program is located. At the DOS prompt, enter this command to change to the AGENDA directory:

cd agenda <ENTER>

The <ENTER> means you are to press the ENTER key after typing the preceding characters. Then you can start the program by typing

agenda <ENTER>

The program will begin executing.

    Alternatively, if you have executed a PATH command that includes the directory in which the Agenda program is located, you can start Agenda from any directory. Start Agenda simply by typing

agenda <ENTER>

The program will begin executing.

    Agenda first displays its opening screen, shown in Fig. 2-1, on which you must specify the file name of the Agenda database with which you want to work. The file name for the database is entered near the bottom of the screen. The first time you run Agenda, the file name area is empty. After the first time, however, the file name for the database you last worked with appears on the File Name line when you start Agenda.

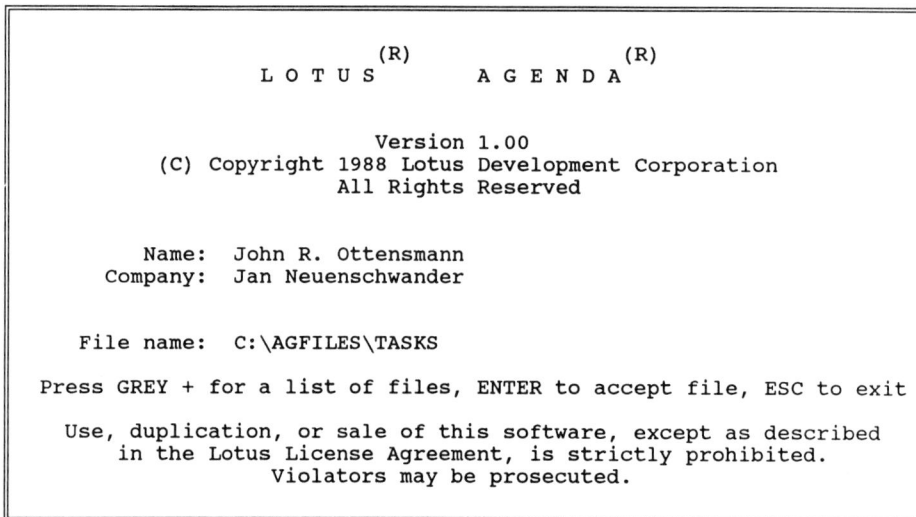

```
                          (R)              (R)
               L O T U S        A G E N D A


                     Version 1.00
         (C) Copyright 1988 Lotus Development Corporation
                  All Rights Reserved


           Name:   John R. Ottensmann
        Company:   Jan Neuenschwander


      File name:   C:\AGFILES\TASKS

    Press GREY + for a list of files, ENTER to accept file, ESC to exit

       Use, duplication, or sale of this software, except as described
          in the Lotus License Agreement, is strictly prohibited.
                     Violators may be prosecuted.
```

Fig. 2-1. *The Agenda opening screen.*

You have three options regarding the database to use when starting Agenda: *(1)* you can work with the Agenda database that you last used, displayed on the File Name line; *(2)* you can work with some other existing Agenda database; *(3)* you can create a new Agenda database.

To begin work with the last-used Agenda database displayed on the File Name line, simply press ENTER. Agenda opens the database and displays the information you were working with when you last worked with Agenda.

To work with some other existing Agenda database, you can either type in the file name (and path, if needed) for the database or you can select the database from lists displayed by Agenda. To directly type in the name of the database, just begin typing the characters. The new characters replace the existing file name on the File Name line. Press ENTER to enter the file name and display the complete path, and press ENTER once again to open that Agenda database. If the database is in the same directory as the last-used Agenda database, you need only enter the file name. If the database is on another drive or in another directory, you have to enter a complete path name.

It is generally much easier to enter another Agenda database by selecting the file name from lists of Agenda databases. To display the list of Agenda databases in the current directory (the one in which the last-used database is stored), press the GREY PLUS key, the plus key on the far right side of the keyboard on the numeric keypad. A window pops up on the screen displaying the file names of the Agenda databases in that directory. You can use the UP and DOWN arrow keys to highlight the desired file name. Press ENTER to select the file name and enter it on the File Name line of the opening screen. Press ENTER one more time to accept this file name and open the database.

If the Agenda database you want is not in the currently displayed directory, you can easily move to the correct directory. The listing displayed by pressing GREY PLUS also includes the parent directory of the current directory and any subdirectories. If you highlight one of these and press ENTER, Agenda switches to that directory and displays any Agenda database file names in that new directory. Once again, you need only highlight the desired file name and press ENTER. Using this capability to change directories, it is possible to move to any directory on your hard disk.

To create a new Agenda database, type in a file name for it. When you begin typing, any file name displayed on the File Name line is erased, and the characters you type are entered there. The file name must be a normal DOS file name, beginning with a letter and consisting of up to eight characters. Do not enter a period or an extension. Agenda automatically provides its own extensions for use in storing the database files. For example, to create a new database named TASKS, type in tasks and press ENTER.

You have the option of entering a path name that includes the drive and/or directory specification for the Agenda database. If you do not enter a path, the new database files will be created in the directory containing the database currently listed on the File Name line. The first time you start Agenda, when the File Name line is blank, the new database files will be created in the directory from which you started Agenda, unless you enter a path.

After typing in the name for the new database, press ENTER once to enter that name and display the complete path name for the new database. Press EN-TER a second time to accept the new database name and begin creating a new Agenda database. At this point, Agenda displays a box prompting for a descriptive title for the database and an optional password, as shown in Fig. 2-2. With the highlighted area to the right of Description, type in any desired text to describe the new database and press ENTER.

If you want password protection, move the highlighted area down by pressing the DOWN arrow, type in the desired password, and press ENTER. This password must be entered each time the database is opened. If you do not want password protection, no action is needed. Press function key F9 (ACCEPT) to accept the information in the box and open the new database. Function key F9 is used frequently throughout Agenda to accept the information in a box and proceed to the next step.

After a database has been opened, a view of the information in it is displayed and you are ready to begin working with Agenda. Figure 2-3 shows the empty Initial View displayed when a new database has been created. You work with Agenda using these views and occasionally other screens displaying other features of Agenda.

When you have finished working with Agenda, you use the Quit command to exit the program. While working with any view, press function key F10 (MENU) to display the menu of view commands and then press Q to select the Quit command. Agenda automatically saves the database with which you have been working and exits to DOS. There is no need to separately save the database prior to exiting Agenda.

To briefly summarize the procedures for running Agenda, first type in AGENDA and press ENTER. Then select the file name of the Agenda database with which you wish to work by accepting the file name displayed, displaying lists of Agenda files by pressing GREY PLUS and selecting from the lists, or typing in the file name. Pressing ENTER opens the database and takes you into the Agenda program, with an intermediate prompt for additional information for new databases. To exit

```
╔══════════════════════════New Database══════════════════════════╗
║ ┌─────────────────────────────────────────────────────────────┐ ║
║ │ Description:                                                  │ ║
║ │ Password:                                                     │ ║
║ │        ══════Press F9 when done, ESC to cancel══════          │ ║
║ └─────────────────────────────────────────────────────────────┘ ║
╚═════════════════════════════════════════════════════════════════╝
```

Fig. 2-2. *The New Database box for the entry of a description and a password for the database.*

```
┌──────────────────────────────────────────────────────────────────────┐
│                                                                        │
│  File: C:\AGFILES\TASKS                              03/09/89   14:03   │
│  View: Initial View                                                    │
│  ════════════════════════════════════════════════════════════════════ │
│  Untitled                                                              │
│                                                                        │
│                                                                        │
│                                                                        │
│                                                                        │
│                                                                        │
│                                                                        │
│                                                                        │
│                                                                        │
│                                                                        │
│                                                                        │
│                                                                        │
│  ═F1══╤══F2══╤══F3══╤══F4══╤══F5══╤══F6══╤══F7══╤══F8══╤══F9══╤═F10══   │
│   Help ║ Edit ║ Copy ║ Done ║ Note ║ Move ║ Mark ║Vw Mgr║Cat Mgr║ Menu │
│                                                                        │
└──────────────────────────────────────────────────────────────────────┘
```

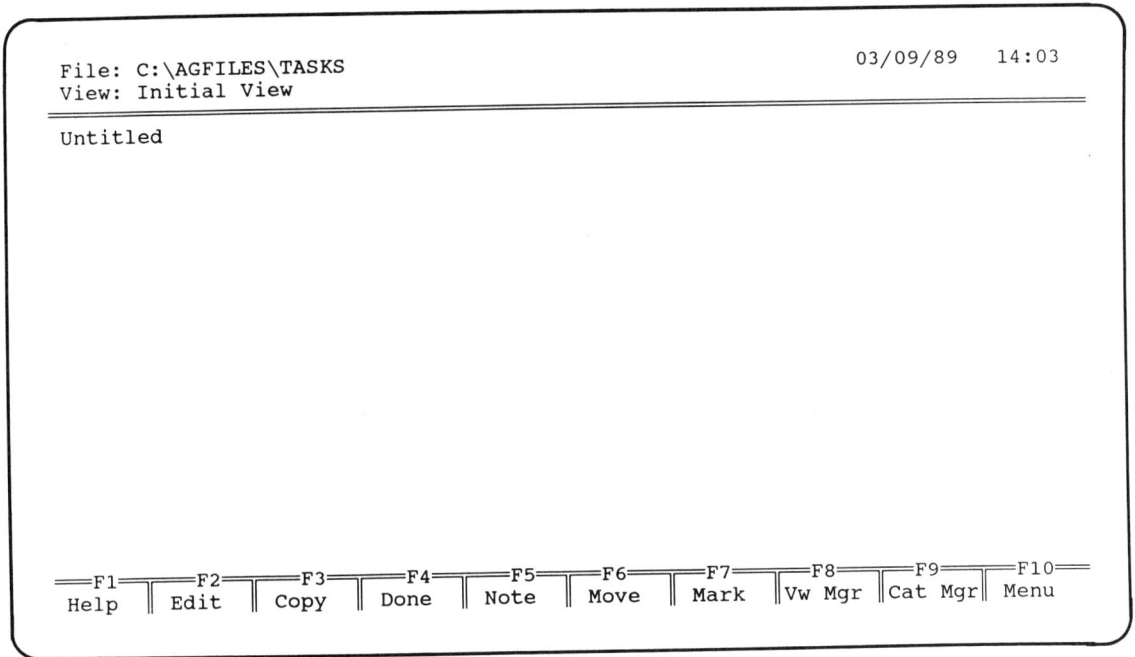

Fig. 2-3. *The Initial view presented after opening a new Agenda database.*

Agenda, press F10 and then Q to select the Quit command. File saving is handled automatically.

## BASIC OPERATIONS

Before actually using Agenda to create databases and manipulate information, you should familiarize yourself with some of the fundamental procedures for accomplishing tasks in Agenda. You should know how to obtain help from the program, how to use the function keys and the other special keys on the keyboard, how to execute Agenda commands, and how to respond to Agenda's prompts for information. By going over these basics first, you will be better able to move ahead in learning Agenda without having to bother with these details.

### Obtaining Help

Function key F1 is the HELP key throughout Agenda. Pressing F1 enters Agenda's help system and displays one page of information on the screen. For example, pressing F1 while examining a view—which is what you are doing when you first enter Agenda—displays the screen of information shown in Fig. 2-4.

Agenda's help system is *context-sensitive*. That is, the information displayed depends upon what you are doing in Agenda at the time you press the HELP key. For example, if you are working with the Print command, pressing F1 displays information discussing printing operations in Agenda.

```
======================= View =======================
  An Agenda database is made up of items assigned to one or more categories.
  An item can be any text up to 350 characters.  For longer text, you can use
  NOTE (F5) to attach a note to an item.

  You work with the items in your database through views.  A view shows items
  grouped into sections.  Each section head is a category in your database. A
  section displays all the items assigned to that category.  Using different
  categories as section heads, you can create many views of the same database.

  A view can also include columns.  Columns show dates for items or list more
  categories to which items are assigned.  Column heads are also categories.

  In a view, press INSERT to add an item, EDIT (F2) to edit an item, DELETE
  to remove an item, and DISCARD (ALT F4) to discard it from the database.
  Menu commands and function keys let you perform many other tasks.   Press
  MENU (F10) to see the view menu.

  View Function Keys          Inserting Items         Inserting Sections
  View Special Keys           Editing Items           Inserting Columns
  View Accelerator Keys       Removing Items          Agenda Overview
  View Menu Commands          Discarding Items        Using Help
  Attaching Notes             Retrieving Items        Help Index
  ================ Press ESC to return to Agenda ================
```

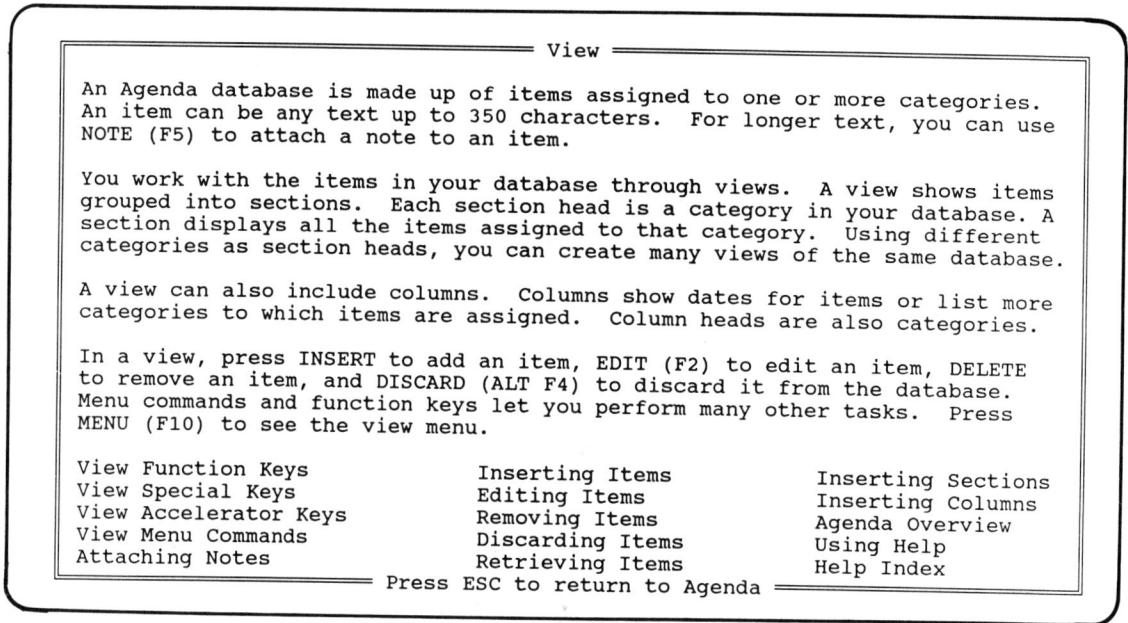

Fig. 2-4. *The help screen displayed when F1 (HELP) is pressed from a view.*

Every help screen contains one or more references to related help screens. This allows you to locate more specific information to address your question. Move the highlighted area to the desired reference using the four arrow keys as appropriate. The END key takes you directly to the last reference, and the HOME key moves you back to the first reference. Pressing ENTER selects the highlighted topic and displays the associated help screen.

You can continue moving around through the help system by selecting topics and pressing ENTER. If you wish to look at the previous help screen, press the BACKSPACE key. BACKSPACE takes you back through the sequence of help screens displayed during the current operation of the help system.

The final reference on every help screen is to the Help Index. The Help Index selection displays a listing of all of the major help topics in the Agenda help system. From the Help Index, you can select other topics and obtain additional information.

To leave the help system and return to your work in Agenda, press ESCAPE, as indicated on the bottom of each help screen. ESCAPE removes the help screen and takes you back to where you were when you initially requested help by pressing F1.

The ESCAPE key is a universal "back out" key throughout the Agenda program. Pressing ESCAPE always takes you out of the current operation and back one step. Thus, if you have gotten to someplace in Agenda where you do not wish to be, ESCAPE will back you out. Sometimes you need to press ESCAPE several times to completely back out of some of the more complex operations.

## Using the Function Keys

Agenda makes extensive use of the function keys F1 through F10 to perform many different operations. In addition, there are alternate-function key combinations in which the function keys are used in conjunction with the ALT key to perform additional operations. The alternate-function key combinations are entered by holding down the ALT key, just as you hold down the SHIFT key, and then pressing the appropriate function key.

The operations performed by the function keys change depending upon just where you are in Agenda and what task is being performed. A complete list of function key operations is provided in Appendix B. To provide assistance in using the function keys, Agenda displays the current operations associated with each of them across the bottom of the screen. The normal display of function keys shows the operations that will be performed when a function key is depressed by itself, without holding down the ALT key. To get the alternate function key combinations, hold down the ALT key. You will see the alternate-function key operations displayed. These are the operations that will be performed when a function key is pressed while holding down the ALT key.

Figure 2-5 illustrates the function key assignments when working in a view in Agenda. The top row is the list of function key assignments normally displayed on the bottom of the screen. For example, function key F10 is the MENU key and is used to display the menu of Agenda commands available from within a View. Pressing F10 displays the menu of View commands at the top of the screen.

The bottom row in Fig. 2-5 shows the alternate-function key assignments when working in a view. Pressing the ALT key while in a view changes the function key map at the bottom of the screen to display these assignments, which are for the function keys used in conjunction with the ALT key. For example, ALT-F4 is the DISCARD key, used to eliminate entries from the database. Holding down the ALT key and pressing F4 causes the currently highlighted entry to be discarded from an Agenda database.

A few of the function keys have the same meaning throughout most of Agenda. F1 is always the HELP key and is used to display information from the help system. F2 is the EDIT key, which allows the editing of text. Function key F10, the MENU

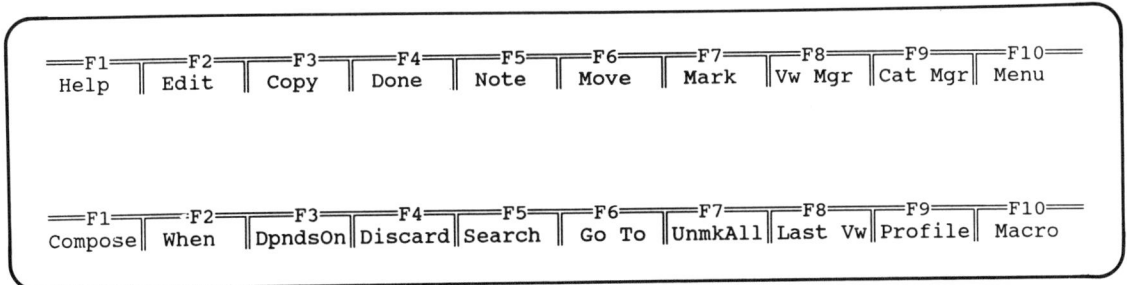

| =F1= | =F2= | =F3= | =F4= | =F5= | =F6= | =F7= | =F8= | =F9= | =F10= |
|------|------|------|------|------|------|------|------|------|-------|
| Help | Edit | Copy | Done | Note | Move | Mark | Vw Mgr | Cat Mgr | Menu |

| =F1= | =F2= | =F3= | =F4= | =F5= | =F6= | =F7= | =F8= | =F9= | =F10= |
|------|------|------|------|------|------|------|------|------|-------|
| Compose | When | DpndsOn | Discard | Search | Go To | UnmkAll | Last Vw | Profile | Macro |

Fig. 2-5. *The View function key designations as normally displayed (top) and as displayed when the ALT key is pressed (bottom).*

key, serves to display a menu of commands (assuming that you are not already working with a command).

Three alternate-function key combinations also perform the same operations throughout most of Agenda. ALT-F1 (COMPOSE), is used to enter international and special characters. ALT-F4 is the DISCARD key, used to eliminate information from the database. ALT-F10 is the MACRO key, used to create, edit, and run Agenda macros.

The specific use of the function keys to perform various tasks is explained throughout the chapters addressing the use of Agenda. This overview is just an introduction to explain the function key maps and the use of the ALT key with the function keys throughout Agenda.

## Using the Special Keys

Like the function keys, various other special keys, such as those on the cursor control keypad, sometimes have different meanings depending upon what you are doing in Agenda. Most of the time the functions associated with these keys will be familiar to you if you have used computers. For example, when entering or editing text, the BACKSPACE key deletes the character to the left of the cursor and moves the cursor back. This is exactly the way BACKSPACE works in nearly all personal computer software.

The specific operation of the various keys are discussed in the course of explaining how to perform operations in Agenda. The special key assignments are also summarized in Appendix B.

Many of the special keys have much the same meaning and perform the same kinds of operations throughout most of Agenda. For example, the UP, DOWN, RIGHT, and LEFT arrow keys move the cursor or highlighted area one unit in the appropriate direction. The nature of the movement varies depending on what you are doing at the time, but should be obvious.

The other keys on the cursor control keypad provide for moving up and down through longer sequences of information. PGUP and PGDN move up and down one screen at a time. The HOME and END keys move to the top and bottom of any groups of information that may be displayed. CTRL-HOME and CTRL-END move to the beginning and end of the information, to the extreme top and bottom. These key combinations are entered by holding down the control key (CTRL) and then pressing the HOME or END keys.

The CTRL key can also be used in conjunction with RIGHT and LEFT arrow keys to move as far as possible to the right or left. CTRL RIGHT moves all the way to the right, and CTRL LEFT moves all the way to the left.

The ESCAPE key is always used to go back to the previous step in any operation. It can be employed to back out of virtually any operation in Agenda.

## Commands and Menus

A variety of operations in Agenda are performed using commands selected from menus. Agenda has three distinct sets of menu commands: commands that can be used while working within a view (the largest set of commands), commands that can be used while working within the category manager, and commands that can be used while working with a note.

In all three situations, function key F10 (MENU) displays the menu of commands available at that particular time. While working within a view, for example, pressing F10 displays the menu of View commands on the top lines of the screen, as shown in Fig. 2-6.

The command menu works exactly like the command menu in Lotus 1-2-3 and in many other programs. The top line of the command menu displays the list of command options from which a selection can be made. One of the choices will always be highlighted. In Fig. 2-6, the first command selection, File, is highlighted. The second line displays further information about the highlighted command. In the case of a command for which further selections must be made, the options are listed on the second line. For the File command, the command options Open, Backup, Use-Backup, and so forth are displayed on the second line, as shown in Fig. 2-6. For commands without additional options, the second line describes the highlighted command.

Different commands can be highlighted by using the RIGHT and LEFT arrow keys to move the highlighted area back and forth on the first line. As different commands are selected, the appropriate lists of options or descriptions are displayed on the second line of the menu.

The selection of a command can be accomplished in two different ways. First, the desired command can be highlighted by pressing the RIGHT or LEFT arrow keys, and then that command can be selected by pressing ENTER. Alternatively, a command can be selected directly by pressing the first letter of the command (each of the commands begins with a different letter). Thus, to select the Print command, you can either press the RIGHT arrow key four times to highlight Print and then press ENTER, or you can just press P. The first approach displays the descriptive information on the second line first. The second method is quicker and is favored by experienced users. Both approaches accomplish the same selection. Throughout this book, when you are instructed to select a command, either approach may be employed.

```
File  View  Item  Category  Print  Utility  System  Quit
Open, Backup, Use-Backup, Copy, Delete, Transfer, Note, Info

Untitled
```

Fig. 2-6. *The menu of View commands.*

When a command is selected, one of two things can happen. Either further command choices can be presented in the same menu form or the execution of the command can begin. For those commands for which further options are displayed on the second line, when the command is selected, those options become menu choices on the first line of the menu. For example, when the File command is selected, Open, Backup, Use-Backup, and so forth become the command options displayed on the first line, as choices, with the first highlighted. Information about these commands or about further options is then displayed on the second line. Selecting a command from such a second-level menu works exactly like selecting it from the original menu. The desired command may either be selected by highlighting and pressing ENTER or by pressing the first letter of the command.

Some commands may involve several levels of menus and several levels of selection. At each level, the menu works in exactly the same way. You need to just proceed through the menus until the final selection is made and the command is executed.

When the final command option has been selected, execution of the command begins. Sometimes, the operation commences immediately. For example, when the Quit command is selected, Agenda saves the database file and exits, returning to the DOS prompt. More often, the selection of a command results in prompts for additional information being displayed in boxes in the middle of the screen. The procedures for responding to such selection and dialog boxes are described in the following section. Once the necessary responses have been given, the command is executed.

The complete menu trees for all of the Agenda commands—those executed from views, those available from the category manager, and those used from notes—are presented in Appendix A. The use of the various commands is explained throughout the book as the command functions are required.

## Selection and Dialog Boxes

The entry of a command in Agenda frequently results in prompts for additional information needed to execute it. These requests for further information are presented in boxes of varying sizes displayed in the middle of the screen. These may either be selection boxes requiring you to choose from a list of options, or dialog boxes involving more extended interaction and information entry.

The File Open command involves the use of a selection box. This command is used to save the current Agenda database and open another database, either new or existing. The command is entered by pressing the F10 (MENU) key in a view, selecting the File command from the initial menu, and then selecting the Open command from the subsequent menu. At this point, a selection box for the entry of the database file name is displayed as shown in Fig. 2-7.

The Select File box includes instructions for operation at the top of the box. To open an existing file, highlight that file in the box by pressing the UP and

```
Open  Backup  Use-Backup  Copy  Delete  Transfer  Note  Info
Switch to a new database, saving current database
┌────────────────────────────Select File════════════════════════════┐
U│Highlight file & press ENTER, or press INS to create new file      │
 │                                                                   │
 │  ..\            Parent directory                                  │
 │  SPECFILE\      <DIR>                                             │
 │                                                                   │
 │  APPNTMNT                                                         │
 │  CONTACTS                                                         │
 │  INFO                                                             │
 │  INVEN                                                            │
 │  ORGMGMT1                                                         │
 │  ORGMGMT2                                                         │
 │  PROJMGMT                                                         │
 │  RSRCH                                                            │
 │  TASKS                                                            │
 └═══════════════Current directory: C:\AGFILES\*.AGA════════════════┘


═F1═══╤══F2═══╤══F3═══╤══F4═══╤══F5═══╤══F6═══╤══F7═══╤══F8═══╤══F9═══╤═F10═══
Help  │       │       │Delete │       │Rename │       │       │Accept │
```

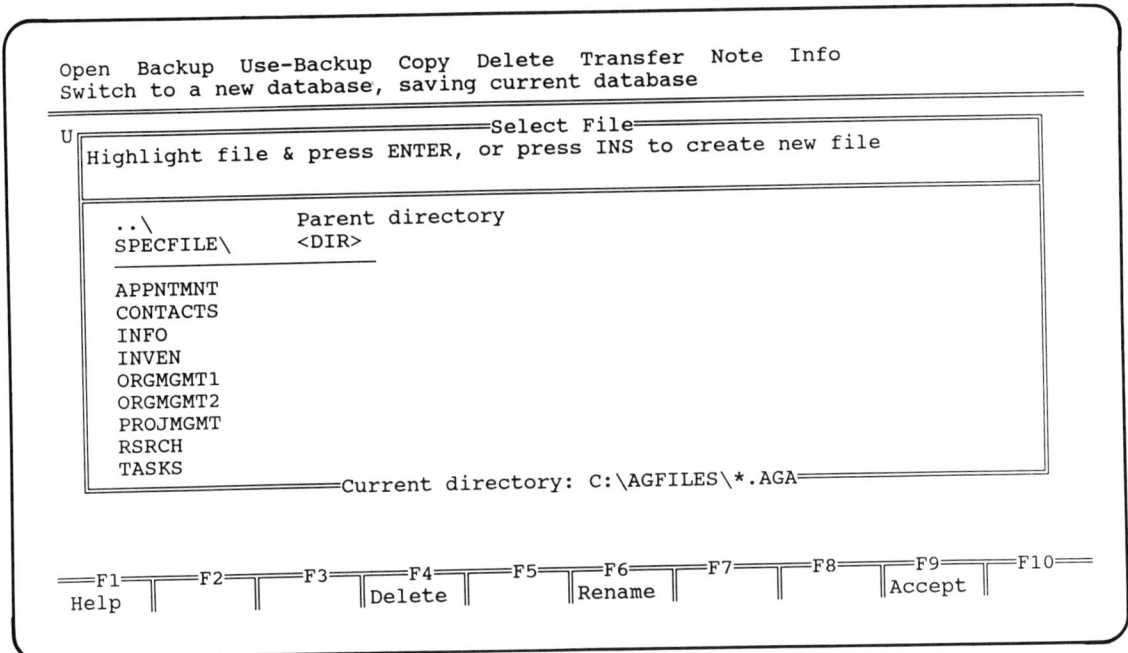

Fig. 2-7. *A selection box for selecting an Agenda file to be opened.*

DOWN arrows and then pressing ENTER. The file will be opened and displayed so that you can work with it. Alternatively, you can press INS (the Insert key) and then type in the file name, with the drive and directory specification, if needed. The latter procedure may be employed to open an existing file and to create a new database from within Agenda. (Obviously no selection from a list of existing database files is possible for the creation of a new database.)

All selection boxes displayed by Agenda commands work in pretty much the same way. You are presented with a list of options. Use the UP and DOWN arrows to highlight the desired option, then press ENTER to select that choice.

Many Agenda commands present dialog boxes that require the specification of multiple settings before the commands can be executed. Suppose, for example, you selected Category Column New to enter a new column into a view. (Information as to how and why you would do this is presented in Chapter 5.) A dialog box with a number of settings is displayed in the middle of the screen, as shown in Fig. 2-8. A highlighted bar may be moved to select the setting to be altered. The highlight is moved by using the UP and DOWN arrows.

To make changes to the *Display Format:* setting, press the DOWN arrow until the Actual Category option is highlighted. Then press the GREY PLUS key to display the list of options available for the *Display Format:* setting. A listing of the possibilities is shown in an additional box, a selection box, displayed on the screen as shown in Fig. 2-9. The current setting, *Actual Category*, is highlighted. To make another selection, use the UP and DOWN arrow keys to move the

New   Remove   Position   Format   Width
Insert a new column
_____
Untitled
_____

                        ══════════════New Column══════════════

                         Position:          Right of current column
                         Column type:       Category
                         Column head:
                         Format:            Actual category

                         Insert in:         All sections

                        ═════Press F9 when done, ESC to cancel═════


══F1══╤══F2══╤══F3══╤══F4══╤══F5══╤══F6══╤══F7══╤══F8════╤══F9═══╤══F10══
 Help  ║ Edit ║      ║      ║      ║      ║      ║Default║Accept║

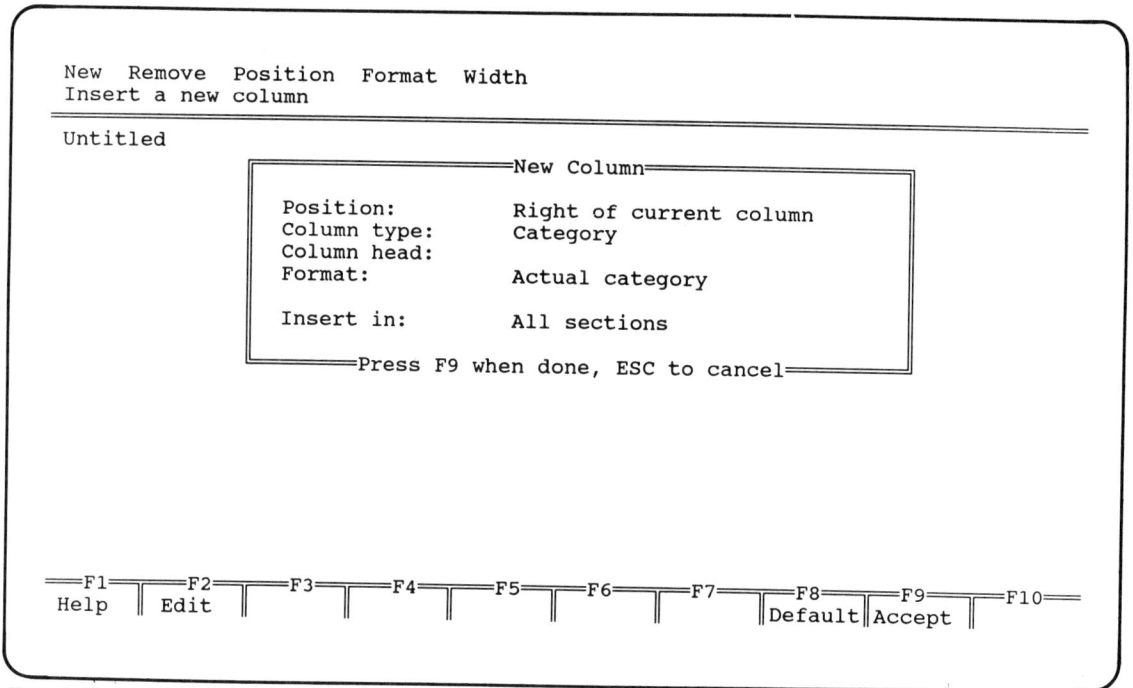

Fig. 2-8. *A dialog box for setting the characteristics for a new column.*

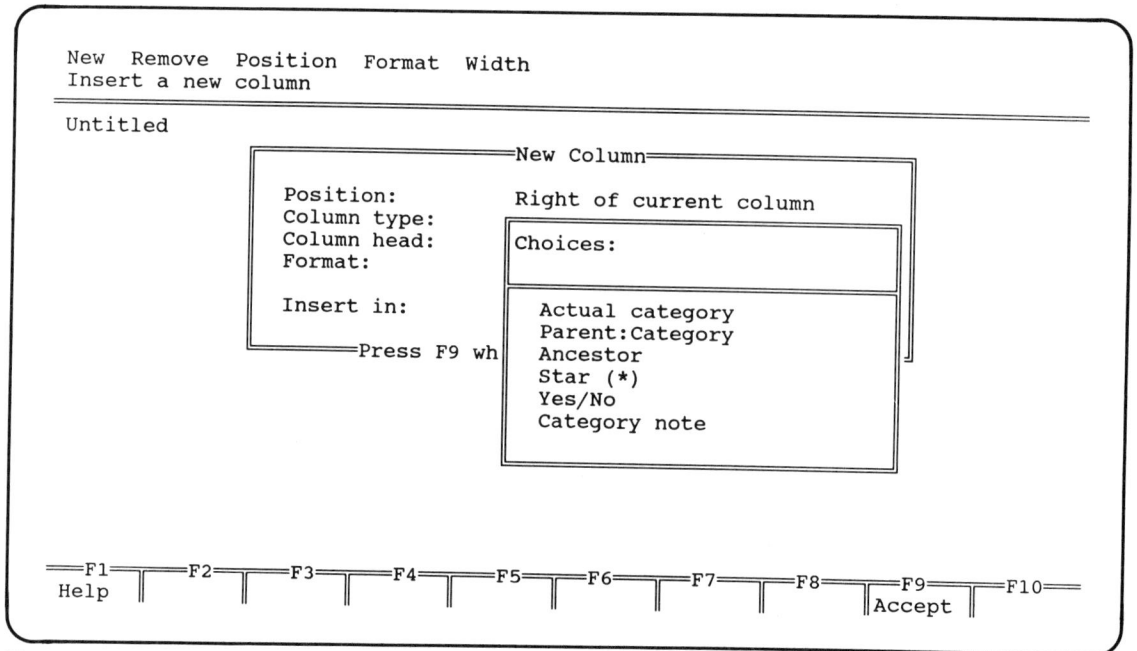

New   Remove   Position   Format   Width
Insert a new column
_____
Untitled
_____

                        ══════════════New Column══════════════

                         Position:          Right of current column
                         Column type:
                         Column head:       ┌─────────────────────────┐
                         Format:            │ Choices:                │
                                            │                         │
                         Insert in:         ├─────────────────────────┤
                        ═════Press F9 wh    │ Actual category         │
                                            │ Parent:Category         │
                                            │ Ancestor                │
                                            │ Star (*)                │
                                            │ Yes/No                  │
                                            │ Category note           │
                                            └─────────────────────────┘


══F1══╤══F2══╤══F3══╤══F4══╤══F5══╤══F6══╤══F7══╤══F8══╤══F9═══╤══F10══
 Help  ║      ║      ║      ║      ║      ║      ║      ║Accept║

Fig. 2-9. *A selection box for selecting the column format.*

highlighted area to select the desired setting. When the appropriate setting has been selected, press ENTER. The selection box disappears, and the new setting is displayed in the dialog box to the right of *Display Format:*.

This procedure is used to alter any of the settings in a dialog box. First, move the highlight to the setting to be changed. Press GREY PLUS to display the selection box with the possible choices. Move the highlight in the selection box to the correct setting, and press ENTER. The newly chosen setting is displayed in the dialog box. You can also change settings by pressing the first letter of the option, or by pressing the SPACE bar to cycle through the options.

When all of the settings in the dialog box are correct, press function key F9 to accept those settings and continue with the execution of the command. Agenda performs the command using the settings specified in the dialog box.

You do not need to be concerned about mastering the operations described in this chapter just now. You will be doing all of these things as you learn and use Agenda in the following chapters. The operations described in this chapter will quickly become second nature when you use Agenda.

# 3
## ENTERING INFORMATION

THE first step in using Agenda to manage information is entering the information to be managed. Information is entered in an Agenda database in the form of items and notes.

The central core of the information in the Agenda database is made up of items. Items are the relatively short text entries, assigned to categories. This assignment allows information in the database to be organized.

If you need to include text that is longer than an item, you can attach longer text entries to an item. These attached text entries are called notes. Notes allow longer text entries to be attached to categories as well as to items. You can look at the information in a note whenever you wish to see the additional text.

This chapter explains the procedures for entering and altering items and notes. The operations described here are necessary for including information in an Agenda database and for modifying that information. This chapter introduces the fundamental procedures for editing information and for dealing with groups of items.

## ENTERING AND EDITING ITEMS

The first step in working with Agenda is entering items into the Agenda database. Items are relatively short text entries, with a maximum of 350 characters (approximately four or five lines). In Agenda, items are always entered and displayed within views. Your hands-on learning in this chapter begins by entering several items into an example database. Since items sometimes need to be changed, the chapter also describes the procedures for editing items. The final part of the chapter explains the ways to discard items from a database, including the methods for working with groups of items and for recovering discarded items.

## Entering Items

The example database you begin to create here will be developed and used throughout the following chapters. You can learn the procedures by actually using Agenda to work through the example as it is developed. In that way, you become familiar with all of the major elements of Agenda by actually working with them.

Throughout the book, all of the instructions for working with the example are set off from the main text with at the beginning and end. If you choose not to work through the example on your computer, however, you can learn the procedures simply by reading the text and looking at the figures.

Begin the Agenda program as described in the preceding chapter. When the initial Agenda screen is displayed, type in

tasks

as the name for the new Agenda database you will be creating. You might want to enter a path specification to store the database in another directory. For example, if you had created a directory named \ AGFILES for all of your Agenda database files, you could type in

\ agfiles \ tasks

for the new database file name. Press ENTER twice to accept this file name and begin creating the new database. A box appears, prompting for a description of the database. In the highlighted box that appears to the right of Description, type in a description such as

Database for Working with Lotus Agenda

and press ENTER. Then press F9 (ACCEPT) to accept the information in the box. Agenda opens the new database.

The initial view of the new database is displayed on the screen. The view contains a single section heading, "Untitled," which is highlighted. You can change this heading to make it more appropriate and informative. Press function key F2 (EDIT) to edit this section heading. The heading appears on the second line, ready for editing. Press the DEL key to delete the original name and type in

Reports

and press ENTER to make the change.

Now you are ready to enter the first item into the database. Agenda always enters items below the current location of the highlighted area. Since the database currently includes only the single section heading ''Reports'' and no items, ''Reports'' is necessarily highlighted and the first item will be entered below this. To begin to enter an item, press INS, the Insert key (think of the process as one of *inserting* an item into the database). When INS is pressed, a dot, called a *bullet*, appears on the next line to mark the item, and the line is highlighted for the entry of text. To create the first item, type in the following text:

Prepare report on Walker project by next Thursday.

If you make a mistake in typing, press the BACKSPACE key to erase the error and make the correction. After the item has been typed in, press either ENTER or F9 (ACCEPT) to enter the item. Figure 3-1 shows the screen as it looks after the entry of the first item.

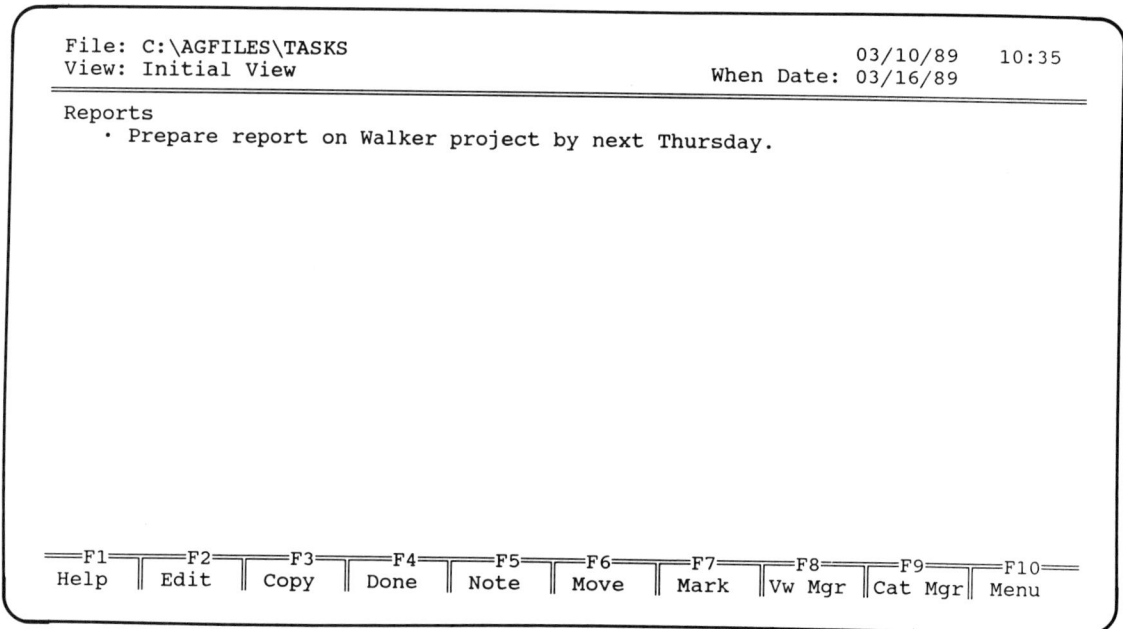

```
File: C:\AGFILES\TASKS                              03/10/89   10:35
View: Initial View                    When Date: 03/16/89
══════════════════════════════════════════════════════════════════
Reports
    · Prepare report on Walker project by next Thursday.




=F1══╤══F2══╤══F3══╤══F4══╤══F5══╤══F6══╤══F7══╤══F8══╤══F9══╤═F10══
Help ║ Edit ║ Copy ║ Done ║ Note ║ Move ║ Mark ║Vw Mgr║Cat Mgr║ Menu
```

Fig. 3-1. *The Tasks database after the entry of the first item.*

This is all that there is to entering items. To review, the steps in entering items are as follows:

- Press INS to start entry of the new item.
- Type in the text of the item.
- Press ENTER or F9 (ACCEPT) to enter the item into the database.

There are two ways to insert new items. The fastest way is to use INS, as shown. A second way is to use the Item New command on the menu of View commands. Selecting that command accomplishes the same thing as pressing INS, but with more work. Since item entry is one of the most common tasks in Agenda, you should learn and use the more direct procedure of pressing INS to insert new items. You will never have any reason to use the Item New command.

The first item you entered in the Tasks database should be highlighted. To enter another item under the first, press INS once again. A bullet appears on the next line for the new item, and that line is highlighted. Now type in this text for the following item:

Meet with Jim to discuss report on the Peters account.

Do not press ENTER or F9 (ACCEPT) to enter this item. Agenda provides a shortcut for entering a list of several items. Just press INS again. INS simultaneously enters the item just typed in and begins the process of entering a new item on the next line. Now type in the text for the next item:

Meeting to discuss project for James next Monday.

As you type items that are longer than one line, the item automatically wraps around to the next line. Press ENTER to enter this item.

As you have seen, Agenda enters items below the location of the highlighted area. If you want to enter an item at a different location, use the arrow keys to move the highlighted area.

To enter an item ahead of the last two items currently under the Reports heading in the Tasks database, move the highlighted block up to the first item by pressing the UP arrow twice. Press INS to begin inserting the new item. Type in the text for this item:

Call Jill Wilson at Walker by Tuesday to discuss the progress of the project.

Press ENTER to enter the item into the database. Figure 3-2 shows the appearance of the screen after the four items have been entered.

To summarize, the entry of new items requires only two special keys, INS and ENTER. The keys needed for item entry are summarized in Table 3-1.

## Editing Items

Errors in items or changes in circumstances might involve modifying items already entered into an Agenda database. Editing involves simple procedures that can be used both to modify items and to change other information as well.

Suppose a change at Walker requires that instead of calling Jill Wilson, as specified in the second item, you are to call Ron Smith instead. This item must be edited to reflect this change. Highlight the item to be edited, then press F2 (EDIT) to begin the editing process. The item highlight disappears and is replaced by a single-character highlight on the first

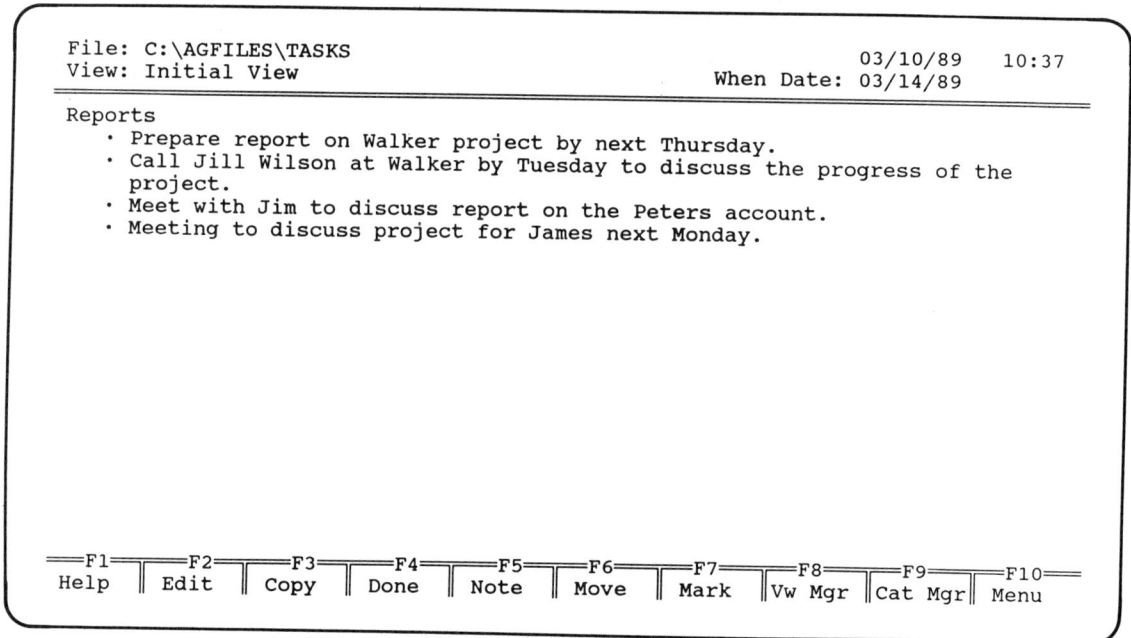

```
File: C:\AGFILES\TASKS                                      03/10/89    10:37
View: Initial View                          When Date: 03/14/89
================================================================================
Reports
    · Prepare report on Walker project by next Thursday.
    · Call Jill Wilson at Walker by Tuesday to discuss the progress of the
      project.
    · Meet with Jim to discuss report on the Peters account.
    · Meeting to discuss project for James next Monday.




=F1=====F2=====F3=====F4=====F5=====F6=====F7=====F8=====F9=====F10==
 Help  || Edit || Copy || Done || Note || Move || Mark ||Vw Mgr||Cat Mgr|| Menu
```

Fig. 3-2. *The Tasks database after the entry of four items.*

### Table 3-1. Special Keys Used for Entering Items.

| Key | Function |
| --- | --- |
| INS | Inserts new items below the highlighted entry. Also can be used to enter list of items without having to press ENTER after each item. |
| ENTER, F9 (ACCEPT) | Enter new item into database. |

letter of the item. This single-character highlight acts as a cursor. It can be moved around to edit the item much as you would use a cursor in a word processing program. Press the RIGHT arrow key until the cursor is on the first letter in ''Jill Wilson.'' Now press the DEL key repeatedly until all of the letters in ''Jill Wilson'' have been deleted. Figure 3-3 shows the Agenda screen at this point. Next, type in

Ron Smith

to insert this text at the cursor. The editing of the item is now complete; press ENTER to conclude the edit and enter the changed item into the database.

```
File: C:\AGFILES\TASKS                              03/10/89   Edit
View: Initial View                      When Date: 03/14/89

Reports
   • Prepare report on Walker project by next Thursday.
   • Call  at Walker by Tuesday to discuss the progress of the project.

   • Meet with Jim to discuss report on the Peters account.
   • Meeting to discuss project for James next Monday.




=F1=====F2======F3======F4======F5======F6======F7======F8======F9======F10==
 Help  | Paste | Copy  | Cut   | Note ||MakeCat| Mark  | Split ||Accept |
```

Fig. 3-3. *Editing the second item in the database.*

The procedure for editing is quite simple, as you have seen. It involves these steps:

- Highlight the item to be edited.
- Press F2 (EDIT) to begin editing.
- Move the character cursor around and insert or delete characters as required.
- Press ENTER to accept the changes made to the item. (If, however, you decide not to make the changes to the item, press ESC to back out of the edit and leave the item unchanged.)

A variety of special keys can be used during editing. The character cursor can be moved around with the arrow keys. The RIGHT and LEFT arrow keys move the cursor one character on the line. The UP and DOWN arrow keys move the cursor up one line or down one line in items with two or more lines. Other keys allow moves to be made more rapidly. CTRL-RIGHT and CTRL-LEFT move the cursor a word at a time. HOME and END move the cursor directly to the beginning and the end of a line. CTRL-HOME and CTRL-END move the cursor to the beginning and the end of the entire item.

Text can be deleted from the item using several special keys. DEL erases the character under the cursor, and BACKSPACE erases the character to the left of the cursor, just as with many word processors. To erase an entire word, use CTRL-BACKSPACE. CTRL-ENTER erases all of the text from the cursor to the end of the line.

To insert text while editing, simply type in the desired characters. The typed characters are inserted at the cursor and the text to the right of the cursor is pushed over. During editing, Agenda always functions in *insert mode*, in which new characters are inserted into the existing text. In insert mode, the new characters typed in do not overtype or replace existing text.

The special keys used for editing items are summarized in Table 3-2. You do not need to learn all of the keys to successfully edit text. Of course, you need to know F2 (EDIT) to begin the editing. The four arrow keys can be used move the cursor to any position in an item, and the DEL key will erase the character at the cursor. ENTER completes the editing.

You can perform any editing function by using F2 (EDIT), the four arrow keys, and the DEL key. All of the other keys merely allow some operations to be performed more quickly.

## Discarding and Marking Items

Sometimes you will want to eliminate items from an Agenda database. Agenda refers to the elimination of items as *discarding*. Items can be discarded one at a time or, alternatively, a number of items can be marked and discarded as a

## Table 3-2. Special Keys Used for Editing Items.

| Key | Function |
| --- | --- |
| F2 (EDIT) | Edit the highlighted item. |
| ENTER | Complete the edit; make the changes permanent. |
| ESC | Terminate edit; leave item unchanged. |
| RIGHT, LEFT | Move cursor one character. |
| UP, DOWN | Move cursor one line. |
| CTRL-RIGHT, CTRL-LEFT | Move cursor one word. |
| HOME, END | Move cursor to beginning, end of line. |
| CTRL-HOME, CTRL-END | Move cursor to beginning, end of item. |
| DEL | Erase character at cursor. |
| BACKSPACE | Erase character to left of cursor. |
| CTRL-BACKSPACE | Erase word. |
| CTRL-ENTER | Erase to end of line. |

group. Marking items in order to work with them as a group is important; it is used not only when discarding items, but in other operations with items as well.

When items are discarded from a database, Agenda places them in *Trash* and holds them for later retrieval in case you change your mind about discarding them. (The Agenda default is to hold items in Trash until midnight.) This section covers both discarding and undiscarding items.

Suppose you want to eliminate the item from the Tasks database beginning "Meet with Jim . . .." Use the arrow keys to highlight that item. Then use ALT-F4 (DISCARD) to eliminate the item, by holding down the ALT key and pressing F4. Agenda uses this alternate key combination to make it more difficult to discard an item accidentally. The discarded item is removed from the screen and is placed into Trash. Do not worry about losing the first item in the Tasks database when you discard it; this item will be retrieved later.

Agenda provides an alternative method of discarding items. The Item Discard command can be used to eliminate highlighted or marked items from a database. This command is entered by pressing F10 (MENU) and then selecting Item from the first menu and Discard from the second menu. This command performs exactly the same operation as pressing the ALT-F4 (DISCARD) function key. The choice of which procedure to use when discarding items is purely a matter of personal preference.

Now retrieve the discarded item from Trash and replace the item in the Tasks database. The Item Undiscard command is used to perform this function. The command inserts the items retrieved from Trash below the currently highlighted item. To replace the discarded item where it was deleted, move the highlight up to the item beginning "Call Ron Smith . . .." Press F10 (MENU) to display the menu of view commands. The list of commands is displayed on the top line of the screen; Item is the third choice. You select Item in one of two ways: either use the arrow keys to highlight Item and then press ENTER, or just press the first letter of the desired command, the letter I. Selecting Item displays the menu of the next level of commands on the top line, as shown in Fig. 3-4. Select Undiscard either by using the arrow keys to highlight it and pressing ENTER, or by pressing U. The item that had been discarded is replaced in the Tasks database.

If more than one item has been discarded, the Item Undiscard command can be used to retrieve either the last item that has been discarded in Trash or all

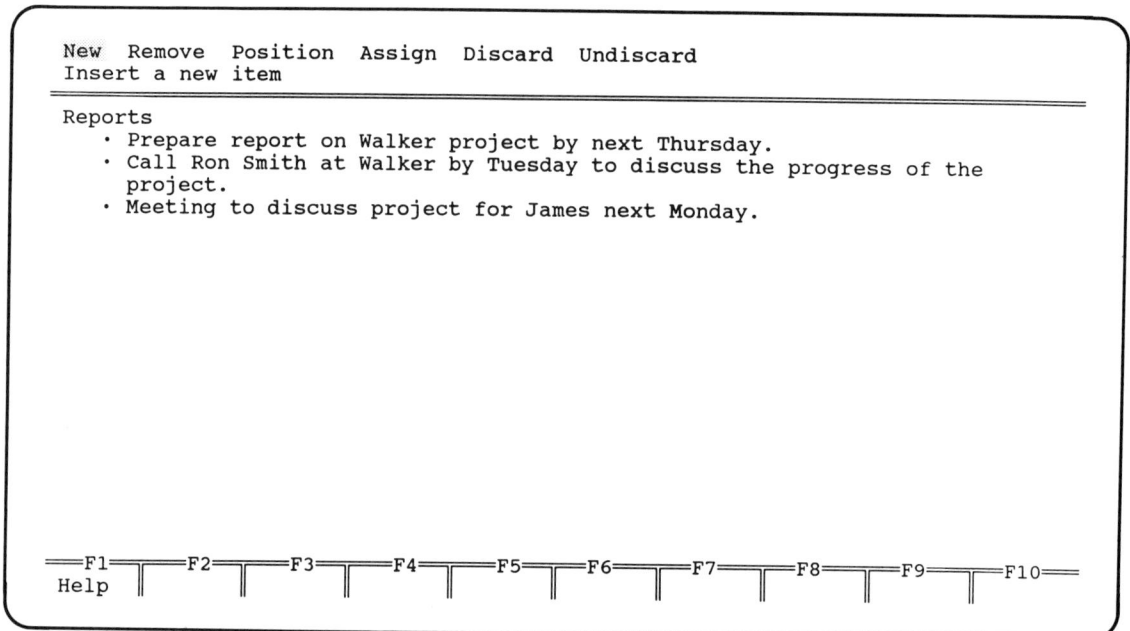

```
 New   Remove   Position   Assign   Discard   Undiscard
 Insert a new item

 Reports
    · Prepare report on Walker project by next Thursday.
    · Call Ron Smith at Walker by Tuesday to discuss the progress of the
      project.
    · Meeting to discuss project for James next Monday.




















 ═F1═══╤═F2═══╤═F3═══╤═F4═══╤═F5═══╤═F6═══╤═F7═══╤═F8═══╤═F9═══╤═F10═
  Help      ║      ║      ║      ║      ║      ║      ║      ║
```

Fig. 3-4. *Retrieving the discarded item from Trash using the Item Undiscard command.*

of the items discarded in Trash. When more than one item has been discarded, Agenda displays a box with the message *Undiscard: All items in Trash*. You press GREY PLUS to display the options. Another box appears showing two options: *Last item in Trash* and *All items in Trash*. If *Last item in Trash* is selected, then only the final item placed in the trash will be restored to the database.

Unless you have specified otherwise, Trash retains items that have been discarded only until the end of the day. After the system clock changes to the next day, Agenda empties the Trash, and discarded items can no longer be recovered. (WARNING: If you work past midnight, keep in mind that you are permanently losing all items in Trash.)

You can direct that the Trash be emptied at any time by using the Utility Trash command, which permanently removes all discarded items from the Trash. The frequency with which Agenda empties the Trash can also be changed using the Utility Preferences Other command to change the *Empty Trash:* setting.

If you want to eliminate several items from a database, the items can be discarded individually by highlighting each item and pressing ALT-F4 (DISCARD). Another way to eliminate several items is to mark them and then discard them as a group in a single operation.

To try marking and discarding, begin by creating two items to be discarded. Move the highlight down to the last item. Press INS and type in Discard 1. Press INS once more, type in Discard 2, and press ENTER.

Highlight the next-to-last item and press F7 (MARK) to mark it. The bullet in front of the item changes to a diamond to show that the item is marked. In addition, a highlighted diamond appears in the upper-right corner of the screen to indicate that one or more items are currently marked. Now highlight the last item by using the DOWN arrow and pressing F7 (MARK) again. This item also is marked with a diamond. The screen with the two last items marked is shown in Fig. 3-5.

Once the items have been marked, they can be discarded in a single operation. Press ALT-F4 (DISCARD) to discard the marked items from the database. Since items are currently marked, a dialogue box appears in the middle of the screen. The box shows the setting *Discard: Marked Items*. The box indicates the desired setting, so you could just press ENTER to discard the marked items. But this is a good time to review the procedures for making settings in dialog boxes, and to see the options available here. Press GREY PLUS to display the list of settings available. A second box pops up showing the two options, *Current item* and *Marked items*. The screen appears as shown in Fig. 3-6. The UP and DOWN arrows are used to select the desired setting. Since the marked items are to be discarded, leave that setting highlighted. Press ENTER to se-

```
┌─────────────────────────────────────────────────────────────────────┐
│   File: C:\AGFILES\TASKS                        03/10/89   10:38      │
│   View: Initial View                                          ♦       │
│  ═══════════════════════════════════════════════════════════════════ │
│   Reports                                                             │
│      · Prepare report on Walker project by next Thursday.             │
│      · Call Ron Smith at Walker by Tuesday to discuss the progress of │
│        the project.                                                   │
│      · Meet with Jim to discuss report on the Peters account.         │
│      · Meeting to discuss project for James next Monday.              │
│      ♦ Discard 1                                                      │
│      ♦ Discard 2                                                      │
│                                                                       │
│  ═F1═══╤═F2═══╤═F3═══╤═F4═══╤═F5═══╤═F6═══╤═F7═══╤═F8══╤═F9══╤═F10═   │
│   Help │ Edit │ Copy │ Done │ Note │ Move │ Mark │Vw Mgr│Cat Mgr│Menu │
└─────────────────────────────────────────────────────────────────────┘
```

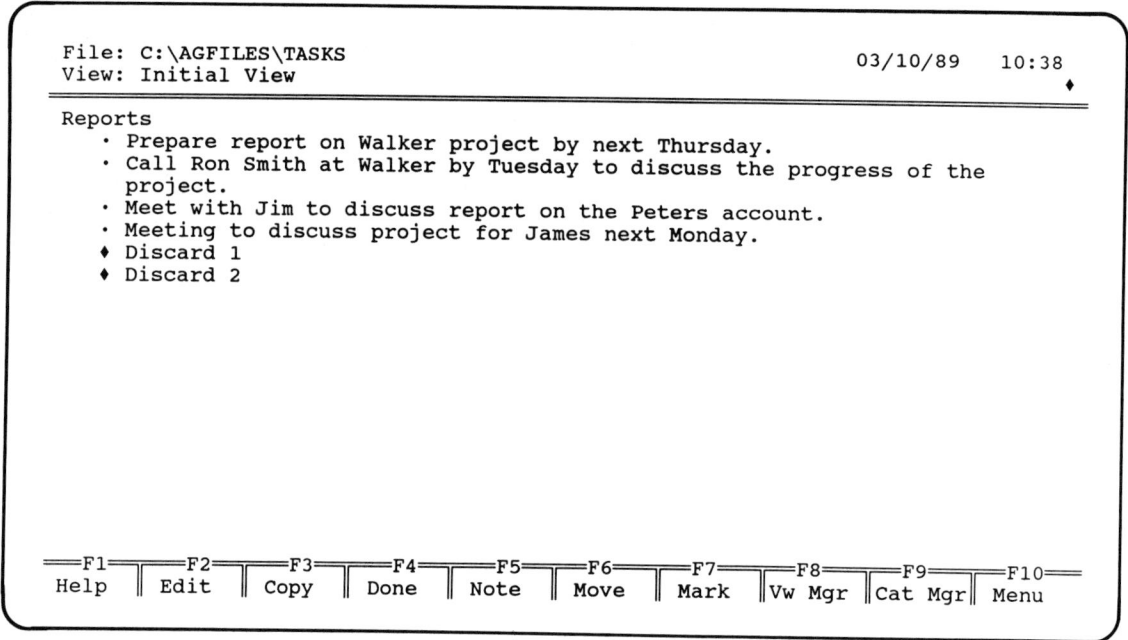

Fig. 3-5. *The Tasks database with two items marked for discard.*

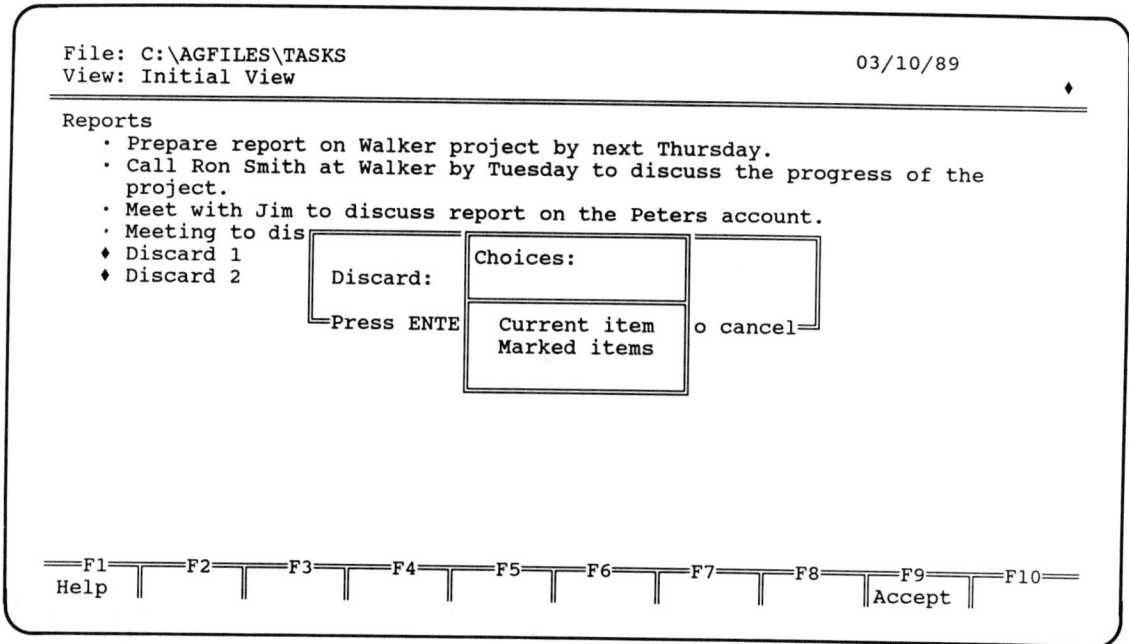

```
┌─────────────────────────────────────────────────────────────────────┐
│   File: C:\AGFILES\TASKS                        03/10/89             │
│   View: Initial View                                          ♦       │
│  ═══════════════════════════════════════════════════════════════════ │
│   Reports                                                             │
│      · Prepare report on Walker project by next Thursday.             │
│      · Call Ron Smith at Walker by Tuesday to discuss the progress of │
│        the project.                                                   │
│      · Meet with Jim to discuss report on the Peters account.         │
│      · Meeting to dis┌──────────┬─────────────┐                       │
│      ♦ Discard 1     │          │ Choices:    │                       │
│      ♦ Discard 2     │ Discard: │             │                       │
│                      └─Press ENTE│Current item│o cancel┘              │
│                                  │Marked items│                       │
│                                  └────────────┘                       │
│  ═F1═══╤═F2═══╤═F3═══╤═F4═══╤═F5═══╤═F6═══╤═F7═══╤═F8══╤═F9══╤═F10═   │
│   Help │      │      │      │      │      │      │     │Accept│      │
└─────────────────────────────────────────────────────────────────────┘
```

Fig. 3-6. *Specifying the discarding of the marked items.*

lect that setting and return to the previous box. Press ENTER again to discard the marked items. The marked items are removed from the database and placed in Trash.

Items are marked so that operations can be performed on them as a group. Marking is a simple procedure: highlight the item and press F7 (MARK). Marked items are indicated with preceding diamonds. To unmark a currently marked item, highlight that item and press F7 (MARK) once more. You can simultaneously unmark all marked items by using function key ALT-F7 (UNMARK ALL).

## ENTERING AND EDITING NOTES

Since items are limited to 350 characters, they can embody your basic ideas, but they cannot always incorporate the detailed information that is needed. To permit inclusion of more information, Agenda lets you attach notes to items (and to categories, as discussed later). Notes are an optional but very useful feature in Agenda.

A note can include up to 10,000 characters—more than seven single-spaced pages of text. Notes are attached to items and can be examined or edited at any time. Agenda includes flexible commands for editing notes and using the text of notes in a variety of ways.

### Entering Notes

The process of creating a note is very easy.

Attach a note with additional information on the Walker report to the first item in the database. In the Initial view, highlight the first item beginning "Prepare report on Walker project," to which you want to attach a note, and press F5 (NOTE). This opens a note screen displaying the contents of the note for this item. The top line reads *Note for:* followed by the text of the item—"Prepare report on Walker project by next Thursday"—to which the note is attached. The function key assignments for working with notes are displayed at the bottom of the screen. The rest of the screen is blank because no text has yet been entered for the note. Enter the text for the note:

The Walker report must include a detailed summary of how we are proceeding on each of the tasks outlined in the work document. We are up to date on most of these. It will be necessary to check with Ron Smith at Walker to determine whether they are satisfied with the layout that we sent them last week.

Have Ann get out the previous Walker project report and begin the process of updating so that we have a draft to work with.

Just type in the text as you would with a word processor. Complete editing capabilities are available when entering notes, but for now, if you make any mistakes, just press BACKSPACE and retype the text. When you reach the end of a line, the text automatically wraps around to the next line, just as in a word processor. At the end of the first paragraph of text, press ENTER twice, once to end the paragraph and the second time to insert a blank line. When you finish typing the second paragraph, the note is complete. The completed note is shown in Fig. 3-7.

Return to the Initial view in the database by pressing F5 (RETURN). Alternatives for returning to the Initial view are to press F9 (ACCEPT) or to use the Note Return command by pressing F10 (MENU) and selecting Return from the menu of commands displayed. The initial view of the database is displayed as shown in Fig. 3-8. Two small changes have been made to the view. The small bullet before the first item has been replaced by a musical note symbol. This musical note indicates that a note has been attached to the item. When an item with a note attached is highlighted, a musical note symbol is also displayed in the upper-right corner of the screen, indicating that the currently highlighted item has a note attached.

```
┌─────────────────────────────────────────────────────────────────────────┐
│                                                                           │
│   Note for:    Prepare report on Walker project by next Thursday.         │
│  ══════════════════════════════════════════════════════════Line 8══Ins═  │
│  The Walker report must include a detailed summary of how we are proceeding on │
│  each of the tasks outlined in the work document.  We are up to date on most of │
│  these.  It will be necessary to check with Ron Smith at Walker to determine │
│  whether they are satisfied with the layout that we sent them last week.   │
│                                                                           │
│  Have Ann get out the previous Walker project report and begin the process of │
│  updating so that we have a draft to work with.                           │
│                                                                           │
│                                                                           │
│                                                                           │
│                                                                           │
│                                                                           │
│                                                                           │
│                                                                           │
│  ═F1═══╤══F2═══╤══F3═══╤══F4═══╤══F5═══╤══F6═══╤══F7═══╤══F8═══╤══F9═══╤═F10══ │
│   Help │ Paste │ Copy  │  Cut  │Return │MakeCat│ Mark  │MakeItm│Accept │ Menu  │
└─────────────────────────────────────────────────────────────────────────┘
```

Fig. 3-7. *The entry of a note attached to an item.*

```
File: C:\AGFILES\TASKS                          03/10/89   10:42

View: Initial View                         When Date: 03/16/89    ♪
═══════════════════════════════════════════════════════════════════
Reports
    ♪ Prepare report on Walker project by next Thursday.
    · Call Ron Smith at Walker by Tuesday to discuss the progress of the
      project.
    · Meet with Jim to discuss report on the Peters account.
    · Meeting to discuss project for James next Monday.




════F1════╤═══F2═══╤═══F3═══╤═══F4═══╤═══F5═══╤═══F6═══╤═══F7═══╤═══F8════╤═══F9════╤═══F10══
 Help     ║ Edit   ║ Copy   ║ Done   ║ Note   ║ Move   ║ Mark   ║Vw Mgr  ║Cat Mgr ║ Menu
```

Fig. 3-8. *The view of the database showing the attachment of a note to the first item.*

To see the text of the note attached to any item, use the same procedure used for entering the note initially: highlight the item and press F5 (NOTE). The note is displayed on the screen. Once again, pressing F5 (RETURN) while looking at the note returns you to the view of the database and the list of items. Thus, F5 (RETURN) can be used to quickly examine the contents of notes and then return to the view.

### General Editing of Notes

Since notes can be much longer than individual items, notes may require additional editing. Agenda provides many of the capabilities of a word processor for use in editing notes. These capabilities are available whenever you are working with a note. (The note-editing capabilities of Agenda are referred to in this book as the *note editor*.) Notes can be edited by highlighting the item that has the attached note and pressing F5 (NOTE). The note is then displayed on the screen.

All of the cursor movement operations provided for editing items are also available for notes. The four arrow keys, UP, DOWN, RIGHT, and LEFT, move the cursor one character in the specified direction. CTRL-RIGHT and CTRL-LEFT move the cursor one word at a time. HOME and END move the cursor to the beginning and the end of a line.

For longer moves, PGUP and PGDN move the cursor up or down one screen at a time, scrolling the text. This is useful for making longer moves in notes that fill more than a single screen. CTRL-HOME moves the cursor to the first character in the note, and CTRL-END moves the cursor to the very end of the note.

The note editor also allows you to use tab settings. TAB moves the cursor to the next tab. SHIFT-TAB moves the cursor back to the previous tab. (Changing the width of tabs is discussed in Chapter 15.)

The text deletion commands that work when editing items also work with notes. DEL erases the characters under the cursor, and BACKSPACE erases the previous character. CTRL-BACKSPACE erases an entire word. CTRL-ENTER erases all of the characters from the cursor to the end of the line.

The note editor allows you to enter text in either insert or overtype modes. The default condition is the insert mode, in which characters that are typed in are inserted into the text at the cursor and the remaining text is pushed over to the right. The designation Ins at the far right of the double line at the top of the screen indicates that the editor is currently working in the insert mode. To change to the overtype mode, you can press the INS key. The indicator changes to *Ovr*. Any text that is typed in replaces (overtypes) the existing text. Pressing INS again changes back to the insert mode.

The ENTER key is used to insert carriage returns into the text of notes. Carriage returns are used to terminate lines of text and to add blank lines.

The note-editing features resemble the procedures used in most word processing programs. Some of the keys used might be different, but the use of these keys will soon become familiar if you do much work with notes. The keys for editing notes are summarized in Table 3-3. As was the case with editing items, you can perform any editing operations with just the four arrow keys to move the cursor and the DEL key to delete characters. The remaining keys just make certain operations faster and easier.

## Moving Text

The note editor includes a variety of commands to move blocks of text, much like many word processors. Movement of text is not confined to just within notes, however.

Suppose you want to move the second paragraph in the note to the beginning of the note. Display the note by pressing F5 (NOTE). Move the cursor to the beginning of the paragraph, to the ''H'' in ''Have.'' Press F7 (MARK) to begin marking a block of text for an operation. Then press the DOWN arrow to move the cursor to the next line and END to move to the end of the line. As the cursor is moved, the marked text is highlighted. Figure 3-9 shows the second paragraph highlighted in preparation for the move operation.

**Table 3-3. Special Keys Used for Editing Notes.**

| Key | Function |
| --- | --- |
| RIGHT, LEFT | Move cursor one character. |
| UP, DOWN | Move cursor one line. |
| CTRL-RIGHT, CTRL-LEFT | Move cursor one word. |
| HOME, END | Move cursor to beginning, end of line. |
| PGUP, PGDN | Move cursor one screen. |
| CTRL-HOME, CTRL-END | Move cursor to beginning, end of note. |
| TAB, SHIFT-TAB | Move to next (previous) tab. |
| ALT-EQUAL, ALT-MINUS | Add (remove) indent to next tab. |
| DEL | Erase character at cursor. |
| BACKSPACE | Erase character to left of cursor. |
| CTRL-BACKSPACE | Erase word. |
| CTRL-ENTER | Erase to end of line. |
| INS | Toggle between insert and overtype modes. |
| ENTER | Insert carriage return. |

```
 Note for:   Prepare report on Walker project by next Thursday.
==============================================================Mark==Line 7==Ins=
The Walker report must include a detailed summary of how we are proceeding on
each of the tasks outlined in the work document.  We are up to date on most of
these.   It will be necessary to check with Ron Smith at Walker to determine
whether they are satisfied with the layout that we sent them last week.

Have Ann get out the previous Walker project report and begin the process of
updating so that we have a draft to work with.




=F1=====F2=====F3=====F4=====F5=====F6=====F7=====F8=====F9=====F10==
 Help  | Paste | Copy | Cut |Return |MakeCat| Mark |MakeItm|Accept | Menu
```

Fig. 3-9. *The last paragraph of the note marked for moving to the beginning of the note.*

Marked text in a note can be placed in a special holding area called the *clipboard* for later insertion into the same or other notes. Two operations can be used to place text into the clipboard. The first operation, F4 (CUT), removes the marked text from the document and places it into the clipboard. The second operation for placing note text into the clipboard is F3 (COPY). This operation makes a copy of marked text in the clipboard, but leaves the original text undisturbed.

Move the marked final paragraph to the beginning of the note by pressing F4 (CUT) to remove the text from its current location and place it in the clipboard. The paragraph disappears from the screen. Now move the cursor to the beginning of the note. (CTRL-HOME will make this move directly.) Press ENTER to insert space for the paragraph being moved in and press the UP arrow to move the cursor to the first line. Now press F2 (PASTE) to insert text from the clipboard into the note at the location of the cursor. The paragraph can be seen in its new location at the beginning of the note in Fig. 3-10.

Text can also be cut or copied from a note for insertion into other notes. Assume that you suddenly realize that the last sentence about checking with Ron Smith at Walker is a detail that should be discussed in the

```
 Note for:   Prepare report on Walker project by next Thursday.
==================================================================Mark==Line 7==Ins=
Have Ann get out the previous Walker project report and begin the process of
updating so that we have a draft to work with.

The Walker report must include a detailed summary of how we are proceeding on
each of the tasks outlined in the work document.  We are up to date on most of
these.  It will be necessary to check with Ron Smith at Walker to determine
whether they are satisfied with the layout that we sent them last week.




=F1====T==F2===T==F3===T==F4===T==F5===T==F6===T==F7===T==F8===T==F9===T=F10===
 Help  | Paste | Copy  | Cut  |Return |MakeCat| Mark |MakeItm|Accept | Menu
```

Fig. 3-10. *The note after moving the last paragraph to the beginning, with the last sentence marked for copying to another note.*

telephone call next Tuesday. That call is the subject of another item. Perhaps the last sentence in the note should also be included as a note attached to the item "Call Ron Smith." Move the cursor to the beginning of the last sentence in the note, press F7 (MARK), and mark the entire sentence. The marked sentence is shown in Fig. 3-10.

Since this sentence is also to remain in the current note, press F3 (COPY) to copy the marked text to the clipboard. Now press F5 (RETURN) to return to the initial view of the database. The item to which the text in the clipboard is to be attached begins "Call Ron Smith at Walker . . . ." Highlight that item and press F5 (NOTE) to create a note. Then press F2 (PASTE) to enter the text from the clipboard into this new note. The marked text copied from the first note is entered and becomes the note attached to this other item.

One more application of the text movement capabilities is to make part or all of a note into an item. Return to the original note. Press F5 (RETURN), to get back to the initial view; highlight the first item; press F5 (NOTE). In looking over the note, you decide that the first paragraph, specifying the job for Ann, would be better included as an item in the database. To create an item from the first sentence in the note, begin by marking the text. Move the cursor to the beginning of the first sentence in the note and press F7 (MARK). Then move the cursor to the end of the sentence. Now press F8 (MAKE ITEM) to make an item out of the marked text. The marked text disappears from the note. Use F5 (RETURN) to return to the initial view of the database. The screen displaying the view at this point is shown in Fig. 3-11. The text from the note has been inserted as a new item under the item to which the note had been attached.

To make an item from text in a note, follow these steps:

- Display the note.
- Press F7 (MARK) and move the cursor to highlight the text.
- Press F8 (MAKE ITEM) to make the marked text an item.

Text can also be moved in the other direction, from items into notes. Use the F7 (MARK) command to mark the item or items to be moved into a note. (Remember that using this command places a diamond in front of the item, to indicate that it is marked.) Then you display the note into which the marked items are to be moved and move the cursor to the location where the text of the items is to be inserted. Press ALT-F3 (GET ITEMS). A dialog box will appear, asking whether you want to discard the item or items after they are copied into the note. Make the appropriate selection, and the marked items and their associated notes, if any, are copied into the note.

```
File: C:\AGFILES\TASKS                          03/10/89    10:46

View: Initial View                      When Date: 03/16/89    ♪
═══════════════════════════════════════════════════════════════
Reports
     ♪ Prepare report on Walker project by next Thursday.
     · Have Ann get out the previous Walker project report and begin the process
       of updating so that we have a draft to work with.
     ♪ Call Ron Smith at Walker by Tuesday to discuss the progress of the
       project.
     · Meet with Jim to discuss report on the Peters account.
     · Meeting to discuss project for James next Monday.




══F1═══╤══F2═══╤══F3═══╤══F4═══╤══F5═══╤══F6═══╤══F7═══╤══F8═══╤══F9═══╤══F10══
 Help  ║ Edit  ║ Copy  ║ Done  ║ Note  ║ Move  ║ Mark  ║Vw Mgr ║Cat Mgr║ Menu
```

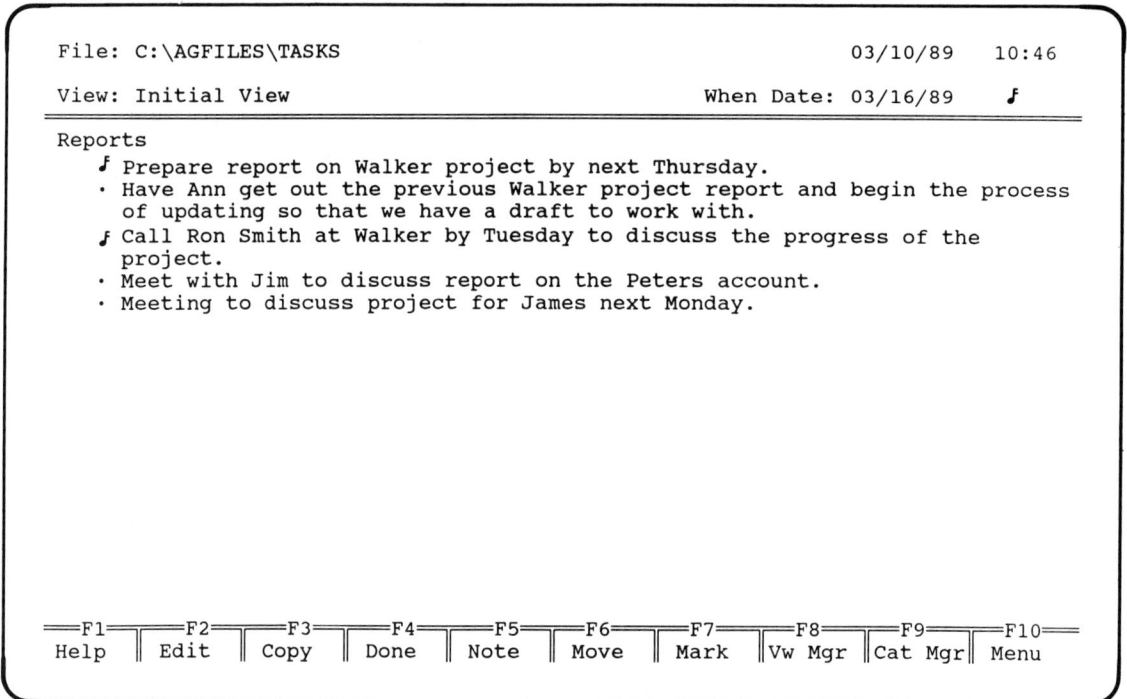

Fig. 3-11. *The view of items after the first paragraph in the note has been changed to an item.*

Agenda provides the capability for copying or moving text within notes, from one note to another, from a note to an item, and from an item to a note. These capabilities are important, because they allow you to adjust your database, moving information to exactly the location where it will be most useful. The first decision on where to put information is not always the best. By moving the information, you can often improve the utility of your database.

## More Note Editing Features

A few additional capabilities of Agenda's note editor will occasionally prove useful. Agenda has a full search-and-replace capability for use with notes. Also, of course, the note editor can be used to delete text.

Search for any references to Ron Smith in the note attached to the first item. In the Initial view, highlight the first item—"Prepare Report on Walker Project by next Thursday"—and press F5 (NOTE). This note is quite short, so you can actually find the reference to Ron Smith quite quickly just by reading through the note. In a note extending over several pages, however, it can be more difficult to find a particular reference.

The Search feature of Agenda's note editor is demonstrated here to illustrate how the feature might be used in such situations.

To begin the search for references to Smith, press ALT-F5 (SEARCH). The Search/Replace dialog box is displayed in the middle of the screen. With the highlight to the right of *Search for:*, type in Smith and press ENTER. The screen should appear as shown in Fig. 3-12. No other settings in the box need to be changed for this simple search, so press F9 to accept the settings and begin the search. Agenda searches the note for the first occurrence of Smith and the cursor is positioned at Smith. To search for additional references to Smith, just press ALT-F5 (SEARCH) again and press F9 to begin the search from that point forward.

You can also perform standard search-and-replace operations within notes to find all occurrences of a specified text string and automatically replace them with another text string. While in the note, you use ALT-F5 (SEARCH) to begin the search/replace operation. A Search/Replace dialog box appears. You enter the text string to be replaced to the right of the *Search for:* setting on the first line of the box. Change the *Replace text:* setting to *Yes*, either by pressing Y or by pressing GREY PLUS to display the list of options (*Yes* and *No*) and selecting *Yes*. A new line prompt appears, *Replace with:*, after which you enter the replacement text. Then press F9 to perform the search-and-replace operation.

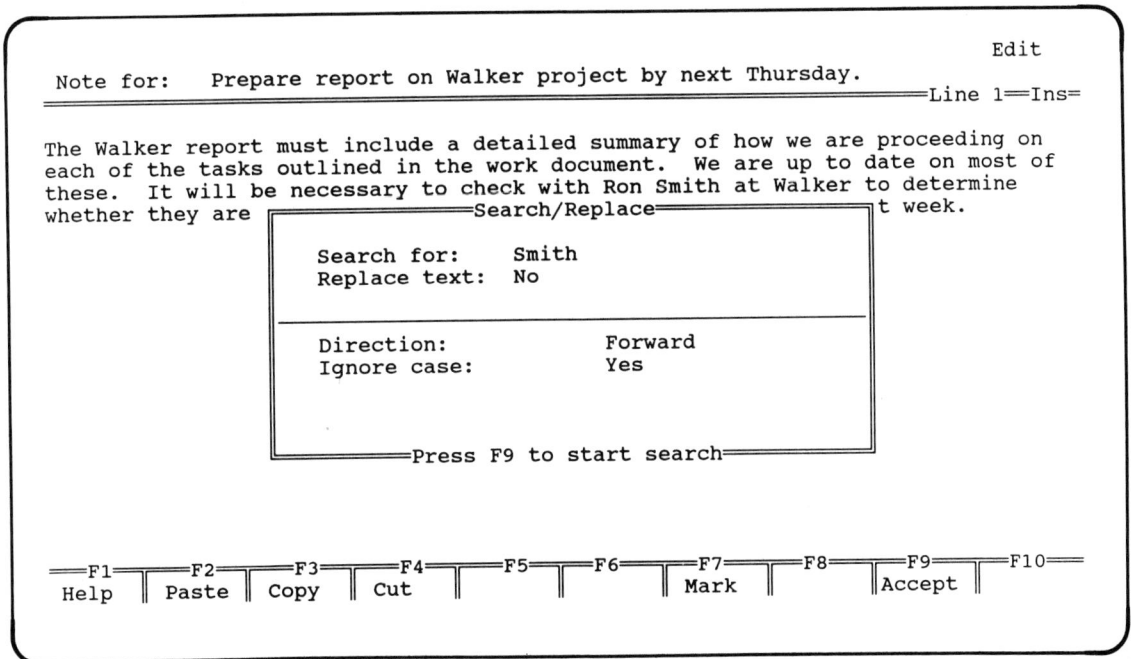

```
                                                            Edit
  Note for:   Prepare report on Walker project by next Thursday.
 ══════════════════════════════════════════════════════════Line 1══Ins══

The Walker report must include a detailed summary of how we are proceeding on
each of the tasks outlined in the work document.  We are up to date on most of
these.  It will be necessary to check with Ron Smith at Walker to determine
whether they are ┌═══════════════════Search/Replace═══════════════════┐t week.
                 │                                                     │
                 │  Search for:    Smith                               │
                 │  Replace text:  No                                  │
                 │                                                     │
                 │ ─────────────────────────────────────────────────  │
                 │                                                     │
                 │  Direction:         Forward                         │
                 │  Ignore case:       Yes                             │
                 │                                                     │
                 │                                                     │
                 └═══════════Press F9 to start search═══════════════════┘


 ══F1══╤══F2══╤══F3══╤══F4══╤══F5══╤══F6══╤══F7══╤══F8══╤══F9══╤══F10══
 Help  ║ Paste ║ Copy ║ Cut  ║      ║      ║ Mark ║      ║Accept ║
```

Fig. 3-12. *Searching for the name "Smith" in the note.*

In addition to the forward search/replace operation just discussed, the search/replace operation provides a *Direction:* setting so you can search backwards from the current location of the cursor. The default operation does not distinguish between upper- and lowercase letters, but a case-sensitive search may be specified if desired. Case-sensitive searches can be made by changing the *Ignore case:* setting in the dialog box. Highlight the setting to be changed, press GREY PLUS to display the list of options, and make the selection.

Text may be deleted from notes in larger chunks than is provided for by the normal editing commands. ALT-F4 (DELETE), F4 (CUT), and the Delete command may be employed to delete varying amounts of text. ALT-F4 (DELETE) can be used to delete words, lines, or all text from a note. When you press ALT-F4, a box appears in which you specify the amount of text to be deleted. The default setting is *Word*. Pressing GREY PLUS displays the additional options of *Line* and *All Text*. After you select the appropriate option, press ENTER and the specified quantity of text is deleted.

To eliminate an extensive section of text, mark the text using F7 (MARK), extending the area to include all of the text to be deleted. Then just press F4 (CUT) to move the text from the note to the clipboard. The text can be left on the clipboard and not used.

To delete an entire note, use either ALT-F4 (DELETE) or the Delete command from the note menu. To use the Delete command, press F10 (MENU) and select Delete. Using the Delete command erases all of the text from the note. When you return to the view, the item is no longer preceded by the note symbol, since there is no longer a note attached to the item.

Having completed this chapter, you have learned about most aspects of entering and editing items and notes in an Agenda database. You have also begun to become familiar with the basic procedures for working with Agenda—using the function keys and the special keys, editing information, entering commands, and making settings in dialog boxes. As you continue working with Agenda, you will be building on this base to become more comfortable with using the program.

# 4

# ORGANIZING INFORMATION USING SECTIONS

THE heart of Agenda's versatility is its ability to assign items to categories. This is how you use Agenda to organize the information in a database. The assignment of items to categories allows information in the database to be selected and displayed in different ways. Understanding the use of categories and the assignment of items to categories is therefore fundamental to learning Agenda.

Learning to use categories can be difficult because a category in Agenda is a very general and powerful concept. Categories and the assignment of items to those categories can be displayed in a number of different ways. A category can be a section head in a view, with the items assigned to that category listed under the section head. Categories and their items can also be displayed in columns within a view. Moreover, it is possible to have categories that are not displayed currently in any view. This flexibility is, of course, one of the strengths of Agenda, but it also makes learning the program more complex.

We will take learning to create and use categories and assigning items to categories one step at a time. This chapter focuses on entering new categories as section heads, assigning items to categories represented by section heads, and working with sections. The next chapter deals with columns and how to use them to create categories and assign items to categories. With the understanding of categories and the assignment of items to categories developed in these two chapters, further uses of categories are explored in subsequent chapters.

This chapter begins with the creation of categories as section heads and the changing of sections. The next part of the chapter describes the procedures for assigning items to those categories by moving them in and out of sections. The last part of the chapter explains how to order items within sections.

## CREATING AND CHANGING SECTIONS

Every item in an Agenda database must be assigned to at least one category. In the last chapter, you assigned items to categories when you created the Tasks database by entering all of the items underneath the Reports section head. Thus, in the Tasks database, all of the items are currently assigned to the Reports category.

Every view of an Agenda database must have at least one section and one section head. When the Tasks database was first created, the initial view automatically included one section head named ''Untitled.'' Your first step in creating the Tasks database was to edit the Untitled section head to the more meaningful ''Reports.''

### Creating Sections

Categories can be created in a number of ways. One way is to create a new section. Any category may, but need not be, a section head in a view. A section head is always a category, and every category can appear as a section head.

In the Tasks database, all of the items are assigned to a single category named Reports; Reports is also the only section head in the Tasks database. Having all of the items in the database assigned to a single category provides very limited opportunities for organizing and using the information. Furthermore, all of the items in the Agenda database are now assigned to the Reports category, and some of those items do not have anything to do with reports.

The next step in developing the Tasks database is to add new categories. These categories will be added as additional sections in the current view of the database.

Work continues in this chapter with the Tasks Agenda database created in the previous chapter. Begin Agenda and specify the Tasks file on the opening screen. The database appears as it did at the conclusion of Chapter 3. (Your screen should appear as in Fig. 3-11.)

The database currently includes a single section, which consists of the section head Reports and the items assigned to the Reports category. Add a new section for Meetings below the existing section by using the Category Section New command. Press F10 (MENU) to display the menu of view commands. Select Category from the first menu, Section from the second menu, and New from the third menu. (Remember that you can select an option from a menu either by moving the highlight to the desired option and pressing ENTER or by pressing the first letter of the desired option.) A box for specifying information about the new section—the New Section box—is displayed in the middle of the screen.

The first setting that appears in the New Section box permits specification of the position at which the new section is to be entered. Since the new section is to be positioned below the current section, this setting does not need to be changed. Press the DOWN arrow or ENTER to move the highlight down to the second setting, *Section Head:*. Here is where the name of the new section head must be specified. Type in the following:

Meetings

Then press ENTER. As you type, the letters are entered in the highlighted area, as shown in Fig. 4-1. Press F9 to accept the settings in the box and create the new section. The section head Meetings is displayed on the screen below the Reports sections with the head and associated items.

Now create several additional sections. Insert a new section called Phone Calls above the Meetings section. First be sure that the Meetings section head is highlighted. Then enter the command Category Section New. Since the new section is to be entered above the current section,

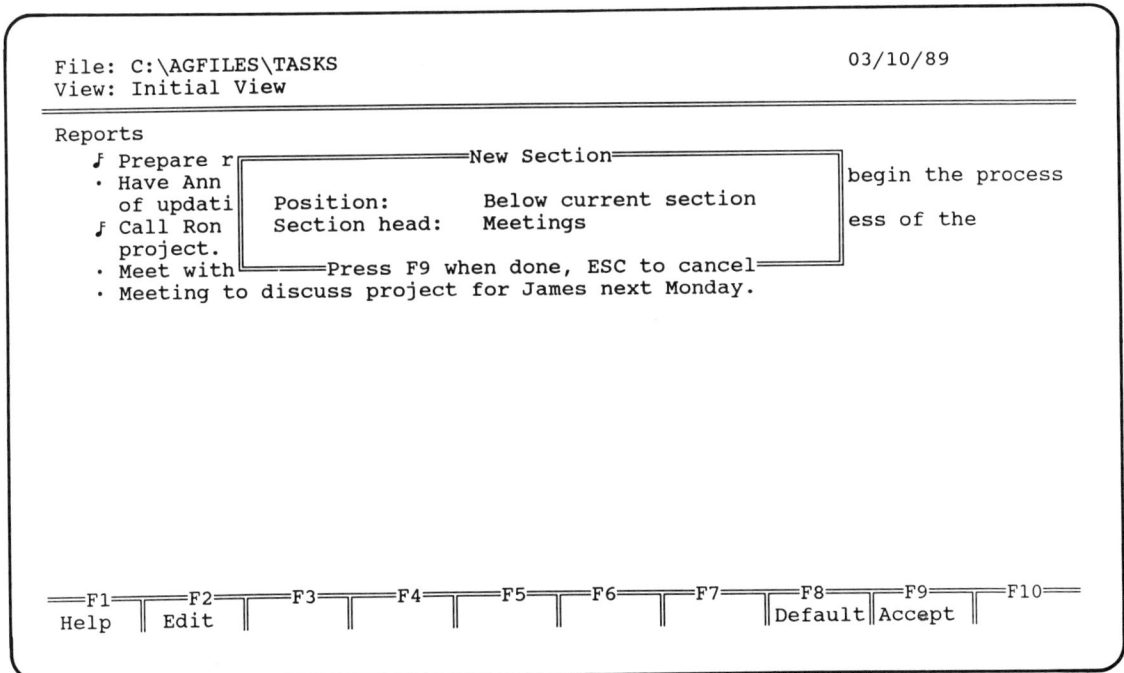

```
File: C:\AGFILES\TASKS                              03/10/89
View: Initial View

Reports
    ♪ Prepare r┌════════════════New Section═══════════┐
    · Have Ann │                                      │begin the process
      of updati│ Position:        Below current section│
    ♪ Call Ron │ Section head:    Meetings            │ess of the
      project. │                                      │
    · Meet with└═══════Press F9 when done, ESC to cancel═══════┘
    · Meeting to discuss project for James next Monday.




═F1═══╤═F2═══╤═F3═══╤═F4═══╤═F5═══╤═F6═══╤═F7═══╤═F8═══════╤═F9═══╤═F10══
Help  ║ Edit ║      ║      ║      ║      ║      ║Default║Accept║
```

Fig. 4-1. *Entering a new section named "Meetings" below the current section.*

the first setting in the box must be changed. With the *Position:* setting highlighted, press GREY PLUS and another box appears with the two options *Below current section* and *Above current section.* Select the option to position the new section head above the current section and press EN-TER. Now move down to the *Section Head:* setting, type in Phone Calls and press ENTER. Press F9 to accept the settings and create the new section.

Create a fourth section in the Initial view of the Tasks database. Call this section "Other," and place it below the Meetings section. (Use the procedures just described.) The screen should appear as shown in Fig. 4-2. The Tasks database now has four categories, displayed as the four section heads shown on the screen. Currently, only the original category, Reports, has items assigned to it.

Section heads can be edited and changed in exactly the same way in which items are edited. To edit a section head, highlight the section head and press function key F2 (EDIT). The section head is displayed on the second line of the screen, where it can be edited using all of the editing functions. When editing is complete, press ENTER to enter the edited text as the new section head.

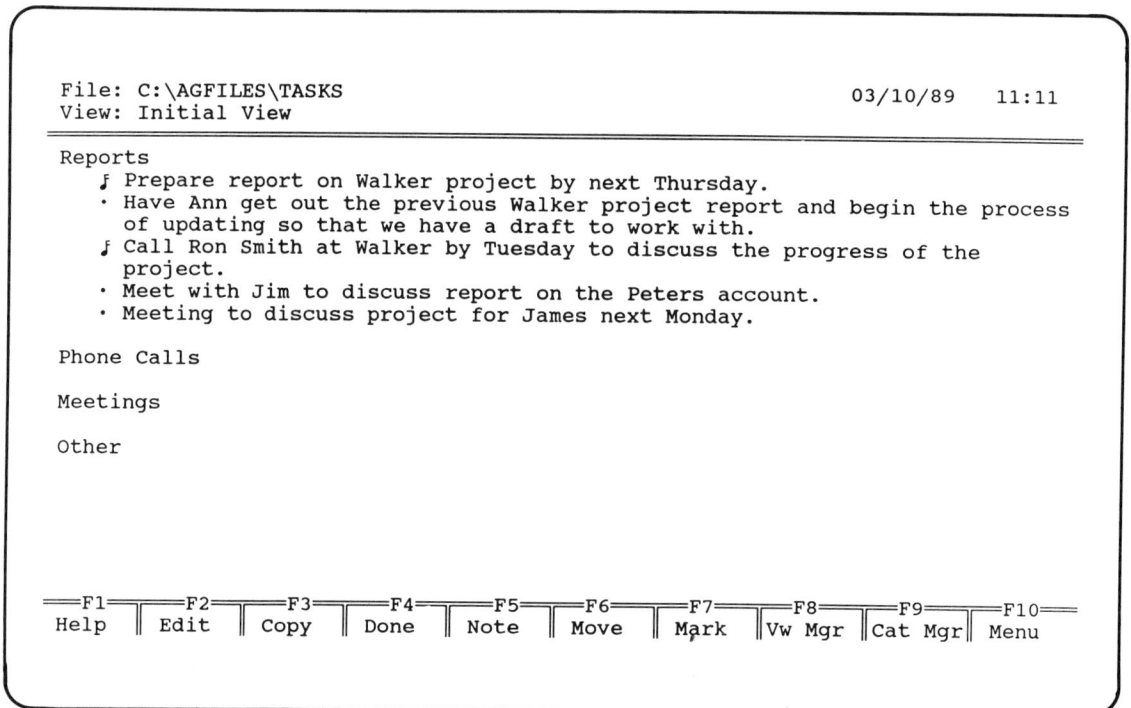

```
File: C:\AGFILES\TASKS                          03/10/89    11:11
View: Initial View
==================================================================

Reports
   ♪ Prepare report on Walker project by next Thursday.
   · Have Ann get out the previous Walker project report and begin the process
     of updating so that we have a draft to work with.
   ♪ Call Ron Smith at Walker by Tuesday to discuss the progress of the
     project.
   · Meet with Jim to discuss report on the Peters account.
   · Meeting to discuss project for James next Monday.

Phone Calls

Meetings

Other




==F1===T==F2===T==F3===T==F4===T==F5===T==F6===T==F7===T==F8===T==F9===T=F10==
 Help  ‖ Edit  ‖ Copy  ‖ Done  ‖ Note  ‖ Move  ‖ Mark  ‖Vw Mgr‖Cat Mgr‖ Menu
```

Fig. 4-2. *The Initial view of the Tasks database after the addition of three sections.*

Now enter several items in the new sections in the Tasks database. First highlight the Phone Calls section head. Press INS to begin entering the new item. You will notice that an additional space is opened up between the Phone Calls and Meetings section heads and that a bullet appears to mark the beginning of the item. Type in the following text:

Call Ann by next Friday to discuss hiring of new assistant.

and press ENTER. This new item is entered into the Phone Calls section and displayed there. Entering a new item into a section assigns that item to the category represented by the section head. Entering the item under the Phone Calls section head results in Agenda assigning the item to the Phone Calls category of the Tasks database.

Enter another new item in the Meetings section. Highlight Meetings, press INS, and type in the text for the item:

Meeting with executive committee 3/24/89 to go over quarterly results.

Press ENTER. The new item is placed in the Meetings section and is assigned to the Meetings category in the Agenda database. Figure 4-3 illustrates the Tasks database at this point.

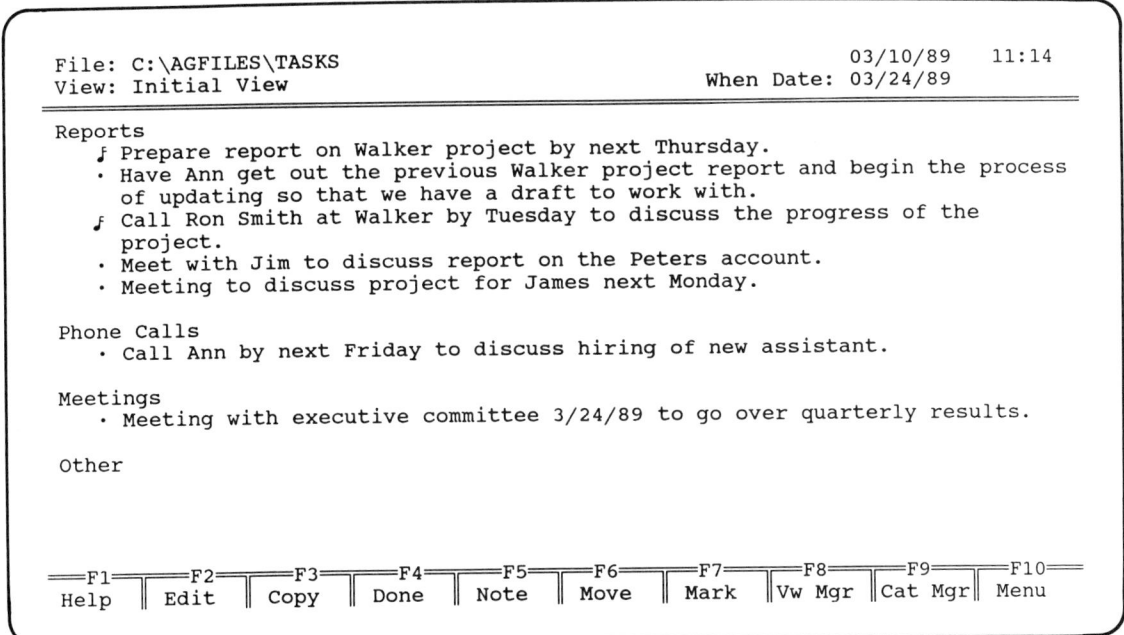

```
File: C:\AGFILES\TASKS                                  03/10/89   11:14
View: Initial View                       When Date: 03/24/89
═══════════════════════════════════════════════════════════════════════
Reports
    ♪ Prepare report on Walker project by next Thursday.
    · Have Ann get out the previous Walker project report and begin the process
      of updating so that we have a draft to work with.
    ♪ Call Ron Smith at Walker by Tuesday to discuss the progress of the
      project.
    · Meet with Jim to discuss report on the Peters account.
    · Meeting to discuss project for James next Monday.

Phone Calls
    · Call Ann by next Friday to discuss hiring of new assistant.

Meetings
    · Meeting with executive committee 3/24/89 to go over quarterly results.

Other


═F1════╦═F2════╦═F3════╦═F4════╦═F5════╦═F6════╦═F7════╦═F8════╦═F9════╦═F10═══
 Help  ║ Edit  ║ Copy  ║ Done  ║ Note  ║ Move  ║ Mark  ║ Vw Mgr║Cat Mgr║ Menu
```

Fig. 4-3. *The addition of new items in the new sections added to the database.*

## Moving Sections

Entire sections—the section head and the items in the section—can be repositioned within a view. The process is very simple and straightforward.

Suppose you want to move the Meetings section up so that it is displayed between the Reports and Phone Calls sections. Begin by highlighting Meetings, the head of the section to be repositioned. Use the Category Section Position command. The screen changes so that only the section heads are displayed. The section that is to be moved remains highlighted. All you need to do is press the arrow keys as instructed to move the highlighted section so that it is between the Reports and Phone Call section heads. The screen appears as shown in Fig. 4-4. Press ENTER to complete the operation and return to the Initial view of the database. The entire Meetings section, both the head and the associated item, are now displayed in the second position in the Initial view, between the Reports and Phone Calls sections.

Repositioning sections only affects the way the information is displayed in a view. It has no other effect on the items or categories in an Agenda database.

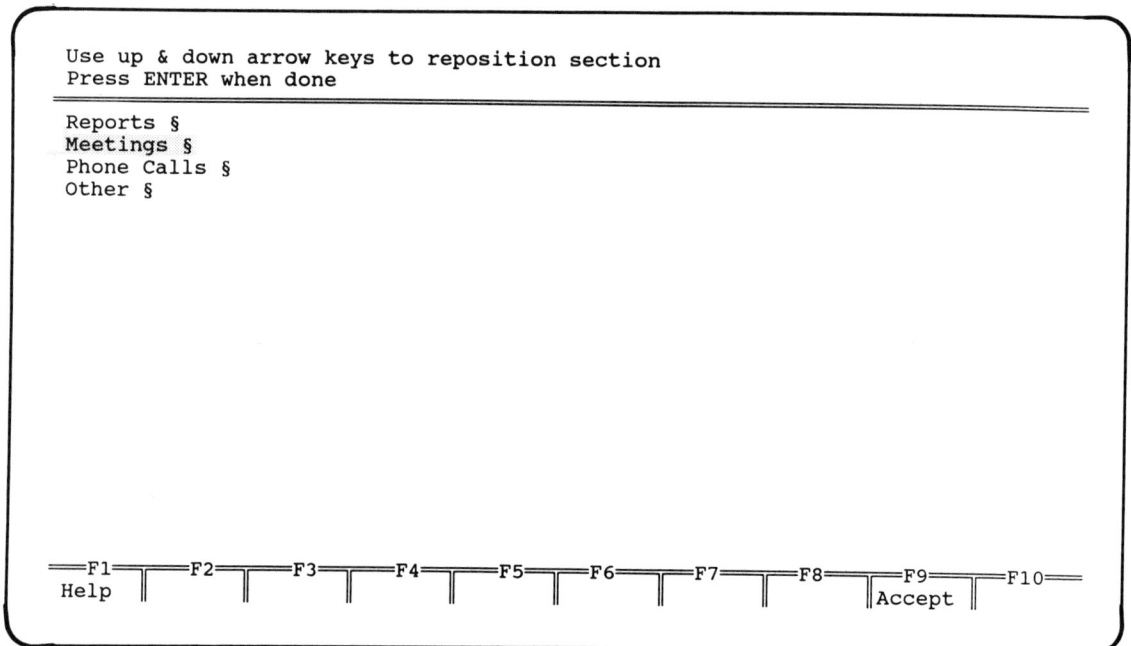

```
Use up & down arrow keys to reposition section
Press ENTER when done

Reports §
Meetings §
Phone Calls §
Other §




F1      F2      F3      F4      F5      F6      F7      F8      F9      F10
Help                                                            Accept
```

Fig. 4-4. *Moving the Meetings section above the Phone Calls section.*

## Discarding and Removing Sections

You might decide that you no longer need a particular section, and want to delete it. Agenda gives you two options for deleting sections. You can *discard* the section from the Agenda database, thereby permanently eliminating it. Alternatively, you can *remove* the section from the current view. If you remove a section, the category represented by the section head continues to exist in the database, and any items assigned to that category remain assigned to it. This will be the case even if the category and the items assigned exclusively to that category are not being displayed in any view in Agenda.

After adding the Other section to the Tasks database, you decide that you have no need for this section after all. Discarding this section from the database is easy. Highlight the Other section head. Press ALT-F4 (DISCARD). The section head is permanently and irretrievably erased from the database. Section heads and other categories are not placed into Trash. They cannot be retrieved later.

A problem arises if you try to discard a section head that has items assigned solely to the category represented by the section head. To illustrate the problem, begin the process of discarding the Phone Calls section head from the database. Highlight Phone Calls and press ALT-F4 (DISCARD). A box appears on the screen warning you that the category selected for discard has items assigned to it, as illustrated in Fig. 4-5. Every item in an Agenda database must be assigned to at least one category. If any items in the database are assigned only to the section head to be discarded, then discarding that section head will also discard those items from the database. Agenda warns you if this is about to happen, and a box appears to give you a chance to change your mind. Press N (for No) to change the setting in the box so as not to discard the category and the items. Press ENTER at this point to return to the view without discarding the information.

If you use the ALT-F4 (DISCARD) command and accept the default *Yes* option, both the section head *and* any items assigned only to the category represented by the section head are eliminated from the database. The items, however, are placed in Trash. Thus, the items could be retrieved with the Item Undiscard command just like any other discarded items.

Instead of discarding a section head from the database, you can just remove it from the current view. When a section head is removed, the entire section is no longer displayed in the current view of the database. The category represented by the section head continues to be a part of the database, however, as do the

```
 File: C:\AGFILES\TASKS                                    03/10/89
 View: Initial View
═══════════════════════════════════════════════════════════════════
Reports
   ♪ Prepare report on Walker project by next Thursday.
   · Have Ann get out the previous Walker project report and begin the process
     of updating so that we have a draft to work with.
   ♪ Call Ron Smith at Walker by Tuesday to discuss the progress of the
     project. ┌─────────────────────────────────────────┐
   · Meet with Jim│
   · Meeting to di│ Category has items. Discard?   Yes
                  └Press ENTER to accept, ESC to cancel═┘
Meetings
   · Meeting with executive committee 3/24/89 to go over quarterly results.

Phone Calls
   · Call Ann by next Friday to discuss hiring of new assistant.




══F1═══╤══F2══╤══F3══╤══F4══╤══F5══╤══F6══╤══F7══╤══F8══╤══F9═══╤═F10══
 Help  ║ Edit ║      ║      ║      ║      ║      ║      ║Accept ║
```

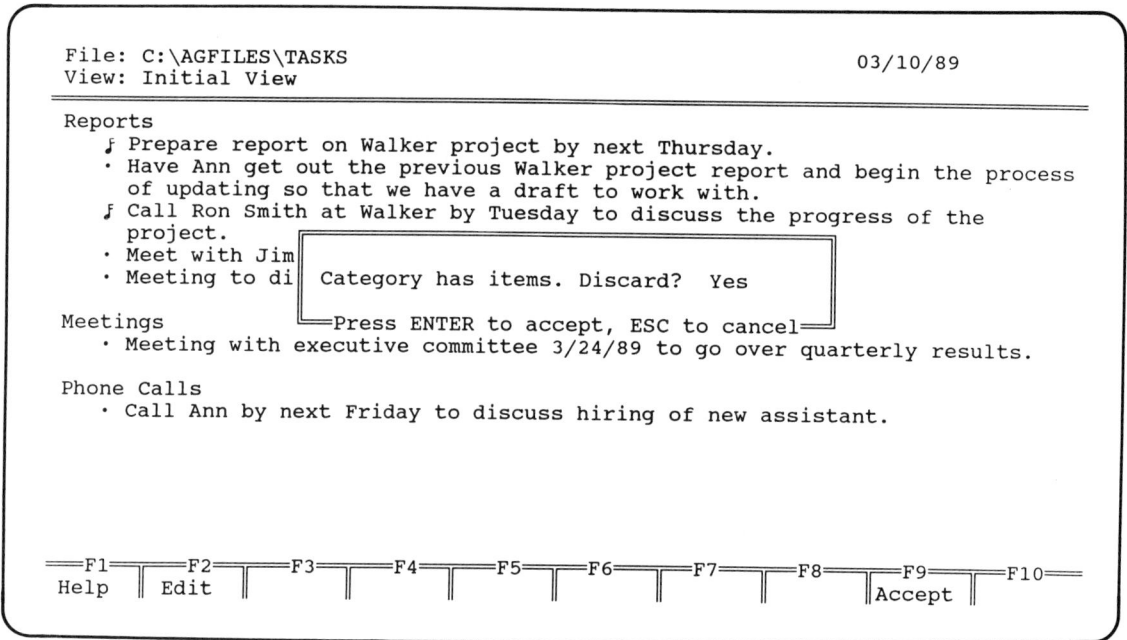

Fig. 4-5. *Attempting to discard a section head to which items are assigned.*

items assigned to that category. The category can later be re-inserted as a section head in the present view or in any other view, or in the category can be used in other ways.

To remove a section from a view, you first highlight the section head. Then either select the Category Section Remove command or press the DEL key. This immediately removes the entire section from the screen. The availability of the DEL key for this operation presents the possibility for one of the scarier mistakes when using Agenda. This can happen when you have a section head highlighted and, while reaching for another key, you accidentally press DEL. The entire section—section head and items—disappears from the screen. Your heart sinks as you worry that you have lost all of this information.

Do not despair, because DEL only *removes* the section from the current view; it does not *discard* it from the database. The mistakenly removed section can be restored to the view by using the Category Section New command to specify that the just-removed category be added as a new section in the current view.

## Collapsing and Expanding Sections

If a large database extends over many screens, you might want only the section heads displayed. Agenda permits you to "hide" the items under the section heads so that you can see more of the structuring of the view into sections. The process of hiding the items under a section head is called *collapsing* the section.

Collapse the Reports section so that all of the items in that section are hidden. Place the highlight anywhere in the Reports section. Then, press SHIFT-GREY MINUS (hold down the SHIFT key and press the GREY MINUS key on the numeric keypad). The section is collapsed immediately. Figure 4-6 shows the Tasks database with the Reports section collapsed. Only the section head, Reports, is displayed. A section symbol (§) is placed after Reports to indicate that this is a collapsed section. This lets you know that the section has been collapsed, and that you could expand the section to see the items assigned to it.

A collapsed section can be expanded to redisplay the items just as easily. Highlight the collapsed section and press SHIFT-GREY PLUS (hold down the SHIFT key and press the MINUS key on the numeric keypad). The screen appears as it did before, with all of the items listed under the Reports section head.

You can collapse or expand all of the sections in a view at the same time without individually performing the operation on each section. Pressing SHIFT-GREY MINUS while an already-collapsed section head is highlighted collapses all of the other sections in the view. This means that you can quickly collapse all of the sections just by pressing SHIFT-GREY MINUS twice: the first press collapses

```
 File: C:\AGFILES\TASKS                          03/10/89   11:16
 View: Initial View

 Reports §
 Meetings
    • Meeting with executive committee 3/24/89 to go over quarterly results.

 Phone Calls
    • Call Ann by next Friday to discuss hiring of new assistant.




==F1==╤══F2══╤══F3══╤══F4══╤══F5══╤══F6══╤══F7══╤══F8══╤══F9══╤══F10══
 Help  ║ Edit ║ Copy ║ Done ║ Note ║ Move ║ Mark ║Vw Mgr║Cat Mgr║ Menu
```

Fig. 4-6. *The Initial view of the Tasks database with the Reports section collapsed.*

the highlighted section, and the second collapses the remainder of the section in the view. Conversely, pressing SHIFT-GREY PLUS with an expanded section highlighted expands all sections in the view. Once again, two quick presses expand all sections.

The ability to collapse and expand sections provides another tool for looking at the information in a view more conveniently. Using these commands does not affect the content of the view or the Agenda database.

## PLACING ITEMS IN SECTIONS

When an item is placed into a section under a section head, the item is assigned to the category represented by that section head. Thus, placing items into sections is one way to assign items to categories in an Agenda database.

In the last chapter you entered new items into the Tasks database, and at the beginning of this chapter you inserted items into the new sections. By inserting the items into sections, you assigned them to the categories represented by the section heads. For an item to be added to an Agenda database, it must be inserted into a section, and therefore assigned to at least one category—the category represented by the section head.

The procedure for entering new items is straightforward, but it is so important that it will be reviewed once again. Highlight the entry—section head or item— below which you wish the new entered. Press INS. Type in the text of the item. Press ENTER. The item is entered into the database, assigned to the category represented by the section head, and displayed in the section under the section head.

The assignment of items to categories can be changed by moving or copying items from one section to another or by removing items from sections. Thus, moving, copying, or removing can change the category assignments of items.

### Moving Items

When the initial items were added to the Tasks database in the preceding chapter, all of them were inserted in the Reports section. Now that additional sections have been added, it is time to move some of the items to more appropriate sections.

The item beginning "Call Ron Smith" in the Reports section obviously refers to a telephone call and belongs in the Phone Calls section. Therefore, the item should be moved from the Reports section to the Phone Calls section. Highlight the item to be moved, then press F6 (MOVE). A box listing all of the sections in the view is displayed, with the instruction to select the section to which the item is to be moved. This box appears as shown in Fig. 4-7. Using the arrow keys, highlight the destination section, Phone Calls. Then press ENTER. The "Call Ron

```
 File: C:\AGFILES\TASKS                              03/10/89
 View: Initial View
═══════════════════════════════════════════════════════════════════
Reports
    ʃ Prepare report on Walker project┌─────────────Move────────────┐
    · Have Ann get out the previous Wa│Select section to move to:    │cess
      of updating so that we have a dr│                              │
    ʃ Call Ron Smith at Walker on Tues│                              │
      project.                        │    Reports                   │
    · Meet with Jim to discuss report │    Meetings                  │
    · Meeting to discuss project for J│    Phone Calls               │
                                      │                              │
Meetings                             │                              │
    · Meeting with executive committee└──────────────────────────────┘

Phone Calls
    · Call Ann by next Friday to discuss hiring of new assistant.



══F1══╤══F2══╤══F3══╤══F4══╤══F5══╤══F6══╤══F7══╤══F8══╤══F9════╤══F10══
Help  ║      ║      ║      ║      ║      ║      ║      ║Accept  ║
```

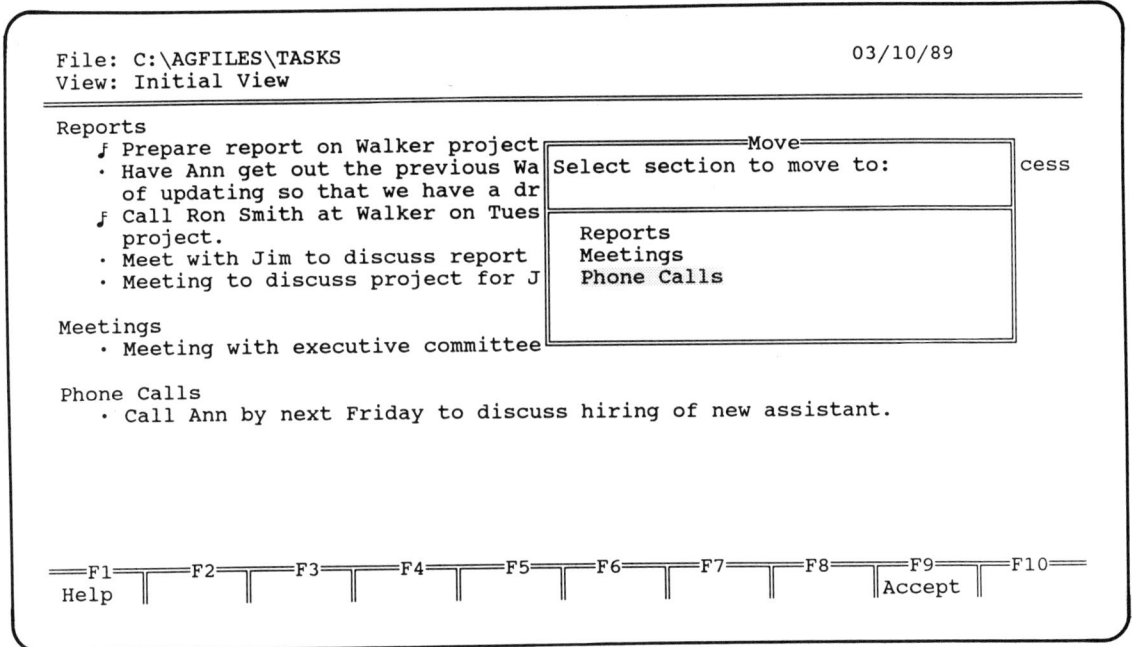

Fig. 4-7. *Moving the ''Call Ron Smith'' item to the Phone Calls section.*

Smith'' item is removed from the Reports section and displayed in the Phone Calls section. When this move was made, the item was assigned to the Phone Calls category and, at the same time, the item was unassigned from the Reports category. The fact that the item is no longer assigned to the Reports category is apparent since the item is no longer listed in the Reports section.

A group of items can be moved from one section to another in a single operation by first marking the items using F7 (MARK) and then moving all of the marked items. The procedure for working with marked items is illustrated in the following discussion of the Copy operation.

## Copying Items

Moving an item removes it from its original section and places it into a new section. Copying an item, on the other hand, does not remove it from its original section, but rather places a copy of it into a new section. After copying, the same item appears in two (or more) sections: the item remains assigned to the category represented by the first section head, and is also assigned to the category represented by the second section head. Thus, copying assigns the item to a new category without unassigning it from its original category.

Agenda's facility for marking multiple items for a single operation was demonstrated in the previous chapter when discarding items from the database. Marking can be used to copy multiple items efficiently. Copying in Agenda is accomplished by using F3 (COPY). The procedures are similar to those for moving items.

In the Tasks database, several items involving both reports and meetings need to be copied simultaneously from the Reports section to the Meetings section. Begin by marking the last three items in the Reports section. (One of the items does not logically belong in the Meetings section, but will be removed later.) Highlight each of the items to be copied and press F7 (MARK) to mark each one. A diamond appears in front of each of the items, indicating that the items are marked.

After you have marked all three items, press F3 (COPY) to begin the copy operation. Because only some items are marked, Agenda first asks you to identify the items to be copied. A box appears on the screen and displays the default copy setting, which is to copy all marked items. In this case, you wish to copy all of the marked items, so simply press EN-TER. (Had you wished to copy only the currently highlighted item, you could have pressed GREY PLUS and selected this option. You might wish to do this if the items have been marked for some other purpose.)

Next, another box appears for the selection of the section to which the items are to be copied, as shown in Fig. 4-8. Highlight Meetings and press ENTER. The three marked items are copied to the Meetings section and are now listed in both the Reports and Meetings sections, as you can see in Fig. 4-9. (Figure 4-9 also illustrates the results of an-other procedure discussed later in this chapter.) This means that these three items are now assigned to both the Reports category and to the Meetings category. After marked items have been copied to another section, the items are unmarked.

The procedures for copying a single item from one section to another are similar to the procedures for moving an item:

- Highlight the item.
- Press F3 (COPY).
- Select the section to which the item is to be copied, from the box displayed on the screen.
- Press ENTER to make the copy.

To copy more than one item, mark each of the items using F7 (MARK) and then follow these procedures.

```
File: C:\AGFILES\TASKS                              03/10/89
View: Initial View                                              ◆

════════════════════════════════════════════════════════════════
Reports
    ♩ Prepare report on Walker project┌──────────Copy──────────┐
    ◆ Have Ann get out the previous Wa│Select section to copy to:│cess
      of updating so that we have a dr│                          │
    ◆ Meet with Jim to discuss report │                          │
    ◆ Meeting to discuss project for J│ Reports                  │
                                      │ Meetings                 │
Meetings                             │ Phone Calls              │
    · Meeting with executive committee│                          │
                                      └──────────────────────────┘
Phone Calls
    · Call Ann by next Friday to discuss hiring of new assistant.
    ♩ Call Ron Smith at Walker by Tuesday to discuss the progress of the
      project.




══F1═══╤══F2═══╤══F3═══╤══F4═══╤══F5═══╤══F6═══╤══F7═══╤══F8═══╤══F9═══╤══F10══
Help   │       │       │       │       │       │       │       ║Accept ║
```

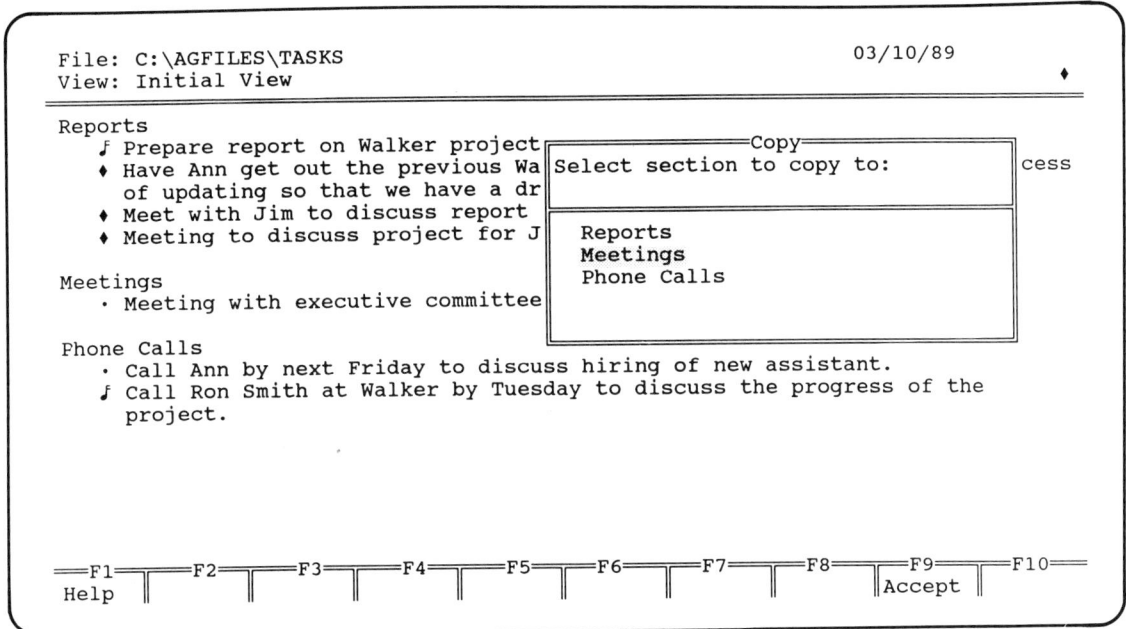

Fig. 4-8. *Copying the marked items to the Meetings section.*

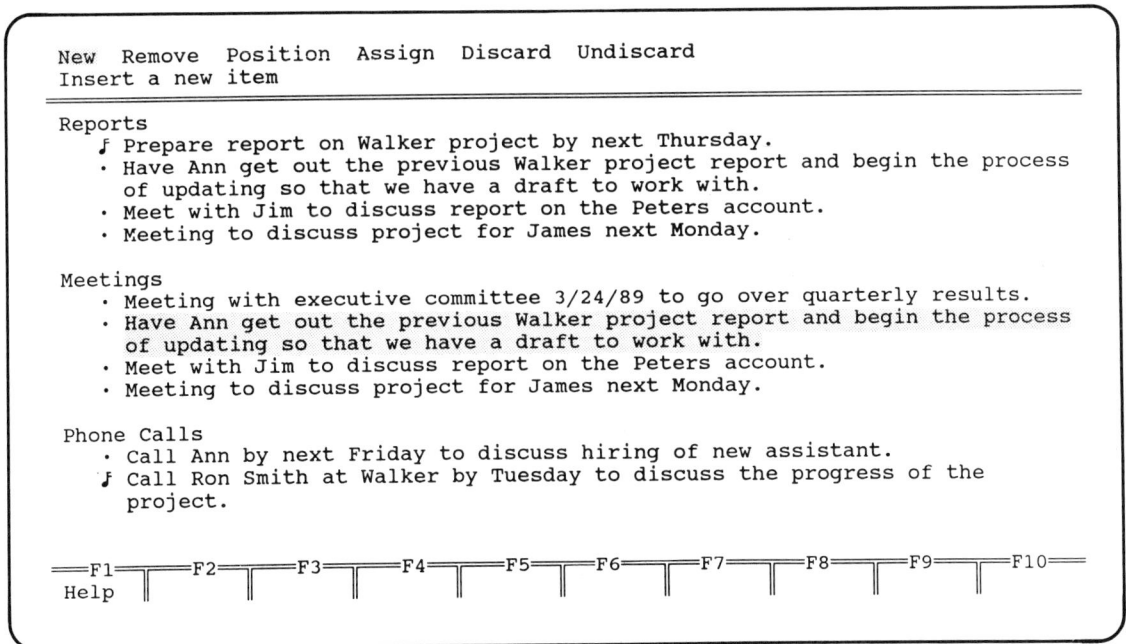

```
 New  Remove  Position  Assign  Discard  Undiscard
 Insert a new item
════════════════════════════════════════════════════════════════
Reports
    ♩ Prepare report on Walker project by next Thursday.
    · Have Ann get out the previous Walker project report and begin the process
      of updating so that we have a draft to work with.
    · Meet with Jim to discuss report on the Peters account.
    · Meeting to discuss project for James next Monday.

Meetings
    · Meeting with executive committee 3/24/89 to go over quarterly results.
    · Have Ann get out the previous Walker project report and begin the process
      of updating so that we have a draft to work with.
    · Meet with Jim to discuss report on the Peters account.
    · Meeting to discuss project for James next Monday.

Phone Calls
    · Call Ann by next Friday to discuss hiring of new assistant.
    ♩ Call Ron Smith at Walker by Tuesday to discuss the progress of the
      project.

══F1═══╤══F2═══╤══F3═══╤══F4═══╤══F5═══╤══F6═══╤══F7═══╤══F8═══╤══F9═══╤══F10══
Help   │       │       │       │       │       │       │       │       │
```

Fig. 4-9. *Removing an item from the Meetings section.*

## Removing Items

Removing an item from a section causes it to be unassigned from the category represented by the section head. Every item must be assigned to at least one category; it cannot simply be removed from the section representing the only category to which the item is assigned. Thus, to remove an item from a section without discarding it from the database, the item must also be assigned to another category. To remove an item from the only section to which it is assigned means discarding it from the database. (Discarding items using ALT-F4 is discussed in Chapter 3. Discarded items are placed in Trash and are eliminated from the database.)

One item currently in the Meetings section—the item beginning ''Have Ann get out the previous Walker project report''—makes no reference to any meetings. This item does not belong in the Meetings section and should not be assigned to the Meetings category. (This item was one of those copied from the Reports section to the Meetings section.) To remove the item, highlight the item and use the Item Remove command. Press F10 (MENU) to display the menu of the view commands; select Item to display the menu of Item subcommands on the top line of the screen, as shown in Fig. 4-9. Select the Remove option from this menu. As soon as Remove is selected, the item is removed from the Meetings section.

An alternative to using the Item Remove command for removing items from sections is to use the DEL key. The ability of the DEL key to remove items from sections can create problems, however. If the DEL key is pressed accidentally while an item is highlighted, the item will disappear from the screen. If that item was assigned only to the category in which it was displayed on the screen, it is discarded from the database and placed in Trash. If, on the other hand, the item had been assigned to a category other than just the one in which it had been displayed, it is still in the database. But you have to find the item in order to reassign it to the section from which it has been removed. DEL is a dangerous key in Agenda. Be careful not to press it accidentally.

It is possible to retrieve the last item removed from a section. Items that have merely been removed rather than discarded from a section are not placed in Trash, because only discarded items are put in Trash. Although the item is not retrievable from Trash, Agenda does keep track of the *last* item (only one item) that has been removed from a section. This item can be retrieved and inserted into any section.

To retrieve the removed item, move the highlight to the entry just above the point where you want the item to be inserted and press the accelerator key, ALT-Y. The item is inserted into the section and is assigned to that category. ALT-Y can be useful if you accidentally remove an item from a section by mistakenly pressing the DEL key. Just press ALT-Y immediately, and the item is restored to its original location.

The information in a section may exist in an Agenda database even if the section is not displayed in the current view. Therefore, even if a section has been removed from a view, the category and the items assigned to it remain in the database and may be displayed as a section in another view. For example, suppose some items are assigned to both the Reports and Meetings categories and are displayed in both those sections. If you were to remove the Reports section from the current view, Reports would remain as a category in the database and the items still would be assigned to it. But you could not see the items, nor their assignment to the Report category in the current view on the screen. If you were to remove one of the items in the Meetings section that also was assigned to the Reports category, the item would be removed from the Meetings section and would not be displayed anywhere on the screen.

Agenda does give you a warning when you give the command to remove an item from the only section to which it is assigned. After you press DEL or issue the Item Remove command, a box appears on the screen with the message *Item not assigned elsewhere. Discard?* This tells you that carrying through the removal of the item means discarding it from the database. If this is what you want, select the given option, *Yes*. Otherwise, choose *No* to keep from losing the information completely.

Moving, copying, and removing items from sections can be used for changing the assignment of items to categories in the database. When an item is copied or moved so that it is displayed in a section, it is assigned to the category represented by the section head. When an item is moved or removed from a section, it is unassigned from that category. In these commands you have learned one set of procedures for managing the assignment of items to categories, and managing the information in your Agenda database.

## ORDERING ITEMS IN SECTIONS

In working with items and sections in Agenda, you might have preferences concerning the order in which the items are listed within a section. Agenda includes capabilities both for moving individual items within sections and for sorting all of the items in one section or in all sections.

### Positioning Items

Moving a single item within a section is a simple procedure using the Item Position command.

Suppose you want to move the item beginning "Prepare report on Walker project" from the beginning of the list of items in the Reports section to the end. Start by highlighting that item. Then enter the Item Position command. You are instructed to use the UP and DOWN arrow keys to reposition the item. Press DOWN until the item is moved to the end of the section. The screen appears as shown in Fig. 4-10. Press ENTER to complete the operation and return to the Initial view.

One restriction is placed on the use of the Item Position command to move items around in sections. You cannot use the command to change the position of items in sections that are sorted (as discussed in the next section).

## Sorting Items

Using the information in an Agenda database is often easier if the items displayed in sections are ordered in some logical fashion. The appropriate ordering might be alphabetical, by date, or according to the assignment of the items to some other categories.

Agenda lets you sort items in all of these ways by using the Category Section Sort command. The command is very flexible, allowing you to specify the type of sorting desired. Options for ordering items include alphabetically, by date, or by category. The orderings can be ascending or descending. Items can be sorted

```
Use up & down arrow keys to reposition item
Press ENTER when done

Reports
    · Have Ann get out the previous Walker project report and begin the process
      of updating so that we have a draft to work with.
    · Meet with Jim to discuss report on the Peters account.
    · Meeting to discuss project for James next Monday.
    ♪ Prepare report on Walker project by next Thursday.

Meetings
    · Meeting with executive committee 3/24/89 to go over quarterly results.
    · Meet with Jim to discuss report on the Peters account.
    · Meeting to discuss project for James next Monday.

Phone Calls
    · Call Ann by next Friday to discuss hiring of new assistant.
    ♪ Call Ron Smith at Walker by Tuesday to discuss the progress of the
      project.


=F1=====F2=====F3=====F4=====F5=====F6=====F7=====F8=====F9=====F10=
 Help                                                   Accept
```

Fig. 4-10. *Using the Item Position command to move an item within a section.*

in individual sections or in all sections. Sorting can be done at several different times: only when specifically requested; each time new items are entered; or when you have completed work with a section.

The Tasks database includes a list of things to do, so it would be appropriate to arrange the items by date. When items are entered into Agenda with a reference to a day, Agenda figures out the date and keeps track of this as a *When Date*. (Chapter 10 addresses working with dates.) You might have noticed as you worked with the Tasks database that when certain items were highlighted, a When Date was displayed on the second line of the screen. For example, the item ''Meeting to discuss project for James next Monday'' has a When Date of 3/13/89 in the Tasks database, as illustrated in the figures.

The When Dates assigned in your database depend upon the actual dates when you entered the items. Sorting the items by date, placing those with the earliest dates first, would make it easier to identify the things to be done first.

To sort the items within the sections by date, use the Category Section Sort command. This command displays a large dialog box—the Sort box—with a number of settings allowing the user to specify how the items are to be sorted. The first setting is *Sort new items: On leaving a section*. This option indicates that new items entered into a section are to be sorted when the highlight is moved from the section. This is an acceptable setting, so do not make any change.

In addition to new items being sorted on leaving a section, you can specify in the Sort box that new items are to be sorted within a section whenever an item is entered, or only on demand (when the Category Section Sort command is invoked). You select one of these alternate settings by moving the highlight to the right of the *Sort new items:* setting and pressing GREY PLUS to display the list of options. You then use the arrow keys to select the desired option and press ENTER.

The Sort box also permits the specification of the sections within which the items are to be sorted. Move the highlight to the right of *Sort items in:*, press GREY PLUS to display the list of choices. Use the arrow keys to move the highlight to the *All Sections* option and press ENTER. Items are sorted in all of the sections of the view. Alternatively, the *Current Section* option allows sorting only in the section where the highlight is located.

The remainder of the Sort dialog box involves specifying the order in which the items are to be sorted. The *primary sort* determines the major ordering of the items in each section. The *secondary sort* determines the ordering of items that have the same value in the primary sort. For example, if a primary sort were to order items by a person's last name, the secondary sort might be used to further order the items by the first name. This would assure that Adam Smith came before John Smith in the listing.

The remaining step involves specifying the primary sort order. The initial setting displayed on the screen for the Primary Sort is used to indicate how the items are to be ordered. Move the highlight to the right of the *Sort on:* setting. Press GREY PLUS to display the selection box with the list of options for sorting. These appear as shown in Fig. 4-11. Items can be sorted based on the text of the items, the assignment of the items to categories, the notes attached to the categories, or upon various dates. To sort the items in the Tasks database by date, select the *When date* option and press ENTER.

When the *Sort on:* setting has been specified, the selection box disappears and an additional setting appears for specifying whether the items are to be sorted in descending or ascending order. Since items with the earlier dates should come first, the sort should be ascending.

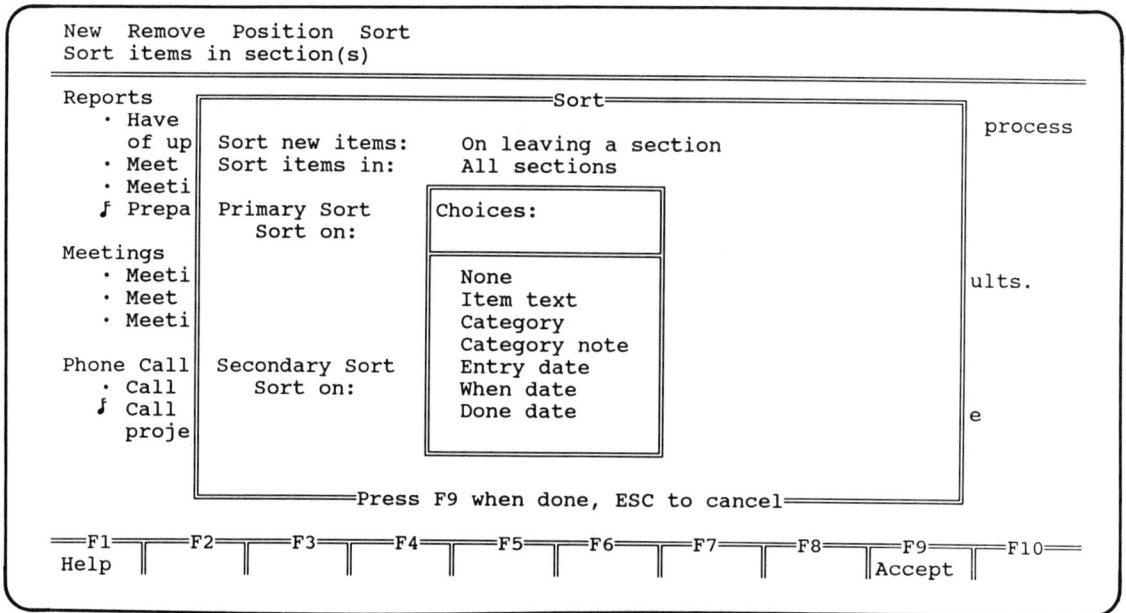

```
 New   Remove   Position   Sort
 Sort items in section(s)

 Reports        ┌────────────────────Sort════════════════┐    process
   • Have       │                                         │
     of up│ Sort new items:    On leaving a section   │
   • Meet │ Sort items in:     All sections            │
   • Meeti│                                             │
   ♪ Prepa│ Primary Sort    ┌─────────────────────────┐ │
          │      Sort on:   │ Choices:                 │ │
 Meetings │                 │                          │ │
   • Meeti│                 │ None                     │ │   ults.
   • Meet │                 │ Item text                │ │
   • Meeti│                 │ Category                 │ │
          │                 │ Category note            │ │
 Phone Call│ Secondary Sort │ Entry date               │ │
   • Call │      Sort on:   │ When date                │ │
   ♪ Call │                 │ Done date                │ │   e
     proje│                 └─────────────────────────┘ │
          └══════════Press F9 when done, ESC to cancel══┘

 ═F1═╤═F2═╤═F3═╤═F4═╤═F5═╤═F6═╤═F7═╤═F8═╤═F9═╤═F10═
 Help │     │     │     │     │     │     │     │Accept│
```

Fig. 4-11. *Specifying the ordering for the primary sort when using the Category Section Sort command.*

Therefore, the current setting is correct. (To change the setting, you could either press GREY PLUS to display the box with the two selections, or just press D to change to descending.)

At this point, all of the settings have been established in the Sort dialog box. The box should appear as in Fig. 4-12. As instructed in the box, press F9 to indicate that you are done. The items in each section of the Tasks database are then immediately sorted by When Date. The view of the Tasks database now appears as shown in Fig. 4-13. Items with the earliest dates come first in each of the sections. For example, in the Reports section, the item referring to a task to be completed by next Monday comes before the task to be done by next Thursday. The first item is currently highlighted. Note the When Date of 3/13/89 displayed on the second line. Items without date references and When Dates come after the items with dates within each section.

Sorting items in sections with the Category Section Sort command raises additional issues, addressed in later chapters as additional features of Agenda are introduced. Any sorting, however, involves the step-by-step specification of requirements in the dialog box. It is basically a matter of working your way through the settings in the Sort dialog box and figuring out the appropriate choice for each setting. This is a good example of a situation where referring to Agenda's

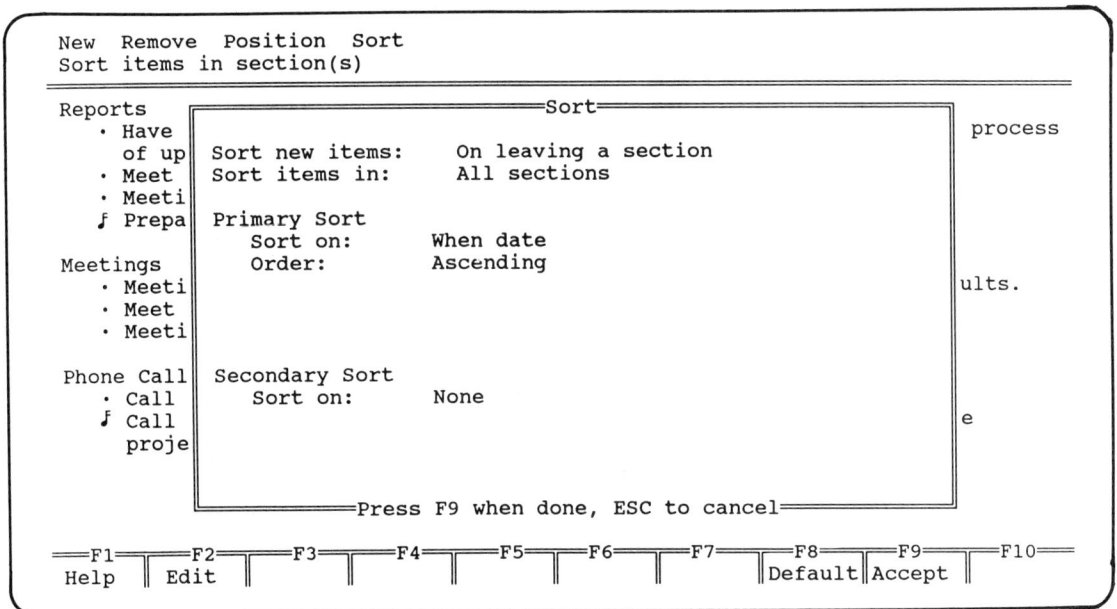

```
 New   Remove  Position  Sort
 Sort items in section(s)
════════════════════════════════════════════════════════════════
 Reports    ┌──────────────────────Sort═══════════════════┐
   · Have   │                                              │  process
     of up  │ Sort new items:    On leaving a section      │
   · Meet   │ Sort items in:     All sections              │
   · Meeti  │                                              │
   ♪ Prepa  │ Primary Sort                                 │
            │     Sort on:       When date                 │
 Meetings   │     Order:         Ascending                 │
   · Meeti  │                                              │  ults.
   · Meet   │                                              │
   · Meeti  │                                              │
            │                                              │
 Phone Call │ Secondary Sort                               │
   · Call   │     Sort on:       None                      │
   ♪ Call   │                                              │  e
     proje  │                                              │
            │                                              │
            └═══════════Press F9 when done, ESC to cancel══┘
═══F1═══╤═══F2═══╤═══F3═══╤═══F4═══╤═══F5═══╤═══F6═══╤═══F7═══╤═══F8═══╤═══F9═══╤══F10══
 Help   ║ Edit   ║        ║        ║        ║        ║        ║Default║Accept  ║
```

Fig. 4-12. *The final settings in the Sort dialog box.*

```
  File: C:\AGFILES\TASKS                          03/10/89   11:46
  View: Initial View                  When Date: 03/13/89
 ══════════════════════════════════════════════════════════════════
  Reports
     · Meeting to discuss project for James next Monday.
     ♪ Prepare report on Walker project by next Thursday.
     · Have Ann get out the previous Walker project report and begin the process
       of updating so that we have a draft to work with.
     · Meet with Jim to discuss report on the Peters account.

  Meetings
     · Meeting to discuss project for James next Monday.
     · Meeting with executive committee 3/24/89 to go over quarterly results.
     · Meet with Jim to discuss report on the Peters account.

  Phone Calls
     ♪ Call Ron Smith at Walker by Tuesday to discuss the progress of the
       project.
     · Call Ann by next Friday to discuss hiring of new assistant.



 ══F1═══╤══F2═══╤══F3═══╤══F4═══╤══F5═══╤══F6═══╤══F7═══╤══F8═══╤══F9═══╤═F10══
  Help  ║ Edit  ║ Copy  ║ Done  ║ Note  ║ Move  ║ Mark  ║Vw Mgr ║Cat Mgr║ Menu
```

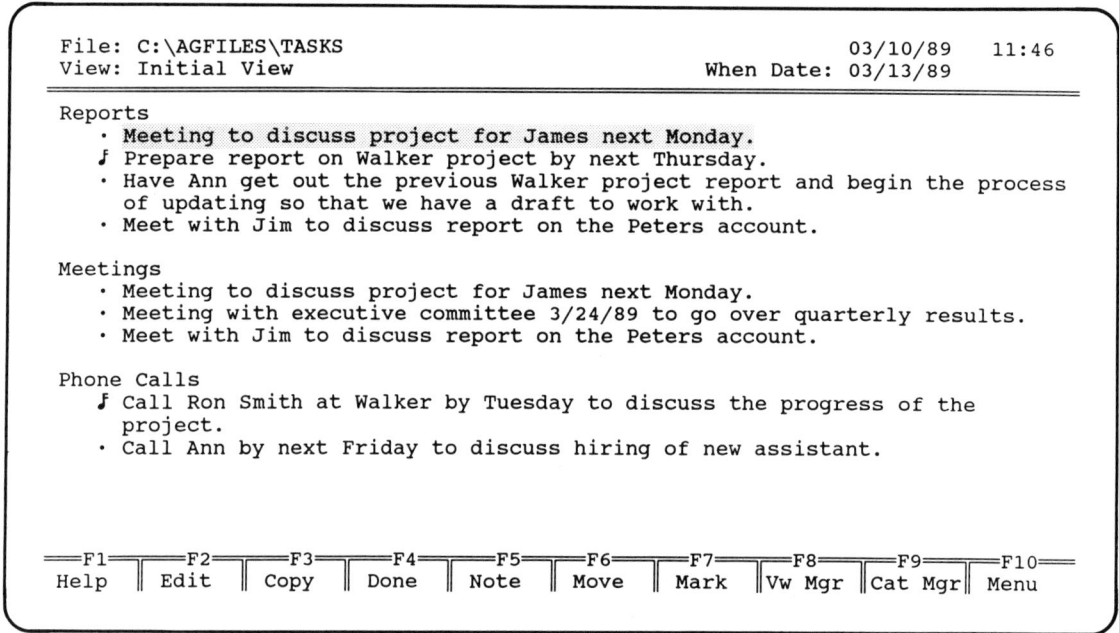

Fig. 4-13. The Tasks database with the items in each section sorted by the When Date.

help system can be useful. When making the settings in the Sort dialog box, press F1 (HELP) to display information on Agenda's sorting procedures.

Using sections is one important method for organizing the information in an Agenda database. Working with the items in the sections provides one means for assigning the items to categories. This is the first step in gaining control over information in your Agenda database.

# 5

# ORGANIZING INFORMATION USING COLUMNS

SECTIONS provide one method for assigning items to categories. The very nature of the division of a view into sections means that sections can provide only a one-dimensional look at the category assignment of items in the database. While many different sections can be displayed in a view, any given section displays only the items assigned to that section, and provides no information on the assignment of those items to other sections.

To display more information on the assignment of items to categories, Agenda allows columns to be added adjacent to the items in the sections of a view. In addition to showing information about the assignment of the items to other categories, columns also facilitate the direct assignment of items to additional categories.

The first part of this chapter explains how to create columns and how to use them to assign items to additional categories. The next part illustrates some of the ways in which columns can display a variety of information. Finally, the last part describes the procedures for managing columns, such as the procedures for changing widths and moving columns.

## CREATING COLUMNS AND ASSIGNING ITEMS

New columns can be added to views to display the assignment of items to additional categories. Columns can also be used to assign existing items to new categories or to change the assignment of items to categories. Columns also help to show the automatic assignment of items to categories that occurs when the items are entered.

## Creating New Columns

New categories can be created and items can be assigned to them without ever displaying the categories or the assignments in any view. Such abstract operations are less than intuitive, however, and are likely to result in errors and omissions. The easiest way to create new categories and category assignments is to display this information on the screen in columns adjacent to the existing items and sections.

You will create columns using the Tasks database developed in the previous chapters. Many of the items in the Tasks database refer to various projects in which the user is involved, such as the Walker project, the James project, and so forth. The information in the database can be organized further by creating separate categories for each of the projects and assigning items to the appropriate project categories. For example, all of the items dealing with the Walker project could be assigned to a Walker category.

Add a Project category column to the initial view of the Tasks database so that items can be assigned to the appropriate project categories. Add the new column by entering the Category Column New command. The New Column box appears in the middle of the screen, as shown in Fig. 5-1. The default options for the first setting in the New Column box specifies that the column is to be entered to the right of the current column. The current column is the one highlighted when you enter the command. In the Tasks database, the current column is made up of section heads and items under those heads. Placing the new Project column to the right is logical, so leave this option unchanged. (The other option is to place the new column to the left of the current column.)

The next setting in the New Column box is for the specification of the column type. The default column type is a *category column*, a column in which information relating to various categories is to be entered and displayed. The Project column is to include categories for the various projects, so the category column type is the appropriate option. Again, no change needs to be made. (Other column types can display date information. These are illustrated later.)

A column head must be entered for a category column. Move the highlight to the right of *Column head:*, type in

Project

```
File: C:\AGFILES\TASKS                              03/10/89
View: Initial View
════════════════════════════════════════════════════════════

Reports
  • Meeting t┌──────────────────────New Column══════════┐
  ♪ Prepare r│                                          │  the process
  • Have Ann  │ Position:       Right of current column  │
    of updati │ Column type:    Category                 │
  • Meet with │ Column head:    Project                  │
            │ Format:         Actual category          │
Meetings     │                                          │
  • Meeting t│ Insert in:      All sections             │
  • Meeting w│                                          │  results.
  • Meet with└═════════Press F9 when done, ESC to cancel═┘

Phone Calls
  ♪ Call Ron Smith at Walker by Tuesday to discuss the progress of the
    project.
  • Call Ann by next Friday to discuss hiring of new assistant.




═F1══════F2═══════F3═══════F4══════F5══════F6═══════F7═══════F8═══════F9═════F10══
Help  │ Edit  │       │       │       │       │       │Default│Accept │
```

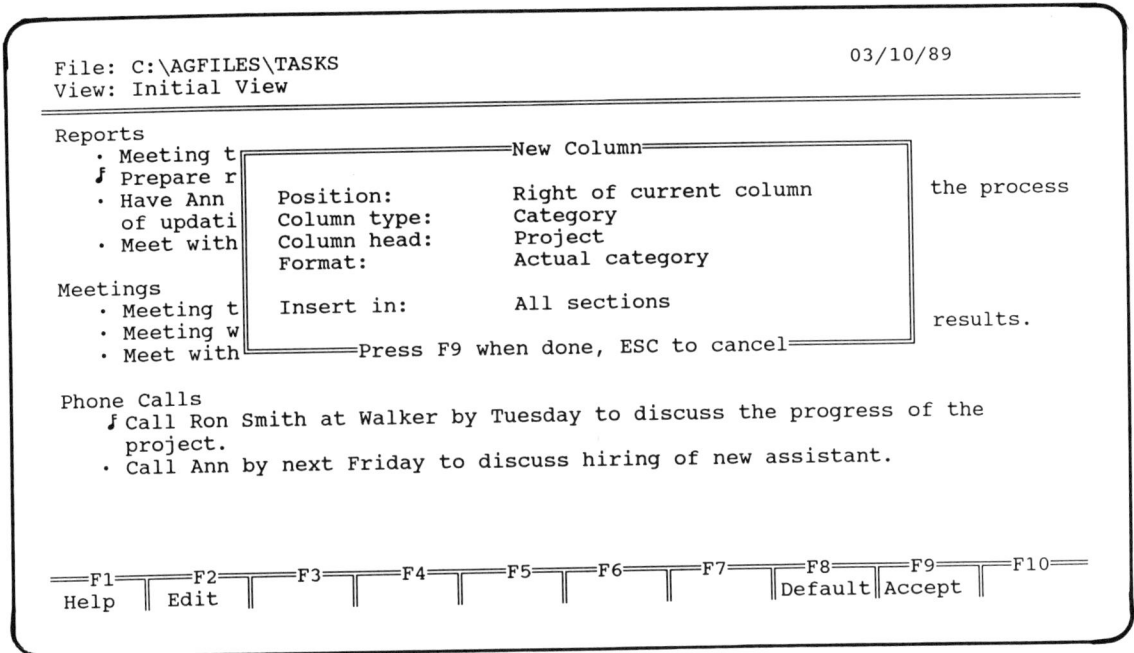

Fig. 5-1. *Entering a new column to be named "Project" in the Tasks database.*

and press ENTER. This creates a new category with the name Project and establishes this category name as the head for the new column being created.

The default display format shown in the New Column box instructs Agenda to display the actual category to which the item is assigned. You want to display the actual category assignment, so leave this setting unchanged. (Additional format options are illustrated in the second part of this chapter.)

The last setting in the New Column box is for specifying the sections in which the column is to be created. The default setting is for the column to be created for all sections of the current view. It is possible to add new columns that will be displayed only in the current section. For the Tasks database, the new column is to be in all of the sections, so no change is necessary.

Press F9 to accept the settings in the box. The new column named Project is created and displayed on the screen. A new category named Project has also been created in the Tasks database. The project categories entered in this column will be subcategories created within the Project category. Using Agenda's terminology, Project is the *parent* category and the specific project categories, such as the Walker project category, are *child* categories.

## Assigning Items to Categories Using Columns

Items can be assigned to categories, and new categories can be created, by placing entries in the Project column. The user must create the new categories and assign the existing items to those categories. When new items are entered subsequently, however, Agenda might be able to figure out the category to which the new items should be assigned and make the assignments automatically.

The first item in the Tasks database refers to the project for James. You need to create a James project category and assign that item to the category. The process is accomplished in a single step. Move the highlight to the Project column, to the right of the first item. Pressing the RIGHT and LEFT arrow keys moves the highlight from one column to the next. (The UP and DOWN arrow keys work in the normal manner.) Note that when the highlight is to the right of the first item, a double arrow on the left side of the screen points to that item. The double arrow indicates the item that is associated with the highlighted entry. These double arrows can be especially helpful in identifying the associated entries in more complex views.

To enter a category name into the Project column, type in James and press ENTER. James appears in the Project column to the right of the first item. Since that item is also assigned to the Meetings category and is displayed in the Meetings section, the assignment of that item to the James category is also shown in the Meetings section. The screen appears as in Fig. 5-2.

The simple action of inserting the James category in the Project column to the right of the first item actually causes three things to happen in the Agenda database. First, a new category named James is created as a child category of the Project category. Second, the first item shown in the database is assigned to this newly created James category. Third, the assignment of this item to the James category is shown by displaying the category name James in the Project column to the right of the item wherever the item appears in the Initial view.

Categories and the assignment of items to categories exist independently of their display in a column of a view. The column helps you create new categories, assign items to categories, and view the category assignments. But the existence of the column is not necessary for the existence of the categories and their items. For example, the Project column could be removed from this view so that the assignment of the item to the James category would no longer be displayed. Nevertheless, the James category would continue to exist in the database, and

```
File: C:\AGFILES\TASKS                                          03/10/89   12:50
View: Initial View                               When Date: 03/13/89
================================================================================
Reports                                                       Project
    » Meeting to discuss project for James next Monday.        ·James
    ♪ Prepare report on Walker project by next Thursday.
    · Have Ann get out the previous Walker project report and
      begin the process of updating so that we have a draft to
      work with.
    · Meet with Jim to discuss report on the Peters account.

Meetings                                                      Project
    · Meeting to discuss project for James next Monday.        ·James
    · Meeting with executive committee 3/24/89 to go over
      quarterly results.
    · Meet with Jim to discuss report on the Peters account.

Phone Calls                                                   Project
    ♪ Call Ron Smith at Walker by Tuesday to discuss the progress
      of the project.
    · Call Ann by next Friday to discuss hiring of new assistant.


==F1==T==F2==T==F3==T==F4==T==F5==T==F6==T==F7==T==F8==T==F9==T=F10==
 Help  ║ Edit ║ Copy ║ Done ║ Note ║ Move ║ Mark ║Vw Mgr║Cat Mgr║ Menu
```

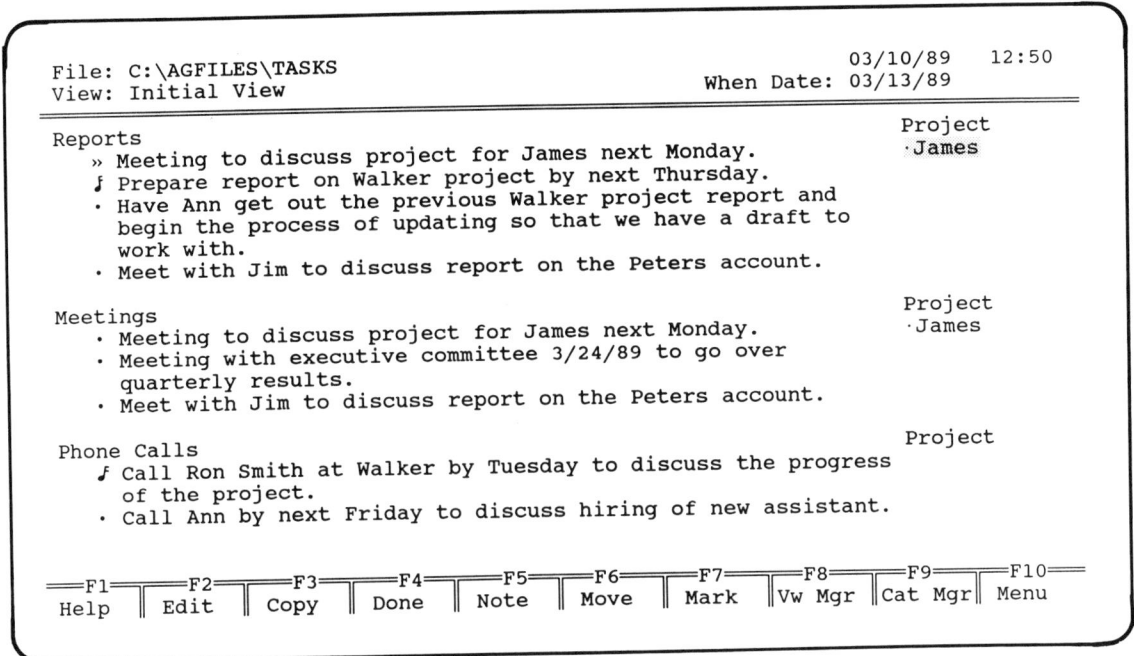

Fig. 5-2. *The assignment of the first item to the James category in the Project column.*

the item would continue to be assigned to that category. Even if steps were taken to unassign the item from the James category, that category would continue to exist as a child of the Project category.

In the Tasks database, assign the second item in the Reports section— "Prepare report on Walker project by next Thursday"—to the Walker category. Use the arrow keys to move the highlight so that it is in the Project category to the right of the second item. Then type in

Walker

and press ENTER. The Walker category is created, the item is assigned to that category, and the Project column shows the assignment of the item to the category.

The third item should also be assigned to the Walker category. Move the highlight down to the right of the third item and just type W. Agenda emits a high-pitched beep and informs you that the database already includes a category, the Walker category, that begins with the letter you have just typed. Figure 5-3 shows the screen at this point. Since the Walker category is the only category beginning with W and this is the

```
┌────────────────────────────────────────────────────────────────────────┐
│                                                                          │
│  1 of 1 matching categories. Current choice: Walker          AutoC       │
│  W                                                                       │
│ ════════════════════════════════════════════════════════════════════    │
│  Reports                                                    Project      │
│     · Meeting to discuss project for James next Monday.      ·James      │
│     ♪ Prepare report on Walker project by next Thursday.     ·Walker     │
│     » Have Ann get out the previous Walker project report and            │
│       begin the process of updating so that we have a draft to           │
│       work with.                                                         │
│     · Meet with Jim to discuss report on the Peters account.             │
│                                                                          │
│  Meetings                                                   Project      │
│     · Meeting to discuss project for James next Monday.      ·James      │
│     · Meeting with executive committee 3/24/89 to go over                │
│       quarterly results.                                                 │
│     · Meet with Jim to discuss report on the Peters account.             │
│                                                                          │
│  Phone Calls                                                Project      │
│     ♪ Call Ron Smith at Walker by Tuesday to discuss the progress        │
│       of the project.                                                    │
│     · Call Ann by next Friday to discuss hiring of new assistant.        │
│                                                                          │
│ ══F1══╤══F2══╤══F3══╤══F4══╤══F5══╤══F6══╤══F7══╤══F8══╤══F9══╤══F10══    │
│  Help ║      ║      ║      ║NewCat║      ║PrevSel║NextSel║Accept║         │
│                                                                          │
└────────────────────────────────────────────────────────────────────────┘
```

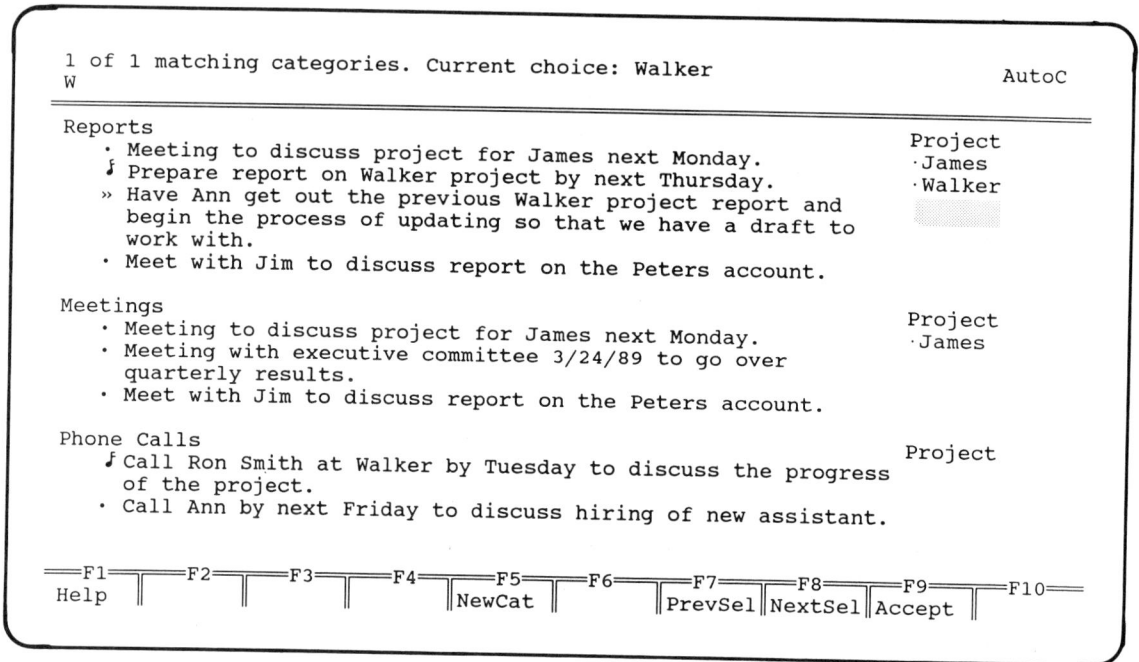

*Fig. 5-3. Selecting the matching category Walker after typing in the W to assign an item to the Walker category.*

category you want, you do not have to type the remainder of the category name. Press ENTER to enter the Walker category.

Whenever you are entering a category name—in a column, as a section head, or in some other position—Agenda provides several automatic completion options. When you begin typing in a category name as you did with the Walker category, Agenda checks to see whether the letters you have typed match those of an existing category. If Agenda finds that one and only one category matches the letters typed, it gives a high-pitched beep and displays the matching category on the top line of the screen. You can choose to accept that category by pressing ENTER, or you can continue typing to enter a new category.

As you enter more categories into a database, several categories might match the letter or letters you have typed in. For example, if you were to add Watson and Wilson categories, a *W* would match three categories: the Walker, Watson, and Wilson categories. As you type in letters for a category name, Agenda tells you the number of matching categories and displays the first matching category. You can use the UP and DOWN arrows to display each of the matching categories or press ENTER to select the desired one. Or you can keep typing. In a database containing Walker, Watson, and Wilson categories, after typing *Wa*, you would have two matching categories, Walker and Watson. After typing the letters *Wal*, Walker would be the only matching category displayed, and Agenda would beep to indicate a match.

At any point in typing in a category name, you can use the UP and DOWN arrow keys to display the other matching categories and you can use ENTER to select and enter the category name displayed. Or you can keep typing and press ENTER after the entire category name has been typed. Typing the entire category name is the only option, of course, when entering a new category.

Another shortcut for entering category names that already have been created is to press GREY PLUS to display a selection box that includes a list of all of the categories in the database. You can highlight the desired category and press ENTER to select and enter that category name.

Assign the remaining items in the database to the appropriate project categories so that the screen appears as shown in Fig. 5-4. Place the highlight opposite the item in the Project category. Type in the category name. After the initial entry of each category name, use the automatic completion capabilities to enter the categories without typing the entire name. Note that some of the items do not have category assignments in the Project column because the items do not refer to any project.

```
File: C:\AGFILES\TASKS                              03/10/89   12:54
View: Initial View                    When Date: 03/15/89
==============================================================================
Reports                                                      Project
   · Meeting to discuss project for James next Monday.        ·James
     Prepare report on Walker project by next Thursday.       ·Walker
   · Have Ann get out the previous Walker project report and  ·Walker
     begin the process of updating so that we have a draft to
     work with.
   · Meet with Jim to discuss report on the Peters account.   ·Peters

Meetings                                                     Project
   · Meeting to discuss project for James next Monday.        ·James
   · Meeting with executive committee 3/24/89 to go over
     quarterly results.
   · Meet with Jim to discuss report on the Peters account.   ·Peters

Phone Calls                                                  Project
     Call Ron Smith at Walker by Tuesday to discuss the progress
     of the project.
   · Call Ann by next Friday to discuss hiring of new assistant.
   · Call Adam Baker at James Wednesday to get his reactions to  »James
     our proposals.
==F1====F2====F3====F4====F5====F6====F7====F8====F9====F10==
 Help   Edit   Copy   Done   Note   Move   Mark  Vw Mgr Cat Mgr Menu
```

Fig. 5-4. *The automatic assignment of a new item to the James category, with the category automatically displayed in the Project column.*

A powerful feature of Agenda is its capability to automatically assign items to the appropriate categories based upon the text of the item. This capability requires no special action on the part of the user.

To illustrate automatic assignment for new items, use the arrow keys to move the highlight to the last item in the Phone Calls section. Enter a new item by pressing INS and typing in the following text:

Call Adam Baker at James Wednesday to get his reactions to our proposals.

Press ENTER and the item is entered in the usual fashion. But look what else has happened. Agenda has assigned the item to the James project category and displays that category assignment in the Project column as shown in Fig. 5-4. When the item was entered, Agenda matched the reference to James in the item with the James category and automatically made the assignment.

If the appropriate categories have been created prior to the entry of an item, Agenda is frequently able to perform the assignment of new items to the correct categories without any action on the part of the user. Agenda is not infallible in its ability to automatically assign items to categories, however.

To illustrate, press INS again to enter a new item below the last item and type in this text:

Call Peter Smith regarding new account proposals for Walker and Acme.

When this item is entered, Agenda automatically assigns the item to two categories, the categories for the Peters and the Walker projects, as illustrated in Fig. 5-5. Agenda incorrectly matches the reference to Peter Smith to the Peters project category. Agenda's automatic category assignment is accomplished simply by the blind matching of strings of text in an item that is entered with the names of the categories. Agenda has no way of determining that the word "Peter" in this item is a reference to Peter Smith, not a reference to the Peters project.

If incorrect assignments become a frequent problem when using Agenda, you can limit the amount of initiative Agenda displays in automatically assigning items to categories. This is discussed in Chapter 11.

```
 File: C:\AGFILES\TASKS                              03/10/89   12:55
 View: Initial View
=Reports ════════════════════════════════════════════ Project═════
        ♪ Prepare report on Walker project by next Thursday.    ·Walker
        · Have Ann get out the previous Walker project report and  ·Walker
          begin the process of updating so that we have a draft to
          work with.
        · Meet with Jim to discuss report on the Peters account.   ·Peters

 Meetings                                                     Project
        · Meeting to discuss project for James next Monday.    ·James
        · Meeting with executive committee 3/24/89 to go over
          quarterly results.
        · Meet with Jim to discuss report on the Peters account.   ·Peters

 Phone Calls                                                  Project
        ♪ Call Ron Smith at Walker by Tuesday to discuss the progress ·Walker
          of the project.
        · Call Ann by next Friday to discuss hiring of new assistant.
        · Call Adam Baker at James Wednesday to get his reactions to  ·James
          our proposals.
        · Call Peter Smith regarding new account proposals for Walker »Walker
          and Acme.                                                »Peters
══F1══╤══F2══╤══F3══╤══F4══╤══F5══╤══F6══╤══F7══╤══F8══╤══F9══╤══F10══
 Help │ Edit │ Copy │ Done │ Note │ Move │ Mark │Vw Mgr│Cat Mgr│ Menu
```

Fig. 5-5. *The automatic assignment of a new item to two categories, with an incorrect assignment to the Peters category.*

In the Tasks database, eliminate the assignment of the new item to the Peters project category and assign the item to a new Acme project category. To drop the assignment of the item to the Peters project, highlight Peters in the Project column. Then press DEL to unassign the item to this category. The assignment is dropped and Peters is no longer displayed in the Project column to the right of the last-entered item.

An item can be assigned to two (or more) categories in a column, assuming that the categories are not mutually exclusive. (The creation of mutually exclusive categories is discussed later, in Chapter 7.)

In the Tasks database, the last item is currently assigned to one category, for the Walker project. However, the item also refers to another project, Acme, and should be assigned to this project category as well. Move the highlight to Walker, in the Project column, to the right of the last item. Press INS to add another category assignment for this item. Then type in Acme, which appears on the top of the screen as shown in Fig. 5-6. Since this is a new category, Agenda displays the message that there are no matching categories. When you press ENTER, the Acme catego-

```
  1 of 1 matching categories. Current choice: Acme                    AutoC
  Acme
 =Reports ==============================================  Project=
       ♪ Prepare report on Walker project by next Thursday.         ·Walker
       · Have Ann get out the previous Walker project report and     ·Walker
         begin the process of updating so that we have a draft to
         work with.
       · Meet with Jim to discuss report on the Peters account.       ·Peters

    Meetings                                                   Project
       · Meeting to discuss project for James next Monday.          ·James
       · Meeting with executive committee 3/24/89 to go over
         quarterly results.
       · Meet with Jim to discuss report on the Peters account.       ·Peters

    Phone Calls                                                Project
       ♪ Call Ron Smith at Walker by Tuesday to discuss the progress ·Walker
         of the project.
       · Call Ann by next Friday to discuss hiring of new assistant.
       · Call Adam Baker at James Wednesday to get his reactions to   ·James
         our proposals.
       » Call Peter Smith regarding new account proposals for Walker ·Walker
         and Acme.
 ==F1====F2====F3====F4====F5====F6====F7====F8====F9====F10==
   Help                         NewCat          PrevSel NextSel Accept
```

Fig. 5-6. *Entering category assignment to the Acme category for the last item entered.*

ry is displayed in the Project column under Walker, to the right of the
final item.

Thus far, this chapter has covered all of the basic procedures needed to use
columns to assign items to categories. To assign existing items to categories in
a column, place the highlight in the column adjacent to the item. If no category
name is currently displayed, enter the category name, either by typing it in or
by making use of Agenda's facilities for entering the names of existing categories. If one or more category names are already shown for the item in the column,
you must first press INS before entering an additional category name.

These procedures can be used to assign the items to as many columns as
desired. To unassign an item from a category in a column, highlight the category
name in the column and press DEL. When new items are entered, Agenda
automatically attempts to assign them to the appropriate category.

## CREATING DIFFERENT KINDS OF COLUMNS

A variety of other column types can be used to display dates and to show
the assignment of items to categories in different ways. The category column was
just discussed. This section of the chapter illustrates the use of When Date, Star,
and Yes/No columns, and discusses the other options available in Agenda.

## Date Columns

As explained in the last chapter, if an item contains a reference to a date, Agenda automatically assigns a When Date to the item. As you have seen, items can be sorted within each section according to date. When an Agenda database is used to keep track of dates, it is helpful to display the dates in a column.

In the Tasks database, begin creating a When Date column by highlighting any entry in the Project column and entering the Category Column New command. The New Column box is displayed on the screen. You want a Date column, so you need to change the *Column type:* setting from Category to When Date. Move the highlight down so that it is across from the *Column type:* setting. Press GREY PLUS to display the list of column options. The screen now appears as shown in Fig. 5-7. Select *When date* and press ENTER. The remainder of the settings in the New Column box can be left at their default values, creating the column to the right of the Project column in all sections. Press F9 to accept the settings and create the When Date column.

The new When Date column is shown in Fig. 5-10. It illustrates the view of the database after the addition of all three new columns in the section. The new column is headed "When." Next to each item that includes a date reference, the When Date is displayed in the When

```
New   Remove   Position   Format   Width
Insert a new column
==============================================================
                                                    Project
Reports                            =New Column=      James
 · Meeting t                                         Walker
 ♪ Prepare r                                         Walker
 · Have Ann    Position:      Choices:      column
   begin the   Column type:
   work with   Column head:
 » Meet with   Format:         Category               Peters
                               Entry date
Meetings       Insert in:      When date              roject
 · Meeting t                   Done date              James
 · Meeting w   =Press F9 wh              ncel=
   quarterly results.
 · Meet with Jim to discuss report on the Peters account.  ·Peters

                                                    Project
Phone Calls
 ♪ Call Ron Smith at Walker by Tuesday to discuss the progress ·Walker
   of the project.
 · Call Adam Baker at James Wednesday to get his reactions to  ·James
   our proposals.
 · Call Ann by next Friday to discuss hiring of new assistant.
=F1===F2===F3===F4===F5===F6===F7===F8===F9===F10==
Help                                            Accept
```

Fig. 5-7. *Inserting a second column for the When Date.*

column. The date in the column is the same as the When Date shown on the second line of the screen when an item is highlighted. ⌨

## Star and Yes/No Columns

Sometimes you might want to use a column to indicate whether an item is assigned to a particular category. Agenda has two column display formats to show this: Star and Yes/No columns. These columns can be used to indicate that an item is assigned to either the parent category, or a child category within that parent category. Star and Yes/No columns will be used to display different aspects of the category assignments in the Tasks database.

⌨ You might wish to use a column to indicate all of the items assigned to the Walker project category. Move the highlight to anyplace in the When column and enter the Category Column New command. The New Column box appears. You want to enter a column to the right of the When column and the new column is to be a category column, so leave the first two settings in the box unchanged. You need to enter a column head, so move the highlight to the third line in the box. The column head will be the category name Walker. Since the Walker category already exists, you do not need to type it in. Instead, press GREY PLUS to display the Category Select box that lists of all of the categories in the database, as shown in Fig. 5-8. Highlight Walker and press F9 to enter this as the column head.

Assume you want to indicate those items assigned to the Walker category by having an asterisk appear in the new column. To accomplish this, use the Star display format. In the New Column box, move the highlight down to *Format:* and press GREY PLUS to display the list of all of the display format options for category columns. The screen should appear as shown in Fig. 5-9. Select *Star (*)* and press ENTER. This completes the settings for the creation of the Walker Star column. Press F9 to accept all of the settings and create the column.

Figure 5-10 shows the new Star column to the right of the When column (the figure also shows the Yes/No column). When Star columns are created, they are two characters wide, so the column head is simply *Wa*, the first two letters in Walker. The width of the column can be expanded to display the entire head, if desired. The procedures for expanding columns are explained in the final section of this chapter.

In the Walker column, an asterisk is displayed if the associated item is assigned to the Walker category. The column is empty for items not assigned to the Walker category. This allows you to quickly glance down the column and identify those items relating to the Walker project. ⌨

```
 New  Remove  Position  Format  Width
 Insert a new column
╔══════════════════════════════════════════════════════════════╗ject    When
║                      ═Category Select═                         ║         ·03/13/89
║ Select a category                                              ║
║ Press F9 when done, ESC to cancel                              ║mn       ·03/16/89
║                                                                ║
║ MAIN                                                           ║
║   Project                                                      ║
║     James                                                      ║
║     Walker                                                     ║
║     Acme                                                       ║
║     Peters                                                     ║
║   Reports                                                      ║ject    When
║   Meetings                                                     ║mes      ·03/13/89
║   Phone Calls                                                  ║
║                                                                ║         ·03/24/89
║                                                                ║
║                                                                ║ters
╚══════════════════════════════════════════════════════════════╝
        account.

  Phone Calls                                         Project    When
 ══F1════╤══F2════╤══F3════╤══F4════╤══F5════╤══F6════╤══F7════╤══F8════╤══F9════╤══F10══
  Help   ║ Edit   ║                                             ║Accept  ║
```

Fig. 5-8. *Selecting the existing category Walker as the name of a new column.*

```
 New  Remove  Position  Format  Width
 Insert a new column
═══════════════════════════════════════════════════════ Project    When
 Reports                                                          ·03/13/89
   · Meeting t╔═══════════════════New Column═══════════════════╗
     Monday.  ║                                                ║ ·03/16/89
   ♪ Prepare r║  Position:          Right of current column    ║
     Thursday.║  Column type:                                  ║
   » Have Ann ║  Column head:   ╔═════════════════════════════╗║
     report an║  Format:        ║ Choices:                    ║║
     that we h║                 ║                             ║║
   · Meet with║  Insert in:     ╟─────────────────────────────╢║
     account. ║                 ║  Actual category            ║║
             ═╚═════Press F9 wh  ║  Parent:Category            ║║
                                 ║  Ancestor                   ║║  When
   Meetings                      ║  Star (*)                   ║║  ·03/13/89
     · Meeting to discuss project fo║  Yes/No                  ║║
       Monday.                   ║  Category note              ║║  ·03/24/89
     · Meeting with executive commit║                          ║║
       over quarterly results.   ╚═════════════════════════════╝║
     · Meet with Jim to discuss report on the Peters    ·Peters
       account.

   Phone Calls                                        Project    When
  ══F1════╤══F2════╤══F3════╤══F4════╤══F5════╤══F6════╤══F7════╤══F8════╤══F9════╤══F10══
   Help   ║                                                     ║Accept  ║
```

Fig. 5-9. *Selecting the Star (*) format for the Walker column.*

```
┌─────────────────────────────────────────────────────────────────────────┐
│                                                                           │
│  File: C:\AGFILES\TASKS                                                    │
│  View: Initial View                              03/10/89    13:02         │
│  ═══════════════════════════════════════════════════════════════════════  │
│  Reports                              Project      When        Wa   Pr     │
│     · Meeting to discuss project for James  ·James      ·03/13/89          Y │
│       next Monday.                                                         │
│     ♪ Prepare report on Walker project by   ·Walker     ·03/16/89     *    Y │
│       next Thursday.                                                       │
│     » Have Ann get out the previous Walker  ·Walker                   *    Y │
│       project report and begin the process of                             │
│       updating so that we have a draft to                                 │
│       work with.                                                          │
│     · Meet with Jim to discuss report on the  ·Peters                       Y │
│       Peters account.                                                     │
│                                                                           │
│  Meetings                              Project      When        Wa   Pr   │
│     · Meeting to discuss project for James  ·James      ·03/13/89          Y │
│       next Monday.                                                         │
│     · Meeting with executive committee                  ·03/24/89          N │
│       3/24/89 to go over quarterly results.                               │
│     · Meet with Jim to discuss report on the  ·Peters                       Y │
│       Peters account.                                                     │
│  ═══╤═════╤═════╤═════╤═════╤═════╤═════╤═════╤═════╤═══════  │
│  =F1═╤═F2══╤═F3══╤═F4══╤═F5══╤═F6══╤═F7══╤═F8═══╤═F9═══╤═F10══  │
│  Help │ Edit │ Copy │ Done │ Note │ Move │ Mark │Vw Mgr│Cat Mgr│ Menu      │
│                                                                           │
└─────────────────────────────────────────────────────────────────────────┘
```

Fig. 5-10. *The Tasks database with three new columns: When Date, Walker in Star format, and Project in Yes/No format.*

A Star column can be employed to assign items to categories and to unassign items in the same manner that the Project column is used. For example, to assign an item to the Walker category, you would move the highlight to the blank position in the column adjacent to that item and enter Walker. You could either press GREY PLUS to display the list of categories and make the selection, type the W and press ENTER to accept the matching category, or type in the entire category name. When you assigned the item to the Walker category, an asterisk would appear in the column and the assignment to the Walker category would also be indicated in the Project column.

To unassign an item from the Walker category, you would move the highlight to the asterisk and press DEL. Then, the assignment of the item to the Walker category would be eliminated. The asterisk would be removed from the Walker column and the Walker category assignment would be removed from the Project column. The assigning and unassigning of items from a category works exactly the same in Star columns as in regular category columns.

Another projects column can be added to distinguish between those items assigned to one of the project categories and those items not related or assigned to any project.

To add the new Project column, check to see that the highlight is in the rightmost column. Then execute the Category Column New command. The New Column box appears. The column head is to be Project, so place the highlight to the right of the *Column head:* setting, press GREY PLUS, select the Project category, and press ENTER. Now specify the format. Move the highlight down to the *Format:* setting and press GREY PLUS to show the list of column format options. You could indicate which items were assigned to some project by using the Star format again. Another option, however, is to use the Yes/No format. Select *Yes/No* and press ENTER. Now press F9 to create the column.

Figure 5-10 shows the Yes/No Project column at the right edge of the display. Like the Star format, Yes/No columns are initially two characters wide. Thus, the column head is limited to Pr for Project. The Yes/No display format places a Y in the Project column if the item is assigned to the Project category or to any of the child categories of that category. All of the individual project categories— James, Walker, and so forth—are child categories of the Project category. Thus, items referring to the individual projects and assigned to those categories will have a Y for Yes in the new Project column. If the item has not been assigned to any of the project categories, an N for No appears in the column.

The Yes/No column works exactly like the Star column, except that a Y (for Yes) is displayed in place of the asterisk and an N (for No) is displayed for items where a Star column would be blank. Assignments and unassignments of items can be made in the same way as with any category column. If you highlight a Y in the Yes/No column and press DEL, the item is unassigned from the specific project category to which it had been assigned. The Y changes to N and the category assignment displayed in the first Project category disappears.

To assign an item to a project category where there was no such assignment, highlight the N and enter the category name—James, Walker, or whatever. The N changes to Y and the category name also appears in the first Project column.

## Additional Category Column Formats

As you undoubtedly noticed on the list of format options, Agenda includes three additional column formats: *Parent:category, Ancestor*, and *Category note*. These additional formats are described briefly here. Since they are used less frequently by most Agenda users, examples of their application to the Tasks database are not provided.

The Parent:category and Ancestor column formats are useful only for databases with a more complex category structure than the current Tasks database.

In the Tasks database, items referring to projects are assigned to specific categories (such as the Walker category) that are child categories of the overall Project category, which is the parent category. Suppose that this breakdown were taken a step further: each of the specific project categories, such as Walker, could have its own child categories specifying particular tasks to be accomplished within that project category. For example, the Walker category might have child categories such as Proposal and Research relating to tasks to be performed for Walker. Then items relating to the tasks to be performed for the Walker project would be assigned to those task categories of Proposal, Research, and so forth. The same creation and assignment to task categories would be carried out for each of the other project categories.

Suppose you included a Project column and used the *Actual category* format to display the category to which an item is assigned. Take an item referring to the preparation of the Proposal for the Walker project. The item would be assigned to the Proposal category, which would be a child category of the Walker category. Since the item is assigned to the Proposal category, Proposal would be displayed as the Actual category in the Project column. You would see information on the task name, but you would not necessarily know the project for which the task was to be completed.

Here is where the Parent:category and Ancestor column formats become useful. The Parent:category format shows not only the category to which the item is assigned, but its parent category as well. For the item involving the preparation of the proposal for the Walker project, the Project column could then display Walker:Proposal rather than just Proposal. You could see the parent category for which the task is to be completed as well as the task category itself.

Alternatively, you might not even be interested in knowing the specific task, but only the project for which the task is to be completed. In this instance, you could use the Ancestor format for the Project column. This would display the project category, such as Walker, without showing the task category. The Ancestor format shows the parent (or the parent of the parent, etc.) of the category to which the item is assigned.

Another category format option is the *Category note* column. Instead of displaying the category to which an item is assigned, the Category note column displays the first line of any note attached to that category. Necessarily, such a column can be used only when notes are attached to the categories and when the information in the notes is structured. For example, suppose that for each of the projects, you attached a note to the project category with the name of your contact at the client firm. Ron Smith might be the contact person at Walker. You attach a note to the Walker category with Ron Smith on the first line. Then you can create a Project column and use the Category note format. Ron Smith would be displayed for each project assigned to the Walker category.

*Table 5-1. Column Types and Display Formats.*

| Column Type | Format | Displays |
|---|---|---|
| Category | | |
| | Actual category | Category to which item is assigned. |
| | Parent:category | Parent category and category to which item is assigned. |
| | Ancestor | Child category of column head category that is parent or ancestor of category to which item is assigned. |
| | Star (*) | Asterisk for items assigned to category of column head or assigned to child or descendent category. |
| | Yes/No | Y for items assigned to category of column head directly or assigned to child or descendent category; N for other items. |
| | Category note | Line of note attached to category to which item is assigned. |
| Entry date | | Date item entered. |
| When date | | Date reference within item. |
| Done date | | Date item set to done. |

The various column types and formats are summarized in Table 5-1. In most situations, it is easy to try several column formats until you get the presentation you want. Just remember that the Parent:category and Ancestor formats are generally useful only when you have two or more levels of categories beneath the column category. The Category note format makes sense only when you have notes attached to the categories.

## MANAGING COLUMNS

The Category Column commands provide tools for managing the columns you create in a view. You can change column widths, remove columns, move columns around in sections, and otherwise closely control the display of columns. This section describes the use of these commands.

## Changing Column Widths

The Walker Star column and the Project Yes/No column were created as two-character columns. This means that the first two letters of the column heads are displayed. The columns must be widened to display the entire column heads. The Category Column Width command is used to change the width of columns in a view.

To expand the width of the Walker Star column, first move the highlight to that column—anywhere in the column will do. Select the Category Column Width command. Agenda prompts you to enter the number for the column width or use the arrow keys to adjust the width. The RIGHT and LEFT arrow keys make the column wider and narrower, respectively. It is generally easier to adjust column widths using the arrow keys, observing the results on the screen. Press the RIGHT arrow four times. The column is expanded to a width of six characters and the entire Walker column head is now displayed, as shown in Fig. 5-11. Press ENTER to make the new column width permanent and complete the command.

## Removing Columns

The Category Column commands can also be used to remove columns.

```
Enter number, or use arrow keys to indicate width
6

Reports                                     Project      When        Walker  Pr
  · Meeting to discuss project for          ·James       ·03/13/89           Y
    James next Monday.
  ♪ Prepare report on Walker project by  ·Walker         ·03/16/89      *     Y
    next Thursday.
  » Have Ann get out the previous          ·Walker                      *     Y
    Walker project report and begin the
    process of updating so that we have
    a draft to work with.
  · Meet with Jim to discuss report on     ·Peters                            Y
    the Peters account.

Meetings                                    Project      When        Walker  Pr
  · Meeting to discuss project for          ·James       ·03/13/89           Y
    James next Monday.
  · Meeting with executive committee                     ·03/24/89           N
    3/24/89 to go over quarterly
    results.
  · Meet with Jim to discuss report on     ·Peters                            Y
    the Peters account.
=F1==T==F2===T===F3===T===F4===T===F5===T==F6===T==F7===T==F8===T==F9===T==F10==
Help                                                           Accept
```

Fig. 5-11. *Increasing the width of the Walker Star column.*

The Yes/No Project column on the far right edge of the screen adds little information. It should be removed. Move the highlight to that column and enter the Category Column Remove command. Since this column was created in all sections, a box appears asking whether you wish to remove the column from all sections. The screen should appear as shown in Fig. 5-12. Changing the setting to No by pressing N causes the column to be removed only from the current section in which the highlight is located. Since this column should be removed from all sections, leave the setting unchanged and press ENTER. The Yes/No Project column is immediately removed from all sections.

You can also remove columns from views by highlighting the column head in any section and pressing DEL. If the column is in more than one section, the same box will appear as in Fig. 5-12 asking whether you want to remove the column from all sections. Respond exactly as with the Category Column Remove command.

## Moving Columns

Columns can be moved around within individual sections by using the Category Column Position command.

```
New   Remove   Position   Format   Width
Remove current column from View
_____
Reports                              Project      When        Walker  Pr
   · Meeting to discuss project for   ·James       ·03/13/89            Y
     James next Monday.
   ♪ Prepare report on Walker project by ·Walker    ·03/16/89      *     Y
     next Thursday.
   » Have Ann get  ┌─────────────────────────────────────┐     *       Y
     Walker projec │                                      │
     process of up │ Remove column from all sections:  Yes │
     a draft to wo │                                      │
   · Meet with Jim └═Press ENTER to accept, ESC to cancel═┘            Y
     the Peters account.

Meetings                             Project      When        Walker  Pr
   · Meeting to discuss project for   ·James       ·03/13/89            Y
     James next Monday.
   · Meeting with executive committee              ·03/24/89            N
     3/24/89 to go over quarterly
     results.
   · Meet with Jim to discuss report on  ·Peters                        Y
     the Peters account.
═F1══╤══F2══╤══F3══╤══F4══╤══F5══╤══F6══╤══F7══╤══F8══╤══F9══╤══F10══
Help  ║ Edit  ║      ║      ║      ║      ║      ║      ║Accept ║
```

Fig. 5-12. *Removing the Yes/No Project column from the view.*

Move the Walker column in the Reports section to the left of the When column. First, move the highlight into the Walker column within the Reports section. Then enter the Category Column Position command. As instructed, use the RIGHT and LEFT arrow keys to move the column. This works just like using the appropriate Position commands to move items and sections around. Press the LEFT arrow once to move the Walker column to the left of the When column. The screen appears as shown in Fig. 5-13. Press ENTER to complete the operation.

    The Walker column was added to the Tasks database only to illustrate the use of certain column operations in Agenda. It should be removed. With the highlight in the Walker column, issue the Category Column Remove command. Accept the default option to remove the column from all sections and press ENTER. The Walker column disappears.

    The Category Column Position command only allows the movement of a column within a single section. If you want to reposition the column in all sections of a view, you need to use the command to make the move within each section. With a large number of sections this can be quite tedious. It might be easier to create a new column in the correct position in all sections and remove the incorrectly positioned column.

```
 Use right & left arrow keys to reposition column
 Press ENTER to accept, ESC to cancel
 ─────────────────────────────────────────────────────────────────
 Reports                                  Project      Walker When
    · Meeting to discuss project for James  ·James             ·03/13/89
      next Monday.
    ♪ Prepare report on Walker project by   ·Walker        *    ·03/16/89
      next Thursday.
    » Have Ann get out the previous Walker  ·Walker        *
      project report and begin the process of
      updating so that we have a draft to
      work with.
    · Meet with Jim to discuss report on the ·Peters
      Peters account.

 Meetings                                 Project      When         Walker
    · Meeting to discuss project for James  ·James       ·03/13/89
      next Monday.
    · Meeting with executive committee                   ·03/24/89
      3/24/89 to go over quarterly results.
    · Meet with Jim to discuss report on the ·Peters
      Peters account.
 ══F1══╤══F2══╤══F3══╤══F4══╤══F5══╤══F6══╤══F7══╤══F8══╤══F9══╤══F10══
 Help  │      │      │      │      │      │      │      ║Accept║
```

Fig. 5-13. *Moving the Walker column in the Reports section.*

## Changing Column Formats and Linkage

The Category Column Formats command is used to perform two functions. Use it to change the format of an existing column, and to control the linking of columns across sections so that certain actions affect the column throughout the view or only in the current section. When this command is invoked, a Column Format dialog box with two settings is displayed on the screen as shown in Fig. 5-14.

The first setting in the Column Format box displays the current format of the column and is used to change the format. With this setting highlighted, pressing GREY PLUS displays the same list of format options presented when the column was created, shown in Fig. 5-9. To select another format, make the selection and press ENTER. This makes it easy to experiment to find the most useful format for a column.

When a new column is created in all sections of a view, the portions of the column in each section are linked to one another so these are all treated as a single column. Linking columns affects the changing of column heads, column widths, and column formats. With the columns linked globally, any of these changes will affect the column throughout the view. With the columns unlinked, it is possible to make changes to the column head, column width, and column format within a single section while leaving the column unchanged in all other sections. The setting in Fig. 5-14 indicates that the columns are linked globally. Changing the

```
New   Remove   Position   Format   Width
Specify current column type
═══════════════════════════════════════════════════════════════════════
Reports                                          Project      When
   • Meeting t┌════════════════Column Format════════════════┐03/13/89
     Monday.  │                                             │
   ♪ Prepare r│  Format:           Actual category          │03/16/89
     Thursday.│                                             │
   » Have Ann │  Link column globally:  Yes                 │
     report an│                                             │
     that we h└════════Press F9 when done, ESC to cancel════┘
   • Meet with Jim to discuss report on the Peters    ·Peters
     account.

Meetings                                         Project      When
   • Meeting to discuss project for James next   ·James     ·03/13/89
     Monday.
   • Meeting with executive committee 3/24/89 to go        ·03/24/89
     over quarterly results.
   • Meet with Jim to discuss report on the Peters    ·Peters
     account.

Phone Calls                                      Project      When
══F1══╤══F2══╤══F3══╤══F4══╤══F5══╤══F6══╤══F7══╤══F8═══╤══F9══╤══F10══
Help  ║ Edit ║      ║      ║      ║      ║      ║Default║Accept║
```

Fig. 5-14. *Using the Category Column Format command to change column formats and to unlink or link columns across sections.*

setting from *Yes* to *No* unlinks the columns so that certain changes can be made to columns within individual sections.

A new column can be created in just one section. Later, the same column also can be created in one or more additional sections. These individually created columns are not linked to one another. The Category Column Format command can be used to link these columns globally by changing the linkage setting from *No* to *Yes*

Linking columns does not affect removing them from views or repositioning them. When you give the command to remove a column, Agenda gives you the option of removing it from all sections or only from the current section. The Category Column Position command allows the movement of a column only within the current section, whether or not it is globally linked. Thus, linkage is irrelevant to these operations.

Knowing how to use sections and columns enables you to create a variety of categories, assign the items in a database to those categories, and indicate relationships among categories. With information entered into the Tasks database and structured through assignment to categories in sections and columns, the time has come to begin using that information.

# 6

# EXAMINING
# INFORMATION

AGENDA'S real power lies in its ability to display the information entered in a database in a variety of ways. In working with sections and columns, items can be assigned to many different categories. Assigning items to categories lets you organize information in ways that are very different from the way the information was initially entered into the database.

Agenda displays information in a database in views. You can create multiple views of a database that display some or all of the information in different ways. You work with the database through views, adding or deleting items, creating categories, assigning items to categories, and so forth. Each view can be considered to be a window through which you look at information contained in a database.

For each view, you can specify which of the categories in the database are to be used as section heads to provide the initial organization of the information in that view. Columns can always be added to show additional category assignments or dates. Views can also be *filtered* so that they display only items assigned to certain categories, or items with specified dates. These capabilities enable you to create views that display exactly the information you need for a particular purpose.

This chapter explains how to use views to examine the information in a database in different ways. The first portion of the chapter shows how to create and use multiple views, and how to change the basic contents of views. The next part of the chapter covers the basic operations for managing the assortment of views included in a database. The final section shows how to further refine views by selecting specified information and controlling its display.

# CREATING AND CHANGING VIEWS

The Tasks database currently contains a variety of items listing things to do. These items were initially assigned to the categories represented by the section heads—Reports, Meetings, and Phone Calls—classifying the items according to the type of task. Since many of the items also refer to different projects, a Project column was created and used to assign the items to specific project categories such as Walker and James. The database has become sufficiently complex so that it now makes sense to create and use additional views to examine and work with the information in the database.

This section shows several methods for creating new views, the methods for selecting and displaying the different views, and the basic procedures for changing the information displayed in views.

## Creating New Views

Many of the items in the database refer to specific projects and have been assigned to appropriate project categories. To help focus on the tasks required for each of the projects, you can create a view in which the items are organized and displayed by the project categories.

Begin by opening the Tasks database. You are looking at the information displayed in the Initial view, which is the view in which all of the information was entered, all of the additional categories were created, and assignments were made. This is currently the only view of the Tasks database.

Use the View New command to begin creating the new view by pressing F10 (MENU) and selecting View and New. A New View box is displayed in the middle of the screen. The first step is to enter a name to be used in referring to this new view. With the highlight opposite *View Name:*, type

Current Projects

and press ENTER.

The next step is to specify the category or categories to be used as section heads to display information in this new view. Move the highlight down to the *Category:* line. You want all of the specific project categories to be used as section heads. The specific project categories are all child categories of the Project category, which was used as the column head for assigning the items to the specific categories. Therefore, you need to enter the Project category. Press GREY PLUS to display the list of categories in the database. Move the highlight to the Project category, press the SPACE bar to include the category, and then press F9.

Alternatively, you could enter the Project category by typing in the name. Begin typing in Project. After the P is typed, Agenda informs you that three categories match the entry, and the Peters category is displayed as a possible match. You can proceed to enter the Project category in one of three ways: First, you can press the UP or DOWN arrows until the Project category is displayed as the match (the categories are in alphabetical order) and then press ENTER. Second, you can continue typing the second letter of the desired category name, r. At this point, the Project category is displayed as the match because it is the only category beginning with Pr; pressing ENTER will enter this category name. Third, you can type out the entire category name, Project, and then press ENTER. All three methods result in the Project category being entered on the second line in the New View box.

After Project has been entered, a third line appears in the New View box, asking whether you want to display child categories. Agenda provides this option whenever a category is entered that has child categories. The Project category has the child categories Walker, James, and so forth. Agenda provides the option of using child categories as the section heads for the display of the information instead of the parent category. You want to use the child categories as section heads in this view, so accept the default options for the *Display child categories:* setting of *Yes.*

Had you instructed Agenda not to display child categories, the new view would have contained only one section for the Project category. All of the items assigned to one or more of the child categories would have been listed in that one Project section, but there would be no indication about the specific project category to which the item had been assigned.

All of the settings have been correctly specified for the creation of the new view. The screen should appear as shown in Fig. 6-1. Accept these settings by pressing F9. The Current Projects view is created and is now displayed on the screen as shown in Fig. 6-2. The section heads in this view are James, Acme, Peters, and Walker, the child categories of the Project category. The items are displayed in the sections under the category heads to which the items had been assigned. For example, all of the items assigned to the James category are displayed in the first section under the James section head.

Not all of the items in the database are displayed in this view; it only displays those items that are assigned to the categories used as section

```
  File: C:\AGFILES\TASKS                                      03/10/89
  View:
 ═══════════════════════════════════════════════════════════════════════
  Reports                                           Project        When
     · Meeting to discuss project for James next     ·James        ·03/13/89
       Monday.
     ♪ Prepare report on Walker project by next      ·Walker       ·03/16/89
       Thursday.
     · Have┌══════════════════════New View══════════════════════┐
       repo │                                                    │
       that │   View name:    Current Projects                   │
     · Meet │   Category:     Project                            │
       acco │   Display child categories:    Yes                 │
             │                                                    │
  Meetings  └════════════Press F9 when done, ESC to cancel═══════┘
     · Meeting to discuss project for James next     ·James        ·03/13/89
       Monday.
     · Meeting with executive committee 3/24/89 to go              ·03/24/89
       over quarterly results.
     · Meet with Jim to discuss report on the Peters  ·Peters
       account.

  Phone Calls                                       Project        When
 ══F1═══╤══F2═══╤══F3═══╤══F4═══╤══F5═══╤══F6═══╤══F7═══╤══F8═══╤══F9═══╤══F10══
  Help  ║ Edit  ║       ║       ║       ║       ║       ║       ║Accept ║
```

Fig. 6-1. *Creating a new Current Projects view to display tasks using specific project categories as sections.*

```
  File: C:\AGFILES\TASKS                              03/10/89    14:05
  View: Current Projects
 ═══════════════════════════════════════════════════════════════════════
  James
     · Meeting to discuss project for James next Monday.
     · Call Adam Baker at James Wednesday to get his reactions to our proposals.

  Walker
     ♪ Call Ron Smith at Walker by Tuesday to discuss the progress of the
       project.
     · Have Ann get out the previous Walker project report and begin the process
       of updating so that we have a draft to work with.
     ♪ Prepare report on Walker project by next Thursday.
     · Call Peter Smith regarding new account proposals for Walker and Acme.

  Acme
     · Call Peter Smith regarding new account proposals for Walker and Acme.

  Peters
     · Meet with Jim to discuss report on the Peters account.


 ══F1═══╤══F2═══╤══F3═══╤══F4═══╤══F5═══╤══F6═══╤══F7═══╤══F8═══╤══F9═══╤══F10══
  Help  ║ Edit  ║ Copy  ║ Done  ║ Note  ║ Move  ║ Mark  ║Vw Mgr ║Cat Mgr║ Menu
```

Fig. 6-2. *The Current Projects view.*

heads. Items that do not refer to any specific project and are not assigned to one of the four project categories are not shown.

Items can be added, edited, or deleted in this view, just as in the Initial view. However, since items must be entered into sections, any item entered in the Current Projects view must be assigned to one of the four project categories. It is impossible to enter an item without assigning it to a project category. Any changes made to items in this view are reflected when the information is displayed in any other view.

Agenda provides several different methods for creating new views. To try out some alternatives, create a third view to display only information on meetings and phone calls. This time, begin the creation of the new view using Agenda's *View Manager*. Press F8 (VIEW MGR) to display the View Manager in a box in the middle of the screen. The View Manager displays a list of the views that have been created, along with instructions to press INS to create a new view. To create the new view, press INS. The New View box is displayed, just as before.

The View New command was the first method used for creating a new view. Using this command is completely equivalent to pressing INS to create a new view from the View Manager. The selection of the procedure to be used is purely a matter of personal preference. The same is true for accomplishing many of the other view operations discussed in this chapter.

There are several additional View commands, but all of those operations can also be accomplished by using the View Manager. In addition, the View Manager can be used to perform several other view operations that cannot be done with View commands. Therefore, you can perform all view operations using the View Manager and ignore the View commands if you wish. The View Manager is used for the remaining examples in this chapter, but equivalent View commands are described when available.

The new view is to be named *Calls and Meetings*, so enter that name in the New View box. Move the highlight down to the *Category:* setting. Press GREY PLUS to display the View Define box, which lists all of the categories in the database. (Only a partial list of the categories can fit on the screen at one time. Use the arrow keys to scroll through the list.) You want both the Meetings category and the Phone Calls category to be used as section heads in the new view. Press the DOWN arrow to move down the list of categories until the Meetings category is highlighted. The View Define instructions say to press SPACE to include a section, so press the SPACE bar once. An asterisk appears in the S column (for *section*) to the left of the Meetings category. This asterisk indicates that the category will be included as a section in the view. Press the DOWN arrow once more to highlight the Phone Calls category and press SPACE to include this section as well. The screen now appears as shown in Fig. 6-3.

Unlike most boxes, the View Define box does not tell you what key to press when you are finished. Pressing ENTER just moves the highlight down one. As you can probably figure out, F9 (ACCEPT), is the proper key to use to move back to the New View box. Once there, press F9 again to accept the settings and create the new view. The new Calls and Meetings view is shown in Fig. 6-4.

## Switching Among Views

As you create multiple views of the information in an Agenda database, you will want to switch from one view to another to look at the information organized in different ways. The primary function of the View Manager is to allow the selection of the view that is to be displayed by Agenda.

After the Calls and Meetings view is created, it is displayed on the screen. To return to the Currents Projects view, first press F8 (VIEW MGR) to display the View Manager on the screen. A list of all of the views created for the database is displayed in the box, as shown in Fig. 6-5. Highlight

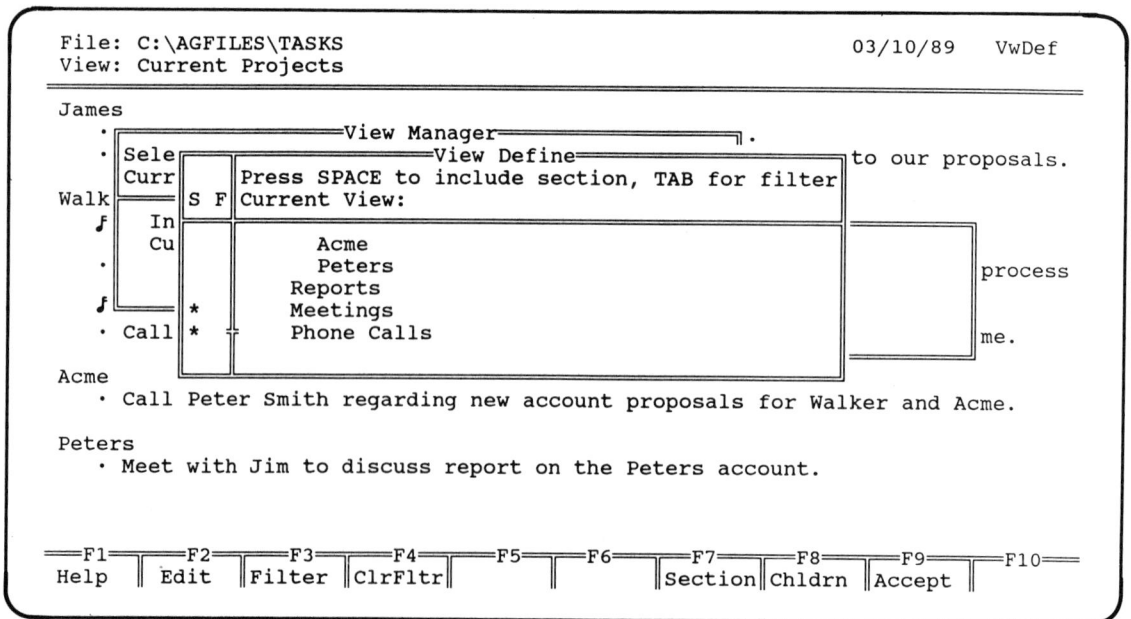

```
 File:  C:\AGFILES\TASKS                              03/10/89    VwDef
 View:  Current Projects
═══════════════════════════════════════════════════════════════════════
 James
    •  ┌Sele┌──────────────View Manager═══════════════════════╖.
       │Curr┌───────════════════View Define════════════════════┐to our proposals.
 Walk  │────│S F│Press SPACE to include section, TAB for filter│
    ♪  │   In│Current View:                                     │
    •  │   Cu│                                                  │
       │     │      Acme                                        │process
    ♪  │     │      Peters                                      │
    •  │─────│*│    Reports                                     │
    • Call│*│ ┤    Meetings                                     │me.
       └────│*││   Phone Calls                                  │
 Acme       └──────────────────────────────────────────────────┘
    •  Call Peter Smith regarding new account proposals for Walker and Acme.

 Peters
    •  Meet with Jim to discuss report on the Peters account.


═F1════╤═F2═══╤══F3═══╤══F4══╤═F5══╤═F6══╤══F7════╤═F8═══╤═F9═══╤═F10══
 Help  ║ Edit ║Filter ║ClrFltr║     ║     ║Section║Chldrn║Accept║
```

Fig. 6-3. *Creating a new Calls and Meetings view from the View Manager, selecting categories to be displayed as sections in the View Define box.*

```
  File: C:\AGFILES\TASKS                         03/10/89    14:06
  View: Calls and Meetings
 ═══════════════════════════════════════════════════════════════════

  Meetings
      • Meeting with executive committee 3/24/89 to go over quarterly results.
      • Meet with Jim to discuss report on the Peters account.
      • Meeting to discuss project for James next Monday.

  Phone Calls
      • Call Ann by next Friday to discuss hiring of new assistant.
      • Call Adam Baker at James Wednesday to get his reactions to our proposals.
      • Call Peter Smith regarding new account proposals for Walker and Acme.
      ♪ Call Ron Smith at Walker by Tuesday to discuss the progress of the
        project.




 ══F1══╤══F2══╤══F3══╤══F4══╤══F5══╤══F6══╤══F7══╤══F8══╤══F9══╤══F10══
  Help ║ Edit ║ Copy ║ Done ║ Note ║ Move ║ Mark ║Vw Mgr║Cat Mgr║ Menu
```

Fig. 6-4. *The Calls and Meetings view.*

```
  File: C:\AGFILES\TASKS                         03/10/89
  View: Calls and Meetings
 ═══════════════════════════════════════════════════════════════════

  Meetings
      •┌══════════════════View Manager═══════════════════┐ver quarterly results.
      •│Select view, or press INS to create new view      │count.
      •│Calls and Meetings                                │.
       │                                                  │
  Phon │   Initial View                                   │ assistant.
      •│   Current Projects                               │actions to our proposals.
      •│   Calls and Meetings                             │ for Walker and Acme.
      •│                                                  │he progress of the
      ♪└══════════════════════════════════════════════════┘




 ══F1══╤══F2══╤══F3══╤══F4══╤══F5══╤══F6══╤══F7══╤══F8══╤══F9══╤══F10══
  Help ║ Edit ║Copy ║Delete║Prefs ║ Move ║      ║Define║Accept║
```

Fig. 6-5. *Selecting the Current Projects view for display using the View Manager.*

the Current Projects view and press ENTER. The view selected is
displayed on the screen.

The View Select command may also be used to change views. This command displays exactly the same list of views as displayed when you use F8 (VIEW MGR). However, using the command requires at least three keystrokes: press F10 to display the menu of commands, and choose View and Select. Only a single key—F8—needs to be pressed to use the View Manager.

A function key is available for switching to the previous view. Just press ALT-F8. (LAST VIEW) to switch to the previous view. This can be handy for switching back and forth between two views of the database while you are working with Agenda.

## Changing Sections in Views

After the initial creation of a new view, you might wish to make changes to the information displayed in that view. For example, you might decide to add or remove sections from the view to display exactly the information desired. Agenda provides a variety of ways in which you can proceed.

Once a view has been created, all of the commands for managing sections and columns described in the preceding chapters may be employed to modify that view. The Category Section New command can be used to add sections for new categories or for existing categories in the database. The Category Section Remove command removes a section from a view. This provides one way of making changes to the sections included in any view.

Another way to change views is to use View Define. The View Define procedure allows you to directly modify the set of sections included in a view. More than one section can be added or removed as part of a single operation.

The Current Projects view has sections for four projects. The Acme project is only tentative; the item refers to making a proposal to Acme, but no project has yet been undertaken. You decide to remove the Acme section from the Current Projects view. Begin by pressing F8 (VIEW MGR) to display the View Manager. When you press F8, the function key assignments at the bottom of the screen change to include operations that may be performed on views. To make changes, press F8 (DEFINE) to display the View Define box, shown in Fig. 6-6. This is the same box used to specify the sections to be included in creating the views. When you first display the View Define box for the Current Projects view, asterisks are shown in the S (for *section*) column to the left of

```
File: C:\AGFILES\TASKS                              03/10/89   VwDef
View: Current Projects
══════════════════════════════════════════════════════════════════
James
  •    ┌─────────────════View Manager════════════════════╗ •
  •    │Sele┌──────────════View Define════════════════┐   posals.
       │Curr│ Press SPACE to include section, TAB for filters
Walk   ├────┤S F│ Current View: Current Projects
  ♪    │ In │
       │ Cu │    MAIN
  •    │ Ca │      Project                               process
  ♪    │    │ *      James
       └────┤ *      Walker
  •         │ *      Acme                                me.
            │ *      Peters
Acme        │      Reports
  • Call    │      Meetings                              me.
            │      Phone Calls
Peters
  • Meet└───┘
```

```
═F1══╤═F2══╤═F3═══╤═F4═══╤═F5═══╤═F6══╤═F7═════╤═F8════╤═F9═══╤═F10══
Help │ Edit│Filter│ClrFltr│     │     │Section│Chldrn│Accept│
```

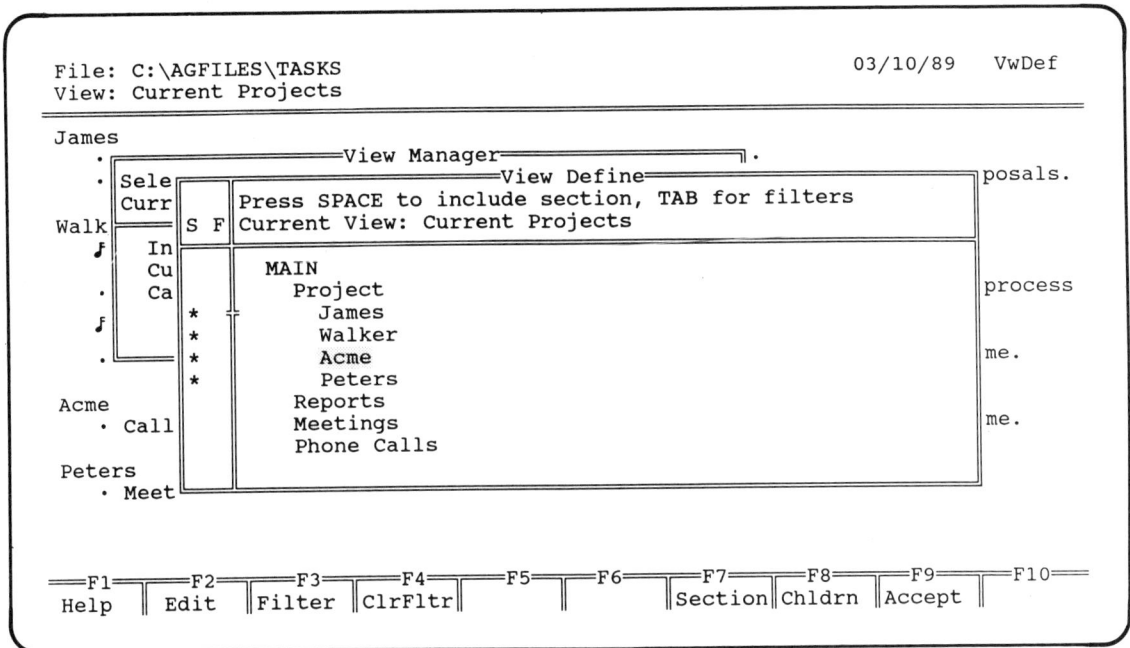

Fig. 6-6. *Using the View Define box to eliminate the Acme category from the Current Projects view.*

all four of the Project child categories. This indicates that these four categories are currently included as sections within the view.

To remove the Acme category from the Current Projects view, move the highlight down to Acme. Then press SPACE, which removes the asterisk from the section column. The Acme category has been removed as a section in the Current Projects view. Press F9 to accept the settings and return to the View Manager. Then press ENTER to redisplay the Current Projects view. The Acme section is no longer included.

The View Define procedure can be employed to make as many changes as desired in the set of sections included within a view. When a category is not currently included within the view, no asterisk will be shown in the Section column. Highlighting the category and pressing SPACE puts in an asterisk and includes the category as a section in the view. When a category is included in the view, an asterisk is shown in the Section column. Highlighting the category and pressing SPACE deletes the asterisk and removes that section from the view. You can use the arrow keys to move up and down the list of categories, and then you can include or remove any category just by pressing the SPACE bar.

Function key F7 (SECTION) may be employed instead of the SPACE bar to make the same changes. In addition, function key F8 (CHILDREN) includes all of the child categories of the highlighted category in a view. In other words, while in the

View Define box, highlighting Project and pressing F8 would include the four children categories, James, Acme, Peters, and Walker, in the view.

The View Define command may also be used to perform exactly the same operations. This command is equivalent to using the F8 (DEFINE) function key from the View Manager.

Adding, removing, and changing columns in views can only be accomplished using the Category Column commands. There are no view operations equivalent to View Define that allow you to work with columns in views as you work with sections in views.

Add a column displaying the When Date to the Current Projects view. To accomplish this, execute the Category Column New command. The New Column Box is displayed. Change the column type to When Date by moving the highlight to the *Column type:* line, pressing GREY PLUS, and selecting *When date*. Press F9 to accept the settings and add the column. (These procedures for creating a column are exactly the same as those described in the last chapter.) Figure 6-7 shows the Current Projects view after removing the Acme section and adding the When column.

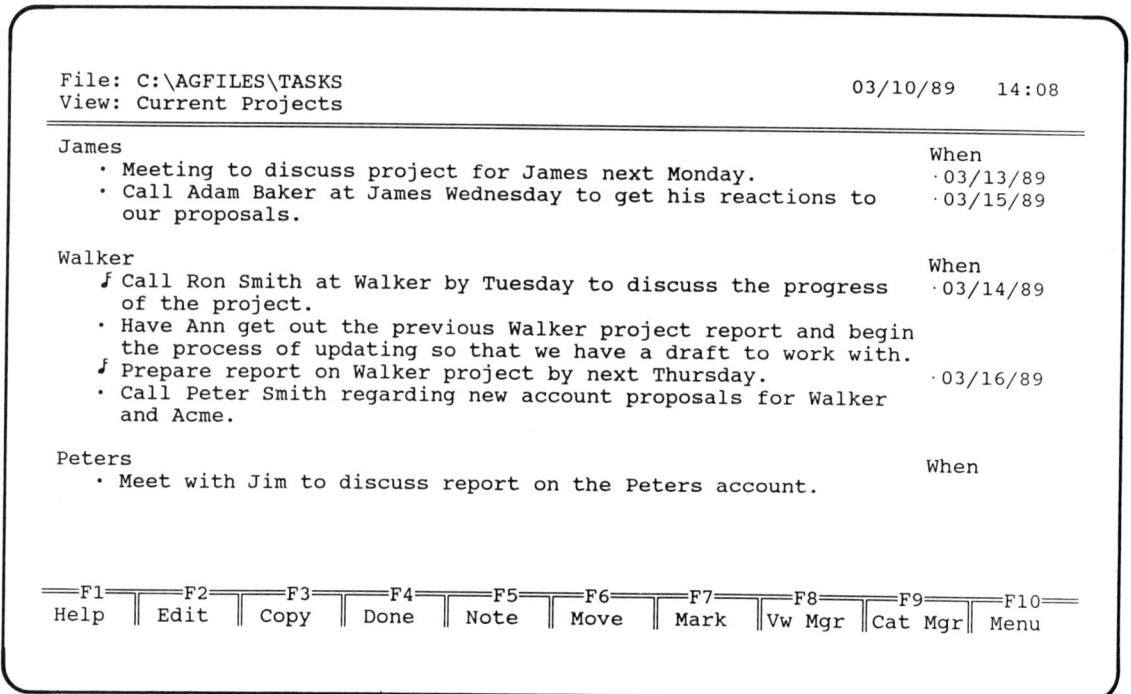

```
File: C:\AGFILES\TASKS                                    03/10/89    14:08
View: Current Projects
==============================================================================
James                                                           When
   • Meeting to discuss project for James next Monday.            ·03/13/89
   • Call Adam Baker at James Wednesday to get his reactions to   ·03/15/89
     our proposals.

Walker                                                          When
   ♪ Call Ron Smith at Walker by Tuesday to discuss the progress  ·03/14/89
     of the project.
   • Have Ann get out the previous Walker project report and begin
     the process of updating so that we have a draft to work with.
   ♪ Prepare report on Walker project by next Thursday.           ·03/16/89
   • Call Peter Smith regarding new account proposals for Walker
     and Acme.

Peters                                                          When
   • Meet with Jim to discuss report on the Peters account.


==============================================================================
 =F1=====F2=====F3=====F4=====F5=====F6=====F7=====F8=====F9=====F10==
 Help  ‖ Edit ‖ Copy ‖ Done ‖ Note ‖ Move ‖ Mark ‖Vw Mgr‖Cat Mgr‖ Menu
```

Fig. 6-7. *The Current Projects view after the elimination of the Acme category as a section and the addition of a When column.*

# MANAGING VIEWS

If a database contains only a few views, managing them is hardly a problem. As you create more elaborate Agenda applications with large numbers of views, however, you will need and appreciate the capabilities available for managing views. Agenda provides procedures that allow you to delete unwanted views, copy views, rename existing views, and reorder the list of views displayed for selection by the View Manager.

## Deleting Views

For whatever reason, a particular view of the database might no longer be needed. The view might have served its purpose, or it might have been a bad idea in the first place.

Delete the Calls and Meetings view from the Tasks database. To eliminate the view, first press F8 (VIEW MGR) to enter the View Manager. Highlight the view to be deleted, in this case, Calls and Meetings. Press DEL or function key F4 (DELETE). A box appears asking whether you really want to delete this view, as shown in Fig. 6-8. Press ENTER to delete the view. It is now removed from the list displayed by the View Manager. Exit the View Manager by selecting any view and pressing ENTER.

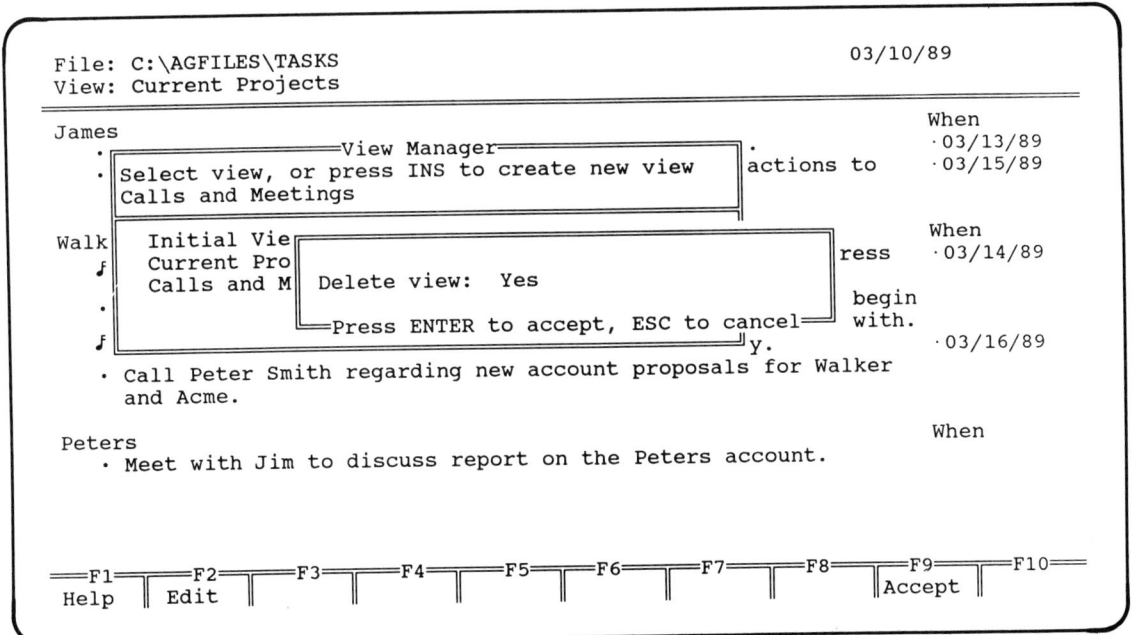

```
  File: C:\AGFILES\TASKS                          03/10/89
  View: Current Projects

  James                                                When
    ·                                              · 03/13/89
    · ┌────────────View Manager────────────┐  .    · 03/15/89
      │ Select view, or press INS to create new view │actions to
      │ Calls and Meetings                  │
                                                     When
  Walk │ Initial Vie┌──────────────────────────┐ress  · 03/14/89
     ♪ │ Current Pro│                          │
       │ Calls and M│ Delete view:  Yes        │   begin
    ·  └────────────│                          │   with.
     ♪              └─Press ENTER to accept, ESC to cancel─┘y.  · 03/16/89
    · Call Peter Smith regarding new account proposals for Walker
      and Acme.

  Peters                                               When
    · Meet with Jim to discuss report on the Peters account.



  ═F1══╥══F2═══╥══F3═══╥══F4═══╥══F5═══╥══F6═══╥══F7═══╥══F8═══╥══F9═══╥══F10══
  Help ║ Edit  ║       ║       ║       ║       ║       ║       ║ Accept ║
```

Fig. 6-8. *Discarding the Calls and Meetings view.*

Deleting a view completely eliminates it from the database, including its name and all information as to how it was defined. The view cannot be retrieved. If it turns out that you later need the same view, you must recreate it.

Deleting a view does not delete any information on items, categories, or the assignment of items to categories from the database, however. Even if an item or category were displayed only in the view that was deleted, that item or category remains in the database. The item or category will not be displayed in any current view, but may be added to existing views or included in new views.

For example, several items in the Tasks database do not involve specific projects, and are not assigned to any of the project categories. These items are therefore not displayed in the Current Projects view, but only (after the deletion of Calls and Meetings) in the Initial view. If the Initial view were deleted, those items would no longer be displayed anywhere. They would continue to be assigned to the Reports, Meetings, and Phone Calls categories. Re-creating a view similar to the Initial view with those categories as sections would result in these items again being displayed.

## Copying Views

In using Agenda, you will frequently need to create new views with formats similar to those of existing views. In such cases, it is easier to start with the existing view and then make necessary modification than to create the view from scratch. The *view copy* operation creates a new view that is the copy of an existing view, facilitating this process.

For use in the next section of this chapter, you need a copy of the Initial view in the Tasks database. Begin making the copy by using F8 (VIEW MGR) to enter the View Manager. Highlight Initial view, which is the view to be copied. Then press F3 (COPY). A box is displayed prompting you for the name to be given to the new view. Type in

Current Tasks to Do

and press ENTER. The screen appears as in Fig. 6-9. Then press F9 as instructed by the box. A new view named Current Tasks to Do is created and displayed on the screen. This view is an exact copy of the Initial view. You will see exactly the same information, displayed in the same manner, as in the Initial view. This view also appears in the list of views displayed by the View Manager.

## Changing View Names

Agenda named the first view the Initial view. When the Tasks database was originally created, Agenda assigned this name because there must be a view in

```
File: C:\AGFILES\TASKS                                  03/10/89
View: Current Projects
═══════════════════════════════════════════════════════════════
                                                        When
James                                              .    ·03/13/89
   .  ┌───────────────View Manager═══════════┐      actions to  ·03/15/89
      │Select view, or press INS to create new view│
      │Initial View                          │
      │  ┌─────────────────New View══════════════════════┐
Walk  │In│                                               │14/89
   ♪  │Cu│   View name:   Current Tasks to Do            │
      │  │                                               │
      │  │                                               │16/89
  ♪ Prep│                                               │
   · Call└──────────Press F9 when done, ESC to cancel════┘
      and Acme.
                                                        When
Peters
    · Meet with Jim to discuss report on the Peters account.


══F1════╤══F2════╤══F3════╤══F4════╤══F5════╤══F6════╤══F7════╤══F8════╤══F9════╤══F10══
 Help   ║ Edit   ║        ║        ║        ║        ║        ║        ║Accept  ║
```

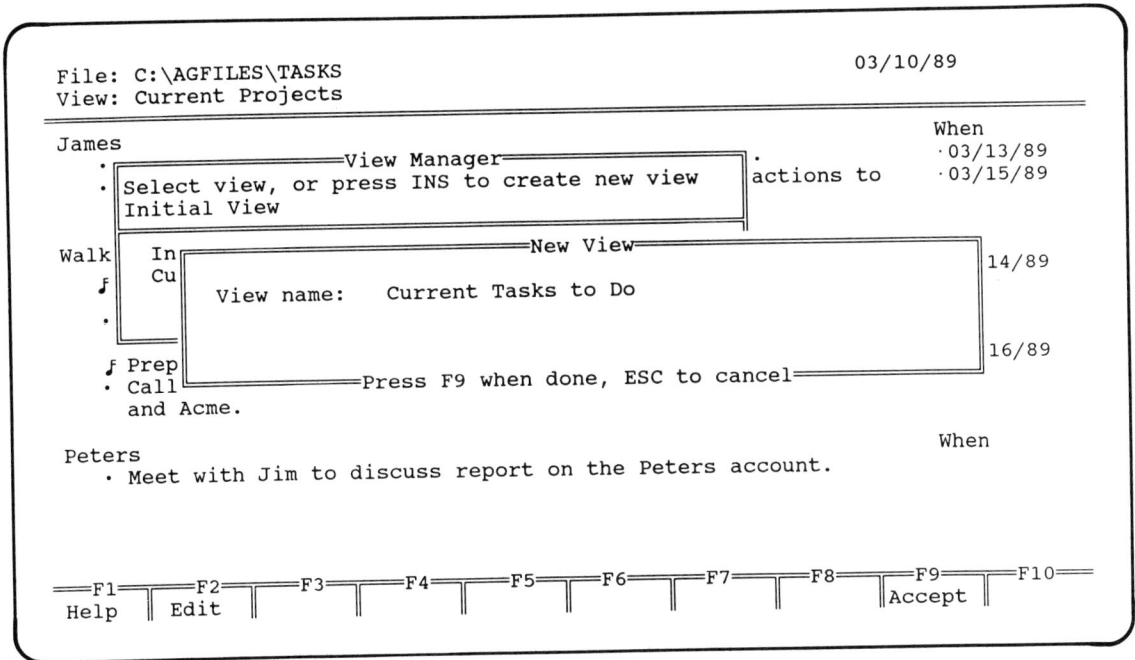

Fig. 6-9. *Copying the Initial view to a new Current Tasks to Do view.*

order to enter any information. You can change the name of the Initial view or any other view at any time.

While in the View Manager, change the view name Initial view to Tasks to Do. Press F8 (VIEW MGR), highlight Initial view, and press F2 (EDIT). Delete the name Initial view by pressing CTRL-ENTER, and type in

Tasks to Do

which will appear on the same line in the View Manager as the characters just deleted. Press ENTER and the name of the view is permanently changed.

View names are changed by using editing procedures, just as with any other entry in Agenda. Enter the View Manager by pressing F8. Highlight the name of the view to be changed. Press F2 (EDIT). Edit the view name and then press ENTER to enter the new name. You can edit the name by using the normal editing procedures.

## Rearranging Views in the View Manager

With only three views, the order in which the views are displayed by the View Manager is hardly important. Any view can be found and selected quickly and without difficulty. After more have been created, however, finding the desired view might be difficult.

Selecting views is easier if the list of views can be rearranged into some more logical order. Two procedures are available to rearrange views in the View Manager: individual views can be repositioned in the list of views, or the entire list can be sorted alphabetically.

You might wish to move individual views on the list of views displayed by the View Manager in order to place the more frequently used views at the beginning and the less frequently used views at the end. Suppose you wish to move the Tasks to Do view to the bottom of the list of views displayed by the View Manager. Press F8 (VIEW MGR) to display the View Manager if necessary. Highlight the Tasks to Do view, and press F6 (MOVE). A double arrow appears to the left of the Tasks to Do view. You are instructed to move the highlight cursor (using the UP and DOWN arrows) to the position in the list where you want the Tasks to Do view placed. After moving the highlight to the bottom of the list, the screen appears as shown in Fig. 6-10. Press ENTER and the Tasks to Do view

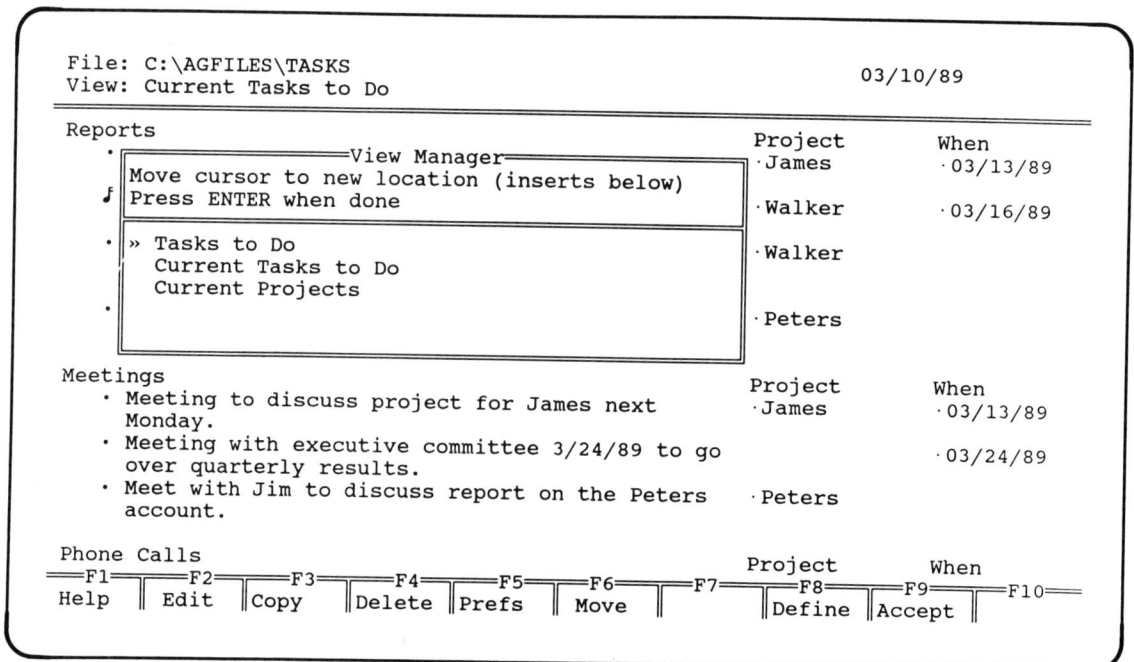

```
 _____
/                                                                        
| File: C:\AGFILES\TASKS                                      03/10/89    
| View: Current Tasks to Do                                              
| ══════════════════════════════════════════════════════════════════════
| Reports                                       Project        When      
|   ·    ╔════════════View Manager════════════╗ ·James      ·03/13/89    
|        ║ Move cursor to new location (inserts below)                   
|     ♪  ║ Press ENTER when done             ║ ·Walker     ·03/16/89    
|        ╟──────────────────────────────────╢                          
|   ·    ║ » Tasks to Do                     ║ ·Walker                  
|        ║   Current Tasks to Do             ║                          
|        ║   Current Projects                ║                          
|   ·    ║                                   ║ ·Peters                  
|        ╚══════════════════════════════════╝                          
| Meetings                                      Project        When      
|   · Meeting to discuss project for James next ·James      ·03/13/89    
|     Monday.                                                            
|   · Meeting with executive committee 3/24/89 to go                     
|     over quarterly results.                                ·03/24/89    
|   · Meet with Jim to discuss report on the Peters  ·Peters            
|     account.                                                           
| Phone Calls                                   Project        When      
| ══F1═══╤══F2═══╤══F3═══╤══F4═══╤══F5═══╤══F6═══╤══F7═══╤══F8═══╤══F9═══╤══F10══
|  Help  │ Edit  │Copy   │Delete │Prefs  │ Move  │       │Define │Accept │
_____
```

Fig. 6-10. *Moving the Tasks to Do view in the View Manager list.*

is moved to the bottom of the list. As you can see, the view is relocated *below* the view name in the list that is highlighted. Exit the View Manager by pressing ENTER.

The procedure for moving views in the View Manager works differently from (and not as well as) the procedures for moving sections within views and items within sections. The Category Section Position and Item Position commands both highlight the element to be moved. Then as the UP or DOWN arrows are pressed, the section head or item is actually moved and remains highlighted. You just move the section or item to the appropriate position.

When moving views, however, the view to be moved is marked with the double arrows. As you move the highlight, the view does not actually move. You are only designating the position to which it is to be moved—below the highlighted view. This is not as intuitive as the other move commands, and produces a serious limitation. A view cannot be moved to the top of the list of views, because the view being moved is always inserted *below* the view name selected. The only way to move a view to the top of the list is to first move it into second position. Then the view move operation must be repeated to move the first view lower in the list, leaving the second view at the top.

An alternative arrangement for making the views easy to locate in the View Manager is to order them alphabetically. This can be accomplished very easily. In the View Manager, press ALT-F9 (SORT). This immediately sorts the views in alphabetical order.

## FILTERS AND VIEW PREFERENCES

Agenda includes additional capabilities for refining both views and the information displayed in them. Most important is the ability to select the items that are to be displayed in a view. Agenda refers to this selection as filtering. Views can be filtered based upon the categories to which items are assigned and the dates associated with items. In addition, further options are available for setting view preferences that will automatically affect the display of items and the format of the view.

### Filtering by Category

Items can be displayed in views or excluded from views based upon their assignment to various categories. This allows views to be created that display selected information from an Agenda database. Such selection can be broad, to display a general class of items of interest. Or the selection can be highly specific, so that a view can be effectively used to locate specific pieces of information within the database. With the filtering capabilities for the selection items based upon category assignment, Agenda can select information from a database much like traditional database management programs locate information meeting certain criteria.

The Current Tasks to Do view is intended to provide information on tasks that need to be done within the next week or so. The view was created by copying the Tasks to Do view (formerly the Initial view), which displayed all of the information in the Agenda database. The Peters project has begun to require extra time, so you have assigned an assistant to be responsible for all of the tasks associated with that project. This means that you do not have to worry about any tasks related to the Peters project in the immediate future. Therefore, such tasks should be excluded from your Current Tasks to Do view. (You might also wish to create another view listing just those tasks associated with the Peters project to give to your assistant, but that is a separate job.)

The ability to filter views by category is part of the definition of a view. The View Define procedure, illustrated previously for specifying the sections to be included in a view, is also used for category filtering. You enter the View Define procedure either by entering the View Manager and then pressing F8 (DEFINE) or by using the View Define command. In either case, the View Define box listing all of the categories in the database is displayed on the screen as shown in Fig. 6-11.

```
File: C:\AGFILES\TASKS
View: Current Tasks to Do                            03/10/89    VwDef

Reports                                        Project        When
  .                                             ·James         ·03/13/89
  ╔═══════════════View Manager═══════════════╗
 ♪║Sele╔════════════════════View Define════════════════════╗
   ║Task║Press SPACE to include section, TAB for filters     ║  16/89
   ║    ║S F║Current View: Tasks to Do                       ║
  .║ Cu ║
   ║ Cu ║   MAIN
   ║ Ta ║      Project
  .║    ║         James
   ║    ║         Walker
   ║    ║         Acme
Meetings        Peters
  · Meet║ *║   Reports
   Mond║ *║   Meetings                                          13/89
  · Meet║ *║   Phone Calls
   over ║                                                       24/89
  · Meet╚════════════════════════════════════════════════════╝
   account.

Phone Calls                                    Project        When
═F1═══╤═F2═══╤═F3═══╤═F4═══╤═F5═══╤═F6═══╤═F7═══╤═F8═══╤═F9═══╤═F10═══
Help  ║ Edit ║Filter║ClrFltr║     ║     ║Section║Chldrn║Accept║
```

Fig. 6-11. *Using View Define to set a profile filter to exclude the items assigned to the Peters project from the Current Tasks to Do view.*

The objective is to filter out items assigned to the Peters category so that they will not be displayed in the Current Tasks to Do view. The Current Tasks to Do view should be displayed by Agenda. From this view, enter the View Define procedure. Use the arrow keys to move the highlight to the Peters category. Press the TAB key *twice* so that an arrow pointing down is displayed in the F column to the left of the Peters category. The F stands for *filters* and the downward-pointing arrow indicates that items assigned to this category will *not* by displayed in the view. They will be filtered out of the view. The View Define box now should look like Fig. 6-11. Press F9 to accept the settings and return to the View Manager. Then press ENTER to display the Current Tasks to Do view and see the effects of filtering out items assigned to the Peters category. No Peters project items are displayed in the view, as a quick look at the Project column confirms.

You can set category filters in the View Define box to include or exclude items assigned to any category or categories in the database. The default condition when a view is created is the inclusion of all items; no filters are set, and there are no entries in the F (filter) column of the view define box.

Category filters are established by placing arrows to the left of the category name in the F column of the View Define box. An arrow pointing up indicates that items assigned to the category are to be *included* in the view (and other items are not). An arrow pointing down indicates that items are to be *excluded* from the view (and other items are to be included). The absences of an arrow in the F column indicates that assignment to this category is not to be considered in determining which items are to be displayed in the view.

Arrows can be added to or deleted from the F column. First highlight the appropriate category name. Then use either the TAB key or F3 (FILTER) to change the filter. When no arrow is displayed, pressing either key once displays the up-arrow in the column to indicate the inclusion of the items assigned to the category. When the up-arrow is displayed, pressing either TAB or F3 changes to the down-arrow to indicate exclusion. Finally, when the down-arrow is displayed, pressing either key removes the arrow from the column. In other words, repeated pressing of TAB or F3 (FILTER) cycles through no filter (blank), inclusion (up-arrow), exclusion (down-arrow), and back to no filter. Just press TAB or F3 to change the filter until you get what you want.

When in View Define, press F4 (CLEAR FILTER) to eliminate all filters from a view. All arrows are deleted from the F column. This is useful if you have set multiple filters for a view and simply wish to start over from scratch in setting new filters.

When a category filter is established for a single category, the effect of that filter is easy to understand. An up-arrow next to a category name causes only those items assigned to that category to be displayed in the view. A down-arrow next to a category name causes all items except for those assigned to that category to be displayed. The items assigned to that category are excluded from the view.

Things become a bit more complicated when filters are used for two or more categories in a view (indicated by two or more arrows in the F column). In most situations, an item must satisfy *all* of the filtering criteria in order to be included within a view. For example, if up-arrows would be placed next to the Peters and Reports categories, an item would have to be assigned to both the Peters *and* the Reports categories in order to be included. This is equivalent to using a logical AND connecting the various criteria: the criterion established by the first filter AND the second filter (AND any additional filters) must all be satisfied for an item to be displayed.

Agenda makes one exception to this procedure for handling multiple filters, however; this might cause some confusion. A set of categories may be specified as being mutually exclusive. In such a case, an item may be assigned to only one of the categories in the set. (The procedures for doing this are discussed in the next chapter.)

It would be impossible for an item to be assigned to one of these mutually exclusive categories AND another one of the categories. So if two mutually exclusive categories are both designated as filtering categories, with up-arrows indicating that items are to be included for those categories, new rules apply. An item is included in the view if it is assigned to one of the mutually exclusive categories OR if it is assigned to another of the mutually exclusive categories.

If filtering a view requires that an item be assigned to a particular category, then entering a new item into that view results in the item being automatically assigned to that category. Thus, a view filtered to include only items assigned to the Walker category (with an up-arrow next to Walker) would be assumed to deal only with Walker. An item entered into that view would therefore be assigned to the Walker category. As long as you are logical in using views and entering items, this automatic assignment should not result in any problems.

## Filtering by Date

A date filter makes the selection of items for the view according to a date associated with each item. While category filters are established within the View Define procedure, date filters are specified along with other settings in the View Preferences procedures. This difference in how the filters are set might seem somewhat illogical. Presumably the rationale is that category filters involve categories, which are handled within View Define. Date filters, on the other hand, do not involve categories and thus must be dealt with in another context.

The Current Tasks to Do view was created to display only those current tasks. Assume that current tasks are those that must be completed within the next week and a half, and assume that this would result in a completion deadline of March 17. You have already added a When Date column that displays the dates by which the various tasks are to be completed. Now the objective is to select only those items with dates up through March 17 for display in this view. (Note that you will want to use a cutoff date appropriate to the When Dates in your database, which will be different from those shown here.)

To set a date filter for the Current Tasks to Do view, begin by invoking the View Preferences procedure. This can be accomplished in two different ways. One way is to enter the View Manager with F8 and then press function key F5 (PREFERENCES). Alternatively, enter the View Preferences command directly from the view. In either case, the View Preferences box is displayed on the screen.

Setting a date filter is accomplished in the middle portion of the View Preferences box. When you begin, the line *Type of date:* setting shows the option *None*, indicating that currently no date filter is established for the view. Highlight *None* and press GREY PLUS to display the list of options. Since the view is to be filtered by the When Date, make that selection and press ENTER.

After the indication that the view is to be filtered by a date, four more settings appear in the Date Filter section of the box. These settings are used to specify how to select items by their When Dates. First specify the range of dates to be selected. All items with When Dates up to and including March 17 are to be included in the view. Since you want to include all items with dates prior to March 17, a start date need not be specified. This setting can therefore be left blank. The selection begins with the earliest When Dates in the database.

The latest date to be included is March 17 (or whatever date makes sense for the When Dates in your database). Place the highlight next to the *End date:* setting, type in

3/17/89

(or whatever cutoff date is appropriate given the When Dates in your database) and press ENTER. This specifies that this is to be the latest date for selection.

Actually, a date filter can be used to either include or exclude items within the specified date range in the view. The default setting results in the inclusion of the items in the date range. This setting can be changed to include the items outside of the date range. For the current problem, items in the date range from the earliest date up through March 17 are to be included in the view, so this setting can be left unchanged.

The final issue in specifying a date filter involves what to do with those items that do not have When Dates. In the Tasks database, not all of the items have When Dates. If the items without dates are not time-critical, they probably do not need to be displayed in the Current Tasks to Do view. Only items with actual dates falling in the range should be displayed. Thus, the *Display:* setting in the View Preferences box should be *Dated items only.* This is the default and can be left unchanged.

Figure 6-12 illustrates the settings for the When Date filter to be used for the Current Tasks to Do view. After all of the settings have been made, press F9 to accept the entries in the View Preferences box. Then display the Current Tasks to Do view. The Current Tasks to Do view using the category and date filters is shown in Fig. 6-13. No items assigned to the Peters category are displayed. They have been excluded by the category filter. And only items with When Dates up through March 17 are included in the view because of the date filter. A double arrow appears in the upper-right corner of the screen, indicating that the view is filtered by category. The notation *(When date: - 3/17/98)* indicates that the view is filtered to include items with When Dates up through March 17. This view presents a concise summary of those tasks to be accomplished during the next week and a half.

```
File: C:\AGFILES\TASKS                                          03/10/89
View: Current Tasks to Do
                                                                        ‡
═══════════════════════════════════════════════════════════════════════
Report┌─────────────────────────=View Preferences=─────────────────────┐
  • ┌─┐ Display Preferences                                             │ /89
    │S│   Hide done items:              No                             │
 ♪ │T│   Hide dependent items:         No                             │ /89
    └─┘   Hide inherited items:         No                             │
  •                                                                     │
        Date Filter                                                    │
          Type of date:           When date                           │
          Start date:                                                  │
Meet└─┐   End date:               03/17/89                            │
  •  └─  Display:                 Dated items only                    │ /89
     M    Include items:          In date range                       │
  • M  Other                                                          │ /89
     o    View name:              Tasks to Do                         │
          Section separator:      No                                  │
Phone └───────────────────=Press F9 when done, ESC to cancel=─────────┘ /89
  ♪ C   the progress of the project.
  • Call Adam Baker at James Wednesday to get his      ·James      ·03/15/89
    reactions to our proposals.
═F1═╤═F2═╤═F3═╤═F4═╤═F5═╤═F6═╤═F7═╤═F8═══╤═F9═══╤═F10══
Help ║ Edit ║    ║    ║    ║    ║    ║Default║Accept║
```

Fig. 6-12. *Using View Preferences to set a date filter to include only items with When Dates up through March 17.*

```
                                                        03/10/89   14:23
File: C:\AGFILES\TASKS
View: Current Tasks to Do                (When date:  - 03/17/89)     ↕
════════════════════════════════════════════════════════════════════════
                                              Project      When
Reports
  · Meeting to discuss project for James next ·James       ·03/13/89
    Monday.
  ♪ Prepare report on Walker project by next  ·Walker      ·03/16/89
    Thursday.

                                              Project      When
Meetings
  · Meeting to discuss project for James next ·James       ·03/13/89
    Monday.

                                              Project      When
Phone Calls
  ♪ Call Ron Smith at Walker by Tuesday to discuss ·Walker  ·03/14/89
    the progress of the project.
  · Call Adam Baker at James Wednesday to get his  ·James   ·03/15/89
    reactions to our proposals.
  · Call Ann by next Friday to discuss hiring of            ·03/17/89
    new assistant.


═F1═══╤═F2═══╤═F3═══╤═F4═══╤═F5═══╤═F6═══╤═F7═══╤═F8═══╤═F9═══╤═F10══
Help  │ Edit │ Copy │ Done │ Note │ Move │ Mark │Vw Mgr│Cat Mgr│ Menu
```

Fig. 6-13. *The Current Tasks to Do view with items referring to the Peters projects excluded by the profile filter and with only items with When Dates up to April 20 included.*

### View Preferences

You undoubtedly noticed that the View Preferences box used for date filters (shown in Fig. 6-12) includes a number of additional settings. These settings are used to further specify details about the current view.

The *View name:* setting may be used to change the name of the view. Editing the view name by highlighting it in the View Manager and pressing F2 (EDIT) allows you to accomplish the same thing, and is a more direct way of accomplishing the change.

The section separator is a line across the screen separating sections within a view. The default is to display sections without separators. If you want the line, simply change the setting in the View Preferences box to *Yes.* The effect of including the section separator is purely cosmetic. Section separators have no effect on the information actually shown in a view.

The Display Preferences at the top of the View Preferences box allow you to specify whether certain types of items are to be displayed in the view. Agenda treats items that are not displayed as *hidden.* (Done items and dependent items involve aspects of Agenda that have not yet been discussed. They are described in later chapters, and the use of Display Preferences with those items will be addressed then.)

*Inherited items* are those considered to be assigned to a category because they have been assigned to a child category of that category. In the Tasks database, the Walker, James, Peters, and Acme categories are child categories of the Project category. The Project category "inherits" the assignments of those items assigned to the child categories. For example, an item assigned to the Walker category is also considered to be assigned to the Project category by inheritance.

The *Hide inherited items:* display preference allows you to specify whether items assigned to categories by inheritance are to be displayed. Suppose you created a view of the Tasks database with the Project category entered as a section in the view. With inherited items not hidden, all of the items assigned to Walker, James, Peters, and Acme would be displayed in the Project section. However, if you were to hide inherited items, then no items would be assigned to the Project section, because no items would be directly assigned to this category.

Obviously, hiding inherited items makes no sense in the current database. However, you might have a situation with a project that had subprojects, with child categories. Some items might refer to the individual subprojects and be assigned to those. Other items might refer to the overall project and be assigned to that category. The *Hide inherited items:* preference allows you to display the major project as a section head and specify whether the list of items to be displayed are those assigned to both the project and the subprojects, or only those items assigned specifically to the project.

As you work with views, you begin to realize how the possibilities associated with an Agenda database are determined by the categories and the assignment of items to those categories. The idea of subprojects, the distinction of inherited items, and the notion of mutually exclusive categories begin to suggest the further possibilities associated with the category structure of a database. The next chapter addresses these possibilities, showing how you can work directly with the category hierarchy of an Agenda database.

# 7

# MANAGING THE CATEGORY HIERARCHY

THE set of categories and the assignment of items to those categories represents the heart of structuring the information in an Agenda database. In views, categories can be used as section heads, column heads and column entries. Categories can also be employed to filter the items to be displayed in specific views.

Given the importance of the categories to any Agenda database, eventually you might want to examine and work with the entire list of categories for the database. This list of categories is called the *category hierarchy*, because it displays the structure of the relationships among the categories as well as listing the names of the categories. As you become increasingly sophisticated in using Agenda, the category hierarchy will show more detailed information about how the information within the database is structured.

This chapter introduces the basic procedures for managing the category hierarchy. The first section illustrates the use of the Category Manager for working with the category hierarchy, and explains the concept of families and the interrelationships within the hierarchy. The second section covers adding, removing, and moving of categories within the hierarchy.

For some purposes it is useful to make a set of categories mutually exclusive, and it is sometimes necessary to promote or demote categories within the hierarchy. These operations are discussed in the final two sections of the chapter.

# UNDERSTANDING THE CATEGORY HIERARCHY

The best way to understand the structure of the categories in an Agenda database is to directly examine the category hierarchy. The Category Manager is Agenda's tool for doing just that. This section looks first at the use of the Category Manager and then examines the structuring of categories in the hierarchy.

## The Category Manager

The Category Manager is used to display and work directly with the category hierarchy.

Continue working with the Tasks database developed in the preceding chapters. Enter Agenda's Category Manager from any view by pressing F9 (CAT MGR). The category hierarchy, showing all of the categories currently created for the Tasks database, is displayed on the screen. Figure 7-1 shows the Category Manager and the current list of categories. (When you enter the Category Manager, Agenda highlights the category or section that you were using in the view.)

Like the View Manager, the Category Manager has its own display and operations. The map of function key assignments at the bottom of the screen has changed to reflect the procedures available for working with the category hierarchy. The Category Manager even has its own

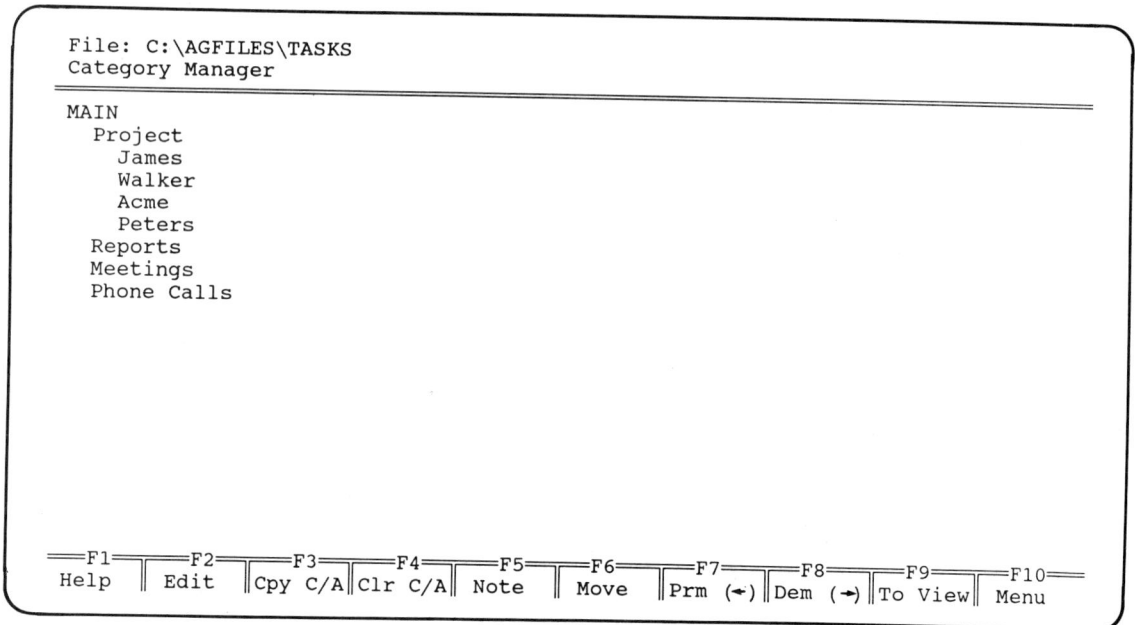

```
File: C:\AGFILES\TASKS
Category Manager

MAIN
   Project
     James
     Walker
     Acme
     Peters
   Reports
   Meetings
   Phone Calls




=F1=======F2=======F3=======F4=======F5=======F6=======F7=======F8=======F9=======F10==
 Help  ‖ Edit  ‖Cpy C/A‖Clr C/A‖ Note  ‖ Move  ‖Prm (←)‖Dem (→)‖To View‖ Menu
```

Fig. 7-1. *The category hierarchy for the Tasks database displayed in the Category Manager.*

set of commands for specifying operations on categories. Press F10 (MENU) to display the first menu of category command options available from within the Category Manager. Press ESC to back out of the menu.

Function key F9 (TO VIEW) returns you from the Category Manager to the view from which you entered it. Since F9 was also the function key that selected the Category Manager, F9 can be employed to conveniently switch back and forth between a view and the Category Manager.

The highlight identifies one of the categories in the list displayed by the Category Manager. The highlight may be moved up and down to scroll through the list of categories if the list is longer than a single screen. The highlight is also used to select categories for various operations.

The basic operations for moving the highlight up and down in the Category Manager are the same as in other parts of Agenda. The UP and DOWN arrows move the highlight up or down one category. PGUP and PGDN move the highlight up or down a full screen at a time. This is helpful for moving quickly through long category lists.

You will notice that some of the categories are indented beneath others. The child categories are indented beneath their parent category to display their relationship. The Category Manager includes several movement operations geared to this structure. CTRL-PGUP and CTRL-PGDN move to the next category at the same level in the hierarchy, called a *sibling*. For example, if Project were highlighted in the Tasks database category hierarchy, pressing CTRL-PGDN would move the highlight down to the Reports category, the next category at the same level.

If the highlight is in the midst of a list of child categories, pressing HOME moves it up to the parent category. Pressing END moves it down to the last of these child categories. Suppose Acme were highlighted in the Tasks database category hierarchy. HOME would move the highlight up to Project, the parent category. END would move the highlight down to Walker, the last of the child categories in that list.

Table 7-1 lists the special keys used to move the highlight through the list of categories displayed by the Category Manager. Remember that the UP and DOWN arrows can always be used to move the highlight to any category in the hierarchy. The other operations exist only to expedite the process.

Agenda provides shortcuts for finding categories in the category hierarchy. You can search for and highlight a particular category name simply by typing some or all of its letters. This is hardly an issue with the short category hierarchy for the Tasks database, but might be very helpful in long lists extending over multiple screens.

*Table 7-1. Special Keys for Movement in the Category Hierarchy.*

| Key | Function |
| --- | --- |
| UP | Move up one category. |
| DOWN | Move down one category. |
| PGUP | Move up one screen. |
| PGDN | Move down one screen. |
| CTRL-PGUP | Move up one sibling. |
| CTRL-PGDN | Move down one sibling. |
| HOME | Move to parent. |
| END | Move to last sibling. |
| CTRL-HOME | Move to first category. |
| CTRL-END | Move to last category. |

The Tasks database will be used to illustrate these shortcuts. Assume that you are looking for a particular category, the name of which begins with *r*. While in the Category Manager, press r. The first category (alphabetically) beginning with the letter *r* is highlighted. *Reports* is highlighted, as shown in Fig. 7-2. This is the only category in the Tasks database that begins with this letter. Press ENTER to conclude the search. If a database contains more than one categories with names beginning with *r*, keep typing the letters until the category you are looking for is highlighted, and then press ENTER.

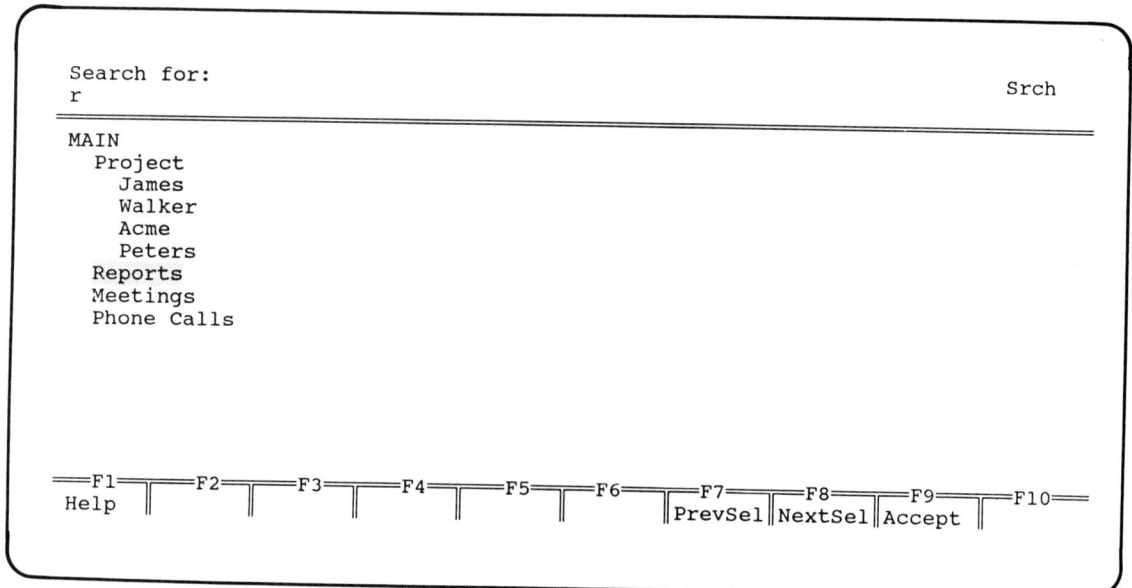

```
Search for:                                                          Srch
r
═══════════════════════════════════════════════════════════════════════
MAIN
  Project
   James
   Walker
   Acme
   Peters
  Reports
  Meetings
  Phone Calls




══F1══╤══F2══╤══F3══╤══F4══╤══F5══╤══F6══╤══F7══╤═F8══╤══F9══╤══F10══
 Help  ┃     ┃     ┃     ┃     ┃     ┃ PrevSel┃NextSel┃Accept┃
```

Fig. 7-2. *Searching for a category beginning with the letter* r.

Agenda also provides several procedures for changing the display of the Category Manager and for using it to change relationships between categories.

Especially in long, complex category hierarchies, listings of child categories might sometimes be distracting and unnecessary. Agenda allows you to "collapse" a family of categories so that child categories are not displayed. Move the highlight to the Project category. Now press SHIFT-GREY MINUS (hold down SHIFT and press the GREY MINUS key on the numeric keypad). The four child categories under the Project category disappear and the screen appears as shown in Fig. 7-3. An ellipsis ( . . . ) is displayed following the Project category to indicate that this category has child categories that are not currently displayed.

When you have multiple levels of indentation and multiple levels of parent-child relationships, pressing SHIFT-GREY MINUS collapses one level. Repeated presses will collapse additional levels.

Reverse the collapsing process by using SHIFT-GREY PLUS to expand the family of categories. Highlight the parent category (followed by the ellipsis) and press SHIFT-GREY PLUS. The child categories are displayed as before.

```
File: C:\AGFILES\TASKS
Category Manager
======================================================================

MAIN
  Project...
  Reports
  Meetings
  Phone Calls




=F1==========F2==========F3==========F4==========F5==========F6==========F7==========F8==========F9==========F10==
 Help    ||  Edit   ||Cpy C/A||Clr C/A||  Note   ||  Move   ||Prm (←)||Dem (→)||To View|| Menu
```

Fig. 7-3. *The category hierarchy with the Project category collapsed and no child categories displayed.*

## Category Families

The Category Manager displays the hierarchical structuring of categories within a database. Certain categories may be subcategories of others, as the specific project categories James, Acme, Peters, and Walker are all subcategories of the Project category. Agenda refers to these as *parent-child relationships*. The entire structuring of categories is in familial terms in Agenda.

In the Tasks database, James, Acme, Peters, and Walker are all child categories to the Project category, which is their parent category. When a category is a child of some other category (the parent), this means that the child category is considered to be a more specific subcategory of the broader parent category. Thus, the Project category encompasses all of the individual projects, while the James category refers specifically to one project, the James project. Project is the parent category to the child category James (and the other three specific project categories).

Parent-child relationships are shown in the category hierarchy through indentation. Child categories are indented two spaces under their parent category.

The combination of a parent category with its associated child categories is referred to as a *family*. In the Tasks database, the categories Project, James, Acme, Peters, and Walker constitute a family. The Project category, of course, is the parent of this family.

Child categories of the same parent category are called siblings. In the Category Manager, siblings having a common parent category are indented the same amount under the parent. James, Acme, Peters, and Walker are siblings in the Tasks database.

The *Main* category is established by Agenda as the highest level category under which all other categories are organized. Main is the parent category of Project, Reports, Meetings, and Phone Calls. Project, Reports, Meetings and Phone Calls are siblings. They are all child categories to the Main category; this is indicated by their being indented to the same extent under the Main category.

If Main is the parent of Project and Project is the parent of James, then Main could be considered the grandparent of James in the category hierarchy. For relationships extending beyond the parent-child level, reference is more often made to *ancestors* and *descendants*. Main is an ancestor of James (as is Project, for that matter). James is a descendant of Main (and is also a descendant of Project). Agenda allows twelve levels of descendants to be included within a category hierarchy.

Understanding category relationships is fundamental to using Agenda. Assignment through inheritance is critical to knowing what items can be displayed and how in various circumstances. As you saw back in Chapter 5 working with columns, a Yes/No column headed with the Project category can be employed to show whether an item is associated with any project. The information displayed in the column is based upon the inheritance of the assignment of items to the specific child project categories.

Not only is it important to understand the relationships, it is necessary to follow Agenda's familial terminology. At various places in the operation of Agenda, the program refers to parents, children, ancestors, descendants, and inheritance in prompting for information and providing options. Working with Agenda requires understanding these terms.

When an item is assigned to any child category, it is also considered to be assigned to its parent category through inheritance. Thus, an item assigned to the James category is also treated as if it were assigned to the Project category. A Project section in a view, for example, would include the item assigned to the James category, even though the item is not directly assigned to the Project category.

Agenda does not permit an item to be assigned to both a parent category and one of its child categories. For example, an item referring to the James project and assigned to the James project category may not also be assigned directly to the Project category. Items that are not assigned to any of the children of the Project category may be assigned to the Project category.

This inheritance of assignments extends beyond the parent category to grandparents and all ancestors of the category to which the item is assigned. All ancestor categories have the item assigned to them through inheritance.

## MANIPULATING THE CATEGORY HIERARCHY

You might wish to work directly with the category hierarchy to add or delete categories from a database and rearrange the way the categories are displayed. The Category Manager allows you to do this. The procedures are described in this section.

### Adding Categories

Structuring the information in a database in a new way might require adding a set of new categories. New categories can be added in a view when new sections or columns are created or when categories are entered into columns. You might, however, know the complete set of categories required before you begin creating a database. If you know all of the categories in advance, it might be more efficient to create the set of categories first, before working with the individual items.

For certain Agenda applications, you might want to create a detailed category hierarchy for a new database prior to entering any items. Although Agenda allows the flexibility of creating new categories at any time, you still have the ability to structure a database in advance. Developing a fairly detailed category hierarchy is sometimes the first step in figuring out where you are going.

New categories may always be created simply by inserting the categories into the list known as the category hierarchy. Once a category has been created, items may be assigned to that category just like any other category.

To illustrate, assume that you have several assistants, and you want to delegate most of the tasks in your Task database to these assistants. New categories could be created for each of the three assistants—Ann, Jim, and George. It would make sense to create these as child categories of a single parent category. The parent category could be called "Staffing," and could be used to assign the tasks to the various assistants. Items could be assigned to the child categories for the three assistants. As the parent category, Staffing would inherit any item assigned to one of the assistant categories, so it could be used to indicate which tasks had been assigned and to which assistant they had been assigned.

If the Category Manager is not on the screen, press F9. Move the highlight down to Phone Calls. To insert the new category, Staffing, below the highlighted item and at the same level as that item (as a sibling), press INS. A row of dots is displayed at the location where the new item is to be entered. (The row of dots indicates the indentation.) Type in the new category name

Staffing

It appears on the second line of the screen in the highlighted area. The screen appears as shown in Fig. 7-4. Press ENTER to create the new category and include it in the category hierarchy, at the bottom of the list.

Next, create the three categories Ann, Jim, and George as child categories under Staffing. To enter the Ann category directly as a child category, highlight Staffing and press ALT-R to create a new category below and to the right (indented, a child category) of the highlighted category. The row of dots appears under Staffing, indented. Type in Ann and press ENTER. Ann is created as a new category, indented, indicating that it is a child Staffing.

The remaining child categories can be entered more directly. With the highlight on Ann, press INS to insert another category at the same level, as a sibling of Ann and a child of Staffing. Type in Jim and press ENTER. Likewise, highlight Jim and press INS to enter George as the final member of the Staffing family. The category hierarchy should now appear as shown in Fig. 7-5.

```
Category name:                                              Edit
Staffing
═══════════════════════════════════════════════════════════════

MAIN
  Project
    James
    Walker
    Acme
    Peters
  Reports
  Meetings
  Phone Calls
  . . . . . . . .




═F1═══╤═F2═══╤═F3══╤═F4══╤═F5══╤═F6══╤═F7══╤═F8══╤═F9═══╤═F10═══
Help  ║Paste║Copy ║Cut  ║     ║     ║Mark ║     ║Accept║
```

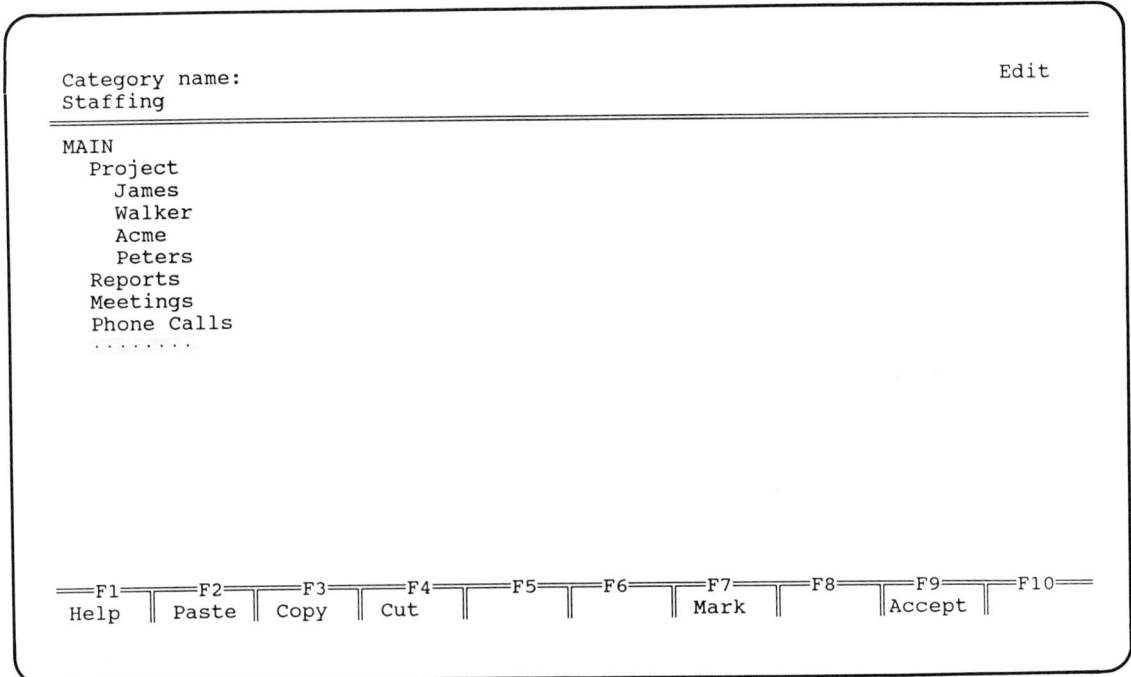

Fig. 7-4. *Entering the new category Staffing at the end of the category hierarchy.*

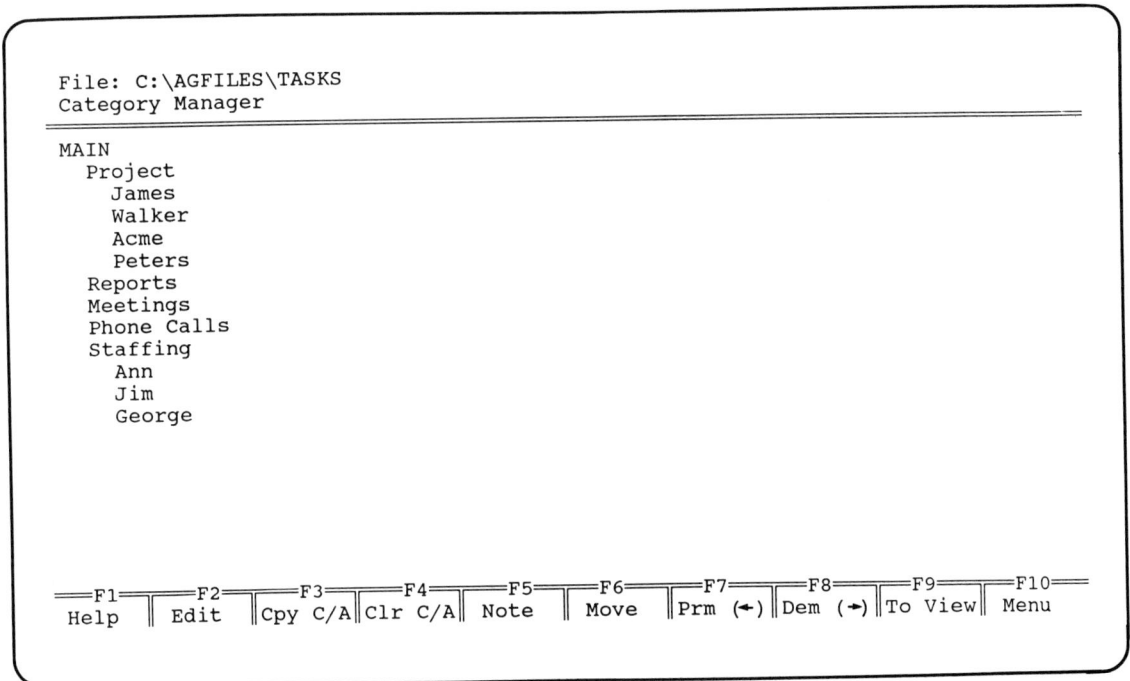

```
File: C:\AGFILES\TASKS
Category Manager
═══════════════════════════════════════════════════════════════

MAIN
  Project
    James
    Walker
    Acme
    Peters
  Reports
  Meetings
  Phone Calls
  Staffing
    Ann
    Jim
    George




═F1═══╤═F2═══╤═F3═════╤═F4═════╤═F5═══╤═F6═══╤═F7══════╤═F8══════╤═F9═════╤═F10══
Help  ║ Edit ║Cpy C/A║Clr C/A║ Note ║ Move ║Prm (←)║Dem (→)║To View║ Menu
```

Fig. 7-5. *The category hierarchy after the entry of the four new categories for the Staffing family.*

Several options are available for specifying where new categories are to be inserted into the category hierarchy. The most basic is the use of the INS key, which works like INS in other parts of Agenda: it inserts the new category directly below the highlighted category in the hierarchy. The new category is a sibling of the category above it.

The INS key is all that you really need for inserting new categories at the appropriate level in the category hierarchy. After the INS key has been used to insert a category, the category can be promoted to parent status or demoted to child status by using F7 (PROMOTE) or F8 (DEMOTE). These commands are listed on the function key map at the bottom of the screen.

Alternatively, new categories can be directly inserted into the correct positions using *accelerator keys*—letters pressed in conjunction with the ALT key. ALT-R inserts the new category below and to the right of the highlighted category, as a child of that category. Complementing this, ALT-L inserts the new category below and to the left of the highlighted category. This starts a new family. With several levels of indentation, even this might not allow the correct positioning of a new category, however. Therefore, you might need to use ALT-U which inserts a new category above (up from) the highlighted category as a sibling to that category.

These three keys, plus INS, cover nearly all the possibilities. They allow the insertion of almost any new category in the desired position. The keys for inserting new categories in the category hierarchy are summarized in Table 7-2.

## Discarding Categories

Eliminating a category from the category hierarchy is accomplished like many other discard operations in Agenda. First you highlight the category to be discarded in the category hierarchy. Then you press either ALT-F4 (DISCARD) or the DEL key.

**Table 7-2. Special Keys for Inserting New Categories in the Category Hierarchy.**

| Key | Function |
| --- | --- |
| INS | Insert new category below the highlighted category as a sibling category. |
| ALT-R | Insert new category below and to the right of the highlighted category as a child category. |
| ALT-L | Insert new category below and to the left of the highlighted category starting a new family. |
| ALT-U | Insert new category above (up from) the highlighted category as a sibling. |

If the category being discarded has no items currently assigned to it and is not the parent of another category, it is immediately eliminated from the screen and from the database. For example, if you were to highlight one of the categories just added to the database and press DEL or ALT-F4 (DISCARD), the category would disappear.

If, on the other hand, items are currently assigned to the category being discarded, Agenda gives you a second chance. A box appears on the screen informing you that items are assigned to that category and asking if you really want to discard it. Accept the setting of *Yes* and press ENTER to discard the category.

Obviously, when a category is discarded, no items can remain assigned to that category. If the items are also assigned to other categories that remain in the database, however, these items will remain in the database.

Items assigned only to the discarded category are themselves discarded, since every item must be assigned to at least one category. These discarded items are placed in Trash and can be recalled in the usual fashion. Only the *items* are placed in Trash, however. The category itself and the assignment of the items to that category are permanently eliminated from the database when the category is discarded.

If the category to be discarded has child categories, Agenda warns you of this fact. A box indicates that the category has children, and asks whether you really want to discard it. Also, the parent or child categories might have items assigned to them, but this will not be indicated. If you specify that a category with children is to be discarded, you eliminate not only the highlighted parent category, but also all of the child categories. The entire family is discarded by the discard operation. Furthermore, any items assigned only to categories within this family are discarded to Trash as well. Therefore, be very careful and make sure that you are performing the desired operation when discarding a category with children.

It is important to distinguish between discarding categories and removing sections or columns headed by categories from a view. When a category is discarded, it is totally eliminated from the database. In contrast, when a category that is used as a section head or for a column is removed from the view, the category and the item assignments to the category remain in the database.

Discarding a category also removes all references to that category from all views in the database. If the category is used as a section head, the section is removed. If the category is used as a column head, the column is removed. If the category is an entry in a column, that entry is removed.

## Rearranging Categories

You might want to rearrange the way categories are displayed in the Category Manager, to present the information in a more logical fashion and make the categories easier to find. You can either move individual categories and families within the category hierarchy or sort the child categories alphabetically within a family.

The Walker and the James projects are both being done for the Walker firm. You want to move the Walker category to the top of the list in the Project family, before James. To move an individual category, begin by highlighting the category to be moved, in this case Walker. Press F6 (MOVE). Figure 7-6 indicates what category is being moved and gives the instruction to perform the move. Using the UP arrow, move the highlight up until James is highlighted. Then press CTRL-ENTER to insert the Walker category above the James category in the list of Project child categories.

The basic move procedure is simple enough: highlight the category to be moved, press F6, and move the highlight to where you want the category inserted. Pressing CTRL-ENTER inserts the category being moved above the highlighted category; pressing ENTER inserts it below the highlighted category. These move procedures insert a category at the same level in the hierarchy as the highlighted category. This is the reason for having the options to insert above or below. In the example, Walker was to be placed between the Project and James categories, but as a child to the Project category at the same level as the James category.

```
Move cursor to position for:    "Walker"
Press ENTER to insert below, CTRL-ENTER to insert above highlighted category
─────────────────────────────────────────────────────────────────────────
MAIN
  Project
    James
    Walker
    Acme
    Peters
  Reports
  Meetings
  Phone Calls
  Staffing
    Ann
    Jim
    George




═F1═══╤══F2══╤══F3══╤══F4══╤══F5══╤══F6══╤══F7══╤══F8══╤══F9══╤══F10═
Help  │      │      │      │      │      │      │      │      │
```

Fig. 7-6. *Moving the Walker category in the category hierarchy.*

Thus, it was necessary to highlight James and use CTRL-ENTER to insert Walker above James but at the same level as James.

In moving the Walker category, had you highlighted the Project category and pressed ENTER to insert the category below, an apparently strange thing would have happened. The Walker category would have been moved below the Project family, and to the same level as the Project category. What is going on here? When you specify that a category is to be inserted below a category that is a parent to child categories, Agenda inserts the category at the level of the parent but beneath the entire family, to avoid disrupting the family.

If you specify that a parent category is to be moved, Agenda moves the entire family. Thus, suppose you had highlighted Project, pressed F6, moved the highlight down to Phone Calls, and pressed ENTER. The entire Project family—the Project category and the four child categories—would have been moved as a block to the position below the Phone Calls category.

Agenda might appear to present a variety of different responses to attempts to move categories within the hierarchy. However, the responses represent logical approaches to preserving the integrity of category families so that moves do not inappropriately disrupt family relationships. As you can see, moving categories is fairly straightforward.

The Category Manager can also be used to sort categories. It sorts the child categories of any parent category in alphabetical order. To sort categories, you first highlight the parent category of the child categories to be sorted, and then press ALT-F9 (SORT). The categories are rearranged. Any children to the categories are moved along with them in a family unit, so no parent-child relationships are changed by the sort operation. Sort the names of the staff members in alphabetical order under the Staffing category. Highlight Staffing and press ALT-F9 (SORT). The child categories are immediately alphabetized.

Sorting only affects the ordering of the first level of categories in the family being sorted. That is, the child categories are alphabetized, but any children of those categories are not rearranged. For example, had Ann had several child categories, their ordering would not have been affected by the sort. To sort at the lower levels, it is necessary to highlight the parent of the categories to be sorted and repeat the sort procedure.

## USING MUTUALLY EXCLUSIVE CATEGORIES

Sometimes the nature of the child categories in a family makes it logical for you to indicate in the database that certain items can be assigned to only one of those child categories. For example, suppose you wished to organize the tasks in the database according to the length of time each task was expected to take. You might create a Duration parent category and create child categories for Short,

Medium, and Long tasks, perhaps as follows:

Duration
    Short (1-2 days)
    Medium (3-5 days)
    Long (over 5 days)

    With such a classification, each task can logically be assigned to only one of the three child categories in the family. No task could be, for example, of both Short and Medium duration. A task would be expected to take either two days (or less), placing it into the Short category, or it would be expected to take 3 days or more, placing it either in the Medium or Long categories.

    Agenda allows you to specify that all of the child categories in a family are to be mutually exclusive. The program then prevents the assignment of items to more than one of the mutually exclusive categories.

## Making Categories Mutually Exclusive

    The Staffing category was created with the child categories for each assistant to allow the assignment of tasks to a specific assistant. Assume that only one assistant will be assigned to a given task; the assigned assistant will have the primary responsibility for completing that task. No task will be assigned to more than one assistant. Thus, the child categories of the Staffing category should be designated as mutually exclusive.

    Making the child categories in a family mutually exclusive is very easy. Within the Category Manager, move the highlight to the Staffing category, the parent category of the family to be designated mutually exclusive. Then execute the Category Manager's Exclusive command. Press F10 (MENU) to display the menu of Category Manager commands and select Exclusive in the normal manner. The child categories, Ann, George, and Jim, are marked with a bracket to indicate that they are now mutually exclusive categories. This is shown in Fig. 7-7.

    Complications arise if items are already assigned to two or more of the categories being made mutually exclusive. To see what happens, highlight Project and issue the Exclusive command. A box appears on the screen informing you that items are assigned to more than one of the categories in the family. Three options are provided for resolving the conflict: the items assigned to multiple categories may be reassigned to the parent category; they may be left assigned to the first category in the family to which they are assigned and unassigned from any other categories; or you may specify that the items be assigned to some other

```
  File: C:\AGFILES\TASKS
  Category Manager
═════════════════════════════════════════════════════════════════════════
MAIN
   Project
     Walker
     James
     Acme
     Peters
   Reports
   Meetings
   Phone Calls
   Staffing
    ┌Ann
    ├Jim
    └George




  ═F1══════F2══════F3══════F4══════F5══════F6══════F7═══╤═F8═══╤═F9═══╤═F10══
   Help  │ Edit ║Cpy C/A║Clr C/A║ Note ║ Move ║Prm (←)║Dem (→)║To View║ Menu
```

Fig. 7-7. *The child categories of the Staffing category made mutually exclusive.*

category. You select the option for resolving the conflict by pressing GREY PLUS and selecting from the list displayed, in the usual fashion. In this case, since you do not need to make the categories in the Project family mutually exclusive, simply back out of the Exclusive command by pressing ESC.

Changing mutually exclusive categories back to the original nonexclusive status is just as easy. Highlight the parent category and issue the Exclusive command once more. The brackets will be removed. No possibility of conflict exists when making the categories nonexclusive. The Exclusive command simply changes the status of the child categories, from nonexclusive to exclusive and back again.

When you are working with a view rather than in the Category Manager, the Category Management Exclusive command is available to change a family of categories from nonexclusive to exclusive or vice versa. You just highlight the parent category in the view and issue the command.

For example, you might have created a view with a Staffing column, in which you are entering the child categories for the individual staff members. To make this mutually exclusive, you would highlight Staffing and enter the Category Management Exclusive command. The same procedure can be used to change an exclusive family back to nonexclusive.

No brackets or other symbols are displayed to indicate the effect of the change when it is made in a view. The only indication appears when you either enter the Category Manager or attempt to make multiple assignments in the view.

## Using Exclusive Categories

You have now created the Staffing category and the child categories for the three staff members, and have made those child categories mutually exclusive. Using these categories requires the assignment of items to the categories.

Return from the Category Manager to a view by pressing F9 (TO VIEW) or ESC. If you are not currently in the Tasks to Do view, press F8 (VIEW MGR) to display the list of views. Select the Tasks to Do view and press ENTER. To assign items to the various Staffing categories, begin by creating a Staffing column. With the highlight on any item, use the Category Column New command. The column head will be Staffing. In the New Column box, move the highlight down to the *Column head:* setting. Begin typing Staffing and press ENTER to accept the match when it is displayed. (Alternatively, you could press GREY PLUS and select Staffing from the category hierarchy.) The remaining new column defaults are appropriate, so press F9 to accept the setting and display the Staffing column.

Newly entered items that refer to the staff members will automatically be assigned to the appropriate category. Move the highlight down to the last item in the Phone Calls section and press INS to insert a new item. Type in the following item

Call Ann to go over report to Walker Inc. on Walker and James projects.

Press ENTER. The item is assigned automatically to the Ann category, which appears in the Staffing column. The item is also assigned automatically to both the Walker and James categories in the Project column. Agenda also automatically assigns the new item to the Reports category and displays it in the Reports section. This is shown in Fig. 7-8.

Items can have multiple assignments to categories, as long as the categories in question have not been designated mutually exclusive. If the categories are mutually exclusive, Agenda only assigns an item to one of the two mutually exclusive categories. Agenda's choice between the two categories is arbitrary.

```
File: C:\AGFILES\TASKS                              03/10/89    15:22
View: Tasks to Do
=Meetings ========================= Staffing===== Project===== When=====
        3/24/89 to go over quarterly
        results.
      • Meet with Jim to discuss report              ·Peters
        on the Peters account.

  Phone Calls                          Staffing       Project       When
      ♪ Call Ron Smith at Walker by                   ·Walker       ·03/14/89
        Tuesday to discuss the progress
        of the project.
      • Call Adam Baker at James                      ·James        ·03/15/89
        Wednesday to get his reactions to
        our proposals.
      • Call Ann by next Friday to                                  ·03/17/89
        discuss hiring of new assistant.
      • Call Peter Smith regarding new                ·Walker
        account proposals for Walker and             Acme
        Acme.
      • Call Ann to go over report to    »Ann         ·Walker
        Walker Inc. on Walker and James              James
        projects.
==F1====F2====F3====F4====F5====F6====F7====F8====F9====F10==
 Help  │ Edit │ Copy │ Done │ Note │ Move │ Mark │Vw Mgr│Cat Mgr│ Menu
```

Fig. 7-8. *The automatic assignment of a new item to multiple categories.*

Existing items can be assigned to a category by making the entries in a column headed by the category. In the Tasks to Do view in the Tasks database, most of the items should be assigned to one of the three staff members by making entries in the Staffing column. Some of the items already refer to these staffers, so the assignment is obvious. For the other items, Ann is to be assigned the tasks involving the Walker project, George is to be assigned to the tasks involving the James project, and Jim is to be assigned the tasks involving the Peters project.

In the Tasks database, assign existing items to the Staffing category by making entries in the Staffing column. Move the highlight over to the Staffing column, to the right of any item. The easiest way to enter one of the staff name categories is to type the first letter or two of the name until that category is displayed as a match. Then press ENTER. The staff member's name is displayed and the item is assigned to that category.

Normally, items can be assigned to a second category in a column by highlighting the first category and pressing INS. Agenda will not allow you to assign an item to a second category in the Staffing column, however, because the categories are mutually exclusive. For example, if you highlight an entry in the Staffing column and press INS, Agenda produces a low beep and does nothing else. Agenda will not allow an assignment to a second category because the categories are mutually exclusive. The only way you could assign that item to another category would be to first delete the existing assignment and then make the new assignment.

## PROMOTING AND DEMOTING CATEGORIES

Structuring categories into families, with parent-child relationships, is a fundamental part of the organization of an Agenda database. Depending on the type of database, it might become necessary to change the family structure. In some databases, once you create the family structure in the category hierarchy, you might have little need to change it. Indeed, any changes might be entirely illogical. On the other hand, working with other databases might involve nearly constant juggling of the parent-child relationships in the category hierarchy. This might be the case, for example, if you are using Agenda to create an organizational framework for managing the information in the database.

Agenda allows you to directly change the level of a category in the hierarchy through promotion or demotion. You simply highlight the category and press either F7 (PROMOTE) or F8 (DEMOTE). Promoting a category moves it to the next higher level, to the left, making it the parent of the category below. Demoting a category moves it to the next lower level, to the right, making it the child of the category above.

In the Tasks database, assume that the Walker project and the James project are being performed for different divisions of Walker, Inc. You have decided to consolidate these two projects into a single Walker project, with the James project being managed as a subproject. Therefore, the James category should now be made a child category of the Walker category.

If you are not already in the Category Manager, press F9 (CAT MGR). The James category is immediately below the Walker category. Highlight the James category and press F8 (DEMOTE) to move the James category down one level, making it a child category of the Walker category.

The promotion and demotion of categories can frequently create conflicts, most often because of the restriction that items cannot be directly assigned to both a parent category and a child category.

The item most recently entered into the Tasks database refers to a report on both the Walker and James projects. This item was assigned to both of the project categories. Thus, a conflict arises if the James category is demoted. When such a conflict arises, Agenda informs you of the conflict by displaying a box on the screen, as shown in Fig. 7-9.

The box indicates that one or more items now assigned to the current category being demoted (the James category) are also assigned to the category that will become its new parent (the Walker category). Options are provided for dealing with the conflicting items. The default, shown in Fig. 7-9, is to remove the items from the current category (the James category).

Since items assigned to both Walker and James involve the entire project and not just the James subproject, they should be assigned to the Walker category. Thus, the current option to remove the items from the current category, James, represents the appropriate choice. Press F9 to accept the setting. The item in question is unassigned from the James category, and the James category is demoted to a child category of the Walker category. Figure 7-10 shows the category hierarchy after this change has been made. If you return to the Tasks to Do view, you will see that the last item entered, the offending item that had been assigned to both the Walker and James categories, is now assigned only to the Walker category.

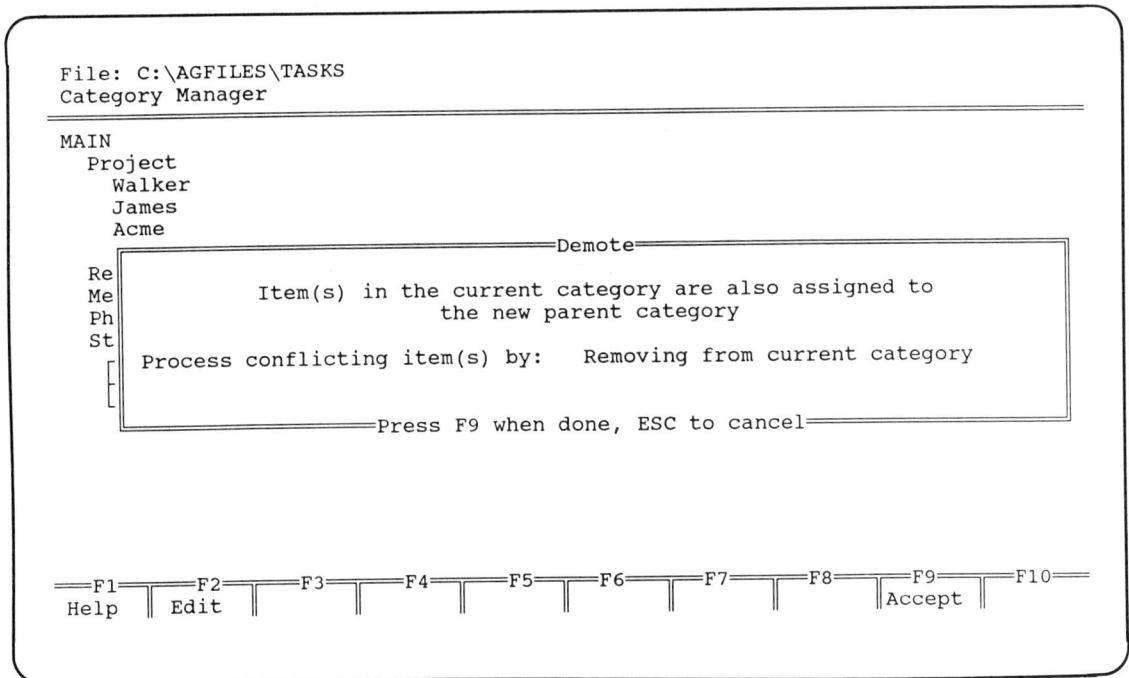

```
File: C:\AGFILES\TASKS
Category Manager
═══════════════════════════════════════════════════════════════
MAIN
   Project
      Walker
      James
      Acme
  ┌─────────────────────────────────Demote═══════════════════════┐
Re│                                                                │
Me│        Item(s) in the current category are also assigned to    │
Ph│                   the new parent category                      │
St│                                                                │
  │ Process conflicting item(s) by:   Removing from current category │
  │                                                                │
  │                                                                │
  └══════════════════Press F9 when done, ESC to cancel═══════════┘



═F1═══╤═F2═══╤═F3═══╤═F4═══╤═F5═══╤═F6═══╤═F7═══╤═F8═══╤═F9═══╤═F10═══
Help  ║ Edit ║      ║      ║      ║      ║      ║      ║Accept║
```

Fig. 7-9. *Dealing with items assigned to both the Walker category and the James category when demoting James to be a child of Walker.*

```
 File: C:\AGFILES\TASKS
 Category Manager
═══════════════════════════════════════════════════════════

MAIN
   Project
     Walker
        James
     Acme
     Peters
   Reports
   Meetings
   Phone Calls
   Staffing
     ┌Ann
     ├Jim
     └George




═F1═══╤═F2══╤═F3═══╤═F4══╤═F5══╤═F6═══╤═F7══╤═F8═══╤═F9═══╤═F10═
 Help │ Edit │Cpy C/A│Clr C/A│ Note │ Move │Prm (◄)│Dem (►)│To View│ Menu
```

Fig. 7-10. *The category hierarchy after the demotion of the James category.*

Conflicts can occur both when demoting categories and when promoting categories. In both situations, conflicts arise because items would be assigned to both a parent category and a child category, which is not allowed. When promoting a category, another type of conflict can arise if the promotion would result in items being assigned to two categories in a family of mutually exclusive categories.

Whenever a conflict arises in promotion or demotion, Agenda displays a box describing the nature of the conflict and presenting options for its resolution. The options are the same for all three types of conflicts. You can choose from the following:

• Remove the item from the current category—the one being promoted or demoted—leaving the item assigned to the conflicting category.
• Remove the item from the conflicting category, leaving the item assigned to the current category being promoted or demoted.
• Remove the item from both the current category and the conflicting category and assign it to a new category, which you specify.

The third option is an alternative if you are not certain what you should do with the item. Create a new category and assign the conflicting items there. Then you can display that category and the items assigned to it in a view, individually examine the items, and determine the appropriate assignment.

To select one of the options for dealing with conflicts when promoting or demoting items, press GREY PLUS to display the list of options. Select the desired option and press ENTER. If your choice is to assign the item to a third category, you will be further prompted for the name of that category.

Not all promotions or demotions are allowed. You may not promote a category above the level of being a child to Agenda's Main category. You may not demote a category more than one level below the category immediately above. That is, a category cannot become a grandchild to a category without an intervening parent. Agenda informs you when you attempt an invalid promotion.

Promoting a category with children results in the promotion of the entire family. All of the family members are moved to the left and the family structure is preserved intact. Demoting a parent category, on the other hand, does not result in the entire family being demoted.

The promotion and demotion operations are actually quite logical. As you use these features in working with the category hierarchy, you will begin to understand the way things work and be comfortable with the possibilities. In general, the Category Manager is an easy place to experiment, moving categories around and changing the category structure. If the results are not exactly what you anticipated, you can usually return to the preceding situation quite easily, just as long as the assignment of items has not been changed in the course of the operation.

When boxes are displayed informing you that conflicts exist and that items' assignments must be altered to resolve the conflicts, be careful to assure that the change being made is what you desire. Otherwise, experiment with the Category Manager freely.

# 8

# PRINTING INFORMATION FROM A DATABASE

ALL users of Agenda need to print out information from their databases. Printing is a fundamental capability that all users must learn.

To do a basic printout of the information in a view requires only a few keystrokes. The new user of Agenda who is interested only in the basic procedures for printing from a view can find out everything he or she needs to know by reading the first part of the first section of this chapter.

Agenda provides an extremely wide range of options for controlling the manner in which information is printed. Mastering these options can take some effort. The second part of this chapter presents options, refinements, and other information that may be useful for users needing more sophisticated options.

The first section of the chapter addresses the basic processes involved in printing information from a view. Next come sections that address the control of page formats and the control of the printer when printing information from Agenda. The procedure for printing to files is covered in the fourth section. The final two sections of the chapter address specific issues relating to printing information from the Category Manager and from notes.

The various sections in this chapter address separate, distinct topics associated with the control of printing in Agenda. The latter sections are generally not dependent upon the earlier sections. Thus, you can go directly to a section covering a topic of interest and learn how to proceed from the information in that section.

# PRINTING INFORMATION FROM A VIEW

Printing information from an Agenda database usually involves printing a view. Selecting and arranging information are accomplished when you create the view. The print operation then essentially prints the information displayed in the view, though some selection is possible.

## The Basic Printing Operation

The basic procedures for printing a view are straightforward: display the view, invoke the Print command, and start the printing. Although many options are available, they can be ignored if all you need is a simple printout of the information in the view.

Print out the main, Tasks to Do view of the Tasks database. After opening the database, display the Tasks to Do view by using F8 (VIEW MGR) and selecting the Tasks to Do view. Enter the Print command by pressing F10 (MENU) and then P. A large dialog box for print settings is displayed on the screen as shown in Fig. 8-1. You can ignore all of the options in the box for now. Be sure your printer is turned on and is ready to print (*online*) and that the paper is set to the top of the page. Press F9 to accept the default settings and begin the printing. (If the view is not

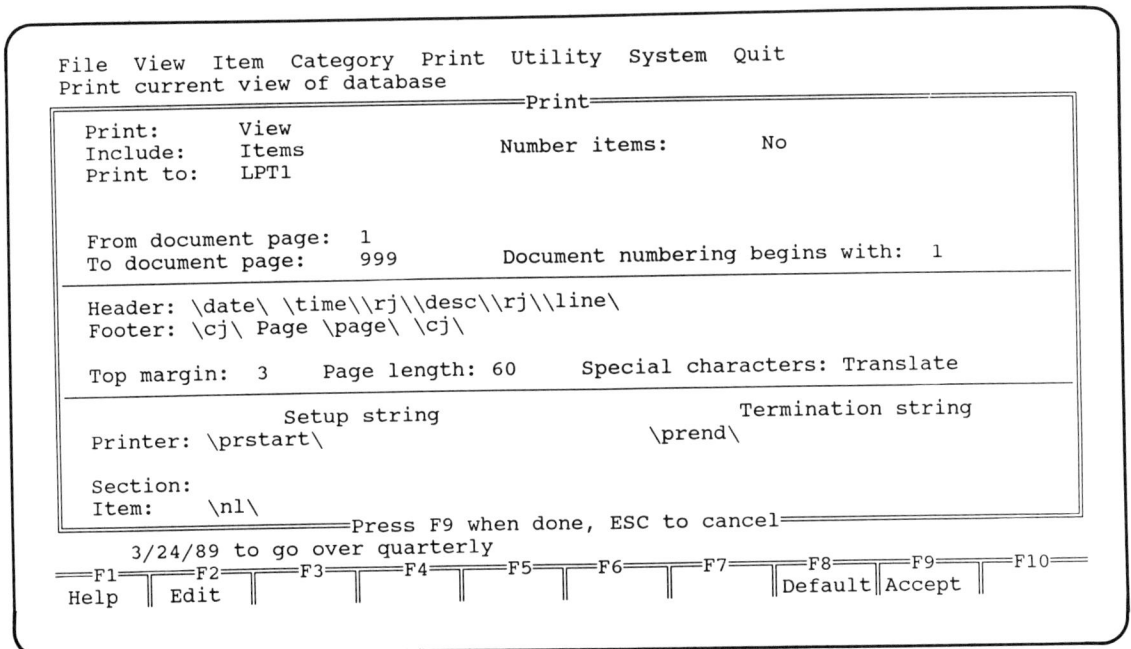

```
 File  View  Item  Category  Print  Utility  System  Quit
 Print current view of database
═══════════════════════════════════════════Print═══════════════════════════════
┌──────────────────────────────────────────────────────────────────────────────┐
│ Print:      View                                                               │
│ Include:    Items            Number items:      No                             │
│ Print to:   LPT1                                                               │
│                                                                                │
│                                                                                │
│ From document page:   1                                                        │
│ To document page:     999      Document numbering begins with:   1             │
├────────────────────────────────────────────────────────────────────────────── │
│ Header: \date\ \time\\rj\\desc\\rj\\line\                                       │
│ Footer: \cj\ Page \page\ \cj\                                                   │
│                                                                                │
│ Top margin:  3    Page length: 60    Special characters: Translate             │
├────────────────────────────────────────────────────────────────────────────── │
│              Setup string                  Termination string                  │
│ Printer: \prstart\                            \prend\                           │
│                                                                                │
│ Section:                                                                        │
│ Item:     \nl\                                                                  │
└═══════════════════════Press F9 when done, ESC to cancel═══════════════════════─┘
      3/24/89 to go over quarterly
══F1══╤══F2══╤══F3══╤══F4══╤══F5══╤══F6══╤══F7══╤══F8══════╤══F9═════╤══F10══
 Help ║ Edit ║      ║      ║      ║      ║      ║Default║Accept ║
```

Fig. 8-1. *The dialog box for printing from a view.*

printed out, read the next section of this chapter to make sure that you are using the correct port.)

When the printing of the view is complete, you are returned to the Tasks to Do view. If you ever need to interrupt printing while it is in progress, press CTRL-BREAK as indicated in the box on the screen. Agenda stops printing and returns you to the view. Your printer might, however, keep printing for a while, depending upon the amount of text stored in the printer's buffer.

Figure 8-2 shows the printout of the Tasks to Do view from the Tasks database. Agenda places a header on the printout with the date, time, and description of the database and a line separating this information from the information in the view. The description in the header is the text that was entered when the Tasks database was first created. Then comes the information that was displayed in the view. The information is printed out almost exactly as it is shown on the screen. The major difference is the double-spacing between the heads and the items.

## Specifying the Output Device

If the above procedure resulted in Agenda's printing out the view, then you probably do not need to worry about specifying the appropriate output device for printing. At issue is the port to which the printer is attached. Most users of IBM PCs and compatibles have their printers hooked to the first parallel port, which is designated LPT1. This is Agenda's default, so Agenda will print properly for those users. If printing works for you and you know nothing about different ports, you may safely skip this section.

If, however, your printer is attached to another port or if you have two printers hooked to different ports and wish to select the printer to be used, you might need to specify a different device. After giving the Print command, the Print box is displayed as shown in Fig. 8-1. Move the highlight down to *Print to: LPT1* and press GREY PLUS to display the box with the list of options. This box shows the list of ports which may be selected for printing. It includes three parallel ports, LPT1, LPT2, and LPT3, and two serial ports, COM1 and COM2 (the File option is used for printing to a file, which is discussed later in this chapter). Select the port to which your printer is connected and press ENTER.

If you select one of the serial ports, COM1 or COM2, Agenda makes no provision for specifying the baud rate or other communications parameters associated with this port. This will have to be done using the DOS MODE command before entering Agenda. Most users with printers connected to serial ports have this operation automatically performed by a MODE command in their AUTOEXEC.BAT file.

If you will usually be printing to a printer connected to a port other than LPT1, this other port can be made the default for all of your work with Agenda.

```
03/10/89 15:32                        Database for Working with Lotus Agenda
----------------------------------------------------------------------------
 Reports                          Staffing      Project       When

    · Meeting to discuss project for   ·George       ·James        ·03/13/89
      James next Monday.

    · Prepare report on Walker project ·Ann          ·Walker       ·03/16/89
      by next Thursday.

    · Have Ann get out the previous    ·Ann          ·Walker
      Walker project report and begin
      the process of updating so that
      we have a draft to work with.

    · Meet with Jim to discuss report  ·Jim          ·Peters
      on the Peters account.

    · Call Ann to go over report to    ·Ann          ·Walker
      Walker Inc. on Walker and James
      projects.


 Meetings                         Staffing      Project       When

    · Meeting to discuss project for   ·George       ·James        ·03/13/89
      James next Monday.

    · Meeting with executive committee                            ·03/24/89
      3/24/89 to go over quarterly
      results.

    · Meet with Jim to discuss report  ·Jim          ·Peters
      on the Peters account.


 Phone Calls                      Staffing      Project       When

    · Call Ron Smith at Walker by      ·Ann          ·Walker       ·03/14/89
      Tuesday to discuss the progress
      of the project.

    · Call Adam Baker at James         ·George       ·James        ·03/15/89
      Wednesday to get his reactions to
      our proposals.

    · Call Ann by next Friday to       ·Ann                        ·03/17/89
      discuss hiring of new assistant.

    · Call Peter Smith regarding new   ·Ann          ·Walker
      account proposals for Walker and               Acme
      Acme.

    · Call Ann to go over report to    ·Ann          ·Walker
      Walker Inc. on Walker and James      ·
      projects.
                              Page 1
```

Fig. 8-2. *The printout of the Tasks to Do view of the Tasks database.*

Select the appropriate port in the Print box and press F9 to print the view. (You must press F9 to accept the new port setting.) After returning to the view, issue the Utility Preferences Update command to record this new port setting as a permanent preference for use with Agenda. From then on, every time you print, the new port will be displayed as the default. You may still change ports at print time if you wish to print to a device connected to a different port.

## Specifying the Information to Be Printed

The major task in specifying the information to be printed is defining the view. In creating a view, you indicate the sections and columns to be included and any filters to be used in selecting items for inclusion in the view. Agenda provides options for specifying exactly what information is to be printed out.

The Print command displays the box with all of the print settings. The first setting is *Print:* and the selected option is *View,* to print all of the information in the view. With *View* highlighted, you can press GREY PLUS to display the list of options. These options are shown in Fig. 8-3. As you can see, it is not necessary to print the entire view. You can print just the current item, all of the items that have been marked (once you have marked them), or the current section. In addition, you can choose to print the item profile, which indicates the categories to which the highlighted item is assigned. Just highlight the selection for the information you wish to print and press ENTER.

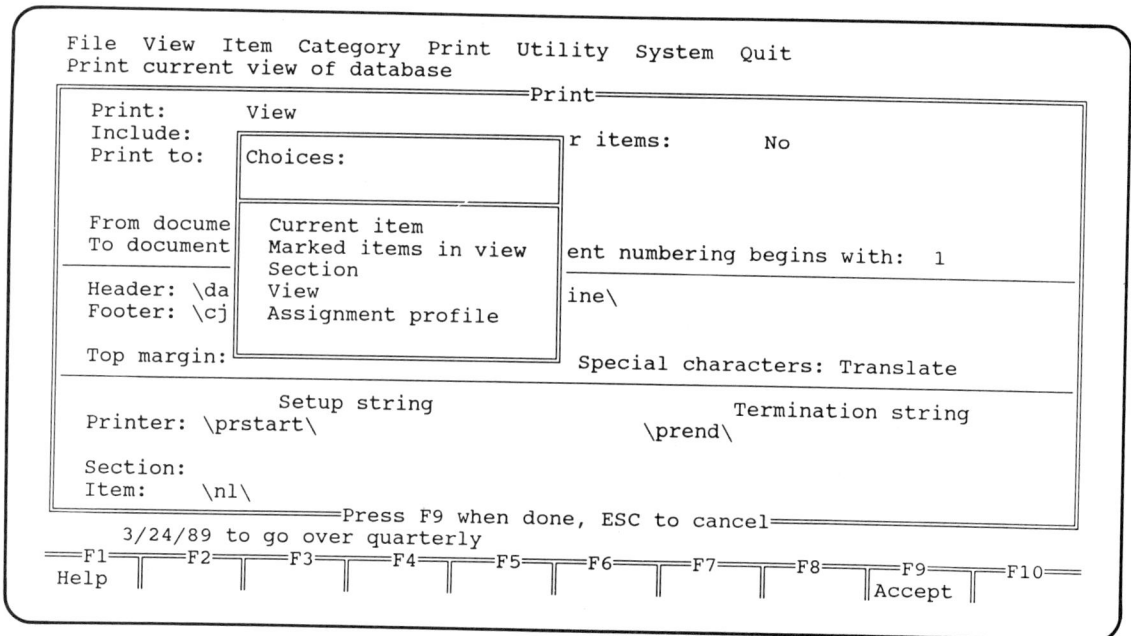

```
 File   View   Item   Category   Print   Utility   System   Quit
 Print current view of database
                                        =Print=
  Print:       View
  Include:                             r items:        No
  Print to:   Choices:

  From docume   Current item
  To document   Marked items in view   ent numbering begins with:   1
                Section
  Header: \da   View                   ine\
  Footer: \cj   Assignment profile

  Top margin:                          Special characters: Translate

                Setup string                       Termination string
  Printer: \prstart\                       \prend\

  Section:
  Item:      \nl\
                    =Press F9 when done, ESC to cancel=
        3/24/89 to go over quarterly
 =F1=    =F2=    =F3=    =F4=    =F5=    =F6=    =F7=    =F8=    =F9=    =F10=
  Help                                                         Accept
```

Fig. 8-3. *Selecting the information to be printed when printing from a view.*

Further options are provided by the *Include:* setting on the second line. The default setting is to print only the items displayed in the view. You can also choose to print the items together with the notes attached to those items. The note attached to an item will be printed under that item. You can even specify that only the notes be printed, without the associated items. Make the choice in the normal way by highlighting the setting, pressing GREY PLUS to display the list of options, selecting the option, and pressing ENTER.

For printing multipage documents, Agenda allows you to control page numbering and to specify the pages to be printed. Normally, documents are numbered beginning with page one. In some instances, however, when printing out information from two views or databases for a single document, you might want the printout of a view to begin with some other page number. To do this, move the highlight to the *Document numbering begin with:* setting in the lower-right corner of the top section of the Print box. For settings like this one with a number, the value can be changed in two different ways. You can press GREY PLUS to increment the setting by one, or you can just type in the new number and press ENTER.

You can also specify which pages of a multipage document are to be printed out. The first time you print a view, you do not know just what information will be on which page, so this is not an effective tool for controlling which information is to be printed. This is useful, however, when you are forced to interrupt the printing of a long document and want to resume printing where you left off.

The two settings *From document page:* and *To document page:* are used to specify the range of pages to be printed. The defaults of 1 and 999 indicate that Agenda should start printing at the beginning and print until the entire document has been printed. (The assumption is that you will not be printing more than 999 pages.) To begin printing on page 3 of a document, change the *From document page:* setting to 3. To stop printing on page 7, change the *To document page:* setting to 7.

If you have changed the *Document numbering begins with:* setting to start page numbering with a value other than one, the *From document page:* and *To document page:* settings will refer to those new page numbers. For example, suppose *Document numbering begins with:* had been changed to 16 to begin the page numbering of the printout with page 16. If you then set *From document page:* to 17, printing would begin with the page to be numbered 17, the second page of the document.

## CONTROLLING PAGE FORMATS

Agenda provides several options for controlling the format in which the information is printed on the page. You can control the top and bottom margins and specify headers and footers to be printed on each page.

## Vertical Alignment

With its default settings, Agenda allows half-inch margins—three blank lines—at the top and bottom of each page. This is determined by the *Top margin:* and *Page length:* settings in the middle of the Print box. The default for the top margin is three lines, which creates the half-inch margin at the top. The page length is the number of lines to be printed from the start of printing at the top margin to the last line of printing. The default is 60 lines. At the normal six lines per inch, 11-inch paper can accommodate 66 lines. Thus, the bottom margin ends up being at 63 (66 lines minus 3 lines for the top margin and 60 lines for the text), or 3 lines from the bottom of the page.

Suppose you wanted more generous margins of one inch at the top and bottom of each page. You would move to the *Top margin:* setting and change the 3 to 6, giving one inch at the top before starting printing on a page. Margins of one inch (6 lines) top and bottom leave 66 minus 12, or 54, lines for printing text. So you would then change the *Page length:* setting to 54 lines. These new settings are shown in the Print box in Fig. 8-4.

With some printers, you might be able to specify that output is to be printed at eight lines per inch rather than six lines per inch. The *Top margin:* and *Page length:* settings refer to numbers of lines, whatever the spacing. They will need to be changed to place the proper amount of text on the page and produce desirable top and bottom margins.

```
 File   View   Item   Category   Print   Utility   System   Quit
 Print current view of database
┌─────────────────────────────────Print════════════════════════┐
│   Print:        View                                          │
│   Include:      Items            Number items:      No        │
│   Print to:     LPT1                                          │
│                                                               │
│                                                               │
│   From document page:    1                                    │
│   To document page:      999     Document numbering begins with:  1 │
├───────────────────────────────────────────────────────────────┤
│   Header: \cj\Printout of View from Tasks Database\cj\        │
│   Footer: \cj\ Page \page\ \cj\                               │
│                                                               │
│   Top margin:  6     Page length: 54     Special characters: Translate │
├───────────────────────────────────────────────────────────────┤
│                  Setup string                 Termination string │
│   Printer: \prstart\                            \prend\       │
│                                                               │
│   Section:                                                    │
│   Item:     \nl\                                              │
└═══════════════════════Press F9 when done, ESC to cancel═══════┘
        3/24/89 to go over quarterly
═F1══╤══F2══╤══F3══╤══F4══╤══F5══╤══F6══╤══F7══╤══F8═══╤══F9═══╤═F10══
 Help ║ Edit ║      ║      ║      ║      ║      ║Default║Accept ║
```

Fig. 8-4. *The settings for printing out a view with larger top and bottom margins and alternate text in the header.*

## Headers and Footers

Agenda allows for headers and footers to be printed at the top and bottom of each page of output. The first two lines and the last line of the printed output shown in Fig. 8-2 were printed as the header and footer using the default settings provided by Agenda. They do a reasonably nice job of formatting the page, but you can specify your own headers and footers as an alternative.

The basic idea of the header and footer operations is quite simple: whatever text is entered in the header or footer box is printed at the top or bottom of each page. The procedures are made more complicated, however, because Agenda has many special commands that can be used to specify what information is to be printed and how to format the information. Each of these commands is enclosed between pairs of backslash characters ( \ ) and directs a certain operation to be performed when the header or footer is printed. These commands are summarized in Table 8-1.

The use of the backslash commands in headers and footers and their effects can best be introduced by examining the default headers and footers provided by Agenda. First consider the default header:

\ date \   \ time \ \ rj \ \ desc \ \ rj \ \ line \

The first entry is the backslash command \ *date* \ , which causes the current date to be printed at the beginning of the header on the first line of the header. This is followed by a space, which is printed after the date to separate the date from the time, which is printed by the command \ *time* \ . Next comes the first of a pair of \ *rj* \ commands. The text between the two \ *rj* \ commands is right-justified on the line.

The command \ *desc* \ prints out the description associated with the current database. Because of the \ *rj* \ commands, the description is right-justified on the line. Last is the command \ *line* \ to print a line of hyphens on the second line to serve as a separator.

The default footer is somewhat simpler, but illustrates the use of some additional backslash commands. The footer is as follows:

\ cj \ Page \ page \   \ cj \

It begins and ends with the commands \ *cj* \ , indicating that the information between is to be centered on the bottom line. The first entry is *Page*, which instructs the Agenda to print that word. This is followed by the backslash command \ *page* \ , which instructs Agenda to print the current page number. So when the current page number is 3, this footer will print

**Table 8-1. Backslash Commands for Print Formatting and Printing.**

| Command | Function |
|---|---|
| *Formatting Commands* | |
| \cj\ | Center enclosed text. |
| \lcj[*char*]\ | Center text and print hyphen or optional *char* on each side. |
| \mgn [*left col width*] | Set margins for printing notes where *left col* is the column in which printing begins and *width* is the line width. |
| \nl\ | Insert carriage return to start new line. |
| \pgbk[*number*] | Start new page; if *number* is specified, start new page if that number of lines cannot be printed on current page. |
| \rj\ | Right justify enclosed text. |
| *Printing Commands* | |
| \date\ | Print current date. |
| \desc\ | Print database description. |
| \fname\ | Print database file name. |
| \line[*char*]\ | Print line of hyphens or optional *char* to right. |
| \ *nnn* \ | Print character with decimal value *nnn*. |
| \page\ | Print current page number. |
| \rem\ | Do not print remaining text on line; used for remarks. |
| \sect\ | Print section and column heads. |
| \time\ | Print current time. |
| \view\ | Print name of view. |
| \ \ | Print backslash character. |

centered at the bottom of the page.

You can construct your own custom headers and footers by combining the backslash commands in Table 8-1 with any text. For example, you might want your printout to have a centered header saying Printout of View from Tasks Database. Move the highlight to the Header: setting and type in the following entry:

\cj\Printout of View from Tasks Database\cj\

As soon as you type the first character, the default header disappears. While you are entering the header, you can move the cursor around and edit the text in the normal fashion. Press ENTER when you are finished. This new heading is shown in the Print box in Fig. 8-4. To print the view with the larger top and bottom margins and the new header, press F9.

After making several changes, particularly to complex entries like the headers or footers, you might wonder how to get back to the original default settings. When the Print box is displayed, just highlight the setting to be returned to its original value and press F8 (DEFAULT). The default setting is restored. For example, with the highlight on the header entry, pressing F8 reenters the original header provided by Agenda. To restore all of the settings in the Print box to their default values at once, press ALT-F8 (DFLTALL) (for Default All).

## CONTROLLING THE PRINTER

You might wish to control various print attributes such as print quality, size, or boldfacing when printing information from Agenda. The program gives you the ability to do this. Agenda also attempts to work with specific printers to make the control of printing easier. This means that certain features are available only if Agenda provides support for your particular printer and if you have selected the proper printer definition file. Even if features are not provided for your printer, however, Agenda allows considerable control over any printer.

### Specifying the Printer Definition File

For certain printers, Agenda allows the use of simple backslash commands to control common print attributes, and does the translation required for printing any special international characters entered into a database. To use these capabilities, the printer definition file for your specific printer must be specified. If you have not specified a printer definition file or if Agenda has not provided a printer definition file for your printer, then you cannot use certain features.

The various printer definition files were copied to the directory with the Agenda program files when Agenda was originally installed. The easiest way to select a printer definition file is to start Agenda from the directory with these files. This saves you problems associated with changing to the correct directory.

Suppose you installed Agenda in a directory named AGENDA, which is a subdirectory of the root directory. At the DOS prompt, give the command

```
CD AGENDA<ENTER>
```

to change to that directory. Then start Agenda in the usual manner. Open any Agenda database—the choice really does not matter.

From any view, give the Utility Preferences Environment command. With the highlight to the right of the *Printer definition file:* setting, press GREY PLUS. A file selection box listing all of the printer definition files is displayed as shown in Fig. 8-5. Printer definition files have the main portion of the file name describing

```
 Auto-Assign  Date  Other  Environment  Update
 Specify display & other system preferences

 R┌──────────────────────────Select File════════════════════┐
  │Highlight file & press ENTER, or type file name or directory│
  │                                                             │
  │    ..\             Parent directory                         │
  │    ───────────────────────────────────                     │
  │    BROTHER.PDF                                              │
  │    CITOHPRO.PDF                                             │
  │    CNNLBP82.PDF                                             │
  │    DBLO630.PDF                                              │
  │    EPSON86E.PDF                                             │
  │    EPSONFX.PDF                                              │
  │    EPSONMX.PDF                                              │
  │    FUJDPL24.PDF                                             │
  │    HPLASER.PDF                                              │
 M│  ↓ IBMPRO.PDF                                               │
  └───────────────────Current directory: C:\AG\*.PDF═══════════┘
    James next Monday.
  · Meeting with executive committee
    3/24/89 to go over quarterly               ·03/24/89
 ══F1══╤══F2══╤══F3══╤══F4══╤══F5══╤══F6══╤══F7══╤══F8══╤══F9══╤══F10══
  Help │     │     │Delete│     │Rename│     │     │Accept│
```

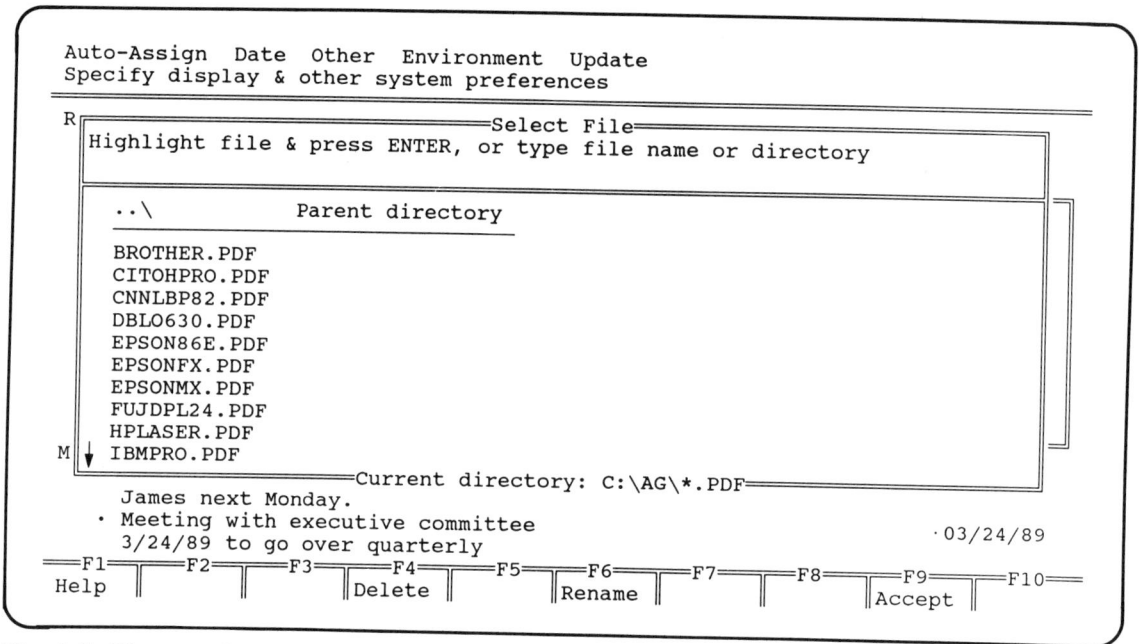

Fig. 8-5. *The specification of the printer definition file with the Utilities Preferences Environment command.*

the printer and the file name extension .PDF. Scroll through the list to find the file for your printer. Since we are using an IBM Proprinter, we selected the file IBMPRO.PDF. Highlight the desired file and press ENTER.

When you have returned to the Environment settings box, press F9 to accept the new settings. Then, to make the change permanent, issue the Utility Preferences Update command to record your choice on the disk for future use. Agenda will now use the printer definition file specified for all future printing operations.

What do you do if your printer is not on the list? Many printers emulate other common models. If you can find a printer that yours emulates, select the appropriate printer definition file. If you do not know whether your printer emulates some other printer, you could experiment. Many dot-matrix printers emulate Epson printers, so try EPSONFX.PDF if you have a dot-matrix printer. Many daisywheel printers emulate Diablo 630 printers, so try DBLO630.PDF for a daisywheel printer. Many laser printers emulate the Hewlett Packard LaserJet, so you might try HPLASER.PDF with a laser printer.

If none of these options works, you need to go back to the generic printer definition file, PRINTER.PDF. With this file, you cannot use the backslash printer attribute commands or print the special characters. All other printing operations should work well, however.

For the adventurous, Agenda allows you to write and use your own printer definition file. Instructions are in the Agenda documentation.

## Printer Backslash Commands

With a printer definition file specified for your particular printer, you can employ various printer backslash commands to control a number of print attributes. These commands can be entered in setup strings in the Print options box, in headers and footers, and in the text of notes entered into an Agenda database.

The backslash commands for printer control are summarized in Table 8-2. They are entered at the points where you want the particular attributes turned on or off. The primary commands are *toggles*; they turn the attribute on if it is off and off if it is on.

Suppose you were entering a header with the text "Special Example Output" and wanted the word "Special" to be printed boldfaced. You would enter the backslash command \b\ before and after the word "Special" as follows:

\b\Special\b\ Example Output

This would cause the text between the two \b\ commands to be printed bold.

The \u\ command is used for underlining. Most printers can print bold text and underline text. Most dot-matrix and laser printers can also print very narrow letters, often referred to as *compressed text*. The \c\ command turns compressed printing on or off. Likewise, letters wider than normal might also be an option, to be used primarily for headings. Use the \e\ command for such expanded printing.

The standard default for vertical spacing is six lines per inch. The \l8\ (the lowercase L, not the number 1) command changes vertical line spacing to eight lines per inch. The \l6\ command changes line spacing back to six lines

### Table 8-2. Backslash Commands for Printer Control.

| Command | Function |
| --- | --- |
| \b\ | Bold on/off. |
| \u\ | Underline on/off. |
| \c\ | Compressed printing on/off. |
| \e\ | Expanded printing on/off. |
| \l6\ | Six lines per inch vertical spacing. |
| \l8\ | Eight lines per inch vertical spacing. |
| \prstart\ | Printer initialization codes. |
| \prend\ | Printer termination codes. |
| \reset\ | Printer reset codes. |

per inch. You might have to experiment with the use of these commands to determine the precise effects they have when employed with your particular printer.

## Setup and Termination Strings

The backslash printer control commands and the actual codes used to set print attributes for the printer may be entered to control overall printing and the printing of section heads, items, and notes. To specify print attributes, you need to enter a *setup string* containing the backslash commands or printer control codes. The appropriate codes are sent to the printer to turn the print attribute on prior to printing the specified elements of text (for example, before printing all section heads or all text). You must also enter a corresponding *termination string* containing the appropriate backslash commands or printer control codes after printing the specified elements of text.

An example will illustrate the setting of these print attributes. The example illustrates the use of an IBM Proprinter. Assume you want the entire document to be printed near letter quality, with the section and column heads boldfaced. Start the Print command to display the box with the print settings. First, specify that the section heads be printed bold. Move the highlight to the right of *Section:* on the second line from the bottom of the box, under the column head *Setup String*. This is where you enter the command to turn on boldface printing for section and column heads. Type in the backslash command ╲ b ╲ to begin boldface printing and press ENTER.

Now move the highlight to the right, under the column head *Termination String*. This is where you enter the command to turn off the print attribute. Type in ╲ b ╲ to turn off boldface printing. The termination string must be entered for sections and items. Otherwise, the attribute is turned on for the first section head and is not turned off for the remainder of the document.

Now it is time to specify near letter quality printing for the entire document. Move the highlight to the right of *Printer:* in the *Setup String* column. (The setup and termination strings for *Printer:* are sent to the printer at the beginning and end of the entire printing process and control the printing of the entire document. The ╲*prstart*╲ and ╲*prend*╲ backslash commands send codes for beginning and ending printing.)

No backslash command is available to specify near letter quality printing, so you must enter the actual printer codes to initiate near letter quality printing for the Proprinter after the ╲*prstart*╲ command. From the manual, you determine that the command is Escape G (having, respectively, the decimal values 27 and 71). Decimal values of commands can be sent to the printer by placing three-digit values between backslashes. Therefore, you can press F2 (EDIT) to edit the printer setup string, adding

╲027╲ ╲071╲

at the end to turn on near letter quality printing. (Since G is a normal keyboard character, you could have just entered the letter G instead of $\setminus$071$\setminus$.)

Figure 8-6 shows the Print box with the settings for printing section and column heads bold and for printing the entire document near letter quality. This near letter quality command is specific to the IBM Proprinter, and will not work with most other printers. When you wish to enter such commands, you need to look up the values in the manual for your particular printer.

Many of the backslash commands discussed earlier and listed in Table 8-1 may also be included in the setup strings to control printing. You can, for example, set margins for notes, print line separators for notes, sections, or items, and insert blank lines or even page breaks. The Agenda documentation provides further details concerning which backslash commands can be used in which situations.

When you specify that notes are to be printed, an additional line is displayed in the bottom section. This enables you to enter setup and termination strings for notes as well.

## Using Printer Commands Within Notes

Various backslash commands can be entered into the text of notes to control print attributes within those notes. Perhaps the most frequent application is for underlining or boldfacing words or phrases.

To underline a word in a note, simply enter the command $\setminus u \setminus$ before and after the text to be underlined. When printed, the text will be underlined.

```
File  View  Item  Category  Print  Utility  System  Quit
Print current view of database
                              ═Print═
  Print:        View
  Include:      Items          Number items:      No
  Print to:     LPT1


  From document page:    1
  To document page:     999    Document numbering begins with:  1

  Header: \date\ \time\\rj\\desc\\rj\\line\
  Footer: \cj\ Page \page\ \cj\

  Top margin:  3    Page length: 60    Special characters: Translate

            Setup string              Termination string
  Printer: \prstart\\027\\071\          \prend\

  Section: \b\                          \b\
  Item:    \nl\
              ═Press F9 when done, ESC to cancel═
      3/24/89 to go over quarterly
══F1══╤══F2══╤══F3══╤══F4══╤══F5══╤══F6══╤══F7══╤══F8═══╤══F9════╤══F10══
 Help ║ Edit ║      ║      ║      ║      ║      ║Default║Accept  ║
```

Fig. 8-6. *The settings for printing out a view with near letter quality printing and with section and column headings printed boldface.*

## International and Special Characters

Throughout Agenda, the ALT-F1 (COMPOSE) key allows the entry of international and special characters. Agenda does its best to display these characters on your monitor and to print them on your printer. The display and printing will be limited, however, by the capabilities of your hardware.

To enter an international or special character that is not on the keyboard, you must use a *compose sequence*. Begin by pressing ALT-F1 (COMPOSE). Then press the two-character sequence required to produce the desired character. For example, to enter the section symbol §, press ALT-F1, S, O. The two-character compose sequences for all of the available international and special characters are given in Appendix C of the Agenda documentation.

Printing international and special characters requires that a printer definition be specified for your printer, *and* that your printer have the basic capabilities allowing it to print the characters. Using the printer definition files, Agenda prints as many of the international and special characters as possible. If your printer does not have a character, Agenda approximates the character if possible.

The Print box includes a setting for specifying how these special characters are to be printed. You can highlight the *Special Characters:* setting and press GREY PLUS to see the list of options. The first, default option, *Translate*, translates these characters into the special commands necessary to make your printer print them. This requires the appropriate printer definition file. It is the choice to make if you want the special characters printed out. If your printer cannot print these special characters, you can select the third option to print any international characters as spaces. Then you can at least write in the special characters by hand.

The second option for special characters, *Do not translate*, takes whatever command is used to represent the special character and sends it directly to your printer. You can use this to print other characters supported by your printer. This requires you to determine which international character has the same code as the character you want to print. The symbol for the international character will be displayed on the screen, but the other character will be printed.

## PRINTING TO DISK FILES

Agenda can direct the output from the printing operation to disk files rather than to the printer. The information stored in such files can then be printed later or can be used with other programs.

In the Tasks database, assume that you want to include the information in the Tasks to Do view in a memo that you will be preparing with your word processing program. While in the Tasks to Do view, issue the Print command, which displays the Print box on the screen. Press ALT-F8 (DFLTALL) to make sure that all settings are the default settings. Move the highlight down to the *Print to:* setting, press GREY PLUS, and select the *File* option for directing the output to a disk file. When this option is selected, several more settings appear to the right.

The *File:* setting is used to specify the name of the file to which the information is to be printed. The default for the Tasks database is the file TASKS.PRT in the current directory. This is acceptable; you do not have to make any change.

The *Format:* setting immediately below is used to specify the nature of the information sent to the file. Highlight this and press GREY PLUS to see the two options. The first choice sends both the text and printer codes. Everything that would have gone to the printer in a normal print operation is sent to the file instead. You would use this option if you wished to later print out the file directly. The second option sends only the text; it omits the headers and footers and all of the print control codes. This is generally the choice to make if the information in the file is to be used by another program. In particular, any special printer control codes could cause problems in such applications. Select the *Text only* option and press ENTER. The Print box should appear as shown in Fig. 8-7.

Now you are ready to "print" to the file. Press F9. The disk drive runs briefly as the information is recorded in the disk file, and you are returned to the view. Nothing very dramatic happens. To see the results of the operation, quit Agenda. A directory listing of the current directory

```
 File   View   Item   Category   Print   Utility   System   Quit
 Print current view of database
                               ══════════Print══════════
    Print:        View
    Include:      Items              Number items:      No
    Print to:     File               File:      C:\AGFILES\TASKS.PRT
                                      Format:    Text only

    From document page:   1
    To document page:     999         Document numbering begins with:   1

    Header: \date\ \time\\rj\\desc\\rj\\line\
    Footer: \cj\ Page \page\ \cj\

    Top margin:   3     Page length: 60     Special characters: Translate

                   Setup string                  Termination string
    Printer: \prstart\                        \prend\

    Section:
    Item:    \nl\
                        ══════Press F9 when done, ESC to cancel══════
       3/24/89 to go over quarterly
 ═══F1═══╤═══F2═══╤═══F3═══╤═══F4═══╤═══F5═══╤═══F6═══╤═══F7═══╤═══F8═══╤═══F9═══╤═══F10══
   Help  ║  Edit  ║        ║        ║        ║        ║        ║Default║Accept  ║
```

Fig. 8-7. *Printing out the view to the file TASKS.PRT.*

will show that the file TASKS.PRT has been created. To see the contents of the file, enter this DOS command:

type tasks.prt

The contents of the file will be displayed on the screen. Figure 8-8 shows the first portion of the display.

The information from a file may be used with other programs. For example, most word processing programs include an option to load DOS text or an ASCII file. Give the command required by the program, specify the TASKS.PRT file, and the information will be entered into the word processing document.

## PRINTING FROM THE CATEGORY MANAGER

The category hierarchy for a database may be printed out from the Category Manager. The basic printing procedures are the same as those used for printing from a view. Most of the print options are also the same.

### The Basic Printing Operation

Printing out the category hierarchy involves the use of the Print command while in the Category Manager. The procedures are similar to those for printing a view.

```
C:\AGFILES>type tasks.prt
   Reports                            Staffing      Project       When
   · Meeting to discuss project for   ·George       ·James        ·03/13/89
     James next Monday.
   · Prepare report on Walker project ·Ann          ·Walker        ·03/16/89
     by next Thursday.
   · Have Ann get out the previous    ·Ann          ·Walker
     Walker project report and begin
     the process of updating so that
     we have a draft to work with.
   · Meet with Jim to discuss report  ·Jim          ·Peters
     on the Peters account.
   · Call Ann to go over report to    ·Ann          ·Walker
     Walker Inc. on Walker and James
     projects.

   Meetings                           Staffing      Project       When
   · Meeting to discuss project for   ·George       ·James        ·03/13/89
     James next Monday.
   · Meeting with executive committee                              ·03/24/89
     3/24/89 to go over quarterly
     results.
   · Meet with Jim to discuss report  ·Jim          ·Peters
     on the Peters account.
```

Fig. 8-8. *The display of the first part of the file TASKS.PRT on the screen using the DOS TYPE command.*

To begin printing the category hierarchy for the Tasks database, enter the Category Manager by pressing F9 (CAT MGR). (Note that the Category Manager has its own Print command.) Press F10 (MENU) and select the Print command. A box with printing selections is displayed on the screen. This box is very similar to the Print box for printing from a view. This is shown in Fig. 8-9.

Accept the default settings and print out the category hierarchy by pressing F9. The information is printed out as shown in Fig. 8-10. The printed output appears just as the information does on the screen.

## Specifying the Information to Be Printed

The normal use of the Print command from within the Category Manager is to print out the category hierarchy for reference. As in printing views, Agenda provides options as to what you can print out. The options are to print out only the categories, the categories and any attached notes, or the notes only. The choice is made in the same way as for views: highlight the *Include:* setting and press GREY PLUS to display the list of options.

Another option is to print out summary information about the database. Within the Print box displayed by the Category Manager Print command, highlight the *Print:* setting and display the options by pressing GREY PLUS. Select *Database Info* and press ENTER. Now you can press F9 to print out this summary information about the database. The output is shown in Fig. 8-11 and presents

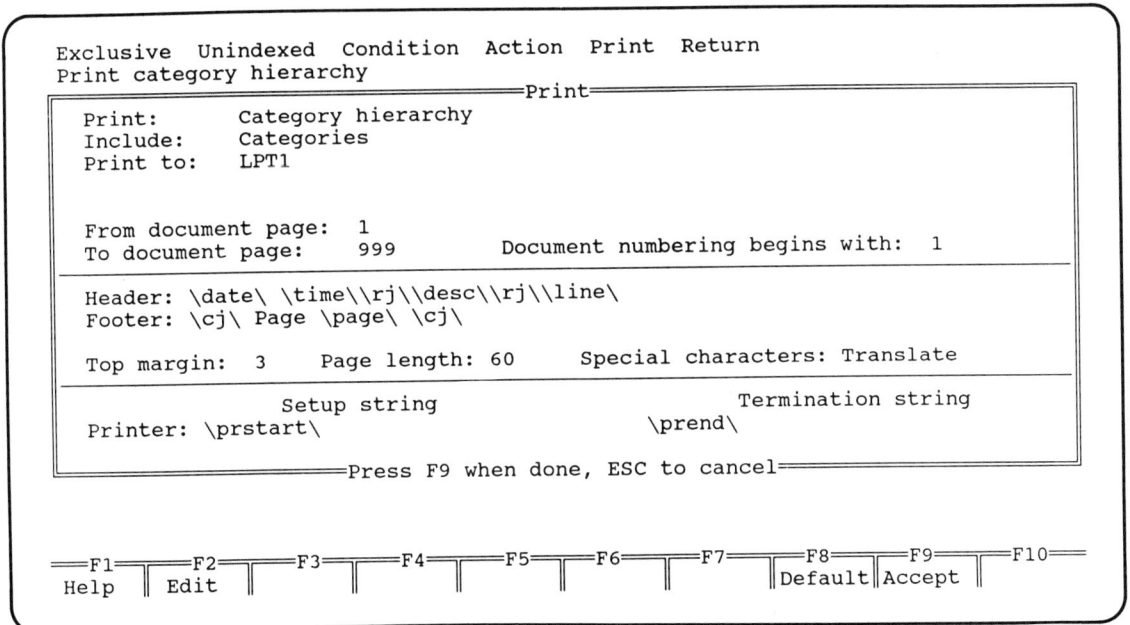

```
Exclusive  Unindexed  Condition  Action  Print  Return
Print category hierarchy
┌──────────────────────────────────Print══════════════════════════┐
│  Print:      Category hierarchy                                   │
│  Include:    Categories                                           │
│  Print to:   LPT1                                                 │
│                                                                   │
│                                                                   │
│  From document page:   1                                          │
│  To document page:     999      Document numbering begins with: 1 │
│                                                                   │
│  Header: \date\ \time\\rj\\desc\\rj\\line\                        │
│  Footer: \cj\ Page \page\ \cj\                                    │
│                                                                   │
│  Top margin:  3    Page length: 60    Special characters: Translate│
│                                                                   │
│              Setup string                    Termination string   │
│  Printer: \prstart\                      \prend\                  │
│                                                                   │
└════════════════════Press F9 when done, ESC to cancel═════════════┘


══F1══╦══F2══╦══F3══╦══F4══╦══F5══╦══F6══╦══F7══╦══F8════╦══F9═════╦══F10══
 Help ║ Edit ║      ║      ║      ║      ║      ║ Default║ Accept  ║
```

Fig. 8-9. *The dialog box for printing from the Category Manager.*

```
03/10/89 15:44                          Database for Working with Lotus Agenda
--------------------------------------------------------------------------------
MAIN
   Project
      Walker
         James
      Acme
      Peters
   Reports
   Meetings
   Phone Calls
   Staffing
    ┌Ann
    ├Jim
    └George




                                 Page 1
```

Fig. 8-10. *The printout of the category hierarchy for the Tasks database.*

```
03/10/89 15:46                          Database for Working with Lotus Agenda
--------------------------------------------------------------------------------
Database information for: C:\AGFILES\TASKS

Description: Database for Working with Lotus Agenda

All files associated with this file are:
C:\AGFILES\TASKS.AGA
C:\AGFILES\TASKS.AGB


File Information

              Unused space: 1%
                     Items: 10
            Items in Trash: 1
         Items with notes: 2
                Categories: 13
       Average items/category: 2
       Average categories/item: 3




                                 Page 1
```

Fig. 8-11. *The printout of database information for the Tasks database.*

some useful statistics. (This summary information is printed out but does not appear on the screen. You can display some of the information on the screen, however, by using the File Info command while in a view.)

### Category Manager Printing Options

Most of the printing options work exactly the same when printing from the Category Manager as when printing from a view. The only difference arises from the nature of the information being printed. Because the category hierarchy does not include sections and items, no provision is made for setup and termination strings for these elements. If you choose to print notes in addition to or instead of the categories, however, the option is available to enter setup and termination strings for the notes.

## PRINTING FROM NOTES

The text of an individual note can be printed out while in the note. The basic printing procedures are the same as those used for printing from a view. Most of the print options are likewise the same.

### The Basic Printing Operation

Printing out a note first requires that the note be displayed on the screen. In a view, highlight an item with an attached note (indicated by the little musical note in front of the item.) Press F5 (NOTE) to enter and display the note. The note also has its own Print command. Press F10 (MENU) and select that command.

A box with printing selections is displayed on the screen that is very similar to the Print box for printing from a view. This is shown in Fig. 8-12. Accept the default settings and print out the text of the note by pressing F9.

### Specifying the Information to Be Printed

From within a note, only one option exists for specifying the information to be printed when using the Print command. The default is to print the entire text of the note. By changing the *Print:* setting, you can instead direct Agenda to print out only the marked text in the note. (This, of course, presumes that you have marked some text in the note prior to starting the Print command.)

### Note Printing Options

Most of the printing options work exactly the same when printing from a note as when printing from a view. Because a note does not include sections and items, however, no provision is made for setup and termination strings for these elements. A single printer setup and terminate procedure encompasses setting print attributes for the entire note (or marked text).

```
Print   Import   Export   Delete   Return
Print current note
                                    ═══════Print═══════
  Print:        All text in note

  Print to:     LPT1


  From document page:   1
  To document page:     999       Document numbering begins with:  1

  Header:
  Footer:

  Top margin:   3    Page length: 60    Special characters: Translate

               Setup string                    Termination string
  Printer: \prstart\                       \prend\
  Note:        \mgn 5 74\
                    ═══════Press F9 when done, ESC to cancel═══════



═F1══╤═F2══╤═F3══╤═F4══╤═F5══╤═F6══╤═F7══╤═F8════╤═F9═══╤═F10══
 Help ║ Edit ║    ║     ║     ║     ║     ║Default║Accept║
```

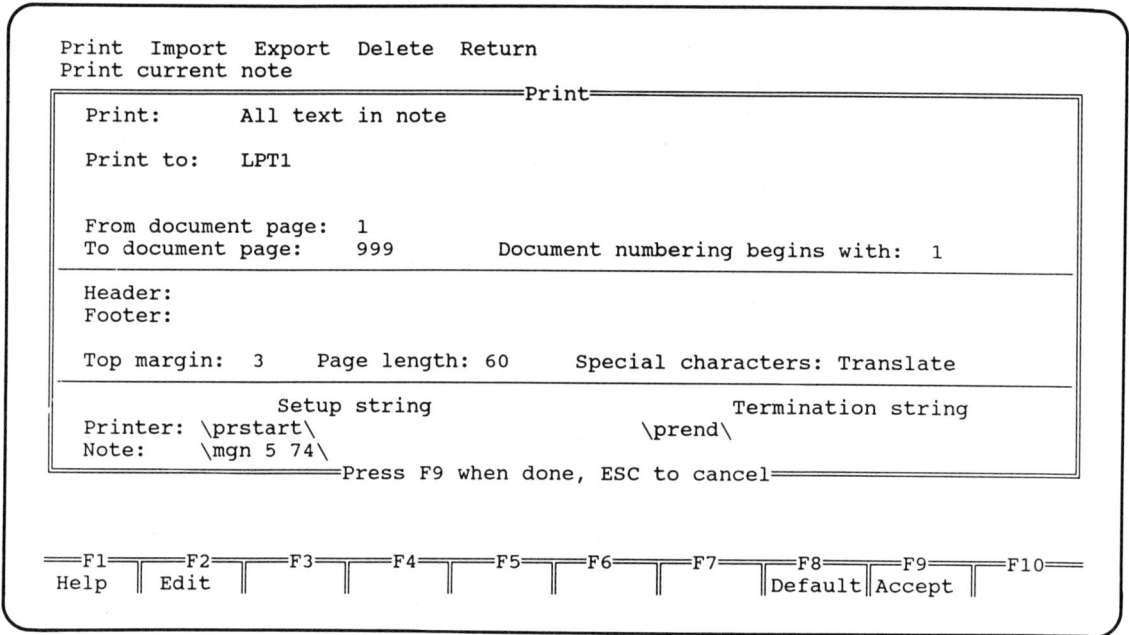

Fig. 8-12. *The dialog box for printing from a note.*

Unlike printing from a view or the Category Manager, printing from a note does not include elaborate headers and footers as defaults. You have the same header and footer capabilities in printing notes as in the other print operations, but you are responsible for entering the information.

All of the information on printing and printing options might seem nearly overwhelming. Just remember that you can print any view, any note, or the category hierarchy just by displaying it on the screen, entering the Print command, and pressing F9 to accept the default settings. Everything else just involves adding options and providing more control over the printing process. You can learn these other features one by one, as you feel a need to add refinements to your printing.

# 9

# MANAGING DATABASE FILES

NEARLY all Agenda users will regularly work with several different Agenda databases. Therefore, most users will need to learn the procedures for creating and working with different database files. Agenda provides the capabilities for managing database files conveniently from within the program.

This chapter explains the procedures for managing database files in Agenda. The first section shows how to create new databases and work with different databases. Next comes the explanation of Agenda's facilities for safeguarding work by using backups. The third section of the chapter demonstrates the procedures for copying and deleting database files. Users with hard disks with many subdirectories will be interested in the fourth section, which explains how to move around through the subdirectories. Finally, the last section covers both the procedures for working with DOS while in Agenda and the manipulation of Agenda database files using DOS.

## CREATING AND OPENING DATABASES

Creating a new Agenda database or selecting any existing database to work with can be made from the opening screen when starting Agenda. Once the program is operating, however, you can also switch to other databases or create new databases from within Agenda without exiting the program. All of these capabilities are illustrated in this section.

You will need an additional directory for the examples described in this chapter. (If you are using a floppy-disk based system, you probably are not using subdirectories, so you will not need to perform the next two operations, so skip this paragraph.) Before starting Agenda, create a new subdirectory. At the DOS prompt, change to the directory which contains your Agenda Tasks database. For example, if the database is in a directory named ＼AGFILES, issue the command

cd ＼agfiles

and press ENTER. Create a new subdirectory of this directory for storing special files by entering the following command:

md specfile

Press ENTER. Now start Agenda in the normal manner, but stop when the opening screen is displayed. Then the complete path, consisting of the disk drive, directories (if any), and file name of the last database used with Agenda is displayed on the screen. If the Tasks database was last used, this database is listed.

If you have been working along with the example in this book, you have created the Tasks database and worked with it on a number of occasions. To allow experimentation with other possibilities, create a second database to be named Tasks2. Just type in the following:

tasks2

This replaces the previous database specification on the screen, as shown in Fig. 9-1. Press ENTER once and this database name is entered and displayed with the complete path specification (drive and directories) from the previously used and displayed database. Press ENTER a second time to accept this new file name and begin the creation of the new database. Agenda will prompt for a description and password. Enter the following description:

Second Tasks Database

Press ENTER, and press F9 to create the new Tasks2 database. Agenda displays the initial view of the new database with the single Untitled section and no items. You may enter some information into this database if desired, but it is not necessary. Exit Agenda using the Quit command.

```
                            (R)                (R)
            L O T U S               A G E N D A


                       Version 1.00
          (C) Copyright 1988 Lotus Development Corporation
                     All Rights Reserved


       Name:   John R. Ottensmann
    Company:   Jan Neuenschwander


  File name:   tasks2

 Press GREY + for a list of files, ENTER to accept file, ESC to exit

   Use, duplication, or sale of this software, except as described
       in the Lotus License Agreement, is strictly prohibited.
                   Violators may be prosecuted.
```

Fig. 9-1. *Creating a new database when starting Agenda.*

Restart Agenda in the usual way. When the opening screen is displayed, the file name Tasks2 is listed because that was the last file used with Agenda. This time you want to work with the original Tasks database. Press GREY PLUS to display the list of Agenda databases in the current directory. Now press GREY PLUS a second time to display the database descriptions associated with each of the databases. These are the descriptions that you entered when the databases were first created.

Figure 9-2 shows the list of Agenda databases displayed along with the database descriptions. Tasks and Tasks2 should both be listed. If any other Agenda databases are stored in this disk and directory, they are also listed. (Other databases might have been created while using Agenda, or there might be tutorial files copied from the Agenda disks.) To open and work with the Tasks database, highlight Tasks and press ENTER. Press ENTER again to open the database. This database is opened and the last view with which you were working is displayed on the screen.

When you start Agenda, you have three options. First, you can open and work with the last-used database, which is listed, simply by pressing ENTER.

Second, you can create a new Agenda database by typing in the name you wish to give to this database. If you want the database to be stored on a different disk or directory, you must enter the entire path name. Otherwise, the new database will be stored on the disk and directory shown for the last-used database.

```
┌──────────────────────────────────────────────────────────────┐
│ ┌────────────────────────────────────────────────────────┐    │
│ │                                                          │    │
│ │ ╔═══════════════════════════Select File═══════════════╗ │    │
│ │ ║Highlight file & press ENTER, or type file name or directory │
│ │ ╟──────────────────────────────────────────────────────╢ │    │
│ │ ║ ..\            Parent directory                      ║ │    │
│ │ ║ SPECFILE\      <DIR>                                  ║ │    │
│ │ ║ ─────────                                            ║ │    │
│ │ ║ TASKS          Database for Working with Lotus Agenda ║ │    │
│ │ ║ TASKS2         Second Tasks Database                 ║ │    │
│ │ ║                                                      ║ │    │
│ │ ║                                                      ║ │    │
│ │ ╚══════════════Current directory: C:\AGFILES\*.AGA════╝ │    │
│ │        Use, duplication, or sale of this software, except as described │
│ │           in the Lotus License Agreement, is strictly prohibited.      │
│ │                    Violators may be prosecuted.       │    │
│ └────────────────────────────────────────────────────────┘    │
└──────────────────────────────────────────────────────────────┘
```

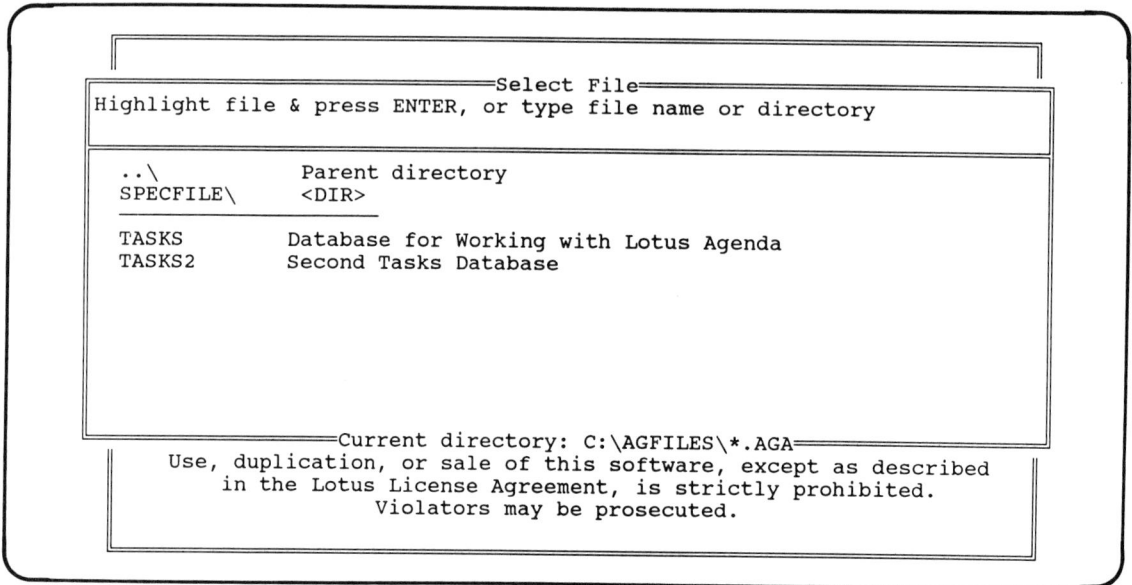

Fig. 9-2. *Selecting a different database to open when starting Agenda.*

Third, you can open and work with another, previously created Agenda database. The normal procedure is to press GREY PLUS to display the list of databases in the current directory. Pressing GREY PLUS a second time causes the database descriptions to be displayed in addition to the database file names. Highlight the database to be opened and press ENTER. You could also type in the name of the existing database to be opened (with the disk and directory specification if different from the current database).

You can open another existing database or create a new database from within Agenda, without exiting the program. Suppose you are working with the Tasks database and decide that you want to use the new Tasks2 database. From any view, enter the File Open command by pressing F10 (MENU) and selecting File and Open. The Select File box will be displayed listing the Agenda databases in the current disk and directory. The box is essentially the same as in Fig. 9-2. Use the DOWN arrow to move the highlight to Tasks2 and press ENTER. Agenda closes and saves the Tasks database, opens the Tasks2 database, and displays a view of that database on the screen. If you have not entered anything in the Tasks2 database, all you will see is the empty Initial View. You might want to enter an item or change the section head to make the Tasks2 database distinctive.

Now create a third, new database. Once again issue the File Open command. This time, when the Select File box is displayed on the screen, follow the instruction to press INS to type in a file name. Type in the name of the new database being created:

tasks3

This will be displayed in the top portion of the Select File box as shown in Fig. 9-3. Press ENTER to create and open this new database. Enter a database description if you desire, and press F9 to create the database. Once again, the empty Initial View is displayed with the Untitled section head and no items entered.

The File Open command may be used to create a new Agenda database or shift to another Agenda database. To create a new database, just issue the command, type in the name for the new database, and press ENTER. If the database is to be stored on a disk or directory other than the one where the current database is stored, the complete path specification must be typed in as well.

To work with an existing Agenda database, enter the File Open command. The Select File box displays an alphabetical listing of the Agenda databases on the current disk or directory. If the listing has more entries than can be displayed

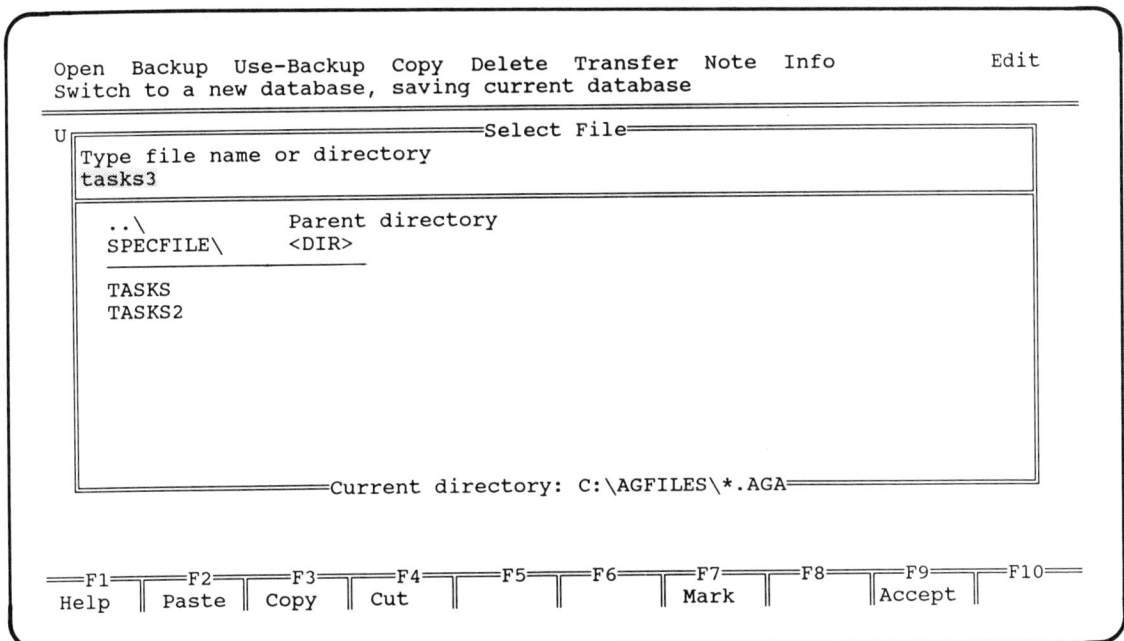

```
Open  Backup  Use-Backup  Copy  Delete  Transfer  Note  Info          Edit
Switch to a new database, saving current database

U┌───────────────────────════Select File═══════════════════════════════┐
 │Type file name or directory                                           │
 │tasks3                                                                 │
 │  ┌────────────────────────────────────────────────────             │
 │  │ ..\            Parent directory                                    │
 │  │ SPECFILE\      <DIR>                                               │
 │  │                         ─────────                                  │
 │  │ TASKS                                                              │
 │  │ TASKS2                                                             │
 │  │                                                                    │
 │  │                                                                    │
 │  │                                                                    │
 │  │                                                                    │
 │  │                                                                    │
 │  └═════════════Current directory: C:\AGFILES\*.AGA═══════════        │
 └──────────────────────────────────────────────────────────────────────┘

══F1══╤══F2══╤══F3══╤══F4══╤══F5══╤══F6══╤══F7══╤══F8══╤══F9══════╤══F10══
 Help ║Paste ║ Copy ║ Cut  ║      ║      ║ Mark ║      ║Accept    ║
```

Fig. 9-3. *Creating a new database from within Agenda using the File Open command.*

at one time, scroll through the listing using the UP and DOWN arrows. The display of small arrows on the screen to the left of the top or bottom file names indicates that there are additional file names that cannot be displayed.

To work with another database, you simply highlight the file name and press ENTER. To move more quickly to a file name in a long list, you can type the first few characters. Agenda moves the highlight to the first matching file name. (Shifting directories and opening a file in another directory are addressed later in this chapter.)

Whenever you use the File Open command to shift to another database, either new or existing, Agenda automatically saves and closes the database with which you had been working. Thus, there is no need to worry about losing your current work by failing to save it. Indeed, Agenda does not even include a Save or Close command for you to use.

## CREATING AND USING BACKUPS

Agenda can automatically save the changes you make to a database as you are working with the program, and Agenda always saves all changes when you switch to other databases and when you exit the program. This provides significant protection to the information in Agenda databases.

What Agenda cannot do for you by itself, however, is to protect you against changes you might inadvertently and erroneously make to a database, such as the deletion of significant information. Agenda's option of automatically saving changes to the disk while working with the database and its procedure of automatically saving changes when exiting Agenda means that you do not have the option of simply abandoning your work and going back to the database as it was when you started (which you can do with many other programs).

As an alternative, Agenda provides the capability for creating and using backup versions of databases. You use the File Backup command to create a backup copy of the database with which you are currently working. This backup version is simply a copy of the Agenda database as it exists at the time you make the backup. The backup version is not changed as you make subsequent changes to the database.

At any later time you can revert to the backup version of the database, replacing the current version with the backup. For example, if you make a serious error in working with a database, just use the File Use-Backup command to go to the backup version. The database is restored to the way it existed the last time you used the File Backup command.

Be careful in using the File Use-Backup command, however. This command makes the backup version of the database the current version. All changes made to the database since the time the File Backup command was last executed are lost.

Try out the backup facilities of Agenda with the Tasks database. If you are still showing the newly created Tasks3 database, shift back to the Tasks database using the File Open command. Select Tasks and press ENTER.

With the Tasks database displayed, make a backup version. Just enter the File Backup command. No messages are displayed when a backup is made. The only indication that anything is happening is the operation of the disk drive as the backup copy is stored on the disk.

Now make a few arbitrary changes to the Tasks database just to prove that the backup process really works. You might add or delete some items, for example. Restore the database to the state at the time you made the backup by entering the File Use-Backup command. A box appears on the screen asking whether you wish to revert to the backup version of the database, as shown in Fig. 9-4. The box also indicates the date when you last backed up the database, which gives you an indication of the amount of work you will lose by going to the backup version. Accept the default, *Yes*, and press ENTER to restore the database to its earlier state. The database is once again displayed, exactly as it was at the time you made the backup. This now becomes the current version of the Tasks database.

```
 Open  Backup  Use-Backup  Copy  Delete  Transfer  Note  Info
 Use backup copy to replace the current database
═══════════════════════════════════════════════════════════════════
 Meetings                            Staffing      Project      When
   · Meeting to discuss project for   ·George       ·James       ·03/13/89
     James next Monday.
   · Meeting with executive committee                            ·03/24/89
     3/24/89 to go over quarterly
     results.
   · Meet with┌─────────────────────────────────────────────┐
     on the Pe│ Revert to backup? (Last backup: 03/10/89)  Yes │
             └════Press ENTER to accept, ESC to cancel════┘
 Phone Calls                                                    When
   ♪ Call Ron Smith at Walker by      ·Ann          ·Walker      ·03/14/89
     Tuesday to discuss the progress
     of the project.
   · Call Adam Baker at James         ·George       ·James       ·03/15/89
     Wednesday to get his reactions to
     our proposals.
   · Call Ann by next Friday to       ·Ann                       ·03/17/89
     discuss hiring of new assistant.
   · Call Peter Smith regarding new   ·Ann          ·Walker
     account proposals for Walker and               Acme
══F1══╤══F2══╤══F3══╤══F4══╤══F5══╤══F6══╤══F7══╤══F8══╤══F9═══╤══F10══
 Help │ Edit │      │      │      │      │      │      │Accept │
```

Fig. 9-4. *Switching to the backup of the current database.*

Making periodic backups of your databases is good protection against the occasional errors you will make that mess up your databases. It can also be used if you just want to "play around" with a database without committing yourself to making the changes permanent. Creating a backup is quick and easy. It only requires the time necessary to make the backup copy of the database on the disk.

## COPYING AND DELETING DATABASES

As you become more involved in working with Agenda, you might need to make copies of existing databases for various purposes. Also, with multiple databases being created, sometimes it is useful to delete unwanted databases from the disk to free up space and reduce clutter. Very straightforward commands are available to perform both of these operations.

You might wish to make a copy of a database in order to permanently preserve the database as it existed at a particular time, independent of any backup versions that you create. A copy is also useful if you want to go in two different directions in working with an existing database.

Make a copy of the Tasks database. First, be sure the Tasks database is the one currently being used in Agenda. Then enter the File Copy command. The Select File box is displayed on the screen. Press INS to create a new file to copy to and type in the name you want for the copy of the database,

taskcopy

as shown in Fig. 9-5. Press ENTER to make the copy. Agenda copies the entire contents of the Tasks database to a new database named Taskcopy. After the operation is completed, you are returned to the Tasks database.

To prove that the copy actually has been made, use the File Open command and select the Taskcopy database. The new database, Taskcopy, is displayed by Agenda, as shown by the file name on the top line. It includes exactly the same information as the Tasks database. So that you can perform further operations on the correct database, use the File Open command once more to switch back to Tasks.

It is important to remember that the File Copy command makes a copy of the Agenda database with which you are currently working and which is currently displayed by Agenda. If you wish to make a copy of a database other than the current one, you must first switch to the database to be copied. Just use the File

```
 Open  Backup  Use-Backup  Copy  Delete  Transfer  Note  Info        Edit
 Make a copy of the current database
===============================================================================
R┌──────────────────────────────Select File══════════════════════════════┐
 │ Type file name or directory                                            │
 │ taskcopy                                                               │
 │ ┌───────────────────────────────────────────────────────────────────┐ │
 │ │  ..\            Parent directory                                   │ │
 │ │  SPECFILE\      <DIR>                                              │ │
 │ │                 ─────                                             │ │
 │ │  TASKS                                                             │ │
 │ │  TASKS2                                                            │ │
 │ │  TASKS3                                                            │ │
 │ │                                                                   │ │
 │ │                                                                   │ │
 │ │                                                                   │ │
M│ └═══════════════════════Current directory: C:\AGFILES\*.AGA═════════┘ │
     James next Monday.
   · Meeting with executive committee                        ·03/24/89
     3/24/89 to go over quarterly
==F1══╤══F2══╤══F3══╤══F4══╤══F5══╤══F6══╤══F7══╤══F8══╤══F9══╤══F10══
 Help │Paste │Copy │Cut  │     │     │Mark │     │Accept│
```

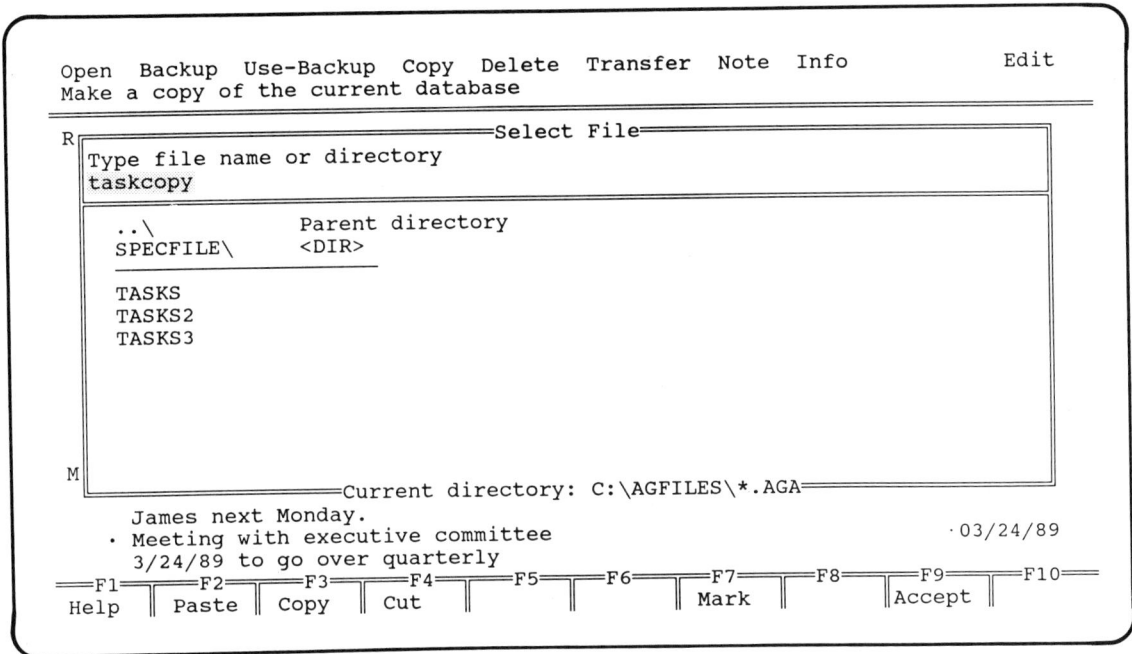

Fig. 9-5. *Making a copy of the current database with the file name Taskcopy.*

Open command and select the database you wish to copy in the normal manner. If you get confused about the direction in which the copying takes place, information can be lost. You might think you are making a copy from an existing database to a new, empty database, when you are actually copying the empty database to the existing database, destroying valuable information.

Most often when making copies of databases, you will create new databases to hold the information copied from the original. After issuing the File Copy command, just type in the name for the new database to which the information is to be copied. If you just type in a file name, the copy will be placed on the same disk and directory as the current database. To copy to another disk or directory, type the complete path specification for the new database.

It is possible to copy the current database to another existing Agenda database. Select the existing database by highlighting it and pressing ENTER, or by typing in the name (including an optional path specification) of the existing database. Copying to an existing database replaces all of the information in that database with the information copied from the current one. The old information is permanently lost when this is done. Agenda warns you when this is about to occur with a message asking whether you wish to replace the information in an existing database.

One note of warning when using the File Copy command: The Select File box instructs you to *highlight* the file to be copied *to*. Remember that if you highlight an existing Agenda database file and press ENTER, you are instructing

Agenda to copy the current database *to* that database. This replaces the original contents, destroying the database. Most often you will not want to copy to an existing database. Therefore, instead of highlighting the file to be copied to as instructed by Agenda, type in the name for the new database file.

New databases and copies of the current database are starting to clutter up the disk with Agenda database files. You have decided that you really do not need the copy of the Tasks database, and wish to delete it. Give the File Delete command. Highlight the database to be deleted, Taskcopy, and press ENTER. The screen should appear as in Fig. 9-6. Agenda responds with a box asking whether you really want to delete the selected database. Accept the *Yes* option and press ENTER. The database files are erased from the disk. The next time you use any File commands that list the Agenda databases, the Taskcopy database will no longer be listed.

Deleting an Agenda database is a permanent, irreversible operation, so use the File Delete command with care. The delete operation erases the database files from the disk. The database is lost and cannot be recovered (except perhaps by using special utilities for unerasing erased files).

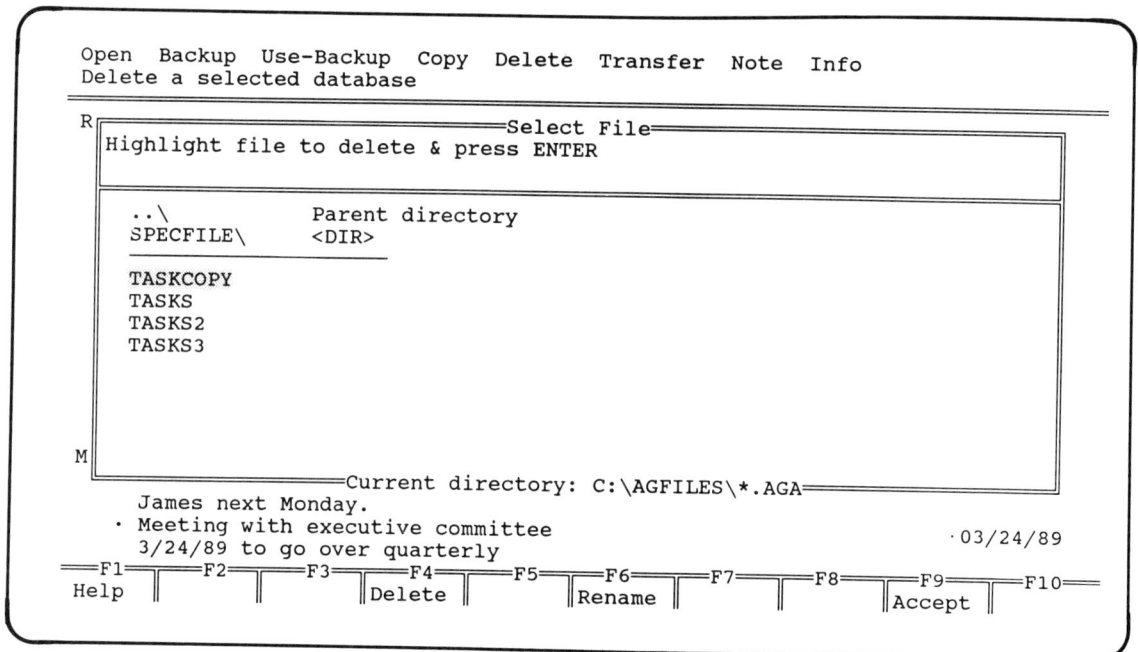

```
 Open  Backup  Use-Backup  Copy  Delete  Transfer  Note  Info
 Delete a selected database

R                              ═Select File═
 Highlight file to delete & press ENTER


   ..\           Parent directory
   SPECFILE\     <DIR>

   TASKCOPY
   TASKS
   TASKS2
   TASKS3

M
                    ═Current directory: C:\AGFILES\*.AGA═
     James next Monday.
   · Meeting with executive committee            ·03/24/89
     3/24/89 to go over quarterly
═F1═══╤══F2══╤══F3══╤══F4══╤══F5══╤══F6══╤══F7══╤══F8══╤══F9══╤══F10═
 Help │     │     │ Delete │     │ Rename │     │     │ Accept │
```

Fig. 9-6. *Deleting the Taskcopy database.*

## MOVING TO DIFFERENT DIRECTORIES

Agenda users with hard disks will undoubtedly have their hard disks subdivided into numerous directories and subdirectories to allow the efficient management of the large numbers of files that can be stored on a hard disk. All of the Agenda File commands conveniently allow you to switch to different directories to create and use databases stored anywhere on a hard disk. (If you are using floppy disk-based systems to run Agenda, you probably do not use subdirectories when storing Agenda databases on your disks. You can skip over the material in this section.)

With the Tasks database displayed by Agenda, enter the File Open command. The Select File box is displayed on the screen as shown in Fig. 9-7. Above the list of Agenda databases and separated from them by a horizontal line is a list of directories directly accessible from the current directory. The first entry is

. . \

which is the standard DOS notation for the parent directory of the current directory. Agenda labels this for you. Below this is the entry

SPECFILE \

```
 Open  Backup  Use-Backup  Copy  Delete  Transfer  Note  Info
 Switch to a new database, saving current database

 R                        ═Select File═
   Highlight file & press ENTER, or press INS to create new file


     ..\              Parent directory
     SPECFILE\        <DIR>

     TASKS
     TASKS2
     TASKS3




 M                   ═Current directory: C:\AGFILES\*.AGA═
      James next Monday.
    · Meeting with executive committee               ·03/24/89
      3/24/89 to go over quarterly
 ═F1═   ═F2═   ═F3═   ═F4═   ═F5═   ═F6═   ═F7═   ═F8═   ═F9═  ═F10═
  Help               Delete        Rename                Accept
```

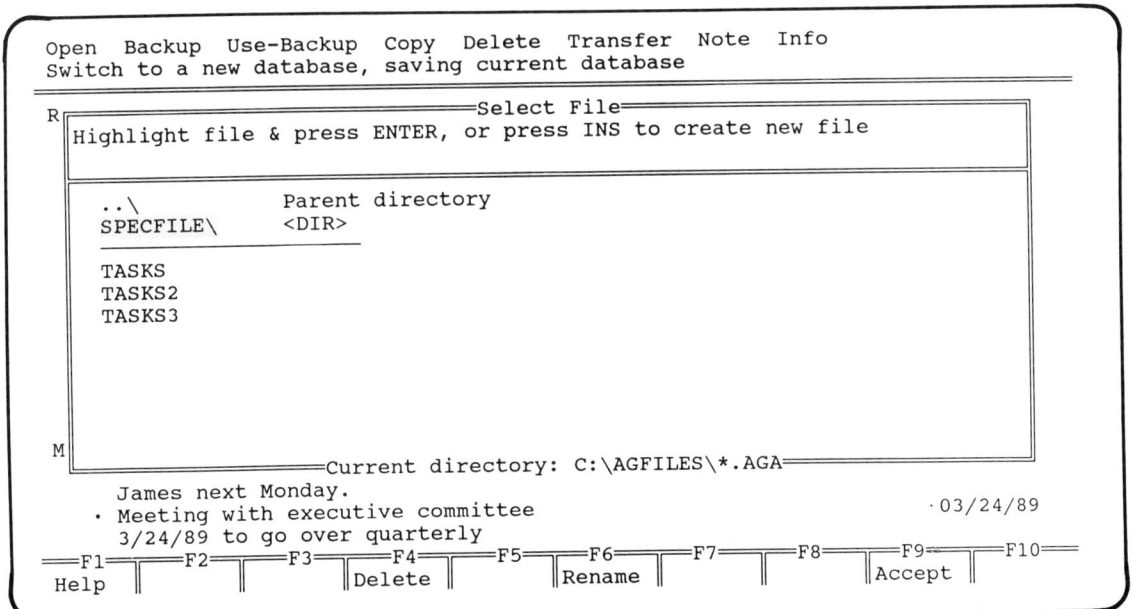

Fig. 9-7. *Switching to the SPECFILE subdirectory in the Select File box.*

which is a subdirectory of the current directory. This is the directory
which you created with the MD (Make Directory) command earlier in
this chapter before starting Agenda. To change to the SPECFILE \
directory, use the UP arrow to move the highlight up until this is
highlighted. Then press ENTER. Agenda switches to that directory and
displays the list of directories and files for the SPECFILE \ directory
as shown in Fig. 9-8. Because this is a new directory in which nothing
has been stored, the only listing is for the parent directory. You could
create a new Agenda database in this directory if you desired, or if you
were using the File Copy command, you could copy a database to this
directory.

The entry for the parent directory, . . \ , is currently highlighted
because this is the only entry. Press ENTER to move back to the directory
from which you entered the SPECFILE \ directory. The screen will
appear as shown in Fig. 9-7.

When using any of the Agenda File commands, you can select and switch
to either the parent directory or any of the child directories of the currently
displayed directory. The operation can be repeated, making it possible to move
up or down through the directory hierarchy into any directory on your hard disk.
For example, repeatedly moving to the parent directory will take you back to

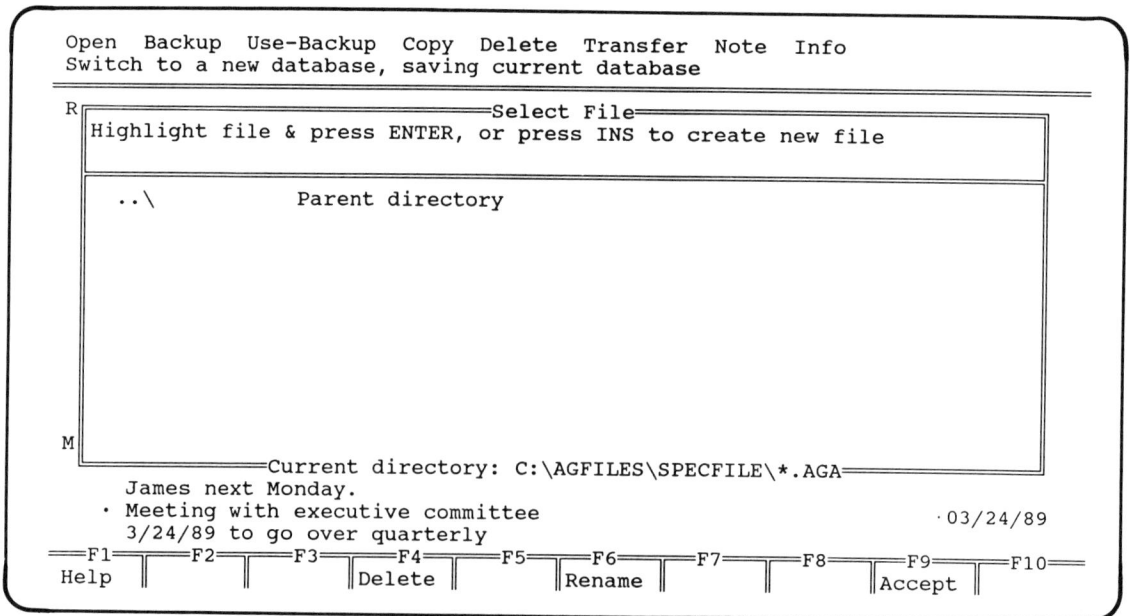

Fig. 9-8. *The display of the Agenda databases in the SPECFILE subdirectory.*

the root directory of the disk. From there, you can select any child directory in the root directory and progressively select child directories until you reach the desired directory.

You can also move directly to any directory on the current disk or to any other disk and directory by typing in the appropriate disk and directory specification and pressing ENTER. For example, to switch to the SPECFILE \ subdirectory, you could have typed in

SPECFILE \

and pressed ENTER. The final backslash is necessary to indicate that this is a directory entry, not a file name.

To switch to a directory that is not a descendent of the current directory, type in the entire directory path starting with the root directory specification, \ . For example, to switch to the TUTOR subdirectory of the AGENDA directory which is in the root directory, type in the following:

\ AGENDA \ TUTOR \

You can even switch to another disk drive. Perhaps you want to switch to the floppy disk drive A: to make a copy of an Agenda database on a floppy disk. Just type in

A:

and press ENTER to switch to the floppy disk drive.

Agenda's Select File box displays the parent directory (unless you are in the root directory of a disk, which has no parent), any child directories of the current directory, and the file names of Agenda databases. No other files are displayed by Agenda, and you cannot perform any File operations on other types of files.

## USING DOS FROM
## AGENDA AND WITH AGENDA FILES

Just like any other program for your personal computer, Agenda runs under PC DOS or MS-DOS, the disk operating system for your computer. Most of the time Agenda users can do their work within Agenda and ignore the presence of DOS. In some situations, however, it can be useful to quickly and temporarily exit to DOS to perform some operation. Also, you might need to deal with Agenda database files directly from DOS. These matters are addressed in this section.

## Using DOS from Agenda

Suppose you are working with Agenda and wish to perform a brief operation outside of the program. You might want to format a floppy disk, use the DOS TYPE command to examine the contents of a file, or perform any of a number of functions. You can, of course, exit Agenda with the Quit command, perform the operation, and then restart Agenda. But it takes a considerable amount of time to save the database and then reload the entire Agenda program. Agenda provides an alternative, allowing you to temporarily exit to DOS without exiting Agenda.

While working with the Tasks database, press F10 (MENU) and select the System command to exit to DOS. A box is displayed on the screen with the name of the program you wish to run. COMMAND.COM, the DOS command interpreter which provides for the entry of all DOS commands, is displayed as the default, as shown in Fig. 9-9. Press ENTER to accept this and you are temporarily placed in DOS. The Agenda display disappears and is replaced by the introductory message that appears when your version of DOS is loaded, and the DOS prompt, such as C>, is displayed.

To illustrate the use of DOS operations, obtain a directory listing for the current directory. Type in

dir

```
File   View   Item   Category   Print   Utility   System   Quit
Exit to DOS (Type EXIT to return to Agenda)
================================================================
Reports                              Staffing      Project      When
   · Meeting to discuss project for  ·George       ·James       ·03/13/89
     James next Monday.
   ♪ Prepare report on Walker project ·Ann         ·Walker      ·03/16/89
     by next Thursday.
   · Have A┌──────────────────────────────────────────────────┐
     Walker │                                                  │
     the pr │  Program to run: C:\COMMAND.COM                  │
     we hav │                                                  │
   · Meet w └────────Press ENTER to accept, ESC to cancel──────┘
     on the Peters account.
   · Call Ann to go over report to    ·Ann          ·Walker
     Walker Inc. on Walker and James
     projects.

Meetings                             Staffing      Project      When
   · Meeting to discuss project for  ·George       ·James       ·03/13/89
     James next Monday.
   · Meeting with executive committee                           ·03/24/89
     3/24/89 to go over quarterly
══F1══╤══F2══╤══F3══╤══F4══╤══F5══╤══F6══╤══F7══╤══F8══╤══F9══╤══F10══
 Help ║ Edit ║      ║      ║      ║      ║      ║      ║Accept║
```

Fig. 9-9. *Temporarily exiting Agenda to go to DOS.*

and press ENTER. The contents of the current directory is listed by DOS in the normal manner. To return to Agenda from DOS, at the DOS prompt type in

exit

The screen display shows your activity in DOS as shown in Fig. 9-10. When you press ENTER after typing exit, you are returned to Agenda and the Tasks database.

The default when using the System command, as you have seen, is the running of COMMAND.COM, the DOS command interpreter. You are literally loading a second copy of DOS on top of the Agenda program, the database, and the original copy of DOS. You can then perform operations as you would whenever the DOS prompt is displayed, except that you will be constrained by the availability of memory.

When you use the System command, Agenda and the original copy of DOS remain in the random access memory (RAM) of your computer. The second copy of DOS and any programs you wish to run have to fit within the remaining RAM. Agenda is a very large program that occupies a significant amount of RAM. Therefore, only shorter programs can be executed while you are in Agenda. For example, you probably will not be able to run a large spreadsheet or word

```
        Microsoft(R) MS-DOS(R) Version 3.20
        (C) Copyright Microsoft 1981-1986
        BLUE CHIP PC Version

        C:\AGFILES>dir

         Volume in drive C has no label
         Directory of   C:\AGFILES

            .               <DIR>        7-26-88   10:00a
            ..              <DIR>        7-26-88   10:00a
         TASKS    AGA        7208        3-10-89    4:31p
         TASKS    AGB        2048        3-10-89    4:31p
         SPECFILE         <DIR>         3-10-89    4:17p
         TASKS2   AGA        3080        3-10-89    4:23p
         TASKS2   AGB         512        3-10-89    4:23p
         TASKS3   AGA        2566        3-10-89    4:23p
         TASKS3   AGB         512        3-10-89    4:23p
         TASKS    BKA        7208        3-10-89    4:25p
         TASKS    BKB        2048        3-10-89    4:25p
             11 File(s)     2088960 bytes free

        C:\AGFILES>exit
```

Fig. 9-10. *The DOS directory showing the Agenda files in the directory.*

processing program when you temporarily exit Agenda. To run such programs, you must quit Agenda entirely and run the other programs in the normal manner.

When you exit to DOS from Agenda using the System command and load COMMAND.COM, this new version of the DOS command interpreter is temporarily in control. To return to Agenda, type in the DOS EXIT command at the DOS prompt and press ENTER.

It is possible to directly execute a program other than COMMAND.COM when using the System command to temporarily exit Agenda. The program must be a directly executable file—a .COM or .EXE file. For example, to format a floppy disk from Agenda, you could issue the System command and enter the file name FORMAT.COM to run the FORMAT program. This would take you directly into the FORMAT program (without going through the DOS prompt). You use FORMAT in the normal manner. When you finish using it, you are returned directly to Agenda and not to the DOS prompt.

When using the System command and operating in DOS, only execute normal programs that perform their functions at that time and then finish. Do not attempt to load programs that are loaded and then remain resident for later use, perhaps to be activated by a special "hot key." Sidekick is a prime example of this type of program. When such programs are loaded from a second copy of DOS, they might not operate correctly and might cause unpredictable results—including "crashing" the system.

## Using DOS with Agenda Database Files

You might need to use DOS commands such as COPY, RENAME, and DEL (or ERASE) with Agenda database files. If so, you need to be aware that every Agenda database is stored in two separate DOS files, which you can observe in the directory listing in Fig. 9-10. Both files have as the main portion of their file names the name given to the Agenda database, but they have the extensions .AGA and .AGB. For example, the Tasks database is stored in the two DOS files

TASKS.AGA
TASKS.AGB

When a backup is created for an Agenda database, this creates two additional files with the extensions .BKA and .BKB.

If you perform any operations on the files that make up an Agenda database, it is important that you deal with all of the relevant files. To copy a database to another disk or directory, you must copy the file with the .AGA extension and with the .AGB extension (and the .BKA and .BKB files if you want the backup version). You can change the name of a database only by renaming all of the files. If you choose to erase a database, you should erase all of the files associated with that database. If you fail to do this, Agenda might be unable to open and work with a database, for the program will be unable to find the necessary files.

Agenda file operations are relatively straightforward. If you have questions, Agenda's help function is likely to provide sufficient information to address your concerns. Even the matter of dealing with subdirectories, which can become a little more involved, can generally be dealt with by trying the various options until you manage to get to the correct directory. Most users will find majority of their needs met by the simpler application of the file operations and should soon be comfortable dealing with Agenda database files.

# 10

## USING DATES

YOU have now covered all of the fundamental features of Agenda and are well on your way to becoming a proficient Agenda user. Agenda includes many advanced features and capabilities beyond these fundamentals. These advanced features can extend your power in using Agenda and can make certain tasks easier.

Beginning with this chapter through Chapter 15, you learn how to use many of the advanced features of Agenda. Each of these chapters covers a related group of Agenda capabilities that extend your ability to use the program in a particular direction. You can work straight through all of the chapters in this section, or you can pick and choose specific chapters as you need to learn and use the specific features covered.

This chapter addresses the use of dates in Agenda. You have already been introduced to When Dates in the course of working through the fundamentals of Agenda. The When Dates are only one of three types of dates available for use in Agenda. The capabilities for using these dates are more extensive than presented up to now.

The first section of this chapter introduces the three types of dates in Agenda. The next three sections of the chapter discuss uses of the three dates. The options available for date formats and for the display of dates are addressed in the following section of the chapter. The chapter concludes by reviewing the use of dates when sorting items in sections and filtering views.

## TYPES OF DATES AND THEIR USES

Agenda provides the capability to work with three kinds of dates: *Entry Dates, When Dates,* and *Done Dates.* For each type, a specific date can be associated with each item in an Agenda database. These dates can be displayed in columns included within any view. Items can be sorted within sections by any of these dates, and can be included within sections using date filters based upon any of these dates.

The three date types differ in their intended function within Agenda. Each is designed to serve a specific purpose. To reflect its function, each type has the date values assigned in a different way. Different entry and display options are also available for the three types. Furthermore, Done Dates also provide options for performing specified actions when those dates are entered.

Each item can have a When Date indicating any date that is significant to that item. A When Date can be used to specify when a task is to be completed, when a report is due, when an event occurred, or any other date you wish to keep track of. You can set any date as the When Date for an item. If the item itself refers to a particular date, that date automatically becomes the When Date for that item.

Entry Dates can be used in different ways. Normally, the Entry Date keeps track of the date on which the item was entered into the Agenda database. This date will be recorded automatically. The Entry Date can also be used to automatically record the last date on which an item was modified or reassigned to categories. Alternatively, you can change a setting so that no date is automatically recorded as the Entry Date; instead, you enter any date you wish as the Entry Date. This allows you to use the Entry Date as a second date associated with an item. For example, you might use the Entry Date to keep track of the starting date for tasks, and use the When Date to keep track of the completion date.

Done Dates record the dates on which tasks described by items have been completed. When an item is designated as Done, the current date is recorded as the Done Date. Options are available to automatically discard Done items from a database and to write them to a separate file.

Agenda uses the current date known to DOS as the basis for its date-keeping abilities. If your computer has a clock-calendar, this date should be correctly set automatically each time you start the computer and load DOS. Users of computers without clock-calendars should be prompted for the date and time each time DOS is booted. It is important to enter the correct date if Agenda is to successfully manage dates.

## USING WHEN DATES

When Dates are specified for items either by direct entry into a When Date column, or by including the dates in the text of the items themselves. Dates may be entered in absolute form, such as the default numerical format MM/DD/YY, where May 17, 1988 would be entered as 5/17/88. Dates may also be entered in relative form, using descriptive terms such as yesterday, today, tomorrow, and next Tuesday. Agenda is able to figure out such date references and assign the proper date.

You will continue working with the Tasks database developed in the preceding chapters. Start Agenda, open the Tasks database, and switch to the Tasks to Do view if it is not currently displayed. (Function key F8 allows you to quickly select any view.)

In working with dates in the Tasks database, your actual dates will necessarily differ from those shown here. A reference to "next Tuesday," for example, will generate a date that depends upon the current date on which you are making the entry. Obviously this will be different for each user.

Relative date references such as "today" and "next Tuesday" can be directly entered into the When Date column. In working with the Tasks database, suppose you want to set "next Tuesday" as the When Date for the third item in the Reports section. You could get out your calendar, check next Tuesday's date, and enter that date in the MM/DD/YY absolute format, but it is much easier to enter the relative date directly. Move the highlight over to the When column, to the right of the item beginning "Have Ann get out the previous Walker project report." Then type in the following:

next Tuesday

The entry appears on the second line of the screen as shown in Fig. 10-1. Press ENTER and this is entered as the When Date. Next Tuesday's date is displayed in the When column. Remember that the actual date entered and displayed depends upon the date when you make the entry. It will be the date of the Tuesday following the current date.

When Dates can also be entered by including a reference to a date within the text of an item. This date can be in either relative or absolute form. Suppose you held a regular staff meeting every Wednesday. Move the highlight so that the Meetings section head is highlighted, for the entry of a new item directly below it. Press INS to insert a new item. Type in the following text:

Staff meeting every Wednesday.

Press ENTER. Next Wednesday's date is automatically entered in the When Date column, as shown in Fig. 10-2.

```
Date:                                                              Edit
next Tuesday
========================================================================
Reports                              Staffing    Project     When
   · Meeting to discuss project for  ·George     ·James      ·03/13/89
   ♪ James next Monday.
     Prepare report on Walker project ·Ann       ·Walker     ·03/16/89
     by next Thursday.
   » Have Ann get out the previous   ·Ann        ·Walker
     Walker project report and begin
     the process of updating so that
     we have a draft to work with.
   · Meet with Jim to discuss report ·Jim        ·Peters
     on the Peters account.
   · Call Ann to go over report to   ·Ann        ·Walker
     Walker Inc. on Walker and James
     projects.

Meetings                             Staffing    Project     When
   · Meeting to discuss project for  ·George     ·James      ·03/13/89
     James next Monday.
   · Meeting with executive committee                        ·03/24/89
     3/24/89 to go over quarterly
==F1====F2======F3======F4======F5=====F6=====F7======F8====F9======F10==
 Help  ‖ Paste ‖ Copy  ‖ Cut  ‖       ‖      ‖ Mark ‖      ‖ Accept ‖
```

Fig. 10-1. *Entering the date "next Tuesday" in the When Date column.*

```
File: C:\AGFILES\TASKS                         03/10/89    16:49
View: Tasks to Do                   When Date: 03/15/89
========================================================================
Reports                              Staffing    Project     When
   · Meeting to discuss project for  ·George     ·James      ·03/13/89
     James next Monday.
   · Have Ann get out the previous   ·Ann        ·Walker     ·03/14/89
     Walker project report and begin
     the process of updating so that
     we have a draft to work with.
   ♪ Prepare report on Walker project ·Ann       ·Walker     ·03/16/89
     by next Thursday.
   · Meet with Jim to discuss report ·Jim        ·Peters
     on the Peters account.
   · Call Ann to go over report to   ·Ann        ·Walker
     Walker Inc. on Walker and James
     projects.

Meetings                             Staffing    Project     When
   · Staff meeting every Wednesday.  »Staffing               ·03/15/89
   · Meeting to discuss project for  ·George     ·James      ·03/13/89
     James next Monday.
   · Meeting with executive committee                        ·03/24/89
==F1====F2======F3======F4======F5=====F6=====F7======F8======F9======F10==
 Help  ‖ Edit  ‖ Copy  ‖ Done ‖ Note ‖ Move ‖ Mark ‖ Vw Mgr ‖ Cat Mgr ‖ Menu
```

Fig. 10-2. *The entry of a new item in the Meetings section referring to a staff meeting every Wednesday.*

The word "every" has special significance when entering When Dates. Agenda recognizes this as referring to a recurring date and continually updates the When Date. For example, when "every Wednesday" is entered, either within the text of an item or directly in the When Date column, Agenda initially assigns the date of the next Wednesday. This remains the When Date through that Wednesday. After that date is passed, however, Agenda automatically changes the date to the following Wednesday. Thus, the When Date column always displays the date for the next occurrence of a recurring event.

If a When Date is assigned based upon a date reference in the item, editing that item to change the date automatically changes the When Date as well. Thus, if the staff meeting were changed to every Thursday, you could just edit the item, changing the Wednesday to Thursday.

When Dates may also be changed by directly changing the date in the When Date column. You can choose either to edit the existing date or to simply enter a new date. The new date replaces the old.

A date entry made directly in the When Date column takes precedence over any date references within the text of the item. For example, an item might include a reference to "next Thursday," with that date displayed in the When Date column. If you move the highlight to the When Date column and enter "next Friday," next Friday's date becomes the When Date and is displayed. Likewise, with a When Date entered directly into the When Date column, editing the item to include a date reference does not result in its becoming the When Date. The directly entered When Date still takes precedence.

Agenda includes a number of date preference settings that control the way dates work. Two of these preferences relate specifically to When Dates. To change the settings, use the Utility Preferences Date command to display the Date Preferences box as shown in Fig. 10-3. The last two settings are used to control the actions relating to When Dates. The first is *Set date from item:* and governs whether When Dates are automatically set when date references are included within the text of the item. The default is *Yes*, which results in the automatic When Date setting you have already used. You can turn off this feature so that When Dates can only be set by making direct entries.

The other When Date preference is *Redate recurring items*. With the default setting of *Yes*, date references including the words "each" or "every" are updated automatically as time passes. This automatic updating can be turned off if desired.

## USING ENTRY DATES

The primary purpose of Entry Dates is to show when changes have been made to a database. The Entry Date can be used to show when an item was originally entered into the database. It can also be employed to store the date when an item was last edited or reassigned to different categories. Alternatively, the Entry Date can be used as a "free" date which you enter and use for other purposes.

```
 Auto-Assign  Date  Other  Environment  Update
 Specify how dates are processed
═══════════════════════════════════════════════════════════════════════
 Reports                                 Staffing    Project     When
   · Meeting to discuss project for       ·George     ·James      ·03/13/89
     James next Monday.
   · Have Ann get out the previous        ·Ann        ·Walker     ·03/14/89
     Walker ┌───────────────────Date Preferences═══════════════════┐
     the pro│                                                       │
     we have│  Default date format:   MM/DD/YY                      │
   ♪ Prepare│  Set Entry date:        When item is entered          │3/16/89
     by next│  Set date from item:    Yes                           │
   · Meet wi│  Redate recurring items: Yes                          │
     on the │                                                       │
   · Call An└──────────Press F9 when done, ESC to cancel════════════┘
     Walker Inc. on Walker and James
     projects.

 Meetings                                Staffing    Project     When
   · Staff meeting every Wednesday.       »Staffing               ·03/15/89
   · Meeting to discuss project for       ·George     ·James      ·03/13/89
     James next Monday.
   · Meeting with executive committee                             ·03/24/89
═F1══════╤═F2═══════╤═F3═══════╤═F4═══════╤═F5═══════╤═F6═══════╤═F7═══════╤═F8═══════╤═F9═══════╤═F10══
 Help    ║ Edit     ║          ║          ║          ║          ║          ║Default║Accept ║
```

Fig. 10-3. *Setting Date Preferences using the Utility Preferences Date command.*

Look at the dates on which you entered various items in the Tasks database (Fig. 10-4). With the Tasks to Do view still displayed, move the highlight over to the When column. Enter the Category Column New command to create a new Entry Date column. In the New Column box, move the highlight down to the *Column Type:* setting, press GREY PLUS to display the list of options, highlight *Entry date*, and press ENTER. Now press F9 to accept the settings and create the new column.

A column headed "Entry" is displayed on the far right side of the screen. For each item, an Entry Date shows the date on which the item was originally entered into the Agenda database. This Entry Date is taken from the current DOS date at the time the item was entered.

Now that you have seen the Entry Date, remove the column to reduce the clutter on the screen. The quickest way to do this is to highlight the column head Entry and press DEL. You will be asked if you wish to remove the column from all sections. Respond with Yes, and the Entry Date column is removed from the view.

The basic operation of the Entry Date is completely straightforward. The Entry Date is automatically assigned when an item is entered. You can then use this date, displaying it in an Entry Date column or sorting or filtering by the Entry Date, as you see fit.

```
┌─────────────────────────────────────────────────────────────────────────────┐
│  File: C:\AGFILES\TASKS                                                        │
│  View: Tasks to Do                                        03/10/89    16:51    │
│ ═════════════════════════════════════════════════════════════════════════════│
│  Reports                    Staffing     Project      When          Entry      │
│    · Meeting to discuss     ·George      ·James       ·03/13/89     ·03/10/89  │
│      project for James                                                         │
│      next Monday.                                                              │
│    · Have Ann get out the   ·Ann         ·Walker      ·03/14/89     ·03/10/89  │
│      previous Walker                                                           │
│      project report and                                                        │
│      begin the process of                                                      │
│      updating so that we                                                       │
│      have a draft to work                                                      │
│      with.                                                                     │
│    ♪ Prepare report on      ·Ann         ·Walker      ·03/16/89     ·03/10/89  │
│      Walker project by                                                         │
│      next Thursday.                                                            │
│    · Meet with Jim to       ·Jim         ·Peters                    ·03/10/89  │
│      discuss report on the                                                     │
│      Peters account.                                                           │
│    · Call Ann to go over    ·Ann         ·Walker                    ·03/10/89  │
│      report to Walker Inc.                                                     │
│      on Walker and James                                                       │
│ ══F1══╤══F2══╤══F3══╤══F4══╤══F5══╤══F6══╤══F7══╤══F8══╤══F9══╤══F10══│
│  Help │ Edit │ Copy │ Done │ Note │ Move │ Mark │Vw Mgr│Cat Mgr│ Menu │
└─────────────────────────────────────────────────────────────────────────────┘
```

Fig. 10-4. *The display of the Entry Date column.*

Several options exist for the use of the Entry Date. Two change the event for which the Entry Date is automatically assigned. A third gives you free use of the Entry Date for other purposes. To see and change these options, use the Utility Preferences Date command. Highlight *Set entry date:* and press GREY PLUS to show the list of options. These are illustrated in Fig. 10-5.

The default option is *When item is entered*. This causes the Entry Date to be set on the day the item is initially entered into the database. When using this setting, the Entry Date for an item will never be changed.

The first two options listed allow the Entry Date to be updated when certain actions are taken involving the item. With the *When item is edited* option, the Entry Date is updated to the current date each time the item is changed by editing. Thus, the Entry Date reflects the last date on which the item has been edited (or the date of initial entry if no changes have been made to the item).

The *When item reassigned* option causes the Entry Date to also be updated whenever the assignment of an item to categories is altered. When an item is assigned to a new category or unassigned from a category, the item's Entry Date is updated. With this setting, the Entry Date will also be updated whenever the item is edited. Thus, this option is used to show the latest date at which any changes have been made involving the items in the database.

The final option, *Do not set*, disables all automatic setting of Entry Dates. When this is selected, Agenda does not enter any Entry Dates. You must manually

```
Auto-Assign  Date  Other  Environment  Update
Specify how dates are processed
─────────────────────────────────────────────────────────────────────
Reports                                Staffing     Project      When
   · Meeting to discuss project for    ·George      ·James       ·03/13/89
     James next Monday.
   · Have Ann get out the previous     ·Ann         ·Walker      ·03/14/89
     Walker ┌───────────────────Date Preferences════════════════┐
     the pro│                        ┌─────────────────────────┐ │
     we have│ Default date format:   │ Choices:                │ │
   ♪ Prepare│ Set Entry date:        │                         │3/16/89
     by next│ Set date from item:    ├─────────────────────────┤ │
   · Meet wi│ Redate recurring items:│ When item reassigned    │ │
     on the │                        │ When item is edited     │ │
   · Call An└────────────Press F9 when│ When item is entered    │ │
     Walker Inc. on Walker and James  │ Do not set              │ │
     projects.                        └─────────────────────────┘ │
                                      └──────────────────────────┘
Meetings                               Staffing     Project      When
   · Meeting to discuss project for    ·George      ·James       ·03/13/89
     James next Monday.
   · Staff meeting every Wednesday.    ·Staffing                 ·03/15/89
   · Meeting with executive committee                            ·03/24/89
══F1═══╤══F2═══╤══F3═══╤══F4═══╤══F5═══╤══F6═══╤══F7═══╤══F8═══╤══F9═══╤══F10══
Help   ║       ║       ║       ║       ║       ║       ║       ║Accept ║
```

Fig. 10-5. *Options for setting the Entry Date in the Date Preferences box.*

enter any dates in the Entry Date column in a view. This lets you use the Entry Date for other purposes. For example, in managing projects, you might wish to record both the start date and the completion date for each task. The Entry Date can be used for the start date and the When Date can be used for the completion date. Unfortunately, there is no way to change the column heading when the Entry Date is used for another purpose such as this. The column will still be headed Entry, and any other uses of this date will still require reference to the Entry Date.

## USING DONE DATES

Done Dates have a very specific function. A Done Date records the current date as the date on which a task has been completed. Options are available to cause specific actions to be taken when items have been recorded as Done.

Using the Tasks database, you will indicate that a task has been completed and then cause Agenda to discard the item from the database. To see the Done Dates in action, first create a Done Date column. In the Tasks to Do view, move the cursor to the rightmost column and enter the Category Column New command. Select the *Category Type:* setting, press GREY PLUS, highlight *Done date*, press ENTER, and press F9 to create the new column. A Done Date column is displayed on the right side of the screen. The column will have no date entries because none of the items in the database have yet been designated as Done.

Assume that the Walker project report has been completed. Move the highlight to the second item, beginning "Prepare report on the Walker project." To specify that the item is Done, just press F4 (DONE). The current date is entered into the Done column, indicating that the item was designated as being done on this date. This is shown in Fig. 10-6. Note the double exclamation points displayed in front of the item. This is a symbol specifying that the item has been designated as Done, providing this information even if you do not have a Done Date column displayed in the view.

Agenda's default conditions cause the Done Date to be assigned and the double exclamation points to mark items when they are designated as Done. But you might not want your database to be cluttered with items that are Done. Issue the Utility Preferences Other command, select the *Process Done Items:* setting, and press GREY PLUS.  Figure 10-7 shows the options for dealing with items that have been marked Done. The current default setting is to take no action. The Done Date is assigned and the item remains in the database.

Since you want to just discard items marked Done, highlight the *Discard* option and press ENTER. The Other Preferences box then displays another setting, *When:*, for specifying when the done items are

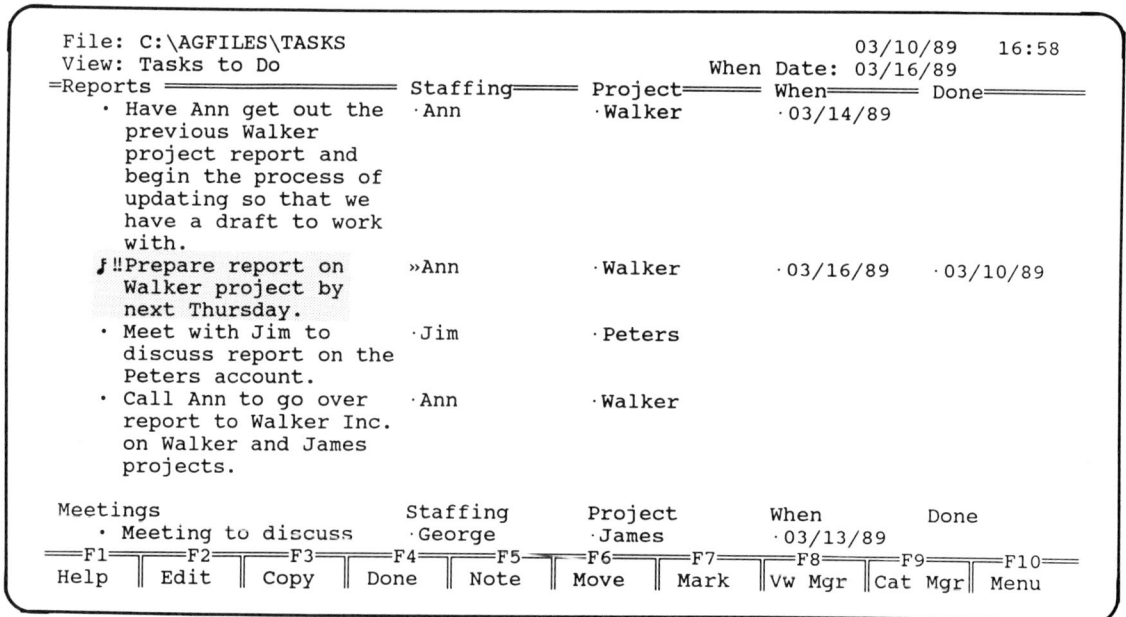

```
 File: C:\AGFILES\TASKS                                    03/10/89   16:58
 View: Tasks to Do                              When Date: 03/16/89
=Reports ===================== Staffing==== Project===== When===== Done====
   · Have Ann get out the   ·Ann           ·Walker      ·03/14/89
     previous Walker
     project report and
     begin the process of
     updating so that we
     have a draft to work
     with.
   ♪‼Prepare report on      »Ann           ·Walker      ·03/16/89   ·03/10/89
     Walker project by
     next Thursday.
   · Meet with Jim to       ·Jim           ·Peters
     discuss report on the
     Peters account.
   · Call Ann to go over    ·Ann           ·Walker
     report to Walker Inc.
     on Walker and James
     projects.

 Meetings                   Staffing       Project      When        Done
   · Meeting to discuss     ·George        ·James       ·03/13/89
==F1======F2======F3======F4======F5======F6======F7======F8======F9======F10==
 Help    Edit    Copy    Done    Note    Move    Mark   Vw Mgr  Cat Mgr  Menu
```

Fig. 10-6. *The second item designated as being Done, with the entry in the Done Date column.*

```
Auto-Assign  Date  Other  Environment  Update
Specify other database preferences
=Reports ════════════════════════ Staffing══ ═ Project══════ When══════ ═ Done════════
   · Have Ann get out the   ·Ann          ·Walker      ·03/14/89
                              ══════════════Other Preferences══════
        ┌─────────────────────────────────────────────────────────────────┐
        │ Insert new columns in:  All sections                             │
        │ Empty Trash:                                                     │
        │ Make backup copy:       ┌──────────────────────────────────┐     │
        │ Process Done items:     │ Choices:                          │     │
    ♪   │                         │                                   │     │
        │                         ├──────────────────────────────────┤     │
        │                         │  No action                        │     │
        │ Tab size:               │  Discard                          │     │
        │ Hide carriage returns:  │  Export to Done file              │     │
    ·   │                         └──────────────────────────────────┘     │
        │ File description:       Database for Working with Lotus Agenda    │
    ·   │ File password:                                                   │
        │ Auto-import file:                                               │
        └═══════════════════════Press F9 when done, ESC to cancel═════════┘
  Meetings                    Staffing      Project        When          Done
     · Meeting to discuss    ·George       ·James        ·03/13/89
  ═F1══╤══F2══╤══F3══╤══F4══╤══F5══╤══F6══╤══F7══╤══F8══╤══F9════╤═F10══
  Help  ║      ║      ║      ║      ║      ║      ║      ║ Accept ║
```

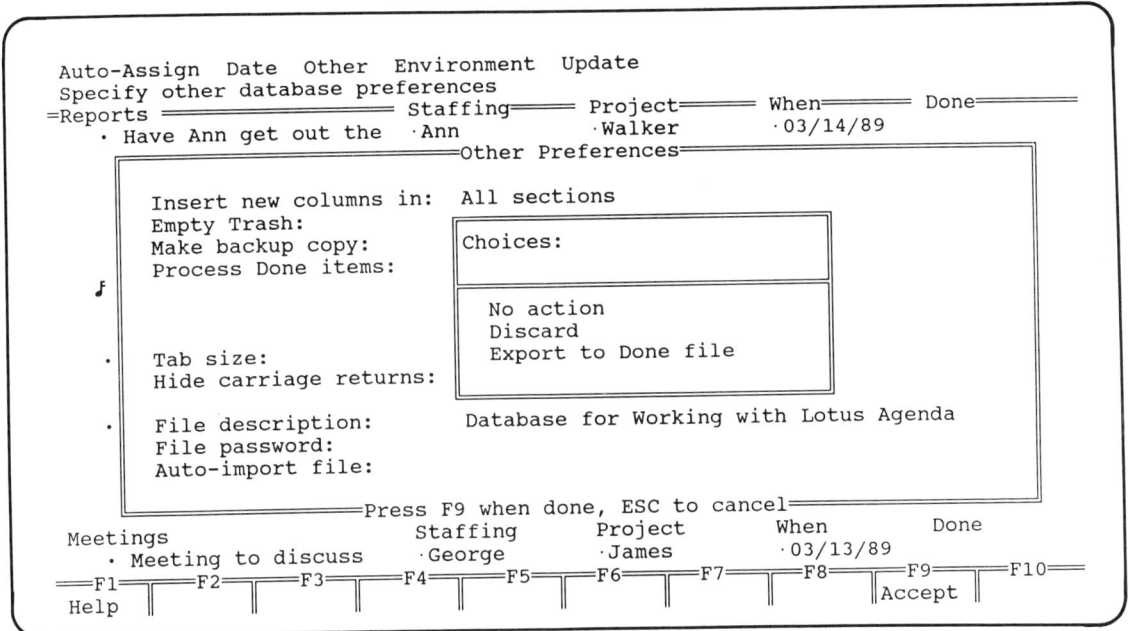

Fig. 10-7. *The options for processing Done items.*

to be discarded. Accept the default option, *Immediately*. Press F9 to accept the settings in the Other Preferences box.

When you are returned to the view, notice that the item that had been marked Done has been deleted from the database. Were you to mark any additional items Done, they would be deleted immediately. Since no Done items will remain in the database, there will be no Done Dates to display, and no need for the Done column. Highlight the column head Done and press DEL to remove the column from the view.

Done items can be discarded from the database immediately as they are marked as being done, when the database is closed, or at the end of the day. These options are available for the *When:* setting when you select the *Discard* option for Done items.

You can also specify that Done items be exported to a separate file. This option provides the best of both worlds; items are removed from the current database but are saved for archival purposes should you need to consult them later. When you select the *Export to Done file* option, you are given the same choices about when this export is to take place: immediately, when the file is closed, or at the end of the day. You are also given the option of specifying the file name for the database to which the Done items are to be exported. Agenda provides a default file name that is the name of the current database followed by an exclamation point. For the Tasks database, the default file name for the Done items will be *Tasks!*. This can be changed by editing the file name if desired.

Agenda's ability to automatically export Done items to another file can be used for other applications as well. Suppose you are working with a large database and occasionally need to move selected items to another database. You can set the Done item processing to export the items to the new database. Then, whenever you wish to move an item to that new database, simply press F4 (DONE). In this application, Done would mean that you are finished using the item and want to export it to the other database, not that a particular task has actually been completed.

If you choose to keep Done items in the database, you can use the Done Dates just like the other Agenda dates. Done Dates can be displayed in columns and used for filtering and sorting data. Nothing requires that you use Done Dates only to keep track of completed activities. You can enter any date in a Done Date column in the usual manner. Of course, pressing F4 (DONE) will automatically enter the current date as the Done Date in the normal manner. When the date entered as the Done Date is either the current date or any earlier date, the double exclamation points will be displayed in front of the item.

As an example of one possible alternative use of the Done Date column, you could enter as Done Dates the future dates by which tasks are supposed to be completed. Then, when a date entered as a Done Date arrives, the item will be marked with the double exclamation points, indicating that the task is either due to be completed or is past due. This automatically marks the items as tasks that need to be dealt with immediately. When an item is completed, it can then be manually discarded from the database using ALT-F4 (DISCARD). Essentially, you are giving up Agenda's capability to automatically discard Done items and using the Done Date to highlight overdue tasks.

The View Preferences command or F5 (PREFERENCES) in the View Manager provides an option that may be used to hide done items. When this is selected, items considered to be done—with Done Dates at or prior to the current date—will not be displayed. This provides an alternative for dealing with the clutter that would be caused by retaining Done items. The items remain in the database but are not displayed in that view. They may be displayed in other views, or you may use the View Preferences command or F5 (PREFERENCES) in the View Manager to change the setting and reveal the Done items.

## DATE FORMATS AND DISPLAY FORMATS

Agenda provides a variety of options for entering and displaying dates to satisfy individual preferences and the differing date conventions used in various countries. Changes can be made to the manner in which dates are displayed and accepted in a specific column in a view, and to the overall format used for dates throughout Agenda.

Take a look at a very different way of displaying the date information in the When Date column. Be sure you are in the Tasks to Do view of the Tasks database. Move the highlight to the When Date column. Issue the Category Column Format command. With the highlight adjacent to the *Format:* setting, press GREY PLUS to display the list of date format options. The screen will appear as shown in Fig. 10-8. Move the highlight down to *Relative* to select that format and press ENTER. Then press F9 to accept the settings and return to the view.

The dates are now displayed in the relative format, that is, in relation to the current date (Fig. 10-9). The current date would be shown as "today," and next Tuesday's date would be shown as "nxt Tues." Dates too far removed from the current date are displayed in the DD-MMM format, such as 24-Mar.

The selection of the date display format is purely a matter of personal preference. I prefer the more mundane MM/DD/YY default format. Therefore, I once again used the Category Column Format command to switch the display format of the When Date column back to the default. You can choose to display the When Dates in whatever format you prefer.

Agenda provides seven date format options that may be employed for entering and displaying dates. These date formats are summarized in Table 10-1. The

Fig. 10-8. *Changing the When Date column display format using the Category Column Format command.*

```
┌─────────────────────────────────────────────────────────────────────┐
│  File: C:\AGFILES\TASKS                            03/10/89   17:05   │
│  View: Tasks to Do                                                    │
│ ═════════════════════════════════════════════════════════════════════│
│  Reports                       Staffing    Project      When          │
│   · Meeting to discuss project for  ·George     ·James     ·nxt Mon   │
│     James next Monday.                                                │
│   · Have Ann get out the previous   ·Ann        ·Walker    ·nxt Tues  │
│     Walker project report and begin                                   │
│     the process of updating so that                                   │
│     we have a draft to work with.                                     │
│   · Meet with Jim to discuss report ·Jim        ·Peters               │
│     on the Peters account.                                            │
│   · Call Ann to go over report to   ·Ann        ·Walker               │
│     Walker Inc. on Walker and James                                   │
│     projects.                                                         │
│                                                                       │
│  Meetings                      Staffing    Project      When          │
│   · Meeting to discuss project for  ·George     ·James     ·nxt Mon   │
│     James next Monday.                                                │
│   · Staff meeting every Wednesday.  ·Staffing              ·nxt Wed   │
│   · Meeting with executive committee                       ·24-Mar    │
│     3/24/89 to go over quarterly                                      │
│     results.                                                          │
│ ══F1═════F2══════F3══════F4══════F5══════F6══════F7══════F8═════F9═════F10══│
│  Help │ Edit │ Copy │ Done │ Note │ Move │ Mark │ Vw Mgr│ Cat Mgr│ Menu│
└─────────────────────────────────────────────────────────────────────┘
```

Fig. 10-9. *The When Date column format changed to Relative.*

### Table 10-1. Date Formats.

| Format | Example |
|---|---|
| MM/DD/YY | 06/15/89 |
| DD/MM/YY | 15/06/89 |
| DD.MM.YY | 15.06.89 |
| YY-MM-DD | 89-06-15 |
| DD-MMM | 15-Jun |
| DD-MMM-YY | 15-Jun-89 |
| Relative | today (assuming that the date is June 15) |

MM/DD/YY format is most commonly used in the United States, and is Agenda's default format when the program is first used. The date *June 15, 1989* would be entered as 6/15/89 and displayed as 06/15/89. The leading zeros before single-digit months and dates are optional when entering the date.

You have already seen the display of Agenda's relative date format, in which dates are described relative to the current date. Agenda will always accept relative date references when entering dates, no matter what default or display formats are established.

For most Agenda users in the United States, the DD-MMM and DD-MMM-YY date formats will be the only other options of interest. Some might prefer dates to be displayed in the format 15-Jun provided by these formats (with the year optional). The remaining date formats are primarily for Agenda users in other countries where dates are expressed in other ways.

The default date format used throughout Agenda can be changed by using the Utility Preferences Date command and changing the *Default date format:* setting. Agenda will present a list of all of the date format options shown in Table 10-1 except for Relative. (Relative dates are always available for entry and can always be specified for display.) For example, if you want to always enter dates in the DD-MMM format (15-June), make that selection. Agenda always interprets dates in items (for assignment of When Dates) according to the default format, and will always recognize relative dates.

Whenever a date column is added to a view, Agenda normally displays the date in the default format specified with the Utility Preferences Date command. Agenda recognizes dates entered in the column in that default format or in the relative date format.

The format used to display a date in any particular column can be changed by altering the *Column Format:* setting either when the column is created or later, by using the Category Column Format command. This command displays the list of choices shown in Fig. 10-8. You can choose to use the default format or specifically select any of the available date formats. This selection applies only to the specific date column in the view that was selected when the *Column Format:* setting was changed.

In addition to displaying the date in the column in the selected format, the specification of a date format for the column governs the format in which dates may be entered into that column. Dates can be entered either in the relative format or in the display format selected for that column. For example, if the DD.MM.YY format were selected as the display format for a column, date entries into that column would have to be either in that format or in the relative date format.

Agenda occasionally recognizes date entries in formats other than the column display format and correctly enters the date into a date column. However, when you attempt to enter the date in a different format, Agenda might inform you that it is unable to interpret the date entry and will give you the opportunity to correct it.

When items are entered, Agenda expects date entries either in the default format or in relative format. If you make a date entry within an item that Agenda cannot understand, Agenda will ignore the entry and will not assign a When Date. When you use a column display format other than the default, Agenda employs different formats for interpreting dates in the column and in related items. Use different date formats only when necessary, when they help to clarify the situation and not confuse it.

## USING DATES FOR SORTING AND FILTERING

All three of Agenda's date types may be employed in sorting items within sections and in filtering the items to be included within views. The procedures for accomplishing these tasks were explained and demonstrated in earlier chapters. They are just reviewed briefly here.

### Sorting by Date

The items in the sections of the Tasks to Do view were sorted by date back in Chapter 4. Any sorting operation is begun with the Category Section Sort command, which displays the box listing all of the sort settings, shown in Fig. 10-10. To sort by any of the three dates, first move the highlight to the *Sort on:* setting (for either the primary or the secondary sort, as appropriate). Use GREY PLUS to display the list of choices. All three of the dates are included among the options. Select the date type to be employed in the sort. Agenda then presents the option to specify the sort order. An ascending sort places the earliest dates first, while a descending sort places the last dates first. Change this setting if necessary.

In any sort (whether by date or by something else), you need to specify which sections are to be sorted and when new items entered into the database are to be sorted. These options are no different for date sorts as opposed to other kinds of sorts. They were discussed in Chapter 4 and will not be repeated here.

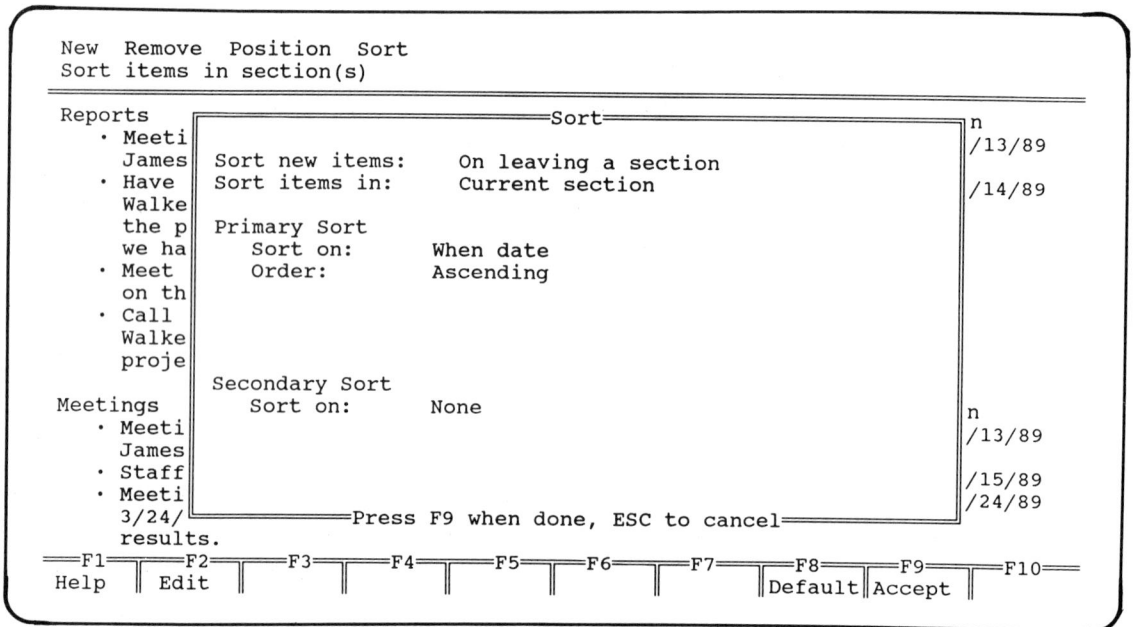

```
New  Remove  Position  Sort
Sort items in section(s)
==========================================================================
Reports   ==================Sort=========================================  n
  • Meeti||                                                            ||  /13/89
    James|| Sort new items:    On leaving a section                    ||
  • Have || Sort items in:     Current section                         ||  /14/89
    Walke||                                                            ||
    the p|| Primary Sort                                               ||
    we ha||    Sort on:       When date                                ||
  • Meet ||    Order:         Ascending                                ||
    on th||                                                            ||
  • Call ||                                                            ||
    Walke||                                                            ||
    proje||                                                            ||
         || Secondary Sort                                             ||
Meetings ||    Sort on:       None                                     ||  n
  • Meeti||                                                            ||  /13/89
    James||                                                            ||
  • Staff||                                                            ||  /15/89
  • Meeti||                                                            ||  /24/89
    3/24/=============Press F9 when done, ESC to cancel=================
    results.
==F1====F2====F3====F4====F5====F6====F7====F8=======F9=======F10==
Help  | Edit |    |    |    |    |    |Default|Accept |
```

Fig. 10-10. *Sorting all sections by the When Date in ascending order using the Category Section Sort command.*

With all of the sort settings selected, pressing F9 accepts the settings and causes the database to be sorted. Note that the items in a section or sections can be sorted by any date whether or not that date is displayed in a column in the view. For example, the items could be placed in the order in which they were entered into the database by sorting on the Entry Date, even though the entry date is not displayed.

Items without date entries are placed *after* all of the items with dates. This could prove useful in certain situations. For example, a sort of items by Done Dates would place the items with Done Dates (designated as being done) at the beginning, followed by all of the items without Done Dates.

## Filtering by Date

Items can be included or excluded from any view based upon any of the three dates assigned to the items. This is accomplished by setting a date filter. Date filters are considered to be among the preference features associated with a view. You set a date filter for a view by pressing F5 (PREFS) while in the View Manager or by using the View Preferences command while in a view.

Setting a date filter was described in Chapter 6, which dealt with views. In that chapter, a Current Tasks to Do view was created and a date filter was set so that only items with When Dates occurring within the next several weeks were displayed. To see the settings for this date filter, first switch to the Current Tasks to Do view. Press F8 (VIEW MGR), highlight that view, and press ENTER. Then issue the View Preferences command to display the View Preferences box shown in Fig. 10-11.

Using a date filter involves specifying the date to be used for the filtering and the manner in which items are to be included or excluded from the view based upon those dates. The first setting is the *Type of date:*, which allows you to select whether Entry, When, or Done Dates are to be employed in filtering the view.

The *Display:* setting provides the most basic choices regarding the inclusion or exclusion of items from the view. The first option is to include only dated items in the view. For example, if you were filtering on Done Dates, only those items with Done Dates assigned to them would be included. Alternatively, you can include only undated items in the view. In this case, when filtering on Done Dates, those items that have not been assigned Done Dates would be included. Finally, you can choose to include both dated and undated items. This will, of course, make sense only if you are further restricting the range of dates to be included for the dated items. Otherwise all items would be included.

```
 New  Select  Define  Preferences  Info
 Specify date filters & display preferences for current view
┌───────────────────────────────────────────────────────────────────────┐
 Report ┌─────────────────────────View Preferences════════════════════┐ /89
   • M ║ Display Preferences                                          ║
     M ║    Hide done items:                  No                      ║ /89
   • H ║    Hide dependent items:             No                      ║
     r ║    Hide inherited items:             No                      ║
     t ║                                                              ║
       ║ Date Filter                                                  ║
 Meetin ║    Type of date:             When date                      ║
   • M ║    Start date:                                               ║ /89
     M ║    End date:                 03/17/89                        ║
   • S ║    Display:                  Dated items only                ║ /89
       ║    Include items:            In date range                   ║
 Phone  ║ Other                                                        ║
   ♪ C ║    View name:                Current Tasks to Do             ║ /89
     t ║    Section separator:        No                              ║
   • C ║                                                              ║ /89
     r └══════════════════Press F9 when done, ESC to cancel═══════════┘
   • Call Ann by next Friday to discuss hiring of          ·03/17/89
     new assistant.

 ══F1══╤══F2══╤══F3══╤══F4══╤══F5══╤══F6══╤══F7══╤══F8══════╤══F9═════╤══F10══
 Help  ║ Edit ║      ║      ║      ║      ║      ║ Default ║ Accept ║
```

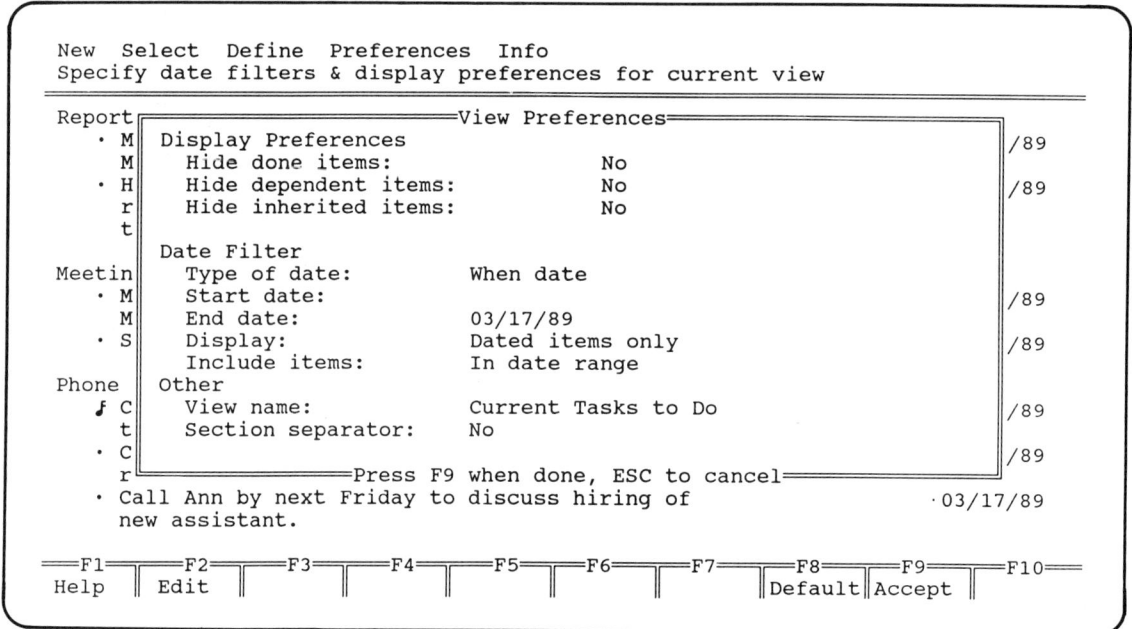

Fig. 10-11. *The View Preferences for the display of Done items and for the setting of a date filter.*

The *Start Date:* and *End Date:* settings are used to specify a range of dates for inclusion in or exclusion from the view. Dates are entered for these settings in the usual manner. If no start date is given, the range of dates begins at the earliest date. If no end date is given, the range of dates ends at the latest date. With no start date or end date, the range would include all of the dates. The example includes no start date, and an end date of 3/17/89. Thus, the range includes all dates up through March 17.

You can use relative dates for the start and end date settings, such as "Today" and "Next Saturday." Relative dates are always interpreted according to Agenda's current date. Thus, a range from today through next Saturday would specify a changing range of dates, always from the current day to the end of the current week. Such date settings could be used in a date filter to always display items with dates during the current week.

If you enter either a start date or an end date to specify a range of dates for the date filter, a final *Include Items:* setting appears. With this setting you can choose to include in the view either those dates within the date range specified or those dates outside of the date range. The latter setting excludes items with dates falling in the range of dates specified, but includes all other dates.

When a view is filtered by date, the range of dates included in the view is always displayed on the second line of the screen. This reminds you of the items being included in and excluded from the current view.

Be careful when entering new items or editing items in views filtered by a range of dates. Agenda might refuse certain entries as being inconsistent with the filter. For example, if the view is filtered by the Entry Date and includes a range of dates that does not include the current date, Agenda will refuse the attempt to enter the item, displaying a message that the entry would be inconsistent with the filter.

In other cases, Agenda will accept an entry and assign a date, but that date will be consistent with the range of dates specified by the view filter. The view filter shown in Fig. 10-11 restricts the view to items with When Dates up through March 17. If, on April 5, you were to enter an item with the relative date reference today or with the absolute date 4/5/89, Agenda would assign a When Date of 3/17/89, the latest date allowed by the date filter.

There might be a few specialized situations where such treatment of new or edited dates by Agenda in views filtered by date would actually be appropriate and useful. In general, however, entering and editing items in date-filtered views can cause strange dates to be assigned. You are better off restricting your item entry and editing to unfiltered views, using the filtered views only to examine the information.

# 11

# ADVANCED CATEGORY ASSIGNMENT FEATURES

A GENDA provides a variety of additional facilities for managing the assignment of items to categories. These include commands allowing assignments to be made directly, as well as settings that allow you to control the automatic assignment of items to categories as they are entered. Other features, called conditions and actions, make it possible for category assignments to be made automatically.

You have already learned a number of ways to assign items to categories. Entering an item in a section assigns the item to the category represented by the section head. Agenda can recognize references to categories within the text of items and automatically make assignments. Copying or moving items to other sections makes category assignments. Making category entries in category columns also results in the assignment of items to the category.

Most of these assignment methods depend upon the presence of the categories as section heads or in columns in particular views. When you use these methods, you actually see the assignment of the item to the category displayed in the view as it is made. The methods for managing category assignment discussed in this chapter do not depend upon the presence of sections or columns within a view. Instead, they deal directly with the categories as categories.

The first section of this chapter describes the procedure for directly assigning items to any category in the database. Agenda helps in category assignment by attempting to automatically assign items to categories; the second section of the chapter describes how you can control this process. The last two sections of this chapter introduce the use of conditions and actions. By using *conditions*, you can specify that items are to be automatically assigned to particular categories whenever these conditions are met. *Actions*, on the other hand, allow you to specify that when an item is assigned to a category, that item is assigned to another category or other actions will be taken.

## DIRECTLY ASSIGNING ITEMS TO CATEGORIES

Until now, explicitly assigning an item to a category required either placing the item in a section or making an entry in the appropriate column. Both of these methods depend upon the presence of the correct section head or column in a view. To assign items, however, it is not necessary to modify a view by adding a section head or column. The Item Assign command allows items to be directly assigned to any category in the database, regardless of the view.

Open the Tasks database and switch, if necessary, to the Tasks to Do view. Move the highlight down to the last item in the Meetings section, press INS, and type in the following new item:

Meeting with Ann and Ron Smith Thursday.

Press ENTER. Ron Smith is the representative for Walker, and the meeting involves the Walker project. You could make the assignment to the Walker project category directly by entering Walker in the Project column. Instead of doing this, use the Item Assign command. Check to be sure that the just-entered item is still highlighted. Issue the Item Assign command. You can type in the Walker category name, or, if you want to see a complete list of categories, press GREY PLUS. Then the Category Select box will appear on the screen. The Category Select box lists the categories in the database (Fig. 11-1). Move the highlight down to the Walker category and press F9. The item is assigned to the Walker category. Walker has been entered in the Project column in the Tasks to Do view. The Project column does not need to be included in the view in order to make the assignment of the item to the Walker category. Its presence merely illustrates that the assignment had in fact been made after the Item Assign command had been employed to make the assignment.

Use of the Item Assign command is straightforward. You highlight the item to be assigned to a category, press F10, and issue the Item Assign command. Se-

```
   File: C:\AGFILES\END10                              03/10/89
   View: Tasks to Do                      When Date: 03/16/89
  =Reports ========================== Staffing===Project=====When=======
  ┌─────────────────Category Select══════════════════════┐
  │Select a category:                                     │
  │Press F9 when done, ESC to cancel                      │
  │                                            ·Peters    │
  │MAIN                                                   │
  │  Project                                   ·Walker    │
  │    Walker                                             │
  │      James                                            │
  │    Acme                                               │
  │    Peters                              Project    When│
  │  Reports                               ·James    ·03/13/89│
  │  Meetings                                             │
  │  Phone Calls                                     ·03/15/89│
  │  Staffing                                        ·03/24/89│
  │   ┌Ann                                                │
  │   └Jim                                                │
  └───────────────────────────────────────────────────────┘
                                              ·Peters
        on the Peters account.
      · Meeting with Ann and Ron Smith     »Ann           ·03/16/89
        Thursday.
  ══F1══╤══F2══╤══F3══╤══F4══╤══F5══╤══F6══╤══F7══╤══F8══╤══F9══╤══F10══
  Help  ║ Edit ║      ║      ║      ║      ║      ║      ║Accept║
```

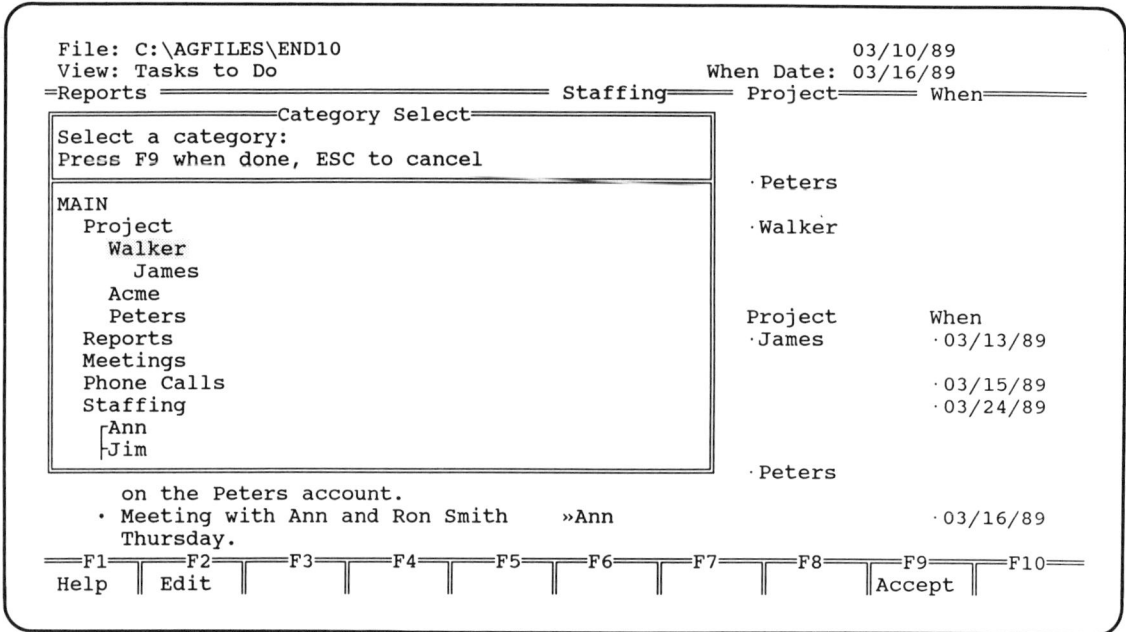

Fig. 11-1. *Using the Item Assign command to directly assign an item to the Walker category.*

lect the category to which the item is to be assigned and press F9. The assignment is made.

Multiple items can be assigned to a category by first marking the items using F7 (MARK) in the usual manner. Then, when you issue the Item Assign command, Agenda asks whether you want to assign the marked items or (after pressing GREY PLUS) only the currently highlighted item. When you specify all marked items, all of the items that are marked will be assigned to the category selected.

Agenda includes another way to directly change the category assignments of items. When any item is highlighted, pressing GREY PLUS will display the Assignment Profile box. Figure 11-2 shows the Assignment Profile box for the item most recently entered into the Tasks database. The asterisks in front of the categories in the column indicate each of the categories to which the item is currently assigned. A ''c'' follows the asterisk preceding the Ann category; this ''c'' indicates that the category assignment was made automatically by Agenda based upon a condition. The other assignments were made directly by the user.

Category assignments can be changed within the Assignment Profile box. To assign an item to a new category, move the highlight to that category and press SPACE. An asterisk appears indicating that the item has been assigned to the category. Items can also be removed, or unassigned, from categories. Highlight a category with an asterisk from which the item is to be removed and press SPACE. The asterisk disappears as the item is unassigned from that category. When you

```
File: C:\AGFILES\END10                            03/10/89   Prof
View: Tasks to Do                        When Date: 03/16/89
=Reports ==================================== Staffing===== Project===== When=====
        Walker project report and begin
        the pro┌════════════Assignment Profile═══════════════════════
        we have│Profile for: "Meeting with Ann and Ron Smith Thur..."
  • Meet wi│Press SPACE to assign to category, F9 to accept
        on the│
  • Call An│  ╫    MAIN
        Walker │        Project
        project│  *        Walker
               │             James
  Meetings     │           Acme
  • Meeting     │           Peters                                   /89
        James n│         Reports
  • Staff m     │  *      Meetings                                   /89
  • Meeting     │         Phone Calls                                /89
        3/24/89 │         Staffing
        results │ *c      ┌Ann
  • Meet wi     │          └Jim
        on the └═══════════════════════════════════════════════════
  • Meeting with Ann and Ron Smith    »Ann        ·Walker     ·03/16/89
        Thursday.
==F1════F2════┬═F3═══┬═F4═══┬═F5═══┬═F6═══┬═F7════┬═F8════┬═F9═══┬═F10══
 Help ║ Edit ║      ║      ║      ║      ║Assign ║       ║Accept ║
```

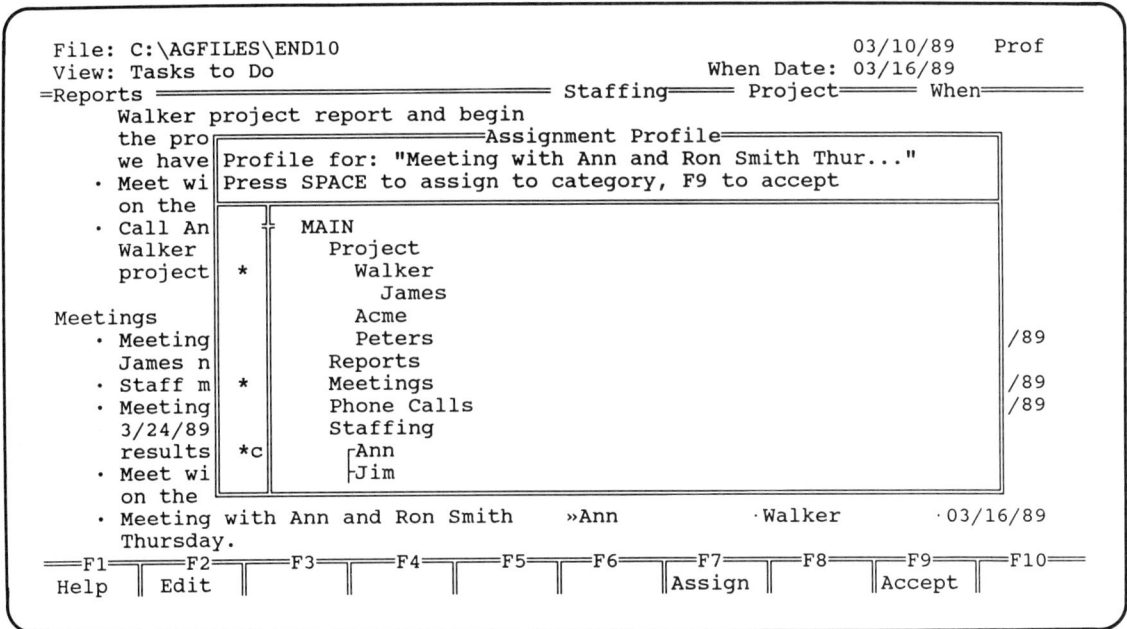

Fig. 11-2. *The Assignment Profile for the item just entered.*

have completed using the Assignment Profile box, press GREY MINUS or F9 to close the box.

The Item Assign command and the use of GREY PLUS to display the Assignment Profile box are alternative methods for directly assigning items to categories. The Assignment Profile box has the advantages of displaying the current assignments, allowing the removal of items from categories as well as assignments to categories, and allowing multiple category assignments to be made. The Item Assign command, on the other hand, might be easier to remember because it appears on the command menus and allows multiple marked items to be assigned to a category in a single operation.

## CONTROLLING AUTOMATIC ASSIGNMENTS

When an item is entered into the database or is edited, Agenda automatically assigns it to any categories referred to within the text of the item. This is a powerful feature that can save you a great deal of effort in assigning items to categories.

Agenda is not infallible, however, and will sometimes make incorrect assignments. It allows you to manage the automatic assignment of items to categories, specifying the extent to which the item text must correspond to categories before assignment is made, and requiring confirmation prior to the actual assignment.

The Tasks database raises several issues in the automatic assignment of items to categories. You have already encountered an instance in which an item referring to a person named Peter was incorrectly assigned to the Peters category. On the other hand, an item that says "Phone Jim," for example, would not automatically be assigned to the Phone Calls category. Changing the settings that control the automatic assignment of items to categories shows one method for managing these problems.

In the Tasks to Do view of the Tasks database, issue the Utility Preferences Auto-Assign command. The box with the automatic assignment preferences is displayed on the screen. To get references to "Phone" assigned to the Phone Calls category, move the highlight down to the *Required match strength:* setting. Press GREY PLUS to display the list of options. Highlight *Partial match* and press ENTER to select this setting.

In order to avoid the problem of erroneous category assignments, such as to the Peters category, require that Agenda confirm all automatic assignments before they are made. Move the highlight down to the *Confirm Assignments:* setting and press GREY PLUS. Highlight *Always* and press ENTER.

The Auto-Assignment Preferences box should now appear as shown in Fig. 11-3. Press F9 to accept the settings and return to the Tasks to Do view.

```
Auto-Assign  Date  Other  Environment  Update
Specify how auto-assignment works
═══════════════════════════════════════════════════════════════
Reports                          Staffing      Project      When
  · Meeting to discuss project for  ·George      ·James     ·03/13/89
    James next Monday.
  · Have An┌══════════Auto-Assignment Preferences══════════┐89
    Walker │                                               │
    the pro│ Enable text conditions:      Yes             │
    we have│   Match on:                  Item text        │
  · Meet wi│   Required match strength    Partial match    │
    on the │   Confirm assignments:       Always           │
  · Call An│   Skip text enclosed by:     " "              │
    Walker │   Ignore suffixes:           Yes             │
    project│   Ignore accents:            Yes             │
           │ Enable date conditions:      Yes             │
Meetings   │ Enable profile conditions:   Yes             │
  · Meeting│ Enable actions:              Yes             │89
    James n│                                               │
  · Staff m└═════════Press F9 when done, ESC to cancel═════┘89
  · Meeting with Ann and Ron Smith    ·Ann        ·Walker   ·03/16/89
    Thursday.
  · Meeting with executive committee                        ·03/24/89
══F1═══╤══F2══╤══F3══╤══F4══╤══F5══╤══F6══╤══F7══╤══F8═══╤══F9═══╤══F10══
Help   ║ Edit ║      ║      ║      ║      ║      ║Default║Accept ║
```

Fig. 11-3. *Using the Utility Preferences Auto-Assign command to change the manner in which items are assigned to categories.*

Now enter a new item to check the effects of these new settings. Move the highlight down to the last item in the Meetings section, press INS, and type in the following item:

Set up phone conference with Jim and Peter Wilson.

Press ENTER to complete the entry of the item. Note that the item has not yet been assigned to the Jim category in the Staffing column, nor to any other category. This is because you have instructed Agenda to require confirmation before making automatic assignments. Agenda displays a question mark in the upper-right corner of the screen, indicating that there are tentative category assignments for one or more items that have not yet been confirmed.

Confirmation is not automatically requested after each item is entered to avoid disturbing you as you enter a series of items. Instead, you must specify when you wish to confirm tentative category assignments. Do that now for the item just entered. Issue the Utility Questions command. A box on the screen shows Agenda's suggested category assignments for the "Set up phone conference" item. The first assignment is to the Jim category, a child category of the Staffing category. This is correct, so highlight this and press SPACE to assign the item to that category. An asterisk appears in the column, indicating that the assignment is to be made. The next assignment is to the Phone Calls category. The partial matching worked to allow Agenda to make this assignment. Highlight this and press SPACE again. On the other hand, the suggested assignment to the Peters category is not correct, so do not mark this one by pressing the SPACE. The Questions box should now appear as shown in Fig. 11-4. Press F9 to accept the choices and make the assignment of the items to the selected categories.

When you return to the view (Fig. 11-5), notice that the item has been assigned to the Jim category in the Staffing column, but has not been assigned to the Peters category in the Project column. If you scroll down to the bottom of the Phone Calls section, you will also see that the item has been assigned to the Phone Calls category, and is displayed there.

Further use of the Tasks database will be easier if you are not required to confirm category assignments for each item that is entered. Issue the Utility Preferences Auto-Assign command. Change the *Confirm Assignments:* setting to *Never*. Press F9 to accept the settings and return to the view.

```
Execute  Show  Questions  Trash  Compress  Preferences
Confirm suggested assignments
=Reports ============================ Staffing==== Project==== When=====
       we have a draft to work with.
   • Meet┌══════════════════════════Questions═══════════════════════════┐
     on t│ Suggested categories for "Set up phone conference wit..."   │
   • Call│ Press SPACE to assign to category, TAB for all categories   │
     Walk│                                                              │
     proj│  *  │  Staffing:Jim                                          │
         │  *  ┤  MAIN:Phone Calls                                      │
  Meetings│     │  Project:Peters                                       │
   • Meet│                                                           │89 │
     Jame└══════════════════════════════════════════════════════════┘
   • Staff meeting every Wednesday.      ·Staffing            ·03/15/89
   • Meeting with Ann and Ron Smith      ·Ann       ·Walker   ·03/16/89
     Thursday.
   • Meeting with executive committee                         ·03/24/89
     3/24/89 to go over quarterly
     results.
   • Meet with Jim to discuss report     ·Jim       ·Peters
     on the Peters account.
   • Set up phone conference with Jim
     and Peter Wilson.
══F1══╥══F2══╥══F3══╥══F4══╥══F5══╥══F6══╥══F7══╥══F8══╥══F9═══╥══F10══
 Help ║     ║     ║     ║     ║     ║     ║     ║Accept ║
```

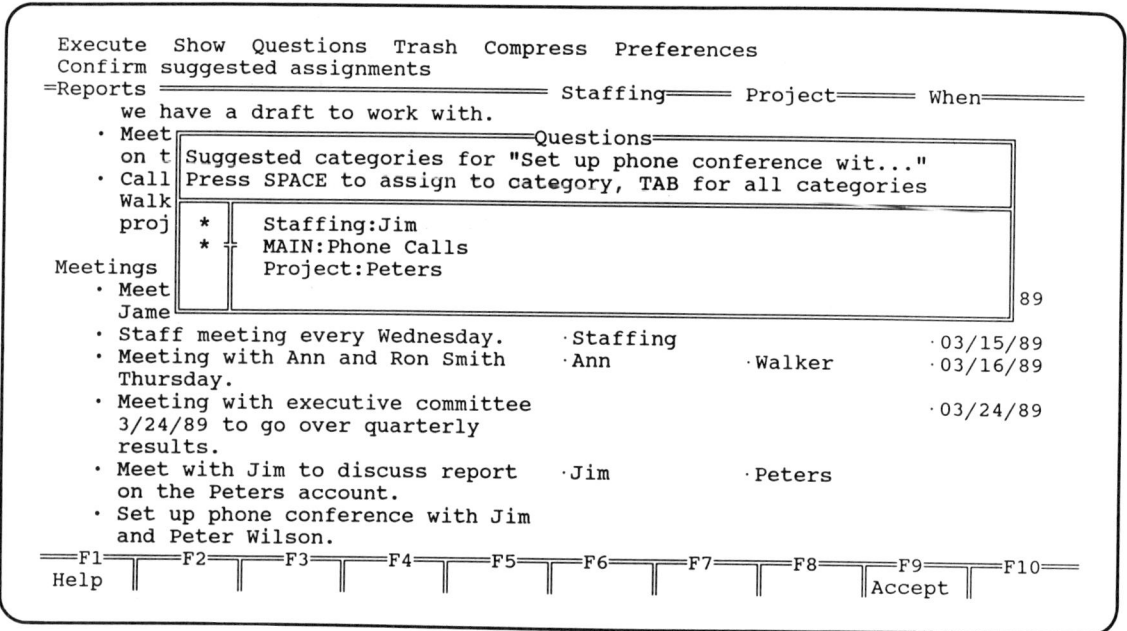

Fig. 11-4. *Using the Utility Questions command to confirm tentative category assignments.*

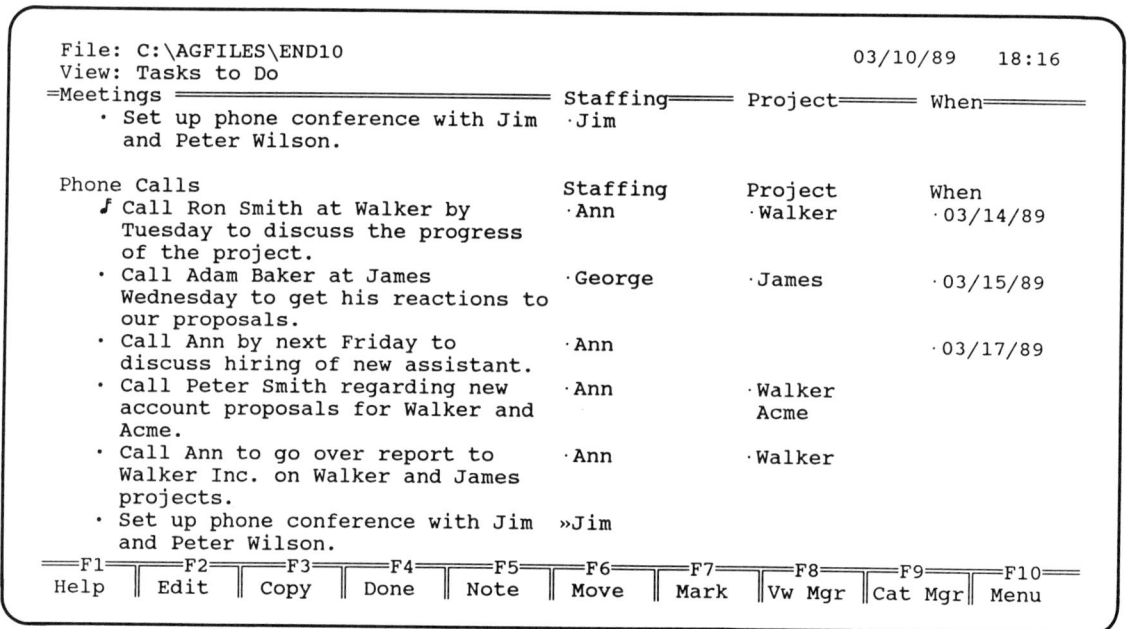

```
 File: C:\AGFILES\END10                        03/10/89   18:16
 View: Tasks to Do
=Meetings ============================= Staffing==== Project==== When=====
   • Set up phone conference with Jim   ·Jim
     and Peter Wilson.

 Phone Calls                            Staffing    Project     When
   ♪ Call Ron Smith at Walker by        ·Ann        ·Walker     ·03/14/89
     Tuesday to discuss the progress
     of the project.
   • Call Adam Baker at James           ·George     ·James      ·03/15/89
     Wednesday to get his reactions to
     our proposals.
   • Call Ann by next Friday to         ·Ann                    ·03/17/89
     discuss hiring of new assistant.
   • Call Peter Smith regarding new     ·Ann        ·Walker
     account proposals for Walker and               Acme
     Acme.
   • Call Ann to go over report to      ·Ann        ·Walker
     Walker Inc. on Walker and James
     projects.
   • Set up phone conference with Jim   »Jim
     and Peter Wilson.
══F1══╥══F2══╥══F3══╥══F4══╥══F5══╥══F6══╥══F7══╥══F8══╥══F9═══╥══F10══
 Help ║ Edit║ Copy║ Done║ Note║ Move║ Mark║Vw Mgr║Cat Mgr║ Menu
```

Fig. 11-5. *The Tasks to Do view showing the category assignments.*

Agenda attempts to give you the greatest possible control over the automatic assignment of items to categories. The settings can be changed using the Utility Preference Auto-Assign command. The major setting, *Enable Text Conditions:*, allows you to specify whether Agenda is to perform *any* automatic assignment of items to categories. Changing this to *No* causes Agenda to stop automatically assigning items to categories. The indented settings disappear, because there is no automatic assignment to control.

The *Match on:* setting is used to specify which text Agenda examines in determining whether to assign an item to a category. The default is to make the assignment based only on the text of the item. This can be changed so that assignments are made based both on the text of the item and any note attached to the item, or just on the text in the note.

Agenda automatically assigns items to categories by attempting to match existing category names to the text of the item (or possibly the note). With the *Required match strength:* setting you specify the degree of the match required for Agenda to make an automatic assignment. The *Exact* setting requires matches to all words in the category name. The *Partial* and *Minimal* settings reduces the extent of the match required before an assignment is made. *Partial* requires that half of the words in the category name be matched, and *Minimal* requires that only one word in the category name be matched.

The *Confirm Assignments:* setting specifies whether or not Agenda will require the confirmation of tentative assignments with the Utility Questions command before actually making those assignments. The choices are *Always, Never,* and *Sometimes* (which requires confirmation only for less than perfect matches).

If you enclose part of the text of an item in double quotes, Agenda will ignore this text in making automatic assignments. Thus, if you know that certain words would trigger an incorrect assignment, you can avoid problems by surrounding the words with the double quotes. The *Skip text enclosed by:* setting allows you to change from double quote marks to other characters for designating text to be ignored.

In attempting to match category names to text, Agenda normally ignores suffixes and accents. This can be changed with the final two settings governing the automatic assignment to categories based on the text of the items or notes.

When you instruct Agenda to require confirmation before making automatic assignments, you must use the Utility Questions command to confirm the assignments. Agenda saves the tentative assignments on all items that you have not yet confirmed. When you give the Utility Questions command, a box is displayed with the initial text of the item (to identify the item in question) and Agenda's suggested category assignments. You can confirm an individual category assignment by highlighting it and pressing SPACE, which places an asterisk in the column. If you change your mind, press SPACE again to remove the asterisk.

If all of the suggested category assignments are acceptable (which is likely to be the case most often), press TAB to accept the assignments for all categories. Function key F9 accepts the settings and makes any specified assignments for the item. If tentative assignments are pending for more than one item after F9 is pressed, the Questions box for the next item appears. Just continue working through until you have addressed the tentative assignments for all of the items.

## USING CONDITIONS TO ASSIGN ITEMS

Two additional features for making assignments as well as performing other operations are conditions and actions. Conditions and actions are closely related in that they depend on category assignments and can cause other operations to be performed automatically. The difference between an action and a condition is in the direction of the causation.

When a *condition* is attached to a category, it means that *if* an item meets the condition, *then* the item will be assigned automatically to the category to which the condition is attached. When an *action* is attached to a category, it means that *if* an item is assigned to that category, *then* some further action will automatically take place involving that item. This section of the chapter focuses on conditions and the next section discusses actions.

Conditions are special criteria associated with specific categories. They are used to cause the automatic assignment of items to those categories. When a condition criterion is met by an item, that item is assigned to the category with the condition. For example, Ann is to be responsible for all of the tasks associated with the Walker project. The Ann category can be given the condition that any item assigned to the Walker category is to be automatically assigned to the Ann category.

Agenda provides for three different kinds of conditions. *Text conditions* cause the assignment of items to categories based upon the text of items or notes. *Profile conditions* cause assignment to categories based upon the items' assignment to other categories. *Date conditions* cause items to be assigned to categories if they have a date that meets specified criteria. All three types of conditions and their uses are explained in the following pages.

### Text Conditions

Text conditions let you extend the automatic assignment of items to categories based upon the contents of items (and, if specified, notes). Text conditions cause text references other than the category name to trigger the automatic assignment to a category. Text conditions can be employed, for example, to use synonyms of the category name as the basis for automatic assignment.

In the first section of this chapter, an item was entered referring to a meeting with Ron Smith, who is a representative of Walker. Therefore, the item was manually assigned to the Walker category. However, since Ron Smith represents Walker, any item referring to Ron Smith should always be assigned to the Walker project category. You can make Agenda do this with a text condition.

In the Tasks database, enter the Category Manager by pressing F9 (CAT MGR). The text condition is to cause the automatic assignment of items to the Walker category, so begin by highlighting that category. Press F2 (EDIT) to edit—actually make additions to—the category name. When the category name Walker appears on the second line of the screen for editing, press END to move the cursor to the end of the name and type in the following text to be inserted at the end:

```
;Ron Smith
```

The text begins with the semicolon. Press ENTER to complete the editing. The complete entry for the Walker category should now be as follows:

```
Walker;Ron Smith
```

The addition of Ron Smith after the semicolon means that any item that is entered or edited with the text "Ron Smith" will automatically be assigned to the Walker category. The demonstration of this automatic assignment is deferred until a profile condition has also been added to the database.

Text conditions are included in the database simply by editing the category name, adding a semicolon followed by the other text for which matching text in an item will trigger an automatic assignment. Multiple text conditions can be added by likewise including further text conditions preceded by semicolons. The text conditions are displayed with the category names in the category hierarchy.

Category names themselves are text conditions. That is, item text that matches the category names will produce the automatic assignment. Additional text conditions following semicolons merely represent additional possibilities for matches that would cause assignment to the categories.

The preferences that are set using Utility Preferences Auto-Assign govern assignment for all text conditions, both the category names and any further text conditions following semicolons. The text to be matched on (notes or items), the strength of the match needed, a confirmation requirement, and all of the other settings apply to the text conditions you add to the category names.

Text conditions (and the other conditions) normally produce the assignment of items to categories only when an item is entered or edited. The entry of new conditions will not change or add to the category assignments of existing items. Agenda does have a special command that allows conditions to be applied retroactively to already entered items. This is described in the part of this section titled ''Executing Conditions.''

## Profile Conditions

Profile conditions cause the assignment of items to a category based upon the assignment of the items to other categories in the database. For example, a profile condition for the Ann category can be used to automatically assign any item assigned to the Walker category to the Ann category as well.

You will be entering a profile condition to automatically assign items assigned to the Walker category to the Ann category. In the Category Manager of the Tasks database, highlight the Ann category. Enter the Condition Profile command from the Category Manager to create this profile condition. A box appears on the screen informing you that you are setting a profile condition for Ann. Move the highlight up to the Walker category (the category now appears as ''Walker;Ron Smith''

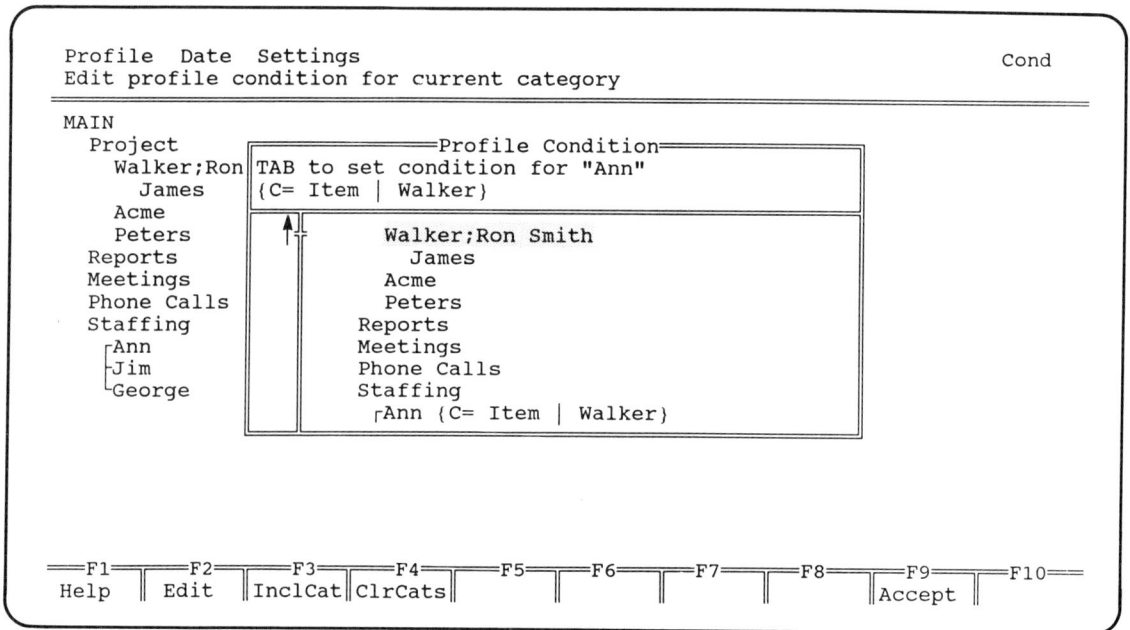

```
 Profile  Date  Settings                                      Cond
 Edit profile condition for current category

 MAIN
   Project            ┌════════════Profile Condition═══════════┐
     Walker;Ron       │TAB to set condition for "Ann"          │
         James        │(C= Item | Walker)                      │
     Acme             ├────────────────────────────────────────┤
     Peters           │ ↑┬        Walker;Ron Smith             │
   Reports            │  ┴           James                     │
   Meetings           │              Acme                      │
   Phone Calls        │              Peters                    │
   Staffing           │            Reports                     │
     ┌Ann             │            Meetings                    │
     ├Jim             │            Phone Calls                 │
     └George          │            Staffing                    │
                      │              ┌Ann (C= Item | Walker)   │
                      └────────────────────────────────────────┘



 ══F1═══╤══F2═══╤══F3═══╤══F4═══╤══F5═══╤══F6═══╤══F7═══╤══F8═══╤══F9═══╤══F10══
  Help  ║ Edit  ║InclCat║ClrCats║       ║       ║       ║       ║Accept ║
```

Fig. 11-6. *Setting a profile condition to assign items that are assigned to the Walker category to the Ann category.*

```
File: C:\AGFILES\END10
Category Manager

MAIN
  Project
    Walker;Ron Smith
      James
    Acme
    Peters
  Reports
  Meetings
  Phone Calls
  Staffing
   ┌Ann {C= Item │ Walker}
   ├Jim
   └George




═F1═══╤══F2══╤═══F3════╤═══F4═══╤══F5═══╤══F6══╤═══F7═══╤══F8═══╤══F9══╤═F10══
 Help │ Edit │Cpy C/A│Clr C/A│ Note │ Move │Prm (◄)│Dem (►)│To View│ Menu
```

Fig. 11-7. *The display of the category hierarchy showing the text and profile conditions.*

with the addition of the text condition in the preceding section). Press TAB once to set the condition that if an item is assigned to the Walker category, it is also to be assigned to the Ann category. A small arrow pointing up appears in the column to the left of the Walker category. Figure 11-6 shows the Profile Condition box as it appears at this point. Now press F9 to accept the settings and create the profile condition.

Figure 11-7 shows the category hierarchy with the text and profile conditions entered. The profile condition is displayed in the category hierarchy following the Ann category as follows:

{C= Item ¦ Walker}

This means that the condition exists (the C) to assign the item to this category if it is assigned to the Walker category. The text condition for the Walker category is indicated by the entry

;Ron Smith

following the category name. That means that any items containing the text "Ron Smith" will be assigned to the category.

Now see how the text and profile conditions operate. Return to the Tasks to Do view by pressing F9 (VIEW). If necessary, use F8 (VIEW MGR) to select the appropriate view. Move the highlight down to the last item in the Meetings section and press INS to enter this new item:

Check with Ron Smith on meeting time.

Press ENTER. When this item is entered, several category assignments are made automatically, as can be seen in Fig. 11-8. The item refers to Ron Smith, and thus it is assigned to the Walker project category because of the text condition that was entered. Because the item is assigned to the Walker category, it is also automatically assigned to the Ann category by the profile condition that was entered. Both of these assignments can be seen in the appropriate columns.

To enter a profile condition, begin by highlighting the category to which the condition is to be applied—the category to which the automatic assignment is to be made. You can highlight the category while in the Category Manager and then issue the Condition Profile command. Alternatively, you can highlight the category in a view and enter the Category Management Condition Profile command. In both instances, the Profile Condition box is displayed on the screen.

In the Profile condition box, highlight the category for which the assignment is to be the condition. Pressing the TAB key once displays an arrow pointing up,

```
  File: C:\AGFILES\END10                                    03/10/89   18:20
  View: Tasks to Do
 =Reports ==============================  Staffing==  Project=====  When=====
        on the Peters account.
      · Call Ann to go over report to     ·Ann         ·Walker
        Walker Inc. on Walker and James
        projects.

   Meetings                               Staffing     Project       When
      · Meeting to discuss project for    ·George      ·James        ·03/13/89
        James next Monday.
      · Staff meeting every Wednesday.    ·Staffing                  ·03/15/89
      · Meeting with Ann and Ron Smith    ·Ann          ·Walker      ·03/16/89
        Thursday.
      · Meeting with executive committee                             ·03/24/89
        3/24/89 to go over quarterly
        results.
      · Meet with Jim to discuss report   ·Jim          ·Peters
        on the Peters account.
      · Set up phone conference with Jim  ·Jim
        and Peter Wilson.
      · Check with Ron Smith on meeting   »Ann          ·Walker
        time.
 ==F1=====T===F2===T===F3===T==F4===T===F5===T==F6===T==F7===T===F8===T==F9===T==F10==
   Help  ║  Edit  ║  Copy  ║  Done ║  Note ║  Move ║ Mark ║ Vw Mgr║Cat Mgr║ Menu
```

Fig. 11-8. *The Tasks to Do view showing the automatic assignment of the new "Check with Ron Smith" item to the Walker and Ann categories.*

which means that an item will be assigned to the category with the condition if the item is assigned to the highlighted category. Pressing TAB a second time displays an arrow pointing down, which means that an item will be assigned to the category with the condition if the item is *not* assigned to the highlighted category. Pressing TAB a third time eliminates the arrow and any assignment based upon the highlighted category.

You can include more than one category in a profile condition. In such cases, the item must be assigned (or not assigned, if specified with the down-arrow) to each of the categories included if the item is to be automatically assigned to the category to which the profile condition is directed. That is, the category entries in a profile condition are assumed to be connected by logical ANDs. All of the individual category conditions must be met for the entire condition to be met. If you need to assign items to a category if they are either assigned to one category or another, use action profiles.

Profile conditions may be disabled using the Utility Preferences Auto-Assign command. When this is done, the conditions are not applied to items and do not produce automatic assignments.

Profile and date conditions and all actions result in the condition or action being displayed in curly braces following the category name in the category hierarchy. The Category Manager has three function keys for manipulating these conditions and actions. Function key F3 (CPY C/A) allows the copying of the condition or action to another category. Highlight the category with the condition or action to be copied. Press F3. Then move the highlight to the category to which the condition or action is to be copied.

Function key F4 (CLR C/A) deletes the conditions and actions for the highlighted category. Function key ALT-F4 (HIDE C/A) turns off the display of conditions and actions in the category hierarchy if they are currently being displayed, and displays the conditions and actions if they are currently hidden.

As with text conditions, profile conditions normally are applied only to items as they are entered or edited. Procedures for applying conditions after the fact are described later.

## Date Conditions

Date conditions are used to assign an item to a category if the item meets a specified criterion for one of Agenda's three dates. Date conditions can be used to automatically create categories based upon dates. These categories can then be used in views. Using date conditions to create new categories might sometimes be an alternative to using a date filter in a view.

Assume that in the Tasks database you want to work with all tasks that have to be done during the month of March. You can use a date condition to assign items with When Dates in March to a new March Activities category. Note that depending upon the dates on which you created your Tasks database and the When Dates assigned to the various items, you will probably choose to use another month.

Begin by creating the March Activities category and a new view to display the items assigned to this category. While in a view, issue the View New command to create a new view. Type in March Activities as the name for the view and also type in March Activities as the name of the category to be included as a section in the view. Press F9 to create the view and the new category. The March Activities category currently has no items assigned to it, so no items are displayed currently in this view. When items are added later, you will want to examine their March When Dates, so use the Category Column New command to enter a When Date column. In the New Column box, change the Column Type setting to When Date and press F9 to add the column.

Now create the date condition. Enter the Category Manager by pressing F9 (CAT MGR). Highlight the March Activities category. Issue the Condition Date command. Press GREY PLUS to see the options for the *Date Type:* setting and select *When date.* Since items with When Dates in the month of March are to be included, set the Start Date at 3/1/89 and set the End Date at 3/31/89. The Date Condition box should

```
 Profile  Date  Settings
 Edit date condition for current category
══════════════════════════════════════════════
 MAIN
   March Activities
   Project
     Walker;Ron Smith
       James
     Acme
     Peter ┌──────────────────Date Condition═══════════════╗
  Reports │                                               │
  Meeting │  Date type:      When date                    │
  Phone C │  Start date:     03/01/89                     │
  Staffin │  End date:       03/31/89                     │
   ┌Ann ( │  Include items:  In date range                │
   ├Jim    │                                               │
   └Georg └═══════════Press F9 when done, ESC to cancel═══╝


══F1══╤══F2══╤══F3══╤══F4══╤══F5══╤══F6══╤══F7══╤══F8════╤══F9═══╤══F10══
 Help │ Edit │      │      │      │      │      │Default│Accept│
```

Fig. 11-9. *Setting a date condition for the assignment of items with When Dates in March to the March Activities category.*

appear as shown in Fig. 11-9. Press F9 to accept the settings and create the date condition.

The date condition is displayed in the category hierarchy following the March Activities category as shown:

$$\{C = \text{Item} \mid W \ 03/01/89\text{-}03/31/89\}$$

This is a condition for which an item is to be assigned to the category if a When Date (specified by the W) of the item falls in the range from March 1 through March 31, 1989.

Return to the March Activities view by pressing F9 (VIEW). Nothing has happened. No items are shown in the view as being assigned to the March Activities category. New items entered with When Dates in March will be assigned automatically, but any existing items will not be assigned to the new category. The assignment of current items with When Dates in March requires an additional operation which is described in the following part of this section.

To enter a date condition, first highlight the category to which the condition is to be applied, either in the Category Manager or in a view. In the Category Manager, give the Condition Date command. In a view, give the Category Management Condition Date command. Both display the Date Condition box. Select the date—Entry, When, or Done—on which the condition is to be based. Enter the beginning and ending dates. These entries can include relative dates. Relative dates would result in the condition changing as the current date advances. Leaving no entry for the beginning date means include the earliest dates; leaving no entry for the ending date means include the latest dates.

Then choose whether items are to be assigned to the category if the date selected falls within the specified range or if it falls outside the specified range. Pressing F9 accepts the settings and creates the date condition.

Like the other conditions, Date conditions can be disabled using the Utility Preference Auto-Assign command. They can also be copied, deleted, and hidden using the function keys in the Category Manager. Normally, Date conditions are applied and assignments are made only when items are entered and edited.

## Executing Conditions

Conditions are normally evaluated to assign items to categories only when items are entered or edited. Items entered prior to the creation of a condition will not be assigned automatically to the category even when they meet the condition. However, the Utility Execute command can be used to ''force'' Agenda to go through previously entered items and automatically assign them to a category if they meet the condition.

All items in the Tasks database that have When Dates in March are to be assigned to the March Activities category. That is, each item with a March When Date satisfies the condition that will result in the item being assigned to the March Activities category. Be sure that you are in the March Activities view so that you can see the consequences of the assignments you will be making.

To begin the process of evaluating all items in the database for possible assignment to the March Activities category, enter the Utility Execute command. An Execute box appears on the screen. Since you want to evaluate the condition for all items, leave the first setting unchanged. Move the highlight down to the *Categories to check:* setting. You only need to check the March Activities category, not the entire hierarchy, so you need to change the default setting. Press GREY PLUS, highlight the *Partial hierarchy* setting, and press ENTER. A *Family:* setting is now displayed in the box. Move the highlight down across from the *Family:* setting, press GREY PLUS, highlight the March Activities category, and press ENTER. The Execute box should now appear as shown in Fig. 11-10. Press F9 to accept the settings and evaluate all items for the date condition on the March Activities category. (An execute message will appear on the screen, indicating Agenda's progress in executing the command.)

You are returned to the March Activities view. All of the items with When Dates in the month of March have been assigned to the March Activities category and are displayed in that section. The results are shown in Fig. 11-11.

You use the Utility Execute command to apply conditions to previously entered items. The Execute box contains the settings for specifying the items and categories for which conditions are to be evaluated (checked to see if they satisfy the condition). In addition to providing for the evaluation of all items, the *Evaluate conditions for:* setting allows you to restrict the evaluation to just the current item, to marked items, or to items in the current section or view.

Likewise, you can evaluate the conditions attached to all categories in the category hierarchy or only to those categories in a specific family. The first level of choice is provided by the *Categories to check:* setting, where you choose to evaluate either the entire hierarchy or a partial hierarchy. If the *Partial hierarchy* option is chosen, a further choice is provided to specify the family to be evaluated. The category hierarchy is displayed and you select a category. Conditions at-

```
Execute  Show  Questions  Trash  Compress  Preferences
Evaluate conditions/actions
══════════════════════════════════════════════════════════════
March Activities                                          When

              ┌══════════════════Execute══════════════════┐
              │                                            │
              │ Evaluate conditions for:   All items       │
              │ Categories to check:       Partial hierarchy│
              │           Family:          March Activities │
              │                                            │
              │ Perform actions:  For new assignments only │
              │                                            │
              └═════════Press F9 when done, ESC to cancel══┘



══F1══╤══F2══╤══F3══╤══F4══╤══F5══╤══F6══╤══F7══╤══F8═══╤══F9═══╤══F10══
 Help ║ Edit ║      ║      ║      ║      ║      ║Default║Accept ║
```

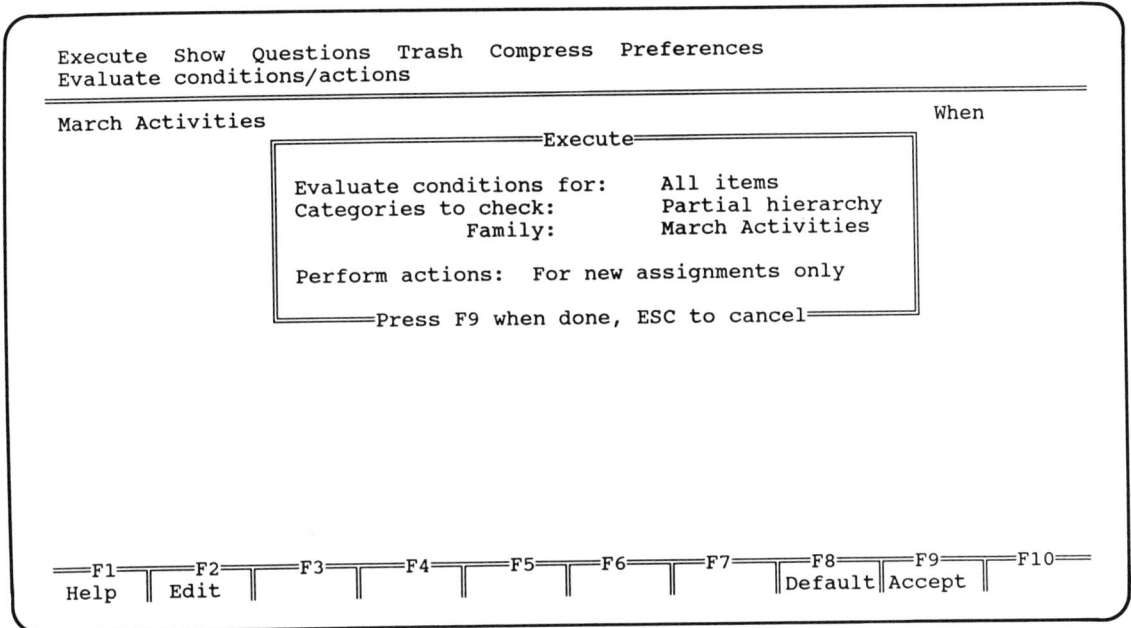

Fig. 11-10. *Using the Utility Execute command to assign existing items with When Dates in March to the March Activities category.*

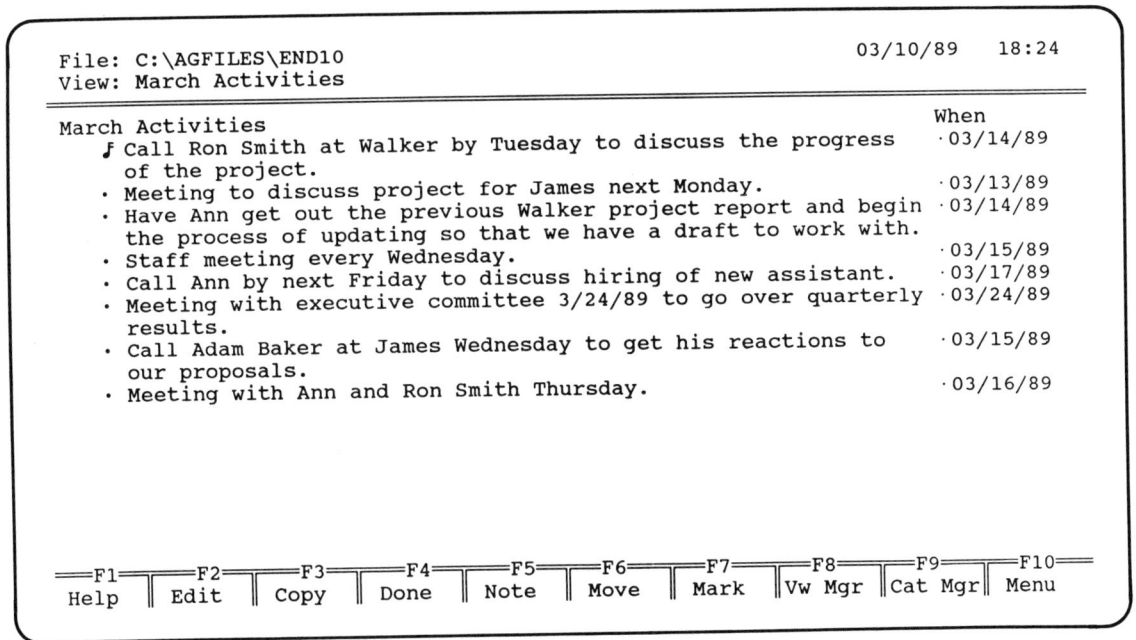

```
File: C:\AGFILES\END10                      03/10/89   18:24
View: March Activities
══════════════════════════════════════════════════════════════
March Activities                                          When
   ♪ Call Ron Smith at Walker by Tuesday to discuss the progress  ·03/14/89
     of the project.
   · Meeting to discuss project for James next Monday.            ·03/13/89
   · Have Ann get out the previous Walker project report and begin ·03/14/89
     the process of updating so that we have a draft to work with.
   · Staff meeting every Wednesday.                               ·03/15/89
   · Call Ann by next Friday to discuss hiring of new assistant.  ·03/17/89
   · Meeting with executive committee 3/24/89 to go over quarterly ·03/24/89
     results.
   · Call Adam Baker at James Wednesday to get his reactions to   ·03/15/89
     our proposals.
   · Meeting with Ann and Ron Smith Thursday.                     ·03/16/89



══F1══╤══F2══╤══F3══╤══F4══╤══F5══╤══F6══╤══F7══╤══F8═══╤══F9═══╤══F10══
 Help ║ Edit ║ Copy ║ Done ║ Note ║ Move ║ Mark ║Vw Mgr║Cat Mgr║ Menu
```

Fig. 11-11. *The March Activities view showing the items assigned to the March Activities category after the execution of the Utility Execute command.*

tached to the family you select, that is, to the chosen category and to any of its child categories, will be evaluated. When the settings in the Execute box have been completed, press F9 to accept the settings and apply the conditions.

In using the Utility Execute command, it is generally a good idea to limit the evaluation of conditions to only those categories for which you really require such evaluation. This is usually preferable to evaluating conditions for all of the categories in the hierarchy for two major reasons. First, for even a modest-sized database, evaluating conditions can take some time. It is much quicker to evaluate conditions just for a single category or for a small family of categories than for all of the categories in a large category hierarchy.

The second reason for restricting the evaluation of conditions to specific categories is to avoid making automatic assignments that you do not want made. Remember that the evaluation of conditions includes all forms of conditions, including text conditions, and that text conditions include the matching of the category name itself.

In the Tasks database, you encountered the problem that the person's name ''Peter'' was inadvertently assigned to the Peters project category. In one case you deleted the automatic assignment; in another you avoided the assignment by requiring confirmation. If conditions were evaluated for all of the categories in the Tasks database, items referring to a person named Peter would again be automatically assigned to the Peters category. By restricting evaluation of conditions only to the March Activities category of interest, this problem is avoided.

## USING ACTIONS

An action indicates that any item assigned to the category to which the action is attached is to be subject to some further operations. Agenda includes two types of actions, *profile actions* and *special actions*. Profile actions are used to automatically assign items to additional categories. Special actions can perform operations involving an item. The use of both types of actions is illustrated in this section.

### Profile Actions

When a profile action is attached to a category, it specifies that when an item is assigned to that category, the item will be assigned automatically to the additional specified categories. Thus, profile actions are another tool for controlling the automatic assignment of items to categories.

The Peters project is Jim's responsibility, so all items assigned to the Peters project should also be assigned to Jim. Use a profile action to make such assignments automatically.

In the Tasks database, enter the Category Manager by pressing F9 (CAT MGR). The profile action is to be created for the Peters project category, so begin by highlighting that category in the hierarchy. Issue the Action Profile command and a box appears to allow the selection of the categories to which items assigned to the Peters category also should be assigned. Move the highlight down to the Jim category and press TAB to set the action. The Profile Action box should appear as shown in Fig. 11-12. Now press F9 to accept the setting and create the profile action.

The category hierarchy displays the newly created action after the Peters category with the following entry:

<A= Jim>

This indicates that items assigned to the Peters category are also to be assigned to the Jim category. (The entry of a new item to demonstrate the operation of this profile action will be deferred until later, after the special action has also been created.)

To begin creating a profile action, you highlight the category for which the assignment of items is to trigger the subsequent action. If you highlight the category in the Category Manager, issue the Action Profile command. If you highlight

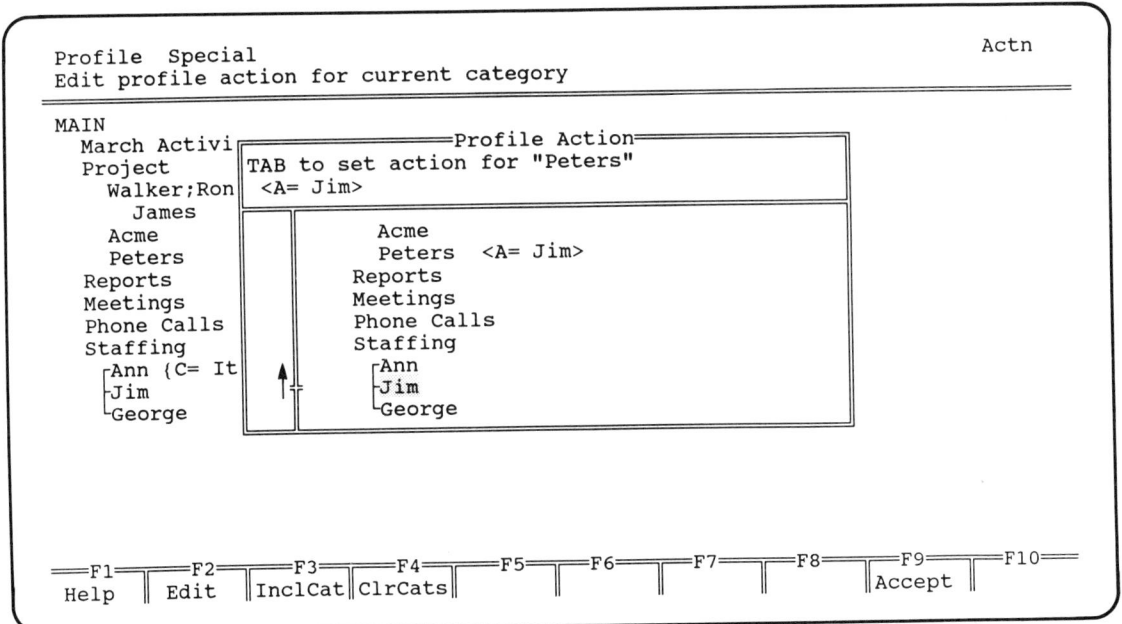

Fig. 11-12. *Setting a profile action to assign items assigned to the Peters category to the Jim category.*

the category in a view, issue the Category Management Action Profile command. In both cases, the Profile Action box is displayed, in which you can specify those categories for which assignments are to be changed based upon the assignment of items to the initial category.

To cause an item to be assigned to a category if it is assigned to the initial category, highlight the category to which the assignment is to be made and press TAB. An up-arrow appears in the column, indicating that the action will automatically assign items to this category when they are assigned to the category with which the action is associated.

Actions can also be used to unassign items from a category once they are assigned to the action category. Highlight the category for which the item is to be unassigned and press TAB twice. A down-arrow appears in the column, indicating that the action will unassign items automatically from this category when they are assigned to the category with which the action is associated. Press TAB a third time to remove the down-arrow and any action for the highlighted category.

A profile action can be used to change assignment to several categories. While in the Profile Action box, you highlight each category in turn and press TAB once or twice to indicate that items are to be either assigned or unassigned to the category. When you have completed the action settings, press F9 to accept the settings and create the action.

Agenda's default is to apply actions to items only as they are entered or edited. While in a view, the Utility Execute command may be used to change this default. The last setting, *Perform actions:*, may be changed from its default, *For new assignments only*, to the alternative value, *For new & old assignments*. The latter option causes actions to be executed for all items assigned to categories with actions. This applies to both profile actions and to special actions, discussed later.

Profile conditions and profile actions both cause items to be assigned automatically to categories based upon their assignment to other categories. A profile condition was attached to the Ann category specifying that any items assigned to the Walker category would also be assigned to the Ann category. A profile action was attached to the Peters category specifying that any item assigned to that category would also be assigned to the Jim category. The only difference was that the profile condition was attached to the category to which the new assignment was to be made, while the profile action was attached to the category that would initiate the assignment.

Simple, one-category profile conditions and actions produce similar results, and you can choose either one. The choice might be based simply upon the way you think about the relationship. For example, if you are focusing on the person to whom all items that are assigned to a project category should be assigned, you might choose to use a profile *condition*. On the other hand, if you are focusing on the items assigned to a specific project category and the person to whom those projects should be assigned, you might choose to use a profile *action*.

The profile conditions and actions differ in more complex situations. A complex profile condition can make the assignment of an item to the category conditional on the assignment and unassignment of the item to numbers of categories. A profile action can cause assignments based only upon the assignment of an item to the category to which the action is attached.

On the other hand, more complex profile actions can be used to cause the assignment or unassignment of items to multiple categories. By their very nature, profile conditions can only cause the assignment of items to the single category to which the condition is attached. The combination of profile conditions and actions allows nearly any conceivable pattern of automatic assignments to be made based upon existing category assignments. (The applications for actions and conditions are illustrated later, in the applications chapters.)

## Special Actions

A *special action* is an operation that can be performed with, or to, an item based upon the item's assignment to a category. The options for special actions are to discard items, mark items as done, set When Dates for items, and export items.

You are competing for a new project, the Baxter project, and the major presentation will be held on March 20. You will be entering new items to be assigned to the Baxter project and want all of those items to be automatically given a When Date of 3/20/89. You will use a special action to accomplish this.

First, create the new category for the Baxter project. In the Category Manager, move the highlight to the Peters category, press INS, type in

Baxter

and press ENTER. Baxter is created as a child category of the Project category.

With Baxter still highlighted, issue the Action Special command. In the Special Action box, press GREY PLUS, highlight *Set When Date:*, and press ENTER. Move the highlight down to the *Date:* setting, type in

3/20/89

and press ENTER. The Special Action box appears as shown in Fig. 11-13. Press F9 to accept the settings and create the special action.

```
Profile  Special
Edit special action for current category
═══════════════════════════════════════════════════════════════════
MAIN
  March Activities {C= Item | W 03/01/89-03/31/89}
  Project
    Walker;Ron Smith
     Jam┌─────────────────────────Special Action═══════════════┐
    Acme│                                                       │
    Peter│   Special action:   Set When date                   │
    Baxte│      Date:          03/20/89                         │
   Reports│                                                     │
   Meeting│                                                     │
   Phone C└─────────────Press F9 when done, ESC to cancel═══════┘
  Staffing
    ┌Ann {C= Item | Walker)
    ├Jim
    └George




══F1══╤══F2══╤══F3══╤══F4══╤══F5══╤══F6══╤══F7══╤══F8══════╤══F9════╤══F10══
Help  ║ Edit ║      ║      ║      ║      ║      ║Default║Accept║
```

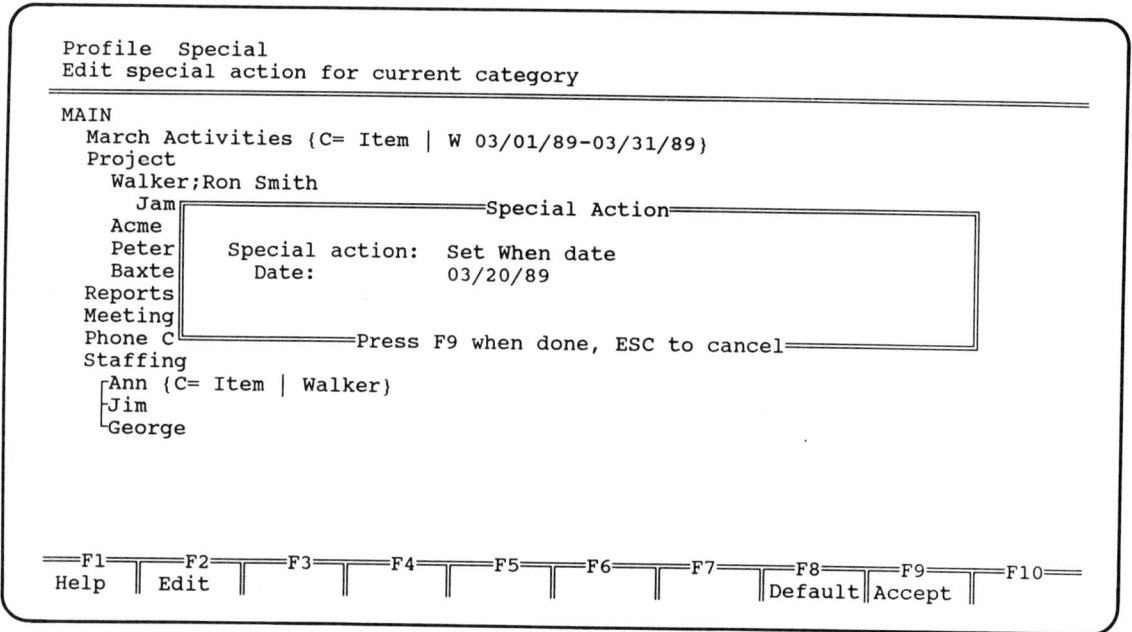

Fig. 11-13. *Setting a special action to assign the When Date of 3/20/89 for items assigned to the Baxter category.*

Figure 11-14 shows the category hierarchy with the profile and special actions entered. The special action to automatically set the When Date is indicated by the entry

<A= When>

following the Baxter category.

Now enter items to see the operation of the profile and special items. Return to a view by pressing F9 (VIEW). If necessary, switch to the Tasks to Do view using F8 (VIEW MGR). Move the highlight down to the last item in the Reports section, press INS to enter a new item, and type in the following text:

Do status report for Peters.

Press ENTER and note that the item is assigned automatically not only to the Peters category in the Project column but also to the Jim category in the Staffing column because of the profile action you have entered.

Press INS to insert an additional item and type in this text:

Prepare proposal for the Baxter project.

```
  File: C:\AGFILES\END10
  Category Manager

MAIN
  March Activities {C= Item | W 03/01/89-03/31/89}
  Project
    Walker;Ron Smith
      James
    Acme
    Peters   <A= Jim>
    Baxter   <A= When>
  Reports
  Meetings
  Phone Calls
  Staffing
   ┌Ann {C= Item | Walker}
   ├Jim
   └George




 ══F1═══╤══F2═══╤══F3═══╤══F4═══╤══F5═══╤══F6══╤══F7═══╤══F8═══╤══F9═══╤══F10══
  Help  ║ Edit  ║Cpy C/A║Clr C/A║ Note  ║ Move ║Prm (←)║Dem (→)║To View║ Menu
```

Fig. 11-14. *The category hierarchy showing the profile and special actions.*

Press ENTER. The item is automatically assigned to the Baxter project, of course, but it is also automatically given the When Date of 3/20/89 because of the special action. The results of these assignments are shown in Fig. 11-15.

A special action can be added to a category when you are either in a view or in the Category Manager. To create a special action, you first highlight the category. In the Category Manager, you issue the Action Special command; in a view, you issue the Category Management Action Special command. In either case, the Special Action box is displayed.

The primary choice to be made is the type of action to be performed on items that are assigned to the category selected. Highlight the *Special action:* setting and press GREY PLUS to see the list of options. The *Discard item* choice does exactly that: items assigned to the category are discarded from the database. Needless to say, the category will not be accumulating additional new items.

The *Mark item as done* selection causes the date on which items are assigned to the category to be set as the Done Date. This assignment could be useful for keeping track of completed tasks. The use of the *Set When Date:* action has already been illustrated.

Finally, the *Export item* selection causes items assigned to the category to be exported to a structured text file. Items may be discarded or not when they

```
File: C:\AGFILES\END10                                    03/10/89   18:28
View: Tasks to Do                              When Date: 03/20/89
```

| Reports | Staffing | Project | When |
|---|---|---|---|
| · Meeting to discuss project for James next Monday. | ·Ann | ·James | ·03/13/89 |
| · Have Ann get out the previous Walker project report and begin the process of updating so that we have a draft to work with. | ·Ann | ·Walker | ·03/14/89 |
| · Meet with Jim to discuss report on the Peters account. | ·Jim | ·Peters | |
| · Call Ann to go over report to Walker Inc. on Walker and James projects. | ·Ann | ·Walker | |
| · Do status report for Peters. | ·Jim | ·Peters | |
| · Prepare proposal for the Baxter project. | | ·Baxter | ·03/20/89 |

| Meetings | Staffing | Project | When |
|---|---|---|---|
| · Meeting to discuss project for James next Monday. | ·Ann | ·James | ·03/13/89 |
| · Staff meeting every Wednesday. | ·Staffing | | ·03/15/89 |

```
=F1==┬══F2══┬══F3══┬══F4══┬══F5══┬══F6══┬══F7══┬══F8═══┬═F9═══┬══F10═
Help  ║ Edit ║ Copy ║ Done ║ Note ║ Move ║ Mark ║Vw Mgr║Cat Mgr║ Menu
```

Fig. 11-15. *A new item assigned to the Peters category then automatically assigned to the Jim category and a new item assigned to the Baxter category then automatically given the When Date 3/20/89.*

are exported, as desired. This might be useful for automatically splitting a portion of a large database. As the items are assigned to the category with the Export item special action, they are written to the structured text file which is then imported into the new database.

As was the case with profile actions, the default is to execute special actions only when items are entered or edited. However, the Utility Execute command may be employed to cause special actions to also be executed for items currently assigned.

You can assign items to categories simply by using the methods learned in the earlier chapters. The procedures discussed in this chapter are purely optional features that enhance your power in working with Agenda. They are included in Agenda to make your work easier when you need them, not to make your life more difficult by requiring that you learn all of them. Use the features that will make working with Agenda easier for you. The power and desirability of these features in certain applications is illustrated in the applications chapters.

# 12

# IMPORTING AND EXPORTING INFORMATION

INDIVIDUAL Agenda databases need not be used in isolation. As you work with Agenda, you will soon find yourself wanting to move information from one Agenda database to another. You might also need to move information created outside of Agenda into an Agenda database. Agenda provides the capabilities for performing these operations. (Moving information from Agenda to files for use with other programs was discussed in Chapter 8.)

Agenda imports and exports information to and from specially formatted files called *structured text files*. These files are employed to transfer information among Agenda databases. Bringing in information from outside Agenda requires the use of a special utility to translate external files into the structured text files used by Agenda.

This chapter begins with the procedures for creating structured text files from files of information produced outside of Agenda. The next section addresses the actual importing of structured text files into an Agenda database. Agenda can also export structured text files for transfer to other agenda databases, and this is described in the third section. The fourth section shows how to generate a database template that can be used to recreate Agenda applications with new information. The chapter concludes with a discussion of importing and exporting text from notes.

## CREATING STRUCTURED TEXT FILES

Information to be imported into Agenda from outside sources must be in the form of *ASCII text files*. These are files that include only the printable ASCII characters with no special formatting information included by the program that generates the files.

Files obtained from outside sources such as online databases and electronic mail systems generally will be in this form. Applications programs such as word processors, spreadsheets, and database managers generally store their information in their own unique formats. However, most programs include options for creating ASCII text files.

## Using the TXT2STF Conversion Program

ASCII text files must be converted into Agenda's special structured text files in order for the information contained in those files to be imported into an Agenda database. A utility program named TXT2STF (for *Text to Structured Text File*) is included with Agenda to do this conversion.

The TXT2STF program converts ASCII text files into structured text files so that each paragraph of information can be imported into an Agenda database as a separate item. A *paragraph of information*, in this context, means a block of text separated from other text by two carriage returns. Thus, an examination of the ASCII text file will show a blank line separating each of the paragraphs of information.

Suppose you have been using your word processor to write down a number of tasks that must be completed for the proposed Baxter project. You want to import this information to the Tasks database with each task becoming an item in the Baxter category.

The first step is to create the ASCII file. For this example, I used the WordPerfect word processing program. I typed in the text of the items shown in Fig. 12-1. At the end of each item, I pressed ENTER twice to place a blank line between the items.

WordPerfect normally stores information in files using its own special format. Creating an ASCII text file requires the use of a special command to save the information in that format. With WordPerfect, you must press function key CTRL-F5, Text In/Out. Then enter 1 to save the document as an ASCII text file (called a "DOS text file" by WordPerfect) and enter the name for the file. I entered the file name BAXTER.TXT.

If you are using WordPerfect to create the file, you can follow this procedure. If you are using another word processor, enter the information in the same manner, but use that program's command to save the

```
C:\AGFILES>type baxter.txt
Create working group to generate proposal for the Baxter project.

Prepare for and hold staff meeting with division heads to discuss
contributions on Baxter proposal.

Assign at least two staffers to do background research for the
Baxter proposal.  This research should address current
developments in the field, similar types of work we have done for
other firms, the resources we would have available for the Baxter
project, and a general assessment of our strengths and weaknesses
compared with other firms that might also be preparing proposals
for Baxter; we also need to get all of the information we can on
the Baxter firm itself.

Prepare regular status reports on Baxter proposal for top
management.

C:\AGFILES>
```

Fig. 12-1. *The ASCII text file BAXTER.TXT with items for entry into the Tasks database.*

information as an ASCII text file. If you have a text editor that produces ASCII text files directly, it can be used to create the BAXTER.TXT file.

ASCII text files can be displayed on the screen using the DOS TYPE command. At the DOS prompt, enter the command

type baxter.txt

and press ENTER. (DOS does not distinguish between uppercase and lowercase letters.) The contents of the file is listed on the screen as shown in Fig. 12-1.

Now you are ready to convert the file BAXTER.TXT into a structured text file. At the DOS prompt, enter the command

txt2stf baxter.txt

and press ENTER. (Note that you must either be in the directory with the Agenda program files or that directory must be included in your DOS PATH in order to execute the program. If the file BAXTER.TXT is not in the directory from which you are executing TXT2STF, you must include the path for that file along with the file name.)

The program TXT2STF converts the ASCII file BAXTER.TXT into the structured text file BAXTER.STF. The file extension .STF is used by Agenda to denote structured text files. The structured text file is a specialized ASCII text file with markers to indicate how the text is to be interpreted by Agenda. If you wish, you can examine the contents of the structured text file with the DOS TYPE command.

The creation of a structured text file from outside information begins with an ASCII text file. The information in the file must be divided into paragraphs for each Agenda item to be entered in the database. The paragraphs must be separated by blank lines (two carriage returns in a row).

Most applications programs have options for creating ASCII text files from their information. You can usually manage to format the ASCII text files from programs into paragraphs separated by blank lines. If this is not possible, you might be able to use a text editor to add the blank lines after the ASCII text file has been created.

Converting the ASCII text file to a structured text file is accomplished by running the program TXT2STF. Just enter the program name followed by the name of the ASCII text file to be converted (with the DOS path, if necessary). The program TXT2STF creates the structured text file with the same file name but with the extension .STF. This file is in a form that can be imported by Agenda.

If a paragraph of information in the ASCII text file is too long to fit into an Agenda item, the first portion of the paragraph is designated as the item, and the remaining text in the paragraph becomes a note attached to that item. This is taken care of automatically by the TXT2STF program.

## A Comment on Definition Files

The default operation of the TXT2STF program is to convert paragraphs in an ASCII text file into items for the Agenda database, with notes if the paragraphs are too long. For text files with regular, repeating formats, TXT2STF can convert the information into categories, items, and notes that can be imported into an Agenda database. Performing these more complex conversions requires the use of definition files that specify precisely the format of the information in the ASCII text files and the manner in which that information is to be entered into the Agenda database.

The Agenda documentation describes the conversion of Lotus Express Email electronic mail files into structured text files. Such files are in a memo format. They are converted so that the text on the Subject line becomes the item, the To and From lines become categories, the Date line becomes the Entry date, and the text of the memo becomes a note attached to the item. The Agenda package includes a definition file named EMAIL.DEF that is used with TXT2STF to perform this conversion.

The name of the definition file to be used in interpreting an ASCII text file must be included after the name of the ASCII text file when invoking TXT2STF. The TXT2STF program then creates a structured text file with all of the information required for Agenda to import the information correctly.

Agenda users can write their own definition files for use by TXT2STF in converting ASCII text files to structured text files. Unfortunately, learning how to write these definition files is not an extension of the abilities you have learned for operating Agenda. TXT2STF essentially has its own programming language for definition files to use in directing the conversion process.

Definition files must be created in a rather rigid format by using a text editor to enter the commands. Writing definition files is not particularly easy to learn. Providing instruction in writing definition files is beyond the scope of this book, which is intended as in introduction to Agenda for new users.

As more people work with Agenda, TXT2STF definition files for various applications will undoubtedly be written. Some definition files probably will be appearing in computer magazines, as public domain or user-supported software which can be downloaded from information services and bulletin boards, and as commercial software for Agenda users.

## IMPORTING STRUCTURED TEXT FILES

Once a structured text file has been created, the information can be imported directly into an Agenda database by using the File Transfer Import command. Just move to the section where you want the information inserted, issue the command, specify the name of the file name to be imported and, if necessary, adjust the settings appropriately. The information in the file is inserted into the database just as if you had typed it in yourself.

You will now import the information in the structured text file BAXTER.STF into the Tasks database. Open the Tasks database and switch to the Current Projects view by using F8 (VIEW MGR). Move the highlight down to the last section and add a section for the Baxter project by issuing the Category Section New command. For the *Section head:* setting enter Baxter. Press F9 to add the Baxter section, which appears at the bottom of the view.

With the highlight remaining in the Baxter section, issue the File Transfer Import command. In the Import Structured File box, move the highlight down across from the *From file:* setting to specify the structured text file from which information is to be imported. Press GREY PLUS to display a list of the structured text files in the current directory. (If the file BAXTER.STF is not in the current directory, change to the directory where that file is stored.) Highlight the file BAXTER.STF and press ENTER.

The only other setting that needs to be changed is *Strip new carriage returns:*, which must be changed to *Yes*. This eliminates the carriage returns that come at the ends of lines in those items with multiple lines. Otherwise, these carriage returns would cause the text of the imported items to begin on new lines at each carriage return, whether or not the line divisions fall at the natural ends of lines as the item is displayed.

The settings in the Import Structured File box should now appear as shown in Fig. 12-2. Press F9 to accept the settings and import the file. A box is displayed briefly, showing the progress of the import process. You are then returned to the Current Projects view.

Move the highlight down in the Current Projects view and look at the new items that have been added to the Baxter section. Figure 12-3 shows the new items in the view. Observe that all of the items have been assigned When Dates of 3/20/89 as a result of the Date condition created in the previous chapter.

The item beginning ''Assign at least two staffers'' has a musical note preceding it, indicating that a note is attached to the item. This item was the first sentence of the long paragraph in the original file. Because all of the text would not fit within an item, Agenda has entered the remaining text in the paragraph as a note attached to that item. To see the note, highlight the item and press F5 (NOTE). Figure 12-4 shows the note created with the text that was not included in the item. If any of the text in this note would more appropriately be included as an item in the database, you could use function key F8 (MAKE ITEM) to create one or more items.

```
 Import  Export  Template
 Import structured file into current database
=Walker ═══════════════════════════════════════════════════════ When════════
      ♪ Call Ron Smith at Walker by Tuesday to discuss the progress   ·03/14/89
        of the project.
      · Have Ann get out the previous Walker project report and begin ·03/14/89
        the process of updating so that we have a draft to work with.
      · Call ┌════════════════════Import Structured File════════════════┐
        and  │                                                          │
      · Call │ Import:          Items & categories                      │
        proj │ From file:       C:\AGFILES\BAXTER.STF                    │
      · Meet │ Delete file:     No                                      │ 16/89
      · Chec │                                                          │
      · Meet │ Assign to category:       Baxter                         │ 13/89
      · Call │ Combine categories if:    Categories match exactly       │ 15/89
        our  │ Create new categories:    Yes                            │
             │ Strip carriage returns:   Yes                            │
    Peters   │                                                          │
      · Meet └════════════════Press F9 when done, ESC to cancel═════════┘
      · Do status report for Peters.


    Baxter                                                          When
      · Prepare proposal for the Baxter project.                    ·03/20/89
═══F1═══╤═══F2═══╤═══F3═══╤═══F4═══╤═══F5═══╤═══F6═══╤═══F7═══╤═══F8════╤═══F9═══╤══F10══
 Help   ║ Edit   ║        ║        ║        ║        ║        ║Default ║Accept  ║
```

Fig. 12-2. *Importing the structured text file BAXTER.STF into the Tasks database.*

```
File: C:\AGFILES\TASKS                          03/10/89   18:38
View: Current Projects                When Date: 03/20/89
=Walker ════════════════════════════════════════════ When═══
   · Meeting with Ann and Ron Smith Thursday.           ·03/16/89
   · Check with Ron Smith on meeting time.
   · Meeting to discuss project for James next Monday.  ·03/13/89
   · Call Adam Baker at James Wednesday to get his reactions to ·03/15/89
     our proposals.

Peters                                                 When
   · Meet with Jim to discuss report on the Peters account.
   · Do status report for Peters.

Baxter                                                 When
   · Prepare proposal for the Baxter project.          ·03/20/89
   · Create working group to generate proposal for the Baxter ·03/20/89
     project.
   · Prepare for and hold staff meeting with division heads to ·03/20/89
     discuss contributions on Baxter proposal.
   ♪ Assign at least two staffers to do background research for ·03/20/89
     the Baxter proposal.
   · Prepare regular status reports on Baxter proposal for top »03/20/89
     management.
═F1═════╤═F2═════╤═F3═════╤═F4═════╤═F5═════╤═F6═════╤═F7═════╤═F8═════╤═F9═════╤═F10══
Help    ║ Edit   ║ Copy   ║ Done   ║ Note   ║ Move   ║ Mark   ║Vw Mgr ║Cat Mgr║ Menu
```

Fig. 12-3. *The items imported from the BAXTER.STF file displayed in the Baxter section.*

```
Note for:   Assign at least two staffers to do background research for
══════════════════════════════════════════════════════════════Line 1══Ins═
  This research should address current developments in the field, similar types
of work we have done for other firms, the resources we would have available for
the Baxter project, and a general assessment of our strengths and weaknesses
compared with other firms that might also be preparing proposals for Baxter; we
also need to get all of the information we can on the Baxter firm itself.




═F1═════╤═F2═════╤═F3═════╤═F4═════╤═F5═════╤═F6═════╤═F7═════╤═F8═════╤═F9═════╤═F10══
Help    ║ Paste  ║ Copy   ║ Cut    ║Return ║MakeCat ║ Mark   ║MakeItm║Accept ║ Menu
```

Fig. 12-4. *The note created from the long item imported from the BAXTER.STF file.*

Importing information from a structured text file begins with the File Transfer Import command. The most important setting is the name of the structured text file. The file name TRANSFER.STF is provided as the default because that file is also employed as the default for exporting structured text files from Agenda. This allows you to perform an export operation followed by an import using the TRANSFER.STF file without specifying other file names. If you are importing information from another structured text file, press GREY PLUS to display the list of structured text files in the current directory. Highlight the file from which you wish to import information and press ENTER to change the setting. (If necessary, you can change to another directory with the desired file in the usual manner.)

The Import Structured File box includes a number of settings. The *Delete file:* setting defaults to *No*. This can be changed so that the structured text file is deleted automatically after the information is imported.

The *Assign to category:* setting is used to specify the category to which the imported items are to be assigned. It defaults to the section highlighted when you entered the File Transfer Import command. It may be changed to any other category by pressing GREY PLUS and selecting the desired category from the category hierarchy.

Structured text files created by using TXT2STF without a definition file will have no category information. However, structured text files created with a definition file or exported from Agenda may have information on categories and category assignments in addition to the text of items and notes. Several of the settings govern how this information is to be handled during the import process.

The initial *Import:* setting allows you to specify whether you wish to import only items, only categories, or both. The default is to import all of the information in the structured text file. The *Combine categories if:* setting governs when imported categories from the structured text file are combined with similar categories that are already in the database. You can require either exact or partial matches. The *Create new categories:* setting specifies whether new categories in the structured text file are to be created as categories in the Agenda database.

It might be necessary to strip carriage returns from structured text files created by TXT2STF. This should not be needed when importing structured text files that were originally exported by Agenda.

Importing and exporting information will be a somewhat tricky process with most programs. If possible, experiment with a small test file before attempting to import a very large file. It is frequently advisable to import files into their own new sections to avoid corrupting the existing database. In that way, you can visually check the results of the import process to be certain that the information was imported in the manner you expected. Also, if a problem did occur, you can easily get rid of all of the imported information by discarding the section head and all of the items assigned to it.

# EXPORTING STRUCTURED TEXT FILES

Agenda exports information to structured text files for transfer to other Agenda databases. When Agenda is exporting information, it can include categories and category assignments along with items and notes, if that additional information is desired. The structured text files created by Agenda can be directly imported into other Agenda databases using the import procedures described in the preceding pages.

Ann has become a confirmed Agenda user and wants to create her own Agenda database that will include the information in the Tasks database pertaining to her activities. You want to export just that information relating to the Ann category. You will give Ann this information so that she can include it in the new Agenda database she is creating.

To make the process as clear as possible, begin by creating a new view with the items assigned to the Ann category. In the Tasks database, issue the View New command. Enter Ann's Tasks as the name of the view and Ann as the category to serve as section head. Press F9 to create the view. On the screen you will see the Ann section, listing all of the tasks assigned to Ann.

Now issue the File Transfer Export command to export the information from this view to a structured text file. Figure 12-5 shows

```
Import  Export  Template
Export current database to a structured file
─────────────────────────────────────────────────────────────
Ann
    • Have Ann get out the previous Walker project report and begin the process
      of updating so that we have a draft to work with.
    ♪ Call Ron Smith at Walker by Tuesday to discuss the progress of the
      projec┌──────────────────Export Structured File──────────────────┐
    • Call A│                                                           │
    • Call P│  Items to export:      Items in section          Acme.    │
    • Call A│  Assignments:          Family                    rojects. │
    • Meetin│  Discard items:        No                                 │
    • Check │                                                           │
    • Call A│  Categories to export: None                      proposals.│
    • Meetin│                                                           │
            │                                                           │
            │  To file:              C:\AGFILES\TRANSFER.STF            │
            │                                                           │
            └─────────────Press F9 when done, ESC to cancel────────────┘


──F1══╤══F2══╤══F3══╤══F4══╤══F5══╤══F6══╤══F7══╤══F8══╤══F9══╤══F10══
Help  │ Edit │      │      │      │      │      │Default│Accept│
```

Fig. 12-5. *Exporting the items in the Ann section into a transfer file.*

the default settings, which are appropriate for this task. All items in the section are to be exported to the default file TRANSFER.STF. Press F9 to accept the settings and export the information to the structured text file.

Of course, you will need to import the information in order to see how the process worked. Create a new database by giving the File Open command, pressing INS, typing in the file name Annfile for the new database, and pressing ENTER. In the New Database box, type in Ann's Tasks for the description and press F9. The new, empty database is displayed.

Import the structured text file (which you just created) by issuing the File Transfer Import command. You can return to the default settings by pressing ALT-F8, (DFLTALL). The default settings are shown in Fig. 12-6. Note that the file TRANSFER.STF, the file to which the information had been exported, is listed as the default. No changes are needed in the settings, so press F9 to accept the setting and import the information. (An import message will appear on the screen, indicating Agenda's progress in importing the file.)

Figure 12-7 shows the items that have been imported into the new Annfile database. All of the items that were in the Ann's Tasks view in the original Tasks database are listed here. More has been accomplished in the transfer, however. Press F9 (CAT MGR) to display the category hierarchy for the new database, which is shown in Fig. 12-8. All

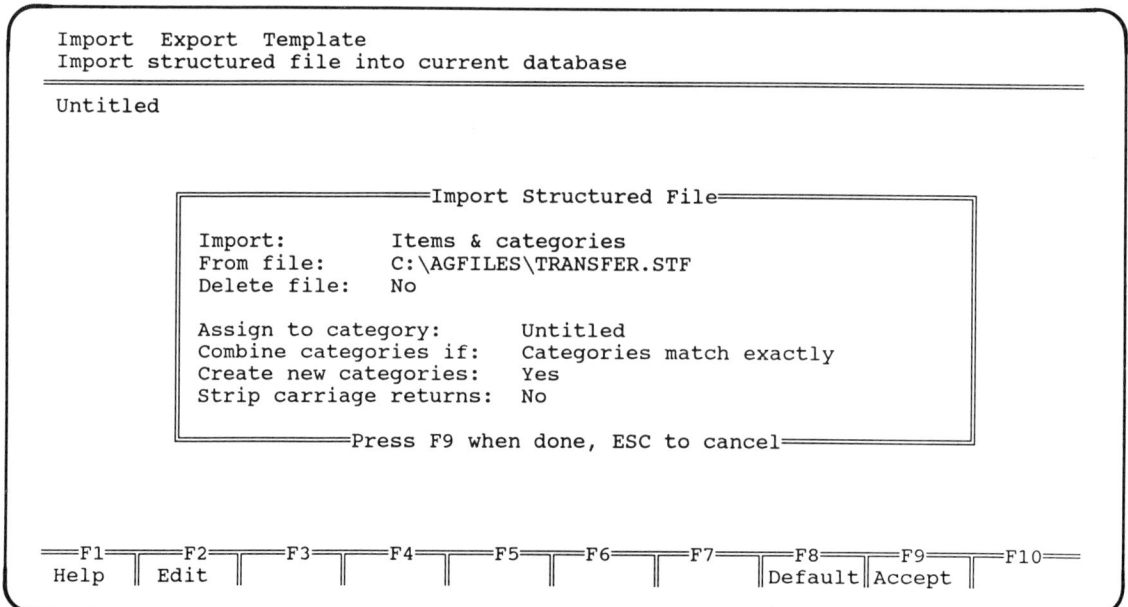

```
 Import   Export   Template
 Import structured file into current database
═══════════════════════════════════════════════════════════════════════

 Untitled



                    ┌════════════Import Structured File════════════┐
                    │                                              │
                    │  Import:          Items & categories         │
                    │  From file:       C:\AGFILES\TRANSFER.STF     │
                    │  Delete file:     No                          │
                    │                                              │
                    │  Assign to category:      Untitled            │
                    │  Combine categories if:   Categories match exactly │
                    │  Create new categories:   Yes                 │
                    │  Strip carriage returns:  No                  │
                    │                                              │
                    └════════Press F9 when done, ESC to cancel═════┘



 ══F1══╤══F2══╤══F3══╤══F4══╤══F5══╤══F6══╤══F7══╤══F8════╤══F9════╤══F10══
 Help  ║ Edit ║      ║      ║      ║      ║      ║Default ║Accept  ║
```

Fig. 12-6. *Importing the information from the transfer file into the new Annfile database.*

```
File: C:\AGFILES\ANNFILE                          03/10/89   18:43
View: Initial View
════════════════════════════════════════════════════════════════════
Untitled
   • Have Ann get out the previous Walker project report and begin the process
     of updating so that we have a draft to work with.
   ♪ Call Ron Smith at Walker by Tuesday to discuss the progress of the
     project.
   • Call Ann by next Friday to discuss hiring of new assistant.
   • Call Peter Smith regarding new account proposals for Walker and Acme.
   • Call Ann to go over report to Walker Inc. on Walker and James projects.
   • Meeting with Ann and Ron Smith Thursday.
   • Check with Ron Smith on meeting time.
   • Call Adam Baker at James Wednesday to get his reactions to our proposals.
   • Meeting to discuss project for James next Monday.




══F1══╤══F2══╤══F3══╤══F4══╤══F5══╤══F6══╤══F7══╤══F8══╤══F9══╤══F10══
 Help │ Edit │ Copy │ Done │ Note │ Move │ Mark │Vw Mgr│Cat Mgr│ Menu
```

Fig. 12-7. *The display of the items imported into the Annfile database.*

```
File: C:\AGFILES\ANNFILE
Category Manager
════════════════════════════════════════════════════════════════════
MAIN
  "Untitled"
  Staffing
    Ann
  Project
    Walker;Ron Smith
      James
    Acme
  Reports
  March Activities
  Phone Calls
  Meetings




══F1══╤══F2══╤══F3══╤══F4══╤══F5══╤══F6══╤══F7══╤══F8══╤══F9══╤══F10══
 Help │ Edit │Cpy C/A│Clr C/A│ Note │ Move │Prm (←)│Dem (→)│To View│ Menu
```

Fig. 12-8. *The category hierarchy imported into the Annfile database.*

of the categories to which the items had been assigned have been imported as well, along with their parent categories. All of the category hierarchy of the original Tasks database that is relevant to the items transferred has been transferred as well. The items in the new database remain assigned to these categories as they were before. The categories can be used to create columns and views having the same format as in the original database.

To export structured text files from Agenda, issue the File Transfer Export command. If you wish to transfer the items in the current section, the default settings probably will be acceptable. In these cases, you need only press F9 to generate the structured text file TRANSFER.STF.

The first setting in the Export Structured File box, *Items to Export:*, allows you to specify the items that are to be written to the structured text file. You can choose to export all of the items in the current section, all of the items in the current view, all of the items in the database, or only the current item or the marked items. You may also specify that no items are to be exported if you wish to export only the categories to another database. In that case, you will need to specify the categories to be exported using that setting.

If you are exporting items, Agenda provides options governing whether the category assignments of those items are to be exported as well. The *Assignments:* setting has the default option *Family*, which exports the maximum amount of information. When this option is used, not only are the categories to which the items are assigned exported, but the ancestor categories (parents, grandparents, etc.) are also exported. This preserves the structure of the category hierarchy as it relates to the items being exported. Thus, if an item in the Tasks database assigned to the Walker category is exported, not only is the Walker category exported, but the Project category is also exported as the parent of the Walker category.

The *Assignments:* setting can be changed to *Category* so that only the categories to which the items are assigned are exported, not ancestor categories. In this case, exporting an item assigned to the Walker category would export Walker, but not the Project category. Finally, you can choose to export no category assignments for the items. The transferred database will then include no category information at all, unless the categories themselves are exported separately.

Categories may be exported independently of any items assigned to them by changing the *Categories to Export:* setting. You can choose to export the entire category hierarchy or only a part of the hierarchy. When the partial hierarchy option is selected, another setting, *Family:*, appears. You specify the parent category of the portion of the category hierarchy you wish to export. Exporting categories using these settings does not result in the export of any items assigned to those categories. Exporting items (and optionally the categories to which those items are assigned) is governed by the *Items to Export:* and *Assignments:* settings.

Agenda's default setting is to export the information to a structured text file named TRANSFER.STF, stored in the current directory. You may change this by typing in a new file name (and path specification if the file is to be stored in a different directory). Type in only the main part of the file name; Agenda automatically appends the extension .STF to all structured text files. If you wish to use an existing file, you may either type in the file name or press GREY PLUS and select the file from the list of existing structured text files.

If the specified file already exists, Agenda gives you the option of either appending the information exported to that file or replacing the information in the file. You might choose to use the append feature if you wish to export information from two different sections of a database. Simply use the File Transfer Export command twice to export the items from each section, the second time appending the information to the file used the first time.

On the other hand, if the existing file had previously been used for some other purpose and if you no longer need to keep the information in that file, you can simply replace the old information with the newly exported information. This is likely to happen with the default TRANSFER.STF file. The file is used for one transfer. The next time you need to make a simple transfer, the file already exists. You just replace the information for the new transfer.

The *Discard items:* setting can be employed to automatically discard items from the database when they are exported to the structured text file. Once you have made all of the settings in the Export Structured File box, press F9 to accept and export the information specified. The structured text file is written to the disk and you are returned to the view.

Agenda includes two procedures for automatically exporting items from a database. By changing the *Process Done items:* setting reached with Utility Preferences Other command, you can cause items marked as Done to be exported to a structured text file. Special actions may also be employed to automatically export items assigned to particular categories. These actions are created using the Category Management Action Special command in a view or the Action Special command in the Category Manager. Both procedures create structured text files that may be imported into Agenda databases like any such files.

## CREATING A DATABASE TEMPLATE

After creating an elaborate Agenda database for a particular application, you might want to use exactly the same format for future applications involving different information. You might want to retain the categories (and any associated conditions and actions) and the views but eliminate the current items. The File Transfer Template command directly creates this framework for the new database, which Agenda refers to as a *template*. This command is equivalent to making a copy of the existing database and then deleting all of the items from the new database.

Create a template for the Tasks database. Open the Tasks database using the File Open command if you are not currently working with that database. Issue the File Transfer Template command. The Select File box is displayed on the screen. Since you want the template to be a new database, press INS and type in the file name

tasktemp

for task template. The screen appears as shown in Fig. 12-9. Press ENTER to create the template database.

Now open the newly created database to see what Agenda has created by entering the File Open command. Highlight TASKTEMP, and press ENTER. Then press F8 (VIEW MGR). You will see the familiar list of all of the views that were in the original Tasks database. Highlight the Tasks to Do view and press ENTER to display that view, which is shown in Fig. 12-10. All of the section heads and columns included in that view in the original database are still there, but no items are displayed because all of them have been discarded. You are ready to enter new items and use the template database for managing new information.

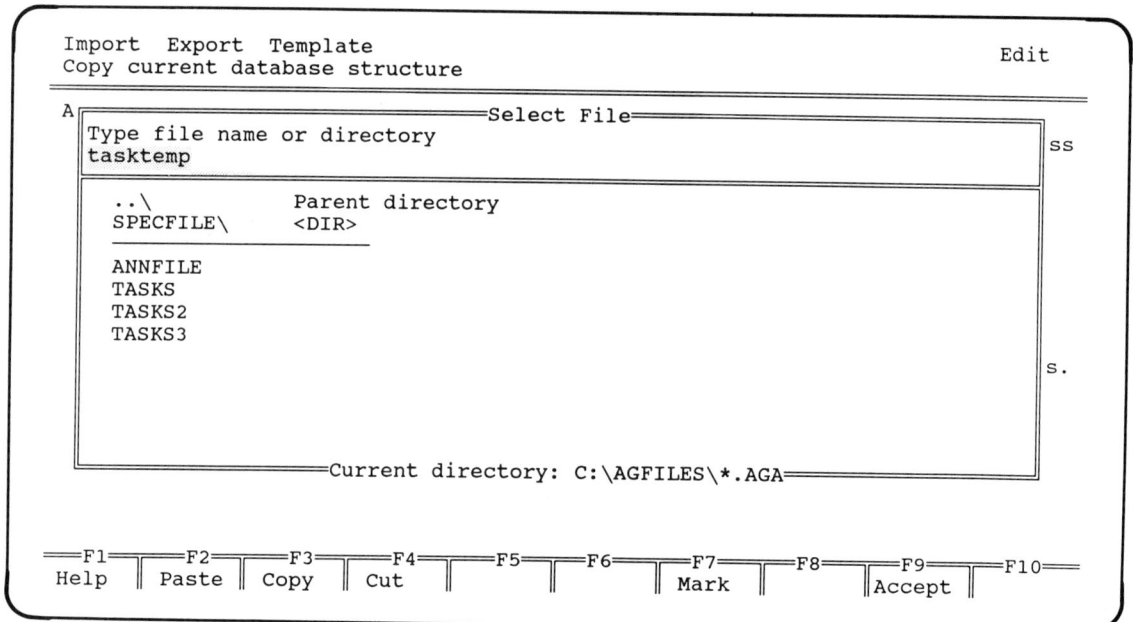

```
 Import  Export  Template                                          Edit
 Copy current database structure

A┌───────────────────────────────Select File────────────────────────────┐
 │Type file name or directory                                         │ss
 │tasktemp                                                            │
 │  ┌──────────────────────────────────────────────────────────────┐ │
 │  │  ..\            Parent directory                             │ │
 │  │  SPECFILE\      <DIR>                                        │ │
 │  │  ─────────────────────                                       │ │
 │  │  ANNFILE                                                     │ │
 │  │  TASKS                                                       │ │
 │  │  TASKS2                                                      │ │
 │  │  TASKS3                                                      │ │
 │  │                                                             │ │s.
 │  │                                                             │ │
 │  └──────────Current directory: C:\AGFILES\*.AGA───────────────┘ │
 └───────────────────────────────────────────────────────────────────┘

═F1═══╤══F2══╤══F3══╤══F4══╤══F5══╤══F6══╤══F7══╤══F8══╤══F9═══╤══F10══
 Help │ Paste│ Copy │ Cut  │      │      │ Mark │      │Accept│
```

Fig. 12-9. *Copying the structure of the Tasks database to the new database Tasktemp.*

```
┌─────────────────────────────────────────────────────────────────────┐
│  File: C:\AGFILES\TASKTEMP                       03/10/89   19:05     │
│  View: Tasks to Do                                                    │
│ ═════════════════════════════════════════════════════════════════════│
│  Reports                          Staffing    Project    When         │
│                                                                       │
│  Meetings                         Staffing    Project    When         │
│                                                                       │
│  Phone Calls                      Staffing    Project    When         │
│                                                                       │
│                                                                       │
│                                                                       │
│                                                                       │
│                                                                       │
│                                                                       │
│                                                                       │
│                                                                       │
│ ══F1══╤══F2══╤══F3══╤══F4══╤══F5══╤══F6══╤══F7══╤══F8══╤══F9══╤══F10══ │
│   Help ║ Edit ║ Copy ║ Done ║ Note ║ Move ║ Mark ║Vw Mgr║Cat Mgr║ Menu │
└─────────────────────────────────────────────────────────────────────┘
```

Fig. 12-10. *The display of the Tasks to Do view in the Tasktemp database.*

A database template created using the File Transfer Template command retains the entire category hierarchy of the original database, including all associated conditions and actions. All of the views in the database are likewise preserved in the new database that is created. No options exist for the File Transfer Template command except for the name of the new database to be created. If you specify the name of an existing database, Agenda asks whether you want to replace all of the information in that database with the new template database.

## IMPORTING AND EXPORTING TEXT INTO AND FROM NOTES

The contents of any ASCII text file may be imported into a note, and the text of a note may be exported to an ASCII text file. Both operations are performed using note commands that you invoked while you are in the note to be used for the import or export operations.

As mentioned earlier in this chapter, ASCII text files contain only the printable characters in the ASCII character set. These files do not include special formatting information inserted by many applications programs in their own files. Information obtained from online databases and electronic mail messages are often in the form of ASCII text files, and many programs provide options for creating ASCII text files. The information in such files may be imported into Agenda notes.

To import information from an ASCII text file, first enter the note into which the text is to be placed by pressing F5 (NOTE). Move the cursor to the point where the new information is to be inserted (if the note already contains some information). Press F10 (MENU) and select the Import command. Enter the file name of the ASCII text file from which the information is to be imported. Also specify whether carriage returns are to be stripped. If the information consists only of text in paragraphs, you might want to select the option to strip carriage returns so that Agenda can wrap the text within its own margins. On the other hand, if the information is in tabular form, such as output from a spreadsheet, do not strip carriage returns. Otherwise, when Agenda rearranges the text, the result could be a mess. Press F9 and Agenda reads the designated file and enters the information into the Note.

Moving in the other direction, you can export the contents of any note to an ASCII text file. Enter the note and issue the Export command. You are prompted for a name for the file to which the information in the note is to be written. After entering the name, press F9. The contents of the note are written to the designated file. This operation creates an ASCII text file. You can import the information into other notes, print the file from DOS, or use the file with any other program that can work with information in ASCII text files. Many word processing programs have special commands that allow them to import text from ASCII text files.

While not strictly an import or export command, Agenda provides one other way to use ASCII text files with notes. The File Note command allows an ASCII text file to be attached to an item or category. That file then becomes the note for the category, and the note information is stored in that file and note in the Agenda database. To attach an ASCII text file as a note, highlight the item or category for which the file is to become the note. Then enter the File Note command. You are prompted for the file name of the ASCII text file to be used as the note. Enter the file name and press F9 to attach the file as the note.

When you look at the note after the File Note command has been executed, you will see the contents of the ASCII text file displayed as the note. The top line of the note screen indicates that an external text file is being used as the note and gives its file name.

You may work with notes created by attaching files exactly like any other notes. Text may be added or deleted, the note may be edited, information may even be imported from or exported to other ASCII files. When you make changes to the note, you are making those changes to the attached file. Essentially, Agenda is serving as a text editor displaying and editing an external ASCII text file. Remember that when you change a note that consists of an attached file, you are permanently changing the contents of that file.

The import and export procedures exist for one purpose: to save you the effort of having to key in information that has already been entered into the computer. When you need to use a significant quantity of information that is in another file, it becomes worthwhile to learn the procedures for importing and exporting information.

# 13

## USING THE ITEMS AND CLIPBOARD ACCESSORIES

W HEN you work with programs other than Agenda, you might encounter a piece of information that should be entered into an Agenda database as an item. Or suppose you think of something that you want to enter as an item. You might think that either you would have to write these items down until you were working with Agenda or you would have to exit your current program, start Agenda to enter the items, and return to what you were doing. However, the Agenda package includes two handy little accessories that you can use to capture or enter information without leaving the program with which you are working.

The Items and Clipboard accessories are programs that you can "pop-up" in the middle of another program. The Clipboard accessory allows you to copy any information appearing on the screen for later pasting into an application. The Items accessory lets you type in items or paste them from the Clipboard and then save them in a structured text file for later importing into Agenda. Together, these accessories serve as a constantly available means for entering information into Agenda.

The first section of this chapter describes the procedures for installing and starting the accessories. The next two sections address the use of Clipboard to copy information from the screen and the use of Items to enter items and save them as structured text files. In the final section, the procedures for importing these items into Agenda are reviewed.

## INSTALLING AND STARTING THE ACCESSORIES

The Agenda accessories are *terminate-and-stay-resident* (TSR) programs that are loaded into memory before using other programs. They remain in the memory of the computer as other programs are being used. When an accessory is invoked with a special ''hot key,'' it pops up in a window on the screen over the current application. You can then work with the accessory. When you exit from the accessory, the window disappears and you can continue your work with the currently running application program.

The Items and Clipboard accessories utilize the core program from the Metro collection of pop-up utilities sold by Lotus. These accessories may be used with other Metro accessories if you have them. However, Metro is not required to use the two accessories that come with Agenda.

The accessories access the disk when they are used. Thus, as a practical matter, you need to have a hard disk to effectively use them, so that the required files are always available.

Using the accessories with Agenda requires that your computer have at least 640K of RAM memory. Although only 512K of RAM is needed to operate Agenda itself, this is insufficient memory once the accessories have been loaded.

### Installing the Accessories

The Items accessory and the Clipboard must be installed on your hard disk before they can be used. Their installation requires a procedure separate from the installation of the Agenda program itself. If you are not certain whether or not you have installed the accessories, check the directory listing of the root directory of your hard disk. The installation procedure copies the file MET-RO.EXE to the root directory and creates the subdirectory METRO. If these are present, the accessories have already been installed.

To install the accessories, insert the Agenda Utilities disk into the A: drive. Change to the A: drive by typing A: and then pressing ENTER. To install the accessories on a hard disk designated as the C: drive, type in

items c:

and then press ENTER. If you wish to install the accessories on a drive other than C:, substitute the appropriate drive specification. The installation program creates the necessary directories, copies the required programs, and performs the configuration for your system.

### Starting the Accessories

To start the accessories, you must be in the root directory of the disk on which the accessories have been installed. Then just type

metro

and press ENTER to load the Metro program that enables you to use the accessories. Messages are displayed indicating that the program has been loaded, and then you are returned to the DOS prompt. The program remains in memory, ready to invoke the accessories whenever you need them. You can proceed to use your computer in the normal manner, loading and running applications programs.

If you want to have the accessories available whenever you work with your computer, you might want to place the command to load the Metro program in your AUTOEXEC.BAT file. Edit the file to include the command to start the accessories. Then, whenever you start the computer or perform a reboot using CTRL-ALT-DEL, the Metro program will be loaded automatically.

The Metro program uses approximately 65K of available RAM, reducing the total amount of RAM available for other programs by that amount. This could be an issue if you use programs that require very large amount of RAM, or if you use other terminate-and-stay-resident programs that also consume memory. If you are using the Agenda accessories with other TSR programs, you might have to experiment with the order in which the programs are loaded if any conflicts arise.

## USING THE CLIPBOARD ACCESSORY

The Clipboard performs two basic functions. When the accessory is invoked, it can copy information appearing on the screen to the Clipboard for temporary storage, and it can paste the information from the Clipboard into any program. Special hot keys recognized by the Clipboard accessory are used to pop up the Clipboard for copying and to paste information from the Clipboard into any application.

To illustrate the use of the Clipboard accessory, assume you are using your word processing program to write a memo about the appointment of staff to the working group for the development of the proposal for Baxter. After starting the text of the memo, you realize that the first sentence should also be included as an item in the Tasks database.

Start your word processor and type in the information as shown in Fig. 13-1. (You really do not need to type in the TO:, FROM:, and SUBJ: lines to perform the operations with the Clipboard. Only the sentence beginning ''I am recommending'' actually needs to be typed.)

Figure 13-1 shows a WordPerfect document. WordPerfect users will recognize the screen display. However, you can use any word processor equally well.

After the text has been typed, press the hot key ALT-SHIFT-D to pop up the Clipboard accessory. Hold down the ALT and SHIFT keys togeth-

TO:         Patricia Sampson, Division Head

FROM:       John Smith

SUBJ:       Baxter Working Group


I am recommending that the working group for the Baxter proposal
include Ann, Jim, and Pete Wilson.



                                    Doc 1   Pg 1   Ln 10        Pos 0

*Fig. 13-1. Marking the text in the word processor memo for copying into the Clipboard.*

er and press D. ALT-SHIFT is the first part of the combination used to
invoke all of the accessories. If you hold down just these two keys, after
about a second a little box appears listing the options for the third key.
The box will remind you that D invokes the Clipboard.

The Clipboard accessory appears in a box across the middle of the
screen. The Agenda accessories use commands that are invoked just as
are commands in Agenda. You want to copy text from the screen to the
Clipboard, so issue the Copy Text command. Press F10 to display the
menu of commands. Select Copy either by highlighting that choice and
pressing ENTER or by typing C. Likewise, select Text either by
highlighting that choice and pressing ENTER or by pressing T.

When the command is completed, the Clipboard window disappears
from the screen and a special blinking, thicker box cursor appears in
the upper-left corner for marking the text to be copied. Use the arrow
keys to move this box cursor down to the first letter in the sentence to
be copied, to the letter *I* beginning the sentence. Then press F7 to anchor
the copy area here. The box cursor changes to an inverse block to mark
the text to be copied, starting here. Press the RIGHT and DOWN arrows
to extend the highlighted area to the end of the sentence, as shown in
Fig. 13-1.

To copy the highlighted text into the Clipboard, press ENTER. The
Clipboard window reappears on the screen and the text that had been

marked is displayed in the lower section, as shown in Fig. 13-2. The Clipboard accessory copies from the left edge of the screen and inserts spaces if the text does not begin at the left edge of the screen.

This completes your work with the Clipboard. Exit the Clipboard with the Quit command, just as in Agenda. The Clipboard window disappears from the screen and you are returned to the word processing program, ready to pick up where you left off.

The information in the Clipboard may be pasted into any program, just as if it had been typed in from the keyboard. You can demonstrate this with your word processor. Move the cursor to any location where you want the information entered. Press ALT-SHIFT-ENTER, and the information from the Clipboard is pasted into the word processing document—repeating the sentence that has already been entered.

The Clipboard accessory has only a small number of commands and options. Its use is fairly straightforward. You pop up the Clipboard by using the hot key ALT-SHIFT-D. This displays the accessory in a window across the middle of the screen. Function key F10 displays the command options, which are used to make selections just as in Agenda. Function key F1 displays the one screen of help information, indicating the functions of the various keys.

To copy information from the screen to the Clipboard, you start with the Copy command and then select the option for determining the information to be

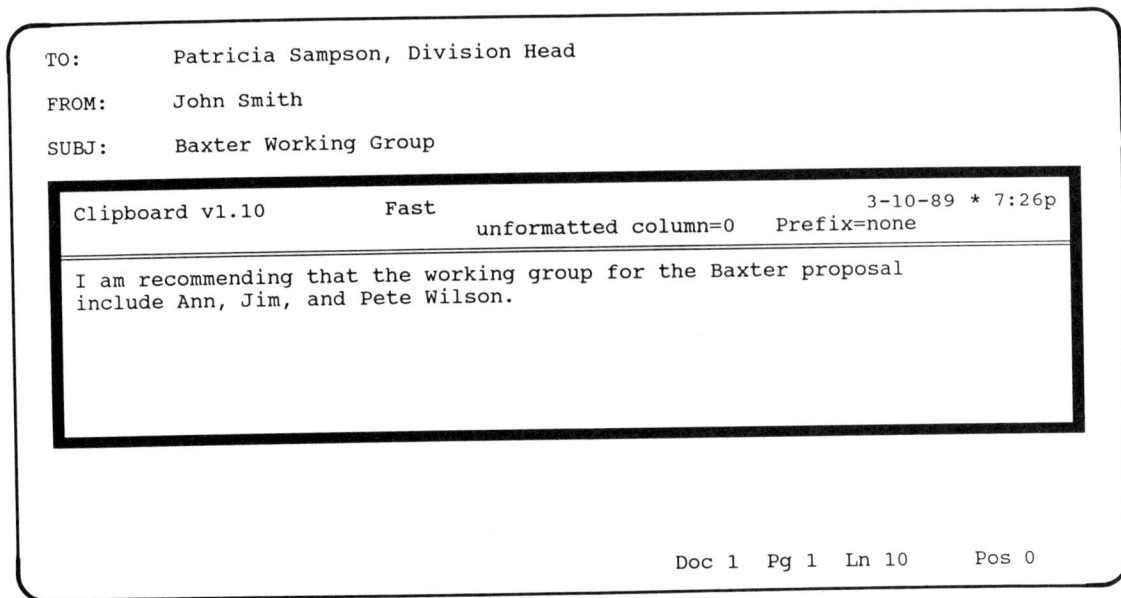

```
TO:        Patricia Sampson, Division Head

FROM:      John Smith

SUBJ:      Baxter Working Group

  Clipboard v1.10          Fast                      3-10-89 * 7:26p
                                unformatted column=0   Prefix=none

  I am recommending that the working group for the Baxter proposal
  include Ann, Jim, and Pete Wilson.




                                        Doc 1   Pg 1   Ln 10    Pos 0
```

Fig. 13-2. *The Clipboard showing the text copied from the word processor memo.*

copied. The Clipboard accessory provides three options for copying information. The Copy Wholescreen command copies all of the text on the screen into the Clipboard. The Copy Text command copies selected lines of text. The Copy Rectangle command copies a specified rectangular block of text, such as one or more columns in a spreadsheet. The Copy Wholescreen and Copy Rectangle commands insert extra spaces for any blank areas that are to the right of the text. This insertion of spaces can cause problems later if you change the format of the text. The Copy Text command does not insert these extra spaces.

If you select either the Text or Rectangle options, the Clipboard window temporarily disappears so you can mark the information to be copied. To mark the information, move the box cursor to the start of the information to be copied. Then press F7 to start the copy at that point and use the arrow keys to extend the highlighted area to encompass all of the information to be copied. The choice of Text or Rectangle governs the manner in which the area is extended. If you select Rectangle, each press of an arrow key will extend the highlight one row or column at a time, allowing you to specify the rectangular area. Press ENTER to copy the information to the Clipboard.

When information is copied to the Clipboard, the copied information replaces anything previously placed there. You can scroll through the information using PGUP or PGDN. If you wish to clear the information from the Clipboard prior to copying some new information, use the Erase command.

The Format command provides three options for formatting the information in the Clipboard. The Normal option ends each line with a carriage return. The WordProcessor(Space) option replaces the carriage returns with spaces separating the words. This is appropriate for text that will be wrapped into lines and formatted by the application into which the text is entered. The Spreadsheet option ends each line with both a carriage return and a line-feed/down-arrow character. This is handy for pasting the information into a spreadsheet down a column. Each line in the Clipboard is entered into a cell, and the down-arrow character moves the cell cursor down to the next cell in the column for the entry of the next line.

The Settings command allows you to specify how the Clipboard operates. The Column setting allows you to enter a column which is the point at which the Clipboard itself will automatically wrap text to the next line. The default of zero means that text will not be wrapped around to the next line. The Prefix setting allows a label-prefix to be included automatically when entering label information into a spreadsheet. The Speed option sets the rate at which information from the Clipboard is pasted into other applications. It slows down the rate of text entry for programs that cannot handle the normal rate at which the Clipboard enters text.

Information copied into the Clipboard may be pasted into the Items accessory or directly into Agenda. The use of the Clipboard is not limited to Agenda, however. It may be used to copy and paste information between any two programs. After information has been copied to the Clipboard, you exit the accessory with the Quit command. Any time thereafter, you can paste the information that is in the Clipboard into any other program, just as if that information had been entered into that program from the keyboard. Move the cursor in the application to the point at which you want the information from the Clipboard entered. Then press ALT-SHIFT-ENTER to enter the information from the Clipboard into the program with which you are working.

## USING THE ITEMS ACCESSORY

The Items accessory allows you to enter items for later importing into an Agenda database. You also can enter categories to which these items are to be assigned. The items entered into the Items accessory are saved in structured text files which may be imported into Agenda. Within any application in which you are working, a hot key pops up the Items accessory.

Earlier you copied text from your word processing program into the Clipboard. Now you want to create one item from that text for import into Agenda. Activate the Items accessory by pressing its hot key combination, ALT-SHIFT-I. (You can be in any program or at the DOS prompt when you use this hot key.) If you press ALT-SHIFT and do not immediately press the I, a small box will pop up reminding you that I is the key for selecting the Item accessory. The Items accessory pops up over your current application in a box in the upper-right corner of the screen.

Create the first item by pasting the contents of the Clipboard into the Items accessory as an item. Just press F2 (PASTE) and the text you had copied from the word processor memorandum is entered into the Items accessory as item number one. Figure 13-3 shows the Items accessory with the Clipboard text entered. The line break on the second line comes from the carriage return copied from the word processor document. It can be stripped when the items are imported into Agenda.

Now you have realized that you will need to call a meeting of the working group and want to enter an item to that effect. Press PGDN to move to the second item. (The item number is shown in the second line and a clear new screen appears.) This time, type in the text of the new item:

Convene first meeting of Baxter working group next Friday.

This item is shown displayed in Fig. 13-4.

Both of these items are to be assigned to the Baxter category. If you choose to make a category assignment, then all items in the Items

```
TO:         Patricia Sampso┌──────────────────────────────────────────┐
                           │ Items v1.00                   3-10-89 * 7:30p │
FROM:       John Smith      │ Note File:                          Item:  1 │
                           ├──────────────────────────────────────────┤
SUBJ:       Baxter Working  │ I am recommending that the working group for the │
                           │ Baxter proposal                            │
                           │ include Ann, Jim, and Pete Wilson.         │
I am recommending that th  │                                            │
include Ann, Jim, and Pet  │                                            │
                           │                                            │
                           │                                            │
                           └──────────────────────────────────────────┘




                                       Doc 1   Pg 1   Ln 10      Pos 0
```

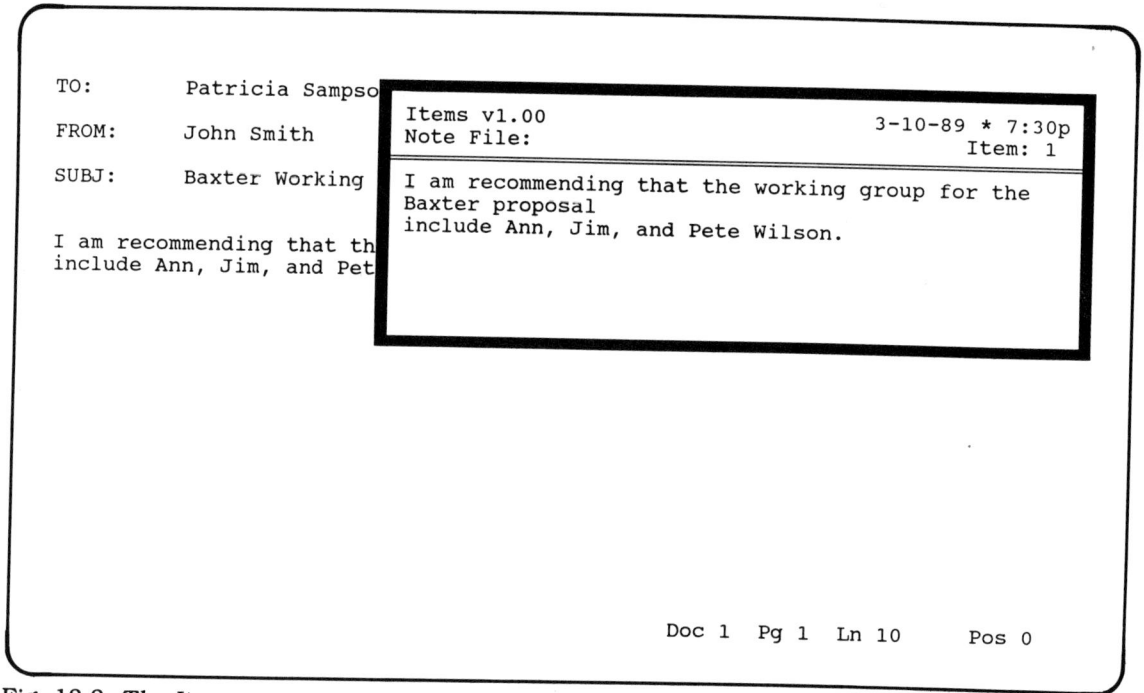

Fig. 13-3. *The Items accessory with the text from the Clipboard pasted in as the first item.*

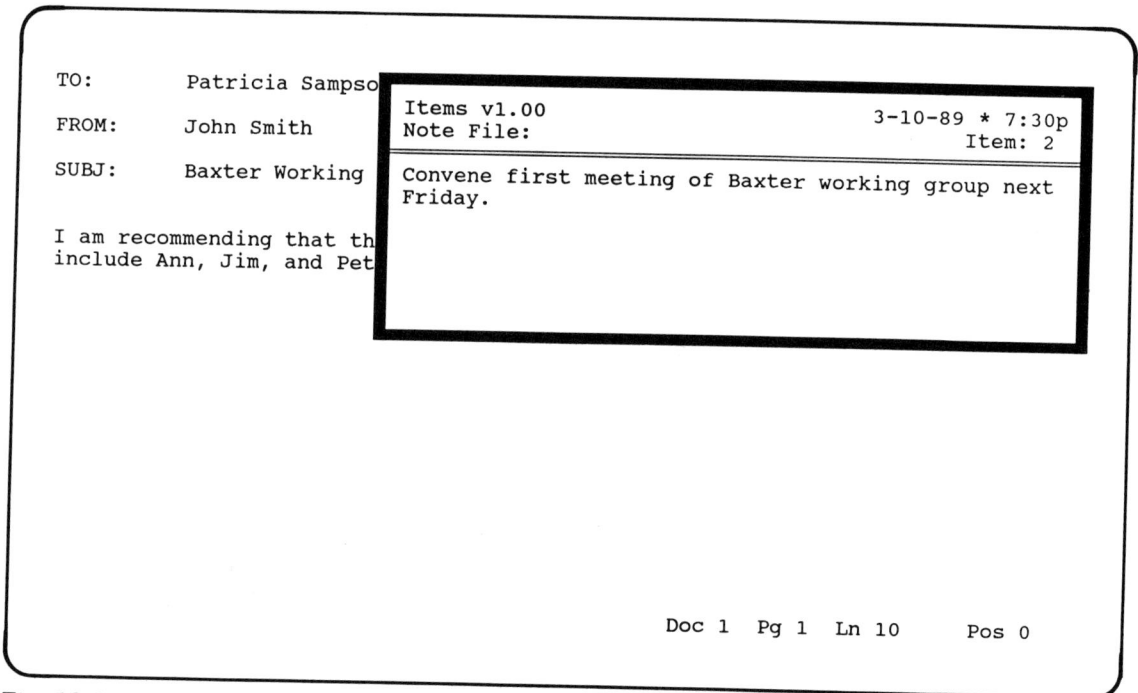

```
TO:         Patricia Sampso┌──────────────────────────────────────────┐
                           │ Items v1.00                   3-10-89 * 7:30p │
FROM:       John Smith      │ Note File:                          Item:  2 │
                           ├──────────────────────────────────────────┤
SUBJ:       Baxter Working  │ Convene first meeting of Baxter working group next │
                           │ Friday.                                    │
I am recommending that th  │                                            │
include Ann, Jim, and Pet  │                                            │
                           │                                            │
                           │                                            │
                           └──────────────────────────────────────────┘




                                       Doc 1   Pg 1   Ln 10      Pos 0
```

Fig. 13-4. *Text typed into the Items accessory for the second item.*

accessory will be assigned to that category. Issue the Category command by pressing F10 and then either by highlighting Category and pressing ENTER or by pressing C. Type in the following:

Baxter

The screen appears as shown in Fig. 13-5. Now press ENTER to assign both of the Items to the Baxter category.

The information entered into the Items accessory may now be saved in a structured text file for import into the Agenda Tasks database. Issue the Transfer All command to save the information on all of the Items that have been entered. Type in the file name

baxter2

as the name to be given to the structured text file. The Items accessory will automatically add the extension .STF. The screen should appear as shown in Fig. 13-6. Press ENTER to accept the file name and write the information in the Items accessory to the transfer file BAXTER2.STF. You can now exit Items with the Quit command.

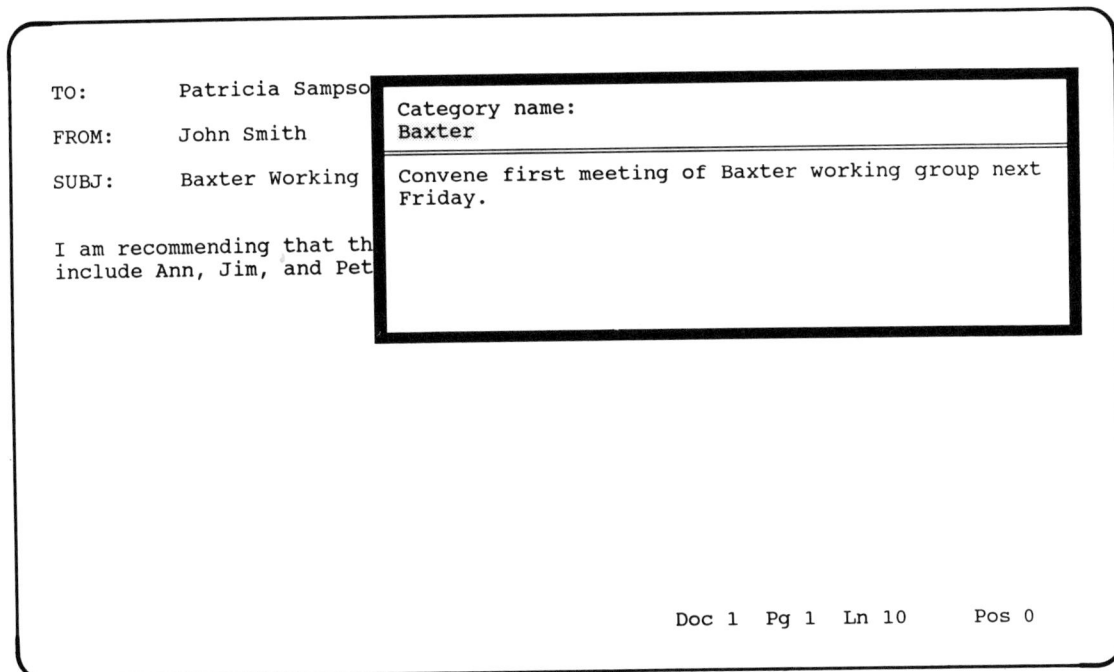

```
TO:        Patricia Sampso┌──────────────────────────────────────────┐
                          │ Category name:                           │
FROM:      John Smith     │ Baxter                                   │
                          ├──────────────────────────────────────────┤
SUBJ:      Baxter Working │ Convene first meeting of Baxter working group next │
                          │ Friday.                                  │
                          │                                          │
I am recommending that th │                                          │
include Ann, Jim, and Pet │                                          │
                          └──────────────────────────────────────────┘




                                    Doc 1   Pg 1   Ln 10      Pos 0
```

Fig. 13-5. *Assigning the items to the Baxter category.*

```
   TO:        Patricia Sampso┌─────────────────────────────────┐
                             │ File name:                        │
   FROM:      John Smith     │ baxter2                           │
                             ├───────────────────────────────────┤
   SUBJ:      Baxter Working │ Convene first meeting of Baxter working group next │
                             │ Friday.                           │
   I am recommending that th│                                   │
   include Ann, Jim, and Pet│                                   │
                             │                                   │
                             │                                   │
                             │                                   │
                             └───────────────────────────────────┘




                                      Doc 1   Pg 1   Ln 10      Pos 0
```

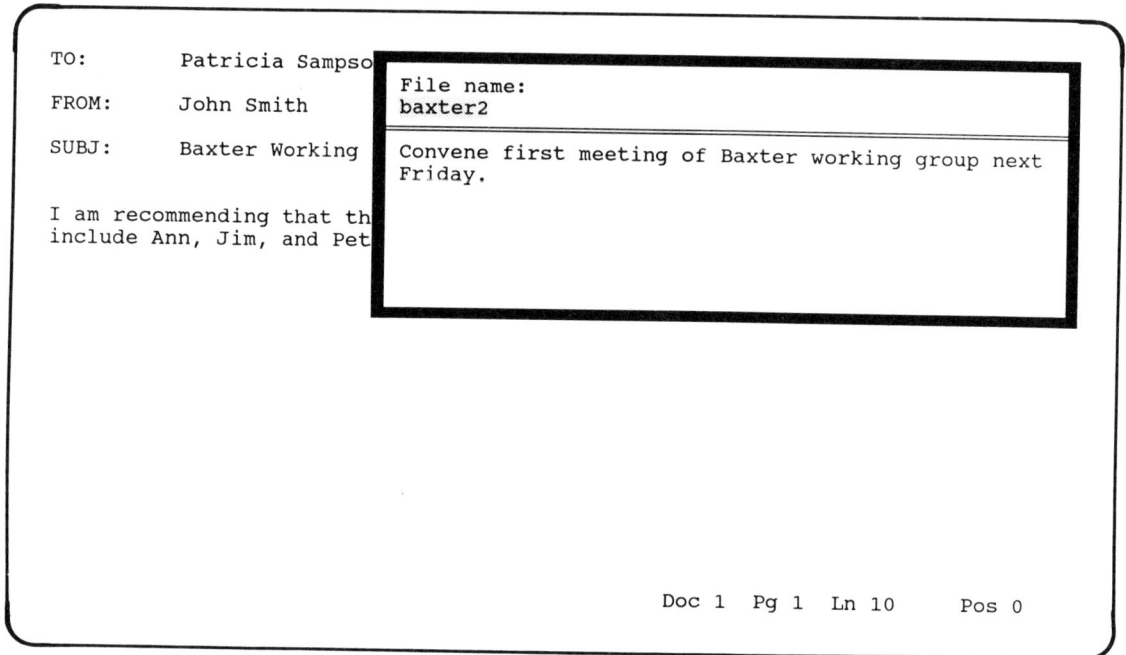

Fig. 13-6. *Exporting the items to the file BAXTER2.STF.*

The Items accessory is invoked using the ALT-SHIFT-I hot key. It has space for ten items of 350 characters or less—the limit on items in Agenda. You move among the items by using PGUP and PGDN. You enter an item in the Items accessory by typing in the text of the item. The cursor movement commands are the same as in Agenda. Function keys may be used to copy an item to the Clipboard (F3), paste information from the Clipboard into the current item (F2), and delete all of the items (F4). Pressing F1 displays one screen of help information listing all of these commands.

As in Agenda, F10 displays the menu of command options. To select a command, either highlight the command and press ENTER or press the first letter of the command.

Two commands are used to add more information to the items. You use the Category command to type in the name of a category to which all of the items in the Items accessory will be assigned when they are imported into the Agenda database. The Category command may be used more than once to assign all of the items to multiple categories. The Note command allows you to attach an ASCII text file to the currently displayed item as a Note file. You give the command and enter the name of the ASCII text file. Using the Note command in the Item accessory has the same effect as using the File Note command within Agenda.

The Delete command allows the deletion of either the current item or all of the items in the Items accessory. The Print command lets you print out the items while you are in the Items accessory.

Before the information entered in Items can be imported by Agenda, it must be saved in a structured text file using the Transfer command. You are first given the option of saving all of the items or just the current item. You then must specify the name of the structured text file to which the information is to be written. The file TRANSFER.STF is provided as the default. You may enter another file name (and an optional path) if desired. Only the main portion of the file name needs to be specified. The Items accessory automatically adds the .STF structured text file extension. If the file specified already exists, you are given the additional option of appending the items being written from the Items accessory to those already in the file or replacing the information in the file.

The Items accessory may be used at any time, in any applications program, to enter new items for Agenda databases. You can save items for multiple databases by using different structured text files. While the accessory holds a maximum of ten items at one time, you can write out the items to a structured text file, delete them, and continue entering more items. The additional items may be appended to the same structured text file or written to a different file.

## IMPORTING ITEMS FROM THE ITEMS ACCESSORY

The structured text files written by the Items accessory may be imported into an Agenda database using the File Transfer Import command, just like any other structured text file. (The procedure is reviewed briefly to complete the example.)

If you are still in your word processor, exit the program now. Start Agenda and open the Tasks database. Use F8 (VIEW MGR) to switch to the Current Projects view. Move the highlight until the Baxter section head is highlighted. This is where the items from the Items accessory are to be entered.

Issue the File Transfer Import command. The *From file:* setting must be entered. Move the highlight down, type in

baxter2.stf

and press ENTER. (If the file BAXTER2.STF created by the Items accessory is not in the current directory, you need to specify the path for that file.) Change the *Strip carriage returns:* setting to *Yes.* All of the other settings for the Import Structure File box should be appropriate for this operation, so you can accept the default settings. Figure 13-7 shows the settings.

Press F9 to accept the settings and import the file BAXTER2.STF. The two new items that have been imported are displayed under the Baxter section head as shown in Fig. 13-8.

```
Import   Export   Template
Import structured file into current database
=Walker ============================================================== When====
   • Meeting with Ann and Ron Smith Thursday.
   • Check with Ron Smith on meeting time.
   • Meeting to discuss project for James next Monday.          ·03/13/89
   • Call Adam Baker at James Wednesday to get his reactions to ·03/15/89
     our ┌══════════════════════Import Structured File═══════════════╗
Peters   ║ Import:          Items & categories                       ║
   • Meet║ From file:       C:\AGFILES\BAXTER2.STF                    ║
   • Do s║ Delete file:     No                                        ║
         ║                                                            ║
Baxter   ║ Assign to category:      Baxter                           ║
   • Prep║ Combine categories if:   Categories match exactly         ║20/89
   • Crea║ Create new categories:   Yes                              ║20/89
     proj║ Strip carriage returns:  Yes                              ║
   • Prep║                                                            ║20/89
     disc╚══════════════════Press F9 when done, ESC to cancel════════╝
   ♪ Assign at least two staffers to do background research for  ·03/20/89
     the Baxter proposal.
   • Prepare regular status reports on Baxter proposal for top   ·03/20/89
     management.
=F1═══╤══F2═══╤══F3═══╤══F4═══╤══F5═══╤══F6═══╤══F7═══╤══F8═══╤══F9═══╤══F10══
Help  ║ Edit ║      ║      ║      ║      ║      ║Default║Accept║
```

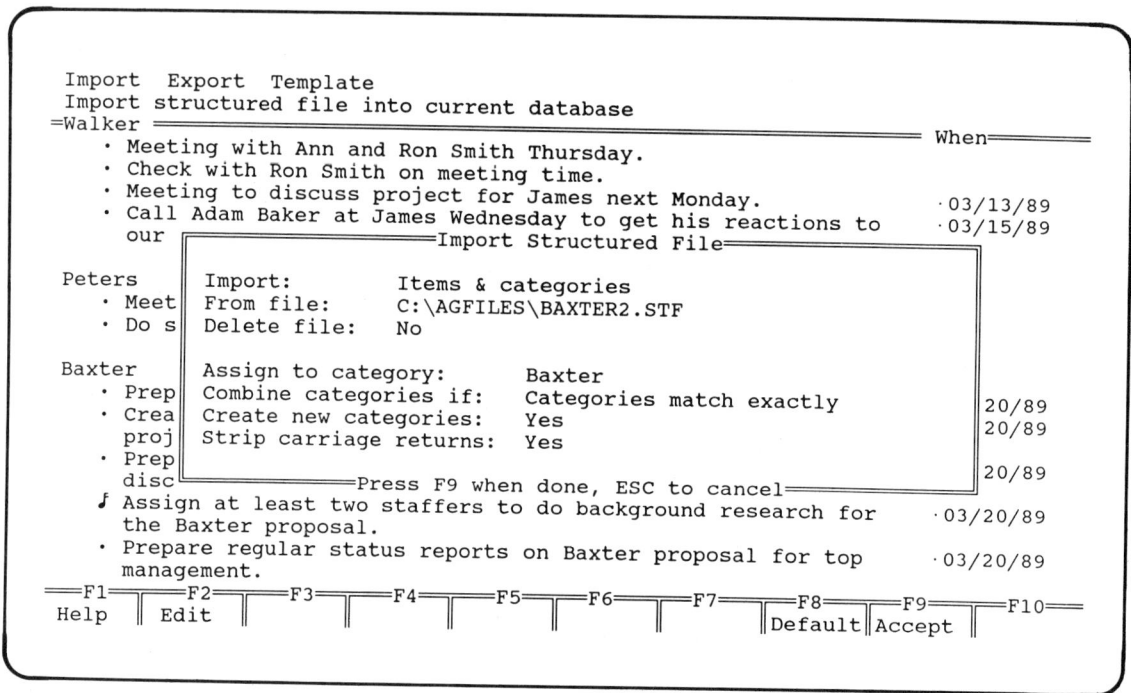

Fig. 13-7. *Importing the file BAXTER2.STF into the Baxter category of the Tasks database.*

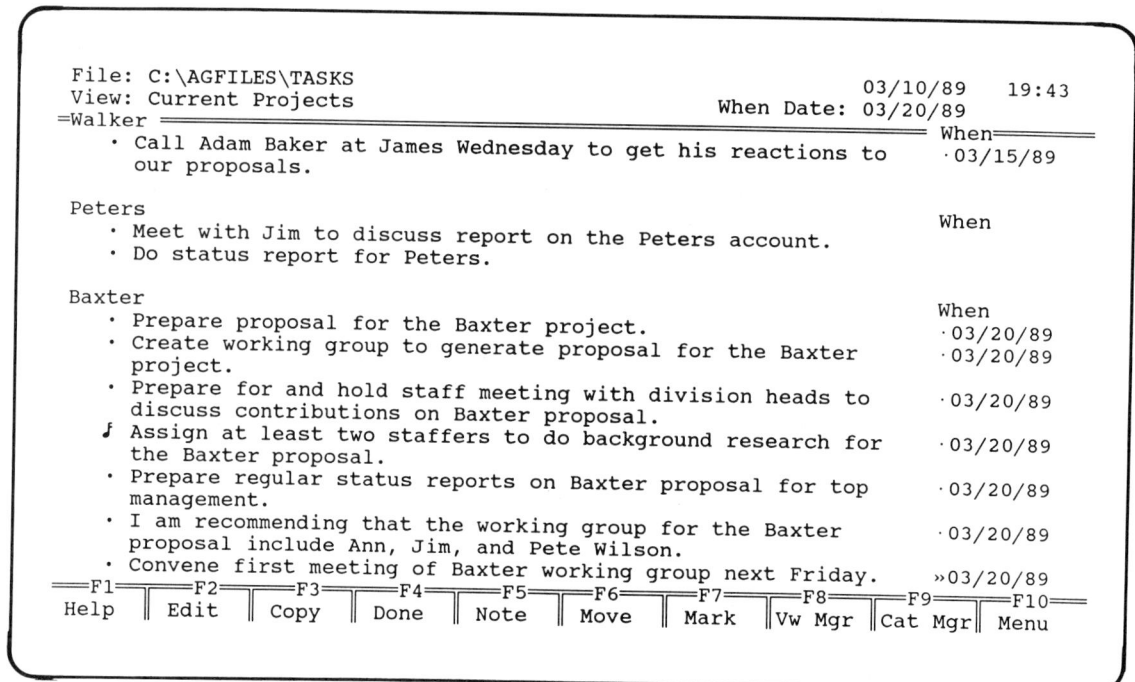

```
File: C:\AGFILES\TASKS                              03/10/89   19:43
View: Current Projects                   When Date: 03/20/89
=Walker ============================================================= When====
   • Call Adam Baker at James Wednesday to get his reactions to  ·03/15/89
     our proposals.

Peters                                                           When
   • Meet with Jim to discuss report on the Peters account.
   • Do status report for Peters.

Baxter                                                           When
   • Prepare proposal for the Baxter project.                    ·03/20/89
   • Create working group to generate proposal for the Baxter    ·03/20/89
     project.
   • Prepare for and hold staff meeting with division heads to   ·03/20/89
     discuss contributions on Baxter proposal.
   ♪ Assign at least two staffers to do background research for  ·03/20/89
     the Baxter proposal.
   • Prepare regular status reports on Baxter proposal for top   ·03/20/89
     management.
   • I am recommending that the working group for the Baxter     ·03/20/89
     proposal include Ann, Jim, and Pete Wilson.
   • Convene first meeting of Baxter working group next Friday.  »03/20/89
=F1═══╤══F2═══╤══F3═══╤══F4═══╤══F5═══╤══F6═══╤══F7═══╤══F8═══╤══F9═══╤══F10══
Help  ║ Edit ║ Copy ║ Done ║ Note ║ Move ║ Mark ║Vw Mgr║Cat Mgr║ Menu
```

Fig. 13-8. *The Current Projects view showing the two items imported into the Baxter section.*

In creating structured text files using the Items accessory, presumably you are entering information that you want to be imported into an Agenda database and you will want to import all of the information entered. Thus, usually most of the default settings for the File Transfer Import command will be appropriate. You might have to change the *Assign to category:* setting if the items are to be assigned to a category other than the currently highlighted one, which is the default.

The correct file name for the structured text file will have to be entered for the *From file:* setting. You will be using the Items accessory to create the structured text files while working with different applications, undoubtedly in different directories. It is not a bad idea to specify the path so that the structured text files are placed in the directory with your Agenda databases. Otherwise, the structured text files created by the Items accessory might be in different directories. You would then have to provide the directory paths to these files when importing them into Agenda. Of course, when you start using the Items accessory regularly to create structured text files for importing into Agenda, you will establish some procedures regarding the directories in which the structured text files will be stored.

Especially for capturing limited numbers of items while working with other applications, the Clipboard and Items accessories are far more flexible and easier to use than creating an ASCII text file and using TXT2STF to convert it into a structured text file. The accessories bring Agenda closer to your other applications, enhancing the power of all.

# 14

# USING MACROS

Macros are sequences of Agenda commands and keystrokes that can be created to perform specified tasks in Agenda. Once created, a macro is invoked simply by selecting its name from the list of macros. Agenda runs the macro, executing the commands and entering the keystrokes to perform the task.

A macro can be a short, simple sequence of commands and keystrokes that performs a basic but often repeated task, such as importing a structured text file or printing a view in a particular format. A macro can also be a long, elaborate program that employs Agenda's special macro commands to automate complex operations in Agenda.

Agenda has a *Learn* feature that makes it easy for even beginning Agenda users to create their own macros. Just tell Agenda to start recording a macro, and then proceed to perform the operation that is to be done by the macro. Agenda records the commands and keystrokes as you do the task and automatically creates the macro. You can then run the macro, which will exactly repeat the actions you performed during the recording.

More advanced users can also write macro programs directly. Agenda includes a variety of special macro commands that may be employed within macros to perform tasks that cannot be accomplished using Agenda in the normal manner. Although this is a form of programming, the basics of macros are not very difficult. Therefore, even relatively inexperienced computer users should at least take a look at the possibilities opened by writing macros.

This chapter begins with a section describing the procedures for recording simple macros and for running macros. The next section explains how to make changes to macros, including the editing of macros to change their operation. The final section addresses the use of macro commands to create more complex macros.

## CREATING AND RUNNING SIMPLE MACROS

The best way to begin understanding macros is to work through the process of creating and running a simple one. Suppose you regularly used the Items accessory to enter new items for your Agenda database. Importing those items using the File Transfer Import command would be a regular activity. You can create a macro to automatically import the structured text files created using the Items accessory.

### Recording Macros

The basic procedure for creating a macro is very easy. You give the macro a name and enter the Learn mode in which Agenda records all of your actions. Then perform whatever actions you want the macro to perform and stop the recording. The macro is created.

Enter the Tasks database and switch to the Current Projects view. Move down to the Baxter section. If you worked through the use of the accessories in the last chapter and imported the two items, they should be the last two items in the section. Use ALT-F4 (DISCARD) to eliminate these items temporarily (you will be importing them again).

In order to complete this example, you will need a structured text file named BAXTER2.STF with one or more items for importing into the database. If you did not work through the last chapter and do not have such a file, you will first have to create one. Use the File Transfer Export command to export some items from the database to such a file. See Chapter 12 if you need further instructions.

Highlight the Baxter section head, since this will be the section into which you will be importing the items from the structured text file. Now begin creating the macro. Enter ALT-F10 (MACRO). In the Macros box that appears, type in

Import Items

as the name for the macro that you will be creating. Then press ENTER. The Macros box is shown in Fig. 14-1. Press F7 (LEARN) to begin recording your actions. From this point forward, Agenda will record

```
  File: C:\AGFILES\TASKS                           03/10/89   Macro
  View: Current Projects
=Walker ═══════════════════════════════════════════════ When═══════
     • Meeting with Ann and Ron Smith Thursday.
     • Check with Ron Smith on meeting time.
     • Meeting to dis┌─────────────Macros═══════════════┐
     • Call Adam Bake│Select macro; INS to create, F2 to edit│to  ·03/13/89
       our proposals.│                                   │    ·03/15/89
                     │                                   │
  Peters             │     Import Items                  │      When
     • Meet with Jim │                                   │
     • Do status repo└═══Press ENTER to run, ESC to cancel═┘
  Baxter                                                        When
     • Prepare proposal for the Baxter project.                ·03/20/89
     • Create working group to generate proposal for the Baxter ·03/20/89
       project.
     • Prepare for and hold staff meeting with division heads to
       discuss contributions on Baxter proposal.              ·03/20/89
     ♪ Assign at least two staffers to do background research for
       the Baxter proposal.                                    ·03/20/89
     • Prepare regular status reports on Baxter proposal for top
       management.                                             ·03/20/89
═F1══════╤═F2═══════╤═F3═══════╤═F4═══════╤═F5══════╤═F6══════╤═F7═══════╤═F8══════╤═F9═══════╤═F10══
 Help    ║EditMac  ║          ║Delete    ║         ║         ║Learn     ║         ║ Run      ║
```

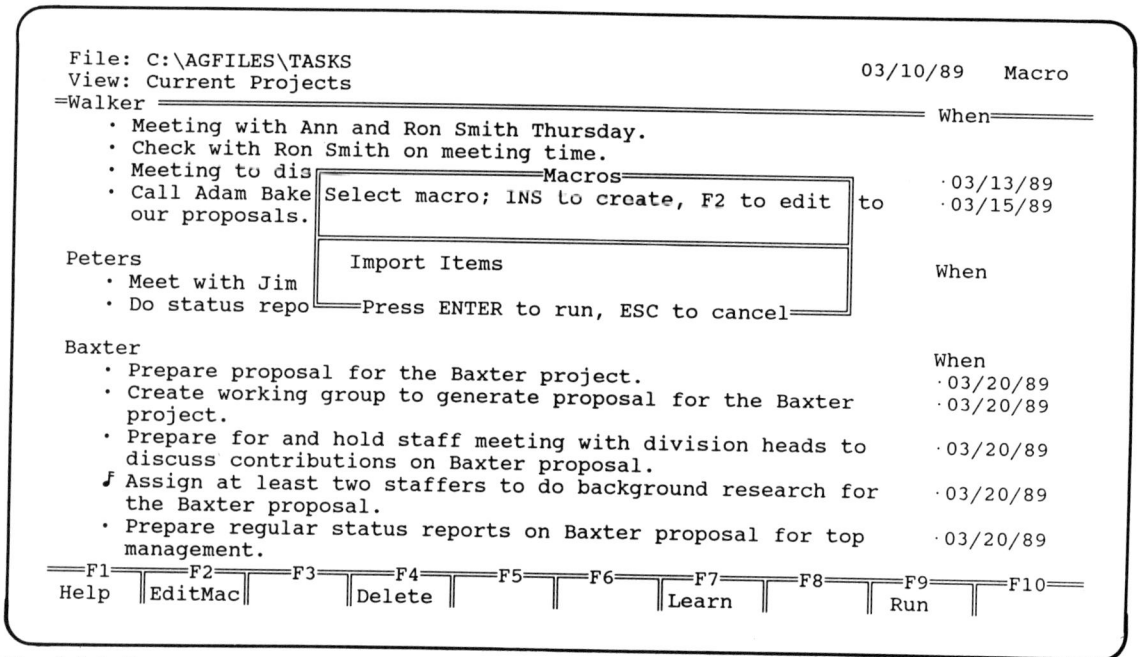

*Fig. 14-1. Beginning the creation of the Import Items macro.*

each keystroke for the Import Items macro. As you press each key, Agenda will emit a low beep to remind you that the keystrokes are being recorded.

Now import the file. Enter the File Transfer Import command by pressing F10 (MENU), F, T, and I. (In recording macros, it is preferable to make selections by typing the first letter rather than by using the arrow keys to highlight the command and pressing ENTER.) The Import Structured File box will be displayed on the screen. To avoid any problems with changed settings, first press ALT-F8 (DEFAULT) to restore the default settings for the Import Structured File box. Designate the correct *From file*: setting. Press the DOWN arrow once to highlight the setting. Enter the complete path and filename for the file to be imported. In this case, it is as follows:

c: \ agfiles \ baxter2.stf

Press ENTER. Press the DOWN arrow until the highlight is to the right of the *Strip Carriage Returns*: setting. Press Y to select the *Yes* option. The settings in the Import Structured File box appear as shown in Fig. 14-2.

Now press F9 to accept the settings and import the information from the structured text file. An Execution box appears briefly, informing you

```
Import  Export  Template
Import structured file into current database
=Walker ══════════════════════════════════════════════  When══════════
      · Meeting with Ann and Ron Smith Thursday.
      · Check with Ron Smith on meeting time.
      · Meeting to discuss project for James next Monday.        ·03/13/89
      · Call Adam Baker at James Wednesday to get his reactions to  ·03/15/89
        our ┌═══════════════════════Import Structured File═══════════════┐
            │                                                            │
Peters      │  Import:            Items & categories                     │
      · Meet │  From file:         C:\AGFILES\BAXTER2.STF                 │
      · Do s │  Delete file:       No                                     │
            │                                                            │
Baxter      │  Assign to category:     Baxter                            │
      · Prep │  Combine categories if:  Categories match exactly          │ 20/89
      · Crea │  Create new categories:  Yes                               │ 20/89
        proj │  Strip carriage returns: Yes                               │
      · Prep │                                                            │ 20/89
        disc └══════════════Press F9 when done, ESC to cancel════════════┘
      ♪ Assign at least two staffers to do background research for    ·03/20/89
        the Baxter proposal.
      · Prepare regular status reports on Baxter proposal for top     ·03/20/89
        management.
══F1══╤══F2══╤══F3══╤══F4══╤══F5══╤══F6══╤══F7══╤══F8═══╤══F9═══╤══F10══
Help  ║ Edit ║      ║      ║      ║      ║      ║Default║Accept ║
```

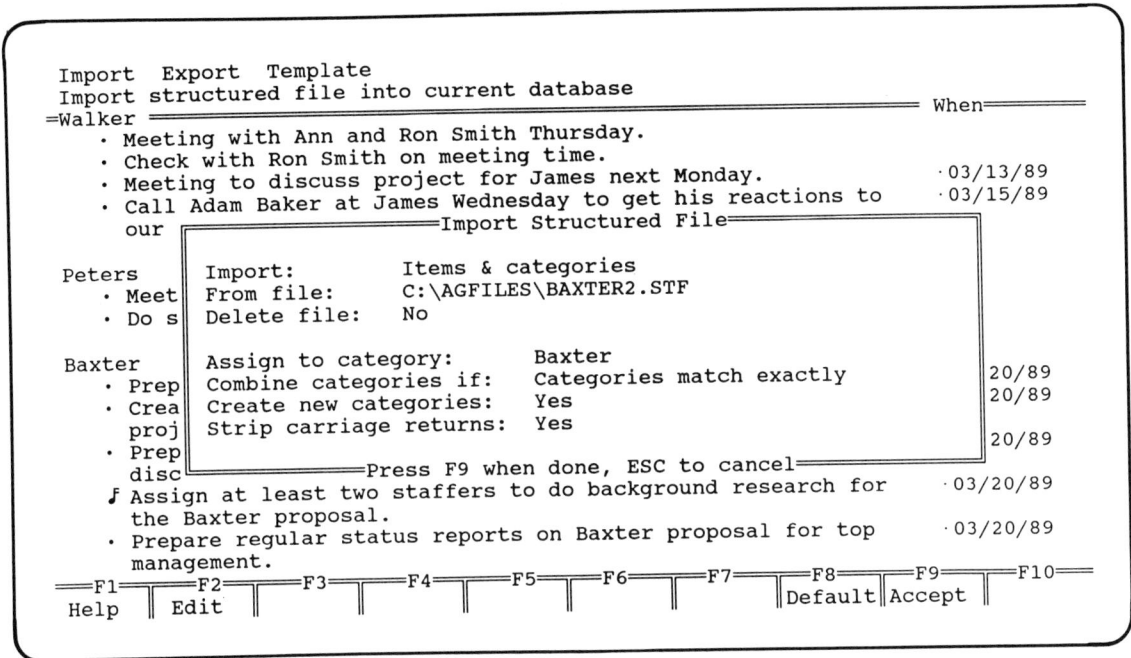

Fig. 14-2. *The settings in the Import Structured File box for the Import Items macro.*

of the progress of the importation. Do not press any other keys. You are returned to the view.

This completes the structured text file import procedure that is to be recorded as the Import Items macro. You must now turn off the recording of the keystrokes. Press ALT-F10 (MACRO) to turn off the Learn mode and terminate the recording. The Macro Learn box appears in the middle of the screen informing you that the recording has been turned off, as shown in Fig. 14-3. Press any key to continue. You can scroll down to see the two items imported into the Baxter section.

The ALT-F10 (MACRO) key is used to begin the creation of a macro. Agenda displays the Macros box. If this is the first macro you are creating in a database, just type in a descriptive name for the macro and press ENTER. If you have already created macros, first press INS and then type in the name and press ENTER. The Macros box provides the appropriate instructions.

With the macro name you have just entered still highlighted, begin recording the macro by pressing F7 (LEARN). From this point forward, every keystroke you enter is recorded until you instruct Agenda to stop. End the recording by pressing ALT-F10 (MACRO).

When recording macros, it is preferable to enter commands and choices of settings by pressing their initial letters rather than by using the cursor arrows

```
    File: C:\AGFILES\TASKS                                   03/10/89
    View: Current Projects
  =Walker ══════════════════════════════════════════════ When══════
      · Meeting with Ann and Ron Smith Thursday.
      · Check with Ron Smith on meeting time.
      · Meeting to discuss project for James next Monday.      ·03/13/89
      · Call Adam Baker at James Wednesday to get his reactions to  ·03/15/89
        our proposals.
                         ┌──────────Macro Learn──────────┐
    Peters               │                               │          When
      · Meet with Jim to │ Learn mode has been turned off │nt.
      · Do status report │                               │
                         └──────Press any key to continue─┘
    Baxter                                                        When
      · Prepare proposal for the Baxter project.                  ·03/20/89
      · Create working group to generate proposal for the Baxter  ·03/20/89
        project.
      · Prepare for and hold staff meeting with division heads to  ·03/20/89
        discuss contributions on Baxter proposal.
      ♪ Assign at least two staffers to do background research for  ·03/20/89
        the Baxter proposal.
      · Prepare regular status reports on Baxter proposal for top  ·03/20/89
        management.
  ══F1═══╤══F2═══╤══F3═══╤══F4═══╤══F5═══╤══F6═══╤══F7═══╤══F8═══╤═F9═══╤═F10══
   Help  ║       ║       ║       ║       ║       ║       ║       ║Accept ║
```

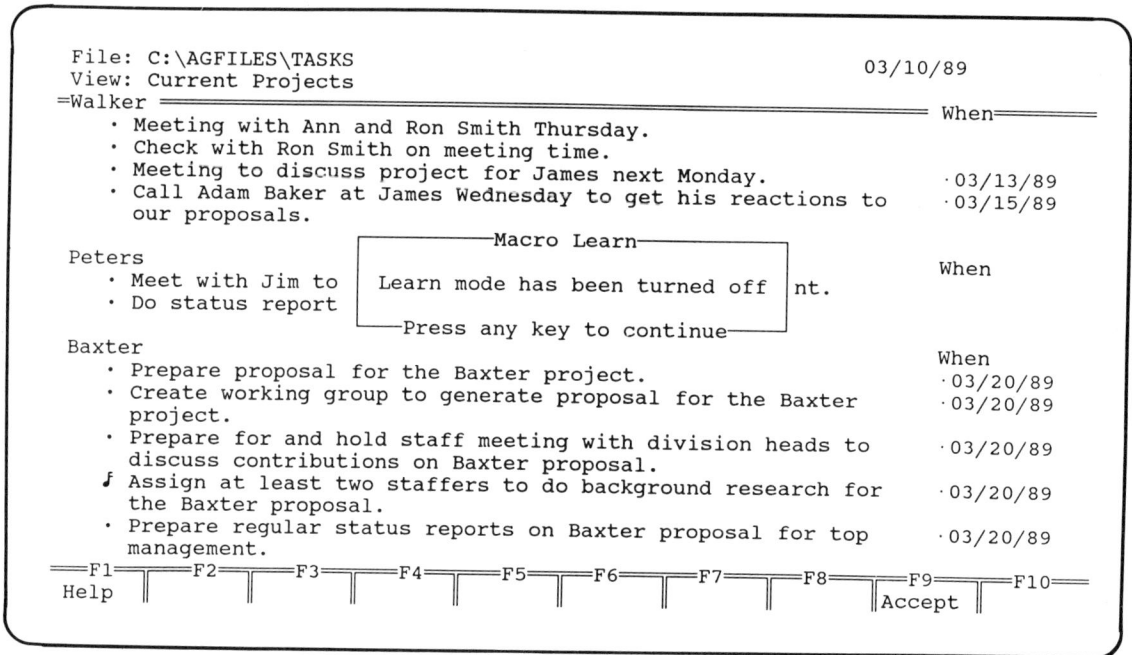

Fig. 14-3. *Completing the recording of the Import Items macro.*

to move the highlight and then pressing ENTER (after using GREY PLUS to open the box with the selections for settings). This makes the recorded macro easier to follow if you edit it later. For example, in the macro just recorded, the keystrokes *fti* clearly indicate that the macro is invoking the File Transfer Import command. If, instead, you had used the arrow keys and ENTER to specify the command, it would be more difficult to interpret the recorded keystrokes.

When entering the name of a file, category, or view while recording a macro, it is very important to type out the name rather than highlighting it and pressing ENTER on a list. This is because the entries on the list might change. For example, in creating the Items Import macro, you were instructed to type in the name of the structured text file BAXTER2.STF. When using the File Transfer Import command, you can also enter the file name for the *From file:* setting by pressing GREY PLUS to display the list of structured text files previously created, pressing the DOWN arrow until the desired file is highlighted, and pressing ENTER. Suppose you did this in recording the Items import macro. After pressing GREY PLUS, you would press the DOWN arrow to highlight the file BAXTER2.STF. If that were the third entry on the list of structured text files, you would press the DOWN arrow twice and then press ENTER. Agenda would record for the macro the keystrokes GREY PLUS, DOWN, DOWN, and ENTER. This sequence would select the third file on the list of structured text files. Later, if structured text files were created or deleted, the third file might no longer be BAXTER2.STF, but the macro would still select and enter the name of the third file.

The same problems can arise in entering category and view names. Whenever the category hierarchy or the list of views is displayed and you need to select a category or view when recording a macro, type in the name. Agenda's search feature will automatically result in the correct category or view name being highlighted. For example, the Reports category might currently be the seventh category in the Category hierarchy. Using the DOWN arrow to select this category in a macro will select Reports as long as it remains seventh. When a preceding category is deleted, however, Reports becomes sixth on the list but the macro still selects the seventh category.

If you make mistakes when recording a macro, you have two options. You can continue, finishing the recording of the procedure, and then edit the macro to correct the changes. Alternatively, you can stop the recording and start over, recording the procedure again. The procedures for editing macros and starting over are explained in the section of this chapter titled "Changing Macros."

## Executing Macros

Executing a macro simply requires that you enter the macro command, select the desired macro, and press ENTER. Agenda automatically executes the recorded keystrokes and any other commands that have been entered into the macro, performing the macro's task.

You have created the Import Items macro. Now it is time to run the macro and see it perform. The macro will import the items from the file BAXTER2.STF. You have already imported these items in creating the macro, so you might wish to discard them from the Tasks database. In the Current Projects view, highlight the newly imported items, which should be the last two items in the Baxter section, and use ALT-F4 (DISCARD) to get rid of them. (This step is not absolutely necessary; if you do not discard the items, you will simply end up with two copies of the same items in the database, and this is only practice.)

Move the highlight to the Baxter section head to import the items into this section. To execute the macro, press ALT-F10 (MACROS) to display the Macros box with the list of macros. Highlight the macro to be executed, Import Items. (Unless you have created other macros, this will be the only macro in the database and will necessarily be highlighted.) Press ENTER to execute the macro. Various boxes flash by on the screen, too quickly to read, as the Import Items macro is executed. The disk drive operates, the items are imported, and Agenda returns you to the Current Projects view. The two new items have been imported from the file BAXTER2.STF and can be seen in the Baxter section.

When a macro is executed, Agenda performs the operations specified by the macro. If the macro was created by recording keystrokes, Agenda attempts to repeat exactly the same keystrokes you used when you recorded the macro. Changes made since the macro was originally recorded occasionally can cause errors, premature termination of the macro, or unexpected consequences. For example, if the Import Items macro were run and no file with the name BAXTER2.STF existed, you would receive an error message to that effect. The macro would terminate execution in the middle of the File Transfer Import operation.

Suppose a macro were created that switched to a particular view and printed it. If that view were deleted from the database, the macro would encounter problems. During execution, the macro presumably would enter the view name in the View Manager. When Agenda recognized the view name as being different from any existing view (because the view had been deleted), it would present the View Define box to allow the definition of a new view. The macro would attempt to enter the print operations as the name for the new view. Things would continue to become more confused until the macro ended or an error was generated.

Probably the most common pitfall for macros in Agenda is the mode problem. Agenda has many modes in which you can operate—in views, notes, the Category Manager, and so on. If, while in one mode, you begin executing a macro that was recorded in another mode, the macro will encounter problems because it will attempt to perform actions that are invalid in that mode. For example, if you execute the Import Items macro while in the Category Manager, you will get a long string of beeps indicating invalid keystrokes as the macro executes. However, the macro will end up executing the Indexed command and will unindex the current category.

You can use macro commands to create macros that will automatically switch to the appropriate mode before continuing execution. Otherwise, remember the mode in which a macro was created and used, and only run the macro while you are in that mode.

## CHANGING MACROS

Once a macro has been created by entering its name in the Macros box, it becomes part of the Agenda database. You can record the keystrokes associated with any operations—as described previously—to produce a macro. However, you might want to make changes to the macros that you have created. You can display and edit the keystrokes in macros and also enter the special macro commands provided by Agenda. You can also add keystrokes to macros, delete entire macros, and perform other related operations with the macros in your database.

## Editing Macros

When you record a macro, Agenda literally records the keystrokes you enter in a long list. The printable characters—letters, numbers, punctuation, and other symbols—are represented by the characters themselves. The other keys on the keyboard are represented by the name of the key enclosed in curly braces. For example, pressing F10 would be represented as {F10}, and pressing HOME would be represented as {HOME}. The representations of special keys within macros is summarized in Table 14-1. It is also possible to create a macro by directly entering each keystroke and the names of the special keys.

### Table 14-1. Representations of Special Keys in Macros.

| Special Key | Macro Representation |
| --- | --- |
| ENTER | {ENTER} |
| HOME | {HOME} |
| END | {END} |
| UP | {UP}*** |
| DOWN | {DOWN} |
| RIGHT | {RIGHT} |
| LEFT | {LEFT} |
| PAGE UP | {PgUp} |
| PAGE DOWN | {PgDn} |
| BACKSPACE | {BS} |
| TAB | {TAB} |
| ESCAPE | {ESC} |
| INSERT | {INS} |
| DELETE | {DEL} |
| GREY PLUS | {Grey +} |
| GREY MINUS | {Grey −} |
| Function Key F1 | {F1} |
| . . . | . . . |
| Function Key F10 | {F10} |
| CONTROL-Key | {CtlKEY} |
|    CONTROL-ENTER | {CtlENTER} |
|    . . . | . . . |
| ALTERNATE-Key | {AltKEY} |
|    ALTERNATE-F1 | {AltF1} |
|    . . . | . . . |
|    ALTERNATE-A | {AltA} |
|    . . . | . . . |

You can view and edit the list of keystrokes that make up a macro. Keystrokes may be added, changed, or deleted. When the macro is run, the keystrokes on the edited list are executed.

The Import Items macro has been serving you well, but you have decided to start using the name ITEMS.STF for the structured text file to be used in transferring items from the Items accessory. The general name ITEMS.STF is more appropriate for repeated importation than the specific name BAXTER2.STF. You will edit the Import Items macro so that it imports the ITEMS.STF files.

Press ALT-F10 (MACRO) and highlight the Import Items macro. Press F2 (EDIT) to edit the macro. Its contents are displayed as shown in Fig. 14-4. The first entry is the name of the macro enclosed within curly braces, followed by the keystrokes recorded in the macro. First comes {F10}fti, the keystrokes used to issue the File Transfer Import command. The {AltF8} represents the pressing of the key to restore all of the settings to their default values. The {DOWN} is the one press of the DOWN arrow that moves the highlight in the Import Structured File box down to the *From file:* setting. Next come the characters

c: \ agfiles \ baxter2.stf

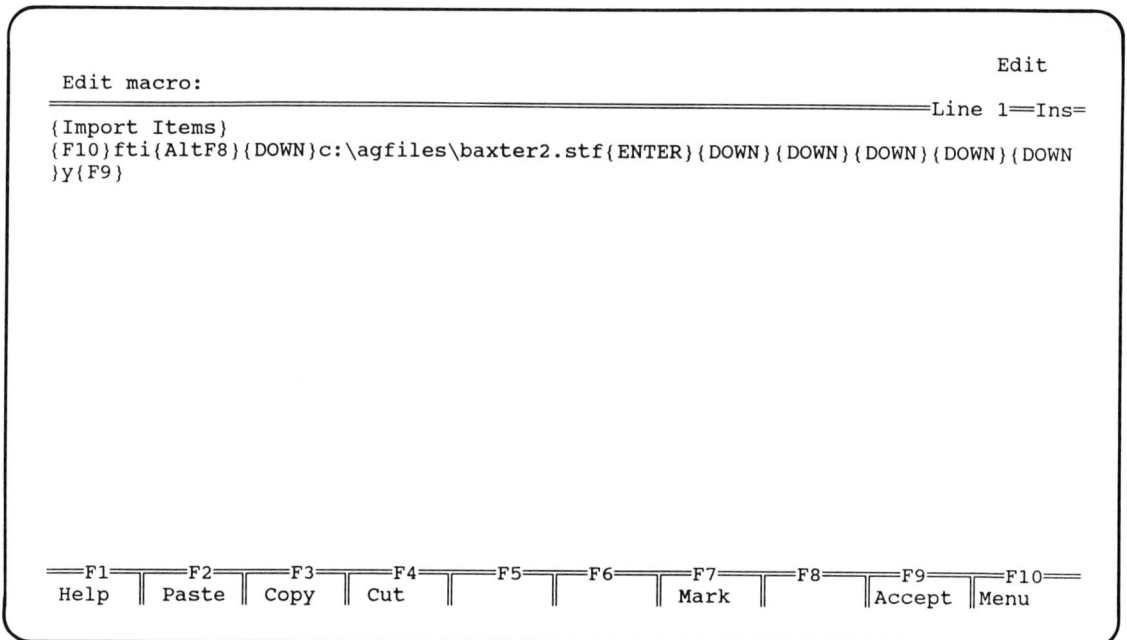

```
                                                                    Edit
   Edit macro:
========================================================================Line 1══Ins═
{Import Items}
{F10}fti{AltF8}{DOWN}c:\agfiles\baxter2.stf{ENTER}{DOWN}{DOWN}{DOWN}{DOWN}{DOWN
}y{F9}








═F1═══╤═F2═══╤═F3═══╤═F4═══╤═F5═══╤═F6═══╤═F7═══╤═F8═══╤═F9═══╤═F10══
 Help ║ Paste║ Copy ║ Cut  ║      ║      ║ Mark ║      ║Accept║Menu
```

Fig. 14-4. *The Import Items macro as it was originally recorded.*

that the macro enters as the file name. The {ENTER} represents the pressing of the ENTER key to enter the file name. Five {DOWN} keypresses move the highlight to the *Strip Carriage Returns:* setting, and the Y changes the option to *Yes*. Finally, the {F9} accepts the settings and imports the file.

The macro may be edited just as any other text in Agenda. To change the macro to import the file ITEMS.STF, use the RIGHT arrow to move the cursor over to the first letter in baxter2. Press DEL to delete the name baxter2. Now type in

items

to insert the new file name. (The assumption is that ITEMS.STF will be stored in the same directory, so the path does not need to be changed.) After this change to the file name, the Import Items macro appears as in Fig. 14-5. Press F9 to accept the results of editing the Import Items macro. You are returned to the Macros box. Press ESC to return to the view.

If you want to try out the revised version of the macro, you need a structured text file named ITEMS.STF. You could use the File Transfer Export command to export some items from the database into a file with that name. However, it is easier to make a copy of the existing file

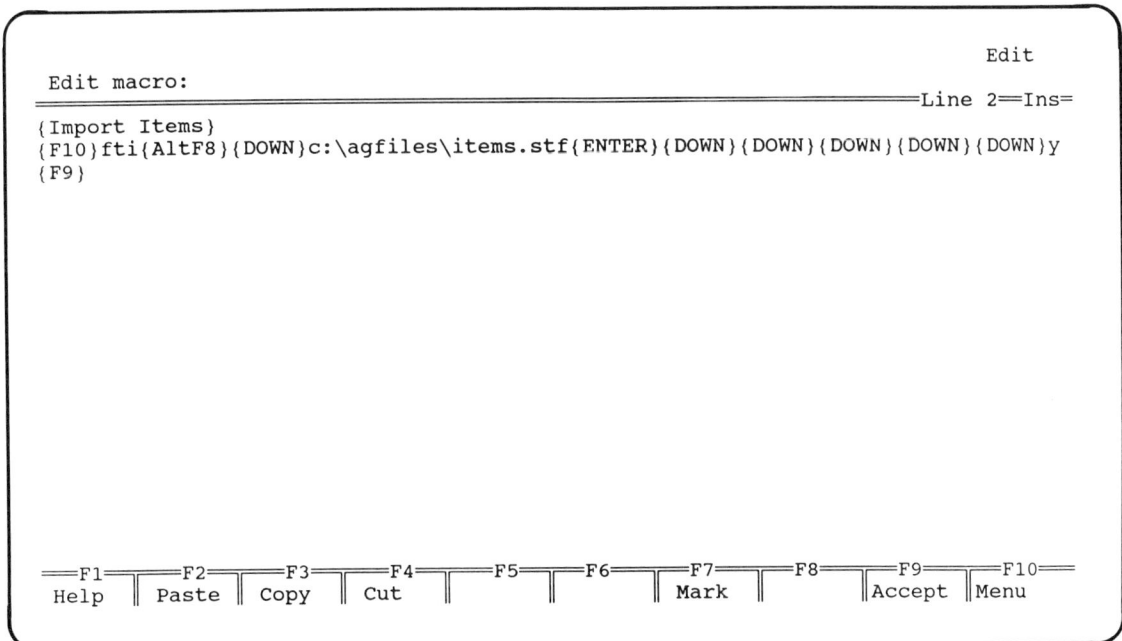

```
                                                                    Edit
 Edit macro:
══════════════════════════════════════════════════════════════════Line 2══Ins══
{Import Items}
{F10}fti{AltF8}{DOWN}c:\agfiles\items.stf{ENTER}{DOWN}{DOWN}{DOWN}{DOWN}{DOWN}y
{F9}




═F1═══╤═F2═══╤═F3═══╤═F4═══╤═F5═══╤═F6═══╤═F7═══╤═F8═══╤═F9═══╤═F10══
Help  ║ Paste║ Copy ║ Cut  ║      ║      ║ Mark ║      ║Accept║Menu
```

Fig. 14-5. *The Import Items macro edited to import items from the file ITEMS.STF.*

BAXTER2.STF and use that. To do that without quitting Agenda, use the System command to temporarily exit to DOS. Accept the running of COMMAND.COM. When the DOS prompt is displayed, issue the following DOS command:

```
copy baxter2.stf items.stf
```

Press ENTER to make a copy of the original structured text file. (If you started Agenda from a directory other than the one containing the file BAXTER2.STF, you either have to include the paths for both file names or change to that directory before issuing the COPY command.) After you have made the copy, return to Agenda by typing this command:

```
exit
```

Then press ENTER. You should have a file named ITEMS.STF that includes the same two items you have been importing from the file BAXTER2.STF.

Switch to the Current Projects view, if necessary. Delete the newly imported items again. (They should be the last two in the Baxter section.) Highlight the Baxter section head. Now run the revised macro. Press ALT-F10 (MACRO), highlight the Import Items macro, and press ENTER. The macro executes and the items are imported into the database, this time from the file ITEMS.STF.

Any macro may be edited by issuing the ALT-F10 (MACRO) command, highlighting the name of the macro, and pressing F2 (EDIT). The macro is displayed on the screen. You edit the macro just like you edit a Note. The cursor movement commands, text deletion operations, and so forth are exactly the same. The copy, cut, and paste capabilities of the note editor are also available. Even the Note commands are available. These are displayed for selection by pressing F10 (MENU), as usual. You can use commands to print out a macro, import or export macros from ASCII text files, and delete all of the information in the current macro.

Special keys are represented in the Edit macro screen by the key name or an abbreviation enclosed within curly braces, as discussed earlier and summarized in Table 14-1. Agenda's special macro commands are also enclosed within curly braces.

Only the special keys and the macro commands enclosed in curly braces are given their special interpretations when a macro is executed. All other characters within the macro actually will be entered as the same characters when the macro is executed. This is the basis for one type of error you can make while editing macros. Suppose a macro was to include pressing the HOME key. You are editing the macro and type in

{HONE}

making a spelling error in entering HOME within the curly braces. When the macro is executed, Agenda will not recognize this as the instruction to press the HOME key. Therefore, it will enter the characters {, H, O, N, E, and }, one by one, instead.

You can insert carriage returns when editing macros to break long lines up into shorter lines. (Do not divide the key equivalents or macro commands within the curly braces, however.) This will not affect the operation of the macro, but can make the macro much easier to follow as you edit it.

Pressing F9 accepts the results of the edit and makes the changes to the macro permanent. If you want to exit the macro editor without making any changes to the macro, press ESC.

## Making Other Changes

Once a macro has been created, you can add more keystrokes to the macro by recording them, or you can re-record the macro from the beginning. If macros are no longer needed, they can be deleted from the database. You can also export macros to move them into other Agenda databases.

To record additional operations for a macro, press ALT-F10 (MACROS), highlight the macro to which you wish to add the keystrokes, and press F7 (LEARN). Agenda gives you two options: to replace the macro or to append the recorded keystrokes to the existing macro. Select the Append option and press ENTER. You are now in the Learn mode. Every keystroke will be recorded and added to the macro until you press ALT-F10 (MACROS) to turn off the recording.

Alternatively, you can start from the beginning when recording operations for an existing macro. The most common use of this will be when you make a mistake while recording the macro initially. Stop the recording. Then re-record the macro by pressing ALT-F10 (MACROS), highlighting the macro to be re-recorded, and pressing F7 (LEARN). Select the Replace option to erase the previously recorded keystrokes and start the macro with the keystrokes you are about the enter. When you press ENTER, recording begins. When you have finished the recording, press ALT-F10 (MACROS).

To deleting a macro from a database, use ALT-F10 (MACROS) to display the Macros box and the list of macros. Then highlight the macro to be deleted and press F4 (DELETE) to delete the macro from the database. Agenda will ask that you confirm that you really do want the macro deleted. Make your choice and press ENTER. The macro is eliminated from the database and cannot be recovered.

You might create a macro in one Agenda database that would be useful in another. Since every macro is stored within a specific database, you will have to copy the macro to the second database. This procedure involves writing the macro information to an ASCII text file and then reading the file back into a macro in the second database.

Begin the process of transferring a macro by entering the edit mode for the macro to be transferred. Press ALT-F10 (MACROS), highlight the macro, and press F2 (EDIT). Next, press F10 (MENU) to display the commands, and select Export. Enter the name to be given to the ASCII text file to which the macro is to be written. Press F9, and the macro is exported.

To import a macro, the procedures are reversed, except that you will need to create a macro if you are importing it as a new macro. Press ALT-F10 (MACROS), press INS to create a new macro, type in the name for the macro, press ENTER, and press F2 (EDIT). You will be viewing an "empty" macro. Press F10 (MENU) and select the Import command. Enter the name of the ASCII text file with the macro to be imported. Press F9, and the macro is copied from the file into the macro editor. Press F9 to accept the results.

Part of a macro may be exported by marking that part before issuing the Export command. Also, you can import macros into existing macros. The information imported will be inserted into the macro at the cursor.

## USING MACRO COMMANDS

Agenda includes 27 macro commands that can be included within macros to perform operations that cannot be performed from the keyboard. These commands significantly extend the power of macros to accomplish significant tasks, but their use involves a form of programming going beyond other skills required to use Agenda. The first part of this section provides an example of the use of several macro commands within a longer macro. The second part gives a brief introduction to the principles of macro programming.

### An Example Using Macro Commands

Developing a sense of the possibilities created by the macro commands is best accomplished by first going through an illustration of their use. This section explains the creation of a longer macro that employs several macro commands.

The Import Items macro is too limited to fully meet your needs. What you really want is a macro that can import structured text files with different file names each time the macro is executed. You also need to create new views and sections into which the items are imported. In that way, you can see the items, check them, and work with them as a group before turning to the remainder of the database. The view and section can be given the same name as the structured text file being imported. When you create files with the Items accessory, you can give the files distinctive names. For example, you can give a third group of items relating to Baxter the name BAXTER3. Then you can import these items into a new Baxter3 section in a new Baxter3 view.

Begin by creating the file BAXTER3.STF for importation. To do this, you can simply make another copy of the BAXTER2.STF structure text file. Use the System command to exit to DOS, and issue the following DOS command:

```
copy baxter2.stf baxter3.stf
```

Press ENTER. Then type exit and press ENTER to return to Agenda.

Macro commands cannot be entered while using the Learn mode to record a macro. You could enter macros that use macro commands by typing in the entire macro while in the macro editor. However, it is often easier to first record a macro that approximates the desired one but does not contain the macro commands. You can then use the macro editor to change the recorded macro, entering the macro commands. You will do that here. From any view of the Tasks database, press ALT-F10 (MACRO), press INS to create a new macro, and type in the name

```
Import Items into New Section
```

and then press ENTER. Begin recording by pressing F7 (LEARN).

You will record the macro to import a file named BAXTER3.STF. Begin by creating the new view and section by entering the View New command and pressing F10, V, N. Type

```
Baxter3
```

and press ENTER to enter the view name. Then enter the same name for the category name by pressing the DOWN arrow once and typing

```
Baxter3
```

and press ENTER. Press F9 to accept the settings and create and enter the view.

Now import the items. Press F10, F, T, I for the File Transfer Import command. Once in the Import Structured File box, press F8 (DFLTALL). Then press DOWN once to move to the *From file:* setting.

Type in the file name, with the appropriate path:

c: \ agfiles \ baxter3.stf

Then press ENTER. (As in the earlier macro, your path might be different.) Press the DOWN arrow until the highlight is to the right of the *Strip Carriage Returns:* setting. Press Y to select the *Yes* option. Press F9 to accept the settings and import the items from the file. The newly imported items are displayed in the new section and view. Press ALT-F10 (MACROS) to stop recording the macro.

Now you need to edit the recorded macro to add the desired features. Press ALT-F10, highlight the Import Items into New Section macro, and press F2 (EDIT). The macro is displayed as it was recorded, as shown in Fig. 14-6. The macro must now be edited to produce the macro shown in Fig. 14-7. You need to make three editing changes:

First, insert carriage returns to break the macro up into shorter lines with a single action on each line. (This is not required, but it makes the macro far easier to read.) Second, insert the following commands into the macro at the locations shown in Fig. 14-7:

```
{INPUT;Structured Text File to be Imported;%a}
{IFEQ;%a;#NULL;end}
{LABEL;end}
{END}
```

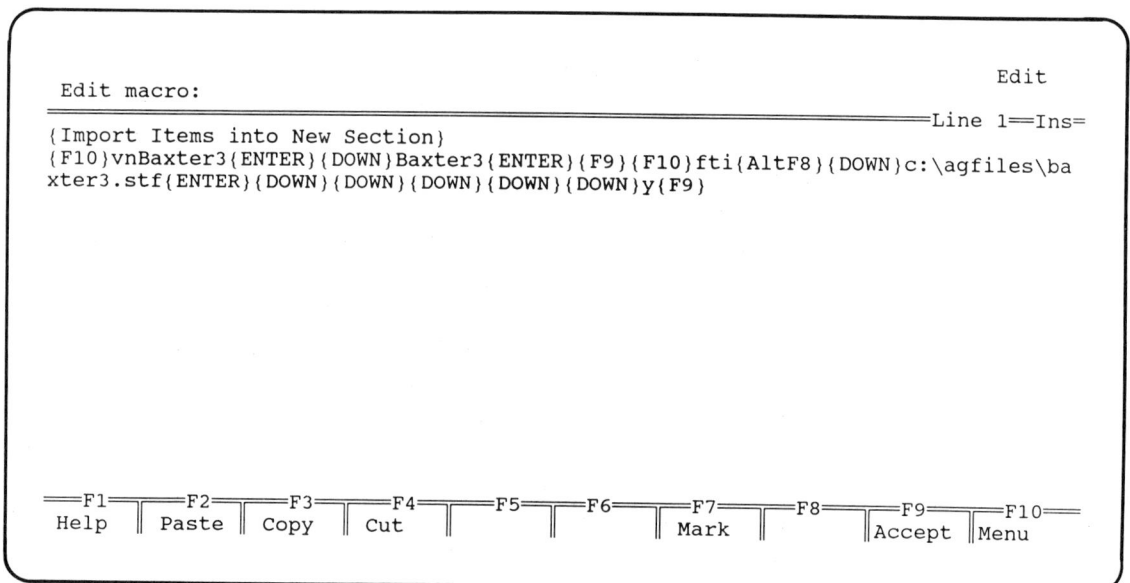

```
                                                        Edit
   Edit macro:
===============================================================Line 1==Ins=
{Import Items into New Section}
{F10}vnBaxter3{ENTER}{DOWN}Baxter3{ENTER}{F9}{F10}fti{AltF8}{DOWN}c:\agfiles\ba
xter3.stf{ENTER}{DOWN}{DOWN}{DOWN}{DOWN}{DOWN}y{F9}




==F1==T==F2==T==F3==T==F4==T==F5==T==F6==T==F7==T==F8==T==F9==T==F10==
Help  | Paste | Copy | Cut  |      |      | Mark |      |Accept|Menu
```

Fig. 14-6. *The Import Items into New Section macro as originally recorded.*

```
                                                                  Edit
  Edit macro:
                                                        ═══Line 10══Ins═
 ═════════════════════════════════════════════════════════════════════
 {Import Items into New Section}
 {INPUT;Structured Text File to be Imported;%a}
 {IFEQ;%a;#NULL;end}
 {F10}vn
 {TYPE;%a}{ENTER}
 {DOWN}{TYPE;%a}{ENTER}
 {F9}
 {F10}fti
 {AltF8}
 {DOWN}c:\agfiles\{TYPE;%a}.stf{ENTER}
 {DOWN}{DOWN}{DOWN}{DOWN}{DOWN}y
 {F9}
 {LABEL;end}
 {END}




 ══F1══╤══F2══╤══F3══╤══F4══╤══F5══╤══F6══╤══F7══╤══F8══╤══F9══╤══F10══
  Help │ Paste│ Copy │ Cut  │      │      │ Mark │      │Accept│Menu
```

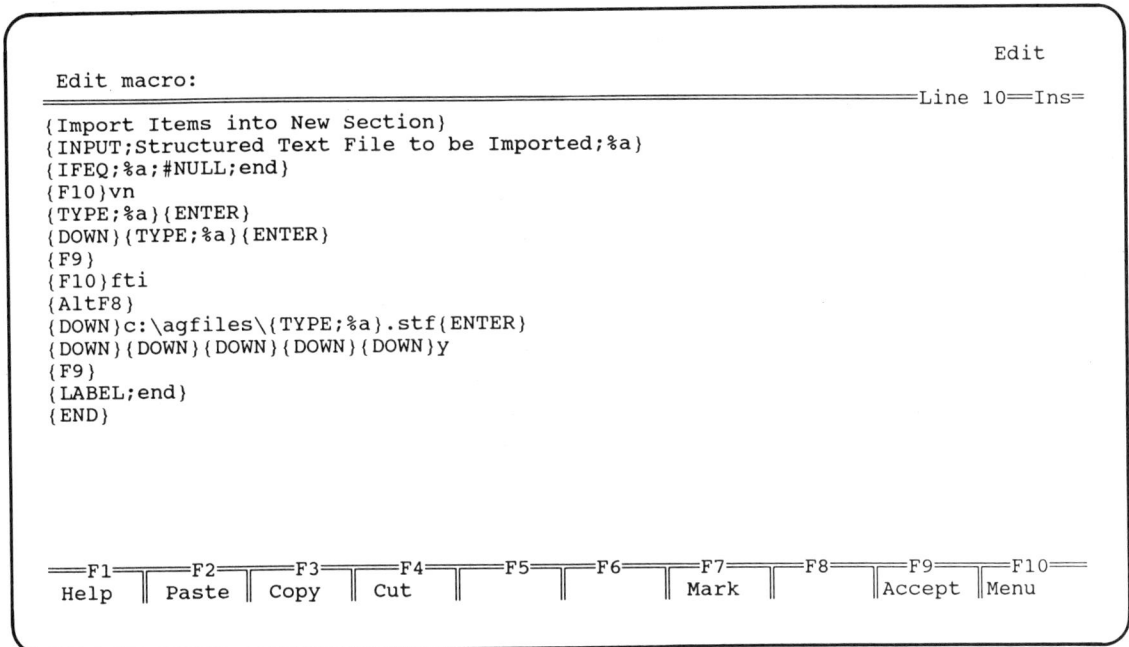

Fig. 14-7. *The Import Items into New Section macro as edited to prompt the user for a file name to use in creating the view and section and importing the file.*

Third, insert the command {TYPE;%a} in place of the word "Baxter3" each time that word appears in the originally recorded macro. You can use ALT-F5 (SEARCH) to perform an automatic search and replace operation. The edited macro should now appear as shown in Fig. 14-7. Press F9 to accept the changes, and press ESC to return to a view.

To try the modified macro, you will need another structured text file to import. Create the file BAXTER4.STF by copying BAXTER3. STF. Use the System command to exit to DOS, issue the DOS command

copy baxter3.stf baxter4.stf

and press ENTER. Then type exit and press ENTER to return to Agenda.

Now begin executing the new macro. Press ALT-F10 (MACRO). Highlight the Import Items into New Section macro in the Macros box. Press ENTER to begin executing the macro. The macro first displays a box on the screen asking you for the name of the structured text file to be imported. Type in

Baxter4

and press ENTER. The screen will appear as shown in Fig. 14-8. Press
ENTER again to accept the entry and continue macro execution. The new
Baxter4 view and Baxter4 section head are created, and the items from
the file BAXTER4.STF are imported into that section. Figure 14-9 shows
the results.

You can see the way macro commands operate by going through the Import
Items in New Section macro step-by-step. An explanation of the operation of the
macro follows. The first operation in the macro is the execution of the following
macro command:

{INPUT;Structured Text File to be Imported;%a}

The INPUT command allows the user to enter information during the execution
of the macro. When the macro is executed, this command displays the box on
the screen that is shown in Fig. 14-8. The user is allowed to enter text into the
box. When the user presses ENTER to accept the text, the command stores the
text in a variable called %a and erases the box. This text is stored in %a for
the duration of the execution of the macro.

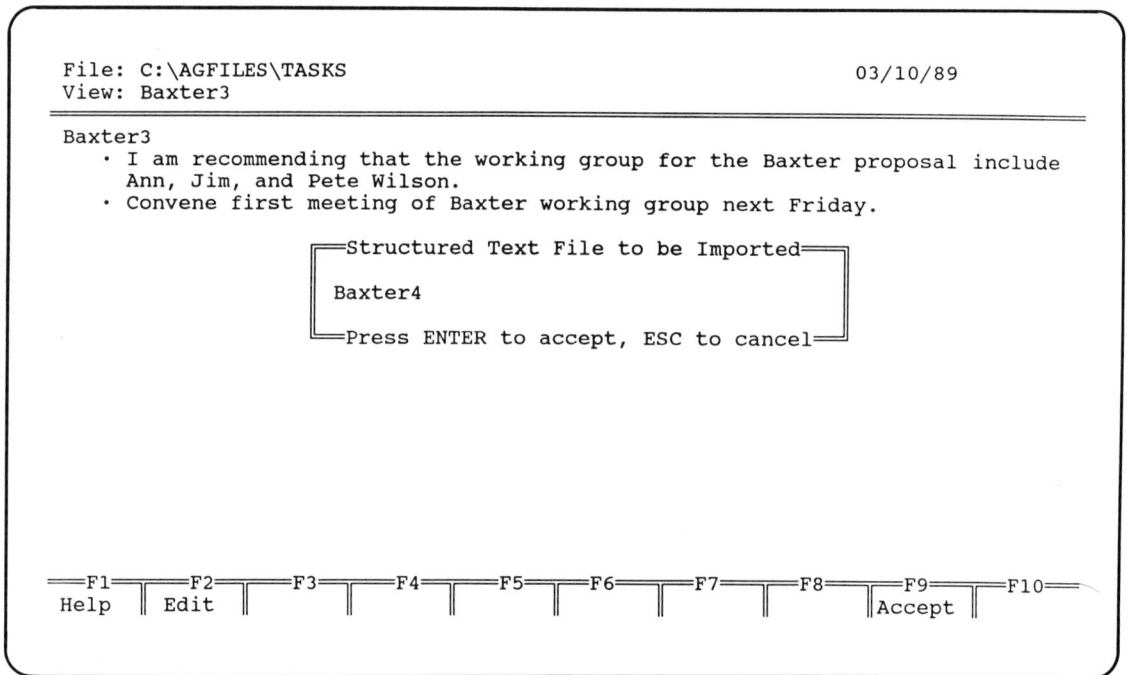

```
 File: C:\AGFILES\TASKS                                      03/10/89
 View: Baxter3
═══════════════════════════════════════════════════════════════════════
 Baxter3
    • I am recommending that the working group for the Baxter proposal include
      Ann, Jim, and Pete Wilson.
    • Convene first meeting of Baxter working group next Friday.

                    ┌═Structured Text File to be Imported═┐
                    │                                     │
                    │ Baxter4                             │
                    │                                     │
                    └═Press ENTER to accept, ESC to cancel═┘




  ═F1══╤══F2══╤══F3══╤══F4══╤══F5══╤══F6══╤══F7══╤══F8══╤══F9═══╤═F10══
  Help ║ Edit ║      ║      ║      ║      ║      ║      ║Accept ║
```

Fig. 14-8. *The prompt for the name of the file to be imported by the Import Items into New Section*
*macro.*

```
File: C:\AGFILES\TASKS                              03/10/89   20:31
View: Baxter4                          When Date: 03/20/89
====================================================================
Baxter4
    • I am recommending that the working group for the Baxter proposal include
      Ann, Jim, and Pete Wilson.
    • Convene first meeting of Baxter working group next Friday.




=F1====F2====F3====F4====F5====F6====F7====F8====F9====F10==
 Help || Edit || Copy || Done || Note || Move || Mark ||Vw Mgr||Cat Mgr|| Menu
```

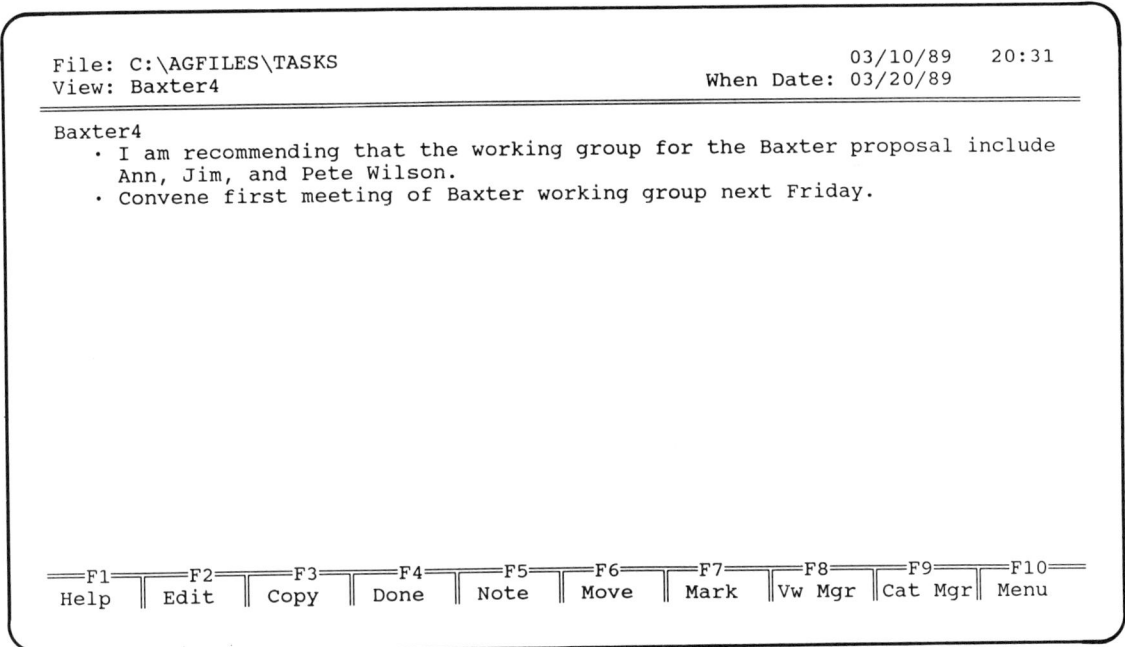

Fig. 14-9. *The new Baxter4 view and the Baxter4 section into which the items in the file BAXTER4.STF have been imported by the Import Items into New Section macro.*

The second command checks to make sure that the user has entered some text and has not just pressed ENTER before making an entry. The second command is

{IFEQ;%a;#NULL;end}

It compares the information stored in the variable %a with the special value #NULL, which means empty. If the values are equal, that is, if no text has been stored in %a, the command transfers execution to the macro label named ''end.'' The label is set by the LABEL command just before the QUIT command. Thus, if the user fails to enter any text into the original box, the IFEQ command causes macro execution to jump directly to the end label, and the execution of the macro terminates.

The keystrokes {F10}vn invoke the View New command. These keystrokes are followed by

{TYPE;%a} {Enter}

The TYPE command enters the text that had been stored in the variable %a exactly as if those characters had been typed in from the keyboard. Thus, the file name

entered in the box in response to the INPUT command and stored in %a is now
entered as the new view name. Likewise, the following command,

{DOWN} {TYPE; %a} {Enter}

moves the highlight down to the *Section head:* setting and enters the same name.
The keystroke {F9} accepts the settings and creates the new view.

Next, the keystrokes {F10}fti invoke the File Transfer Import command.
Then the command

{DOWN}c: \ agfiles \ {TYPE; %a}.stf {Enter}

moves the highlight down to the *From file:* setting and types in the path and file
name for the structured text file to be imported. The TYPE command is used
to enter the main portion of the file name from the variable %a. The keystrokes

{DOWN} {DOWN} {DOWN} {DOWN} {DOWN}y

move the highlight down to the *Strip Carriage Returns:* setting and select the
option *Yes.* Then {F9} accepts the settings and imports the file. The command

{LABEL;end}

performs no action, but merely serves as a location to which macro execution
can be transferred by the IFEQ command when no text has been entered. The
command

{QUIT}

stops macro execution. Execution would stop in any event when the macro runs
out of actions to perform, but the QUIT command helps mark the conclusion
more clearly.

You can run Import Items into New Section again to see the effect of the
IFEQ command. Execute the macro. When the initial box is displayed requesting
the file name, press CTRL-ENTER to clear the previous file name, then press EN-
TER. The macro immediately ends. Without this checking, the macro would have
gone on to create a view called New View with an untitled section (since no entries
were made). There would have been an error when you attempted to import the
nonexistent file for the nonexistent file name.

## Principles of Macro Programming

Agenda's macro commands are combined with Agenda commands and any text that may be entered from the keyboard to create more complex macros. The macro commands must be entered by typing them into a macro using the macro editor. The regular Agenda commands may be entered either by typing them in or by recording them using Agenda's learn mode.

Agenda's macro commands provide a variety of capabilities to the writer of advanced macros. Some of the commands are used to control the order in which the actions in a macro are executed. The example used the IFEQ command to branch to a label specified using the LABEL command. The QUIT command terminated execution.

Another type of macro command provides for input or output from the macro during the course of execution. In the example, the INPUT command displayed a box with a prompt and obtained the name of the structured text file from the user, which was stored in a variable. The TYPE command enters text—in the example, the file name—into Agenda during macro execution.

Macro commands can also provide a variety of other functions. They can set and clear the values of variables and control the speed of macro execution. Special debugging commands allow the single-step execution of macros during development and testing. Comments can be included in macros to explain the procedures.

Macro commands are enclosed in curly braces and begin with the name of the command. Most macro commands have one or more arguments that control the operation of the command. These arguments follow the name of the macro and are separated from the name and from each other by semicolons. Table 14-2 summarizes Agenda's macro commands.

Special macro *variables* may be used within macros to store information. Many of the macro commands can be used either to enter information into the variables or to use the information in the variables in different ways. Each variable can store up to 79 characters of text. Agenda provides 26 macro variables, which are named %a through %z. The example macro uses the variable %a to store the structured text file name entered using the INPUT command. The value of this variable is tested with the IFEQ command and entered into the database several times during macro execution by the TYPE command.

Agenda also includes seven macro *arguments*, which are preestablished values that may be used within macro commands. The example macro employs the argument #NULL in testing whether the variable %a is empty or contains information. These macro arguments are summarized in Table 14-3.

Agenda allows 19 macros to be created and used in any database. Each macro may have more than two thousand characters. Thus, you can develop a considerable number of very complex macros.

### Table 14-2. Macro Commands.

| Macro Command | Function |
|---|---|
| {ALERT;*boxtop message;main message*} | Displays box with messages in top border and inside and awaits keystroke from user to continue. |
| {BRANCH;*labelname*} | Transfers macro execution to LABEL command with *labelname*. |
| {CLEAR:*variable*}, {CLEAR;ALL} | Clears values from *variable* or from all variables. |
| {COMMENT;*text*} | No action; serves to include comments within macro. |
| {DEBUGON} | Begins single-step macro execution, requiring user keypress to execute each step. |
| {DEBUGOFF} | Ends single-step macro execution. |
| {GETKEY;*variable*} | Pauses, awaits user keystroke, which is stored in *variable*. |
| {GOTO;*macroname*} | Transfers execution to another macro. |
| {IFEQ;*value1;value2;labelname*} | If *value1* is equal to *value2*, transfer execution to the LABEL command with *labelname*. |
| {IFKEY;*labelname*} | If user presses key, transfers execution to the LABEL commnd with *labelname*. |
| {IFNOTEQ;*value1;value2;labelname*} | If *value1* is not equal to *value2*, transfers execution to the LABEL command with *labelname*. |
| {INPUT;*prompt message;variable*} | Displays box with prompt at top, awaits user input of text, which is saved in *variable*. |
| {LABEL;*labelname*} | Set location of *labelname* to which other macros can transfer execution. |
| {LET;*variable;value*} | Assigns *value* to *variable*. |
| {QUIT} | Terminates execution of macro. |
| {SPEED;*argument*} | Controls speed at which macro is executed, where *argument* is SLOW, MED, FAST, or NORMAL (fastest). |
| {TYPE;*text*} | Types *text* as if it were entered from keyboard. |

*Table 14-3. Macro Arguments.*

| Argument | Value |
| --- | --- |
| #DATE | Current date in the default date format. |
| #FALSE | FALSE for testing in the IFEQ and IFNOTEQ commands. |
| #KEYHIT | TRUE or FALSE depending on whether user has pressed a key. |
| #MODE | Agenda's current mode: VIEW, CATMGR, NOTE, or OTHER. |
| #NULL | Null or empty value. |
| #TIME | Current system time in HH:MM format. |
| #TRUE | TRUE for testing in the IFEQ and IFNOTEQ commands. |

Learning to use macros in Agenda or in any other program that has a macro capability takes time. It is best approached gradually. Agenda's ability to create macros by recording keystrokes provides a very easy way to get started. When you identify a simple but frequently used activity associated with your database, try recording a short macro.

As you create and use these simple macros, you will develop ideas for more complex tasks that could be done with macros, and you will begin recording longer macros. As you use these macros, you are likely to get ideas for changes and will begin editing them, making additions and changes. This process will become so familiar that you will start thinking about ways to further enhance the macros through the addition of macro commands.

Start by using a few macros, and you will soon become an accomplished Agenda macro programmer.

# 15

## USING SPECIAL
## FEATURES AND
## CUSTOMIZING AGENDA

AGENDA has a number of additional features that have not been discussed in the preceding chapters. Some of these features allow you to quickly display selected information from the database, set and use dependent relationships, and show various database statistics. In addition, Agenda allows you to set a variety of preferences to tailor the operation of the program to your needs. This chapter addresses some of these additional capabilities of Agenda.

### SHOWING INFORMATION IN THE DATABASE

The Utility Show command provides a quick and convenient way to display selected items from your Agenda database in a new view. The command provides options to make a variety of different selections from the database, and it creates a new view to display these items directly.

You are working with the Tasks database and want to look at all of the items that refer to Ron Smith. You could create a Ron Smith category and use the Utility Execute command to assign the items with the text "Ron Smith" to that category. You could then create a new view with Ron Smith as the section head to examine the items assigned to the Ron Smith category. This might be worthwhile if you would have use for the Ron Smith category later. However, the Utility Show Match command may be employed to display the items referring to Ron Smith more directly.

Open the Tasks database. Any view may be displayed. Issue the Utility Show Match command. You first need to enter the text for which to search. In the Show Match box, type in

Ron Smith

and press ENTER to establish this as the *Search for:* setting. You want to look for matches with *Item text*, you want the *Syntax:* to be *Literal* for text matches, and you also want case to be ignored. These should be the default settings. The Show Match box should appear as in Fig. 15-1. Press F9 to search for the matching items.

Agenda finds those items with the text "Ron Smith" and displays them in a new *Show View* (Fig. 15-2). This view was created by the Utility Show Match command to display the items. The Show View is a new view in the Tasks database. It appears when you select views using the View Manager. The view name may be edited in the normal manner. You may add sections to this view, print it, and do most of the things you can do with any view.

The items in Show View are displayed in a section with the head *Show*. This section was created by the Utility Show Match command solely to display the items. The section head *Show* is not a category

```
  Match  Prerequisites  Dependents  ItemsDone  Circular  All
  Show all items containing a specific word or phrase
 ═══════════════════════════════════════════════════════════════════
 Reports                              Staffing    Project    When
   · Meeting to discuss project for    ·Ann        ·James      ·03/13/89
     James next Monday.
   · Have Ann get out the previous     ·Ann        ·Walker     ·03/14/89
     Wa┌──────────────────────Show Match═══════════════════════┐
     th│                                                        │
     we│   Search for:                                          │/89
   · Pr│   Ron Smith                                            │
     pr│                                                        │/89
   · Pr│   Match on:      Item text                             │
     Ba│   Syntax:        Literal                               │
     ma│   Ignore case:   Yes                                   │
   · Me│                                                        │
     on└──────────────────Press F9 when done, ESC to cancel════┘
   · Call Ann to go over report to      ·Ann        ·Walker
     Walker Inc. on Walker and James
     projects.
   · Do status report for Peters.       ·Jim        ·Peters

 Meetings                             Staffing    Project    When
 ═F1═══╤═F2═══╤═F3═══╤═F4═══╤═F5═══╤═F6═══╤═F7═══╤═F8═════╤═F9═════╤═F10══
 Help  │ Edit │      │      │      │      │      │Default │Accept  │
```

Fig. 15-1. *Using the Utility Show Match command to display the items with the text "Ron Smith."*

```
   File: C:\AGFILES\TASKS
   View: *Show View*                                        03/10/89   20:52
  ════════════════════════════════════════════════════════════════════════
   *Show*
       ♪ Call Ron Smith at Walker by Tuesday to discuss the progress of the
         project.
       · Meeting with Ann and Ron Smith Thursday.
       · Check with Ron Smith on meeting time.




  ══F1══╤══F2══╤══F3══╤══F4══╤══F5══╤══F6══╤══F7══╤══F8══╤══F9══╤══F10══
   Help │ Edit │ Copy │ Done │ Note │ Move │ Mark │Vw Mgr│Cat Mgr│ Menu
```

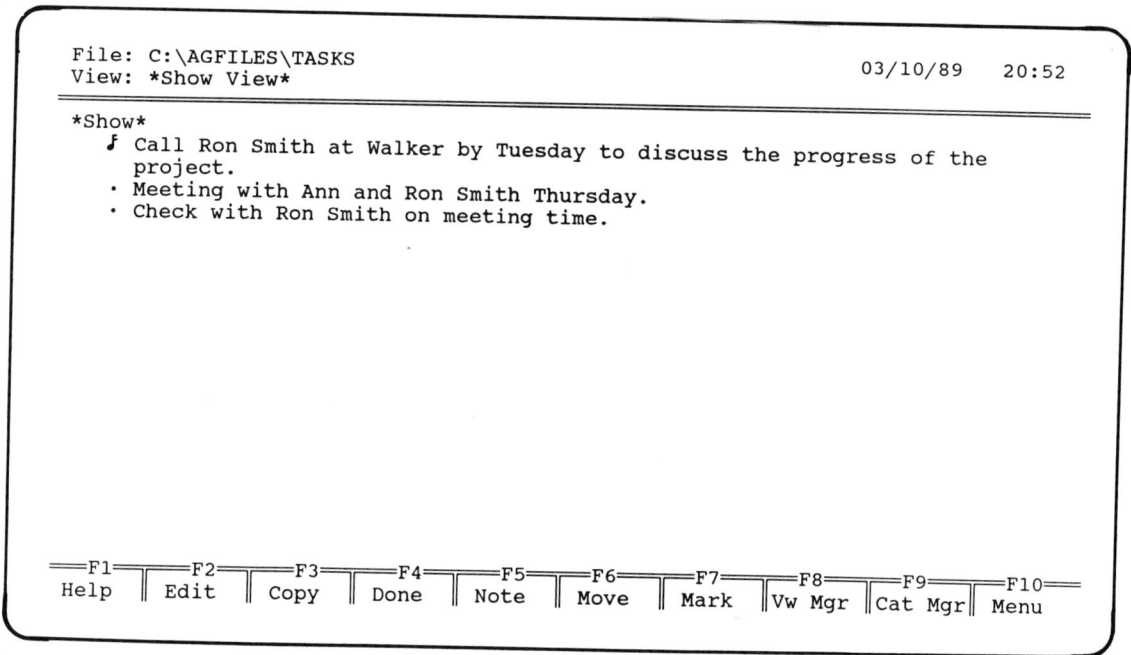

Fig. 15-2. *The Show View displaying the items with the text Ron Smith.*

in the database, however, and does not appear in the category hierarchy.
It just appears as the section head.

The Utility Show Match command is just one of the various Utility Show
commands that can be used to display items in the database. All of these commands
work in much the same way: you issue the command and specify any required
settings. The designated items are displayed automatically in a view called the
Show View. When a Show View is created, you can specify whether the
information is to be added to or is to replace the previous Show View.

The Utility Show All command displays all of the items in the database in
a list. The category Main is displayed as the section head since Main is the ancestor
of all other categories in the database.

The Utility Show Items Done command displays all of the items that are considered to be Done. Thus, it displays items that have Done Dates where those
Done Dates are earlier than or the same as the current date.

The Utility Show Circular command displays the items that are caught in
*circular references*. These are items that are part of a chain in which a condition
or action leads from one item to another and back to the original item. Circular
references can produce inconsistent and ambiguous category assignments. By
displaying such items, you can diagnose problems in the database.

The remaining two Utility Show commands display items involved in dependency relationships with other items. The general topic of dependency relationships and the use of the Utility Show Prerequisites and Dependents commands are discussed in the following section.

After using a Utility Show command, you will have a Show View in the database unless you have either renamed or deleted that view. When you next use a Utility Show command, Agenda asks whether you want to delete the existing Show View. If you choose not to delete it, the items selected by the Utility Show command will be added to the items currently in that view. Deleting the existing Show View causes the new items being selected to be displayed in a new Show View.

A Show View can be given another view name. The view name can be edited while in the View Manager. Renaming a Show View allows the view to be saved permanently. The renamed view will not be deleted when another Utility Show command is executed.

## USING ITEM DEPENDENCIES

Relationships in an Agenda database generally are expressed through the assignment of items to categories. Agenda also allows you to specify relationships between items. Items in a database can be made dependent upon other items. Dependency might be used, for example, to indicate that a task represented by one item—the *dependent* item—could not begin until the task represented by another item—the *prerequisite* item—had been completed. The Utility Show commands can be used to display dependent or prerequisite items.

The Show View just created in the Tasks database includes three items referring to Ron Smith. Prior to the meeting with Ann and Ron Smith on Thursday, you need to check with Ron Smith on the time of the meeting, and you need to call him to discuss the progress of the project. Thus, the item referring to the meeting itself is dependent upon the prior completion of the other tasks. You are going to specify these dependencies and display items based upon the dependent relationships.

Begin by marking the prerequisite items. Highlight the item beginning "Call Ron Smith at Walker" and press F7 (MARK) to mark it. Highlight the item "Check with Ron Smith on meeting time" and again press F7 (MARK). Move the highlight to "Meeting with Ann and Ron Smith" and press ALT-F3 (DPNDS ON) to specify that this item is dependent upon the marked items. Note that a little double-arrow symbol is now displayed in front of the item, indicating that it is dependent on one or more other items. The screen should appear as shown in Fig. 15-3.

```
┌──────────────────────────────────────────────────────────────────────────┐
│  File: C:\AGFILES\TASKS                                                    │
│  View: *Show View*                               03/10/89   20:56          │
│                                            When Date: 03/16/89             │
│ ══════════════════════════════════════════════════════════════════════════│
│  *Show*                                                                    │
│     ♪ Call Ron Smith at Walker by Tuesday to discuss the progress of the   │
│       project.                                                             │
│     ↔ Meeting with Ann and Ron Smith Thursday.                            │
│     · Check with Ron Smith on meeting time.                               │
│                                                                            │
│                                                                            │
│                                                                            │
│                                                                            │
│                                                                            │
│                                                                            │
│                                                                            │
│                                                                            │
│                                                                            │
│                                                                            │
│                                                                            │
│                                                                            │
│ ═F1══╤══F2══╤══F3══╤══F4══╤══F5══╤══F6══╤══F7══╤══F8══╤══F9══╤══F10══       │
│  Help │ Edit │ Copy │ Done │ Note │ Move │ Mark │Vw Mgr│Cat Mgr│ Menu       │
└──────────────────────────────────────────────────────────────────────────┘
```

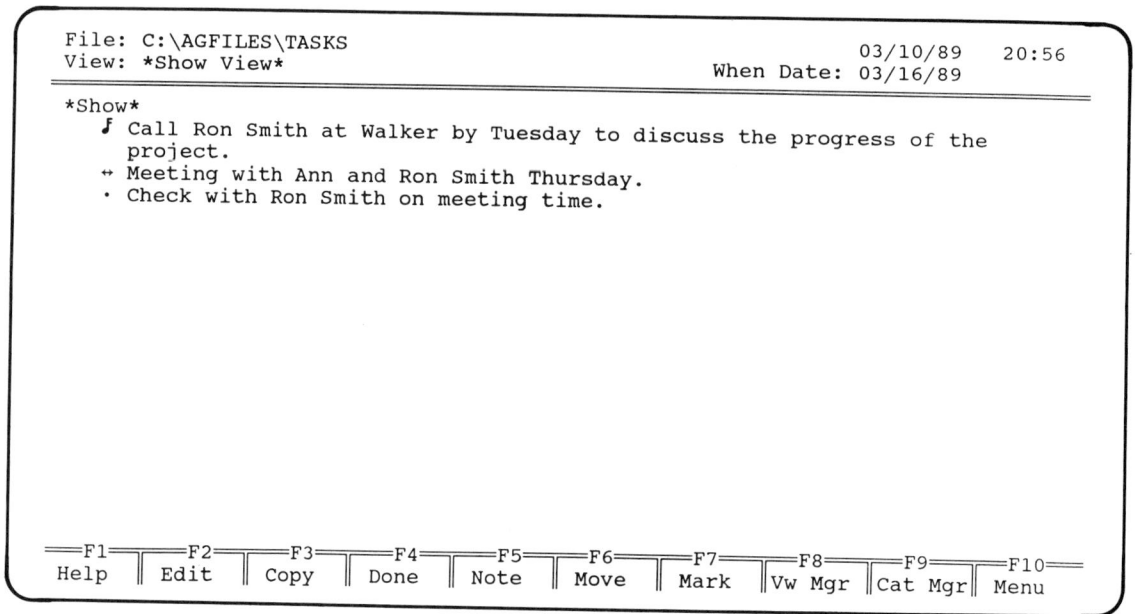

Fig. 15-3. *The second item specified as being dependent upon the first and third items.*

You now want to see what tasks need to be done prior to the meeting with Ron Smith. With the "Meeting with Ann and Ron Smith" item still highlighted, issue the Utility Show Prerequisites One Level command to show all of the items upon which the current item is dependent. Accept the default setting to delete the existing Show View. A new Show View is created, displaying the items that are prerequisites to the "Meeting with Ron Smith" item. This is shown in Fig. 15-4.

To specify that an item is dependent upon other items, mark the prerequisite items and press ALT-F3 (DPNDS ON). A double-arrow symbol appears in front of the dependent item.

Two Utility Show commands may be used to display items involved in dependent relationships. You begin by highlighting an item and then you issue the Utility Show Prerequisites or the Utility Show Dependents command. The Prerequisites option displays items upon which the currently highlighted item is dependent. Use this to show items that must be completed before the currently highlighted item. The Dependents option displays items that are dependent upon the current item. Use this to show those items that cannot be done until the current item is completed.

The Utility Show Prerequisites and the Dependents commands both include three additional options that determine the degree of dependency for items in the

```
File: C:\AGFILES\TASKS                          03/10/89    20:57
View: *Show View*

*Show*
    · Check with Ron Smith on meeting time.
    ♪ Call Ron Smith at Walker by Tuesday to discuss the progress of the
      project.




  ═F1═╤══F2══╤══F3══╤══F4══╤══F5══╤═F6═╤══F7══╤═F8══╤══F9══╤═F10══
  Help ║ Edit ║ Copy ║ Done ║ Note ║ Move ║ Mark ║Vw Mgr║Cat Mgr║ Menu
```

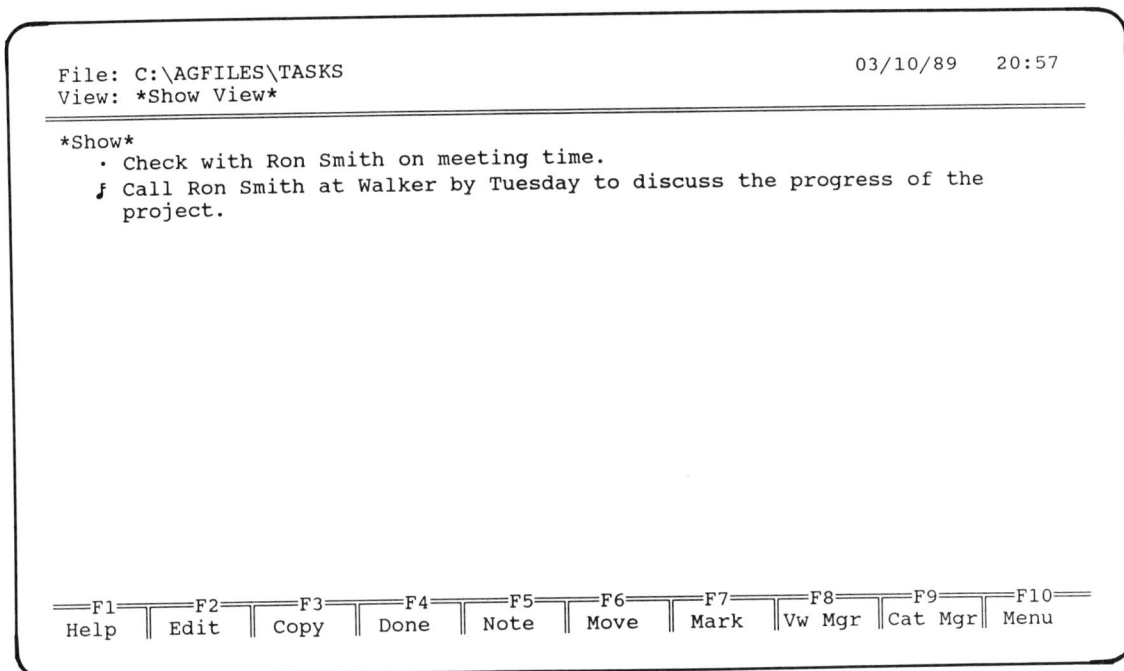

Fig. 15-4. *The Show View displaying the items that are prerequisites of the "Meeting with Ron Smith"*
*item.*

Show View. Selecting One Level causes only the direct prerequisites or dependents of the current item to be displayed. The All Levels selection displays all prerequisite or dependent items, both those directly prerequisite or dependent and those prerequisite to or dependent upon the current item through intermediate items. For example, you might specify that item A is dependent upon item B and also specify that item B is dependent upon item C. In displaying the prerequisites of item A, the One Level option would display only item B. The All Level option would display both items B and C. The third option is Every Item. This option displays all of the items in the database that are either prerequisite to or dependent upon some other item. The selection of items displayed does not depend upon the current item.

The View Preference command includes a setting for specifying whether dependent items are to be displayed in a view. The default for the *Hide dependent items:* setting is *No*, so normally dependency does not affect the display of items. By changing this setting to *Yes*, only items that are dependent upon another item are displayed.

## DISPLAYING DATABASE STATISTICS

Agenda includes three commands for displaying basic statistical summaries for categories, views, and the entire database. You issue the command and the information is displayed on the screen.

Switch to the Tasks to Do view of the Tasks database and move the
highlight to the Reports section head at the top of the view by pressing
CTRL-HOME. Use the Category Info command to display the category
information for the Reports category. Next, display the view information
for the Tasks to Do view by issuing the View Info command. Finally,
display the database information for the entire Tasks database with the
File Info command. Figure 15-5 shows the three boxes of information
displayed by these three commands.

When using the Category Info command, you must first highlight the category for which you want the information displayed. The category to be highlighted
can be displayed either as a section head or in a category column. The View Info
command requires that the view for which you want the information must be
currently displayed. When using the File Info command, you may be in any view.

```
┌────────────Category Information────────────┐
│                                            │
│  Items in category:          7             │
│  Child categories:           0             │
│  Used as section heads:      2             │
│  Included in view filters:   0             │
│  Included in conditions:     0             │
│  Included in actions:        0             │
│                                            │
│        ──Press any key to continue──       │
└────────────────────────────────────────────┘


┌────────────View Information────────────┐
│                                         │
│  Marked items:             0            │
│  Items in current section: 7            │
│  Sections in view:         3            │
│  Items in view:           20            │
│                                         │
│      ──Press any key to continue──      │
└─────────────────────────────────────────┘


┌──────────────File Information──────────────┐
│                                            │
│  Unused space:            14%              │
│  Items:                   25               │
│  Items in Trash:           0               │
│  Items with notes:         2               │
│  Categories:              17               │
│  Average items/category:   5               │
│  Average categories/item:  3               │
│                                            │
│        ──Press any key to continue──       │
└────────────────────────────────────────────┘
```

Fig. 15-5. *The information displayed by the Category Info, View Info, and
File Info commands.*

# SETTING DATABASE PREFERENCES

Agenda allows the setting of a wide variety of preferences that govern the operation of the program. Many of these have been discussed in earlier chapters in conjunction with the activities to which they related. For example, the preferences for default date formats and for the handling of Done Dates are addressed in the chapter dealing with dates. Chapter 11 explains the use of the automatic assignment preferences to govern the way Agenda assigns items to categories.

Additional preference settings are made available by the Utility Preferences Other and Utility Preferences Environment commands. Most of these settings govern the general operation of Agenda and have not been addressed in any of the preceding chapters. They are discussed in the following paragraphs, along with the procedures for changing preferences for all Agenda databases.

## Other Preferences

The first group of settings to be discussed is displayed using the Utility Preferences Other command. This command displays the box with the Other Preferences settings as shown in Fig. 15-6. (The *Process done items:* setting is discussed in Chapter 10; it is not addressed here.)

The *Insert new columns in:* setting determines whether new columns you create are inserted in all of the sections of the view or only in the current section.

```
Auto-Assign  Date  Other  Environment  Update
Specify other database preferences
═══════════════════════════════════════════════════════════════════════
Reports                                  Staffing    Project     When
 •            ═══════════════════════Other Preferences═══════════════════
   •     Insert new columns in:  All sections
         Empty Trash:            End of day
         Make backup copy:       On demand
         Process Done items:     No action
   •


   •     Tab size:               5
         Hide carriage returns:  Yes

         File description:       Database for Working with Lotus Agenda
   •     File password:
         Auto-import file:

   •            ═══════════Press F9 when done, ESC to cancel═══════════
Meetings                         Staffing     Project      When
═F1═══╤═══F2═══╤═══F3═══╤═══F4═══╤═══F5═══╤═══F6═══╤═══F7═══╤═══F8═══╤═══F9═══╤═══F10═══
Help  ║ Edit  ║        ║        ║        ║        ║        ║Default║Accept ║
```

Fig. 15-6. *The Other Preferences set using the Utility Preferences Other command.*

Like all of the settings in dialog boxes, you may display the options by pressing GREY PLUS. Then move the highlight to the selection desired and press ENTER. Alternatively, you can select the option by pressing the first letter. In this case, pressing C changes the setting to Current Section, and pressing A changes back to All Sections.

The *Empty trash:* setting governs when discarded items that have been placed in Trash are permanently eliminated and are no longer accessible with the Item Undiscard command. The default option, *End of Day*, empties Trash when the system date changes to the next day (or the next time the database is opened with a later date). You can change this setting to *When file is closed* so that Trash is emptied each time you finish working with a file. This setting, of course, will not preserve items in Trash for retrieval later in the day if you close a database and then reopen it.

You can control the emptying of Trash by changing the setting to *On demand*. In this case, discarded items are removed from Trash only when you issue the Utilities Trash command to empty Trash. If you use this option, you should occasionally empty Trash to avoid accumulating large numbers of discarded items that waste space. Also, if a lot of discarded items accumulate in Trash, it can complicate the retrieval of items. The Item Undiscard command lets you retrieve either the last discarded item in Trash or all items. Retrieving all items could be difficult if many discarded items have been allowed to accumulate over a long period of time. The setting to empty Trash *When item is discarded* is for those people who do not make errors. It effectively eliminates Trash as a backup against mistakes when discarding items.

The *Make backup copy:* setting can be used to automatically make backup copies of the database. With the default option, *On demand*, backup copies are made only when you issue the File Backup command. The other two options are to automatically make a backup copy either *When file is opened* or *When file is closed*. Both settings automatically give you a backup copy that reflects the state of the database at the time you opened it and began work.

When you use *When file is closed*, the backup version of the file is the same as the current version stored on the disk when you are not working with the file. *When file is opened* delays making the backup until the file is again used. This means that the backup version of the file when you are not working with it will be the file as it existed when you last opened it, or when you last issued a File Backup command. No matter what method is used to create the backup copies of the file, the File Use-Backup command is employed to revert to the most recent backup version of a database.

The next setting, *Tab size:*, allows you to change tab stops. Agenda provides tab stops at periodic intervals across the screen. These may be used with the TAB key to move the cursor when entering text. The default is to place tab stops every five spaces, but this interval may be changed by altering the *Tab size:* setting.

You can type in the desired tab size and press ENTER. Alternatively, you can use GREY PLUS and GREY MINUS to increase or decrease the interval. You can press these keys repeatedly until the desired setting is displayed.

A carriage return, placed in text by pressing the ENTER key, causes text to begin at the start of the next line. Normally, no character is displayed on the screen to indicate the presence of a carriage return. This is the condition when the *Hide carriage returns* setting is set to *Yes*. Changing this to *No* creates visible "hard" carriage returns represented by solid triangles. These triangles are displayed in the text of notes and macros. It might occasionally be useful to show carriage returns when their presence is important to formatting text.

The *File description:* and *File password:* settings in the Other Preferences box can be used to change any description or password that was entered when the database was first created. You can either edit the current settings or type in new settings. If the database is not currently password-protected and has no entry after the *File password:* setting, this can be changed here. When you enter text as the file password, you will be prompted for the password each time you open the database. You must enter the text that was entered as the setting here, or Agenda will not open the database. If you change an existing file password, opening the database will henceforth require this new password.

You can remove password protection from a database by deleting an existing file password. Agenda assumes that anyone working with a database has the authority to use it and therefore should have the authority to make changes to the password protection associated with that database.

Finally, the *Auto-import file:* setting is used to optionally provide the name of a structured text file that will be automatically imported into the database each time the database is opened. To select this option, you must enter the file name and, if necessary, the path specification. When a file name is specified for the *Auto-import file:* setting, each time the database is opened, the File Transfer Import command is invoked automatically to import the information from the designated structured text file. The default settings of the File Transfer Import command will be used for the operation. You might select this option if you routinely use the Items accessory to enter items and save them to structured text files while working outside of Agenda. Then, whenever you start the database, the structured text file containing the most recent items will be imported automatically.

## Environment Preferences

The Utility Preference Environment command is used to make changes to an additional group of settings. This command displays the Environment Preferences box shown in Fig. 15-7. The specification of the *Printer definition file:* setting is addressed in Chapter 8. All of the other settings are briefly discussed here.

```
Auto-Assign  Date  Other  Environment  Update
Specify display & other system preferences
═══════════════════════════════════════════════════════════════
Reports                              Staffing      Project      When
  · Meeting to discuss project for   ·Ann          ·James       ·03/13/89
    James next Monday.
  · Have┌───────────────────────Environment Preferences═══════════════┐
    Walk│                                                              │
    the │  Display key map:            Yes                             │
    we h│  Color:                      Mono                            │
  · Prep│  Beep on auto-completion:    Yes                             │
    proj│  Printer definition file:    C:\AG\IBMPRO.PDF                │
  · Prep│  Item tag character:         ·                               │
    Baxt│  Auto-save interval (mins):  0                               │
    mana│  Character set:              Use Agenda default (CP 850)     │
  · Meet│  Suppress snow:              No                              │
    on t│                                                              │
  · Call└═══════════════════════Press F9 when done, ESC to cancel═════┘
    Walker Inc. on Walker and James
    projects.
  · Do status report for Peters.      ·Jim          ·Peters

Meetings                             Staffing      Project      When
══F1═══╤══F2══╤══F3══╤══F4══╤══F5══╤══F6══╤══F7══╤══F8═══╤══F9═══╤══F10══
Help   ║ Edit ║      ║      ║      ║      ║      ║Default║Accept ║
```

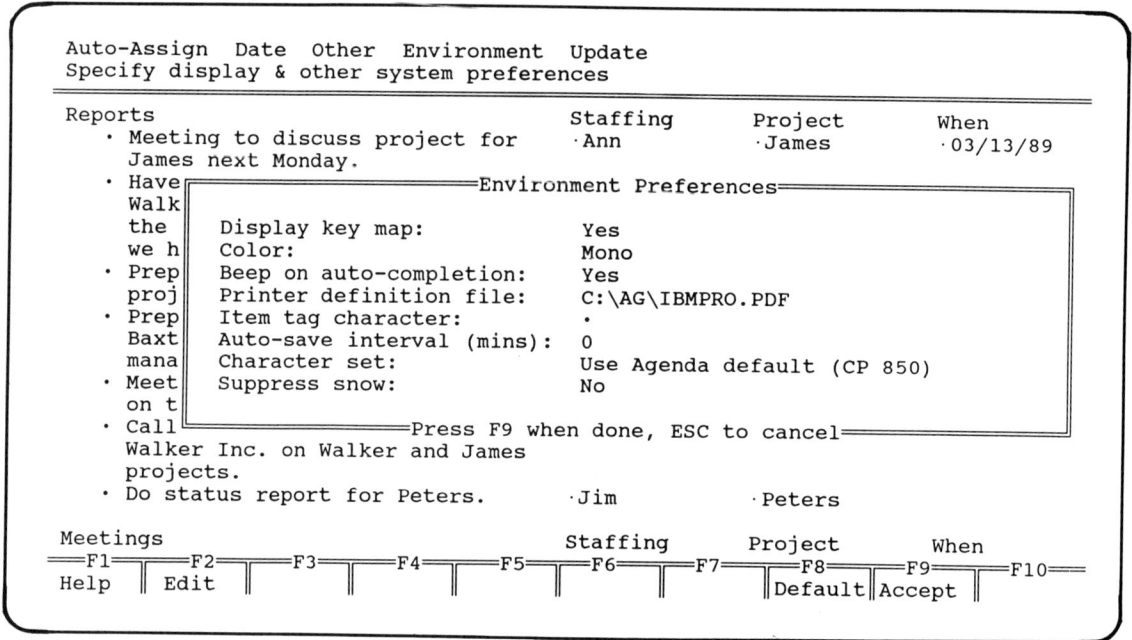

Fig. 15-7. *The Environment Preferences set using the Utility Preferences Environment command.*

Agenda normally displays the function key assignments across the bottom lines of the screen. Changing the *Display key map:* setting to *No* deletes this information and gives several more lines for the display of information from the database. Given the many different function key assignments, which vary depending on the Agenda mode you are in, probably only very experienced Agenda users will choose to eliminate the key map display.

The *Color:* setting controls the way Agenda displays information on your video display. The default is *Mono*, for a monochrome display. Agenda provides two prespecified sets of color combinations that may be selected for color monitors. These options are designated *Set 1* and *Set 2*.

Agenda also allows you to select your own colors with the *Custom* option. When you make this selection, nothing further happens while you remain in the Environment Preferences box. But when you press F9 to accept the settings and leave the box, Agenda presents an additional box which allows you to specify the colors to be used for text, highlighted text, backgrounds, and borders. If you want to later change your custom color settings, you must again issue the Utility Preference Environment command and respecify *Custom* as the option for the setting.

During automatic completion, Agenda normally beeps at you with loud, high beeps to indicate matches and with soft, low beeps to indicate no matches. If the beeping is bothersome, you can turn it off by changing the *Beep on auto-completion:* setting.

Agenda usually displays a small dot on the screen as a bullet in front of each item (unless special symbols are used to designate attached notes, marking, dependency, or Done items). The symbol used for this purpose may be changed using the *Item tag character:* setting. Pressing GREY PLUS displays a list of alternative symbols that may be used. You might want to change the symbol for various reasons. First, you might just prefer the appearance of a different symbol. Second, you might want to use different item tag symbols for different databases to allow you to distinguish instantly between different databases by the general screen appearance. Third, if you regularly use screen dumps to obtain printed output, you might wish to change the symbol if the default symbol does not print out on your printer.

Agenda automatically saves your database whenever you switch to a new database and when you exit the program. You can also set Agenda to save your database automatically to the disk at intervals while you are working with a database. The *Auto-save interval (mins):* setting determines how frequently Agenda performs these automatic saves. The default setting of zero results in no automatic saving of databases during work sessions. Automatic saving helps protect the information in your database in the event of unexpected problems. It does, however, result in periodic interruptions of your work as Agenda automatically saves the database.

IBM personal computers have character sets that can be used to display different characters on the screen other than the normal, printable characters. Agenda selects the character set best able to support special international characters. *If* you use the international characters, and *if* your personal computer does not display the multilingual (code 850) character set, you might wish to instruct Agenda to employ the code 437 extended ASCII characters, translating certain international characters. This is accomplished by changing the *Character set:* setting. The default is *Use Agenda default (CP850).* Changing the character set can slow up screen display, so select this option only if you know what you are doing and need to use the special characters.

Some video display systems (such as the IBM Color Graphics Adapter) might show video interference in the form of snow when writing to or scrolling the screen. If you have this problem, you can change the *Suppress snow:* setting to *Yes.* Doing so will slow the operation of the screen display. Do this only if really necessary.

## Updating Agenda Preferences

Make changes in preferences for the current database using the Utility Preference Other and Utility Preference Environment commands. After making changes to any preference settings, press F9 to accept the changes and return to the view. These changes take effect immediately and will remain in effect for that database when you use it later. These preferences are changed only by using the appropriate command to change the setting and then accepting those changes.

Using the various Utility Preference commands alone affects only the current database. The new preference settings do not affect the operation of Agenda with other databases. However, the Utility Preference Update command may be employed to make the current database preference settings the defaults for all of your Agenda databases. When you execute the Utility Preference Update command, the preference settings currently in effect for the Auto-Assign, Date, Other, and Environment Preferences are made the defaults for all of your Agenda applications.

Thus, to change the way Agenda operates for all databases, use the Utility Preference Auto-Assign, Date, Other, and Environment commands to make change settings. Then issue the Utility Preference Update command. The current database preference, including all of the changes just made using the commands to change the preference settings, will be made the defaults for all further use of Agenda with all databases.

Be careful when using the Utility Preference Update command, however. Executing this command makes *all* of the settings that can be changed with the Utility Preference commands the Agenda defaults. This includes not only changes you might have made just before executing the Update, but also any changes in these settings that you have made for the current database at an earlier time.

For example, you might have specified at some earlier time that Done items in the current database were to be discarded. This was a choice you made for the current database, but it might not represent the desired default for all of your work with Agenda. Now you want to change the colors and change the *Color:* setting using the Utility Preference Environment command. If you were to execute the Utility Preference Update command, both the new *Color:* setting and the previously changed setting for *Process Done Items:* would become the new Agenda defaults.

To avoid these problems, when making changes to Agenda defaults, begin by opening a new database. In that way, there can be no preference setting changes made earlier that you might have forgotten. Use the Utility Preference commands to make the changes to settings that you want to become Agenda defaults. Then issue the Utility Preference Update command to make the new changes the defaults for Agenda. In this way, you avoid inadvertently making some database-specific preferences into defaults throughout Agenda.

## COMPRESSING THE DATABASE

When you add information to an Agenda database, Agenda allocates space for the storage of that information, increasing the size of the database files. When you discard information from the database, however, Agenda does not necessarily reclaim this space. Instead, unused holes are left in the database files.

```
Execute  Show  Questions  Trash  Compress  Preferences          WAIT
Recover unused space in current database
═══════════════════════════════════════════════════════════════════
Reports                              Staffing     Project      When
   · Meeting to discuss project for    ·Ann        ·James       ·03/13/89
     James next Monday.
   · Have Ann get out the previous     ·Ann        ·Walker      ·03/14/89
     Walker project report and begin
     the pr┌═══════════════════Compress═══════════════════┐
     we hav│                                              │
   · Prepar│                                              │      ·03/20/89
     projec│          Recovering space in AGA file        │
   · Prepar│                                              │      ·03/20/89
     Baxter│                66% complete                  │
     manage│                                              │
   · Meet w└═══════════════Press CTRL-BREAK to cancel═════┘
     on the Peters account.
   · Call Ann to go over report to     ·Ann        ·Walker
     Walker Inc. on Walker and James
     projects.
   · Do status report for Peters.      ·Jim        ·Peters

Meetings                             Staffing     Project      When
══F1══╤══F2══╤══F3══╤══F4══╤══F5══╤══F6══╤══F7══╤══F8══╤══F9══╤══F10══
```

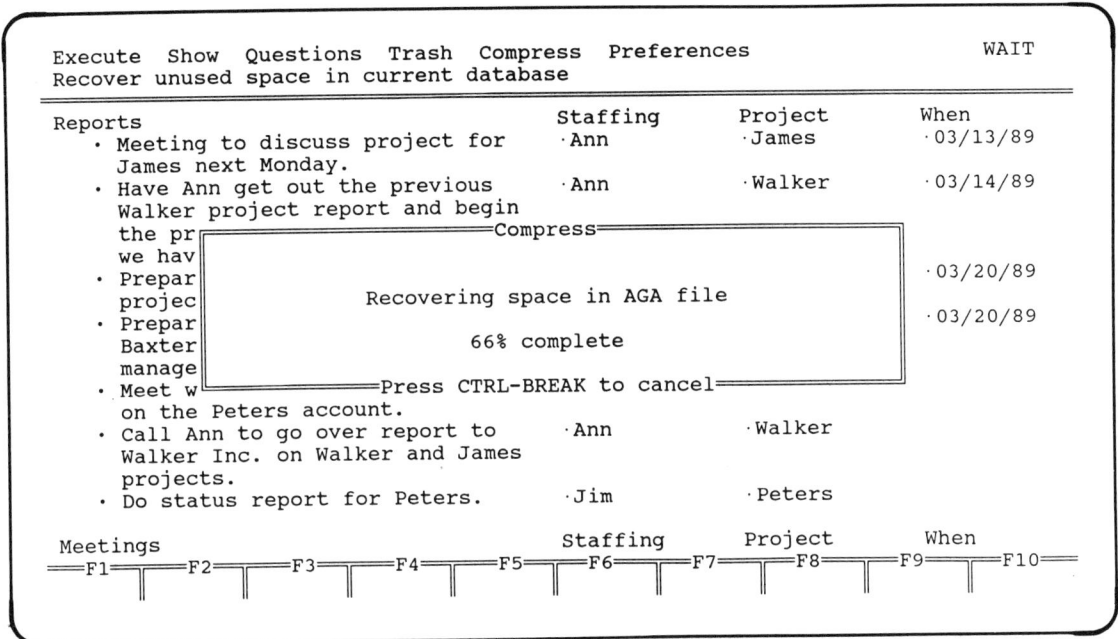

Fig. 15-8. *Using the Utility Compress command to recover unused space in the database.*

You can see how much space in the database is unused by running the File Info command. The first entry is the percentage of the space in the database that is unused. To more efficiently store the database in less space, you can direct Agenda to reclaim any unused space. Eliminating the holes in the database is called *compressing* the database. You will want to do this periodically with large, frequently changed databases to avoid wasted storage.

To compress a database, enter the Utility Compress command. Once you issue the command, the file compression operation begins immediately. Since compressing a database involves rewriting the entire database, it may take some time. Agenda displays a box indicating its progress, as shown in Fig. 15-8.

The preceding chapters have given you a comprehensive introduction to all of the important features of Agenda. A few of the more obscure features and keystroke combinations have been deliberately left out to avoid burdening you with too much specialized detail. Becoming an accomplished user of any powerful piece of software does not require mastery of every last feature in the program. Rather, it requires that you become proficient at the important operations so that you can successfully accomplish your task. You are well on your way to becoming a very proficient Agenda user.

# 16

## STRATEGIES
## FOR DEVELOPING
## APPLICATIONS

By now you have gained considerable proficiency in the use of Agenda. Although there will always be more to learn, you are prepared to use Agenda to accomplish a wide variety of useful tasks. You know how to use Agenda, but what do you use it for?

The power and flexibility of Agenda make it a useful tool for managing everything from your time, to complex projects, to the information with which you work. Perhaps the most important step is just coming up with the ideas of how Agenda might be used.

The final part of this book includes seven chapters presenting ideas for potential applications of Agenda. These ideas for applications are designed to get you started thinking about how Agenda might be used in a range of different settings. Each chapter shows how Agenda can be used for different types of applications. The chapters show how various features of Agenda can be used to extend your power in the particular application.

Every Agenda user will employ the program in a different way, and that is as it should be, for Agenda is a flexible program that allows each user to tailor its operation to meet his or her own preferences and needs. The suggestions for applications presented in the following chapters should not be viewed as prescriptions to be followed exactly, but rather as ideas and points of departure for developing your own Agenda applications.

No matter what your potential Agenda application, it will be worth your while to look through the full range of suggestions offered in the following chapters. Each suggested application highlights certain features of Agenda that are particularly useful for most potential users of that application. Given the diverse ways in which people use Agenda, however, some features of Agenda highlighted for one application may be just what you need to fully develop a very different type of application.

This chapter gets you started thinking about applying Agenda by providing some general suggestions as to how you might proceed in developing applications. These are ideas about how you might approach the application development process, not a fixed set of procedures to be followed in developing an application. Start by considering your approach to problems using Agenda in this chapter, and then add the suggested applications provided in the following chapters.

## IDENTIFY WHAT YOU WANT TO ACCOMPLISH

The first step in developing any application using Agenda (or any other software) is to answer some basic questions: What am I trying to do? What are going to be the products of the application? How is the output from the program going to be employed, and how is it going to help me? How is the application going to be used?

This might all seem so obvious that it does not bear mentioning. However, users of traditional database management software have often started developing databases and entering data because of an ill-formed idea that it would somehow be a ''good thing'' if they could manage that data. Without a clear idea of what was to be accomplished, such noble attempts more than likely lead to an application with very limited utility.

The great flexibility of Agenda gives users the advantage that they do not have to specify all of their requirements at the beginning. Instead, Agenda allows the user to enter information and begin using a database before all specifics have been determined. You can always add new categories and create new views to accommodate additional needs. Nevertheless, the same principle holds: Agenda databases developed by someone with only a vague notion that it would be a ''good thing'' to somehow organize the information are less likely to be useful than those originating with some sense of purpose.

For example, suppose you are responsible for managing a project involving a large number of interrelated tasks. What might you want to accomplish in managing these tasks? You would want to be able to see the various times when the tasks are to be started or completed. You might want to see which people are responsible for the different tasks. If completion of a task is delayed, you would want to see which other tasks are dependent upon that first task so you can take appropriate actions.

How would such an application be used? Probably most of the information on the tasks is known at the beginning of the project and can be entered when the database is created, even though changes are made during the course of the project. The beginning and end dates of the various tasks are likely to change frequently. As the project proceeds, you will want to examine its progress at different points in time. The particular information needed from the database is likely to be dictated by the course of events, such as a delay in the completion of a particular task. Thus, specialized views will probably have to be created as the database is used to manage the project.

Answering the questions about what information you want out of the application and how you are likely to use the application is important to determining how to proceed. Obviously, the answers to these questions determine what types of information must be included in the database, and what relationships must be established among the pieces of information. Furthermore, how you plan to enter and change the information and output results will influence the structure of the database.

The goal here is not to specify in excruciating detail how the application is to be developed. Agenda does not demand this. Rather, attempt to develop a sense of direction so that the choices made in setting up the database and developing the application work toward your objectives, not against them.

## DETERMINE THE STRUCTURE OF THE DATABASE

Having established some idea of what you want to accomplish with your application, you can begin to determine the structure of the Agenda database. You need to determine which information is to be entered into the database as items, as categories, and as notes and the interrelationships among these elements. For many applications, determining the structure of the category hierarchy is also an important part of defining the database structure. There might be other relationships in the database to be concerned with as well. Finally, you need to identify some of the more important views, especially those that are needed for entering and editing information. You need to specify the procedure to be used for entering information and assigning items to categories.

The first task in developing any Agenda database is likely to be identifying the information to be entered as items. You might think this is obvious, and in many instances, it is. For the problem of managing the project, for example, the individual tasks should probably be entered as items. These task items can be assigned dates, can be involved in dependency relationships, and can be assigned to categories relating to the type of task, person responsible, and so forth.

On the other hand, for some applications, the choice of what to enter into the database as an item is not so obvious. For example, suppose you plan to use Agenda to assign many different tasks to many different people. Are the tasks to be entered as items, to be assigned to people categories? Or should the people be entered as the items that can be assigned to task categories? Your prior definition of the application and determination of how the database is to be used will be crucial in making these decisions.

You also have to decide how item notes and category notes are to be used in the database. For some applications, the notes can be reserved for comments or extended explanations that are attached to the items or categories. For other applications, however, it might be useful for notes to have more specific functions. For example, in a database used to keep track of sales prospects, you might choose to put mailing addresses for the prospects into notes.

The categories and the assignment of items to those categories provides the key to managing the information. You might be able to identify some categories, or at least category families, in advance. In managing projects, you want to keep track of the person(s) responsible for each of the tasks. Thus, you would want a family of categories containing the names of everyone with responsibilities for tasks included in the project.

For other applications, developing the category hierarchy might be an integral part of what you are attempting to accomplish in using the database. For example, you might want to use Agenda to develop an organizational structure. The items are to represent the activities to be accomplished. The activities are to be assigned to organizational divisions, represented by a rather complex hierarchical set of categories. This structure is to be developed as you work with Agenda, so much of your work will be with those categories in the Category Manager.

Still other applications involve dealing with information that is entered on a continuing basis. The categories are developed and items are assigned to those categories on an evolving basis, reflecting the information that is entered. This might be the case when you use Agenda to manage unstructured information from various sources, or when you use Agenda to conduct a research project. Still, you are likely to have some idea of the broad, general topics into which the information falls, and these topics perhaps should become parent categories in the category hierarchy.

The point is not that you must specify the set of categories to be included in the database in advance. Agenda does not require this and, indeed, one of Agenda's strengths is that it allows you to create new categories and assign items to those categories as you work with the database. However, if you at least begin the development of an Agenda application with a general idea of the nature of the categories to be included, you might be able to proceed more directly towards your objective than if things developed randomly.

Finally, give some thought to how and when information is to be entered or changed. You will need to provide appropriate views for the entry of items, either at the beginning or on a continuing basis. Would a New Item view aid in entering items, allowing you to avoid jumping to different sections or views? Items must be assigned to categories, and at least some of those assignments will probably not be made automatically by Agenda. Will the database include a view with the necessary columns so that items may be assigned to categories by making column entries? Will the plan be to use the Assignment Profile to make category assignments as items are entered? If so, you need to set up the database appropriately.

Certain views might be such a fundamental part of the proposed application that they should be developed at the beginning. Some of these views might require filtering or sorting. For project management, one view should probably present the tasks sorted in order of their start date. This will be a basic necessity just to look at the relationship of project tasks in the database. As another example, a Today view, filtering items with When Dates equal to the current date, might be a central element in a database used to schedule appointments.

You attempt to determine the structure of your Agenda database in advance for two primary reasons. First, you want to avoid the false starts that might be caused by entering information inappropriately. For example, if certain information is entered as items and you later realize that this information would be more useful in the form of categories, you have some work to do in making that change. Second, a clear definition of the database structure allows you to move more quickly and directly in developing your application. A summary of the issues that need to be addressed in determining the structure of an Agenda database is provided in Table 16-1.

## DETERMINING THE FEATURES
## TO BE USED IN THE DATABASE

You should think about how you will use features such as dates, dependency relationships, and conditions and actions in your Agenda application. For example, you need to decide how to apply the three types of dates provided in Agenda. The When Dates are always available to be associated with date references within items. As a default, Entry Dates records the date of item entry or editing. Is this needed, or do you need this date for some other purpose?

For project management, you might wish to use the Entry Date as the starting date for each task, with the When Date serving as the completion date. In such a case, it is easier to disable the automatic assignment of Entry Dates from the beginning. Otherwise, you have to go back and delete the automatically entered Entry Dates in order to use the Entry Dates in this manner.

The use of Done Dates and the associated determination of how Done items are to be processed should also be addressed early in the planning of a new database.

For some applications, you might want to establish dependency relationships among the items. That is, you want to specify that starting some tasks depends upon completing others. The management of a project would be one situation

**Table 16-1. Considerations in Structuring a Database.**

| Structural Component | Considerations |
|---|---|
| Items | What are the basic units of information you are trying to organize? |
| Notes | Does a certain type of information need to be associated with each item or category? Or are notes available for additional general information for items or categories? |
| Category Families | What are the different general ways in which the items should be organized? Examples would be by project and by type of task. |
| Child Categories | How are the category families to be broken down into subcategories and how much detail is needed? |
| Views | How are items to be entered and assigned to categories? What information is needed for various purposes and how is it to be organized? |

where this would be appropriate. Thus, determining the use and types of dependency relationship is another element in your definition of the database.

Some applications might present natural opportunities to employ conditions or actions that automatically make category or date assignments. You are more likely to identify these possibilities after you begin working with the database. However, especially as you gain more experience in using Agenda, you might see potential conditions or actions while you are defining the database. In these instances, the conditions or actions may be entered immediately, so that they can assist you right from the start. For example, you might design an appointments database so that items are entered into categories by date. In such a database, you might want to use a date condition to automatically assign those items the corresponding When Date.

Agenda's flexibility often makes it easy to make mid-course corrections as you work with a database. It is almost always necessary to make such corrections, but you save time and effort, and have a more useful database, if you consider the use of these features when you create the database. Table 16-2 summarizes some of the questions to be considered in determining the features for an Agenda application.

### *Table 16-2. Agenda Features to Consider for Use in a Database.*

| Considerations | Features |
|---|---|
| Do you need an easy way to make category assignments or do you need to display assignments as they are automatically made? | Category columns |
| Will the database contain multiple levels within category families and will the assignment of items to these categories need to be displayed? | Parent:Child columns Ancestor columns |
| Will the database contain structured information in notes that needs to be displayed within views? | Category note columns |
| Can items be assigned to only one category within certain category families? | Exclusive categories |
| Will category columns contain information that will not be used for organizing the database? | Unindexed categories |
| What types of dates are needed in the database? | When Dates Entry Dates Done Dates |
| Does the information in certain views need to be arranged in any particular order? | Sorting by date, by category, or alphabetically |
| Will it be necessary to select certain items for display in a view? | Category filters Date filters |
| Do you want items assigned to categories based upon the text of the items or notes? | Text conditions |
| Can the assignment of items to certain categories be the basis for the assignment of items to other categories? | Profile conditions Profile actions |
| Will dates be the basis for category assignments or will certain category assignments imply certain dates? | Date conditions Special actions for dates |
| Will items be assigned Done Dates, either manually or based upon the assignment of items to catgories, and how will the Done items be managed? | Special actions for Done items Done item processing options |
| Will certain operations within the database be repeated frequently? | Macros |
| Will there be a need to select and display certain items from the database? | Show Views |
| Are there priority relationships among the items? | Dependencies |

## DEVELOP A SIMPLE PROTOTYPE

Once you have considered the structure and features of a new Agenda database, the best approach might be to work with a simple prototype of the database. You will often learn far more about what works and what does not by actually working with a database. Developing a simple prototype of the proposed application can be a useful tool for refining your ideas about the best database structure.

The idea is to enter a small amount of information—either real or made-up—into an Agenda database. Then you can experiment with different database structures to determine which will be most effective in accomplishing your objectives. Try different possibilities for items and categories. See what is involved in entering information, assigning it to categories, and making changes. Create views that provide you with the information you desire.

In this experimentation, you will learn the problems and limitations associated with various database structures. For example, you might try to create a view, and find out that you cannot get the information you want from the database as it is currently structured. So you work to see how you can change the database so that it can be used to produce the information you want.

The key is to do this experimentation with the prototype, with a small quantity of information. In a small database, you can more readily change things to try out different possibilities—and you will be more willing to experiment. An hour or two spent working with a small prototype database can save countless hours of work later. You might be able to identify a better database structure for your application. This saves you the effort of restructuring your database later and enables you to work with your application more efficiently.

## EXPERIMENT WITH COPIES OF YOUR DATABASE

Even after you have begun developing the database for your actual application, the search for better ways to do things need not cease. You can still experiment with alternative ways of using your database to find better techniques.

Several Agenda commands might facilitate this experimentation with a database application. You can use the File Copy command to make a copy of your Agenda database. Then you can play around with this copy, experimenting to find better ways of accomplishing your objectives. By working with the copy of the database, you run no risk of damaging the working version.

With some very large databases, experimenting with certain possibilities on a copy might be too time-consuming. For example, retroactively applying certain conditions or actions to the entire database might be a very lengthy task that would be worth doing only if the results actually enhanced the database. In such cases, you might use the File Transfer Template command to create a template of your current database structure without the items. Then you can enter a small number of items, either by typing them in directly or by copying selected items from the original database. This in effect creates a small prototype of your actual database. You can then try the conditions or actions to see if they have the desired effect on this prototype database. If the results are positive, you can go through the lengthy process of applying these conditions or actions retroactively to the entire database.

The purpose of this chapter is to offer suggestions for how you might develop applications in the most effective manner possible; it is not intended to present rules for designing Agenda applications. Use the suggestions for specific types of applications presented in the following chapters to develop the Agenda applications that best meet your needs.

# 17

# MANAGING YOUR TIME

MANAGING tasks that you have to complete is perhaps the prototypical Agenda application. The Tasks database used to demonstrate the working of Agenda throughout this book was designed to keep track of things to do. Many of the features included within Agenda, such as the various dates and the advanced date manipulation capabilities, are oriented especially to such applications.

One alternative for managing tasks is to use a database such as the Tasks database developed in the previous chapters of this book. You can sort or filter databases containing tasks to be done by When Dates to display those activities on a day-by-day basis. You can go further and add times to scheduled appointments, and sort the items by time as well as date. (Sorting by time raises some issues that are addressed later in this chapter.)

This chapter presents another alternative for managing tasks, the use of a calendar format. Many people like to schedule their appointments on a traditional calendar that lists the times throughout a day. Using such a calendar, you can see the blocks of time already scheduled and the times that remain free. This chapter shows how to use Agenda to create such an appointments calendar for managing your time. The first section gives an overview of the application. The next section describes how you would go about creating the database. The final section presents some ideas for how the database can be used.

## AN OVERVIEW OF THE APPOINTMENTS CALENDAR

The heart of the appointments calendar database will be the views displaying the times throughout each day and any activities scheduled for those times. Figure 17-1 shows the screen display of a portion of the view for the week from March 13 through March 19. The Time column on the left contains the times throughout the day, and any appointments are entered as items. The items are contained in sections for each day. Parts of the March 16 and March 17 sections are shown in Fig. 17-1.

Additional views might also be created using relative date references such as "today" or "tomorrow" in a date filter to select items for those views. With such views, you could switch instantly to a particular day's calendar without having to scroll through the appointments for a number of days in a larger view.

Appointments can be scheduled on the calendar by making entries directly in such a view. Tasks to be done sometime during the day, but without any specific time, may be entered as items at the beginning or end of the day's section. For example, Fig. 17-1 shows the item "Try to get monthly budget report completed," without any time, at the end of the Thursday, March 16 section.

Of course, you can create additional views to examine activities assigned to other categories. All of the items referring to specific projects, for example, might be displayed in another view. These items can be ordered by date and time. Furthermore, appointments and tasks can be entered as items in the other views.

```
 File: C:\AGFILES\APPNTMNT                              03/11/89    09:17
 View: Week of March 13 to March 19          When Date: 03/16/89
= Time═══════════ Thursday, March 16, 1989 ═══════════════════════════
 ·11:00 am      ‼ Appointment with Ron Smith from Walker.
 ·11:30 am      ·
 ·12:00 noon    ‼ Lunch with Bill and Mary, something informal
 ·12:30 pm      ‼ ...
 ·1:00 pm       ·
 ·1:30 pm       ‼ Meeting of group giving presentation of proposal to Acme to
                  go over presentation.
 ·2:00 pm       ‼ ...
 ·2:30 pm       ‼ Presentation of proposal to Acme at their offices, 410 E.
                  Tenth St., Suite 1100.
 ·3:00 pm       ‼ ...
 ·3:30 pm       ‼ ...
 ·4:00 pm       ‼ ...
 ·4:30 pm       ‼ Report to Ed on Acme's reactions to proposal.
 ·5:00 pm       ·
                ‼ Try to get monthly budget report completed.
 ─Time───────────Friday, March 17, 1989─────────────────────────────
 ·8:00 am       ‼ Appointment with D. George, possible new vendor.
 ·8:30 am       ‼ Quarterly staff review with Jim
 ·9:00 am       ‼ Quarterly staff review with Ann
══F1═══╤══F2══╤══F3══╤══F4══╤══F5══╤══F6══╤══F7══╤══F8══╤══F9═══╤══F10══
 Help  ║ Edit ║ Copy ║ Done ║ Note ║ Move ║ Mark ║Vw Mgr║Cat Mgr║ Menu
```

Fig. 17-1. *A portion of the appointments calendar displayed for the week of March 13 to March 19.*

If the items are given dates (and possibly times), they will also appear in the appointments calendar for the appropriate date.

The categories for the individual days, such as Thursday, March 16, 1989, are Agenda categories, not Agenda dates. This is required in order to employ the dates as section heads. All items assigned to a particular day's category are also given the corresponding When Date. These When Dates can be used with Agenda's sorting and filtering capabilities. Items that have been given When Dates as they were entered elsewhere in Agenda (perhaps by Agenda recognizing date references), are automatically assigned to the appropriate day's category. Date conditions and special actions are used to make these automatic assignments.

## CREATING THE APPOINTMENTS CALENDAR

Creating the appointments calendar requires the use of many of Agenda's capabilities. Some tricks are required to create the blank calendar pages with the times in a reasonable manner. This is the perfect place for the use of a macro to assist in adding new dates to the calendar.

### The Template View and the TIMES File

The first step in creating the appointments calendar is to enter a view that has the blank entries required for each date. Figure 17-2 shows the view created for this purpose. The section is headed by the Template category, because the items are being used as models for the entries in each date category. A category column named Time includes the times as regular intervals throughout the day.

In looking at Fig. 17-2, it appears that only the times have been entered into that column, with no item entries. However, since column entries can be made only for items that actually exist, this view contains a list of empty items. If you press INS to create an item and then press ENTER, an item is created with no text. The appointments database starts out with such empty items. These are later edited to insert text for appointments. You can create a long list of such empty items just by pressing INS repeatedly (and ENTER after the last one).

Once the empty items have been created for each half-hour interval, you can enter the times in the Time column. Figure 17-2 shows half-hour intervals, but any other interval may be employed. The times are entered here in the traditional format, but 24-hour times can be used and have their advantages when sorting. Enter the times in order so that the categories will appear in order in the category hierarchy.

Once you have created the initial set of items and times, you might be tempted to just copy these items into new sections for each day to be included in the calendar. Initially, this will produce results that look all right, but the resulting database will not work. Copying an item causes that item to be assigned to the new category and to be displayed in the new section as well as in the old, but it remains a single item. Then, when such a copied item is edited to enter an

```
File: C:\AGFILES\APPNTMNT                           03/11/89   09:17
View: Template

 Time                Template
 ·8:00  am        ·
 ·8:30  am        ·
 ·9:00  am        ·
 ·9:30  am        ·
 ·10:00 am        ·
 ·10:30 am        ·
 ·11:00 am        ·
 ·11:30 am        ·
 ·12:00 noon      ·
 ·12:30 pm        ·
 ·1:00  pm        ·
 ·1:30  pm        ·
 ·2:00  pm        ·
 ·2:30  pm        ·
 ·3:00  pm        ·
 ·3:30  pm        ·
 ·4:00  pm        ·
 ·4:30  pm        ·
 ·5:00  pm        ·
==F1===T==F2===T==F3===T==F4===T==F5===T==F6===T==F7===T==F8===T==F9===T=F10==
 Help  ‖ Edit  ‖ Copy  ‖ Done  ‖ Note  ‖ Move  ‖ Mark  ‖Vw Mgr‖Cat Mgr‖ Menu
```

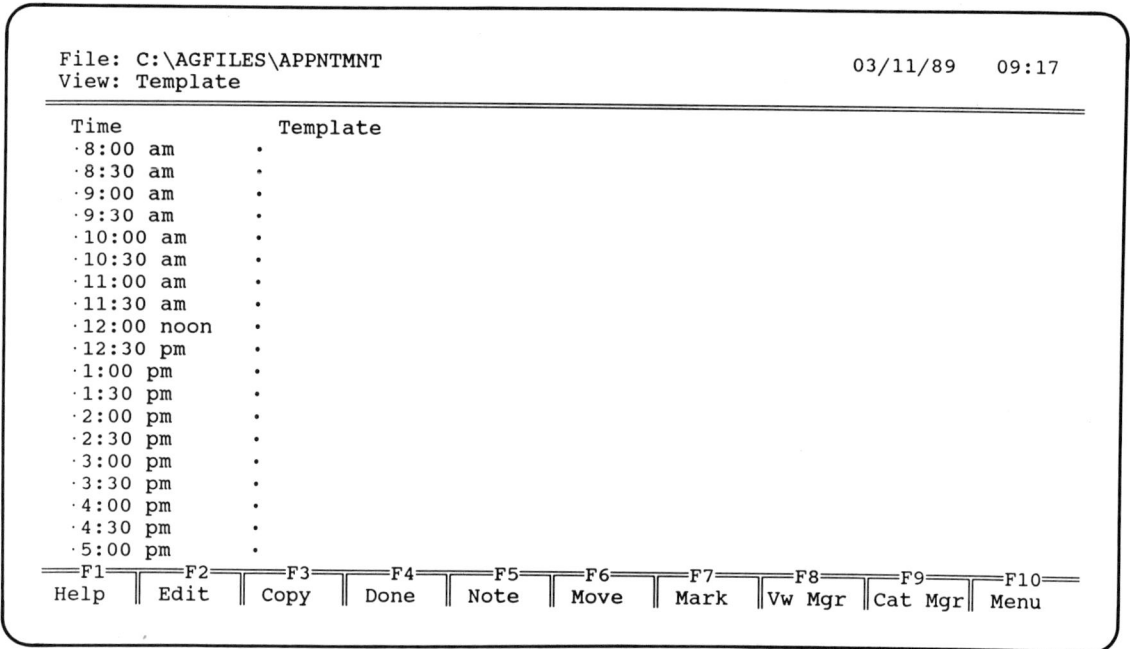

Fig. 17-2. *The Template view showing the blank items and the assigned times in the Time column.*

appointment, that appointment will appear in every occurrence of that item in the database. For example, if you edited the empty item for 11:00 A.M. on one day, entering the text "Staff meeting," this text would be displayed for the 11:00 A.M. time period for all days to which the empty item had been copied.

To provide for the replication of empty items and their assigned times in the Template section, you can use the File Transfer Export command to export the items and their category assignments (including the times) to a structured text file. Then you can use the File Transfer Import command to bring these items back into the database, assigning them to the section for the day being created. The empty items are placed into the section and are assigned to the Time categories as in the original Template section. This creates the blank calendar "page" for a given day.

## Date Categories, Conditions, and Actions

Each day in the calendar is a separate category, used as a section head to display in a section the appointments for that day. Figure 17-3 shows the top portion of the category hierarchy for an appointments calendar database with one week of calendar pages created. Each day is a category. For example, Monday, March 13, 1989 is a category. In the example shown, these individual date categories are entered as child categories of a weekly category to simplify the creation of a view showing the appointments for the seven days.

```
 File: C:\AGFILES\APPNTMNT
 Category Manager
═══════════════════════════════════════════════════════════════════════════

MAIN
  Template
  Week of March 13 to March 19
     Monday, March 13, 1989 {C= Item | W 03/13/89} <A= When>
     Tuesday, March 14, 1989 {C= Item | W 03/14/89} <A= When>
     Wednesday, March 15, 1989 {C= Item | W 03/15/89} <A= When>
     Thursday, March 16, 1989 {C= Item | W 03/16/89} <A= When>
     Friday, March 17, 1989 {C= Item | W 03/17/89} <A= When>
     Saturday, March 18, 1989 {C= Item | W 03/18/89} <A= When>
     Sunday, March 19, 1989 {C= Item | W 03/19/89} <A= When>
  Time
     8:00 am
     8:30 am
     9:00 am
     9:30 am
     10:00 am
     10:30 am
     11:00 am
     11:30 am
     12:00 noon
══F1══╤══F2══╤══F3══╤══F4══╤══F5══╤══F6══╤══F7══╤══F8══╤══F9══╤══F10══
Help  ║ Edit ║Cpy C/A║Clr C/A║ Note ║ Move ║Prm (←)║Dem (→)║To View║ Menu
```

Fig. 17-3. *The display of a portion of the category hierarchy in the Category Manager.*

All of the items in each date category should be given the appropriate When Date to use for sorting and filtering. Likewise, any item entered elsewhere in the database and given a When Date (either automatically or by you) also should be assigned to the appropriate date category. Agenda's conditions and actions can be employed to do these things automatically.

The use of the special action, Set When Date, is required to give items assigned to a date category the appropriate When Date. In entering the special action, you specify the date associated with the category.

To assign items with When Dates to the appropriate date categories, you can use the date condition for a When Date. In entering the date condition, you specify the category date as both the beginning and end dates and include all items with When Dates in that range.

### The Add Date Macro

Adding a new day of pages to the appointment calendar database requires a number of steps. First, you must create a date category to serve as a section head for each day. This can be done directly in the category hierarchy by inserting the category in the appropriate position. Next, the appropriate date condition and special action must be entered for the category to automatically make the assignments involving When Dates. Finally, the information from the TIMES structured text file must be imported into that category to include the empty items with the associated times. These steps must be repeated each time a new day is added to the calendar.

This repetitive process is a perfect candidate for automation using a macro. A relatively simply macro can be created to add a new date category to the database below the highlighted category in the hierarchy. The Add Day macro used to create the calendar is shown in Fig. 17-4.

The Add Day macro begins by obtaining from the user the date for the category to be entered, using the INPUT macro command. The user is asked to enter the date for the calendar in both Agenda's default date format (for use in the condition and action) and in the expanded day and date format used for the date category. These are stored in macro variables.

The macro then creates the new category by "pressing" INS and entering the expanded day and date as the category name. The Category Manager menu commands are then used to add the When Date condition and the special action to set the When Date. The macro enters the date in the Agenda date format to make the necessary settings when creating the condition and action.

Finally, the macro shifts to the view mode and uses the File Transfer Import command to enter the information from the file TIMES.STF into the newly created category. The macro enters the name of the file, specifies that the import is not to be limited to items that have not yet been entered, and enters the name of the newly created date category as the section into which the items are to be imported.

To use the Add Day macro to add another page to the appointment calendar, you must be in the Category Manager and highlight the category below which

```
                                                                    Edit
  Edit macro:
===============================================================Line 4==Ins==
 {Add Day}
 {INPUT;Enter Date in Agenda Date Format;%b}
 {INPUT;Enter Day and Date;%a}
 {INS}{TYPE;%a}{ENTER}
 {F10}cdw
 {DOWN}{TYPE;%b}{ENTER}
 {DOWN}{TYPE;%b}{ENTER}
 {F9}
 {F10}ass{DOWN}
 {TYPE;%b}{ENTER}
 {F9}
 {F9}
 {F10}fti{F8}
 {DOWN}c:\agfiles\times{ENTER}
 {DOWN}{DOWN}n
 {DOWN}
 {TYPE;%a}{ENTER}
 {F9}



==F1===T==F2===T==F3===T==F4===T==F5===T==F6===T==F7===T==F8===T==F9====T==F10==
 Help  ‖ Paste ‖ Copy  ‖ Cut   ‖       ‖       ‖ Mark  ‖       ‖Accept ‖Menu
```

Fig. 17-4. *The Add Day macro to create a new day category and import the items and times.*

the new date category is to be entered. You can then start the macro. The macro prompts for the date for the category to be entered, in both formats. It then creates the category, adds the condition and action, and imports the information to create the blank calendar page. If you use the Add Day macro to add a date category as the child of another category, you will have to use F8 (DEMOTE) to make the new category a child category.

You can use the Add Day macro repeatedly to add a number of date categories and calendar pages to the database. The previously entered dates will be displayed in the boxes by the INPUT command, so you can edit them for the new date entries. The macro could easily be enhanced to automatically loop through the entire set of commands, allowing multiple dates to be added with one execution of the macro.

## Database Views

Several different views may be created to facilitate the use of the appointments calendar database. The primary views are calendar views that display the appointments for one or more days. The example calendar includes the "Week of May 23 to May 29" view, including all of the date categories for that week as section heads. The view includes a category column with the Time category, to the left of the items, listing the appointment times.

Calendar views may be created with as many or as few date categories as desired. The choice is a matter of personal preference, depending upon whether you would prefer to scroll through long views with many dates or switch more frequently between views with fewer dates.

You might also want to create a special calendar view that always displays the appointments for the current day. In that way, you can always display the current day's appointments quickly, by switching views instead of scrolling. To create such a view, include all of the items in the database by specifying the Main category. Then use a When Date filter with the relative date entry "Today" to include the appointments for the current day.

The items in the database may be assigned to other categories, and views may be created to display all of the appointments and other activities relating to those categories. In the example presented here, several of the items have been assigned to the Acme and Walker project categories, just as in the Tasks database. These categories are displayed as sections in a Projects view, shown in Fig. 17-5. The When Date and Time category columns have been included to show when the various activities are scheduled.

## USING THE APPOINTMENTS CALENDAR

The appointments calendar database may be used exactly like any other Agenda database. Items may be entered and assigned to categories. New views

```
┌──────────────────────────────────────────────────────────────────────────┐
│  File: C:\AGFILES\APPNTMNT                          03/11/89   09:23       │
│  View: Projects                            When Date: 03/17/89             │
│  ════════════════════════════════════════════════════════════════════════ │
│  Acme                                          When          Time          │
│     ‼ Meeting of group giving presentation of  ·03/16/89     ·1:30 pm      │
│       proposal to Acme to go over presentation.                            │
│     ‼ Presentation of proposal to Acme at their ·03/16/89    ·2:30 pm      │
│       offices, 410 E. Tenth St., Suite 1100.                               │
│     ‼ Report to Ed on Acme's reactions to proposal. ·03/16/89 ·4:30 pm     │
│     ‼ Meeting with Acme proposal group to discuss »03/17/89  ·10:00 am     │
│       reactions to presentation Friday.                                    │
│                                                                            │
│  Walker                                        When          Time          │
│     ‼ Appointment with Ron Smith from Walker.  ·03/16/89     ·11:00 am     │
│                                                                            │
│                                                                            │
│                                                                            │
│                                                                            │
│                                                                            │
│  ═F1══╤══F2══╤══F3══╤══F4══╤══F5══╤══F6══╤══F7══╤══F8══╤══F9══╤══F10══      │
│  Help ║ Edit ║ Copy ║ Done ║ Note ║ Move ║ Mark ║Vw Mgr║Cat Mgr║ Menu      │
└──────────────────────────────────────────────────────────────────────────┘
```

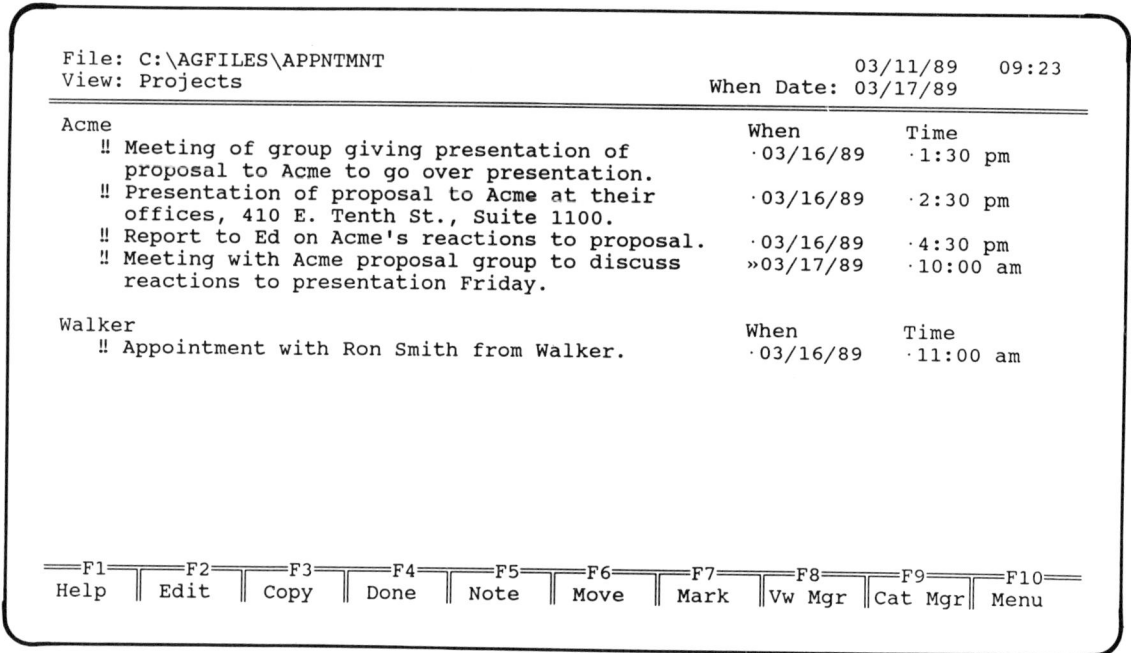

Fig. 17-5. *A Projects view showing the information in the calendar presented in another format.*

may be created to display the information in a variety of ways. The appointments calendar does have several unique aspects that are discussed in detail in the following pages.

## Using the Calendar Views

Appointments most often will be entered in one of the calendar views listing the various time periods throughout a day, such as the view shown in Fig. 17-1. You move the highlight to the item corresponding to the appropriate time and press F2 (EDIT) to edit the empty item. Type in the desired text and press ENTER.

This procedure might take a little getting used to, however. If you have used Agenda for any length of time, you are used to pressing INS to insert new items. When there is no entry for a particular time, you might be tempted to press INS to insert a new item rather than pressing F2 (EDIT) to edit the empty item. Doing so will create a new item without a time, and leave the item associated with that time empty.

When an appointment is scheduled to last longer than a single half-hour time interval, you will probably want to make entries for those later time periods to indicate this continuation. In the example, we just entered three dots to indicate that the preceding activity was scheduled into that time period. Choose whatever is clearest to you.

The times of appointments cannot be changed simply by moving the items, because the time is a category assignment that will be moved right along. To move an appointment, begin editing the item in which the appointment was entered, and move the entire text of the item to the Clipboard. Then edit the (presumably empty) item for the date and time to which the appointment is to be moved and paste in the text from the Clipboard.

You might have activities you want to do sometime during a given day that are not scheduled for any particular time. You can insert new items, without times, into the appropriate date category section. The example shown in Fig. 17-1 includes the item ''Try to get monthly budget report completed'' at the end of the Thursday, March 16, 1989 section. You will probably want to insert such items either at the beginning or the end of the section, before or after the scheduled activities. Note that sorting items in a section by time might place items without times at the end of the section.

Other conventions may be adopted to further refine your use of the calendar views. In the example shown in Fig. 17-1, each of the items for which appointments are scheduled has been marked as Done by pressing F4 (DONE) after editing the item to enter the appointment. Since Done items are marked with double exclamation points, you can more easily distinguish between scheduled times and times still available for appointments.

If you have a very full schedule and often have to search for open appointment times, you can go further and use the View Preferences command to hide Done items. Then only the items not marked as done—the available appointment times— are displayed. The setting can be changed temporarily in your working calendar views, or you can create additional calendar views with Done items hidden to facilitate the search for open appointment times.

## Using Other Views

You might want to display the items in your calendar database in other types of views, such as the Projects view shown in Fig. 17-5. This view shows the activities associated with various projects and their scheduled dates and times, allowing you to see what is to be done for each project.

Additional activities may be entered as new items in these other views. A When Date may be assigned automatically by Agenda in response to a date reference in the item, or it may be assigned directly by entry into the When column. If a new item is assigned a When Date, the item will be assigned to the corresponding date category by the date condition and will be displayed in the calendar views in the appropriate date section.

A time may also be entered for new items by making the entry into the Time column. Of course, to determine whether something is already scheduled for that date and time, you will have to look at a calendar view. However, some activities might take priority over others, requiring any conflicting appointments to be rescheduled.

In Fig. 17-5, a new item has been entered at the end of the Acme section referring to a meeting tomorrow. Agenda automatically assigns Friday's date, 3/17/88, as the When Date. Additionally, a time of 10:00 A.M. has been entered in the Time column for this meeting. When you look at a calendar view with appointments for March 17, the newly entered item will be displayed in addition to the previously existing item for 10:00 A.M. This existing item could be an empty item if no appointment has been made for that time, or it could already have an entry, which would indicate a scheduling conflict. If necessary, an existing appointment would have to be rescheduled and moved to another time. Once the information is no longer needed, the original item for the 10:00 A.M. time slot can be discarded from the database, being replaced by the new item.

## A Note on Sorting by Time

The day's section in the calendar view will have to be sorted by the Time categories in order for the new item to be displayed in its proper sequence. The Category Section Sort command is used to set the sort parameters and invoke the sort. After it is used initially to sort by Time, the settings made will remain as the defaults so the command can be used quickly to re-sort a date category whenever it is necessary. This is probably preferable to specifying a re-sorting operation every time an item is entered, because the time associated with doing the sort can be considerable.

Sorting the items in order by Time categories can present some problems. Agenda includes sophisticated date-recognition capabilities but, ironically, the program is ignorant when it comes to times. To Agenda, the categories entered in the Time category are just strings of characters. If you sorted on those categories either alphabetically or numerically, Agenda would misorder the items, placing an item with a 1:00 P.M. time before an item with an 8:00 A.M. time. This is because Agenda knows nothing about times and the meaning of A.M. or P.M.

You can, however, sort on the Time categories by ordering them according to the way they appear in the category hierarchy. If the times were originally entered in the correct order, they will be in order in the category hierarchy. If they are not, they can be individually moved to place them in the correct order in the category hierarchy. Then, when you sort the Time categories by the order in which they appear in the category hierarchy, they will be ordered correctly.

This use of the category hierarchy ordering for sorting on the Time categories works well as long as you only use times that have already been entered and appear in the hierarchy. Should you enter a new item with a different time, such as 8:15 A.M., the new category would be placed out of order in the list of Time categories and Agenda would sort the new item incorrectly. If you want to use times in the formats shown in this chapter and you want to sort items by time, you have to restrict yourself to using only the times originally entered when creating the database.

An alternative is to use 24-hour time for the appointments calendar database. A time of 7:30 A.M. would be entered as 07:30 (including the leading zero) and a time of 3:30 P.M. would be entered as 15:30. These times can be correctly sorted using an alphabetical ordering. (Numeric sorting does not work because of the colon.) An item with any intermediate time, such as 15:33, would also be correctly ordered when the items in a section are sorted.

The selection of the time format poses a tradeoff. Twenty-four-hour times might be more convenient for sorting all possible time entries, but they are also less familiar to most people. More normal time entries can be sorted only according to the category hierarchy ordering, limiting time entries to the discrete interval values included in the database. The choice is yours.

This chapter, like all of the following chapters discussing possible applications of Agenda, does not begin to exhaust the possibilities. Rather, it is intended to serve as a point of departure, showing you how an Agenda database may be employed as an appointments calendar to assist in managing time. Possible extensions of these ideas are as diverse as the possibilities of Agenda itself.

# 18

# MANAGING PROJECTS

MANAGERS frequently confront the problem of managing projects that involve multiple, interrelated tasks. Managing a project involves keeping track of the starting and completion times of each task, knowing which tasks depend upon the completion of other tasks, and managing the resources needed to accomplish the various tasks. Agenda can effectively assist in such project management.

Special-purpose project management software is available for these jobs and, quite honestly, these programs can do more for managing projects than can be accomplished using Agenda. For very large, complex projects, specialized programs would be the tools of choice. However, project management software is complex, and requires considerable effort to learn and use. For more modest projects, the use of such programs might be overkill. Agenda provides a familiar environment for a manager to use in keeping track of the major aspects of more modest projects.

This chapter illustrates the ways Agenda might be used to manage projects. Each of the sections of the chapter illustrates a particular application of Agenda, focusing on the different views you might create and use. The first section shows how you can enter and view the basic information on each of the tasks associated with the project. The next two sections present examples of using Agenda to manage a project by examining the allocation of staff resources and the consideration of task dependencies. Finally, the last section demonstrates how Agenda can be used to create a simple Gannt chart for displaying the scheduling of tasks over time.

# ENTERING AND VIEWING
# THE INFORMATION ON THE TASKS

The example presented here focuses on the use of Agenda to manage a population survey. The overall project consists of three major phases. The first is the design, in which the survey is planned and the survey instrument (the questionnaire) is developed and tested. Next comes the actual administration phase, with the hiring and training of interviewers, the administration of the survey, and the follow-up checking of the results. Then, in the final phase, the results must be analyzed and presented.

The basic information on the project is entered into a Tasks view shown in Fig. 18-1. The items in the database are the specific tasks that have to be accomplished in carrying out the project. These items are entered into sections representing the three phases of the project—design, administration, and analysis. Such a division is not necessarily required, but it can aid in organizing the project tasks.

Different types of information about each of the tasks have been entered into the Tasks view. The areas covered include task length and scheduling, the assignment of personnel resources to the tasks, and the task dependencies.

The Duration column and the Entry and When Date columns are employed for the entry of information on tasks scheduling. The Duration column includes the estimated length of time that each task will take to complete. The Entry Date column is used to display the planned starting dates for each of the tasks.

```
File: C:\AGFILES\PROJMGMT                         03/11/89    10:12
View: Tasks View

Design                                Duration  Entry      When       Staffing
    · Establish objectives            ·6 days   ·03/13/89  ·03/20/89  ·All
                                                                      Bob
                                                                      Gina

    ↔ Develop survey instrument       ·7 days   ·03/21/89  ·03/29/89  ·Gina
    ↔ Develop survey procedures       ·5 days   ·03/21/89  ·03/27/89  ·Bob
    ↔ Developing sampling frame       ·9 days   ·03/28/89  ·04/07/89  ·Bob
    ↔ Test survey instrument          ·9 days   ·03/30/89  ·04/11/89  ·Gina
    ↔ Develop final instrument        ·5 days   ·04/12/89  ·04/18/89  ·Gina

Administration                        Duration  Entry      When       Staffing
    ↔ Have survey instrument printed  ·3 days   ·04/19/89  ·04/21/89
    ↔ Hire and train interviewers     ·10 days  ·04/10/89  ·04/21/89  ·Bob
    ↔ Administer survey               ·14 days  ·04/24/89  ·05/11/89  ·Bob
    ↔ Survey checking and followup    ·6 days   ·05/12/89  ·05/19/89  ·Gina

Analysis                              Duration  Entry      When       Staffing
    ↔ Edit and code survey results    ·6 days   ·05/22/89  ·05/30/89  ·Bob
    ↔ Conduct statistical analysis    ·7 days   ·05/31/89  ·06/08/89  ·Gina
    ↔ Prepare final report            ·7 days   ·06/09/89  ·06/19/89  ·All
═F1═══════F2═══════F3═══════F4═══════F5═══════F6═══════F7═══════F8═══════F9═══════F10══
Help   ║ Edit   ║ Copy   ║ Done   ║ Note   ║ Move   ║ Mark   ║Vw Mgr ║Cat Mgr║ Menu
```

Fig. 18-1. *The Tasks view showing the basic information on the project tasks.*

Remember that since the Entry Date is being used in this manner, you must use the Utility Preferences Date command to change the setting so that the Entry Date is not automatically set by Agenda. The When Date column displays the planned completion date for each task. (The Entry and When Dates are dates that you calculate by looking at the tasks, determining the order in which the tasks must be undertaken, and estimating the duration of each task.)

The Staffing column is used to specify which staff members will be assigned to the various tasks. For this simple example, only a small staff of two people—Gina and Bob—is available. This use of the Staffing column should be quite familiar to any Agenda user who has been following along in this book.

One feature has been added to demonstrate one of the advanced capabilities of Agenda. For several of the tasks, including the first, the entire staff (both Gina and Bob) is assigned. A child category named All is created under the Staffing category, along with Gina and Bob. A profile action is attached to this All category so that any items assigned to the All category are also automatically assigned to the Gina and Bob categories. Thus, when entering staff assignments in the Staffing column, the assignment of the entire staff can be accomplished simply by entering the category All. The profile action then assigns the tasks to the Gina and Bob categories, which are automatically displayed in the Staffing column. Admittedly, in this small example with the staff of only two persons and only two assignments of that entire staff, the use of the profile action is probably not worth the effort. However, in more complex situation in which numbers of staff groups are routinely assigned to tasks, such actions can simplify the assignment of persons to tasks.

Staff personnel are not the only resources that might be assigned in the management of projects. Special equipment and work space are examples of other resources that can be crucial to the completion of a project, and that might need to be managed in carrying out the project.

Note the double arrows in front of every one of the tasks items except the first. Item dependencies have been entered to specify which other tasks have to be completed before work on the given task can begin. For example, the actual administration of the survey cannot begin until the sampling frame has been developed, the survey instrument has been printed, and the interviewers have been hired and trained. Therefore, the items referring to these tasks are marked, the "Administer survey" item is highlighted, and ALT-F3 (DPNDSON) key is used to specify the dependency. These dependencies will be important and useful when managing the project.

## VIEWING THE ALLOCATION OF STAFF RESOURCES TO THE TASKS

An important function in managing any project is allocating and managing the resources required for the completion of the project. Figure 18-2 shows the

```
┌─────────────────────────────────────────────────────────────────────────┐
│ File: C:\AGFILES\PROJMGMT                            03/11/89   10:13     │
│ View: Staffing View                                                       │
│ ═══════════════════════════════════════════════════════════════════════ │
│ Bob                                  Duration     Entry       When        │
│   · Establish objectives             ·6 days     ·03/13/89   ·03/20/89    │
│   ↵ Develop survey procedures        ·5 days     ·03/21/89   ·03/27/89    │
│   ↵ Developing sampling frame        ·9 days     ·03/28/89   ·04/07/89    │
│   ↵ Hire and train interviewers      ·10 days    ·04/10/89   ·04/21/89    │
│   ↵ Administer survey                 ·14 days    ·04/24/89   ·05/11/89    │
│   ↵ Edit and code survey results     ·6 days     ·05/22/89   ·05/30/89    │
│   ↵ Prepare final report             ·7 days     ·06/09/89   ·06/19/89    │
│                                                                           │
│ Gina                                 Duration     Entry       When        │
│   · Establish objectives             ·6 days     ·03/13/89   ·03/20/89    │
│   ↵ Develop survey instrument        ·7 days     ·03/21/89   ·03/29/89    │
│   ↵ Test survey instrument           ·9 days     ·03/30/89   ·04/11/89    │
│   ↵ Develop final instrument         ·5 days     ·04/12/89   ·04/18/89    │
│   ↵ Survey checking and followup     ·6 days     ·05/12/89   ·05/19/89    │
│   ↵ Conduct statistical analysis     ·7 days     ·05/31/89   ·06/08/89    │
│   ↵ Prepare final report             ·7 days     ·06/09/89   ·06/19/89    │
│                                                                           │
│ ══F1══╤══F2══╤══F3══╤══F4══╤══F5══╤══F6══╤══F7══╤══F8═══╤══F9═══╤══F10══   │
│  Help │ Edit │ Copy │ Done │ Note │ Move │ Mark │Vw Mgr │Cat Mgr│ Menu    │
└─────────────────────────────────────────────────────────────────────────┘
```

Fig. 18-2. *The Staffing view showing the tasks assigned to the various staff members.*

Staffing view with the tasks assigned to the two staff members, Bob and Gina. (The resource categories are used as the section heads in the resource views.)

Added to the Staffing view are the Duration, the Entry, and the When Date columns, specifying the planned start and completion times for each of the tasks. To aid in examining the requirements placed on each of the resources, the items in the sections in this view have been sorted using the Entry Date (start time) as the primary sort and the When Date (completion time) as the secondary sort.

The Staffing view shows how resources are committed to the project tasks. You can see if any resource is overcommitted (scheduled to do too many things at one time). You can also find the times when resources are not committed to project tasks and would be available for use on other tasks or even other projects.

Looking at the Staffing view in Fig. 18-2, you see that Bob is fully committed to the project until the middle of May, at which time there are several gaps in his task assignments. Gina, on the other hand, is committed to the project through April 18, and then has a gap until May 12. This suggests that Gina might be assigned to work on some other project during this time. Alternatively, if you want to get the survey research project completed as quickly as possible, this might present an opportunity for moving up the schedule. By assigning Gina to help Bob in administering the survey, it might be possible to complete the job more quickly. Also, it might be possible to get Gina started earlier on the survey checking and follow-up, overlapping this task somewhat with the actual administration of the survey.

Resource views of the project tasks—such as this Staffing view—give the manager the opportunity to see how the various resources are being allocated and to consider their possible reallocation. Changes in assignments can be made in the resource views. For example, a task can be reassigned from one staff member to another simply by moving it from section to section. The starting or completion dates can be changed by changing the entries in the Entry or When columns. Of course, any changes in these columns are reflected in the Tasks view and all other views of the project database.

## USING ITEM DEPENDENCIES IN MANAGING THE PROJECT

The project database includes information on the relationships among the tasks, in the form of item dependencies. A given task is designated as dependent upon other tasks if those tasks must be completed prior to the start of the given task. This information can be useful in managing a project, especially when problems arise and the schedule has to be adjusted.

Suppose that while carrying out the example project, problems arise during the development of the sampling frame (to be used in selecting the households to be interviewed). Because of the problem, it now appears that this task will take longer to complete than the nine days originally planned. A look at the Staffing view indicates that this is likely to pose problems for Bob, who has a full schedule of responsibilities. Will a delay in the development of the sampling frame result in a delay of the entire project?

To answer this question, you can create a view showing the tasks that are dependent upon the completion of the "Develop sampling frame" task. You would use the Utility Show Dependents All command to create a view containing all of the items that are dependent upon that item and that cannot be started until that task is completed.

Figure 18-3 shows the view that has been created to show these dependencies. The Utility Show command generates a Show View containing the dependent items. The name of the view has been edited to "Tasks Dependent Upon Sampling Frame" to describe the view contents. The Duration category and the Entry and When Date columns have been added to the view so that the scheduling of these dependent tasks may be examined.

The sampling frame task was scheduled for completion by April 7, but no task dependent upon that task is scheduled to begin until April 24. There is considerable slack, so running late on the sampling frame task will not necessarily cause delays to other aspects of the project. When you refer back to the Staffing view, however, you see that Bob is completely scheduled for other tasks between the completion of the sampling frame task and the administration of the survey. If he is to devote more time to the sampling frame task, it might be necessary

```
File: C:\AGFILES\PROJMGMT                    03/11/89    10:13
View: Tasks Dependent Upon Sampling Frame
══════════════════════════════════════════════════════════════════
                                  Duration     Entry      When
*Show*
    ↔ Administer survey            ·14 days   ·04/24/89  ·05/11/89
    ↔ Survey checking and followup  ·6 days   ·05/12/89  ·05/19/89
    ↔ Edit and code survey results  ·6 days   ·05/22/89  ·05/30/89
    ↔ Conduct statistical analysis  ·7 days   ·05/31/89  ·06/08/89
    ↔ Prepare final report          ·7 days   ·06/09/89   ·06/19/89




══F1════╤══F2════╤══F3════╤══F4════╤══F5════╤══F6════╤══F7════╤══F8════╤══F9════╤══F10═══
  Help  │  Edit  │  Copy  │  Done  │  Note  │  Move  │  Mark  │ Vw Mgr │Cat Mgr│ Menu
```

Fig. 18-3. *The view created to show the tasks dependent upon the development of the sampling frame.*

to find additional staff members to help out with the tasks to which Bob had been assigned. Otherwise, completion of the tasks could be delayed.

This is a simple example of how the information on task dependencies may be used in managing a project. When a task takes more or less time to complete than was originally planned, you will want to see which of the succeeding tasks will be affected by the change. Use the Utility Show Dependents command to display the tasks dependent upon the task that has changed. Meeting the planned starting date might be critical for certain tasks. In such cases, use the Utility Show Prerequisites command to display the tasks upon which this task depends.

As illustrated in the example, views showing task dependencies can be used in conjunction with resource allocation views to provide the basis for making project management decisions in the face of changing circumstances. The project management database is designed to provide the information necessary to make such decisions as the project evolves, and changes take place.

## VIEWING THE SCHEDULING
## OF TASKS WITH A GANNT CHART

A frequently used tool in project management is a visual display of the time periods taken up by the various project tasks. Such displays are called *Gannt charts.* Even if you have not heard the name, you might have seen such charts, with the tasks listed on the vertical axis, at the left, and dates listed on the horizontal axis. Horizontal bars are placed on the chart for each task, extending from the starting date to the finishing date.

Agenda can be used to create such Gannt charts. Figure 18-4 shows the Gannt Chart view for the survey research example. The tasks are listed in the order in which they are scheduled to begin. Moving across in each section are weekly time intervals for the periods when the activities in that project phase are to be completed. The entry .>>. for each task indicates that the task is scheduled to begin sometime during that week. The entry .<<. indicates that the task is scheduled to be finished sometime during that week.

For example, Fig. 18-4 shows that the first task is scheduled to begin during the week of 9/5, and that it is scheduled to be completed during the week of 9/12. The pair of entries then shows the interval over which each task is scheduled to be carried out. The Gannt Chart view allows you to see how the various tasks in the project relate to one another across time.

Because of limitations on the space available and the numbers of weeks that can be displayed on the screen, different ranges of weeks are shown for each of the three project phases. The initial design phase comes first, and is to be carried out during the range of weeks from March 13 through April 17. The administration phase begins during the week of April 10 and extends through the week of May 15. Analysis goes from the week of May 22 through the week of June 19.

The Gannt Chart view is integrated with the rest of the project management database. If changes are made to the start or completion dates of any of the tasks

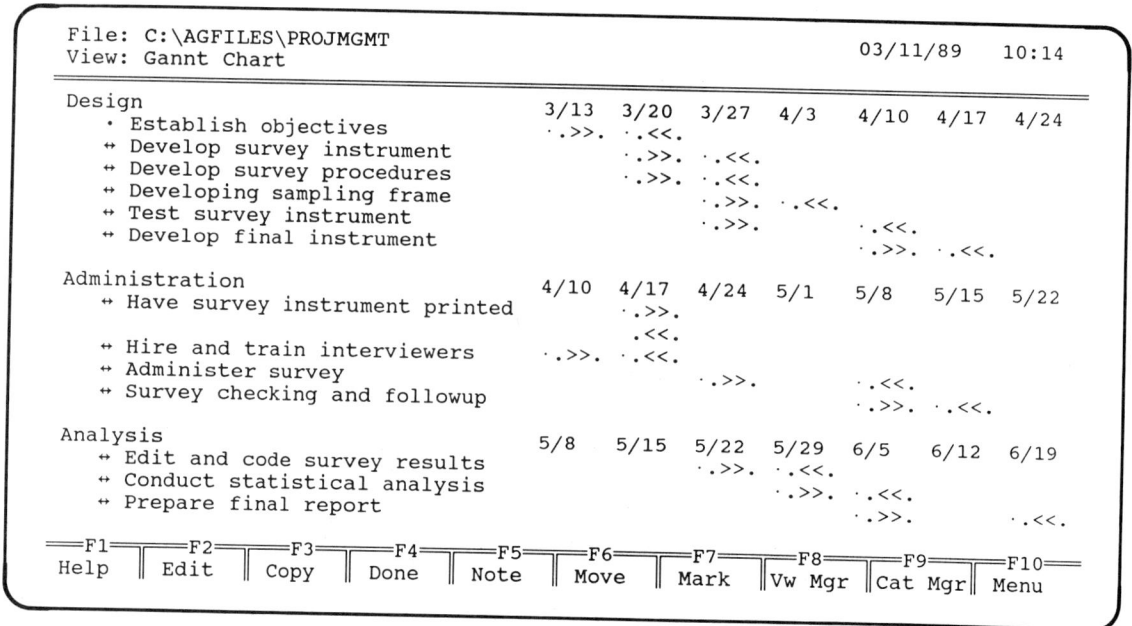

```
 File: C:\AGFILES\PROJMGMT
 View: Gannt Chart                                    03/11/89    10:14
═══════════════════════════════════════════════════════════════════════
 Design                               3/13  3/20  3/27  4/3  4/10  4/17  4/24
    · Establish objectives            ·.>>. ·.<<.
    ↔ Develop survey instrument             ·.>>. ·.<<.
    ↔ Develop survey procedures             ·.>>. ·.<<.
    ↔ Developing sampling frame                   ·.>>. ·.<<.
    ↔ Test survey instrument                      ·.>>.        ·.<<.
    ↔ Develop final instrument                                 ·.>>. ·.<<.

 Administration                       4/10  4/17  4/24  5/1  5/8  5/15  5/22
    ↔ Have survey instrument printed        ·.>>.
                                            .<<.
    ↔ Hire and train interviewers     ·.>>. ·.<<.
    ↔ Administer survey                            ·.>>.       ·.<<.
    ↔ Survey checking and followup                             ·.>>. ·.<<.

 Analysis                             5/8   5/15  5/22  5/29  6/5  6/12  6/19
    ↔ Edit and code survey results                ·.>>. ·.<<.
    ↔ Conduct statistical analysis                      ·.>>. ·.<<.
    ↔ Prepare final report                                    ·.>>.       ·.<<.
══F1════╤═F2════╤═F3════╤═F4════╤═F5════╤═F6════╤═F7════╤═F8═════╤═F9═════╤═F10══
 Help   │ Edit  │ Copy  │ Done  │ Note  │ Move  │ Mark  │Vw Mgr │Cat Mgr│ Menu
```

Fig. 18-4. *The view showing the times during which the various tasks are scheduled to be carried out in the form of a Gannt chart.*

in any other view, those changes are reflected in the Gannt Chart view. Thus, using such a chart provides a dynamic tool for examining the effects of changes in task schedules on the relationships of the various tasks.

Creating a Gannt chart is not a built-in feature of Agenda. In fact, it requires a fair amount of effort, but if Agenda is to be used over an extended period of time for the management of the project, such effort may be time well spent.

The key to creating the Gannt Chart view can be found in the category hierarchy, shown in Fig. 18-5. Categories are created for each of the weekly periods over the duration of the project. Thus, the category 3/13 represents the week beginning March 13.

Each of the weekly categories has two child categories with the unusual names .>>. and .<<. These unusual category names have been selected to create the visual display shown in the Gannt Chart view. Items are assigned to a .>>. category if they are scheduled to start (have Entry Dates) during the week associated with the parent category. Items are assigned to a .<<. category if they are scheduled to be completed (have When Dates) during the week associated with the parent category.

Items are assigned to these categories automatically through the use of date conditions. Figure 18-5 shows these conditions. The first date condition specifies that an item is assigned to the category .>>. as the child category of 3/13 if the Entry Date of the item falls into the range 3/13/89 through 3/19/89. The When Date conditions are used with the .<<. categories.

```
File: C:\AGFILES\PROJMGMT
Category Manager
==========================================================
MAIN
  Survey Tasks
    Design
    Administration
    Analysis
  Staffing
    Bob
    Gina
    All    <A= Bob,Gina>
  Weeks
    3/13
      .>>.  {C= Item | E 03/13/89-03/19/89}
      .<<.  {C= Item | W 03/13/89-03/19/89}
    3/20
      .>>.  {C= Item | E 03/20/89-03/26/89}
      .<<.  {C= Item | W 03/20/89-03/26/89}
    3/27
      .>>.  {C= Item | E 03/27/89-04/02/89}
      .<<.  {C= Item | W 03/27/89-04/02/89}
    4/3
=F1===F2===F3===F4===F5===F6===F7===F8===F9===F10==
Help | Edit |Cpy C/A|Clr C/A| Note | Move |Prm (←)|Dem (→)|To View| Menu
```

Fig. 18-5. *The category hierarchy showing the form of the categories and conditions used in creating the Gannt chart.*

Creating all of the categories and the corresponding date conditions can be rather tedious. Even so, the categories and conditions could be entered in a half-hour or so. This might be a worthwhile investment of time for a project management database to be used over a period of months.

A relatively simple macro could be created to automate the creation of the categories and conditions. The macro might use the INPUT macro command to allow the user to specify the beginning and ending dates of the week for which the work is to be accomplished, such as 9/5 and 9/12. The macro could then create the weekly category, create the .>>. category as a child category and enter the Entry Date condition, and then create the .<<. category as a child category and enter the When Date condition.

If the categories and conditions for the Gannt chart are created after the tasks and their Entry and When Dates have been entered, you must use the Utility Execute command to assign existing items to categories. From then on, whenever any changes are made to the Entry or When Dates in managing the project, the appropriate category reassignments are made automatically.

Once the categories and conditions have been created and the items have been assigned to these unusual categories, creating the Gannt Chart view is relatively straightforward. The appropriate weekly categories need only be added as category columns in the various sections. The actual category assignments to the child categories (that is, the .>>. and .<<. categories) are displayed if the item (task) is assigned to those weekly categories. Thus, if an item has an Entry Date during the week beginning September 5, it is assigned to the .>>. child category and the category .>>. is displayed in the 9/5 column.

In order to display the maximum number of weeks as columns and still see the column headings and column entries, the column widths should be set to four. Seven weekly columns were entered into each section. One or two more could be reasonably accommodated before the space left for the item itself became too constrained.

The selection of the category names to be used as symbols in the Gannt chart was made to best convey the sense of a Gannt chart within the framework of Agenda. Obviously, other choices can be made to better accommodate individual preferences.

The project management example presented in this chapter is intended to serve as a set of ideas for ways in which Agenda can assist in the management of projects with multiple tasks. Every user is likely to vary the implementation of these ideas to best meet the needs of specific projects.

# 19

## MANAGING PERSONAL CONTACTS

NEARLY everyone has occasion to manage personal contacts, varying from clients to sales prospects to prospective donors. In doing this, you will have a variety of information for each person. Each time you need to use information about one of these contacts, you must look it up and select particular individuals or pieces of information. Agenda can be used effectively for selecting information about personal contacts.

The use of Agenda for managing personal contacts raises the issue of how the database can most effectively be structured. The first section of this chapter discusses the alternatives for structuring a database. The following sections of the chapter discuss and illustrate three approaches for structuring a personal-contact Agenda database. One approach is to enter each person as an item in the database. This approach is applied in illustrating how you can produce mailing labels for personal contacts. A second approach is to create a database in which the persons are entered as categories. A third, hybrid approach combines features of the first two approaches.

### STRUCTURING THE DATABASE

A database for managing personal contacts will obviously include the names of those contacts, and a variety of information about each of those contacts. There are two fundamentally different approaches for structuring an Agenda database for such an application. First, the names may be entered as the items in the database. The information about each of those people can then be entered as categories, in category columns in one or more views. Alternatively, the names may be entered as categories which would be used as section headings in a view. Then, information about each of those people can be entered as items in the appropriate sections.

Entering the names of persons as items makes sense when you have more or less the same information about each individual. Then a common set of category columns works well for entering that information. This arrangement makes it easy to select individuals based upon the information entered in columns by using category filters.

On the other hand, entering the names of persons as categories and using those categories as section heads makes sense when you have many pieces of dissimilar information about the different people. These varying pieces of information about each person can be entered and displayed as items in the appropriate sections.

The two different approaches allow you to see and work with the information in distinctly different ways. Each approach has its advantages and disadvantages. Thus, for certain applications, it might be appropriate to use a hybrid of the first two choices. Choosing the structure for the database depends upon both the nature of the information you intend to enter and how you wish to manage that information.

## ENTERING PERSONS AS ITEMS

The first example illustrates the development of an Agenda database in which persons are entered as items in the database and information about those persons is entered and displayed in category columns. The problem to be addressed throughout this chapter involves the needs of a sales manager working for a vendor selling personal computer software to businesses. The sales manager needs to keep track of the contact persons at the different firms using the software. Some basic information is needed for each person, such as the company name and telephone number. The sales manager also needs to know which of the software firm's products are being used by that company, and on which computer systems.

Figure 19-1 shows a small Agenda database in which the names of the contact persons have been entered as items in the database. The view has a single section, with the heading Contacts. The names of the persons have been entered as items in this section. Four category columns are included in the view: Company, Phone, Applications, and Systems. Information about each of the persons has been entered into those columns.

This simple tabular format makes it easy to look up the information on any of the contacts. The information can be sorted in alphabetical order by either

```
File: C:\AGFILES\CONTACTS                    03/11/89   11:24
View: Persons as Items
════════════════════════════════════════════════════════════════

Contacts            Company        Phone          Applications  Systems
   ♪ Anderson, Susan  ·Acme         ·(818)275-3821 ·Basic Acctng ·IBM PC
                                                    Mgmt Anal
   ♪ Baker, Martha    ·Walker       ·(317)872-1466 ·Adv Acctng   ·IBM PC
                                                    Mgmt Anal      Macintosh
                                                                   LAN
   ♪ Donaldson, Jim   ·Superior     ·(212)945-2133 ·Basic Acctng ·IBM PC
   ♪ Forbush, George  ·Four-Way     ·(608)234-6000 ·Mgmt Anal    ·Macintosh
   ♪ Hatfield, James  ·New Designs  ·(201)382-2733 ·Basic Acctng ·IBM PC
   ♪ Martin, Gina     ·Diversified  ·(408)654-7351 ·Adv Acctng   ·IBM PC
                                                    Mgmt Anal
   ♪ Peters, Wanda    ·Geosys       ·(719)239-5687 ·Adv Acctng   ·Macintosh
                                                                   LAN
   ♪ Smith, John      ·Acme         ·(818)275-3776 ·Adv Acctng   ·IBM PC
                                                                   LAN
   ♪ Watson, Bill     ·Wallston     ·(303)783-8534 ·Basic Acctng ·IBM PC
   ♪ Wilson, Paula    ·Bridgeport   ·(213)892-4726 ·Basic Acctng ·IBM PC


=F1==╤=F2==╤=F3==╤=F4==╤=F5==╤=F6==╤=F7==╤=F8===╤=F9===╤=F10==
Help  ║ Edit ║ Copy ║ Done ║ Note ║ Move ║ Mark ║Vw Mgr║Cat Mgr║ Menu
```

Fig. 19-1. *A database for managing personal contacts with individual persons entered as items.*

the contact name or by the name of the company to facilitate quickly looking up the information for any person or company.

With the persons as items and the information entered as category entries in the category columns, it is easy to use category filters to select out persons that meet specific criteria. Suppose the sales manager wants a list of the contacts at the firms using the Basic Accounting software package, perhaps to begin an effort to get those firms to upgrade to the Advanced Accounting Package. A new view can be created by copying the Persons as Items view. Then the View Define procedure can be used to set a category filter so that only those items (names of persons) assigned to the Basic Acctng category will be displayed in the view. This simple procedure yields the selection of the persons desired, as shown in Fig. 19-2.

In addition to the structured information shown in Fig. 19-1, the sales manager might have miscellaneous comments relating to some of the contacts in the database. An additional category column can be used to record such comments. The original Persons as Items view does not have sufficient room for such an additional column, so a new view is created with a single, wide comments column, as shown in Fig. 19-3. Comments are entered into this column for various persons. The comments are limited to a single line of text as wide as the column. However, multiple comments can be entered for any of the contacts.

Creating this view for the comments illustrates several of the limitations of using persons as items. The tabular display of the information in columns limits

```
┌─────────────────────────────────────────────────────────────────────────────┐
│  File: C:\AGFILES\CONTACTS                              03/11/89   11:25       │
│  View: Persons as Items, Basic Acctng                                 ↕       │
│ ═══════════════════════════════════════════════════════════════════════════  │
│  Contacts             Company        Phone          Applications  Systems     │
│     ♪ Anderson, Susan  ·Acme          ·(818)275-3821 ·Basic Acctng ·IBM PC     │
│                                                       Mgmt Anal                │
│     ♪ Donaldson, Jim   ·Superior      ·(212)945-2133 ·Basic Acctng ·IBM PC     │
│     ♪ Hatfield, James  ·New Designs   ·(201)382-2733 ·Basic Acctng ·IBM PC     │
│     ♪ Watson, Bill     ·Wallston      ·(303)783-8534 ·Basic Acctng ·IBM PC     │
│     ♪ Wilson, Paula    ·Bridgeport    ·(213)892-4726 ·Basic Acctng ·IBM PC     │
│                                                                               │
│                                                                               │
│                                                                               │
│ ══F1══╤══F2══╤══F3══╤══F4══╤══F5══╤══F6══╤══F7══╤══F8══╤══F9══╤══F10══         │
│   Help │ Edit │ Copy │ Done │ Note │ Move │ Mark │Vw Mgr│Cat Mgr│ Menu        │
└─────────────────────────────────────────────────────────────────────────────┘
```

*Fig. 19-2. A view of the database using persons as items with a category filter to include only those items assigned to the Basic Acctng category.*

```
┌─────────────────────────────────────────────────────────────────────────────┐
│  File: C:\AGFILES\CONTACTS                              03/11/89   11:26       │
│  View: Persons as Items, Comment Column                                       │
│ ═══════════════════════════════════════════════════════════════════════════  │
│  Contacts              Comments                                               │
│     ♪ Anderson, Susan   ·They are planning on implementing a LAN              │
│                          Company is developing new offices                    │
│     ♪ Baker, Martha                                                           │
│     ♪ Donaldson, Jim    ·Needs a lot of support                              │
│                          Company is large, could use multiple applications    │
│                          Wants us to send all promotional material            │
│     ♪ Forbush, George   ·Expressed interest in accounting application         │
│                          Operation is large, could use Advanced Accounting    │
│     ♪ Hatfield, James                                                         │
│     ♪ Martin, Gina      ·They have agreed to be test site for new versions    │
│     ♪ Peters, Wanda                                                           │
│     ♪ Smith, John       ·Company is developing new offices                    │
│     ♪ Watson, Bill      ·Has expressed interest in Advanced Acctng package    │
│                          They may be adding Macintosh LAN                     │
│     ♪ Wilson, Paula                                                           │
│                                                                               │
│ ══F1══╤══F2══╤══F3══╤══F4══╤══F5══╤══F6══╤══F7══╤══F8══╤══F9══╤══F10══         │
│   Help │ Edit │ Copy │ Done │ Note │ Move │ Mark │Vw Mgr│Cat Mgr│ Menu        │
└─────────────────────────────────────────────────────────────────────────────┘
```

*Fig. 19-3. The use of a Comments category as a column in the database with individual persons as items.*

the amount of information that can be displayed for each person in any view. Thus, the comments must be placed into a second view, and a user of the database would have to switch back and forth between views containing different pieces of information about the contacts. Furthermore, comments are limited to a single line of text; they cannot be as long as items. Finally, Agenda does not allow the searching of category names (which the comments are) for the occurrences of text. It is not possible to search through the comments to locate references to specific topics.

Notes can be used to overcome some of the limitations of the persons-as-items approach. Notes may be employed to associate additional information with the persons as items in the database. Notes, of course, can include large amounts of text. They can be immediately displayed whenever the associated item is highlighted. Agenda also allows searching through notes for the occurrences of text. This makes it possible to identify those items with notes referring to specific topics.

## PRINTING NAMES AND ADDRESSES

A user of a database with personal contacts might well need to keep track of the addresses of the persons entered into the database. The names and addresses could then be printed out on mailing labels for use in mailings to some or all of the contacts in the database.

Agenda is not the software to use for managing large mailing list applications, however. Conventional database management software, or programs specifically designed for handling mailing lists, can manage such applications far more easily and flexibly than Agenda. But when the ability to produce mailing labels would be a useful adjunct to another Agenda application, it is possible to get Agenda to perform this task.

The mailing label capability can be added to the database for keeping track of sales contacts, described in the preceding section. The complete name and address has been added as a note for each person in the database. Figure 19-4 shows the name and address in the note for the first person.

To print out uniformly spaced mailing labels, each of the notes must have the same number of lines. Four lines are probably sufficient for most business addresses, and that is the number of lines included in the note shown in Fig. 19-4. If you have any three-line addresses, you must add an extra, blank line after the three lines of the address. Press ENTER at the end of the third and final line of the address and then press ENTER a second time to add the blank line.

Normally, you would not be able to see such blank lines in a note to check for their presence. However, the Utility Preferences Other command includes the *Hide carriage returns:* setting, which may be changed to No. This causes the hard carriage returns placed into a note to be displayed as solid triangles by

```
┌─────────────────────────────────────────────────────────────────────────┐
│  Note for:    Anderson, Susan                                       ↕     │
│  ═══════════════════════════════════════════════════════════Line 1═Ins═  │
│  Susan Anderson◄                                                          │
│  Acme Corporation◄                                                        │
│  15 Needleman Blvd.◄                                                      │
│  LaCrescenta, CA  90276◄                                                  │
│                                                                           │
│                                                                           │
│                                                                           │
│                                                                           │
│                                                                           │
│                                                                           │
│                                                                           │
│                                                                           │
│                                                                           │
│  ═F1══╤══F2═══╤══F3══╤══F4══╤══F5══╤══F6═══╤══F7══╤══F8═══╤══F9═══╤══F10═  │
│   Help │ Paste │ Copy │ Cut │Return│MakeCat│ Mark │MakeItm│Accept │ Menu   │
└─────────────────────────────────────────────────────────────────────────┘
```

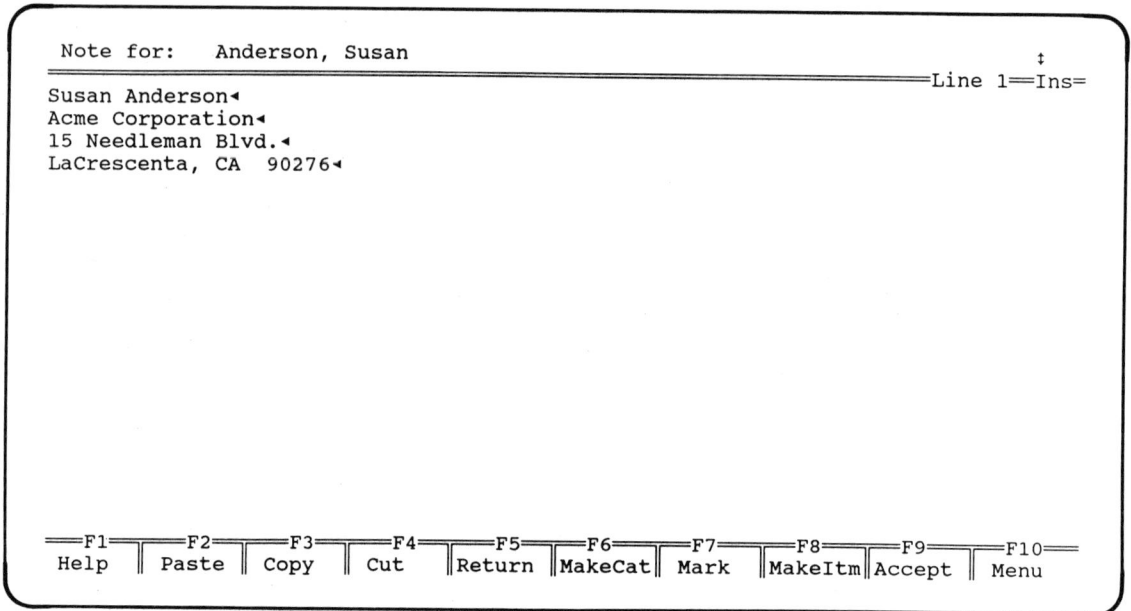

Fig. 19-4. *The note with the name and address for a mailing label for Susan Anderson.*

pressing the ENTER key. By using this option, it is possible to easily check that every note includes exactly four lines.

Mailing labels may be printed out for all of the contacts displayed in any view. For example, the sales manager might want to print out mailing labels for the persons whose companies use the Basic Accounting software, shown in the filtered view in Fig. 19-2.

To print out mailing labels, display the view with the persons for whom mailing labels are to be printed and enter the Print command. The *Include:* setting must be changed so that only the text of notes are to be printed. Headers and footers are not desired when printing out mailing labels, so those settings should be changed so that no headers and footers are printed.

If one-inch–high mailing labels are to be printed, a total of six lines must be used for each mailing label. The notes with the names and addresses all contain four lines of text. Thus, two extra blank lines have to be printed for each note to obtain the correct vertical spacing. The new-line backslash command \ nl \ inserts a carriage return and starts a new line, so two of these commands should be used, as follows:

\ nl \ \ nl \

This instructs Agenda to insert two blank lines after printing each note.

Finally, if more than one ''page'' of mailing labels is to be printed, the Top Margin and Page Length settings will need to be changed so that an even multiple of six lines are printed before skipping to the top of the next page. Agenda prints at least one line for the header and one for the footer at the top and bottom of each page, even if they are blank. Thus, at least one mailing label will have to be skipped in going from one page to the next. Setting Top Margin to zero and Page Length to 61 allows ten mailing labels to be printed on a page before skipping six lines so that the next mailing label will begin printing at the top of the next page.

The printout of the mailing labels with the names and address of the contacts at the companies using the Basic Accounting software is shown in Fig. 19-5. The names and addresses are uniformly spaced and could be printed on mailing-label stock for use on letters.

An alternative approach for creating mailing labels is to create the notes with the names and addresses in the format required by the mail-merge feature of your word processor. Some word processors require that commas be used to separate elements in a record to be used for mail-merging; others require the use of control characters. If the notes can be created in the appropriate format, Agenda can be used to print the notes to a file on the disk. This file can then be used with your word processor's mail-merge function to incorporate the names and addresses into form letters or to print out mailing labels, formatted by the word processor.

Fig. 19-5. *The mailing labels printed from the view with the items assigned to the Basic Acctng category.*

```
Susan Anderson
Acme Corporation
15 Needleman Blvd.
LaCrescenta, CA  90276


Jim Donaldson
Superior Services
P.O. Box 4609
Chicago, IL  60634


James Hatfield
New Designs, Inc.
P.O. Box 98347
New York, NY  10098


Bill Watson
Walston Group
9976 Corporation Drive
Baltimore, MD  23947


Paula Wilson
Bridgeport, Inc.
19034 Century Blvd.
Los Angeles, CA  90062
```

## ENTERING PERSONS AS CATEGORIES

An alternative approach for developing the database to manage personal contacts is the entry of contact names as categories in the database. These person categories can be used as section heads, with the information pertaining to each person being entered as items in the appropriate section.

A portion of a database with person categories is shown in Fig. 19-6. This database contains the same information as that included in the previous database, in which the persons were entered as items. In the database illustrated in Fig. 19-6, items are entered for the company name, telephone number, applications software being used, and types of systems on which the software is used. Additional comments regarding any of the contacts are entered as additional items in the section.

This organization for a personal contacts database makes it easy to see all of the information for a particular person at one time. There is no need to switch from one view to another if all of the information cannot be displayed in the columns of a single view. On the other hand, you forego the convenience afforded by a tabular view, which lets you scan down a column to compare individuals.

In the database in which persons are entered as items, it is possible to select persons who meet certain criteria and are assigned to specific categories by using category filters. The database with persons entered as categories does not allow this type of filtering to be used. However, it is still possible to select out persons meeting specific criteria by using the Utility Show Match command to display

```
File: C:\AGFILES\CONTACTS                        03/11/89   11:30
View: Persons as Categories

Anderson, Susan
    · Acme Corporation
    · Phone:  (818)275-3821
    · Uses the Basic Accounting and the Management Analysis applications
    · Uses IBM PCs and compatibles
    · They are planning on implementing a LAN
    · Company is developing new offices

Baker, Martha
    · Walker Products
    · Phone:  (317)872-1466
    · Uses the Advanced Accounting and the Management Analysis applications
    · Uses IBM PCs and Macintoshes on a LAN

Donaldson, Jim
    · Superior Services
    · (212)945-2133
    · Uses the Basic Accounting application
    · Uses IBM PCs
    · Needs a lot of support
==F1===F2===F3===F4===F5===F6===F7===F8===F9===F10==
 Help   Edit  Copy  Done  Note  Move  Mark  Vw Mgr Cat Mgr Menu
```

Fig. 19-6. *A database for managing personal contacts with persons entered as categories.*

those items containing specified text. For example, to determine the contacts at companies using the Basic Accounting application, you could use the Utility Show Match command to display those items including the text "Basic Accounting." The Show View would display just the items selected. Then you could add a Name column to display the names of the contacts to whom those items are assigned. (Categories that are the names of the contacts would have to be made child categories of a Name category.)

## DEVELOPING A HYBRID APPROACH

Databases with persons entered as items and databases with persons entered as categories both have their advantages. This suggests that some sort of hybrid approach might be taken that could capture the best features of both. One possible hybrid approach is described in this section.

The first view of a hybrid database for managing the contacts for a sales manager is shown in Fig. 19-7. The names of the contact persons have been entered as categories, and are used as the section headings in this view. Items reflecting the miscellaneous comments are entered in some of the sections, for some of the contacts. In addition, each of the sections has a specialized item with the text "Info>" used for organizing the more structured information.

The Info> items have all been assigned to an Info> category. (This can, of course, be done automatically, as there is a perfect text match.) An Info>

```
File: C:\AGFILES\CONTACTS                           03/11/89   11:30
View: Hybrid, Person Categories
==============================================================================
Anderson, Susan
  ♪ ↔Info>
    · They are planning on implementing a LAN
    · Company is developing new offices

Baker, Martha
  ♪ Info>

Donaldson, Jim
  ♪ ↔Info>
    · Needs a lot of support
    · Company is large, could use multiple applications
    · Wants us to send all promotional material

Forbush, George
  ♪ ↔Info>
    · Expressed interest in accounting application
    · Operation is large, could use Advanced Accounting

Hatfield, James
==F1====╤==F2===╤==F3===╤==F4===╤==F5===╤==F6===╤==F7===╤==F8===╤==F9===╤=F10===
 Help   ║ Edit  ║ Copy  ║ Done  ║ Note  ║ Move  ║ Mark  ║Vw Mgr ║Cat Mgr║ Menu
```

Fig. 19-7. *A hybrid database for managing personal contacts with persons entered as categories but with a special Info> item for assigning category information.*

view can be created in which the Info> category is used as the section head, and all of the Info> items are displayed under the section head in that section. A column can be added to that view to show the Name category, the name of the contact person to whom the individual Info> items are assigned. (The individual name categories will have to be made child categories of the Name category.)

Columns can also be added to the Info> view for the entry and display of structured information for each of the contacts. Figure 19-8 shows the Info> view of the hybrid database with columns for the company, telephone number, applications, and systems. This tabular view looks very much like the view in Fig. 19-1, in which the persons were entered as items. In this case, however, the actual items are the Info> items, each of which is assigned to a category that is the name of the particular contact person.

The Info> items in the Info> view can be filtered based upon category assignments to find contacts meeting certain criteria, just as the items were filtered when persons were entered as items. Notes with names and addresses can be attached to the Info> items to print out mailing labels using the same procedures discussed in the previous section.

The Utility Show Match command can be used to select out items from the miscellaneous comments entered into the person sections and shown in Fig. 19-7. For example, to generate a listing of all of the contacts using or planning to use an LAN (local area network), the items could be displayed in a Show View that

```
  File: C:\AGFILES\CONTACTS                          03/11/89    11:31
  View: Hybrid, Info> View
 ══════════════════════════════════════════════════════════════════════
  Info>            Name            Company      Phone         Application Systems
    ♪ ↔Info>       ·Anderson, Susan ·Acme        ·(818)275-3776 ·Basic Acct ·IBM PC
                                                                 Mgmt Anal
    ♪  Info>       ·Baker, Martha   ·Walker      ·(317)872-1466 ·Adv Acctng ·IBM PC
                                                                 Mgmt Anal  Macinto
                                                                            LAN
    ♪ ↔Info>       ·Donaldson, Jim  ·Superior    ·(212)945-2133 ·Basic Acct ·IBM PC
    ♪ ↔Info>       ·Forbush, George ·Four-Way    ·(608)234-6000 ·Mgmt Anal  ·Macinto
    ♪  Info>       ·Hatfield, James ·New Designs ·(201)382-2733 ·Basic Acct ·IBM PC
    ♪ ↔Info>       ·Martin, Gina    ·Diversified ·(408)654-7351 ·Adv Acctng ·IBM PC
                                                                 Mgmt Anal
    ♪  Info>       ·Peters, Wanda   ·Geosys      ·(719)239-5687 ·Adv Acctng ·Macinto
                                                                            LAN
    ♪ ↔Info>       ·Smith, John     ·Acme        ·(818)275-3776 ·Adv Acctng ·IBM PC
                                                                            LAN
    ♪ ↔Info>       ·Watson, Bill    ·Wallston    ·(303)783-8534 ·Basic Acct ·IBM PC
    ♪  Info>       ·Wilson, Paula   ·Bridgeport  ·(213)892-4726 ·Basic Acct ·IBM PC


 ══F1═══════F2═══════F3═══════F4═══════F5═══════F6═══════F7═══════F8═══════F9═══════F10══
   Help  ║  Edit  ║  Copy  ║  Done  ║  Note  ║  Move  ║  Mark  ║ Vw Mgr ║Cat Mgr║  Menu
```

Fig. 19-8. *The Info> view of the hybrid database displaying the Info> items and the category information in columns.*

included the text "LAN." A Name column could be added to such a view to
show the names of the contacts associated with those selected items. This capability
was also provided in the database in which persons were entered as categories.

One remaining issue is how to relate the information associated with the Info>
items with the other items assigned to the contact person categories. To accomplish
this, each of the Info> items is made dependent upon all of the other items in
their respective sections. This is indicated by the double-arrow symbol appearing
to the left of each of the Info> items.

Now suppose that the sales manager wants to select the contacts that are
planning LAN installations, and wants complete information on those contacts.
The first step is to use the Utility Show Match command to select out those items
that included the text "LAN." These items could be displayed in a Show View.

Now, to include the rest of the information about the contacts planning LAN
installations in that new view, the Info> items associated with those persons need
to be added to that view. This is where the item dependencies play a role. Since
each Info> item depends upon the other items assigned to the same person categories, they can also be selected. You need to highlight one of the items referring to an LAN in the new view and use the Utility Show Dependents One-Level
command to obtain the Info> item associated with that item. When the option
is presented, choose the option to add the new item to the existing Show View
rather than to create a new Show View. The appropriate Info> item is added.
This process can be repeated to add the Info> for all of the other items.

```
File: C:\AGFILES\CONTACTS                        03/11/89   11:32
View: Hybrid, LAN Selection
================================================================
*Show*              Name          Company   Phone           Applications
 ♪ ↔Info>          ·Anderson, Susan ·Acme    ·(818)275-3776 ·Basic Acctng
                                                              Mgmt Anal
  · They are       ·Anderson, Susan
    planning on
    implementing a
    LAN
 ♪ ↔Info>          ·Watson, Bill  ·Wallston ·(303)783-8534 ·Basic Acctng
  · They may be     ·Watson, Bill
    adding Macintosh
    LAN



=F1===F2===F3===F4===F5===F6===F7===F8===F9===F10==
Help   Edit  Copy  Done  Note  Move  Mark  Vw Mgr Cat Mgr Menu
```

Fig. 19-9. *A view of the hybrid database created by using the Utility Show commands to select items
with the text "LAN" and the Info> items dependent upon those items.*

Columns can be added to the view to display the name and any of the desired information available for the Info> items, and the view can be sorted into an appropriate order. The result is the view shown in Fig. 19-9. The text of the items—the Info> items and those referring to the LAN—are shown in the left column of the view. The Name column shows the names of the contacts, for each item, because each item is assigned to a Name category. The Company, Phone, and Applications category columns show information that results from the assignment of the Info> items to those categories in the Info> view.

The hybrid database begins with persons entered as categories. The specialized Info> item provides capabilities equivalent to the database in which persons were entered as items. By making each of the Info> items dependent upon the other items assigned to the same person category, the advantages of both approaches can be combined.

Most applications of Agenda for the management of personal contacts probably can be accomplished by using one or the other of the two simpler approaches—entering persons as items or entering persons as categories. However, it does pay to give some consideration to what information you plan to include within the database, and how you intend to use that information, before selecting a structure for the database. For more complex applications, the additional capabilities provided by using a hybrid approach such as the one described in the final section of this chapter might be worth the extra effort.

# 20

## MANAGING PEOPLE AND ORGANIZATIONS

MANAGERS have the responsibility for determining which people in an organization are to perform which functions. From a broader perspective, managers must also determine the organizational structures that will be most effective in enabling their organizations to perform required functions. Agenda can be a useful tool for managing people and organizations.

The applications presented in this chapter demonstrate how to use Agenda to make decisions about assigning tasks and personnel. The first section of this chapter illustrates the use of Agenda to assign specific tasks to the persons responsible for them. The second part considers the reverse—the use of Agenda to assign persons to the functional areas for which they will be responsible. The third section considers the more complex problem of developing an organizational structure, with both functions and people assigned to units of an organization.

### ASSIGNING TASKS TO PEOPLE

One problem faced by a manager is the assignment of numbers of different tasks to the people who must perform those tasks. Such assignments frequently require balancing conflicting concerns. On the one hand, managers want to assign tasks to the people best qualified to perform them. On the other hand, the amount of work assigned to the various people must be balanced, to avoid the problem of some people having too much work and some having too little. Agenda can be used to facilitate the process of making such assignments, allowing the easy reassignment of tasks until an appropriate outcome is achieved.

The example used to illustrate this application of Agenda involves developing a simple new product and bringing it to market quickly. A fair number of tasks have to be performed in order to do this. Three staff members have the responsibility for carrying out these tasks. The problem is to assign the tasks to the three staff members.

The first consideration in developing an Agenda database for this application is determining the best structure for the database—that is, how is information to be divided between items and categories? In the example, a larger number of tasks are to be assigned to a smaller number of people. Thus, it makes the most sense for the tasks to be the items in the database and for the people to be categories, to which those task items are assigned.

The three people to whom the tasks will be assigned should be entered as section heads in a view of the Agenda database. An additional section can then be added to this view for the initial entry of the tasks to be assigned to those people. The various tasks required for the project are then entered as items in this section of the view. This view for assigning tasks to people appears as shown in Fig. 20-1, prior to the assigning of the tasks.

Making the assignments involves moving the task items from the task section to one (or more) of the person sections. Function key F6 (MOVE) can be used to move the highlighted items or a group of marked items from one section in the view to any other section.

```
File: C:\AGFILES\ORGMGMT1                          03/11/89    12:01
View: Assigning Tasks to People
═══════════════════════════════════════════════════════════════════

Kathy Baker

Mark Matthews

Sally Randall

Tasks to Be Assigned
    · Conduct initial marketing survey (3 weeks)
    · Develop initial product design (2 weeks)
    · Develop product prototypes (2 weeks)
    · Test market prototypes (4 weeks)
    · Develop marketing plan (2 weeks)
    · Develop manufacturing plan (2 weeks)
    · Develop distribution procedures (3 weeks)
    · Contact potential distributors and retailers with prototypes (2 weeks)
    · Start up manufacturing operations (3 weeks)
    · First phase of manufacturing
    · First phase of marketing
    · First phase of distribution

══F1═══╤══F2══╤══F3══╤══F4══╤══F5══╤══F6══╤══F7══╤══F8══╤══F9══╤══F10══
 Help  ║ Edit ║ Copy ║ Done ║ Note ║ Move ║ Mark ║Vw Mgr║Cat Mgr║ Menu
```

Fig. 20-1. *The view showing the tasks to be assigned and the people to whom those tasks are to be assigned.*

The results of assigning task items to people sections can be seen in Fig. 20-2. The assignment process is likely to involve repeated movements to balance responsibilities among the staff members, a process that cannot be well-illustrated by showing the view of the database at any given point. For example, a large number of the task items might be assigned to one of the people. Seeing that this person has been given too much responsibility, some of those task items might then have to be reassigned to other people by moving them into other sections. It might be appropriate for two or more people to share the responsibility for carrying out a particular task. In this case, the task item will have to be copied using F3 (COPY) from one section to another so that the task is assigned to several people.

Agenda makes this assignment process easier by allowing task assignments to be balanced and juggled simply by moving or copying the task items from one person section to another. At each point in the process, the user sees the entire pattern of task assignments and can judge whether additional changes are required.

The simple assignment of twelve tasks to three persons shown in this example only begins to illustrate the utility of Agenda for such problems. The assignment illustrated in this example could probably be carried out just as easily using pencil and paper, because the amount of juggling of assignments required is just not that great for three people. However, with larger numbers of tasks and people, balancing assignments is likely to become far more complex, with many more changes required before an acceptable task assignment is determined. Agenda's

```
File: C:\AGFILES\ORGMGMT1                        03/11/89   12:02
View: Assigning Tasks to People

Kathy Baker
    · Develop initial product design (2 weeks)
    · Develop product prototypes (2 weeks)
    · Develop manufacturing plan (2 weeks)
    · Start up manufacturing operations (3 weeks)
    · First phase of manufacturing

Mark Matthews
    · Conduct initial marketing survey (3 weeks)
    · Test market prototypes (4 weeks)
    · Develop marketing plan (2 weeks)
    · First phase of marketing

Sally Randall
    · Test market prototypes (4 weeks)
    · Develop distribution procedures (3 weeks)
    · Contact potential distributors and retailers with prototypes (2 weeks)
    · First phase of distribution

Tasks to Be Assigned
=F1=====F2=====F3=====F4=====F5=====F6=====F7=====F8=====F9=====F10==
Help  || Edit || Copy || Done || Note || Move || Mark ||Vw Mgr ||Cat Mgr|| Menu
```

Fig. 20-2. *The view showing the assignment of the tasks to the different people.*

flexibility, allowing the easy, continual modification of assignments, becomes far more important for these more complex problems.

## ASSIGNING PEOPLE TO TASKS

A similar problem emerges for a manager faced with the need to assign numbers of people to perform various tasks. Once again, the people need to be matched up with the tasks to be performed. However, if larger numbers of people are to be assigned to a lesser number of tasks, the approach to be taken in developing an Agenda database must differ from that demonstrated in the previous example.

Suppose a new product is to be developed, manufactured, and marketed. Three major functions need to be accomplished: product development, manufacturing, and sales and marketing. A manager has twelve people to carry out these tasks, and confronts the problem of assigning the people to the tasks.

This time, since the larger number of people are to be assigned to the smaller number of tasks, it is appropriate that the people be entered as the items in the Agenda database and the tasks be the categories. To start out, a view is created with the three tasks as section heads and a personnel section head for the initial listing of the available people.

The twelve employees are entered as items in the personnel section. In addition to an employee's name, brief information on each employee's background or experience is included in each item to provide guidance to the manager in making appropriate assignments. The view of the database at this point is illustrated in Fig. 20-3. Such a view could also include additional features, such as columns for beginning and completion dates.

The manager using the Agenda database to make personnel assignments then begins moving people items from the personnel section into one of the three task sections. The backgrounds or experience of some people makes the selection of the task to which they are to be assigned relatively obvious. The backgrounds of other people, however, make assignment to several different tasks reasonable. The manager can make a tentative assignment, moving the person to one of the appropriate task sections. Then, if too many people are assigned to one task and too few to another, people can be reassigned until the overall pattern of the assignments is appropriate. Figure 20-4 shows the assignments of the people to the three tasks, but of course it cannot illustrate the use of Agenda to experiment with different assignments, moving people around, until a suitable result is obtained.

## DEVELOPING AN ORGANIZATIONAL STRUCTURE

The preceding examples discussed the assignment of tasks to people and people to tasks. A more complex job for a manager would be the determination of an appropriate structure for an organization. Such a structure could provide for the

```
┌─────────────────────────────────────────────────────────────────────────┐
│  File: C:\AGFILES\ORGMGMT1                        03/11/89   12:04        │
│  View: Assigning People to Tasks                                          │
│ ═════════════════════════════════════════════════════════════════════════│
│  Sales and Marketing                                                      │
│                                                                           │
│  Product Development                                                      │
│                                                                           │
│  Manufacturing                                                            │
│                                                                           │
│  Personnel                                                                │
│     • Joe Smith (exper. in development and marketing on Star product)     │
│     • Ann Walters (exper. in manufacturing with Star product)             │
│     • Jill Martin (exper. in all phases of Cosmos product)                │
│     • George Thomas (exper. in marketing on Cosmos, mfg. on Mars product) │
│     • Jim Beech (new, MBA in marketing)                                   │
│     • Sandra Johnson (new, engineering degree)                            │
│     • John Koch (oversaw manufacturing operation of Mercury product)      │
│     • Bill Glass (product development specialist on several products)     │
│     • Michelle Clayton (has primarily worked in manufacturing)            │
│     • Karen Schultz (exper. in development and mfg. of Mercury product)   │
│     • Tom Hastings (exper. in all phases of Mercury product)              │
│     • Elizabeth Wilson (directed product development for Cosmos product)  │
│ ══F1══╤══F2══╤══F3══╤══F4══╤══F5══╤══F6══╤══F7══╤══F8══╤══F9══╤══F10══     │
│  Help ║ Edit ║ Copy ║ Done ║ Note ║ Move ║ Mark ║Vw Mgr║Cat Mgr║ Menu     │
└─────────────────────────────────────────────────────────────────────────┘
```

Fig. 20-3. *The view showing the personnel to be assigned and the functions to which those people are to be assigned.*

```
┌─────────────────────────────────────────────────────────────────────────┐
│  File: C:\AGFILES\ORGMGMT1                        03/11/89   12:05        │
│  View: Assigning People to Tasks                                          │
│ ═════════════════════════════════════════════════════════════════════════│
│  Sales and Marketing                                                      │
│     • George Thomas (exper. in marketing on Cosmos, mfg. on Mars product) │
│     • Jim Beech (new, MBA in marketing)                                   │
│     • Joe Smith (exper. in development and marketing on Star product)     │
│     • Tom Hastings (exper. in all phases of Mercury product)              │
│                                                                           │
│  Product Development                                                      │
│     • Bill Glass (product development specialist on several products)     │
│     • Elizabeth Wilson (directed product development for Cosmos product)  │
│     • Sandra Johnson (new, engineering degree)                            │
│     • Jill Martin (exper. in all phases of Cosmos product)                │
│                                                                           │
│  Manufacturing                                                            │
│     • John Koch (oversaw manufacturing operation of Mercury product)      │
│     • Michelle Clayton (has primarily worked in manufacturing)            │
│     • Ann Walters (exper. in manufacturing with Star product)             │
│     • Karen Schultz (exper. in development and mfg. of Mercury product)   │
│                                                                           │
│  Personnel                                                                │
│ ══F1══╤══F2══╤══F3══╤══F4══╤══F5══╤══F6══╤══F7══╤══F8══╤══F9══╤══F10══     │
│  Help ║ Edit ║ Copy ║ Done ║ Note ║ Move ║ Mark ║Vw Mgr║Cat Mgr║ Menu     │
└─────────────────────────────────────────────────────────────────────────┘
```

Fig. 20-4. *The view showing the assignment of personnel to functions.*

assignment of both people and tasks to the various units within the organization. In developing an organization structure, a manager must decide how the organization is to be divided into units, and which functions and employees are to be assigned to each of those units. Agenda can be an effective tool for addressing this problem as well.

The Agenda database must include the units within the organization's structure, the various functions that must be performed within the organization, and the personnel needed to carry out those functions. The functions and the personnel are to be assigned to the various units. Therefore, the database should have both the organization functions and the personnel entered as items, while the units of the organization will be categories within the database to which those items eventually will be assigned.

The categories reflecting the units into which the organization is structured can be entered in a hierarchy, reflecting the hierarchical relationships among the units in the organization. The Category Manager allows you to work directly with the category hierarchy, and this is where the organizational structure can be entered, displayed, and manipulated. This application of Agenda involves working directly with the category hierarchy, since the manager deals with the organizational structure.

Indeed, the development of the application might well begin with the entry of the current or proposed organizational structure in the category hierarchy. Function key F9 (CAT MGR) takes you into the Category Manager and displays the category hierarchy. Once there, you can enter new categories directly. For

```
File: C:\AGFILES\ORGMGMT2
Category Manager

MAIN
  Organization
    Chief Executive Officer
      Research and Development
      Operations
        Manufacturing
        Marketing
        Distribution
      Administration
        Financial Affairs
        Legal Affairs
        Information Systems
        Personnel
  Functions
  Staff




   =F1=====F2======F3======F4======F5======F6======F7======F8======F9======F10===
   Help  ||  Edit  ||Cpy C/A||Clr C/A|| Note  || Move  ||Prm (◄)||Dem (►)||To View|| Menu
```

Fig. 20-5. *The category hierarchy showing one possible organizational structure for the organization.*

example, pressing INS allows you to enter a new category directly below the highlighted one. Categories may be promoted and demoted using F7 (PROMOTE) and F8 (DEMOTE), and they may be moved to other positions in the category hierarchy using F6 (MOVE).

The example presented in this section addresses the development of an organizational structure for a high-technology manufacturing company that is very dependent upon research and development. The first step is the entry of a possible organizational structure in the category hierarchy. Figure 20-5 shows the hierarchy of categories that have been entered. The organizational structure is displayed under the Organization category. At the top of the structure—the only child category to the Organization category—is the Chief Executive Officer. The company has three major units that report to the Chief Executive Officer—Research and Development, Operations, and Administration. These are entered as child categories to the Chief Executive Officer category. Finally, the Operations and Administration units are subdivided into lower-level units. These units are child categories to the Operations and Administration categories.

This portion of the category hierarchy, shown in Fig. 20-5, constitutes an organizational chart for the company, showing all of the units and the hierarchical relationships among those units. It conveys exactly the same information as the traditional organizational chart using boxes connected by lines; it is just in a different format.

Having an organizational chart expressed in the Agenda category hierarchy provides flexibility that is not available with a traditional chart printed on paper. The organizational structure can be readily modified within the Category Manager. Units can be added, deleted, and moved to other positions within the structure. This makes it easy to examine alternative organizational forms, which may be especially useful in assigning functions and personnel to the various units within the organization.

The next step in the development of the organizational structure involves assigning organization functions and personnel to the various units within the organization. The procedures for making these assignments are very similar to those used in assigning tasks to people and people to tasks, described earlier in this chapter.

Consider the assignment of the various organizational functions to the units within the organization. You begin by creating a view in which the organizational units are section heads. An additional Functions section can be added for the entry of the various functions that need to be performed within the organization. The organization's functions are entered into the database as items. These items can be moved to different sections, to assign the functions to the various units within the organization.

If functions are being assigned to units at all levels of the organization, a decision must be made as to whether the functions are to be displayed in the sections for the higher-level units, or only in the sections to which they are directly assigned. For example, suppose a function were assigned to the Manufacturing unit and the item were placed into the Manufacturing section. The Manufacturing category is a child of the Operations category, the next higher-level unit in the organizational structure. Thus, in Agenda, the item also would be assigned by inheritance to the Operations category, and normally would be displayed in that section as well. In most cases, you probably would want to display in each section only those functions directly assigned to the unit, not items assigned by inheritance. The View Preferences command can be used to change *Hide inherited items:* to *Yes* if you only want to show those items assigned directly. This causes the inherited items not to be displayed within sections. The only items representing functions that will be displayed for a unit will be those directly assigned to the category.

Figure 20-6 displays a portion of the view showing the assignment of functions to the sections representing the various organizational units. This allows the manager to see which functions are to be carried out by which units, and to judge whether the particular organization of those functions is logical.

The manager using an Agenda database to develop the organization structure can, of course, move items around from section to section to change the functional responsibilities of the various units. In addition, however, the manager can consider alternative arrangements for the organizational structure itself. By entering the Category Manager, organizational units can be moved around, changed, added, and deleted within the category hierarchy. These changes can be accompanied by reassigning functions from one organizational unit to anoth-

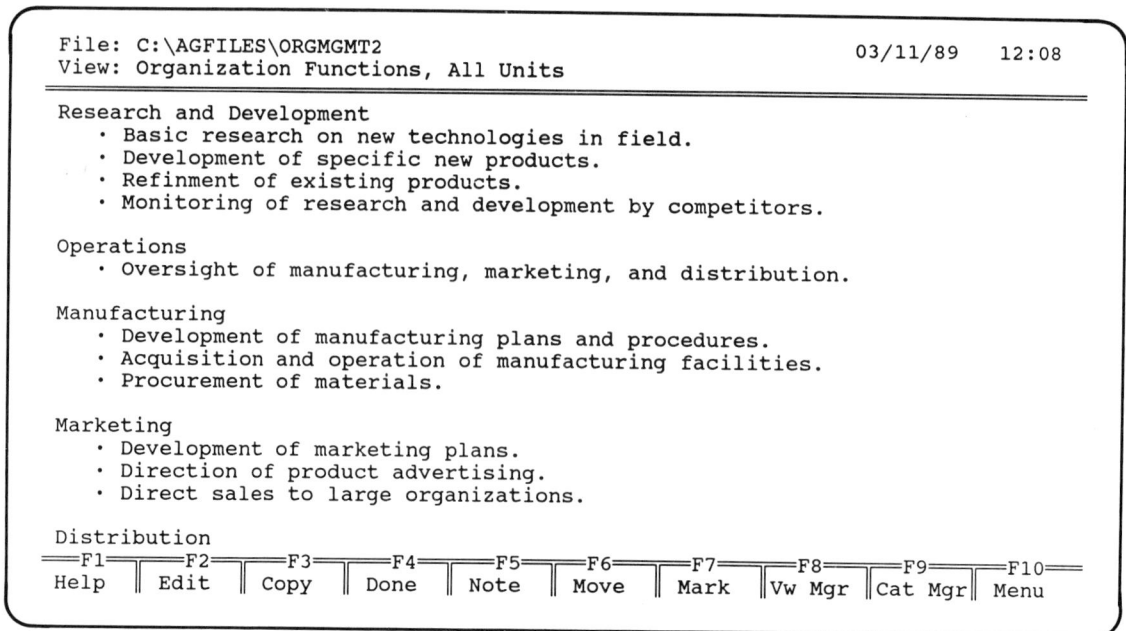

```
File: C:\AGFILES\ORGMGMT2                        03/11/89    12:08
View: Organization Functions, All Units
═══════════════════════════════════════════════════════════════════
Research and Development
    · Basic research on new technologies in field.
    · Development of specific new products.
    · Refinment of existing products.
    · Monitoring of research and development by competitors.

Operations
    · Oversight of manufacturing, marketing, and distribution.

Manufacturing
    · Development of manufacturing plans and procedures.
    · Acquisition and operation of manufacturing facilities.
    · Procurement of materials.

Marketing
    · Development of marketing plans.
    · Direction of product advertising.
    · Direct sales to large organizations.

Distribution
══F1══╤══F2══╤══F3══╤══F4══╤══F5══╤══F6══╤══F7══╤══F8══╤══F9══╤══F10══
 Help ║ Edit ║ Copy ║ Done ║ Note ║ Move ║ Mark ║Vw Mgr║Cat Mgr║ Menu
```

Fig. 20-6. *The view showing the functions directly assigned to each of the units in the organization.*

er. In this way, a manager can readily examine different structural alternatives in designing the organizational structure that makes the most sense.

In trying out alternative organizational arrangements, it might be necessary to modify the functions, perhaps breaking them down so that they can be appropriately assigned to a new set of organizational units. For example, certain sales functions might be currently assigned to the marketing unit. Suppose that a manager decides that it is more appropriate to organize the sales function on a regional basis, with East, South, Midwest, and West Sales units. Then a function such as direct sales to large organizations might have to be broken down into direct sales in the east, direct sales in the south, and so forth. Alternatively, the direct sales item might be assigned to each of the regional sales units, with the understanding that each is responsible for those sales in its own region.

Additional views can be created to examine different ways of assigning the functions to the organizational units. For example, a manager might wish to see all of the functions assigned to each of the three major divisions of the organization, including those functions assigned to their subdivisions. A view can be created in which Research and Development, Operations, and Administration are the three section heads. All of the items assigned to those categories can be displayed without hiding inherited items. In this way, all of the functions associated with each of the major divisions can be easily examined and compared. A portion of such a view is illustrated in Fig. 20-7.

```
File: C:\AGFILES\ORGMGMT2                           03/11/89   12:08
View: Organizational Functions, Major Units
================================================================
Research and Development
    · Basic research on new technologies in field.
    · Development of specific new products.
    · Refinment of existing products.
    · Monitoring of research and development by competitors.

Operations
    · Oversight of manufacturing, marketing, and distribution.
    · Development of manufacturing plans and procedures.
    · Acquisition and operation of manufacturing facilities.
    · Procurement of materials.
    · Development of marketing plans.
    · Direction of product advertising.
    · Direct sales to large organizations.
    · Manage shipping of products to distributors.
    · Handle direct orders from end users.
    · Direct shipping to end users.

Administration
    · Oversee functions of all administrative units.
==F1==╥==F2==╥==F3==╥==F4==╥==F5==╥==F6==╥==F7==╥==F8==╥==F9==╥==F10==
 Help ║ Edit ║ Copy ║ Done ║ Note ║ Move ║ Mark ║Vw Mgr║Cat Mgr║ Menu
```

Fig. 20-7. *The view showing the functions assigned directly and indirectly, by inheritance from subunits, to the three major units in the organization.*

A manager might also wish to address the assignment of personnel within the organization to these different units. The employees of the company would be entered as items, and assigning personnel to organizational units would be carried out in exactly the same fashion as assigning functions to those units. If the manager wanted to examine either personnel assignments or function assignments to the organization units, but not both in a particular view, an appropriate filter could be used to select the appropriate items to be displayed in the view.

The advantage of developing an organizational structure using an Agenda database arises from Agenda's flexibility. You are not limited to just entering the organizational hierarchy into the Category Manager and then assigning the function and personnel items to these categories. Rather, you can experiment with and revise any and all aspects of the organizational design. The organizational hierarchy can be readily changed. You can move units around, adding and deleting units as necessary for the new structure. Functions and personnel may be easily shifted from one organizational unit to another.

Agenda provides the manager with a tool for working with the organizational design, enabling him or her to try out various alternatives until the most satisfactory result is obtained.

# 21

## MANAGING COLLECTIONS OF THINGS

AGENDA can be used effectively to keep track of diverse products, services, or other things with varying characteristics. A user can store different kinds of information about the things in a database, readily select things that meet certain requirements, and easily group things for different purposes.

Such applications of Agenda would be useful for people who sell products that differ from each other in many ways. For example, a car dealer might use an Agenda database to keep track of the inventory of vehicles. The dealer could use the database to select vehicles meeting individual customer's specific requirements. A real estate salesperson could employ an Agenda database in a similar way to organize information on different properties.

For those selling goods or services as packages of individual things to meet customer's needs, Agenda can be used to develop these packages and to locate the most appropriate packages for a customer. For example, a computer dealer might sell packaged computer systems consisting of collections of components to meet specific requirements. A travel agent might sell packaged tours consisting of transportation, accommodations, and other elements.

Using Agenda to manage collections is not limited to business applications. Agenda is the ideal tool for keeping track of personal collections such as those of records or stamps. Agenda can also be used effectively to keep an inventory of possessions for insurance purposes.

Agenda will not always be the most appropriate tool for managing information about things, however. For large inventories of relatively simple items, conventional database management software would be far more appropriate. Agenda's strength lies in keeping track of diverse things with varying characteristics.

This chapter presents simple examples of using Agenda to manage collections of things. The first section shows how one might establish an inventory of vehicles for a car dealer, and the second section shows how vehicles meeting specified requirements can be selected from that inventory. The use of Agenda to store inventory information is demonstrated in the third section. The final section of this chapter illustrates the manner in which packages of things can be developed in an Agenda database.

## CREATING AN INVENTORY

When you wish to keep track of information on large numbers of things, each thing can be entered as an item in a view. Category columns can then be used to enter information about each of the items. This is the type of application for which Star or Yes/No column formats are especially useful, because they indicate whether an item has a particular attribute.

As an example, consider a used car and truck dealer who wants to keep track of all of the vehicles in the inventory. Each vehicle might have a unique identification number used by the dealer. Those identification numbers can be entered as the items in a Vehicle section in an Inventory view.

Category columns can be added to the Inventory view for the entry of information about each of the vehicles. Figure 21-1 shows the Inventory view with six columns of information about each of the vehicles. Four columns are displayed in the Actual Category format, with the child category assignments under the parent category column heading being displayed. In the Vehicle Type column, for example, category assignments of the vehicles to either Auto or Truck have been entered. Similar entries have been made in the Year column, the Manufacturer column, and the Color column.

The child categories in the Vehicle Type, Year, and Manufacturer columns are mutually exclusive. A vehicle can be assigned to only one of the child categories. For example, any vehicle is either an auto or a truck, but not both. Thus, it is appropriate to designate the child categories of these columns as exclusive, to prevent multiple category assignments. This can be accomplished using the Exclusive command in the Category Manager.

The Auto Trans (Automatic Transmission) and P/S (Power Steering) columns are displayed in the Star column format. This is used to indicate whether or not a vehicle has the specified feature. An asterisk in the Auto Trans column, for example, indicates that the item has been assigned to that category; the vehicle has an automatic transmission.

```
┌─────────────────────────────────────────────────────────────────────────────┐
│  File: C:\AGFILES\INVEN                              03/11/89   12:13          │
│  View: Inventory View                                                         │
╞═══════════════════════════════════════════════════════════════════════════════╡
```

| Vehicles | Veh Type | Year | Manufacturer | Color | Auto Trans | P/S |
|---|---|---|---|---|---|---|
| · 07614 | ·Auto | ·1988 | ·Uranus | ·Red | * | * |
| · 18331 | ·Auto | ·1987 | ·Neptune | ·White | * | * |
| · 29347 | ·Truck | ·1988 | ·Cosmos | ·Blue | * | * |
| · 30662 | ·Auto | ·1985 | ·Neptune | ·Beige | | |
| · 34788 | ·Truck | ·1984 | ·Cosmos | ·Red | | |
| · 38962 | ·Truck | ·1987 | ·Neptune | ·White | | |
| · 47354 | ·Auto | ·1984 | ·Jupiter | ·Yellow | * | |
| · 59112 | ·Auto | ·1986 | ·Uranus | ·Brown | | * |
| · 60347 | ·Auto | ·1988 | ·Cosmos | ·Grey | * | |
| · 63287 | ·Truck | ·1988 | ·Neptune | ·Red | * | * |
| · 65661 | ·Auto | ·1983 | ·Neptune | ·Blue | * | * |
| · 68789 | ·Auto | ·1987 | ·Uranus | ·Brown | | * |
| · 72458 | ·Auto | ·1986 | ·Uranus | ·White | * | * |
| · 81236 | ·Truck | ·1987 | ·Neptune | ·Blue | * | |
| · 83475 | ·Truck | ·1984 | ·Cosmos | ·Red | | |
| · 87881 | ·Truck | ·1988 | ·Cosmos | ·White | | * |
| · 90993 | ·Auto | ·1988 | ·Neptune | ·Beige | * | |
| · 91437 | ·Auto | ·1987 | ·Jupiter | ·Red | * | * |

```
═F1═══╤═F2═══╤═F3═══╤═F4═══╤═F5═══╤═F6═══╤═F7═══╤═F8═══╤═F9═══╤═F10══
Help  │ Edit │ Copy │ Done │ Note │ Move │ Mark ║Vw Mgr│Cat Mgr║ Menu
```

Fig. 21-1. *The Inventory view providing basic information on all of the vehicles in a dealer's inventory.*

The Inventory view is used to display the basic information on all of the vehicles in the dealer's inventory. The view may be sorted in any order desired. Figure 21-1 shows the view ordered by the identification numbers, which are the item entries. A user might instead wish to sort the items by the category assignment in a particular column. Thus, the vehicles might be sorted by Vehicle Type, placing all of the autos together and all of the trucks together.

## SELECTING THINGS FROM THE INVENTORY

One important aspect of using an inventory database is selecting those things that meet certain requirements. Category filters are used to filter a view so that only those items assigned to the proper categories are retained in the view. Filters can be extremely useful, allowing a user to search for things having the desired characteristics.

The vehicle database described in the previous section may be searched to find those vehicles meeting the needs of a particular customer. The first step in doing this is to create a new view, called the Vehicle Selection view, for doing the necessary filtering. Initially, this view was created by copying the Inventory view, and was identical to it. A second view is used for the selection process so that the complete, unfiltered Inventory view is always available for reference.

Selecting out specified vehicles involves setting a category filter to include only those items with the proper characteristics in the view. The View Define procedure is entered either by using the commands from the view or by pressing F8 (VIEW DEF) in the View Manager. In either case, the View Define box appears on the screen, displaying the categories in the category hierarchy.

Suppose a customer wanted a truck built in 1987 or 1988 that was neither grey nor red (perhaps those were a competitor's colors). To find the trucks in the database that matched the criteria, you first highlight the Truck category and press TAB to insert an arrow pointing up, indicating that an item must be assigned to the Truck category for it to be included in the view. The TAB key is pressed twice to enter down arrows for both the Red and Grey categories, to specify that items assigned to these categories (vehicles with these colors) should not be included. The View Define box as it appears after the entry of these category filters is shown in Fig. 21-2. In a similar manner, up arrows have to be entered for the 1987 and 1988 categories to include only items assigned to those categories. Note that since the Year categories are mutually exclusive, items are selected if they are assigned to either of the designated categories.

After setting the category filter, the Vehicle Selection view displays only those vehicles meeting the requirements specified by the filter. Figure 21-3 shows the listing of trucks built in 1987 or 1988 that are neither red nor grey.

This selection procedure can be employed quickly whenever it is necessary to select vehicles meeting certain criteria. You can switch to the Vehicle Selection view and begin the View Define procedure. Function key F4 (CLRFLTR) deletes all of the category filter arrows set with the previous selection. Then you can

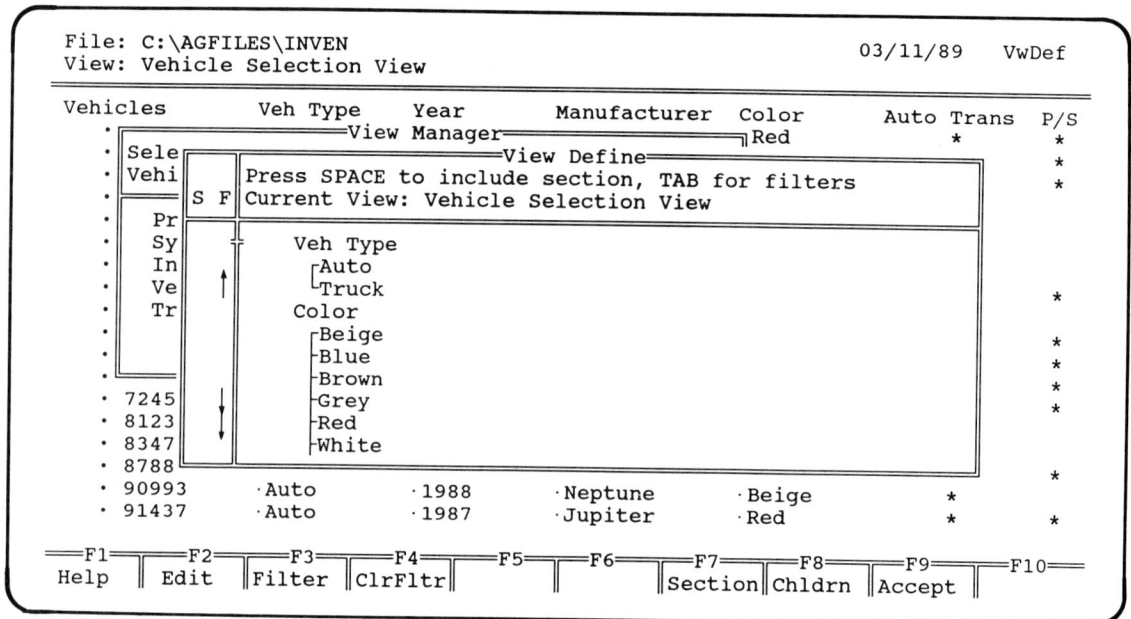

```
 File: C:\AGFILES\INVEN                           03/11/89    VwDef
 View: Vehicle Selection View

 Vehicles          Veh Type    Year     Manufacturer  Color    Auto Trans  P/S
   •                       ═══View Manager═══════════════════╗Red      *        *
   •  ┌Sele┌═══════════════════View Define══════════════╗            *
   •  │Vehi│ Press SPACE to include section, TAB for filters        *
   •  │    │S F│Current View: Vehicle Selection View  │
   •  │ Pr │
   •  │ Sy │  ┬      Veh Type
   •  │ In │  │      ┌Auto
   •  │ Ve │  ↑      └Truck                                         *
   •  │ Tr │         Color
   •  │    │         ┌Beige                                        *
   •  │    │         ├Blue                                         *
   •  │    │         ├Brown                                        *
   •  7245│  │       ├Grey                                         *
   •  8123│  ↓       ├Red
   •  8347│  ▼       ├White
   •  8788└══════════├White                                        *
   •  90993    ·Auto     ·1988    ·Neptune      ·Beige      *
   •  91437    ·Auto     ·1987    ·Jupiter      ·Red        *        *

 ═F1═══╤═F2═══╤═F3═══╤═F4═══╤═F5══╤═F6══╤═F7═══╤═F8═══╤═F9═══╤═F10══
 Help  ║ Edit ║Filter║ClrFltr║     ║     ║Section║Chldrn║Accept║
```

Fig. 21-2. *Setting a category filter to find trucks that are not grey or red and were built in the model years 1987 and 1988.*

```
 File: C:\AGFILES\INVEN                              03/11/89   12:17
 View: Vehicle Selection View                                    ↕
 ════════════════════════════════════════════════════════════════════
 Vehicles       Veh Type    Year     Manufacturer  Color    Auto Trans  P/S
   · 29347      ·Truck      ·1988     ·Cosmos       ·Blue        *        *
   · 38962      ·Truck      ·1987     ·Neptune      ·White
   · 81236      ·Truck      ·1987     ·Neptune      ·Blue        *
   · 87881      ·Truck      ·1988     ·Cosmos       ·White                *




 ══F1════╤══F2════╤══F3════╤══F4════╤══F5════╤══F6════╤══F7════╤══F8════╤══F9════╤══F10══
  Help   ║ Edit   ║ Copy   ║ Done   ║ Note   ║ Move   ║ Mark   ║Vw Mgr ║Cat Mgr║ Menu
```

Fig. 21-3. *The Vehicle Selection view showing the trucks selected using the category filter.*

move through the category hierarchy in the View Define box, setting filters to specify the inclusion or exclusion of items based upon the category assignments. The desired vehicles are displayed in the Vehicle Selection view.

## STORING SPECIALIZED INFORMATION

The storage and selection of information described thus far could also be accomplished using conventional database management software. Each vehicle would be a record in a database, and the attributes of the vehicles would be entered into separate fields. Records could be selected based upon the information entered into those fields.

The greater flexibility provided by Agenda becomes important, however, when more diverse forms of information are to be stored for selected items in the database. New views can be created for various classes of items, and specialized information can be entered that is relevant only to that class of item.

Consider the example discussed in the previous sections. The Vehicle Inventory view contains information that is relevant to all of the vehicles in the database. Additional information might be entered, however, that is relevant only to some of the vehicles. For example, the dealer might want to include additional information for the trucks in the database.

The first step might be to create a Trucks view, with the Trucks category being entered as the section head. This would display all of the items (vehicles) assigned to the Trucks category. New columns could be added to this view for

```
┌─────────────────────────────────────────────────────────────────────────────┐
│  File: C:\AGFILES\INVEN                                                        │
│  View: Trucks                                       03/11/89    12:18          │
│ ═══════════════════════════════════════════════════════════════════════════  │
│  Truck          Year      Manufacturer Truck Type    Eng type      Payload    │
│     • 87881     ·1988     ·Cosmos      ·Pickup       ·Gasoline     ·1 ton     │
│     • 83475     ·1984     ·Cosmos      ·Van          ·Gasoline     ·1/2 ton   │
│     • 81236     ·1987     ·Neptune     ·Van          ·Diesel       ·1 ton     │
│     • 63287     ·1988     ·Neptune     ·Delivery     ·Diesel       ·2 1/2 ton │
│     • 38962     ·1987     ·Neptune     ·Pickup       ·Gasoline     ·3/4 ton   │
│     • 34788     ·1984     ·Cosmos      ·Pickup       ·Gasoline     ·1/2 ton   │
│     • 29347     ·1988     ·Cosmos      ·Van          ·Gasoline     ·3/4 ton   │
│                                                                               │
│                                                                               │
│                                                                               │
│  ═F1══╤══F2══╤══F3══╤══F4══╤══F5══╤══F6══╤══F7══╤══F8══╤══F9══╤═F10══          │
│  Help │ Edit │ Copy │ Done │ Note │ Move │ Mark │Vw Mgr│Cat Mgr│ Menu         │
└─────────────────────────────────────────────────────────────────────────────┘
```

Fig. 21-4. *The Trucks view showing additional information entered only for trucks.*

the entry and display of information significant to trucks. Figure 21-4 shows such a Trucks view of the database. The Year and Manufacturer columns duplicate the information included in the original Inventory view. Three new category columns have been added, however, for truck-specific information: Truck Type, Eng Type, and Payload. Entries are made in these columns in the usual manner.

With this additional information, specific trucks can be selected from the inventory based upon the category assignments displayed in both the Inventory view and the Trucks view. When making a selection, category filters can be set for any of the categories to which trucks may be assigned. The breadth of the information in the database has thus been extended specifically for trucks.

Agenda databases can be easily extended in this way. Information on the items in the database is entered by the making category assignments. Such category assignments can be made and the information entered only for selected items in the database. Thus, it is possible to store different kinds of information for different items in the database, providing the Agenda user with flexibility that is not found in traditional database management software.

## GROUPING THINGS WITHIN A COLLECTION

For some applications, it might be useful to be able to specify groupings of things in a database. This might be the case, for example, when products or services are sold to customers as a package rather than individually. The capabilities of Agenda allows the flexible assignment of items to different categories, making Agenda ideally suited for such applications.

As an example, consider a computer dealer in the business of selling complete computer systems. Each system would include the basic computer and the necessary accessories to constitute a fully functional system. The computer dealer would have large numbers of different components which could be combined and packaged in various ways to form the complete systems.

An Agenda application could begin with a Products view showing the individual products contained in the computer dealer's inventory. Such a view is illustrated in Fig. 21-5. The items are brief descriptions of the individual products. Further information is entered in category columns indicating the type of product, the vendor, the quantity in stock, and the price.

The Quantity and Price columns contain specific attributes of the individual products, and the information in those columns would not be used as categories in the traditional sense. For example, one is unlikely to want to use a "65" child category of the Quantity category as a section head for displaying information. Thus, the Quantity and Price categories should be unindexed so that information entered in the columns is not treated as traditional Agenda categories. This can be accomplished by using either View or Category Manager commands.

Unindexing the Quantity and Price categories serves three purposes. First, it relieves Agenda of the responsibility of keeping track of certain category indexing information, which reduces storage requirements and speeds up certain operations. Second, it keeps the entries in the Quantity and Price columns from being displayed in the category hierarchy, so that it is not cluttered with useless information. Third, it disables automatic category completion. This disabling is critical in creating the Products view shown in Fig. 21-5. Consider the entries

```
File: C:\AGFILES\INVEN                              03/11/89   12:18
View: Products View

Products                      Type          Vendor      Quantity  Price
  · Turbo XT Computer        ·Computer     ·Acme        ·65       ·$499
  · Turbo AT Computer        ·Computer     ·Acme        ·43       ·$899
  · Turbo 386 Computer       ·Computer     ·Acme        ·9        ·$1899
  · Turbo Laptop Computer    ·Computer     ·Acme        ·14       ·$1199
  · Monochrome Graphics Board ·Video Board ·Multicomp   ·38       ·$89
  · Color Graphics Board     ·Video Board  ·Multicomp   ·29       ·$79
  · EGA Video Board          ·Video Board  ·Multicomp   ·56       ·$249
  · Amber Monochrome Monitor ·Monitor      ·Triax       ·31       ·$109
  · Standard RBG Monitor     ·Monitor      ·Triax       ·22       ·$319
  · Multimode RGB Monitor    ·Monitor      ·Triax       ·61       ·$489
  · 20 Meg Hard Disk Drive   ·Disk Drive   ·Shumi       ·44       ·$289
  · 40 Meg Hard Disk Drive   ·Disk Drive   ·Shumi       ·51       ·$469
  · 70 Meg Hard Disk Drive   ·Disk Drive   ·Shumi       ·13       ·$899
  · LIM Memory Expansion Card ·Memory      ·Multicomp   ·16       ·$299
  · AT Memory Expansion Card ·Memory       ·Multicomp   ·22       ·$399
  · 1200 Baud Internal Modem ·Modem        ·Solo        ·39       ·$129
  · 2400 Baud Internal Modem ·Modem        ·Solo        ·21       ·$249
  · Budget Dot Matrix Printer ·Printer     ·Quanto      ·68       ·$319
  · Laser Printer            ·Printer      ·Quanto      ·34       ·$1499
=F1=====F2======F3======F4=====F5======F6======F7======F8=====F9=====F10==
 Help  || Edit || Copy || Done || Note || Move || Mark ||Vw Mgr||Cat Mgr|| Menu
```

Fig. 21-5. *The Products view of the computer store inventory showing the separate items available.*

in the Price column. A price of $899 is entered for the second item. Suppose you move down and enter a price of $89 for another item. If the Price category were indexed, Agenda would recognize the entry of $89 as a match for the existing category $899. It would automatically assign the item to the $899 category and display that value. That would obviously be incorrect. After the price category has been unindexed, Agenda does not make this match. The price of $89 can be entered without problems.

To create complete computer system packages, you can assign the product items to the system categories. This can be done easily by marking the items to be included in a given system and then using the Item Assign command to assign the marked items as a group.

For example, suppose the computer dealer begins by creating a Basic Economy System. The first step is to mark those products to be included in the system—the Turbo XT computer, the monochrome graphics board, the amber monitor, the 20 megabyte hard disk, and the budget printer. When the Item Assign command is entered, it provides the option of assigning all of the marked items as a group, as shown in Fig.21-6. When this option is accepted, the dealer enters the name of the new category to which the items are to be assigned, the Basic Economy System category.

Figure 21-7 shows the Systems view of the computer dealer's database in which this Basic Economy System is displayed as a section. Included in this section are the items—the individual products—that were assigned to this category. Together they make the Basic Economy System.

```
New   Remove   Position   Assign   Discard   Undiscard
Assign item(s) to an additional category

Products                        Type         Vendor        Quantity   Price
   ♦ Turbo XT Computer          ·Computer    ·Acme          ·65       ·$499
   · Turbo AT Computer          ·Computer    ·Acme          ·43       ·$899
   · Turbo 386 Computer         ·Computer    ·Acme          ·9        ·$1899
   · Turbo Laptop Computer      ·Computer    ·Acme          ·14       ·$1199
   ♦ Monochrome Gra┌───────────────────────────────────┐·38       ·$89
   · Color Graphics │                                   │·29       ·$79
   · EGA Video Boar │ Assign:   Marked items            │·56       ·$249
   ♦ Amber Monochro │                                   │·31       ·$109
   · Standard RBG M └═Press ENTER to accept, ESC to cancel═┘·22     ·$319
   · Multimode RGB Monitor      ·Monitor     ·Triax        ·61       ·$489
   ♦ 20 Meg Hard Disk Drive     ·Disk Drive  ·Shumi        ·44       ·$289
   · 40 Meg Hard Disk Drive     ·Disk Drive  ·Shumi        ·51       ·$469
   · 70 Meg Hard Disk Drive     ·Disk Drive  ·Shumi        ·13       ·$899
   · LIM Memory Expansion Card  ·Memory      ·Multicomp     ·16      ·$299
   · AT Memory Expansion Card   ·Memory      ·Multicomp     ·22      ·$399
   · 1200 Baud Internal Modem   ·Modem       ·Solo          ·39      ·$129
   · 2400 Baud Internal Modem   ·Modem       ·Solo          ·21      ·$249
   ♦ Budget Dot Matrix Printer  »Printer     ·Quanto        ·68      ·$319
   · Laser Printer              ·Printer     ·Quanto        ·34      ·$1499
═F1══╤══F2══╤══F3══╤══F4══╤══F5══╤══F6══╤══F7══╤══F8══╤══F9══╤══F10══
 Help ║ Edit ║     ║     ║     ║     ║     ║     ║Accept ║
```

Fig. 21-6. *Assigning the marked items to the Basic Economy System category.*

Additional system packages can be created in the same manner, and can be displayed as additional sections in the Systems view. This gives the computer dealer the ability to look at the available computer equipment both from the perspective of the individual products and from the perspective of the packaged systems to be offered to customers.

Agenda's flexibility allows the computer dealer to adjust the makeup of the various system packages to provide the best range of customer offerings. For example, after a series of systems had been developed and displayed in the Systems view, the dealer might be interested in comparing and adjusting the various packages. In some cases, systems might be too similar, so that it would make sense to upgrade one or downgrade another by changing one or more of the products included. Gaps might exist in the product line, so new systems might be required. Such juggling can be accomplished easily in an Agenda database.

Likewise, changes in the products available to the computer dealer will require changes to the system packages. Old products are discontinued, new products become available, and prices change. As this happens, the products used in the line of systems offered by the dealer must be changed.

One significant limitation of Agenda, however, is that it is not capable of performing even the simplest mathematical computations. After assembling the products into the systems, the dealer would undoubtedly want to add up the prices of those products to arrive at a total price for the system. This total price would be used as the starting point for setting the system price.

```
File: C:\AGFILES\INVEN                              03/11/89   12:23
View: Systems View

Basic Economy System           Type          Vendor      Quantity  Price
  · Turbo XT Computer           ·Computer     ·Acme        ·65      ·$499
  · Monochrome Graphics Board   ·Video Board  ·Multicomp   ·38      ·$89
  · Amber Monochrome Monitor    ·Monitor      ·Triax       ·31      ·$109
  · 20 Meg Hard Disk Drive      ·Disk Drive   ·Shumi       ·44      ·$289
  · Budget Dot Matrix Printer   ·Printer      ·Quanto      ·68      ·$319




  =F1=====F2=====F3=====F4=====F5=====F6=====F7=====F8=====F9=====F10==
   Help    Edit   Copy   Done   Note   Move   Mark  Vw Mgr Cat Mgr Menu
```

Fig. 21-7. *The Systems view showing the individual items assigned to the Basic Economic System category.*

```
            A                    B              C            D          E
 1
 2
 3
 4   Basic Economy System    Type           Vendor      Quantity    Price
 5   Turbo XT Computer       Computer       Acme              65      499
 6   Monochrome Graphics Board Video Board  Multicomp         38       89
 7   Amber Monochrome Monitor Monitor       Triax             31      109
 8   20 Meg Hard Disk Drive  Disk Drive     Shumi             44      289
 9   Budget Dot Matrix Printer Printer      Quanto            68      319
10
11   Total Price                                                    1305
12
13
14
15
16
17
18
19
20
E11:  @SUM(E5..E9)
11-Mar-89   12:46 PM
                                                                  READY
```

Fig. 21-8. *The information from the Systems view imported into a spreadsheet for analysis.*

Although numerical analysis cannot be done in Agenda, it is not too difficult to move the information from an Agenda view into a spreadsheet for numerical analysis. You begin by printing the information in a view (such as the Systems view) to a file. Print out text only—do not include printer codes. Then exit Agenda and start your spreadsheet program. Most powerful spreadsheet programs such as Lotus 1-2-3 and Quattro include capabilities for importing ASCII files and parsing the information from tables into cells in the spreadsheet.

You could import the text file printed from Agenda using the File Import command in either 1-2-3 or Quattro. You could then parse the text information that has been imported as cell labels, moving the information into individual cells by using the Data Parse commands in 1-2-3 or the File Parse commands in Quattro. This produces a spreadsheet with the information contained in the Agenda database. All of the analytical capabilities of the spreadsheet can be used with the information. For example, the prices of the individual products can be added using the @SUM function. Figure 21-8 shows the information from the Systems view imported into a Quattro spreadsheet.

The ability to create groupings of products or services is a powerful feature of Agenda that is valuable to many users managing collections of things. Even when products or services are not sold in packages, a user might wish to group them in various ways for special promotions or for store displays.

Agenda can be used effectively when you want to keep track of different kinds of information for different things, and when you want to organize and group the things in different and changing ways. In these situations, Agenda can surpass traditional database management software for managing collections.

# 22

## MANAGING UNSTRUCTURED INFORMATION

A dilemma faced by all professionals is the management of the flood of information that confronts them in a typical day. Such information can arrive in many forms and from many different sources—memos, reports, newspapers, and magazines all contain important information. The problem is keeping track of the important ideas and being able to find the information later when you need it.

Agenda can be used effectively to manage those unstructured bits and pieces of information with which everyone must deal. Summaries of the information can be entered into a database as items and notes. Once entered, Agenda allows you to organize and examine the information in a variety of ways.

This chapter illustrates the use of Agenda for managing unstructured information. The first section addresses the entry of information into an Agenda database. The next section presents strategies for organizing this information. The final section considers the ways in which you can access and use specific information when you need it.

### ENTERING THE INFORMATION

When using Agenda to manage unstructured information, the items in the database should be brief summaries of the information. More detailed information can be incorporated into notes attached to those summary items. This will generally be the most effective strategy for finding and using the information as easily as possible.

If the source of information is a newspaper or magazine article, the item entered into the database would probably be the headline or other brief description of the article. A note attached to the item could include a longer summary of the article or actual text from the article. If the source is a memo, the item could be the subject line of the memo and the text could be attached in a note.

As an example, consider the job of an analyst for a real estate firm. The analyst comes across many articles and reports about the real estate market. The challenge is to keep track of all of the information so that the appropriate pieces of information can be retrieved when they are needed. Figure 22-1 shows some of the items that the analyst might enter into a database on a typical day. All of the items are concise summaries of the source. Often the items might be the actual headlines for the articles.

Notes are attached to each of the items in Fig. 22-1. The notes include additional details beyond the summary provided in the items. The notes could also include complete references to the sources of the information. The references make it possible to find the original source if additional information is needed.

The Information view of the database shown in Fig. 22-1 includes several additional columns, illustrating information one might wish to include in that view of such a database. The Source category column includes the name of the source from which the information was obtained. This would be useful in indicating the

```
 File: C:\AGFILES\INFO                                03/11/89    13:14
 View: Information View
═══════════════════════════════════════════════════════════════════════
 Information                         Source         Subject       Entry
   ♪ Alpha Corporation wins big      ·Wall St J     ·Alpha          ·07/01/88
     government contract for major                   Contracts
     housing study.                                  Government
                                                     Housing
   ♪ Mortgage interest rates show    ·Business Wee  ·Interest Rat  ·07/01/88
     slight rise over preceding weeks.               Mortgages
                                                     Housing
   ♪ Thrift industry increases       ·Wall St J     ·Thrifts        ·07/01/88
     residential lending in response                 Housing
     to pressure by regulators.                      Mortgages
   ♪ HUD issues new regulations for  ·Fed Register  ·Mortgages      ·07/01/88
     certain mortgage insurance                      Housing
     programs.                                       HUD
                                                     Government
   ♪ Beta Real Estate Company releases ·Hometown Tim ·Beta          ·07/01/88
     report on local market for office               Offices
     space.
   ♪ Zoning restrictions are posing  ·HUD Report    ·Government     ·07/01/88
     problems for new residential                    Housing
══F1══╤══F2══╤══F3══╤══F4══╤══F5══╤══F6══╤══F7══╤══F8══╤══F9══╤══F10══
 Help │ Edit │ Copy │ Done │ Note │ Move │ Mark │Vw Mgr│Cat Mgr│ Menu
```

Fig. 22-1. *The Information view showing items describing various pieces of information entered into the database.*

nature of the information included in the source. An Entry Date column identifies the date on which the information was entered into the database. The Subject category column is used for organizing the information in the database and is discussed in the following section.

One major decision is how to enter the relevant information into Agenda. Most users will simply type the information in as items and notes directly. For many people, in many situations, this might be the only option. This will, of course, favor the entry of rather concise summaries into the notes in order to reduce the amount of work required.

For some users, however, the information to be entered into the database might come in machine-readable form in a relatively standardized format. For example, memos could be received through electronic mail systems. Articles might be routinely downloaded from information systems such as CompuServe. In these cases, you might be able to use the TXT2STF program with special definition files to convert this information into structured text files with the appropriate items and notes that can be imported into an Agenda database. Obviously, if this approach for getting the information is feasible, it makes for the easiest way of managing the information. It would be worth a considerable expenditure of effort writing a definition file for TXT2STF and getting the bugs out of the procedures if the entire process could be automated.

An intermediate situation might confront many Agenda users, in which at least some of the information to be managed in an Agenda database is available in machine-readable form. The information might be in diverse formats, however, so that conversion and importation using TXT2STF would not be feasible. The information could still be brought into notes in a database without retyping.

If information is to be imported into an Agenda database, the information must be in the form of ASCII text files. These files can be created by downloading information from other sources, or they can be produced by other applications programs. Usually, this information is too detailed and lengthy to be an item, so a useful strategy probably would be to first import it into notes. The information in these files can be inserted into notes by using the Note Import command. Alternatively, the files themselves may be used as the notes by using the File Note command from a view.

You do not have to decide on the final text of an item before you import information into an attached note. If you want to wait before deciding on the text, it might be easier to begin by creating a one-character "dummy" item. Then import the file as a note attached to the item. Look over the text of the note, and then go back and edit the dummy item to enter the appropriate summary. It might even be possible to cut or copy appropriate summary text from the note and paste that text into the item to serve as the descriptive summary.

You might have a file consisting of many separate pieces of information that need to be entered as separate items and notes. Such a file can still be imported into the Agenda database as a single note. You can then cut the portions from that note that are to be used to create new items or notes attached to those new items.

Another useful means for transferring information into an Agenda database is to use the Items accessory. You can open the accessory, enter appropriate summary text for an item, and then specify that an ASCII text file is to be attached as a note to that item. The information is then exported from the Items accessory to a structured text file, and can be imported from there into the Agenda database.

This process of bringing ASCII text files into notes involves a certain amount of effort. As you do this on a regular basis, however, the procedures will become fairly routine and can be accomplished rather quickly. Even if the process involves a number of steps, it is far easier than typing the information into the database.

## ORGANIZING THE INFORMATION

The primary method for organizing the information entered into the database is by assigning items to categories. The Information view shown in Fig. 22-1 includes a Subject category column listing the various subject categories to which the items have been assigned. Each of the items is assigned to several subject categories, reflecting the various subjects addressed by each item.

Most Agenda users creating databases to manage information will probably begin establishing the subject categories by entering assignments into a Subject column as the database is created. As more subject categories are entered, text in new items will match existing categories and Agenda will automatically assign the items to those categories. Having the Subject column displayed in the Information view allows the user to see the categories to which items are assigned automatically as they are entered. The user can then determine whether additional subject categories need to be entered to reflect topics addressed by new items. In this way, the set of subject categories for organizing the information is expanded over time as items are entered into the database. As the database grows, more subject category assignments will be made automatically.

Text conditions can be added to provide for the assignment of new items, including terms that are synonymous with existing subject category names. In the example database, Housing is established as a subject category for the very first item. Later, an item is entered that referred to "residential" activity. This item obviously deals with housing, and should be assigned to the Housing category. A text condition can be used to cause Agenda to automatically assign any item containing the word "residential" to the housing category.

Text conditions are established by editing the category name, adding a semicolon and the new text. Figure 22-2 shows the category hierarchy for the example, including several text conditions added to the subject categories.

Agenda normally compares the category names and other text conditions with the text of items when searching for matches that will produce automatic

```
File: C:\AGFILES\INFO
Category Manager
═══════════════════════════════════════════════════════════════════════════════
  Source
     Business Week
     Fed Register
     Hometown Times
     HUD Report
     Wall St J
  Subject
     Alpha
     Beta
     Contracts
     Government
     Housing; residential
     HUD   <A= Government>
     Interest Rates
     Mortgages; lending   <A= Housing>
     Offices
     Savings and Loans; Thrifts
     Zoning
  Information

══F1════╤══F2════╤══F3═══╤══F4═══╤══F5════╤══F6════╤══F7═══════╤══F8═══════╤══F9══════╤══F10══
 Help   ║  Edit  ║Cpy C/A║Clr C/A║  Note  ║  Move  ║Prm (←)    ║Dem (→)    ║To View   ║ Menu
```

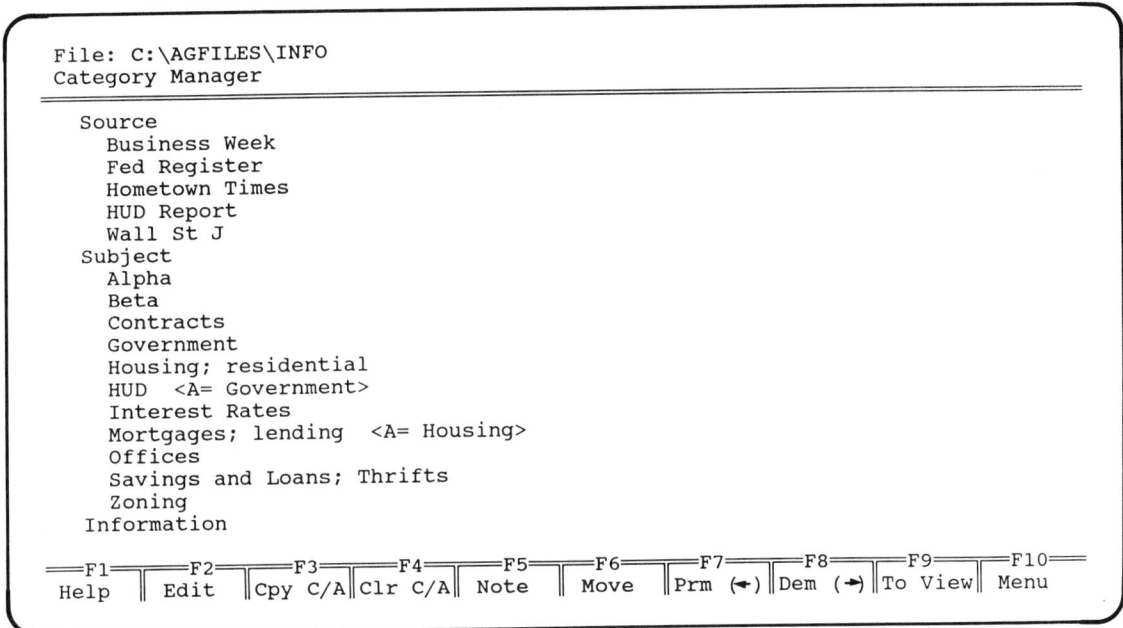

Fig. 22-2. *The Category Manager showing the source and subject categories, including the use of text conditions for synonyms and profile actions to assign items to additional categories.*

assignments. You can use the Utility Preferences Auto-Assign command to cause Agenda to go through the text of both items *and* notes to search for possible category assignments. This increases the likelihood of subject category matches, and increases the number of subject categories to which items are assigned. However, it is also likely to result in somewhat more frequent assignments of items to inappropriate subject categories. The choice is a matter of judgment that depends upon the details of the specific application, and upon personal preferences.

Note that you can also change the automatic assignment preferences to require confirmation before items are automatically assigned to categories. Requiring confirmation might provide an effective way of compromising on the automatic assignment question: match text conditions to both items and notes to get the greatest possible number of assignments, but then require confirmation before those assignments are actually made.

As you develop a database for dealing with unstructured information, you might decide that any items assigned to a certain category should also be assigned to another category. For example, the real estate analyst developing the database might assume initially that any information dealing with mortgage lending also relates to housing. Thus, the database should be designed so that items assigned to the Mortgages subject category are also assigned to the Housing category. This can be accomplished automatically by adding a profile action to the Mortgages category to direct this automatic assignment. The profile action used in the example database is shown in the category hierarchy in Fig. 22-2. An alternative to using a profile action is to place a condition on the Housing category.

As you work with a database—adding new text conditions, profile conditions, and profile actions—you create possibilities for additional category assignments to be made for the existing items as well as for new items entered into the database. After adding a number of conditions and actions, you might wish to run the Utility Execute command in order to retroactively apply these to the existing items.

Some of the subject categories created for managing information might turn out to be more specific subcategories of other subject categories. The example database includes both a Government subject category, for items that refer to government in general, and a HUD subject category, for items that refer to the U. S. Department of Housing and Urban Development. The latter is one unit of government.

The HUD category logically can be made a child category of the Government category. This not only groups the categories together logically, but also means that any items assigned to the HUD category will also be assigned to the Government category by inheritance. To make the HUD category a child of the Government category within the Category Manager, move the HUD category to the position immediately below the Government category. Then demote it. The result is shown in Fig. 22-2.

As a database of unstructured information grows, you are likely to develop a very extensive list of subject categories to which the items are assigned. Remember that while in the Category Manager, the categories within any family can be sorted easily. Just highlight the parent category and press ALT-F9 SORT). This produces an alphabetical listing of the subject categories.

## USING THE INFORMATION

The information database is useful only to the extent to which you are able to find the information you need, when you need it. Agenda provides multiple tools to do just that.

In searching for information, naturally you would first look at the subject categories to which items have been assigned as the database was developed. You could enter the Category Manager to determine if subject categories appropriate to your current query exist. If so, it is a very straightforward task to display those items that have been assigned to that category. One way is to create a new view with the desired category specified as the section head. For example, to examine information on mortgages in the example database, you could create a Mortgages view with the Mortgages category used as the single section head. This is shown in Fig. 22-3. Alternatively, a category filter could be used to restrict a view to those items assigned to the Mortgages category.

As a database becomes very large, the list of items assigned to a single category might be so long that it is difficult to find the desired information. In such

```
 File: C:\AGFILES\INFO                        03/11/89    13:16
 View: Mortgages
═══════════════════════════════════════════════════════════════
Mortgages
    ♪ Mortgage interest rates show slight rise over preceding weeks.
    ♪ HUD issues new regulations for certain mortgage insurance programs.
    ♪ Thrift industry increases residential lending in response to pressure by
      regulators.




═F1══╤══F2══╤══F3══╤══F4══╤══F5══╤══F6══╤══F7══╤══F8══╤══F9══╤═F10══
 Help │ Edit │ Copy │ Done │ Note │ Move │ Mark │Vw Mgr│Cat Mgr│ Menu
```

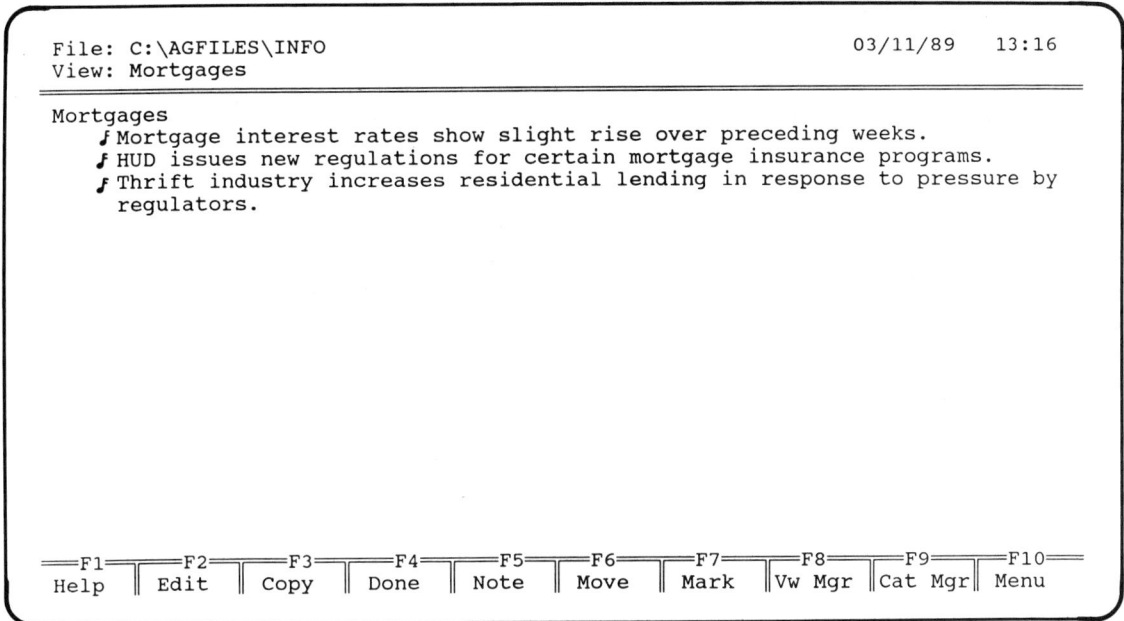

Fig. 22-3. *The Mortgages view showing items referring to mortgages and assigned to the Mortgages category.*

a case, a view restricted to items assigned to a single category can be filtered further, based upon the assignment of items to another category. Thus, if you were specifically interested in actions taken by HUD with respect to mortgages, the Mortgages view could be filtered by the HUD category to find only those items assigned to both categories.

In some cases, the existing subject categories will not enable you to find the information you are seeking. Agenda allows you to search through the items in a view for those with specific information. Suppose you knew there was something in the database dealing with growth control, and wanted to find it. You could switch back to the Information view and search for any occurrences of that text using F5 (SEARCH). In the Search box, you would enter the text, "growth control." Since the desired reference might be either in an item or in a note, the *Match on:* setting would need to be changed appropriately. Figure 22-4 shows the Search box set up for such a search.

The Search function then goes through the items and notes in the view, looking for the specified text. It stops when it finds the text, and highlights the selected item. When you examine the note attached to the selected item, you find that it includes the reference to growth control that you were seeking. Figure 22-5 shows the note attached to the item found using the Search function.

The Utility Show Match command can also be used to search for items. Like the Search function, the Utility Show Match command can search the items, the

```
File: C:\AGFILES\INFO                              03/11/89   Edit
View: Information View
═══════════════════════════════════════════════════════════════════
Information                          Source      Subject      Entry
   ♪ Alpha Corporation wins big     ·Wall St J   ·Alpha       ·07/01/88
     government contract for major               Contracts
     housing study.                              Government
                          ═════════Search═══════════════════
   ♪ Mo  ║                                                    ║  /88
     sl  ║  Search for:                                       ║
         ║  growth control                                    ║
   ♪ Th  ║                                                    ║  /88
     re  ║  Match on:      Both item & note                   ║
     to  ║  Direction:     Forward                            ║
   ♪ HU  ║  Ignore case:   Yes                                ║  /88
     ce  ║                                                    ║
     pr  ╚═══════Press F9 when done, ESC to cancel════════════╝
                                                  Government
   ♪ Beta Real Estate Company releases ·Hometown Tim ·Beta   ·07/01/88
     report on local market for office              Offices
     space.
   ♪ Zoning restrictions are posing    ·HUD Report  ·Government ·07/01/88
     problems for new residential                   Housing
═F1══════F2══════F3══════F4══════F5══════F6══════F7══════F8══════F9══════F10══
Help  ║ Paste ║ Copy ║ Cut ║      ║      ║ Mark ║      ║Accept ║
```

Fig. 22-4. *Searching for the reference to "growth control" in both the items and notes.*

```
Note for:   Zoning restrictions are posing problems for new residential
════════════════════════════════════════════════════════════Line 1═Ins═
The Department of Housing and Urban Development released a report of a study of
the effects of local zoning ordinances on the volume and price of new housing
construction in a sample of twelve large metropolitan areas in the United
States.  The report concludes that the zoning ordinances of suburban
communities in several of the faster-growing metropolitan areas have
significantly increased the prices of new residential construction in those
metropolitan areas and have dramatically reduced the availability of affordable
housing for large segments of the population.  The suggestion is made that the
more stringent zoning ordinances in these communities has arisen as a result of
growth control efforts aimed at addressing the problems of the rapid growth.




═F1══════F2══════F3══════F4══════F5══════F6══════F7══════F8══════F9══════F10══
Help  ║ Paste ║ Copy ║ Cut ║Return║MakeCat║ Mark ║MakeItm║Accept ║ Menu
```

Fig. 22-5. *The note attached to the item on "Zoning restrictions . . ." found searching for the reference to "growth control."*

notes, or both the items and notes for the occurrence of the specified text. The items found are displayed in a Show View. Using the Search function makes sense when you are looking for a single item, while the Utility Show Match command is more useful when you want to find multiple items with certain specified text.

Suppose you have several possible terms that might have been used in the desired items or notes. You can use the Utility Show Match command repeatedly, specifying that the items found each time are to be added to the existing Show View. In this way, you can build up a view of items in which the items or notes contain text matching several different terms.

You might decide that the items selected for a Show View belong to a new subject category that should be added to the database. In such a case, you might want to create this new subject category and assign all of the items found for the Show View to it.

In searching for information in the database, you might realize that the information represents a subject category that should be included in the database. You could create the new subject category, along with any appropriate additional text conditions as synonyms. Then you could use the Utility Execute command to assign matching items in which the text of the items (or the items and notes) matches the specified text conditions. Then the items assigned to this new subject category could be displayed in an appropriate view.

A database for the management of unstructured information evolves over time. As more information is added, more subject categories are likely to be included for organizing that information. The subject categories will be refined with conditions and actions, and by creating child categories so that items are more likely to be automatically assigned to the appropriate categories. Even so, when searching for information you might have to go beyond the existing categories and search through the database for items or notes containing other text. Agenda provides all of the capabilities required to easily accomplish these operations in managing and using the information.

# 23

## MANAGING BUSINESS AND ACADEMIC RESEARCH

CONDUCTING research and organizing what you find for the preparation of a report or paper involves the management of information. You collect information from different sources. Then you need to organize that information and create an outline for the paper or report. Agenda is the ideal tool for managing information while doing research.

Such applications of Agenda are appropriate to people in a wide variety of settings. People in business often have to prepare reports incorporating information from numbers of different sources. Researchers in business, government, and universities regularly write research papers. Students could make effective use of Agenda in developing and writing papers.

The key to applying Agenda in all of these contexts is the development of a structure for the database that will most effectively allow the powers of Agenda to be applied to the task. The first section of this chapter describes the way you might develop an Agenda database and enter the information from the various sources. The next section shows how Agenda can be used to develop an outline for the report. Finally, the last section demonstrates how the information in the database could be used in the actual preparation of the report.

## ENTERING THE RESEARCH INFORMATION

In a typical research project, you go through many different sources of information, identifying specific pieces of relevant information from each source.

The Agenda database must be structured to provide for the entry and use of these pieces of information, as well as for identifying the sources of the information.

The pieces of information obtained from each source should be entered as items into an Agenda database. If more extended information is needed, it can be entered in notes attached to the items. The items can be entered in a section headed by the reference to the source. The complete reference for each source can be entered as a note attached to the source category.

Suppose you were writing a brief history of the development of urban public transportation in the United States. You probably would go through numbers of different books and articles to find information describing the various developments that had taken place. You begin by entering this information into an Agenda database.

Figure 23-1 shows the Agenda database that would be created for such a research project. The first source consulted is an article by James Smith written in 1972. You create a section for this source, with the section head serving as a brief identifier of the source. You might use the author's last name followed by the year, a convention that is common in certain fields, heading the section *Smith, 1972*. However, any other brief identification would be equally satisfactory.

The specific pieces of information obtained from the first source are then entered as items in that section. If more details are required for any item, they can be entered in a note attached to the item. After working through and entering the items for the first source, you would then create another section for the next source, and begin entering items in exactly the same way.

```
File: C:\AGFILES\RSRCH                              03/11/89   13:21
View: Initial View
===================================================================
♪Smith, 1972                                          Subjects
      · The omnibus was the urban equivalent of the stagecoach and  »Omnibus
        was first used for intraurban transportation in New York
        City beginning in the late 1820s.
      · The horsecar, or horse-drawn street railway, became          ·Horsecars
        important beginning in the 1850s, providing faster
        transportation and greater passenger-carrying capacity than
        the omnibus.
      · The cable car was first introduced in San Francisco because ·Cable cars
        horses could not pull streetcars up the steep hills.
      · Cable car systems were developed in numbers of American      ·Cable cars
        cities, especially Chicago, to deal with the increasing
        demands for mass transportation.

♪Jones, 1967                                          Subjects
      · The development of the horsecar expanded the area available ·Horsecars
        for residential development, leading to the growth of the
        first suburbs.
      · Electric streetcars led to further expanses of the city,     ·Streetcars
        creating more "streetcar suburbs" and defining the growth
===F1======F2======F3======F4======F5======F6======F7======F8======F9======F10===
 Help  ‖ Edit  ‖ Copy  ‖ Done  ‖ Note  ‖ Move  ‖ Mark  ‖Vw Mgr ‖Cat Mgr‖ Menu
```

Fig. 23-1. *The entry of information from different sources as items in the source category sections.*

The brief identifier for a source is a category. It is used as a section head in the initial view shown in Fig. 23-1. The complete reference for each source can be entered as a note attached to the category for that source. Figure 23-2 shows the attached note with the reference for the Smith, 1972 category.

As you enter the items of information obtained from the various sources, you might want to begin assigning those items to subject categories that can be used to organize the information in the research report. The view in Fig. 23-1 includes a Subjects column, in which various subject category assignments have been entered. Once those categories have been created, of course, new items with text matching existing subject categories are assigned to the matching categories automatically.

As you work on the research report, you might find it necessary to go back and assign items to new subject categories that represent new ideas for the report. Agenda allows you to make new category assignments at any time, and this flexibility may be important in developing the appropriate organization of the information for the report.

## OUTLINING THE WORK AND ORGANIZING THE INFORMATION

After entering the information items from all of the sources for the research report, you will have a long listing of subject categories to which items have been assigned. The next step is to organize this information into an outline for the report.

Figure 23-3 shows the listing of the category hierarchy in the Category Manager as it might appear after all of the information from the research has been

```
   Note for:    Smith, 1972
 ══════════════════════════════════════════════════════════════Line 2══Ins═
   Smith, James F.   1972.   "Early Developments in the History of Urban Mass
   Transportation in the United States." Review of Urban History, Vol. 19, No. 3
   (Autumn):    371-392.




  ═F1══════F2═══════F3═══════F4═══════F5═══════F6═══════F7═══════F8═══════F9═══════F10══
   Help  ║ Paste  ║ Copy  ║  Cut  ║ Return ║MakeCat║ Mark  ║MakeItm║Accept ║ Menu
```

Fig. 23-2. *A note with the complete bibliographic reference attached to the associated source category.*

```
File: C:\AGFILES\RSRCH
Category Manager
═════════════════════════════════════════════════════════════════
    Subjects
      Omnibus
      Horsecars
      Cable cars
      Streetcars
      Interurbans
      Mass transit
      Subways
      Elevateds
      Buses
      BART
      METRO
      MARTA
      Light rail
      Dial-a-ride
      Vanpooling
    Sources
      Anderson, 1984
      Jones, 1967
      Martin, 1977
══F1═══╤══F2══╤══F3═══╤══F4═══╤══F5═══╤══F6═══╤══F7═══╤══F8═══╤══F9═══╤══F10══
 Help  │ Edit ║Cpy C/A║Clr C/A║ Note  ║ Move  ║Prm (←)║Dem (→)║To View║ Menu
```

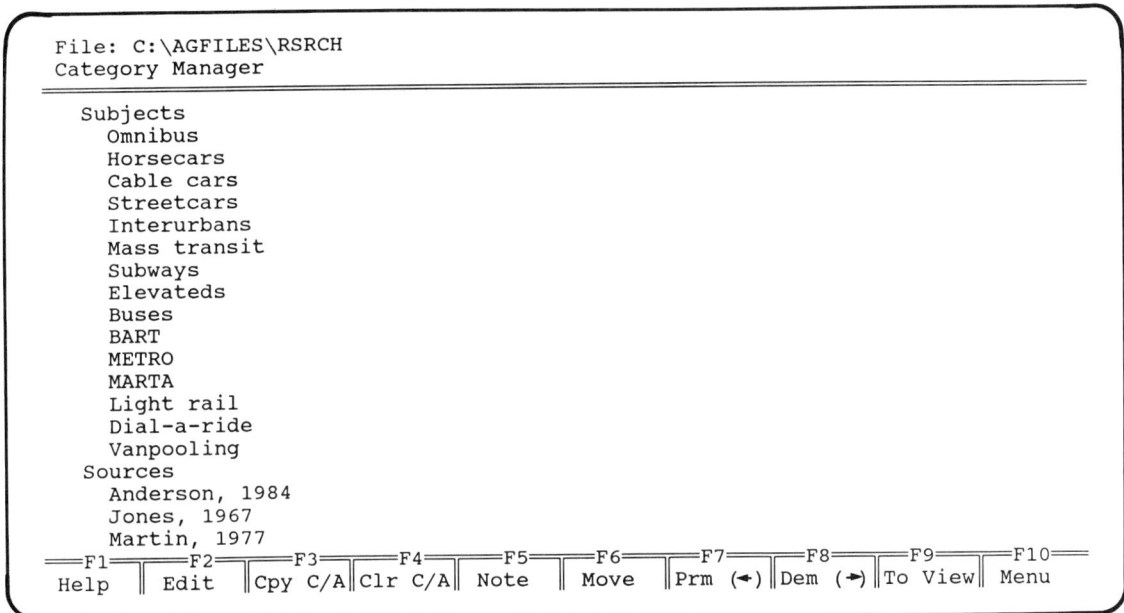

Fig. 23-3. *The category hierarchy displaying the list of subject categories to which the items have been assigned.*

entered. A long list of subject categories has been created in the process of doing the research. The presence of each subject category indicates that one or more items assigned to that category have been entered into the database.

The next step is to develop an outline for the research report. The various subject categories need to be grouped into a smaller number of categories that will serve as the major sections in the report. The outline can be created within the Category Manager by moving categories around, creating new ones, and making some into the child categories of others.

Figure 23-4 shows the outline that might be developed for the research report on the development of public transportation. The Omnibus, Horsecars, and Cable Cars categories all refer to the earliest developments of public transportation in the United States, so they could be grouped together in a new category, "Early Developments in Mass Transportation." This new category could be inserted into the category hierarchy while working in the Category Manager. The Omnibus, Horsecars, and Cable Cars categories would be moved to positions underneath this new category, and would be demoted to child categories of this category.

Likewise, additional categories would be added to the outline for the research report. The specific categories identified in the research would be positioned as child categories under those categories.

Creating the outline for the research is likely to be by trial-and-error, involving the repeated entry of new categories and the movement of existing subject categories until a satisfactory outline is developed. You might decide that certain

```
┌─────────────────────────────────────────────────────────────────────┐
│  File: C:\AGFILES\RSRCH                                               │
│  Category Manager                                                     │
│ ═══════════════════════════════════════════════════════════════════ │
│        Early Developments in Mass Transportation                     │
│          Omnibus                                                     │
│          Horsecars                                                  │
│          Cable cars                                                 │
│        The Application of Electric Power to Mass Transportation      │
│          Streetcars                                                 │
│          Interurbans                                               │
│          Mass transit                                              │
│            Subways                                                 │
│            Elevateds                                              │
│          Buses                                                    │
│        Modern Developments in Mass Transportation                   │
│          Heavy rail                                               │
│            BART                                                   │
│            METRO                                                 │
│            MARTA                                                │
│          Light rail                                             │
│        Paratransit Alternative                                   │
│          Dial-a-ride                                            │
│          Vanpooling                                            │
│ ═F1══╤══F2══╤══F3══╤══F4══╤══F5══╤══F6══╤══F7══╤══F8══╤══F9══╤══F10═ │
│  Help ║ Edit ║Cpy C/A║Clr C/A║ Note ║ Move ║Prm (←)║Dem (→)║To View║ Menu │
└─────────────────────────────────────────────────────────────────────┘
```

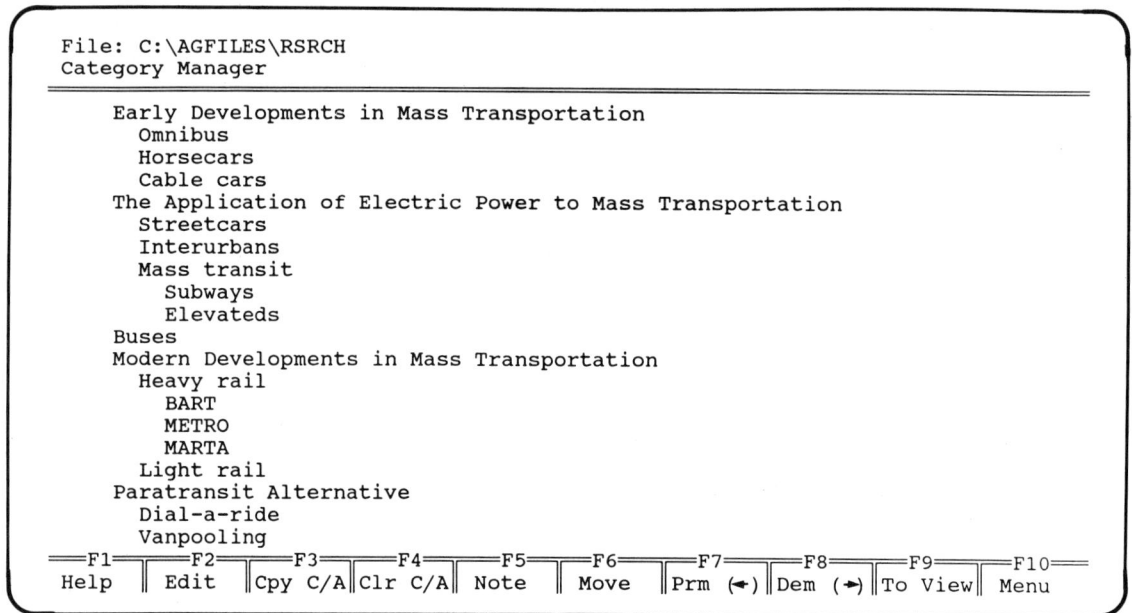

Fig. 23-4. *The revised category hierarchy showing the outline of the paper and the placement of the original subject categories in this outline.*

subjects fall into two different sections of the outline. This might require going back to the items and assigning them to more specific subject categories than were initially employed. In that way, some of the information items can be assigned to one more specific category that will be in one major section, and other items will be assigned to another category that will be in another section. Agenda makes it easy to make such additional assignments and to continue the refinement of the outline until a satisfactory result is obtained.

This process of entering items, assigning them to specific subject categories, and then organizing the categories into more general categories is the reverse of the way most people develop outlines. Most people work from the top down, developing the major topics in the outline first, and then refining those into more specific subtopics. The bottom-up procedure described here, however, can be a powerful method for developing an outline to encompass a large number of diverse topics.

This outlining procedure can be extremely effective and useful. One of our first applications of Agenda was the development of the outline for this book. We entered each of the features of Agenda—each element, command, and procedure—as an item in an Agenda database. The items were assigned to subject categories—in many instances to multiple categories. These categories were then juggled around within the category hierarchy and were made child categories of chapter categories until the outline for the book was developed.

For example, items referring to profile conditions were assigned to the Condition subject category. The Condition category was ultimately positioned as a child category to the Chapter 11 category, which would address additional ways of assigning items to categories.

## USING THE INFORMATION IN WRITING A REPORT

The final step in the process of preparing a report is organizing the information that has been entered into the database. You will want to group the items so that the information can be used in the writing of the report. You will also want to generate a listing of sources for use as the references to be included with the report.

An Outline view can present the information assigned to all of the subject categories in the same order in which those categories are included within the outline of the report. To create an Outline view, you could use the View Define procedure to include all of the categories within your outline. Then, each of the subject categories is displayed as a section head in the view, with the items assigned to each of those categories being displayed in the sections.

You will probably want items to be displayed only in those sections headed by categories to which they have been directly assigned. You will not want the items to also be displayed in the parent categories to which they are assigned by inheritance. Thus, you will want to use the View Preferences procedure to hide inherited items.

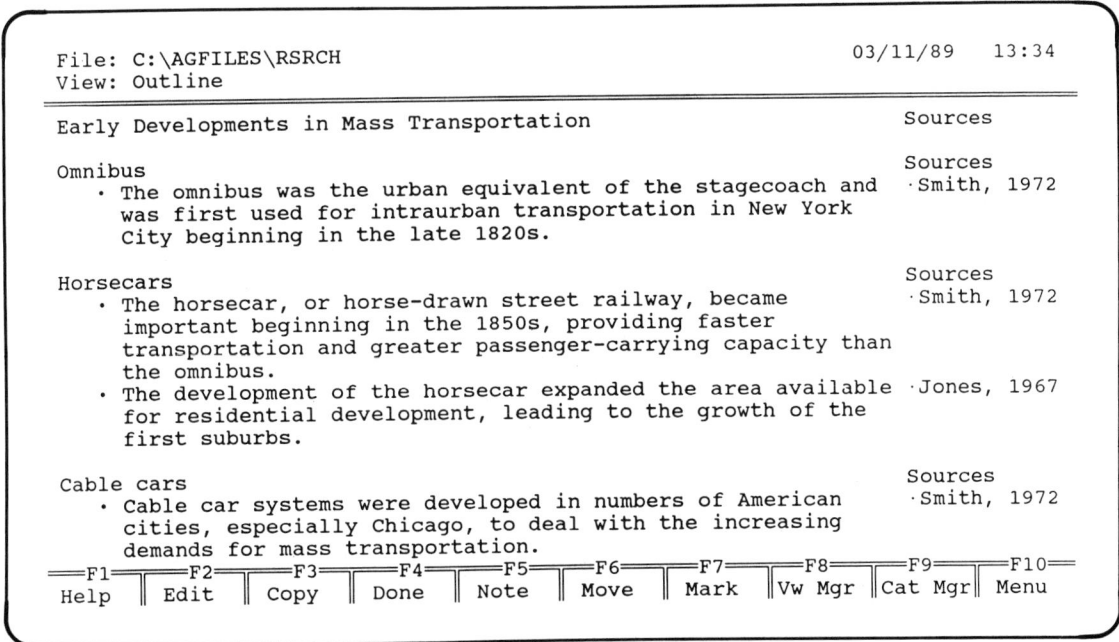

```
File: C:\AGFILES\RSRCH                        03/11/89    13:34
View: Outline
================================================================
Early Developments in Mass Transportation            Sources

Omnibus                                              Sources
   · The omnibus was the urban equivalent of the stagecoach and  ·Smith, 1972
     was first used for intraurban transportation in New York
     City beginning in the late 1820s.

Horsecars                                            Sources
   · The horsecar, or horse-drawn street railway, became         ·Smith, 1972
     important beginning in the 1850s, providing faster
     transportation and greater passenger-carrying capacity than
     the omnibus.
   · The development of the horsecar expanded the area available ·Jones, 1967
     for residential development, leading to the growth of the
     first suburbs.

Cable cars                                           Sources
   · Cable car systems were developed in numbers of American     ·Smith, 1972
     cities, especially Chicago, to deal with the increasing
     demands for mass transportation.
==F1===T==F2===T==F3===T==F4===T==F5===T==F6===T==F7===T==F8===T==F9===T==F10==
 Help  ||  Edit || Copy  || Done  || Note  || Move  || Mark  ||Vw Mgr ||Cat Mgr|| Menu
```

Fig. 23-5. *The Outline view using the categories in the outline as sections, showing the items directly assigned to each category.*

Figure 23-5 shows the Outline view in the example database for research on the development of public transportation. The first section identifies the general topic of early developments in public transportation. No items have been directly assigned to that section. The second section includes the item describing the omnibus, the third section includes the items referring to horsecars, and so forth.

If you require cross-references to items assigned to other sections, it is simple enough to create additional views to display any desired information. Filters can always be used to display only those items assigned to the combinations of categories desired.

After creating the Outline view, you can use it to write the report in one of two ways. The most obvious method is to print out the information in the Outline view and refer to the printout as you are writing the report. Another option is to print the Outline view to a file and import that information into your word processor. You could then use that as the point of departure in writing the report. The information from Agenda would appear in your word processor document. You could refer to that information while writing the report, incorporating some of the text and deleting other information as you write each section.

A report based upon information found in other sources should contain a bibliography or list of references with the sources from which the information in the report has been obtained. In the example, the sources have been included as notes attached to the source categories in the Agenda database. You can output this information by switching to the Category Manager and printing out the notes. In the Category Manager, enter the Print command and specify that only the text of the notes is to be printed out. Since the references should be included within the report, specify that the information is to be printed to a file. You might name this file BIBLIO.PRT. You might wish to enter a \nl\ backslash command to print a blank line between each of the note references printed.

Figure 23-6 shows the contents of this file displayed on the screen using the DOS TYPE command. The notes attached to the categories—the complete references to the sources—will be printed to the file BIBLIO.PRT. This file may

```
Anderson, Katherin.  1984.  "A Survey of Recent Developments in Paratransit."
Journal of Mass Transit.  Vol. 34, No 2 (Spring):  203-224.

Jones, Sally.  1967.  The Role of Streetcars in Shaping the Patterns of Urban
and Suburban Development.  New York:  Gotham Press.

Martin, Thomas.  1977.  The Development of Mass Transportation in Large Cities.
Philadelphia:  The University Press.

Smith, James F.  1972.  "Early Developments in the History of Urban Mass
Transportation in the United States." Review of Urban History, Vol. 19, No. 3
(Autumn):  371-392.
```

Fig. 23-6. *The printout of the bibliographic information from the notes attached to the source categories to the file BIBLIO.PRT.*

be imported into your word processing document to serve as the list of references for your final report.

The procedures described in this chapter for using Agenda for research represent only some ways in which Agenda might be employed to organize research information. Likewise, the examples presented in the preceding applications chapters are only suggestions for possible methods to follow in the application of Agenda.

The most important feature of Agenda is its flexibility. It allows you to organize information in many different ways, enabling you to use information in the manner that best meets your needs. All of the applications have been presented as suggestions for how you might use Agenda to accomplish your tasks. Be creative, and explore the potential of Agenda for most effectively organizing information to meet your own particular needs.

# APPENDIX A

## AGENDA COMMANDS

| VIEW COMMANDS | |
|---|---|
| *Command* | *Description/Settings* |

**FILE**

| | |
|---|---|
| OPEN | Open Agenda database |
| BACKUP | Create backup copy of database |
| USE-BACKUP | Open backup copy of database |
| COPY | Make copy of database |
| DELETE | Erase database |
| TRANSFER | |
|     Import | Import structured file |
| |     Import: |
| |     From file: |
| |     Delete file: |
| |     New data only: |
| |     Assign to category: |
| |     Combine categories if: |
| |     Create new categories: |
| |     Strip carriage returns: |

| Command | Description/Settings |
|---|---|
| Export | Create structured file |
| | Items to export: |
| | Assignments: |
| | Discard items: |
| | Categories to export: |
| | Parent category: |
| | To file: |
| | File already exists: |
| Template | Copy database without items |
| NOTE | Attach text file as note |
| | File name: |
| INFO | Show database statistics |
| **VIEW** | |
| NEW | Create new view |
| | View name: |
| | Category: |
| | Display child categories: |
| SELECT | Display different view |
| DEFINE | Select section heads and filters |
| PREFERENCES | Set View preferences |
| | Display Preferences |
| | Hide done items: |
| | Hide dependent items: |
| | Hide inherited items: |
| | Date Filter |
| | Type of date: |
| | Start date: |
| | End date: |
| | Display: |
| | Include items: |
| | Other |
| | View name: |
| | Section separator: |
| INFO | Show view statistics |
| **ITEM** | |
| NEW | Insert item |
| REMOVE | Removed item(s) from section |
| POSITION | Move item within section |
| ASSIGN | Assign item(s) to category |

| *Command* | *Description/Settings* |
|---|---|
| DISCARD | Eliminate item(s) from database |
| UNDISCARD | Retrieve item(s) from trash |
| **CATEGORY** | |
|  COLUMN | |
|   New | Insert column |
|  | Position: |
|  | Column type: |
|  | Column head: |
|  | Format: |
|  | Line number: |
|  | Insert in: |
|   Remove | Remove column from view |
|   Position | Move column |
|   Format | Specify column format |
|  | Format: |
|  | Line number: |
|  | Link column globally: |
|   Width | Set column width |
|  SECTION | |
|   New | Insert section |
|  | Position: |
|  | Section head: |
|   Remove | Remove section from view |
|   Position | Move section within view |
|   Sort | Set preferences and sort section(s) |
|  | Sort new items: |
|  | Sort items in: |
|  | Primary sort |
|  | Sort on: |
|  | Order: |
|  | Sequence: |
|  | Category: |
|  | Line number: |
|  | Secondary sort |
|  | Sort on: |
|  | Order: |
|  | Sequence: |
|  | Category: |
|  | Line number: |

| *Command* | *Description/Settings* |
|---|---|
| MANAGEMENT | |
|    Exclusive | Make children mutually exclusive |
|    Unindexed | Make children indexed |
|    Condition | |
|       *Profile* | Set profile condition |
|       *Date* | Set date condition |
| |    Date type: |
| |    Start date: |
| |    End date: |
| |    Include items: |
|       *Settings* | Set default condition settings |
| |    Evaluate: |
| |    Text condition match on: |
| |    Condition logic: |
| |    Prevents explicit assignments: |
| |    Override conflicting assignment: |
|   Action | |
|       *Profile* | Set profile action |
|       *Special* | Set special action |
| |    Special action: |
|   INFO | Show category statistics |
| **PRINT** | Print view |
| |    Print: |
| |    Include: |
| |    Number items: |
| |    Print to: |
| |    File: |
| |    Format: |
| |    From page: |
| |    To page: |
| |    Begin numbering with: |
| |    Header: |
| |    Footer: |
| |    Top margin: |
| |    Page length: |
| |    Special characters: |
| |    Printer: |
| |    Note: |
| |    Section: |
| |    Item: |

| *Command* | *Description/Settings* |
| --- | --- |

**UTILITY**

    EXECUTE — Apply conditions and actions
        Evaluate conditions for:
        Categories to check:
        Perform actions:

    SHOW

        Match — Create view with matching items
            Search for:
            Match on:
            Syntax:
            Ignore case:

| Command | Description/Settings |
| --- | --- |
| Prerequisites | Create view with prerequisite items |
| *One Level* | Immediate prerequisite items |
| *All Levels* | All prerequisite items |
| *Every Item* | All items with dependents |
| Dependents | Create view with dependent items |
| *One Level* | Immediate dependents |
| *All Levels* | All dependent items |
| *Every Item* | All items with prerequisites |
| Items Done | Create view with Done items |
| Circular | Create view with circular refs |
| All | Create view with all items |
| QUESTIONS | Confirm assignments |
| TRASH | Empty items from trash |
| COMPRESS | Eliminate unused space in database |

PREFERENCES

    Auto-Assign — Set auto-assignment
        Enable text conditions:
        Match on:
        Required match strength:
        Confirm assignments:
        Skip text enclosed by:
        Ignore suffixes:
        Ignore accents:
        Enable date conditions:
        Enable profile conditions:
        Enable actions:

    Date — Set date format and features
        Default date format:
        Set entry date:

| Command | Description/Settings |
| --- | --- |
| | Set date from item: |
| | Redate recurring items: |
| Other | Set system preferences |
| | Insert new columns in: |
| | Empty Trash: |
| | Make backup copy: |
| | Process Done items: |
| | When: |
| | Done file: |
| | Tab size: |
| | Hide carriage returns: |
| | File description: |
| | File password: |
| | Auto-import file: |
| Environment | Set system and display features |
| | Display key map: |
| | Color: |
| | Beep on auto-completion: |
| | Printer definition file: |
| | Item tag character: |
| | Auto-save interval: |
| | Character set: |
| | Suppress snow: |
| Update | |
| SYSTEM | Temporarily exit to DOS |
| QUIT | Finish session and leave Agenda |

## CATEGORY MANAGER COMMANDS

| *Command* | *Description/Settings* |
|---|---|
| **EXCLUSIVE** | Make children mutually exclusive |
| | Assign conflicting item(s) to: |
| | New category for item(s): |
| **UNINDEXED** | Make children unindexed |
| **CONDITION** | |
| PROFILE | Set profile condition |
| DATE | Set date condition |
| | Date type: |
| | Start date: |
| | End date: |
| | Include items: |
| SETTINGS | Set default condition settings |
| | Evaluate: |
| | Text condition match on: |
| | Condition logic: |
| | Prevent explicit assignments: |
| | Override conflicting assignments: |
| **ACTION** | |
| PROFILE | Set profile action |
| SPECIAL | Set special action |
| | Special action: |
| **PRINT** | Print category hierarchy |
| | Print: |
| | Include: |
| | Print to: |
| | File: |
| | Format: |
| | From page: |
| | To page: |
| | Begin numbering with: |
| | Header: |
| | Footer: |
| | Top margin: |
| | Page length |
| | Special characters: |
| | Printer: |
| | Note: |
| **RETURN** | Return to view |

---

# NOTE COMMANDS

| *Command* | *Description/Settings* |
|---|---|
| **PRINT** | Print note |
| | Print: |
| | Print to: |
| | File: |
| | Format: |
| | From page: |
| | To page: |
| | Begin numbering with: |
| | Header: |
| | Footer: |
| | Top margin: |
| | Page length: |
| | Special characters: |
| | Note: |
| **IMPORT** | Import text from ASCII file |
| | File name: |
| | Strip carriage returns: |
| **EXPORT** | Export text to ASCII file |
| | File name: |
| **DELETE** | Delete text from note |
| **RETURN** | Return to prior activity |

---

# APPENDIX B ———

## AGENDA KEY
## ASSIGNMENTS

## SPECIAL KEY ASSIGNMENTS

| Key | Throughout Agenda | In a View | In Category Manager |
|---|---|---|---|
| UP | Up one unit | Up one unit | Up one category |
| DOWN | Down one unit | Down one unit | Down one category |
| RIGHT | Right one unit | Right one unit | |
| LEFT | Left one unit | Left one unit | |
| CTRL-RIGHT | To extreme right | To rightmost column | |
| CTRL-LEFT | To extreme left | To leftmost column | |
| PGUP | Up one screen | Up one screen | Up one screen |
| PGDN | Down one screen | Down one screen | Down one screen |
| CTRL-PGUP | | Up one section | Up one sibling |
| CTRL-PGDN | | Down one section | Down one sibling |
| HOME | To top of group | To section head | To parent |
| END | To bottom of group | To last item in section | To last sibling |
| CTRL-HOME | To extreme top | To first section head | To first category |
| CTRL-END | To extreme bottom | To last item | To last category |
| INSERT | | Add new item | Add sibling category |
| DELETE | | Remove item from section, section or column from view | Eliminate category |
| ENTER | | Down one unit | Down one category |
| BACKSPACE | | Up one unit | Up one category |
| CTRL-ENTER | | | |
| CTRL-BACKSPACE | | | |
| SPACE | | | |
| TAB | | Right one unit | |
| SHIFT-TAB | | Left one unit | |
| GREY PLUS | Display more information | Select catgory to replace category or assign item | |
| GREY MINUS | Remove display of more information | | |
| SHIFT-GREY PLUS | Expand group | Expand section | Expand family |
| SHIFT-GREY MINUS | Collapse group | Collapse section | Collapse family |
| ESCAPE | Back one step | Back one step | Back one step |

## SPECIAL KEY ASSIGNMENTS

| Key | In a Note | Editing Items and Categories | During Automatic Completion |
|---|---|---|---|
| UP | Up one line | Up one line in item | Show previous matching category |
| DOWN | Down one line | Down one line in item | Show next matching category |
| RIGHT | Right one character | Right one character | Right one character |
| LEFT | Left one character | Left one character | Left one character |
| CTRL-RIGHT | Right one word | Right one word | To end of word |
| CTRL-LEFT | Left one word | Left one word | To beginning of word |
| PGUP | Up one screen | Up one screen | |
| PGDN | Down one screen | Down one screen | |
| CTRL-PGUP | Up one screen | | |
| CTRL-PGDN | Down one screen | | |
| HOME | To beginning of line | To beginning of item line or category | To beginning of line |
| END | To end of line | To end of item line or category | To end of line |
| CTRL-HOME | To top of note | To beginning of item | |
| CTRL-END | To bottom of note | To end of item | |
| INSERT | Toggle insert/overstrike modes | Complete item and insert new item | Insert character string as new category |
| DELETE | Delete character at cursor | Delete character at cursor | Delete character at cursor |
| ENTER | | Complete item or category | Accept category |
| BACKSPACE | Delete character left of cursor | Delete character left of cursor | Delete character left of cursor |
| CTRL-ENTER | Delete to end of line | Delete to end of line | Accept category as parent |
| CTRL-BACKSPACE | Delete word | Delete word | Delete word |
| SPACE | | | |
| TAB | To next tab | Complete and move one column right | Accept category and move right |
| SHIFT-TAB | To previous tab | Complete and move one column left | Accept category and move left |
| GREY PLUS | | | Select category to replace current category |
| GREY MINUS | | | |
| SHIFT-GREY PLUS | | | |
| SHIFT-GREY MINUS | | | |
| ESCAPE | Exit note | Abort edit | Back one step |

SPECIAL KEY ASSIGNMENTS

| In View Manager | In Category Hierarchy | In Dialog Boxes | In Selection Boxes |
|---|---|---|---|
| Up one unit | Up one category | Up one setting | Up one unit |
| Down one unit | Down one category | Down one setting | Down one unit |
| Right one unit when searching | | Right or down one setting | |
| Left one unit when searching | | Left or up one setting | |
| Up one screen | Up one screen | Up one screen | Up one screen |
| Down one screen | Down one screen | Down one screen | Down one screen |
| Up one screen | Up one sibling | Up one category | Up one screen |
| Down one screen | Down next sibling | Down one category | Down one screen |
| To first view | To parent | To first setting | To first selection |
| To last view | To last sibling in family | To last setting | To last selection |
| To first view | To first category | To first setting | To first selection |
| To last view | To last category | To last setting | To last selection |
| Create new view | Add sibling category | | Create new database or macro |
| Eliminate view | Eliminate category | | Delete selection or macro |
| To highlighted view | Down one category | Down one setting; accept on last setting | Accept selection |
| | Up one category | Clear setting | |
| | Include category or assign item to category | Cycle through settings | |
| | Include category in filter, condition, or action | Down one setting | |
| | Remove all categories from filter, condition, or action | Up one setting | |
| | | Display options | |
| | | Remove display of options | |
| | Expand family | | Display database descriptions |
| | Collapse family | | Hide database descriptions |
| Back one step | Back one step | Back one step | Back one step |

## FUNCTION KEY ASSIGNMENTS

| Key | Throughout Agenda | In a View | In Category Manager |
|---|---|---|---|
| F1 | HELP<br>Show help information | HELP<br>Show help information | HELP<br>Show help information |
| F2 | EDIT<br>Edit information | EDIT<br>Edit item, section or column head | EDIT<br>Edit category name |
| F3 | | COPY<br>Copy item or marked items | COPY<br>COND/ACTIONS<br>Copy conditions and actions |
| F4 | | DONE<br>Mark item done | CLEAR<br>COND/ACTIONS<br>Clear conditions and actions |
| F5 | | NOTE<br>Display and edit note for item | NOTE<br>Display and edit note for category |
| F6 | | MOVE<br>Move item or marked items | MOVE<br>Move category |
| F7 | | MARK<br>Mark items | PROMOTE<br>Move category left |
| F8 | | VIEW MANAGER<br>To View Manager | DEMOTE<br>Move category right |
| F9 | ACCEPT<br>Accept entry or all settings | CATEGORY MANAGER<br>To Category Manager | TO VIEW<br>Go to view |
| F10 | MENU<br>Display menu | MENU<br>Display View Menu | MENU<br>Display Category Manager Menu |
| ALT-F1 | COMPOSE<br>Enter international characters | COMPOSE<br>Enter international characters | COMPOSE<br>Enter international characters |
| ALT-F2 | | WHEN<br>Set When date | |
| ALT-F3 | | DEPENDS ON<br>Set to depend on marked items or remove dependency | HIDE<br>COND/ACTIONS<br>Shift to hide or display conditions and actions |
| ALT-F4 | DISCARD<br>Eliminate from database | DISCARD<br>Eliminate item or marked items from database | DISCARD<br>Eliminate category from database |
| ALT-F5 | | SEARCH<br>Search for text string | |
| ALT-F6 | | GO TO<br>Go to different section | |
| ALT-F7 | | UNMARK ALL<br>Unmarks all items | |
| ALT-F8 | | LAST VIEW<br>Go to last view | |
| ALT-F9 | | PROFILE<br>Display assignments for item or marked items | SORT<br>Sort children of category |
| ALT-F10 | MACRO<br>Create, edit, run macro | MACRO<br>Create, edit, run macro | MACRO<br>Create, edit, run macro |

## FUNCTION KEY ASSIGNMENTS

| **In a Note** | **Editing Items and Categories** | **During Automatic Completion** | **In View Manager** |
|---|---|---|---|
| HELP<br>Show help information | HELP<br>Show help information | HELP<br>Show help information | HELP<br>Show help information |
| PASTE<br>Insert text from clipboard | PASTE<br>Insert text from clipboard | | EDIT<br>Edit view name |
| COPY<br>Copy text to clipboard | COPY<br>Copy text to clipboard | | COPY<br>Copy current view |
| CUT<br>Move text to clipboard | CUT<br>Move text to clipboard | | DELETE<br>Eliminate current view |
| RETURN<br>Go back to view | NOTE<br>Display and edit note for item | NEW CATEGORY<br>Insert character string as new category | PREFERENCES<br>Set view preferences |
| MAKE CAT<br>Make word or marked text a category | MAKE CAT<br>Make word or marked text a category | | MOVE<br>Move current view to new position |
| MARK<br>Set start of text marking | MARK<br>Set start of text marking | PREVIOUS SELECTION<br>Shows last category that matches character string | |
| MAKE ITEM<br>Make text an item | SPLIT<br>Split item into two items | NEXT SELECTION<br>Shows next category that matches character string | DEFINE<br>Set sections and filters for current view |
| ACCEPT<br>Save changes, return to view | ACCEPT<br>Save changes, return to view | ACCEPT<br>Accept given matching category | ACCEPT<br>Display current view |
| MENU<br>Display Note Menu | | | |
| COMPOSE<br>Enter international characters | COMPOSE<br>Enter international characters | COMPOSE<br>Enter international characters | COMPOSE<br>Enter international characters |
| GET ITEMS<br>Copy marked items and attached notes | | | |
| DELETE<br>Eliminate text | DELETE<br>Eliminate marked text | | DELETE<br>Eliminate current view |
| SEARCH<br>Search for specified string | | NEW PARENT<br>Insert character string as new parent | |
| APPEND<br>Append text to item | | | |
| | | ACCEPT PARENT<br>Accept current category as parent | SORT<br>Sort list of views |
| MACRO<br>Create, edit, run macro | | | |

## Function Key Assignments

| Key | In Category Hierarchy | In Dialog Boxes | In Selection Boxes |
|---|---|---|---|
| F1 | HELP<br>Show help information | HELP<br>Show help information | HELP<br>Show help information |
| F2 | EDIT<br>Edit current category name | EDIT<br>Edit setting or display options | EDIT MACRO<br>Edit highlighted macro |
| F3 | FILTER; INCLUDE CATEGORY<br>Include category in filter, condition, or action | | |
| F4 | CLEAR FILTER; CLEAR CATEGORIES<br>Remove all categories from filter, condition, or action | | DELETE<br>Delete highlighted macro |
| F5 | | | RENAME<br>Rename highlighted database |
| F6 | | | |
| F7 | SECTION; ASSIGN<br>Include category or assign items | | |
| F8 | CHILDREN<br>Include children of current category as sections | DEFAULT<br>Restore setting to default | LEARN<br>Begin macro keystroke recording |
| F9 | ACCEPT<br>Accept changes and return | ACCEPT<br>Accept options and exit | ACCEPT; RUN<br>Accept values in selection box or run macro |
| F10 | | | |
| ALT-F1 | COMPOSE<br>Enter international characters | COMPOSE<br>Enter international characters | COMPOSE<br>Enter international characters |
| ALT-F2 | | | |
| ALT-F3 | | | |
| ALT-F4 | DISCARD<br>Eliminate category | | |
| ALT-F5 | | | |
| ALT-F6 | | | |
| ALT-F7 | | | |
| ALT-F8 | | DEFAULT ALL<br>Restore all settings to defaults | |
| ALT-F9 | | | |
| ALT-F10 | | | |

ACCELERATOR KEY ASSIGNMENTS

| Key | Throughout Agenda | In a View | In Category Manager |
| --- | --- | --- | --- |
| ALT-A | | Assign item or marked items | Establish profile action |
| ALT-B | | | |
| ALT-C | | | Establish profile condition |
| ALT-D | Insert down | Insert section down | Insert sibling category down |
| ALT-E | | Evaluate conditions, perform actions for item | |
| ALT-F | | Close file, open last file | |
| ALT-G | | | |
| ALT-H | | Hop to next occurrence of same item | |
| ALT-I | Insert next place | Insert new item | Insert category down |
| ALT-J | | Jump to next marked item | |
| ALT-K | Function key map on or off | Function key map on or off | Function key map on or off |
| ALT-L | Insert left | Insert column left | Insert category left |
| ALT-M | | | |
| ALT-N | Go to next | Go to next view | |
| ALT-O | | | |
| ALT-P | Go to previous | Go to previous view | |
| ALT-Q | | Execute Utility Questions command | |
| ALT-R | Insert right | Insert column right | Insert child category right |
| ALT-S | | Sort sections | |
| ALT-T | | | |
| ALT-U | Insert up | Insert section up | Insert sibling category up |
| ALT-V | | Hop to same item in same section in other view | |
| ALT-W | | | |
| ALT-X | | Evaluate conditions, perform actions for all items | |
| ALT-Y | | Get last removed item | |
| ALT-Z | Run current macro | Run current macro | Run current macro |

## ACCELERATOR KEY ASSIGNMENTS

| Key | In a Note | Editing Items and Categories | During Automatic Completion |
|---|---|---|---|
| ALT-A | | | |
| ALT-B | | | |
| ALT-C | | | |
| ALT-D | | | |
| ALT-E | | | |
| ALT-F | | | |
| ALT-G | | | |
| ALT-H | | | |
| ALT-I | | Complete or insert new item | |
| ALT-J | | | |
| ALT-K | Function key map on or off | Function key map on or off | Function key map on or off |
| ALT-L | Insert outdented area | | |
| ALT-M | Insert hard return | Insert hard return | |
| ALT-N | Go to note for next item | Go to next item | Display next category |
| ALT-O | | | |
| ALT-P | Go to note for previous category or item | Go to previous item | Display previous category |
| ALT-Q | | | |
| ALT-R | Insert indented block | | |
| ALT-S | Repeat last search | | |
| ALT-T | | | |
| ALT-U | | | |
| ALT-V | | | |
| ALT-W | | | |
| ALT-X | | | |
| ALT-Y | | | |
| ALT-Z | Run current macro | | |

**ACCELERATOR KEY ASSIGNMENTS**

| In View Manager | In Category Hierarchy | In Dialog Boxes | In Selection Boxes |
| --- | --- | --- | --- |
| | Insert sibling category down | | |
| Function key map on or off | Function key map on or off<br>Insert category left | | |
| | Insert child category right | | |
| | Insert sibling category up | | |

# GLOSSARY

**accelerator keys**—Combinations of the ALT key and other keys that, when pressed together, allow the user to perform various functions.

**accessory**—Terminate-and-stay-resident program that is loaded before using other programs so that the user can, without exiting other programs, enter information for later importing into an Agenda database.

**action**—Causes some action to be performed for all items assigned to that category to which it is attached. See *profile action* and *special action*.

**automatic assignment**—The assignment of items to categories by Agenda without action on the part of the user. Automatic assignment is caused by conditions and actions.

**bullet**—A dot or other marker that appears before each item in a view.

**category**—The organizational unit in an Agenda database to which items are assigned. Categories can be section heads in views, with all items assigned to that category being displayed in that section. Categories and category assignments can also be displayed in category columns.

**category family**—A parent category together with its child categories.

**category hierarchy**—The list of all of the categories in a database. It displays the structure of the relationships among the categories.

**Category Manager**—The section of the Agenda program used for working directly with the category hierarchy.

**child category**—A subcategory of a parent category.

**Clipboard accessory**—A pop-up utility program allowing the user to copy information from one application to another.

**column**—An element of a view adjacent to the items. It is used to display information on category assignments or dates.

**collapsing categories**—In the Category Manager, causing the child categories in a category family to be hidden.

**collapsing sections**—In a view, causing the items in a section to be hidden.

**command**—Agenda function invoked by its selection from a menu. Different sets of commands are available in views, in notes, and in the Category Manager.

**condition**—Attached to a category, causes an item to be assigned to that category when the specified criteria are met. See *profile condition* and *date condition*.

**cursor highlight**—A single-character highlight that indicates the position when editing text.

**date condition**—A condition attached to a category that causes an item to be assigned to that category when the date meets certain criteria.

**demotion**—The movement of a category to a lower position in the category hierarchy.

**dialog box**—A box appearing in the middle of the screen for the specification of additional information required for the execution of a command.

**discard**—To eliminate an item or category from an Agenda database. Discarded items are placed in Trash and can be retrieved later.

**Done Date**—A date associated with an item that records the date on which the item has been marked as Done. Done items are marked with double exclamation points. They can be automatically exported from or discarded from a database. Done dates can also be used for other purposes.

**Entry Date**—A date associated with an item that indicates the date on which the item was originally entered into the database. Entry dates can also be used for other purposes.

**filter**—A selection criterion used to specify which items are to be displayed in a view. Items can be selected based upon either category assignments or dates.

**hidden items**—Items with certain characteristics that are not displayed in a view or in the database.

**hot key**—A key or group of keys used to invoke one of the Agenda accessories while working with another program.

**inherited item**—An item assigned to a parent category based on its assignment to a child category.

**item profile**—A list specifying the categories to which an item is assigned.

**item**—A fundamental unit of information in an Agenda database containing up to 350 characters of text. An item must be assigned to at least one category. Items are displayed in views in the sections headed by categories to which the items are assigned.

**Items accessory**—A pop-up utility program allowing the user to enter items for later importing into an Agenda database while working with other programs.

**macro**—A sequence of Agenda operations that are performed automatically when the macro is executed.

**macro argument**—One of the required elements of information in a macro command.

**macro command**—Instructions for performing special operations that may be included within macros.

**Main**—The highest-level category, under which all other categories are organized.

**marking**—Specifying certain items as part of a group so that an operation may be performed simultaneously on all of the items in the group.

**note**—Additional text (up to 10,000 characters) that can be attached to items and categories.

**options**—The possible choices for a setting in a dialog box.

**parent category**—A category that has subcategories. The subcategories are called child categories of the parent category. A parent category inherits the assignment of items to its child categories.

**pop-up**—A terminate-and-stay-resident accessory program that may be invoked while working with another program.

**profile actions**—An action attached to a category that causes items assigned to that category to be assigned to one or more other categories.

**profile condition**—A condition attached to a category that causes items to be assigned to that category when they are assigned to the categories specified in the condition.

**promotion**—The movement of a category to a higher position in the category hierarchy.

**remove**—To eliminate an item, section, or column from a view, without discarding the items or category from the database.

**section**—A division of a view headed by a category and containing the items assigned to that category.

**section head**—A category or the special head Show View that appears at the top of each section.

**section separator**—A line marking the divisions between sections in a view.

**selection box**—A box appearing in the middle of the screen allowing the user to select from a list of options for a setting.

**setting**—A specification for the operation of a command appearing in a dialog box. The user must select the desired option for the execution of the command.

**siblings**—Child categories of the same parent category.

**sorting**—The process of arranging items within sections, sections within a view, view names within the View Manager, or categories within the category hierarchy.

**special action**—An action attached to a category that causes items assigned to that category to be discarded, marked as Done, exported, or given a specified date.

**special key**—Any key that does not enter characters. See Appendix B.

**structured text file**—An ASCII text file in a special format suitable for importing into an Agenda database. Can be created by exporting from an Agenda database or by converting a file using the TXT2STF utility.

**text condition**—A condition attached to a category that causes an item be assigned to that category when the item or its note includes specified text.

**Trash**—The place in which discarded items are stored for possible later retrieval.

**TXT2STF**—*Text to Structured Text File*, utility program for converting ASCII text files into structured text files.

**view**—The general mode for the display of information in an Agenda database.

**View Manager**—The section of the Agenda program used for selecting, creating, and modifying views.

**When Date**—A date of significance associated with an item, such as the date on which a task is to be completed. If the text of an item includes a reference to a particular date, Agenda automatically assigns that as the When Date unless the user specifies otherwise.

# INDEX